Russian, Book 1

Russian Through Propaganda

by Mark R. Pettus, Ph.D.

Russian, Book 1: Russian Through Propaganda
by Mark R. Pettus, Ph.D.

ISBN 979-8-6493-4599-6

about this series

This series is intended for students who are serious about learning Russian, and favors a thorough, grammar-centric, long-term approach over simple but ultimately misleading "rules of thumb." In my experience, many beginner's textbooks strive to simplify Russian in order to make it seem more approachable. Of course, if the student's goal is to "learn a bit of Russian," simplifaction and short-cuts are well justified. However, for students whose long-term goal is real mastery of the language, early simplifications may result in lingering confusion. This series was designed for students who are looking for an in-depth knowledge of the language, and, eventually, genuine fluency.

Based on my own experience as a learner and teacher of Russian, I believe that the best approach to take with such students is to confront difficulties as thoroughly as possible from the very beginning. Examples include verbal aspect and verbs of motion. We will look at such topics in great depth, emphasizing an imaginative understanding of the Russian idiom. Often, we will contrast an "unpacking" of the Russian idiom (saying, in English, everything that the Russian really conveys) with a simple "translation" that often results in a loss of information — and tremendous confusion!

This book is also meant to be practical — for one thing, it contains a large number of tables, including full tables of conjugated forms for all verbs, to help students as they drill the vocabulary and eliminate many "guessing games" regarding correct forms. All relevant grammatical information is included — for example, what case and/or preposition follows a given verb. All verbs are tagged by verb type, using a system (modified somewhat) that I learned from Prof. Charles Townsend at Princeton. Here again, becoming familiar with these "tags" and verb types requires a bit of extra effort at first, but is, in the long run, extremely profitable — particularly when we begin reading literary texts in the original and need to assimilate new vocabulary in an efficient and systematic manner.

Of course, this is neither a reference grammar nor a linguistics textbook, and presupposes no prior knowledge of Slavic languages or grammar in general. Grammatical and other technical terms are used, to the extent that they are all but unavoidable (examples include subject and object, predicate nouns and adjectives, determinacy and animacy, etc.), but such terms are explained carefully as they are introduced. All Russian words are grouped very carefully according to type.

The series consists of two first-year texts (*Russian, Books 1 and 2: Russian through Propaganda*) which focus on the Soviet era and feature a large number of Soviet posters, whose short, pithy slogans serve to illustrate points in each day's grammar. Students generally find these posters very amusing and memorable, and they provide short but authentic bursts of Russian from the very beginning. Certainly, these posters present a triumphalist vision of Soviet life that is very one-sided, and, amidst the inevitable chuckles, students are encouraged to critique this vision and contrast it with what they know of the historical reality. Much could be said about the enduring pernicious effect of much of this propaganda in post-Soviet reality; but, inasmuch as this is a language textbook, and I am not a historian, I'll refrain from further comment and leave it for readers to draw their own conclusions regarding this highly problematic content.

The series continues with two second-year texts (*Russian, Books 3 and 4: Russian through Poems and Paintings*), whose focus is the Imperial era, including classical Russian poetry and prose. These books are illustrated with famous Russian paintings, many of them depicting important cultural phenomena and historical events. Meanwhile, some of the finest poems in the Russian canon are used to illustrate topics in the grammar. As we go, we'll continue to develop our reading ability, and prepare ourselves for extended units on Pushkin and Lermontov (most importantly, Pushkin's *The Bronze Horseman*). It is hoped that immersion in a Russian novel of this caliber will serve as a genuine reward for students. All texts are marked up with vocabulary, including aspectual pairs for all new verbs, flagged according to type. At this point, the legwork done as early as Book 1 in terms of classifying nouns and verbs really begins to pay off. Book 3 pays special attention to such advanced "literary" forms as verbal adverbs, adjectives (participles), and nouns, and Book 4 has extensive word formation material to help students expand their vocabulary and approach new Russian words in a rigorous fashion. In recent years, I've published a series of dual-langauge Russian readers that should be very accessible to students who have completed this 4-book course.

so, how hard is Russian?

Beginning students often ask for an honest assessment of how difficult Russian really is.

The answer: hard, but doable. Any student who sincerely wants to learn Russian should not be frightened off — least of all by the intimidating alphabet, which can be learned in a matter of days! But, every student should set realistic expectations, and be prepared to put in plenty of work.

What makes Russian so much harder than, say, Spanish, French, or German? First, it is highly **inflected** (that is, it has many grammatical **endings** that change depending on a word's role in the sentence). A good portion of first-year Russian (Books 1 and 2 in this series) will involve learning the endings for nouns, adjectives and verbs, and how to use them. This does involve its share of drudgery, since we have to know the endings in order to practice them, and vice versa!

In time, through a combination of memorization and practice, manipulating these endings will come more naturally, but they still account for much of the frustration felt by beginning students. Many have the feeling that despite excellent knowledge of the grammar, and solid passive knowledge of Russian (reading and even listening), they still have great difficulty actually speaking the language, since even relatively simple utterances may involve a number of cases and tricky verb forms.

Moreover, simply learning Russian **vocabulary** will require a lot more work than learning Spanish, French or German vocabulary. Not only are we working with a new alphabet, but we have far fewer words that are cognate with words in English (such as the German "Haus"). It's extremely important to spend time every day "drilling" your Russian vocabulary — particularly verb forms. Find what works for you. Writing out vocabulary and repeating verb conjugations can help you to develop a kind of "muscle memory" that, over time, will allow you to speak Russian more spontaneously.

What else makes Russian difficult? In terms of pronunciation, Russian has **shifting stress**. Not only must we grow accustomed to stressing just one syllable in each word, but we must also learn about the patterns by which stress may shift about in a given word, depending on how we manipulate its endings. Secondly, in terms of grammar, Russian has **verbal aspect**, a category that English lacks. Here and elsewhere, Russian idioms may be very different from their English counterparts. So, relying on translations will often be of little help; we'll have to use our imagination, and even think about the world in new ways in order to talk about it in a distinctively Russian manner.

On the other hand, some features of Russian are simple, even compared to the "easy" languages we mentioned. For example, Russian has only three tenses, and no difficult subjunctive forms.

Try to avoid the unrealistic expectations that may carry over from your previous study of an "easy" language. Be patient — but realize that by the end of this Book 4 you will have all the tools necessary to read, say, Dostoevsky, Pushin, or Tolstoy in the original. Along the way, we'll read some outstanding peices of Russian poetry and prose, from Akhmatova to Pushkin. The ability to work with these texts in the original is what draws many students to study Russian in the first place, and this series was written with that goal in mind. In short, achieving a solid **reading** ability in Russian within a year or two (or, by Book 4 in this series) is a very reasonable goal.

However, if your goal is to achieve advanced proficiency in **spoken** Russian, then, in my view, and based on my personal experience, you should make it a priority to **spend time in an immersive, Russian-speaking environment**. I believe it is all but impossible to attain spoken proficiency in Russian in a classroom, no matter how good the instruction may be. Students are often nervous when they are first "forced" to speak Russian: they "don't know how to say anything," despite even a full year — or two! — of study. This is a very common feeling (I felt the same way when I first arrived in Russia!). But students who take the plunge often find that their speaking ability begins to catch up surprisingly quickly with their knowledge of grammar. They know more than they often realize; they just need practice. In many ways, the real goal of this series is to equip serious students with all of the grammar and cultural background they need to spend time in Russia, or anywhere Russian is spoken, productively. By the time you complete Book 4, you will be ready to deal with just about anything Russian can throw at you.

how to use this book

Each lesson (or, "day") is presented in the form of a "lecture" — that is, a complete prose explanation of the day's grammar topic, of the sort you might expect to hear in a classroom, along with all necessary tables and examples. When reviewing the material, students are advised to focus on the examples — if you are comfortable with them, move on; if not, try re-reading the prose explanations. These explanations take into account questions asked by past students, and carefully try to eliminate sources of confusion; if you have a question, chances are it is addressed somewhere!

As you study, try to dedicate as much time as possible to drilling the vocabulary and forms, especially verb conjugations. It will take time for these unfamiliar forms to sink in. Repetition, on a daily basis, is really the only way to master Russian vocabulary!

Pay particular attention to the method used to "tag" verbs by conjugation type. Learning this system will require more work at first, but will pay great dividends down the road. Every time you come across a new verb, note the "tag," and drill yourself: can you conjugate it? A full table of verb types is provided in the back of the book for reference.

Stress is marked throughout the book — watch for the underlined vowels in each word. Paying attention to these stress marks is an essential part of learning Russian.

Exercises include grammar drills (fill-in-the-blank, translation, etc.) — marked by a the number of the Day, plus a letter, with an answer key in the back — and questions for free responses and simple discussions, which are unmarked.

The conversational materials also invite you to use the day's grammar in more creative and practical ways — for example, to tell about yourself, answer simple questions, etc.

Watch for black boxes in the reference tables, which highlight forms that, for one reason or another, cause special problems for students. Often, these forms are not what we might expect based on general rules. So, focus on the "black boxes" as exceptions.

While the posters and proverbs have been carefully selected to illustrate the grammar at hand, you shouldn't expect to understand every last nuance right away. See how much you can make of them. Down the road, when you come back to review old material, you may be surprised to find how much more you suddenly understand. These daily bits of "real Russian" will gradually help prepare you to read real prose and poetry in the original, beginning in Book 2.

Remember to bookmark the series web site at **www.russianthroughpropaganda.com.** There you can also easily access the free video lessons available at YouTube, as well as a number of resources — worksheets, speaking activities, and more. I hope to continue to add to and improve these resources in the future.

As you learn, do your best to seek out real Russian wherever you can find it — movies, music, etc. Hearing Russian as often as possible, especially in ways that are meaningful for you, is essential to learning — even when you might think that you aren't understanding a thing, your mind is learning, bit by bit, to make sense of unfamiliar sounds and structures. As you learn more grammar and vocabulary, what once seemed impenetrable will gradually begin to make sense, and Russian will become more and more enjoyable.

Удачи! (Good luck!)

Chapter I

Chapter 2

people & activities

verbs, the genitive, and the accusative

Chapter 3   food & feelings

the dative case and reflexive forms

Chapter 4

going places

motion verbs and the prepositional case

Chapter 5

work, study & interests

the instrumental case and case review

Билет Государственного

Сто ру

ВАНКОВСКИЕ БИЛЕТЫ ОБЕСПЕЧИВАЮТСЯ ЗОЛ
МЕТАЛЛАМИ И ПРОЧИМИ АКТИВАМИ ГОСУ

100

33 069539

СТО КАРБОВАНЦІВ · СТО РУБЛЕ
ЙУЗ МАНАТ · ҙҕо ҙҙбоооо · ᲖᲘᲠᲒᲚᲘᲠ ᲒᲘᲚᲙᲠ
ЮЗ СӮМ · САД СӮМ · ЖУЗ СОМ · ЖУЗ СОМ
0 СУТЭ РУБЛЕ · SIMTAS RUBLIŲ · SIMTS RUBL

1947

I

everyday items

nouns and adjectives

In this chapter, we'll learn how to pronounce, read, and write Russian and its Cyrillic alphabet. We'll learn how to introduce ourselves. Finally, we'll learn how to use nouns and adjectives in the nominative case to name basic everyday items, describe them, and tell whose they are.

1. the alphabet and basic pronunciation
2. pronunciation in detail
3. more on pronunciation
4. handwriting
5. learning names and getting acquainted
6. nouns and the nominative case
7. adjectives
8. adverbs, conjunctions, and the verb "to be"
9. possessive pronouns
10. demonstrative pronouns

day 1: the alphabet and basic pronunciation

stress, vowels, consonants, and the basics of pronunciation

ша-лаш | му-хо-мор | су

су-ха-ри | ах | мох
са-хар | ах-нул | о-си-

У осины мох. Сыро.
У осины рос мухомор.
Ахнул Шура.

A Soviet **Букварь** (ABC book) from 1978.

1.1 Before learning a single letter — a word on stress and vowel purity

A typical Russian word has **only one stressed syllable**; unfortunately, in words of more than one syllable, it's all but impossible to guess the stress just by looking. For learning purposes, we'll mark the <u>**stressed**</u> syllable by <u>**underlining**</u> its vowel. For example: the word **студент** (student) is stressed on the **second** syllable, whose vowel is "e." Watch for the stress carefully, and be sure to "hit" the stressed syllable with **extra force** and emphasis.

To pronounce a Russian vowel correctly, we must first find the proper **tongue position**, and then resist the temptation to **move our tongue** (or any part of our mouth) in order to produce an **unchanging** vowel sound. English vowels that are spelled using a single letter ("o," "u" etc.) may actually consist of more than one sound when pronounced, if we listen very closely. But a Russian vowel consists of **one sound only**. It is, so to speak, "**pure.**"

1.2 Our first three letters: two vowels (и, ы) and a consonant (й)

Instead of presenting the letters in alphabetical order, we'll begin by grouping them for learning purposes. Let's start out with three letters that are easily confused. The consonant **й**, like English letter "y," is used in combination with vowels. Note the "hat" above the **й**, which distinguishes it from the vowel **и**. Finally, the vowel **ы** does not occur at all in English, and is clearly distinct from **и**! It will likely take some practice to master this vowel.[1]

Й й	y		И и	i		Ы ы	y
like "y" in "yes" or "boy" (must combine with a vowel!)			like the "i" in machine			tongue position between "ee" and "oo" (not the "ooey" in "gooey"!)[2]	
йога	yoga		**и**	and		**ты**	you (singular)
Нью-Йорк	New York		**или**	or		**вы**	you (plural)
ой!	oy!		**идея**	idea		**мы**	we
война	war		**блин**	pancake		**музыка**	music
музей	museum		**икра**	caviar		**новый**	new
давай!	OK, let's do it!		**история**	history; story		**блины**	pancakes

[1] The tables show the English letter typically used to **transliterate** the Russian letter — but don't rely on them as guides to **pronunciation**!
[2] Again, this is a pure vowel sound in between "ee" and "oo" (or, try "ee" and "ah") — not a sequence of the two separate sounds "oo + ee." Because we tend to process unfamiliar sounds in terms of familiar ones, students often first pronounce this like the "ooey" in "gooey."

1.3 Four more vowels: а, у, э, о — and a preview of vowel reduction

When any Russian vowel is **stressed**, we will always hear its **"true"** sound. However, some vowels — notably "a" and "o" — may sound differently when **unstressed**, depending on their position with regard to the stressed syllable. This principle is called **vowel reduction**: we say that certain vowels are **reduced** when unstressed.[1]

To practice reduction, we may transcribe Russian vowels as **ah / oh / uh / eh / ih** (as in: open up and say "ah!") — but keep in mind that these are only rough approximations, for convenience only. Take careful note of the actual **sound** of each Russian vowel as described below, without relying entirely on English transliterations.

А а	a	У у	u	Э э	e	О о	o
• stressed: "ah" ("a" in father) • just before stress: "ah" • everywhere else: "uh"		like the "oo" in what the owl says: "hoo, hoo!" — with lips rounded		"eh" (like "e" in set)		• stressed: "oh" ("o" in more) • just before stress: "ah" • everywhere else: "uh"	
да	yes	университет	university	это	this	вино	wine
автор	author	урок	lesson	экзамен	exam	он	he
страна	country	учебник	textbook	этажерка	bookshelf	она	she
Америка	America	курс	course	поэзия	poetry	вопрос	question
литература	literature	русский	Russian (m)	эхо	echo	ответ	answer
группа	group	русская	Russian (f)	экстремизм	extremism	оценка	grade
машина	car	студент	student (m)	эгоист	egotist	пока!	bye!
газета	newspaper	студентка	student (f)	энтузиазм	enthusiasm	дело	matter

1.4 Four "soft" vowels: я, ю, е, ё

As we mentioned, the Russian consonant **й** (like English "y") combines with vowels. If the **й** sound comes **after** a vowel, Russian represents the resulting combination using **two letters**, as in **ой** (much like the "oy" in "boy").

However, if the **й** sound **precedes** a vowel sound, Russian represents the resulting combination using one of the **single letters** shown below. Note how their pronunciation mirrors that of the four vowels above: adding the **й** sound before the basic vowel sound produces a so-called **"soft"** version, as in: й + а = **я**, й + у = **ю**, etc.

We will refer to these four new vowels, shown below — plus a fifth, **и**, that we've already learned — as Russian's five **soft vowels**. They are "soft" in the sense that they **mark a preceding consonant as soft.** Hold that thought!

Я я	ya	Ю ю	yu	Е е	ye	Ё ё	yo
• stressed: like "yah" • end of word: "yuh" • unstressed 1st syllable: "yih" • everywhere else: "ih"		like "yoo" (remember: the vowel sound is like the "oo" in "hoo!")		• stressed: "yeh" • end of word: "yeh" • unstressed 1st syllable: "yih" • everywhere else: "ih"		Like "yoh." Can only occur in stressed positions. Typically written without the dots in actual Russian texts.[2]	
я	I	юг	south	нет	no	ещё	still
язык	language	юмор	humor	все	everyone	ёлка	fir tree
Россия	Russia	компьютер	computer	совет	advice	всё	everything
Япония	Japan	рюкзак	backpack	советский	Soviet	лёд	ice
ясно!	that's clear!	союз	union	еда	food	актёр	actor
простыня	bedsheet	рюмка	shot glass	Европа	Europe	осёл	donkey
лекция	lecture	говорю	I say	занятие	activity	живёт	he/she lives
одеяло	blanket	уютный	cozy	Петербург	Petersburg	ёж	hedgehog

like "э" after ц
полотенце towel

Note: in French and English borrowings, Russians typically write "e" but say "э."
интернет Internet
кафе cafe
but: кофе coffee

[1] This and other tricky details of pronunciation will be treated more thoroughly tomorrow. Today, just try to grasp the basics.
[2] Russians "just know" where to pronounce ё and where e; for learning purposes, we will try to always dot the ё in these textbooks.

1.5 The hard and soft signs

Most Russian consonant sounds come in two varieties: **hard** and **soft**. These sounds are very distinct, but the Russian alphabet uses the same letter for both: for example, the letter **т** can represent both **hard t** and **soft t**.

So, how do we know if a given consonant is soft? **By what follows it.** If a consonant is followed by a **soft vowel** (**е, ё, ю, я, и**) or a **soft sign** (**ь**), then we know the consonant itself is **soft**, and must be pronounced as soft.

Otherwise, however, we simply **assume that consonants are hard**. Before the Bolshevik spelling reforms of 1918, this assumption wasn't made; instead, Russians wrote (quite superfluously, one might argue!) a **hard sign** (**ъ**) after hard consonants. The hard sign *is* still used today, but only to **mark a consonant as hard despite being followed by a soft vowel** — a combination that sometimes occurs when prefixes are added to words. This is relatively rare, especially in beginner's Russian. One example is **въехать** (to drive into; that is, в + ехать).

In short, our next two letters — the soft sign and hard sign — **have no sound of their own**. They simply tell us how to pronounce preceding consonants. Take note of the difference in these letters: the **hard sign** has a "hat."

ь	/

soft sign: marks a preceding consonant as soft

мать	mother
Русь	(ancient) Rus'
мед**ведь**	bear

ъ	//

hard sign: marks a preceding consonant as hard

	в	into (prefix)
+	<u>е</u>хать	to drive
=	въ<u>е</u>хать	to drive into

Stress and the **hard/soft** distinction are essential for good Russian pronunciation. Ignore them at your peril!

Compare:

мать	mother
мат	vulgar language (!)[1]
пис<u>а</u>ть	to write
п<u>и</u>сать	to piss (!)[2]

1.6 Pronouncing soft consonants

How do we **soften** a consonant? Technically speaking, we **palatalize** it. That is, a **soft (palatalized)** consonant is pronounced with the front of our tongue raised up against the **hard palate** (or "roof") of our mouth.

So, <u>tongue position</u> is key! The position required for softening is <u>the same one used to pronounce **и** or **й**</u>. Pin down this position by saying "**и**" several times, taking note of where your tongue is positioned while you say it. Now, **without letting your tongue drop** from this position, move it **just enough** to pronounce the given consonant. The result is a **"soft" version** of that consonant. This is not easy, and will definitely take time to master!

Of course, a **soft** sound is related phonetically to its **hard** counterpart, but it must be thought of as a **distinct, single sound** — not as the "hard consonant" **plus** a separate "y" sound (that is, **нет** is not simply "n + yet").

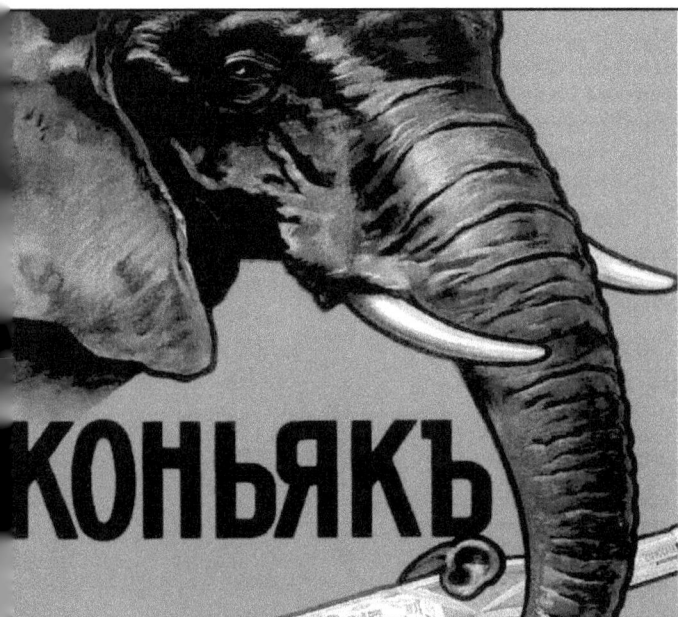

The orthographical reform of 1918

In the wake of the Bolshevik Revolution, the following four letters were eliminated from the official alphabet.

Ѣ ѣ	called **ять**; pronounced like **е**
I i	pronounced like **и**
Ѳ ѳ	pronounced like **ф**
V v	pronounced like **и**

As we noted above, the hard sign (**ъ**) was also written much more frequently. To the left, we have an Imperial-era advertisement for **коньякъ** (cognac / brandy); today, this word would be written **коньяк**. That is, we continue to write the soft sign to mark the **н** as soft,[3] but we simply **assume that the final к is hard**, and don't write the hard sign.

Nowadays, you may on occasion see such archaic orthography in stylized "old-fashioned" store signs and the like (something along the lines of the English "Ye Olde Shoppe," etc.). One good example is the name of a leading daily newspaper: **Коммерс<u>а</u>нтъ**, which often refers to itself as "**ъ**" for short in its articles.

---

[1] The term "mat" refers to the worst Russian obscenities. For a detailed look, consult my book *Cursing in Russian with Lenin*.
[2] Pardon my crudity, but this mistaken placement of stress is extremely common among students! Do avoid embarrassing yourself!
[3] In fact, this word involves a **soft consonant** (нь) followed by a **soft vowel**. We'll discuss this combination tomorrow; it is relatively rare.

1.7 Consonants

Some Russian consonants can be grouped into pairs of "voiced" and "unvoiced" consonants. If a consonant is **voiced**, it means that your **vocal cords** must be **vibrating** in order to pronounce it. When pronouncing its **unvoiced** counterpart, they'll remain **motionless**.

As we learn the consonants and read the examples below, notice that **final voiced consonants** in Russian are **devoiced**— that is, they are pronounced as their unvoiced counterpart (for example: **народ** is pronounced **нарот**). We'll discuss this in detail in tomorrow's lesson.

в → ф   з → с   ж → ш
б → п   г → к   д → т

К к	k
like "k" in kit (no aspiration/breath)	
кот	cat (m)
кошка	cat (f)
кто?	who?
комната	room
книга	book
кольцо	ring
кухня	kitchen
квартира	apartment

М м	m
like "m" in mother	
Москва	Moscow
музыка	music
мобильник	cell phone[1]
место	place
машина	car
мир	world
ум	intellect
проблема	problem

Т т	t
like "t" (tongue against upper teeth)	
театр	theater
студент	student
привет!	hi!
тарелка	plate
свет	light; world
анекдот	joke, story
автор	author
зонт	umbrella

Д д	d
like "d" (tongue against upper teeth)	
друг	friend (m)
подруга	friend (f)
дело	a matter
ладно!	ok, fine!
день	day
неделя	week
до свидания!	goodbye!
задача	task

Н н	n
like "n" (tongue against upper teeth)	
ноутбук	laptop
нет	no
новый	new (m)
неделя	week
напиток	beverage
вино	wine
народ	people
зонт	umbrella

Л л	l
like "l" (tongue against upper teeth)	
ладно!	ok, fine!
лекция	lecture
ложка	spoon
плохой	bad (m)
Ленинград	Leningrad
проблема	problem
журнал	magazine
начало	beginning

В в	v
like English "v"	
вот	here is...
вид	view
вопрос	question
вода	water
водка	vodka
привет!	hi!
век	century
вечер	evening

Б б	b
like English "b"	
большой	big (m)
большая	big (f)
большое	big (n)
билет	ticket
будильник	alarm clock
блог	blog
дуб	oak tree
бельё	laundry

Г г	g
like "g" in game	
группа	group
город	city
герой	hero
блогер	blogger
глупый	stupid (m)
глупая	stupid (f)
книга	book
магазин	store

З з	z
like English "z"	
занятие	class
золото	gold
газ	gas
знать	to know
знаю	I know
газета	newspaper
закуска	snack
зонт	umbrella

П п	p
like English "p"	
папа	dad, papa
проблема	problem
профессор	professor
плохой	bad (m)
поле	field
пиво	beer
поэзия	poetry
группа	group

Р р	r
trilled "r" (tongue should flap against teeth, as with "tt" in English "better")[2]	
работа	work
роман	novel
рюкзак	backpack
Россия	Russia
театр	theater
рубль	rouble
картина	picture
брат	brother

С с	s
like "s" (_never_ like English "k"!)	
спорт	sports
студент	student (m)
студентка	student (f)
семестр	semester
писать	to write
писатель	writer
союз	union
сестра	sister

Ф ф	f
like English "f"	
футбол	soccer
философия	philosophy
флаг	flag
физика	physics
фраза	phrase
Франция	France
фильм	a movie
телефон	telephone

[1] A colloquial term for **мобильный телефон**. You may also hear the adjective alone (**мобильный**), or simply **телефон**.
[2] If you can't produce a trilled or "rolled" r, this may take a lot of practice — you might try consulting YouTube for tips.

X x	kh	Ж ж	zh	Ц ц	ts	Ч ч	ch

like German "ch" in Bach (this sound should help clear your throat!)	like "s" in "measure" or "pleasure"	like English "ts" as in "cats" (but think of it as a single letter and a single sound!)	like "ch" in "chair"

хорошо!	good!	журнал	magazine	царь	tsar	читать	to read
плохо!	bad!	журналист	journalist	полотенце	towel	ручка	pen
хороший	good (m)	журнализм	journalism	страница	page	начало	beginning
хорошая	good (f)	жаль!	what a pity!	солнце	sun	учебник	textbook
хорошее	good (n)	жук	beetle	месяц	month		
хостел	hostel	жить	to live	конец	end		
храм	church	живу	I live	сердце	heart		
кухня	kitchen	гараж	garage	отец	father		
запах	a smell	нож	knife	лекция	lecture		

like "ш" (sh) in these common words

что?	what?
конечно!	of course!

Ш ш	sh	Щ щ	shch

like "sh" in shoot (with tongue further back)	a double-length[1] "sh" as in "sheet" (with tongue further forward)

шутка	a joke	борщ	borshch
шутить	to joke	щенок	puppy
шутник	a joker	ещё	still
машина	car	товарищ	comrade
карандаш	pencil		
кошка	cat		
большой	big (m)		
большая	big (f)		
большое	big (n)		

the combination "сч" is typically pronounced like "щ"

счастье	happiness
счастливо!	take it easy!

Now that we've been through all the letters, go back and practice each word again. Of course, working with a native speaker would also be a great idea, if possible. But keep in mind: developing good pronunciation *will take time*.

At this point, having a good feel for each letter's basic sound is sufficient; tomorrow we'll look more closely at some important subtleties of pronunciation, particularly those which cause certain letters to be pronounced somewhat differently from what we'd expect based on today's lesson.

See page 15 for the entire alphabet, in order!

ПЕРВЫЙ ПАССАЖИР СПУТНИКА - СОБАКА „ЛАЙКА"

What's the Russian for bow-wow?

Ever wondered what animals say in Russia? Ask and answer, using the following model:

— Что говорит **кошка**?   — What does a cat say?
— **Кошка** говорит "**мяу-мяу**"!   — A cat says "meow!"

1. кошка (cat):   "мяу-мяу"
2. собака (dog):   "гав-гав"
3. лягушка (frog):   "ква-ква"
4. петух (rooster):   "ку-ка-ре-ку"
5. свинья (pig):   "хрю-хрю"
6. корова (cow):   "му-му"
7. лошадь (horse):   "и-го-го"

Первый пассажир спутника — собака "Лайка"
The first satellite passenger (literally, "passenger of a satellite") — "Laika" the dog.

The name **Лайка** is related to the verb **лаять** (to bark) and the noun **лай** (barking). So, its literal meaning is something like "barker!"

[1] That is, this sound should be held for roughly twice as long as a normal consonant; this is the key to pronouncing it properly. This is unusual for Russian, which doesn't feature long or "double" consonants as a regular feature of its phonetics (as, say, Hungarian does). Where double consonants do occur, you may notice a slight lengthening (as in **группа**: group), but this rarely occurs, and usually in borrowed words.

day 2: pronunciation in detail

more on vowel purity, stress, vowel reduction, and
devoicing and softening of consonants

Книги! Books! (detail from a very famous 1924 poster by **Александр Родченко**.

2.1 Five keys to good Russian pronunciation

Now that we have a general feel for the Russian alphabet, let's revisit some of the points we introduced yesterday in greater detail. We will focus on five features of Russian phonetics that are essential for good pronunciation: 1) vowel **purity**; 2) **stress**; 3) vowel **reduction**; 4) consonant **devoicing**; and 5) consonant **softening**.

2.2 Vowel purity

Russian vowels are "**pure,**" in the sense that they consist of **one sound only.** To avoid contaminating this pure sound with another, we must **avoid moving** any part of our mouth while pronouncing a given Russian vowel.

Take particular care when pronouncing the Russian vowels **y** (like the "oo" in "hoo!") and **o** (like the "o" in **more**), as English speakers tend to have the most trouble maintaining purity in these two vowels.[1] For an exaggerated example, say "**Ewww, gross!**" as obnoxiously as you can.[2] Listen carefully to the sounds you actually produce; if you pronounce a Russian **y** or **o** in this "impure" fashion (even the slightest bit!), it will grate on a Russian ear!

ну well...	**живу** I live	**кто** who	**урок** lesson
ручка pen	**университет** university	**метро** subway	**всё** everything

2.3 Stress

In English, stress is relatively **weak**. Even native speakers can have trouble pinning it down, since longer words may have both primary and secondary stress. For example, where's the stress in the English word **independent**?

In Russian, stress is **strong** and unambiguous, and falls on **one syllable only** in any given word. This textbook will mark a stressed syllable by **underlining** its vowel. Note that Russian words typically have as many syllables as they have vowels. There are **no silent vowels** in Russian! For example, **ударение** ("stress") has 5 vowels and 5 syllables: **у-да-ре-ни-е**. The underlined vowel tells us that, in this word, the **third syllable** is stressed.

If a word has only **one syllable**, it usually won't be marked for stress in this textbook.

---

[1] This feature of certain English vowels — which you have probably never noticed — is called "offglide."
[2] That is, compare "ewww!" to Russian "y" and the "o" in "gross!" to Russian "o." If your Russian "y" or "o" sounds anything like these English examples, you will sound almost as silly to a Russian as this somewhat ridiculous English example suggests.

Without question, knowing **where the stress falls** in Russian words presents one of the language's greatest challenges for learners. In our textbook, stress will be **marked**, but in "real" Russian, it isn't! It can be tempting to try to evade this difficulty by giving each syllable roughly equal emphasis and hoping no one will notice. But this is **always incorrect**, and ultimately disastrous for proper pronunciation! Better to stress the wrong syllable occasionally as you're learning Russian than to overlook this principle altogether. By the way: being able to hear and pronounce stress is essential for appreciating Russian poetry, as we'll begin to learn in Book 2.

As you practice, try "getting physical" when reading or speaking: nod your head or pump your first as you "hit" the stressed syllable — whatever it takes to bring out a little more "umph."[1] Try it with these words:

гру́ппа group   **студе́нт** student   **маши́на** car   **университе́т** university

One way to practice stress

One easy exercise for understanding how stress affects pronunciation is to imagine how a word would sound if the stress fell on another syllable. Mispronounce it in every possible way, and notice the difference!

Incorrect: **у́ниверситет   уни́верситет,**
                        универси́тет   универ́ситет

Correct: **университе́т**

As we'll see next, **stress** and **vowel reduction** are closely linked. This means that stressing the wrong syllable can cause a kind of cascading breakdown in the pronunciation of a given word!

Ста́нция метро́ "Университе́т" (the "University" subway station in Moscow)

2.4   Vowel reduction

Four Russian vowels (**о, а, е, я**)[2] are pronounced differently ("reduced" to other vowel sounds) when they are **unstressed**; how they are pronounced depends on where they are **relative to the stressed syllable**. Remember, the transcriptions used here ("ah," "oh," "uh," etc.) are rough approximations, provided for convenience only!

Here are some examples of words containing each vowel, broken down by syllable. Note each vowel's position relative to the **stressed** syllable (in **black**). At first, this may seem like a lot to think about every time you say a word! In time, though, you will come to reduce vowels more intuitively. Just continue to keep in mind: just because we see an "o" on the page, for example, we will not necessarily pronounce a pure "o" sound!

А а			"ah"	"ah"			
	"uh"	"uh"			"uh"	"uh"	
1. **да** (yes):				да			= **dah**
2. **фра́за** (phrase):				фра	за		= **frah**-zuh
3. **страна́** (country):			стра	на			= strah-**nah**
4. **Кана́да** (Canada):			Ка	на	да		= Kah-**nah**-duh
5. **каранда́ш** (a pencil):		ка	ран	даш			= kuh-rahn-**dahsh**

О о			"ah"	"oh"			
	"uh"	"uh"			"uh"	"uh"	
1. **кот** (cat):				кот			= **koht**
2. **го́род** (city):				го	род		= **goh**-ruht
3. **зо́лото** (gold):				зо	ло	то	= **zoh**-luh-tuh
4. **кольцо́** (ring):			коль	цо			= kahl'-**tsoh**
5. **пло́хо** (bad, badly):				пло	хо		= **ploh**-khuh
6. **хорошо́** (good, well):		хо	ро	шо			= khuh-rah-**shoh**

---

[1] This may sound silly, but it can be a huge help. When it comes to Russian stress, it's very hard to "overdo" it.

[2] The vowel **и** may be reduced somewhat from the "ee" in "feet" to the short "i" in "sit" when unstressed, but this tends to happen naturally and doesn't require the same attention as the four examples examined here.

Е е

word	"yih" (initial unstressed)	"ih"	"ih"	"yeh" (stressed)	"ih"	"yeh" (final position)	
1. **нет** (no):				н**е**т			= **nyeht**
2. **медведь** (bear):			мед	в**е**дь			= mihd-**vyeht'**
3. **о медведе** (about the bear):			мед	в**е**		де	= ah mihd-**vyeh**-dye
4. **лебедь** (swan):				л**е**	бедь		= **lyeh**-biht'
5. **о лебеде** (about the swan):				л**е**	бе	де	= ah **lyeh**-bih-dye
6. **о серебре** (about silver):		се	ре	бр**е**			= ah sih-rih-**bryeh**
7. **о еде** (about food)	е			д**е**			= ah yih-**dyeh**

Я я

word	"yih" (initial unstressed)		"yah" (stressed)	"ih"		"yuh" (final position)	
1. **ряд** (row):			р**я**д				= **ryaht**
2. **дядя** (uncle):			д**я**			дя	= **dyah**-dyuh
3. **Яп<u>о</u>ния** (Japan):	Я		п**о**	ни		я	= Yih-**poh**-ni-yuh
4. **серебряная** (silver, f):		се	р**е**	бря	на	я	= sih-**ryeh**-brih-nuh-yuh

Try these examples.[1] Focus on vowel reduction (you may also notice examples of devoicing of consonants).

он	ohn	**карандаш**	kuh-rahn-**dahsh**	**п<u>о</u>ле**	**poh**-lyeh
он<u>а</u>	ah-**nah**	**к<u>о</u>шка**	**kohsh**-kuh	**Евр<u>о</u>па**	yih-**vroh**-puh
отв<u>е</u>т	aht-**vyeht**	**соб<u>а</u>ка**	sah-**bah**-kuh	**ед<u>а</u>**	yih-**dah**
д<u>е</u>ло	**dyeh**-luh	**раб<u>о</u>та**	rah-**boh**-tuh	**нед<u>е</u>ля**	nih-**dyeh**-lyuh
г<u>о</u>род	**goh**-ruht	**пл<u>о</u>хо**	**ploh**-khuh	**ещё**	yih-**shchoh**
з<u>о</u>лото	**zoh**-luh-tuh	**л<u>а</u>дно**	**lahd**-nuh	**философ<u>и</u>я**	fih-lah-**soh**-fi-yuh
золот<u>о</u>й	zuh-lah-**toy**	**хорош<u>о</u>**	khuh-rah-**shoh**	**Росс<u>и</u>я**	Rah-**si**-yuh
сов<u>е</u>тский	sah-**vyeht**-ski	**медв<u>е</u>дь**	mihd-**vyet'**	**Яп<u>о</u>ния**	Yih-**poh**-ni-yuh
больш<u>о</u>й	bahl'-**shoy**	**леб<u>е</u>дь**	**lyeh**-biht'	**в Петерб<u>у</u>рге**	f Pih-tihr-**bur**-gyeh[2]

2.5 Voiced and unvoiced consonants

Recall from yesterday's lesson the **pairs** of unvoiced/voiced consonants below. The two consonants in a given pair are formed similarly — the only difference is that the vocal cords **vibrate** when we pronounce the first (**voiced**) consonant, but not when we pronounce the second (**unvoiced**) consonant. Press a finger against your neck, near your voicebox: you should feel a slight vibration (buzzing) when pronouncing a voiced consonant.

в — ф   з — с   ж — ш   б — п   г — к   д — т

2.6 Devoicing of final consonants

Devoicing is most noticeable at the end of Russian words: if a **final consonant** (that is, a consonant that is the final letter in the word) is itself a **voiced** consonant, it will actually be pronounced as its **devoiced** counterpart.

лев → say: "леф"	lion	**ёж** → "ёш"	hedgehog	**сад** → "сат"	garden
газ → "гас"	gas	**дуб** → "дуп"	oak tree	**блог** → "блок"	blog

The "soft" versions of these voiced consonants are also devoiced at the end of words:

кровь → "крофь"	blood	**ложь** → "лош"[3]	falsehood	**медв<u>е</u>дь** → "медв<u>е</u>ть"	bear
грязь → "грясь"	filth	**рябь** → "ряпь"	ripple		

[1] It must be said that the proper reduction of "**а**" and "**о**" is much more noticeable and important than that of "**е**" and "**я**."
[2] The degree of reduction in longer words like **Петербург**, **карандаш**, etc. may vary slightly, but that need not concern beginners!
[3] The letter **ш** is considered inherently hard; since there is no "soft" version, a soft sign does not affect its pronunciation (see p. 11).

2.7 Devoicing (and voicing) in consonant clusters

In consonant clusters, an initial consonant will **assimilate** (that is, become similar) to the consonant that follows. That is, if a **voiced** consonant is followed by an **unvoiced** consonant, then the former is also **devoiced**:

в → ф	з → с	ж → ш	б → п	г → к	д → т

автор → "афтор"	author	**ложка** → "лошка"	spoon	**ногти** → "нокти"	fingernails
сказка → "скаска"	fairy tale	**общество** → "опщество"	society	**водка** → "вотка"	vodka

Likewise, three **unvoiced** consonants become **voiced** when followed by these voiced consonants: **б г д ж з**.[1]

с → з	т → д	к → г

сдача → "здача" change[2]	**футбол** → "фудбол" soccer	**вокзал** → "вогзал" train station

Try some more words — and don't forget to keep both **vowel reduction** and **consonant devoicing** in mind! Again, the transcriptions provided are for convenience only — don't rely on them entirely!

город	**goh**-ruht	city	**ёж**	yohsh	hedgehog
Петербург	Peh-tihr-**burk**	Petersburg	**нож**	nohsh	knife
союз	sah-**yus**	union	**лев**	lyehf	lion
дуб	dup	oak tree	**газ**	gahs	gas
ряд	ryaht	row	**медведь**	mihd-**vyet'**	bear
сад	saht	garden	**лебедь**	**lyeh**-biht'	swan
Чехов	**Cheh**-khuhf	Chekhov	**ложь**	losh'	falsehood, lie
народ	nah-**roht**	people, nation	**ложка**	**lohsh**-kuh	spoon
вид	vit	view	**автор**	**ahf**-tuhr	author
водка	**voht**-kuh	vodka	**сказка**	**skahs**-kuh	fairy tale
лёд	lyoht	ice	**вокзал**	vahg-**zahl**	train station
снег	snyehk	snow	**сдача**	**zdah**-chuh	change[2]

2.8 Soft consonants (palatalization)

Soft consonants are difficult for English speakers, because English doesn't really have them. So, for example, a **hard** Russian "н" is no problem to pronounce; it's just like an ordinary English "n." A **soft** Russian "н," however, is a very different story. Realize that when you go to pronounce a **soft** Russian consonant, every bone in your body will be longing to pronounce a **hard** consonant instead, of the sort you're used to hearing and saying.

A detailed look at softness

The word **нет** begins with **н**. The following soft vowel, **е**, tells us that the **н** is soft. We might unpack this a bit as follows: **нь + (й) + эт**. That is, [soft **н**] + [й] + [the vowel **э**]. The role of **й** here can lead to misunderstandings, especially regarding the nature of softness. It's as if the **й** is lurking in between the **soft consonant** (pronounced with our tongue in the **и/й position**) and the soft vowel **е** (which we could break down into **й + э**). Depending on how emphatically "**Нет!**" is said, the **й** sound itself may be more or less noticeable. If someone's being extremely emphatic, we may even hear an **и** — something like "**Ни-ет!**" In any case, note well: **the н is soft!**

But regardless of how prominent this "**й**" may or may not be, we can say very clearly: a soft "**н**" is **not** simply **[hard "н"] + [й]**, as might be suggested by the English transliteration "nyet." If we simply pronounce a hard English "n," then follow it with a "y" sound, we won't pronounce the Russian word properly. We must fully palatalize (soften) the consonant itself. To put it another way, **soft н** (or "**нь**") is a distinct sound that can't be produced by "**combining**" other sounds. Remember: **tongue position** is the key.

It's sometimes said that a soft "**н**" is like the "n" in the English "**canyon**" or "**onion**." Well, yes and no. While *some* softening is all but inevitable (thanks to the following "y" sound), these English "n's" are certainly not softened to the degree that a true Russian soft "**н**" is.

НЕТ!

[1] Here too, it must be said that: 1) devoicing of final consonants is very noticable and very important, while 2) devoicing in clusters is less somewhat less important for beginners, and 3) voicing in clusters is quite unusual and therefore even less important for beginners.
[2] As in, getting change at the cash register.

Listen carefully for the difference in the following pairs of hard and soft consonants, and remember that the key to pronouncing soft consonants properly is to <u>keep the tongue in the **й/и** position</u>,[1] moving it just enough to pronounce the given consonant without first allowing the tongue to lazily "**drop**" down from its palatalized position. With some practice, you'll be able to both hear and pronounce soft consonants more clearly.

Remember: according to spelling conventions, a consonant is **soft** when followed by: **и, е, ё, ю, я** or **ь**.
Also, continue to **watch out for devoicing**. For example, the final **д** in **сад** will actually be pronounced as **т**.

We'll begin with those soft sounds that are arguably the most conspicuous. Spend plenty of time practicing them!

Н		НЬ		Д		ДЬ	
ноутб<u>у</u>к	laptop	д<u>е</u>нь	day	сад	garden	д<u>е</u>нь	day
нар<u>о</u>д	people	ж<u>и</u>знь	life	нар<u>о</u>д	people	буд<u>и</u>льник	alarm clock
н<u>о</u>вый	new	нет	no	анекд<u>о</u>т	story	л<u>ю</u>ди	people
он	he	он<u>и</u>	they	л<u>а</u>дно	ok	студ<u>е</u>нт	student
студ<u>е</u>нт	student	Яп<u>о</u>ния	Japan	м<u>о</u>да	fashion	д<u>е</u>ло	matter

Т		ТЬ		Л		ЛЬ	
нет	no	мать	mother	л<u>а</u>дно	OK, fine!	рубль	rouble
прив<u>е</u>т	hi	пис<u>а</u>ть	to write	плох<u>о</u>й	bad	жаль!	what a pity!
анекд<u>о</u>т	funny story	смерть	death	ос<u>ё</u>л	donkey	л<u>ю</u>ди	people
з<u>о</u>лото	gold	<u>э</u>ти	these	журн<u>а</u>л	magazine	нед<u>е</u>ля	week
бил<u>е</u>т	ticket	т<u>ё</u>ща	mother-in-law	блог	blog	больш<u>о</u>й	big

С		СЬ	
р<u>у</u>сский	Russian	Русь	Rus'
сон	dream/sleep	<u>о</u>сень	fall
стих<u>и</u>	poetry	лос<u>о</u>сь	salmon
пис<u>а</u>ть	to write	м<u>е</u>сяц	month

Try these additional consonants as well; you may hear a more distinct "**й**" sound trailing the soft versions.

В		ВЬ		Б		БЬ	
лев	lion	люб<u>о</u>вь	love	уч<u>е</u>бник	textbook	рябь	ripple
вопр<u>о</u>с	question	сов<u>е</u>т	advice	дуб	oak	пр<u>о</u>рубь	hole cut in ice[2]
дав<u>а</u>й	ok, let's!	вид	view	боль	pain	бил<u>е</u>т	ticket

П		ПЬ		М		МЬ	
гр<u>у</u>ппа	group	пить	to drink	м<u>а</u>ма	mom	семь	seven
п<u>о</u>ле	field	п<u>и</u>во	beer	м<u>у</u>зыка	music	в<u>о</u>семь	eight
суп	soup	пять	five	ум	intellect	медв<u>е</u>дь	bear

Р		РЬ		З		ЗЬ	
<u>а</u>втор	author	слов<u>а</u>рь	dictionary	газ	author	зять	son-in-law
под<u>а</u>рок	present	царь	tsar	з<u>о</u>лото	gold	зим<u>а</u>	winter

NOTE: **ж**, **ш**, and **ц** are considered **hard** by definition, while **ч** and **щ** are considered **soft**.[3] So, a soft sign following these letters cannot affect the pronunciation. It is written by convention, and often serves as a kind of **visual marker** for certain noun types and verb endings. We'll get a better idea of what this means later. For now, note simply that there is **no difference in the pronunciation** of these final consonants, despite the difference in spelling:

Ч		ЧЬ		Ж		ЖЬ	
матч	match	ночь	night	нож	knife	ложь	falsehood

Ш		ШЬ		Щ		ЩЬ	
каранд<u>а</u>ш	pencil	мышь	mouse	борщ	borshch	вещь	thing
		чит<u>а</u>ешь	you read				

[1] One hears a lot of convoluted talk about pronouncing soft consonants. Ultimately, this tongue position is really all there is to it!
[2] For example, a hole for fishing (or swimming!) in winter.
[3] On a practical level, this is of little consequence. Note that other Slavic languages may still retain hard *and* soft versions of these sounds.

day 3:   more on pronunciation

special situations and exceptions to general rules of pronunciation;
practice with pronouncing our chapter vocabulary

3.1   Russian "e" is never silent!

We've already noted that Russian, unlike English, has **no silent vowels**, and that a Russian word therefore has **as many syllables as it has vowels**. English speakers are especially prone to treating Russian **e** as a silent vowel, since English "e" is often silent, as in "toe" or "site." But Russian "e" is **always pronounced** and always constitutes a full **syllable** — including at the **end of words**. Also remember: it begins with a "y" (**й**) sound!

п**о**ле field	м**о**ре sea	зан**я**тие activity	с**е**рдце heart[1]

3.2   Adjectival endings

As we'll soon learn, Russian adjectives **change their endings** depending on the grammatical **gender** of the noun they're modifying (masculine, feminine, or neuter). For now, pay special attention to their **pronunciation**, as some endings feature multiple vowels. Again: each vowel is a **full syllable**, and the "e" is **never silent**!

н**о**вый new (m)	ст**а**рый old (m)	хор**о**ший good (m)	плох**о**й bad (m)
н**о**вая new (f)	ст**а**рая old (f)	хор**о**шая good (f)	плох**а**я bad (f)
н**о**вое new (n)	ст**а**рое old (n)	хор**о**шее good (n)	плох**о**е bad (n)
больш**о**й big (m)	м**а**ленький small (m)	ск**у**чный boring (m)	лёгкий easy (m)
больш**а**я big (f)	м**а**ленькая small (f)	ск**у**чная boring (f)	лёгкая easy (f)
больш**о**е big (n)	м**а**ленькое small (n)	ск**у**чное boring (n)	лёгкое easy (n)

3.3   Russian "e" at the beginning of words

The soft vowels **я, ю, е, ё** begin with the sound **й**, especially at the beginning of words. In the case of "e" (and "ё"), this can take some getting used to. Take careful note of the difference between "**e**" and "**э**."

ещё still	ед**а** food	ёж hedgehog	экз**а**мен exam

[1] While **e** typically begins with a **й** sound, recall that after **ц** it is pronounced as **э**. Thus, **с**е**рдце** is pronounced "**с**е**рдц-э**"

3.4 Russian has no silent letters — except for the exceptions!

Not only does Russian have no silent vowels; we can also say, generally, that it has no silent consonants either. In this sense, Russian **spelling** is much more straightforward than English; with Russian, "what you see is what you get," as long as you allow for vowel reduction and consonant devoicing. Exceptions in which a letter is simply **not pronounced** at all are **extremely rare** in Russian. Here are a few common examples.

здравствуйте → say: "здраствуйте"	hello (no **в**)	**чувство** → "чуство"	feeling (no **в**)	**солнце** → "сонце"	sun (no **л**)
счастливый → "щасливый"	happy (no **т**)	**поздно** → "позно"	late (no **д**)	**пожалуйста** → "пожалста"	please (no **уй**)

3.5 Certain consonants can sound like others

You may have noticed that the word for "happy" — **счастливый** — sounded more like **щасливый**. The cluster **сч** is typically pronounced like a **щ**.

счастье → "щастье"	joy	**счастливый** → "щасливый"	happy	**счёт** → "щёт"	bill

In these two extremely common words, the **ч** sounds like **ш**.

что → "што"	what?	**конечно** → "конешно"	of course

Finally, **г** sounds like **х** in front of **к** (as in the two adjectives below), and, often, when final in the word **Бог** (God).

лёгкий → "лёхкий"	light, easy	**мягкий** → "мяхкий"	soft	**Бог** → "Бох"	God

Слушай, говорит Москва!
Listen, Moscow speaking!

3.6 Syllabic consonants

In general, Russian must have a **vowel** in order to have a **syllable**. Take, for example, **собака** (dog): со-ба-ка = three syllables). Some Slavic languages (Czech and Serbian, for example) feature certain **syllabic consonants** that can themselves constitute a syllable when pronounced: to produce this syllable, an almost unnoticeable vowel sound ("uh") is inserted in front of the syllabic consonant.[1]

Strictly speaking (e.g. for purposes of counting syllables in poetry), Russian does **not** have such syllabic consonants, but in everyday pronunciation some letters may sound much **like full syllables** at the **end** of words.

театр "te-ah-t(uh)r"	theater	**рубль** "ru-b(uh)l'"	rouble	**жизнь** "zhi-z(uh)n'"	life
семестр "se-mes-t(uh)r"	semester	**Кремль** "Kre-m(uh)l'"	Kremlin	**коммунизм** "kom-mun-i-z(uh)m"	Communism

3.7 Difficult consonant clusters

Aside from the examples we've just seen, we must resist the urge to insert even the slightest vowel sound in order to break up consonant clusters that may strike us as difficult (if not impossible!) to pronounce otherwise. Fortunately, it must be said that the clusters found in Russian are not too hard, if we just practice a bit.[2]

птица	bird	**мгла**	fog, mist	**тьма**	darkness
взгляд	gaze	**ткань**	fabric	**ртуть**	mercury

[1] Note four such examples in the famously "vowel-less" Czech phrase, "**Strč prst skrz krk!**" (Stick your finger through your throat).
[2] If you think these are hard, compare them, for example, to Georgian clusters, as in: გვფრცქვნი (gvprtskvni): "you peel us" (!)

3.8 Soft consonants *plus* soft vowels

Let's look at one final (and relatively infrequent) combination that causes lingering confusion for many students: words in which a **soft consonant** (marked with the **soft sign** "ь") is directly followed by a **soft vowel**. This is pronounced as written — with what one might call "double softness."

So, first pronounce the **soft consonant**, then, as a **separate sound**, pronounce the **soft vowel**, beginning with the **й** sound. For beginners, it may help to **pause**, ever so slightly, after the **soft consonant** in order to "reset" and "start over" with a fully-fledged **soft vowel**. To take the first example below: *first* say "**ть**" and *then* say "**е**."

It's very important to note that the **soft sign** here is not merely ornamental or superfluous — this spelling is necessary to capture the actual pronunciation of the word. These words would indeed be **pronounced differently** if the soft sign weren't there, as shown below. Still, it can be very difficult for beginners to hear this distinction!

счастье	joy	= "щасть + е"	(not simply "щасте")
платье	dress	= "плать + е"	(not simply "плате")
семья	family	= "семь + я"	(not simply "семя")
статья	article	= "стать + я"	(not simply "статя")
скамья	bench	= "скамь + я"	(not simply "скамя")

Why does this often confuse learners? In short, since they know that soft vowels like "е" and "я" mark a preceding consonant as soft, they think that the "ь" must be superfluous. But it's not! The combination -**тье** is different from -**те**.[1]

3.9 Practice pronouncing this chapter's vocabulary

For more practice, let's look at this chapter's vocabulary, beginning with nouns. As we do so, we'll preview the concept of **grammatical gender**. Generally, we can determine a Russian noun's gender by looking at its **ending**.

Let's begin with **feminine** nouns. **Hard** feminine nouns end in -**а**, while **soft** feminine nouns end in -**я**.

книга	book	**проблема**	problem	**футболка**	t-shirt	**страница**	page
комната	room	**задача**	problem[2]	**этажерка**	bookshelf	**газета**	newspaper
одежда	clothes	**ручка**	pen	**машина**	car	**сумка**	purse
работа	work	**лампа**	lamp	**передача**	TV show	**тема**	topic
картина	picture	**рубашка**	shirt	**ошибка**	mistake		
идея	idea	**простыня**	bedsheet	**фотография**	photo	**фамилия**	last name
неделя	week	**статья**	article	**история**	story	**семья**	family

Next come **neuter** nouns. **Hard** neuter nouns end in -**о**, while **soft** neuter nouns end in -**е** (sometimes -**ё**).

дело	matter	**зеркало**	mirror	**одеяло**	blanket	**пальто**	coat
окно	window	**кресло**	easy chair	**мыло**	soap	**кино**	cinema
место	place	**письмо**	letter	**утро**	morning	**имя**	first name[3]
платье	dress	**бельё**	laundry	**упражнение**	exercise (in textbook)		
полотенце	towel	**расписание**	schedule	**задание**	assignment		

Finally, we have **masculine** nouns, which, strictly speaking, have **no ending** (also called "zero ending"). More practically, we might say that they end in a **consonant**: hard masculines end in a **hard** consonant, while soft masculines end in a **soft** consonant (with ь). Some **soft** masculines end in **й** (which, remember, is a **consonant**).

стол	table	**телевизор**	television	**мяч**	ball	**фильм**	film, a movie
стул	chair	**плакат**	poster	**ключ**	key	**журнал**	magazine
велосипед	bicycle	**карандаш**	pencil	**вечер**	evening	**вопрос**	question
телефон	phone	**рюкзак**	backpack	**зонт**	umbrella	**ответ**	answer
компьютер	computer	**ковёр**	carpet	**сериал**	TV series	**кошелёк**	wallet
шампунь	shampoo	**день**	day	**кафетерий**	cafeteria	*Another term for "cafeteria"*	
словарь	dictionary	**музей**	museum			*is the feminine* **столовая.**	

---

[1] Note that it can be all but impossible for beginners to hear this difference, especially if people are speaking at normal speed.

[2] **задача** refers to an assignment or task — for example, a math or physics problem. Otherwise, the word for "problem" is **проблема**.

[3] A special group of neuters end in -**мя**. This group is small in number; we'll discuss their unusual declension pattern on Day 162.

Now, let's practice some of this chapter's **adjectives**, in all three **grammatical genders**. Watch those endings!

masculine	feminine	neuter	
но́вый	но́вая	но́вое	new
ста́рый	ста́рая	ста́рое	old
чи́стый	чи́стая	чи́стое	clean
гря́зный	гря́зная	гря́зное	dirty
дорого́й	дорога́я	дорого́е	expensive
дешёвый	дешёвая	дешёвое	cheap
тру́дный	тру́дная	тру́дное	difficult
лёгкий	лёгкая	лёгкое	easy, light

masculine	feminine	neuter	
плохо́й	плоха́я	плохо́е	bad
хоро́ший	хоро́шая	хоро́шее	good
большо́й	больша́я	большо́е	big
ма́ленький	ма́ленькая	ма́ленькое	small
ва́жный	ва́жная	ва́жное	important
люби́мый	люби́мая	люби́мое	favorite
ужа́сный	ужа́сная	ужа́сное	horrible
ру́сский	ру́сская	ру́сское	Russian

3.10 The alphabet

Here is the full Russian alphabet, in alphabetical order. Pronouncing the letters themselves is easy enough — just add a vowel to the consonants (usually **э**, but note the **а** in **ка, ха, ша, ща**. Three letters — **й** and the hard and soft signs — are referred to by name (the Russian for "short **и**," "hard sign," and "soft sign," respectively).

Аа	Бб	Вв	Гг	Дд	Ее	Ёё	Жж	Зз	Ии	Йй
"а"	"бэ"	"вэ"	"гэ"	"дэ"	"е"	"ё"	"жэ"	"зэ"	"и"	"и краткое"

Кк	Лл	Мм	Нн	Оо	Пп	Рр	Сс	Тт	Уу	Фф
"ка"	"эл"	"эм"	"эн"	"о"	"пэ"	"эр"	"эс"	"тэ"	"у"	"эф"[1]

Хх	Цц	Чч	Шш	Щщ	Ъъ	Ыы	Ьь	Ээ	Юю	Яя
"ха"	"це"	"че"	"ша"	"ща"	"твёрдый знак"	"ы"	"мягкий знак"	"э"	"ю"	"я"

Pronouncing acronyms

Just for fun, here are a few important acronyms, many of them from Soviet history. Most are pronounced letter-by-letter, but a few are pronounced almost as if they were ordinary words.

СССР	"эс-эс-эс-эр"	The USSR, Сою́з Сове́тских Социалисти́ческих Респу́блик
КПСС	"ка-пэ-эс-эс"	Коммунисти́ческая па́ртия Сове́тского Сою́за
ЧК	"че-ка́"	The "Cheka," Чрезвыча́йная коми́ссия
НКВД	"эн-ка-вэ-дэ́"	The NKVD, Наро́дный комиссариа́т вну́тренних дел
КГБ	"ка-гэ-бэ́"	The KGB, or Комите́т госуда́рственной безопа́сности
ФСБ	"фэ-эс-бэ́"	The FSB, Федера́льная слу́жба безопа́сности
ГУЛаг	"гу-ла́г"	The GULAG, Гла́вное управле́ние лагере́й
США	"сэ-шэ-а́"[2]	The USA, Соединённые Шта́ты Аме́рики
НАТО	"на́-то"	NATO (the Russian acronym is adopted from the English)
ООН	"о-о́н"	The UN, Организа́ция Объединённых На́ций
МИД	"мид"	Ministry of Foriegn Affairs, Министе́рство иностра́нных дел
ГАИ	"га-и́"	State Auto Inspectorate, Госуда́рственная автоинспе́кция
ВДНХ	"вэ-дэ-эн-ха́"	The VDNKh, a Soviet-era exhibition park in Moscow

[1] "**фэ**" is also heard   [2] Typically sounds more like **сэ-ша** when said quickly, in everyday speech.

day 4: handwriting

the Russian cursive alphabet; general handwriting principles;
forming "tails," "hooks" and "humps"; examples to practice

Неграмотный ребёнок — позор для матери. An illiterate child is a disgrace for a mother. An unenlightened mother is trying to prevent her child from going to school!

4.1 Russian cursive script

Cursive is commonly used in Russia (more so than in the United States, at least), so it's very important to learn how to write and read this script. The best way to learn is simply to dive in and practice writing out words — then check your work to be sure you're minding the few tricky details mentioned below (connections, "hooks," etc.).

Of course, you'll encounter **variations** on the models shown on the next page — and, in time, you'll also develop your own inimitable style! The "rules" emphasized here are those that, if violated, can seriously **affect legibility**.

Although **stress** will be marked in this textbook, don't include stress marks in your written work, unless specifically asked to as part of an exercise.[1] Ordinarily, Russians would never include stress marks in their writing![2]

4.2 Write each word continuously

The basic principle of cursive is to write each word in **one continuous stroke**, to whatever extent possible. Most (but not all!) letters will be connected. So, write out the **body** of the word first, then lift your pen and go back to **"dot your i's and cross your t's."** In Russian, this final step may involve the following:

1) Adding the "**hat**" to the letter **й**.

2) Adding the **cross-stroke** to the letter **х**— which initially looks much like a Russian **г**.

3) Optionally, you can add an **understroke** beneath the letter **ш** and an **overstroke** above the letter **т**.

война → война война (war)
плохо → плохо плохо (bad)
шутка → шутка шутка (joke)

The additional strokes mentioned in item 3 can help to further distinguish these letters visually from such letters as **и** and **п**, especially when several such letters occur together (for example, try writing out the word **шишка**: pinecone). However, not all Russians add them; ultimately, it's a matter of preference. But they are strongly recommended for students — especially with **ш**, if only to differentiate it from **щ** (which <u>never</u> has this understroke!).

16
[1] Many instructors expect students to always mark stress, for learning purposes. Personally, I find that this can become a very bad habit!
[2] In rare cases when stress *is* marked, this is done with an accent mark, as in "á." This book has opted for the "underlining" technique, which strikes me as somehow less intrusive — especially since Russian lacks the diacritical marks found in, say, Czech.

4.3 Notes on connecting letters

If a letter requires more than two strokes to write (this is true of many capital letters, and may be true of lower-case **к**, depending on how you write it), then of course you'll have to pick up your pen. Otherwise, strive to **connect** any letters that flow together **naturally**. Possible points of connection are indicated by the **dotted lines** in the chart below. Note which letters **can** connect to preceding or following letters — and, if so, **where**.

If there is **no dotted line** on a given side, this means that the given letter can't connect at all there. For example, **э** never connects, on either side. Nor do many upper case letters, like **Б**, **В**, **Г**, **Д**, **З**, **О**, **Р**, **У**, **Э**, and **Ю**. Some letters never connect to **subsequent** letters. These include — very importantly! — **б** and the soft sign **ь**.

Certain combinations of letters simply can't connect "**naturally**." For example, if one letter ends up high (near the mid-line), and the following letter can only begin down low, from the baseline, then pick up your pen before beginning the next letter. This often happens with lower-case **о** (as in the combo **ол**). Imagine: if we tried to connect it to a following letter that begins at the baseline, the **о** might begin to resemble an **a**, affecting legibility.

In the example to the right, there should be no connection between the **б** and **о**, the **о** and **л**, and the **ь** and **ш**. Note how the **ь** comes to resemble an **ы** if we insist on connecting it to the following letter!

большой   *большой*
incorrect   correct

А а	Б б	В в	Г г	Д д
Е е	Ё ё	Ж ж	З з	И и
Й й	К к	Л л	М м	Н н
О о	П п	Р р	С с	Т т
У у	Ф ф	Х х	Ц ц	Ч ч
Ш ш	Щ щ	ъ	ы	ь Э э
Ю ю	Я я			

1	penstroke number
	penstroke direction
⋯	possible connection to adjacent letters
◯	note the important "hook" or "hump"

4.4 Forming the letter ж

This letter may take practice! Write it in **three strokes** (but without lifting your pen!); notice how the first and third strokes are "mirror images" of each other, separated by a single **straight line**.

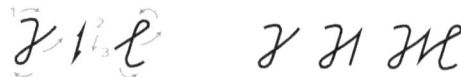

4.5 Minding the midline; forming "tails"; the Russian р

Note how many lower-case letters remain entirely confined to the **bottom half** of the frame — baseline to midline. In some cases this differentiates them from their English counterparts (note the Russian к in particular). Also, the soft sign ь MUST remain below the midline; otherwise, it may come to resemble lower-case в.

Note how the lower-case Russian р extends far below the baseline, and **remains open** at the bottom — unlike English р.

Finally, note that the "tails" on the letters ц and щ should be very short and compact; compare them to the letter у in particular.

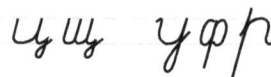

кольцо (ring):

 incorrect

кольцо correct

4.6 "Hooks" when joining л, м, or я to a preceding letter

This is one of the most important details to remember when writing Russian: the letters л, м, and я begin with a tiny **hook**, even when they are the first letter in a word. When they are **joined** to a preceding letter, the hook **must be preserved**. This hook is crucial for distinguishing these letters from other letters; since its absence can severely affect legibility, it is **not optional!**

Namely, if the hook is not apparent, then you'll find that your л will often resemble a г, your м will resemble an и or ч, and, finally, your я may even resemble an е, especially if written quickly.

Practice the examples on the upper right.

Meanwhile, as illustrated on the lower right, resist the urge to go overboard and add an **extra** stroke to the hook of an **initial** л, м or я (or one not connected to a preceding letter)

ладно (OK, fine): *ладно*

ум (mind): *ум*

жаль (it's a pity): *жаль*

грязь (dirt): *грязь*

яма (hole, pit): *яма*

мать (mother): *мать*

incorrect: *мать* *ладно* *роман*

correct: *мать* *ладно* *роман*

4.7 "Humps" when joining н, п, т, ж, and к (but not и, й, etc.)

Note how the lower-case letters н, п, т, ж and к connect to preceding letters via a kind of curved "hump," not via a sharp point as we see in such letters as и, й, ш, and щ.

Note how this results in a total of two "humps" for the completed letter п (which looks just like the English cursive n) and three humps for the completed letter т (which looks just like the English cursive m).

Students often confuse the cursive м and т.

Take a special look at Russian н, which is written in a single stroke, beginning with the "hump." The example to the right shows a couple of ways in which students sometimes write н. In these cases the result is not illegible, but can still look odd. So remember to include a curving "hump," just as for п or т.

папа (papa): *папа*

тут (here): *тут*

шум (noise): *шум*

они (they): *они*

роман (novel):

incorrect

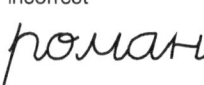

correct

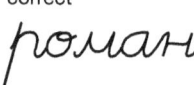

4.4 Some examples to practice

As you practice, be sure to refer to the chart to check that your connections are made correctly, and that you haven't missed any "hooks!" Also check your letters' position relative to the guidelines — e.g., check that a **к** and **л** doesn't extend above the midline, and that the tiny "tails" on your **ц** and **щ** don't extend very far below the baseline (not nearly as far as the tail on **у**).

When printed in italics using traditional "serif" typefaces, many print letters closely resemble the cursive forms we're practicing now (note in particular **т**)! For comparison's sake, each word below is also given in serif italics.

город city	*город*		**ложь** lie, falsehood	*ложь*	
фраза phrase	*фраза*		**поэзия** poetry	*поэзия*	
книга book	*книга*		**союз** union	*союз*	
стихи poetry	*стихи*		**язык** language	*язык*	
неделя week	*неделя*		**борщ** borshch	*борщ*	
сказка fairy tale	*сказка*		**кошка** cat	*кошка*	
большой big (masc.)	*большой*		**студент** student	*студент*	
журнал magazine	*журнал*		**читать** to read	*читать*	
конец end	*конец*		**сдача** change	*сдача*	
ёжик hedgehog	*ёжик*		**плохая** bad (fem.)	*плохая*	
Чехов	*Чехов*		**Толстой**	*Толстой*	
Франция	*Франция*		**Петербург**	*Петербург*	
Германия	*Германия*		**Москва**	*Москва*	
Россия	*Россия*		**Япония**	*Япония*	
Америка	*Америка*		**Пушкин**	*Пушкин*	

day 5: learning names and getting acquainted

Russian names; introductions; more handwriting practice;
overview of classroom Russian; introduction to word endings

До‍бро пожа‍ловать! Welcome! (to the new school year, that is)

5.1 Russian names

Anyone who's read a Russian novel probably knows that Russian names can be confusing: a given character may be referred to in any number of ways, depending on the situation. We'll have more to say about this, in time; for now, let's look at the basics. Full Russian names consist of: 1) a given name, **имя** (note: this word is *neuter*, even though it appears to be feminine!); 2) a patronymic, **отчество** (a name formed from the name of the person's **отец**, father); and 3) a last name, **фамилия**. Let's take two famous Russian poets as examples:

Алекса‍ндр Серге‍евич Пу‍шкин   the patronyimic **Серге‍евич** tells us that his father's **имя** was **Серге‍й**

А‍нна Андре‍евна Ахма‍това   the patronyimic **Андре‍евна** tells us that her father's **имя** was **Андре‍й**

In formal address, we would refer to these poets using **имя** + **отчество**, as in "**Алекса‍ндр Серге‍евич!**" But even if we were their close friends, we'd be unlikely to call them simply by their **имя**. We'd likely use a standard **short** form of the name, expressing familiarity: in this case, we'd say "**Са‍ша!**" instead of "**Алекса‍ндр!**" [1]

20   [1] We'll learn more examples of these short "friendly" names in a later lesson (Day 133). Note that these are not made-up nick-names; any traditional Russian first name will have a standard "friendly" form, along with one or more diminutive forms!

In direct address, these familiar forms are often shortened by dropping the final "a" vowel, as shown below. Truth be told, Russians today are somewhat more likely to refer to each other using the **full first name only** in semi-formal situations (in the workplace, for example), as old formalities give way to more casual practices.

Александр Сергеевич! (formal) →	**Александр!**	**Анна Андреевна!** (formal) →	**Анна!**
	Саша! Саш!		**Аня! Ань!**

However, one should always be prepared to **be polite** by addressing Russians (especially superiors at work, professors, or any older person you don't know well) using **both first name and patronymic!**

A brief history of titles in Russia

Students often ask: what's the Russian for "Mr." and "Ms?" The answer is a bit complicated, and has changed throughout history.

In Imperial days, there were a large number of honorific titles, based on the addressee's rank (**чин**) according to the infamous "Table of Ranks" (**Табель о рангах**) introduced by Peter the Great. For example, if you were in the 3rd or 4th grades of the bureaucracy, you had the privilege of being addressed as "**Ваше превосходительство**" (Your Excellency), but if you made your way to the 1st or 2nd grades, you became "**Ваше высокопревосходительство**" (Your High Excellency). You'll encounter many such tongue-twisting honorifics when you begin reading 19th-century literature (they are sometimes contracted to "**Вашество**" or even "**с**"[1]).

In Soviet times, "comrade" (**товарищ**) could be used with men and women; as a form of address, it is used today (if at all) with varying degrees of irony. Today, the Russian equivalents of "Mr." (**господин**) and "Ms." (**госпожа**) are fairly rare, but may be used in formal contexts, often to refer to someone in the third person ("**Господин Иванов сказал...**" (Mr. Ivanov said...), "**Госпожа Меркель сказала...**" (Ms. Merkel said...). By the way — "ladies and gentlemen" is "**Дамы и господа.**"

What about strangers? It's common to address men (waiters, for example) as "**молодой человек**" ("young man") and women (waitresses, for example) as "**девушка**" (girl, young lady). This may strike us as insulting, but it is perfectly normal in Russian! Generally, though, to get a stranger's attention, simply begin with "**Извините.**" There's no precise Russian equivalent of "Ma'am" or "Sir." You may hear unfamiliar (older) men and women referred to as "uncle" (**дядя**) or "aunt" (**тётя**) — but never as a form of address!

5.2   Introductions

Let's get to know our classmates with a short dialogue. We won't understand much of the grammar yet — but we will soon. For example, in Russian, **меня зовут** literally means "They call me..."

Unfortunately, the Russian for "hello" (**здравствуйте**) is one of the hardest words to pronounce! As we've seen, the first **в** is not pronounced at all. This word literally means "Be healthy!"

Tonight, as part of your homework, you'll learn how to spell your name in Russian. Note that this new spelling (and pronunciation!) will likely differ somewhat from the way you normally say your name in English. Russians will inevitably "Russify" your name, approximating it as best they can using native Russian sounds. Do your best to embrace your "new" Russian name. Don't fight it!

If your name has a standard Russian equivalent, such as **Николай** (**Коля**) for Nicholas (Nick), then you might choose to go with that!

„Товарищ, верь: взойдет она,
Звезда пленительного счастья,
Россия вспрянет ото сна,
И на обломках самовластья
Напишут наши имена!"
— А. С. ПУШКИН

Здравствуйте!	Hello!
Давайте познакомимся!	Let's get acquainted!
Меня зовут _____.	"They call me_____." [2]
А как вас зовут?	"How do they call you?"
Меня зовут _____.	"They call me_____."
Очень приятно познакомиться.	Very nice to get acquainted.
А как ваша фамилия?	And what's your last name?
Моя фамилия _____.	My last name is _____.
А ваша?	And yours?
Моя фамилия _____.	My last name is _____.

Товарищ, верь: взойдёт она,
Звезда пленительного счастья,
Россия вспрянет ото сна,
И на обломках самовластья,
Напишут наши имена.

Comrade,[3] believe: it will rise,
The star of captivating joy;
Russia will awaken from its slumber,
And on the rubble of autocracy,
They will write our names.

from "К Чаадаеву" (To Chaadaev), by А. С. Пушкин, 1818.

---

[1] Short for **сударь** (sir, lord), often appended to other words via a hyphen, as in "**Да-с!**" Of course, this is no longer used!
[2] This book will occasionally resort to "strange" English in order to convey the literal meaning of the Russian.
[3] Of course, Pushkin wrote this long before the term **товарищ** had any Communist connotations!

5.3 More handwriting practice

Let's practice our cursive a bit more, while getting acquainted with just a few of the many outstanding Russian writers who await us! Have you heard of them? We will be reading many of them later in this series of books!

Александр Сергеевич Пушкин

1799-1837. Generally considered Russia's greatest poet, and the founder of modern Russian literature.

Михаил Юрьевич Лермонтов

1814-1841. Another major poet of the "Golden Age" (**Золотой век**). Author of the novel *A Hero of Our Time*.

Николай Васильевич Гоголь

1809-1852. Author of such well-known Petersburg Tales as "The Nose" (**Нос**) and "The Overcoat" (**Шинель**).

Лев Николаевич Толстой

1828-1910. The author of the novels *War and Peace* (**Война и мир**) and *Anna Karenina* (**Анна Каренина**).

Фёдор Михайлович Достоевский

1821-1881. Wrote *The Idiot* (**Идиот**), *Demons* (**Бесы**), and *The Brothers Karamazov* (**Братья Карамазовы**).

Антон Павлович Чехов

1860-1904. A renowned playwright and author of short stories. Plays include *Uncle Vanya* (**Дядя Ваня**).

Анна Андреевна Ахматова

1889-1966. A poet of the Silver Age (**Серебряный век**). Author of "Requiem" (**Реквием**).[1]

Михаил Афанасьевич Булгаков

1891-1940. A Soviet writer best known for the novel *The Master and Margarita* (**Мастер и Маргарита**).[2]

Here's a quick list of some odd sounds you may hear Russians make under various circumstances — for future reference!

ой!	surprise, concern, accidents	**тьфу**!	spitting (three times: тьфу-тьфу-тьфу, to avoid being jinxed)
фу!	in response to a foul odor	**ага**!	uh-huh! (confirmation); a-ha! (I get it!)
опа!	wow, look at what I just did! tah-dah!	**ну**	well...
ах! (эх!)	ah! surprise, fright, "sigh"	**ну-ка**	come on, you can do this!
тсс!	shh! hush!	**бац**!	bang! wham! whack!

[1] This is a cycle of poems dealing with the Stalinist purges; we will read it in its entirety in Book 2!
[2] Many students new to Russian have never heard of this widely beloved novel; if you haven't read it, be sure to check it out!

5.4 An overview of classroom Russian

Let's get some more pronunciation and reading practice while learning a few useful phrases we're likely to use on a daily basis in class. We'll be positioned to understand much of this grammar soon; for now, just practice reading and repeating these phrases. You'll get used to them in time as you hear them over and over in class!

по-ру́сски	in Russian (more generally, "in the Russian way")
по-англи́йски	in English ("in the English way")
У вас есть вопро́сы? Есть вопро́сы?	Do you have questions? Are there questions?
У меня́ есть вопро́с.	I have a question.
Нет, вопро́сов нет.	No, there are no questions.
Кака́я страни́ца?	What page (are we on)?
Поня́тно. Всё поня́тно.	Understood, I get it. Everything is understood.
Как э́то бу́дет по-ру́сски / по-англи́йски?	How do you say that in Russian / English?
Как бу́дет по-ру́сски _____?	How do you say _____ in Russian?
Как бу́дет по-англи́йски _____?	How do you say _____ in English?
Как э́то пи́шется?	How is this spelled (literally, "written")?
Как пи́шется сло́во _____?	How is the word _____ spelled?
Э́то пи́шется че́рез "____".	This is spelled with an _____ (insert name of letter!).
Где ударе́ние?	Where's the stress?
Ударе́ние здесь. Ударе́ние на э́том сло́ге.	The stress is here. The stress is on this syllable.
Чита́йте, пожа́луйста. (say: "пожа́лста")	Read, please.
Повтори́те, пожа́луйста.	Repeat, please.
Переведи́те на ру́сский, пожа́луйста.	Translate into Russian, please.
Переведи́те на англи́йский, пожа́луйста.	Translate into English, please.
Сда́йте, пожа́луйста, свою́ дома́шнюю рабо́ту.	Hand in your homework, please.
Молоде́ц! / Молодцы́!	Great, way to go! (said to one / to several people)
Э́то всё на сего́дня. До за́втра!	That's all for today. Until tomorrow!

Here are some more useful terms for discussing classes and languages — for reference, and passive knowledge.

дома́шняя[1] рабо́та	homework	оконча́ние	(word) ending	грамма́тика	grammar
дома́шнее зада́ние	homework	произноше́ние	pronunciation	паде́ж	case (of nouns)
контро́льная	quiz, test	предложе́ние	sentence	глаго́л	verb
экза́мен	exam	фра́за	phrase	предло́г	preposition
уро́к / на уро́ке	class / in class	констру́кция	construction	существи́тельное	noun
уче́бник	textbook	выраже́ние	expression	прилага́тельное	adjective
страни́ца	page	упражне́ние	exercise	сло́во	word
ударе́ние	stress	интона́ция	intonation	слог	syllable

Nouns versus adjectives: an introduction to word endings in Russian

Ever notice how easily English turns nouns into adjectives (or verbs, for that matter!), often without any changes to the word at all (as in, a **soccer** ball)? In Russian, one of several **adjectival suffixes** would have to be added to a noun to produce a true adjective — which, of course, must have adjectival **endings**. Here are just a few examples formed using a very common adjectival suffix, -ный:

футбо́л soccer, football	➡	футбо́льный "soccer-related"	➡	футбо́льное по́ле soccer field
баскетбо́л basketball	➡	баскетбо́льный "basketball-related"	➡	баскетбо́льный мяч basketball ball (!)[2]
хокке́й hockey	➡	хокке́йный "hockey-related"	➡	хокке́йный матч hockey game (match)

Here are two other examples, with other adjectival suffixes: -ский and -ческий.

студе́нт student	➡	студе́нческий "student-related"	➡	студе́нческий биле́т a student ID
сове́т council, "soviet"	➡	сове́тский "soviet-related"	➡	Сове́тский Сою́з the Soviet Union

In short, **parts of speech** are not interchangeable in Russian, because nouns, adjectives, and verbs each have their own special set of endings, and those endings will also **change**. These changing endings will help convey the role each word plays in a given sentence.

---

[1] This isn't a typo — it's a feminine soft adjectival ending! We will not formally introduce soft adjectives until Book 2 (Day 56).
[2] A student once told of the baffled responses he met with when he went around asking Russians for a "баскетбо́л."

day 6: nouns and the nominative case

greetings; nouns and gender; pronouns; the nominative case and the "pointing word" **это**; expressing possession; negation with **не**

Ты! You! (As in, "Have *you* signed up as a volunteer?")

6.1 Greetings using the formal and informal "you"

Russian has two versions of "you" in the **singular**: one formal (**вы**), one informal (**ты**).[1] You can address close friends (and, in informal settings, anyone of your own age) using **ты**. Otherwise, it's important to err on the side of civility and address everyone using **вы**. **Вы** can also mean "you" **plural** ("you all"), both formal and informal.

formal (using **вы**):	**Здравствуйте!**	Hello! (pronounced **здра́ствуйте** — no **в**!)
informal (using **ты**):	**Здравствуй!**	Hi![2]
"goodbye" isn't affected:	**До свидания!**	Goodbye! ("until we see each other again")

If you are addressing someone "**на ты**" (that is, using **ты**) you can use the following informal expressions:

Приве́т!	Hi!
Здоро́во!	Hey, good to see you!
Пока́!	Bye!
Счастли́во!	Bye, take care!

What if a relationship begins on formal terms, but later becomes more friendly? One of you will need to suggest "transitioning to **ты**." In practice, you can wait for a new Russian friend to suggest this when the time is right.

Дава́йте перейдём на "ты"!	Let's switch ("cross over") to **ты**.
Хорошо́, дава́й!	OK!

6.2 More everyday niceties

Пожа́луйста	Please / You're welcome (say "**пожа́лста**")	**Доброе у́тро!**	Good morning!
Спаси́бо	Thank you.	**Добрый день!**	Good day!
Извини́те / извини́	Excuse me (for **вы** / **ты**)	**Добрый ве́чер!**	Good evening!
Как вы сказа́ли?	What? (literally: How did you say?, using **вы**)	**Мне на́до идти́.**	I've got to go.
Повтори́те, пожа́луйста!	Repeat, please. (using **вы**)	**До за́втра!**	See you tomorrow!

---

24   [1] Similarly to other European languages, like German (du, Sie) or French (tu, vous).
[2] This form, and others below (**извини́те, повтори́те**) are actually imperatives (commands), which add the ending **-те** for the **вы** form.

6.3 Nouns and grammatical gender

Any given noun in Russian is **masculine**, **feminine**, or **neuter**. Even nouns referring to **things** have **gender**. Any other word we use to refer to a given noun (like an adjective or pronoun) will **match the gender** of that noun.

We can almost always determine a noun's gender by **looking at its ending**. Let's begin with **hard** nouns. Hard feminines end in **-a**; hard neuters end in **-o**; and hard masculines end in a **consonant** — that is, with **no vowel**. This is often called "**zero ending**," in the sense that, technically, masculine nouns have **no ending** in the nominative singular. Due to Russian spelling conventions, we can tell that all of these nouns are **hard** just by looking.[1]

hard nouns		
masculine	**feminine**	**neuter**
стол table	книга book	дело matter, business
стул chair	комната room	окно window
велосипед bicycle	одежда clothes	место place
телефон phone	работа work	зеркало mirror
компьютер computer	картина picture	кресло easy chair, armchair
телевизор television	футболка t-shirt	письмо letter
плакат poster	этажерка bookshelf	одеяло blanket
карандаш pencil	машина car	мыло soap
рюкзак backpack	передача TV show	утро morning
ковёр carpet	ошибка mistake	пальто coat
мяч ball	страница page	кино cinema, movie(s)
ключ key	газета newspaper	
вечер evening	сумка purse	
зонт umbrella	тема topic	
сериал TV series	проблема problem	
фильм film, a movie	задача (math) problem, task	
журнал magazine	ручка pen	
вопрос question	лампа lamp	
ответ answer	рубашка shirt	
кошелёк wallet	бумага paper	

Next come **soft** nouns. A soft noun's final stem consonant is inherently soft, and that softness affects the spelling and pronunciation of any ending attached to that stem. Soft **feminines** end in the soft vowel **-я**, and soft **neuters** in the soft vowel **-e** (or **-ё**). Soft **masculines** end in either a **soft consonant** (marked by **-ь**) or in **-й**.[3]

Once again, note that Russian spelling conventions allow us to tell that each of these nouns is **soft** simply by looking. The presence of a **soft vowel** or **soft sign** marks the final stem consonant as soft, and -й is itself soft.

soft nouns		
masculine	**feminine**	**neuter**
шампунь shampoo	идея idea	платье dress
словарь dictionary	неделя week	полотенце towel
день day	простыня bedsheet	бельё laundry
музей museum	статья article	имя first name[3]
	семья family	

Finally, we have a separate set of "**special**" **soft** nouns, ending in **-ий**, **-ия**, and **-ие**. For now, the endings (-**й** / -**я** / -**е**) are indistinguishable from those of ordinary soft nouns, but eventually we'll see that in some cases their endings will differ. For this reason, we should be very careful to group them separately from the very beginning.

Again, take a moment to note how we can tell that each of these nouns is **soft** simply by looking!

special soft nouns		
masculine	**feminine**	**neuter**
кафетерий cafeteria[3]	фамилия last name	расписание schedule
комментарий comment	фотография photo	упражнение exercise (in textbook)
гений a genius	история story, history	задание assignment

[1] Remember, unless a consonant is followed by **и, е, ё, я, ю** or **ь**, we assume it is hard.
[2] Remember: **й** is a consonant — a soft consonant. Students often forget this!   [3] A few special neuters end in **-мя**.
[4] Another, more common term for "cafeteria" is **столовая**. We'll learn it in a later chapter; it's a "stand-alone" feminine adjective.

6.4 Pronouns and grammatical gender

In English we refer to almost any **thing** using the pronoun "it." But in Russian, we'd refer to a book (**кни́га**) using the **feminine** pronoun **она́**, just as we would use **она́** to refer to a woman (say, **А́нна Каре́нина**). And we'd use the **masculine** pronoun **он** to refer to anything masculine, whether a thing (**компью́тер**) or a person (Anna's husband, **Алексе́й Каре́нин**). We'd only use the **neuter** pronoun **оно́** to refer to things that are **grammatically neuter**, like **письмо́**. So, when speaking of any noun whatsoever, we must always be aware of its gender!

6.a. *What pronoun would you use to refer to these things in Russian, and why? Choose between* **он**, **она́**, *and* **оно́**.

телефо́н → _____	шампу́нь → _____	отве́т → _____	плака́т → _____
слова́рь → _____	иде́я → _____	зе́ркало → _____	маши́на → _____
окно́ → _____	пла́тье → _____	зада́ние → _____	мяч → _____
рабо́та → _____	фильм → _____	исто́рия → _____	музе́й → _____

6.5 The nominative case and the "pointing word" (э́то)

The nouns we've seen so far were given in the **nominative** case. Russian has **six cases** in all, with each case marked by special **endings**. Case endings tell us **what role a particular word is playing in a given sentence**.

The **nominative** case (from the Latin *nomen*, name) is used to "name" things in Russian. We can point out things and name them using the "pointing word" (**э́то**), followed by the nominative. The nominative can answer the question "**Что?**" (What?), as in "**Что э́то?**" (What's this?), as well as "**Кто?**" (Who?) or "**Кто э́то?**" (Who's this?)

The nominative is also used for **subjects** and for **predicate nouns and adjectives**, in such simple sentences as "The pen is new" or "It is a pen" or "It is new." Here are some examples with nouns of each gender.

Что э́то?	**Э́то ру́чка.**	**Э́то она́.**	**Она́ но́вая.**	**Ру́чка но́вая.**	**Э́то но́вая ру́чка.**
What's this?	This is a pen.	This is it.	It is new.	The pen is new.	This is a new pen.
А что э́то?	**Э́то зе́ркало.**	**Э́то оно́.**	**Оно́ но́вое.**	**Зе́ркало но́вое.**	**Э́то но́вое зе́ркало.**
And what's this?	This is a mirror.	This is it.	It is new.	The mirror is new.	This is a new mirror.
А что э́то?	**Э́то зонт.**	**Э́то он.**	**Он но́вый.**	**Зонт но́вый.**	**Э́то но́вый зонт.**
And what's this?	This is a umbrella.	This is it.	It is new.	The umbrella is new.	This is a new umbrella.

Note the **arrows** marking gender **agreement**. We must always keep in mind the grammatical gender of the thing we're speaking of; any pronoun or adjective that refers to it must **agree** with it in terms of gender![1]

Also note that the English **linking verb** "is" is not translated in the Russian examples. The Russian equivalent is **есть**. When existence is not in question, or not being emphasized, the verb **есть** is typically **omitted** in Russian.

6.b. *Say "this is it" by supplying the correct pronoun* (**он**, **она́**, **оно́**) *to match the grammatical gender of the noun.*

1. **Э́то кни́га.** Э́то _____.	9. **Э́то фотогра́фия.** Э́то _____.	17. **Э́то телеви́зор.** Э́то _____.
2. **Э́то телеви́зор.** Э́то _____.	10. **Э́то кафете́рий.** Э́то _____.	18. **Э́то плака́т.** Э́то _____.
3. **Э́то окно́.** Э́то _____.	11. **Э́то ключ.** Э́то _____.	19. **Э́то статья́.** Э́то _____.
4. **Э́то слова́рь.** Э́то _____.	12. **Э́то карти́на.** Э́то _____.	20. **Э́то зада́ние.** Э́то _____.
5. **Э́то простыня́.** Э́то _____.	13. **Э́то музе́й.** Э́то _____.	21. **Э́то шампу́нь.** Э́то _____.
6. **Э́то одея́ло.** Э́то _____.	14. **Э́то бельё.** Э́то _____.	22. **Э́то зонт.** Э́то _____.
7. **Э́то пла́тье.** Э́то _____.	15. **Э́то полоте́нце.** Э́то _____.	23. **Э́то кни́га.** Э́то _____.
8. **Э́то расписа́ние.** Э́то _____.	16. **Э́то этаже́рка.** Э́то _____.	24. **Э́то и́мя.**[2] Э́то _____.

---

[1] In time, we'll learn that agreement extends to **number** (singular / plural) and **case** (nominative / genitive, accusative, etc.) as well.
[2] Remember: this is an odd exception: despite ending in **-я**, this noun is neuter!

Что это?	Это компьютер.	Он новый.	Это новый компьютер.
What (is) this?	This (is) a computer.	It (is) new.	This (is) a new computer.
1. Что это?	Это карандаш.	_____ новый.	Это _____ _____.
2. Что это?	Это музей.	_____ интересный.	Это _____ _____.
3. Что это?	Это платье.	_____ новое.	Это _____ _____.
4. Что это?	Это расписание.	_____ интересное.	Это _____ _____.
5. Что это?	Это стул.	_____ старый.	Это _____ _____.
6. Что это?	Это кресло.	_____ старое.	Это _____ _____.
7. Что это?	Это мяч.	_____ новый.	Это _____ _____.
8. Что это?	Это книга.	_____ новая.	Это _____ _____.

6.6 Expressing possession ("I have" = "at me is")

Here are the **nominative** forms of all pronouns, along with a prepositional phrase (**y** + the **genitive** case[1]) used to express **possession**:

pronouns					
singular			plural		
nominative	y + genitive		nominative	y + genitive	
я	I →	у меня at me...	мы	we →	у нас at us...
ты	you →	у тебя at you...	вы	you →	у вас at you...
он	he →	у него[2] at him...			
она she →		у неё at her...	они	they →	у них at them...
оно it →		у него[2] at it...			

This "**y**" construction is our first Russian **idiom**. An idiom is the particular way in which a language expresses a given idea. When learning Russian, it's very important not to assume that we can simply translate English expressions word for word into Russian. Russian may express even a very simple idea in a completely different way.

The preposition **y** literally means "near" or "at." So Russian expresses possession by saying, literally, "**At me is book**" — _not_ "**I have a book**." Note that, in the Russian idiom, "**book**" is the **subject**, _not_ the **direct object**, as it would be in the English "I have a book."

У НАС

РАВНОПРАВИЕ, СВОБОДА, БЛАГОПОЛУЧИЕ.

У нас — равноправие, свобода, благополучие.
_We_ have equal rights, freedom, and prosperity.
(you should see the "**у них**" half of this poster!)

У тебя есть книга?	Да, у меня есть книга.	У вас есть зонт?	Да, у нас есть зонт.
"At you is book?"	Yes, "at me is book."	"At you is umbrella?"	Yes, "at us is umbrella."

These questions and answers emphasize existence (it's the entire point of the question!), so they **do** include the Russian verb for "is" — **есть**. But if existence has been established (or is assumed), we can omit the **есть**:

У тебя **есть** книга?	Да, **есть**. Она новая.	Книга у тебя новая?	Да, новая.
"At you is book?"	"Yes, is. It new."	"Book at you new?"	"Yes, new."

У кого есть книга?	я →	У меня есть книга.	_Say that these people (based on the pronouns) have_	6.d
Who has a book?		I have a book.	_these things. Try asking the same of your classmates._	

1. У кого есть телевизор?	он → У _____ есть _____.	4. У кого есть зонт?	ты → У _____ есть _____.
2. У кого есть телефон?	она → У _____ есть _____.	5. У кого есть окно?	вы → У _____ есть _____.
3. У кого есть машина?	они → У _____ есть _____.	6. У кого есть идея?	мы → У _____ есть _____.

[1] We will discuss the genitive case in detail in Chapter 2; for now, it will be used only in the expressions shown here.
[2] **него** is pronounced as if written **нево**; this same genitive form affects the pronunciation of "today" (сегодня = "севодня").

6.7 Have you noticed? Russian has no articles!

Russian has no equivalent of the English "a" and "the" — the indefinite and definite **articles**. Usually, the context would make clear what article we might need in English. Even without further context, Russian word order may provide a clue: in Russian sentences, **new information** (or whatever is considered "**most interesting**" in the sentence) is usually **saved for the end**. Such a new item would usually take an indefinite article in English.

У теб**я** есть **кн**и**га?**	Do you have **a** book?	(I'm trying to established whether or not you have one at all)
Кни**га** у теб**я** есть?	Do you have **the** book?	(I have a definite book in mind — do you have it with you?)

In questions, Russian **intonation** rises sharply on whatever word is the "**point**" of the question, then falls again. Since these are both questions about existence, the intonation would rise on the verb **есть**.

Again — in these examples, **есть** is emphasized (it's the point of the question), so it is not omitted.

6.8 Negation using не

We can negate an adjective or noun with **не**, as in the following examples. Many adjectives can also create an antonym by adding **не** directly, as in **интер**е**сный** (interesting) → **неинтер**е**сный** (uninteresting).

Это комп**ь**ю**тер.**	This is a computer.	**Э**то не каранд**а**ш.	This isn't a pencil.
Он не н**о**вый.	It's not new.	**Э**то р**у**чка.	It's a pen.
Он ст**а**рый и об**ы**чный.	It's old and ordinary.	Он**а** о**ч**ень необ**ы**чная.	It's very unusual.

---

*Talk about some of your things in a brief dialogue. Choose the right pronoun (***он***, ***он**а*, ***он**о*) and adjective (***н**о**вый**, ***н**о**вая**, ***н**о**вое**).*

У теб**я** есть **телеф**о**н?**	Да, есть.	**Он (не) н**о**вый.**	А у теб**я**?	Да, у мен**я** т**о**же есть.
Do you have a telephone?	Yes, I do.[1]	It's (not) new.	What about you?	Yes, I also have one.
1. У теб**я** есть **маш**и**на?**	Да, есть.	____ _____.	А у теб**я**?	Да, у мен**я** т**о**же есть.
2. У теб**я** есть **к**о**мната?**	Да, есть.	____ _____.	А у теб**я**?	Да, у мен**я** т**о**же есть.
3. У теб**я** есть **комп**ь**ю**тер?	Да, есть.	____ _____.	А у теб**я**?	Да, у мен**я** т**о**же есть.
4. У теб**я** есть **руб**а**шка?**	Да, есть.	____ _____.	А у теб**я**?	Да, у мен**я** т**о**же есть.
5. У теб**я** есть **кошел**ё**к?**	Да, есть.	____ _____.	А у теб**я**?	Да, у мен**я** т**о**же есть.
6. У теб**я** есть **р**у**чка?**	Да, есть.	____ _____.	А у теб**я**?	Да, у мен**я** т**о**же есть.
7. У теб**я** есть **велосип**е**д?**	Да, есть.	____ _____.	А у теб**я**?	Да, у мен**я** т**о**же есть.

*Can you repeat this exchange using the polite pronoun ***вы*** (У **вас** есть...?)*

6.9 How are you?

We can use the same **у** construction to ask how someone's doing. In the Russian idiom, we ask "how things are at someone," using the plural of **д**е**ло** (a piece of business, a matter), **дел**а. Three variations of this question, and simple answers, are given below:

Как у вас дела**?**	How are things? (using **вы**)
Как у тебя **дел**а**?**	How are things? (using **ты**)
Как дела**?**	How are things?

У меня **всё хорош**о**.**	Everything's good with me.
Всё отли**чно.**	Everything's great.
Пло**хо.**	(Things are) bad.
Норма**льно.**	(Things are) OK — nothing to write home about!

Practice greeting someone and asking how they're doing!

Кто **э**то? Он коммун**и**ст? Как у нег**о** дел**а**? У нег**о** есть газ**е**та? Он**а** хор**о**шая и**ли** (or) нет?

---

[1] NOTE: For now, we can't say that we **don't have** something; we need the **genitive** endings first. We'll learn how to say this in Chapter 2.

day 7: adjectives

talking about names; adjectives in the nominative singular; end-stressed adjectives; the question word **какой**; omitting the verb "is"

Военная присяга. Military oath. (The adjective **военный** is from the noun **война**, meaning "war")

7.1 What's your name?

Here's another Russian **idiom**: in English, we ask "What is your name?" In Russian we ask, literally, "What do they call you?" The pronoun "you" is in the **accusative** case, as the **direct object** of the verb "they call."

Как **вас** зовут? / Как **тебя** зовут?
"What do they call you?" (using вы / ты)

Меня зовут Иван.
"They call me Ivan."

Luckily, these new **accusative** pronoun forms (in the **black boxes** below) are identical to the genitive forms we learned yesterday with "**у**." They simply lack the initial "**н**," which appears following prepositions.[1]

Родина-мать зовёт!
The "homeland-mother" calls!

pronouns							
singular			plural				
nominative	у + gen.	accusative		nominative	у + gen.	accusative	
я	I	**у меня**	**меня** me	**мы** we	**у нас**	**нас** us
ты you	**у тебя**	**тебя** you	**вы** you	**у вас**	**вас** you
он he	**у него**[2]	**его**[2] him				
она she	**у неё**	**её** her	**они** they	**у них**	**их** them
оно it	**у него**[2]	**его**[2] it				

он:	Как **его** зовут?	Как у **него** дела?	Очень хорошо. У **него** новая машина!	**7.a**
	"How him they call?"	"How at him things?"	"Very good. At him new car!"	
1. **она**:	Как _____ зовут?	Как у _____ дела?	Очень хорошо. У _____ новая лампа!	
2. **они**:	Как _____ зовут?	Как у _____ дела?	Очень хорошо. У _____ новый шампунь!	
3. **ты**:	Как _____ зовут?	Как у _____ дела?	Очень хорошо. У _____ новое одеяло!	

[1] In short, third-person pronouns that normally begin with a vowel (**е, и**) add an initial **н** when following prepositions.
[2] Just as **него** is pronounced as if written **нево** ("nyeh-voh"), **его** is pronounced as if written **ево** ("yeh-voh").

Rules to live by

Spelling rules tell us: 1) which letter combos **can't** occur, and 2) what to write **instead**. Today we'll introduce **two rules** that affect adjectival endings; we'll add **a third rule** later. Each rule involves some combination of **8 letters**, which we can break down into 4 "hushing" sounds (**ж, ч, ш, щ**), 3 "velars" (pronounced in the back of the throat— **г, к, х**), and 1 "**odd man out**" — **ц**.

	4 "hushings"	3 "velars"	1 "odd man out"		
	ж ч ш щ	**г к х**	**ц**		
7-letter rule: after these 7 letters...	**ж ч ш щ**	**г к х**	_	...write: **и**	...not: **ы**
5-letter rule: after these 5 letters...	**ж ч ш щ**		**ц**	...write: **e**	...not: unstressed **o**

These rules are **universally valid**, since they deal with certain combinations of sounds that simply do not occur in Russian words. Those very few exceptions that do exist reflect sound combinations native to other languages; an example is **Кыргызстан** (Kyrgyzstan).

Не суши у огня вымытую бензином одежду. Don't dry clothes washed with gasoline near a flame.

7.2   Adjectives in the nominative singular

Most **hard**[1] adjectives take the endings **-ый** for masculine, **-ая** for feminine, and **-oe** for neuter. Note how the various endings are added to a common stem. Remember: **-ая** and **-oe** are both **two syllables** (no **silent vow-**

	stem	masculine: -ый	feminine: -ая	neuter: -oe
new:	**нов-**	нов**ый**	нов**ая**	нов**ое**
old:	**стар-**	стар**ый**	стар**ая**	стар**ое**
boring:	**скучн-**	скучн**ый**	скучн**ая**	скучн**ое**
favorite (literally, "loved"):	**любим-**	любим**ый**	любим**ая**	любим**ое**
hard, difficult:	**трудн-**	трудн**ый**	трудн**ая**	трудн**ое**
strange:	**странн-**	странн**ый**	странн**ая**	странн**ое**
clean:	**чист-**	чист**ый**	чист**ая**	чист**ое**
dirty:	**грязн-**	грязн**ый**	грязн**ая**	грязн**ое**
cheap:	**дешёв-**	дешёв**ый**	дешёв**ая**	дешёв**ое**
awful:	**ужасн-**	ужасн**ый**	ужасн**ая**	ужасн**ое**
huge:	**огромн-**	огромн**ый**	огромн**ая**	огромн**ое**
excellent, great:	**отличн-**	отличн**ый**	отличн**ая**	отличн**ое**
hideous, awful:	**безобразн-**	безобразн**ый**	безобразн**ая**	безобразн**ое**
important:	**важн-**	важн**ый**	важн**ая**	важн**ое**
(not) pretty:	**(не)красив-**	(не)красив**ый**	(не)красив**ая**	(не)красив**ое**
(un)usual:	**(не)обычн-**	(не)обычн**ый**	(не)обычн**ая**	(не)обычн**ое**
(un)interesting:	**(не)интересн-**	(не)интересн**ый**	(не)интересн**ая**	(не)интересн**ое**

7.b   Describe these items as **новый**:

1. _____ **книга**
2. _____ **музей**
3. _____ **рубашка**
4. _____ **платье**
5. _____ **рюкзак**
6. _____ **идея**

Describe these items as **старый**:

7. _____ **мяч**
8. _____ **комната**
9. _____ **словарь**
10. _____ **одеяло**
11. _____ **плакат**
12. _____ **машина**

Describe these items as **интересный**:

13. _____ **вопрос**
14. _____ **ответ**
15. _____ **задача**
16. _____ **история**
17. _____ **место**
18. _____ **картина**

"Пожалуйста" — **волшебное слово.** "Please" is the magic word.[1]

[1] As always, we can tell these adjectives are hard **simply by looking**: in all forms, the **spelling** shows the final "**н**" of the stem to be hard.
[2] You'll find common Russian sayings scattered, for fun, throughout the book, illustrating some bit of grammar we've learned. Of course, as with the poster captions, you may not always understand every last word. Ask an instructor or Russian speaker to tell you more about them!

7.3 Adjectives affected by the spelling rules

We should think of the endings we've just seen <u>as the default</u>, while keeping in mind that certain adjectival endings are affected by the **spelling rules** we just learned — depending on their **final stem consonant**.

Such slight "irregularities" happen to be most evident in the **masculine** endings; for this reason, dictionaries usually cite adjectives using their **masculine singular** form, e.g. **больш<u>о</u>й**, **хор<u>о</u>ший**, **н<u>о</u>вый**. From this form, the feminine and neuter forms can easily be derived. The tables below provide all three genders for convenience.

Here and elsewhere, watch out for **black boxes** in our tables. They will help highlight forms that are tricky or exceptional in some way. Here, for example, the forms in the black boxes are those affected by the spelling rules.

		adjectives affected by the 7-letter spelling rule		
		masculine: -ий	feminine: -ая	neuter: -ое
small:	**маленьк-**	маленьк**ий**[1]	маленьк**ая**	маленьк**ое**
easy, light:	**лёгк-**	лёгк**ий**[1]	лёгк**ая**	лёгк**ое**
Russian:	**р<u>у</u>сск-**	р<u>у</u>сск**ий**[1]	р<u>у</u>сск**ая**	р<u>у</u>сск**ое**

		an adjective affected by the 5- *and* 7-letter spelling rules		
		masculine: -ий	feminine: -ая	neuter: -ее
good:	**хор<u>о</u>ш-**	хор<u>о</u>ш**ий**[1]	хор<u>о</u>ш**ая**	хор<u>о</u>ш**ее**

Describe these items as **р<u>у</u>сский**:

1. _____ плак<u>а</u>т
2. _____ кн<u>и</u>га
3. _____ сери<u>а</u>л
4. _____ маш<u>и</u>на
5. _____ фам<u>и</u>лия
6. _____ <u>и</u>мя (n!)

Describe these items as **маленький**:

7. _____ ош<u>и</u>бка
8. _____ зонт
9. _____ окн<u>о</u>
10. _____ семь<u>я</u>
11. _____ ковёр
12. _____ стол

Describe these items as **хор<u>о</u>ший**:   7.c

13. _____ муз<u>е</u>й
14. _____ ид<u>е</u>я
15. _____ м<u>е</u>сто
16. _____ раб<u>о</u>та
17. _____ вопр<u>о</u>с
18. _____ слов<u>а</u>рь

Не дай Бог увидеть р<u>у</u>сский бунт — бесс<u>мы</u>сленный и беспощадный. God forbid we see a Russian rebellion — senseless and merciless. (an oft-quoted line from Pushkin's short story *Капит<u>а</u>нская д<u>о</u>чка* — "The Captain's Daughter")

7.4 End-stressed adjectives

Some adjectives are **end-stressed**, meaning that their **endings** are **always stressed**. They also take a special ending in the masculine singular: -**ой**. Here, since endings that include "o" are always **stressed**, they can never violate the 5-letter spelling rule (note, for example, **больш<u>о</u>й** and **больш<u>о</u>е**, where a **stressed o** follows the **ш**).

		end-stressed adjectives		
		masculine: -ой	feminine: -ая	neuter: -ое
bad:	**плох-**	плох**<u>о</u>й**	плох**<u>а</u>я**	плох**<u>о</u>е**
big:	**больш-**	больш**<u>о</u>й**	больш**<u>а</u>я**	больш**<u>о</u>е**
expensive:	**дорог-**	дорог**<u>о</u>й**	дорог**<u>а</u>я**	дорог**<u>о</u>е**
different, another:	**друг-**	друг**<u>о</u>й**	друг**<u>а</u>я**	друг**<u>о</u>е**
funny:	**смешн-**	смешн**<u>о</u>й**	смешн**<u>а</u>я**	смешн**<u>о</u>е**

Describe these items as **больш<u>о</u>й**:

1. _____ рюкз<u>а</u>к
2. _____ пробл<u>е</u>ма
3. _____ ковёр
4. _____ окн<u>о</u>

Describe these items as **дорог<u>о</u>й**:

5. _____ м<u>ы</u>ло
6. _____ шамп<u>у</u>нь
7. _____ бум<u>а</u>га
8. _____ р<u>у</u>чка

Describe these items as **плох<u>о</u>й**:   7.d

9. _____ день
10. _____ нед<u>е</u>ля
11. _____ газ<u>е</u>та
12. _____ м<u>ы</u>ло

Дурн<u>о</u>е д<u>е</u>ло нех<u>и</u>трое. A bad deed is not clever (that is, it requires no great genius or effort to do bad things; **дурн<u>о</u>й** is an end-stressed adjective).

[1] Note that these adjectives, too, are **hard**, as their feminine and neuter forms make clear. The "и" seen in the masculine forms can be thought of as simply the consequence of a "spelling rule" — it's not marking a stem that is inherently soft.

7.5 The question word как**о**й

Another end-stressed adjective is the question word как**о**й: "What kind of...?" As an **adjective**, it **agrees with the noun** it's modifying (that is, the noun it's asking about). We can answer this question using other adjectives. We can also include the "pointing word" **это** to **point out** something and ask **what kind** of thing it is.

Here are some как**о**й questions, along with follow-up questions using a **pronoun**. Note the **agreement** arrows!

Како**й** это фильм? What kind of film is this?	Это **русский** фильм. This is a Russian film.	Он **интер**е**сный**? Is it interesting?	Да, о**ч**е**нь интер**е**сный**. Yes, very interesting.
Кака**я** это кн**и**га? What kind of book is this?	Это **русская** кн**и**га. This is a Russian book.	Он**а** тр**у**дная? Is it difficult?	Нет, не о**ч**е**нь** тр**у**дная. No, not very difficult.
Како**е** это пальт**о**? What kind of coat is this?	Это **русское** пальт**о**. This is a Russian coat.	Он**о** дор**о**гое? Is it expensive?	Нет, деш**ё**вое. No, (it's) cheap.

Как**а**я у теб**я** к**о**мната?	**Хор**о**шая** или (or) **плох**а**я**?	К**о**мната у мен**я** хор**о**шая.
_____ у теб**я** телеф**о**н?	**Н**о**вый** или **ст**а**рый**?	Телеф**о**н у мен**я** _____.
_____ у теб**я** расписа**н**ие?	**Тр**у**дное** или **л**ё**гкое**?	Расписа**н**ие у мен**я** _____.
_____ у теб**я** рюкз**а**к?	**Ч**и**стый** или **гр**я**зный**?	Рюкз**а**к у мен**я** _____.
_____ у теб**я** семь**я**?	**Больш**а**я** или **м**а**ленькая**?	Семь**я** у мен**я** _____.
_____ у теб**я** шамп**у**нь?	**Дорог**о**й** или **деш**ё**вый**?	Шамп**у**нь у мен**я** _____.
_____ у теб**я** кн**и**га?	**Интер**е**сная** или **ск**у**чная**?	Кн**и**га у мен**я** _____.

7.6 Using как**о**й in exclamations

We can also use как**о**й in such exclamations as "What a good idea!" As always, watch **agreement**!

Кака**я** хор**о**шая ид**е**я! What a good idea!	**Как**о**й** больш**о**й зонт! What a big umbrella!	**Как**а**я** у теб**я** гр**я**зная к**о**мната! What a dirty room you have!

Certain expressions with как**о**й are extremely common. Here are a few typical examples:

Како**й уж**а**с!**	What horror! (How awful!)	**Как**о**е безобр**а**зие!**	What a mess! What an outrage!
Како**й кошм**а**р!**	What a nightmare!	**Как**о**й иди**о**т!**	What an idiot!
Кака**я ерунд**а**!**	What nonsense!	**Как**а**я р**а**зница?**	What's the difference? Who cares?

7.e больш**о**й[1] + крас**и**вый + к**о**мната	➡ Как**а**я больш**а**я и крас**и**вая к**о**мната!
1. дорог**о**й + больш**о**й + **маш**и**на**	_____ маш**и**на!
2. ст**а**рый + интер**е**сный + **плак**а**т**	_____ плак**а**т!
3. крас**и**вый + необ**ы**чный + **пл**а**тье**	_____ пл**а**тье!
4. хор**о**ший + ч**и**стый + **общеж**и**тие**	_____ общеж**и**тие!
5. уж**а**сный + ск**у**чный + **фильм**	_____ фильм!
6. необ**ы**чный + интер**е**сный + **ид**е**я**	_____ ид**е**я!
7. ст**а**рый + безобр**а**зный + **фотогр**а**фия**	_____ фотогр**а**фия!
8. м**а**ленький + гр**я**зный + **окн**о**	_____ окн**о**!

[1] Again, for reasons explained in 7.3, we'll supply adjectives in their **masculine** form by default; change their gender as needed!

7.7 Adjectives grouped in pairs of opposites

Use your imagination to imbue Russian words with real associations; try to "feel" their meaning intensely as you drill the vocabulary — it will help! We can think of words as "positive" or "negative," group them into pairs of opposites, and expand those basic pairs with words expressing more extreme feelings (awful, hideous, huge, etc.):

отли́чный great	**хоро́ший** good	**плохо́й** bad	**ужа́сный** horrible
огро́мный huge	**большо́й** big	**ма́ленький** small	
	но́вый new	**ста́рый** old	
	интере́сный interesting	**неинтере́сный** uninteresting	**ску́чный** boring
	чи́стый clean	**гря́зный** dirty	
	дорого́й expensive	**дешёвый** inexpensive	
	лёгкий light, easy	**тру́дный** hard	
	краси́вый pretty	**некраси́вый** ugly	**безобра́зный** hideous
	обы́чный usual, ordinary	**необы́чный** unusual	**стра́нный** strange

---

Компью́тер у теб́я **но́вый**? Is your computer new?	Нет, **он ста́рый**, к сожале́нию.[1] No, it's old, unfortunately.	Како́й ужас! **7.f** What horror!
1. **Ко́мната** у теб́я **больша́я**?	Нет, _____ _____, к сожале́нию.	Како́й ужас!
2. **Телефо́н** у теб́я **хоро́ший**?	Нет, _____ _____, к сожале́нию.	Како́й ужас!
3. **Маши́на** у теб́я **дорога́я**?	Нет, _____ _____, к сожале́нию.	Како́й ужас!
4. **Рюкза́к** у теб́я **краси́вый**?	Нет, _____ _____, к сожале́нию.	Како́й ужас!
5. **Кафете́рий** у теб́я **хоро́ший**?	Нет, _____ _____, к сожале́нию.	Како́й ужас!
6. **Окно́** у теб́я **большо́е**?	Нет, _____ _____, к сожале́нию.	Како́й ужас!
7. **Зада́ние** у теб́я **лёгкое**?	Нет, _____ _____, к сожале́нию.	Како́й ужас!

7.8 More on omitting the linking verb "is"

A **linking verb** (like "is" or "are") links the **subject** of a sentence to a **predicate noun or adjective**, as in "The car **is** new." The verb "is" is typically omitted in Russian, unless it is being emphasized for some reason. That is, if **existence** is the very point of the statement or question, then **есть** must be included.

In questions like "**У теб́я есть маши́на?**" the very existence of the thing is in question: is there a car, or isn't there? So here we do include the **есть** in Russian.

Meanwhile, questions with **како́й?** assume that the thing exists — they're just asking for more specifics. So **есть** is not included. This is usually true when questions include adjectives:

Кака́я у теб́я маши́на?	**Маши́на у теб́я но́вая?**
What kind of car do you have?	(Is) your car new?

but: **У теб́я есть кра́сная ру́чка?**
         Do you have a red pen (that is, a red one specifically)?

Рели́гия — яд. Береги́ ребя́т! Religion is poison. Protect children! (notice the rhyme!) Yet another innocent child prevented from going to school!

In formal writing, a long dash (called a **тире** in Russian) often stands in for an omitted **есть**. In sentences that provide a kind of definition or explanation, the dash is often followed by **это**:

Моя́ люби́мая ру́сская кни́га — «Война́ и мир».[2]
War and Peace is my favorite Russian book.

«Война́ и мир» — это вели́кий ру́сский рома́н.
War and Peace is a great Russian novel.

---

[1] Pronounce this prepositional phrase as though it were a single word — as though it were written: **ксожале́нию**

[2] Note the "suspense" in the Russian word order — the most interesting information is saved for the end. Often, this is the **subject**!

day 8: adverbs, conjunctions, and the verb "to be"

tenses; infinitives in -ть; past and future forms of the verb **быть**; adverbs of degree; conjunctions and comparisons

Ги́тлеровская Герма́ния. This poster looks forward to the defeat of Hitler's Germany. Remember, Russian has no "h" sound!

8.1 Verb tenses in Russian and English

Russian verbs have only three tenses: **present**, **past**, and **future**.

Note that English, in addition to the three **simple** tenses (*I see, I saw, I will see*) has three additional **perfect** tenses: present perfect (*I have seen*), past perfect (*I had seen*), and future perfect (*I will have seen*).

English also has **emphatic** forms in the past and present with "do" (*I do see, I did see*). These forms are often used in questions (*Do you see? Did you see?*).

English also has **progressive** tenses: present progressive (*I am seeing*), past progressive (*I was seeing*), and future progressive (*I will be seeing*).

Finally, English even has **perfect progressive** tenses: present perfect progressive (*I have been seeing*), past perfect progressive (*I had been seeing*), and future perfect progressive (*I will have been seeing*).

In short, the Russian tense system is **much, much simpler** than that of English. Remembering this simple fact is extremely helpful. Russian verbs help compensate for this dearth of tenses with another grammatical feature that English lacks: that of **verbal aspect**.[2] More on that later!

Так оно́ и бу́дет!
That's how it will be!

8.2 Russian infinitives ending in -ть

We will cite Russian verbs using **infinitives** — **unconjugated** forms that usually end in -ть[1] (the **infinitive ending**). In English, infinitive forms begin with "to": *to see, to hear*, etc. We can **conjugate** a verb (I see, you see, he sees, etc.) and change its **tense** (I saw, I will see, I have seen, etc.). The Russian equivalent of the infinitive "to be" is **быть** (again, note the ending: -ть). In Russian, **Га́млет** asks: **Быть и́ли не быть?** (To be or not to be?)

34   [1] A limited number of verbs have infinitives ending in -чь and -сти. These do not form the past tense straight from the infinitive, as we'll see.
[2] While almost any language has ways of expressing aspectual distinctions, English does not do this in the systematic way that Slavic languages do. As we'll learn, verbal aspect constitutes one of the most distinctive (and most difficult) features of Russian grammar.

8.3 Past-tense forms of the verb быть

Today, Russian has only one present-tense form of the verb **быть**: **есть** (is, are).[1] In the present, this verb is typically omitted unless it is being emphasized. But a full set of forms exists for **быть** in the **past** and **future** tenses.

Forming the **past** tense in Russian is **very simple**. For the vast majority of verbs, we take the **infinitive**, remove the infinitive ending -**ть**, add the letter **л** (the **past-tense marker**), and then add **gender and number markers**.

бы-ть ➡	бы-л ➡	он **был**	masculine singular	Компьютер **был** новый.	The computer was new.
	бы-л-а	она **была**[2]	feminine singular	Машина **была** новая.	The car was new.
	бы-л-о	оно **было**	neuter singular	Кресло **было** новое.	The armchair was new.
	бы-л-и	они **были**	plural (all genders!)	Они **были** новые.	They were new.

So, for any infinitive, there are **only four** possible past-tense forms: one for each gender in the singular, and only one form in the plural. Note that the **singular** forms are marked for **gender only**, not for **person**. So, if our **subject** is **я** or **ты**, the verb form must simply agree with the gender of the person the pronoun refers to. On the other hand, if our **subject** is **plural**, we have **only one form** to use, regardless of the gender of the subject.

Я **был**.	I was. (male speaker)	Ты **был**.	You were. (male subject)	Мы **были**.	We were. (either gender)
Я **была**.	I was. (female speaker)	Ты **была**.	You were. (female subject)	Вы **были**.	You were. (either gender)

This is also true if we use the formal **вы** to refer politely to a **single** person, whether male or female:

Вы **были**. You (singular, formal) were. The **вы** could be male or female. We could **never** say вы был or вы была!

IMPORTANT: To simplify the process of learning case endings, we will almost completely **avoid** the **plural forms** of nouns and adjectives in Book 1. For now, we will only see **plural verbs** after the **plural pronouns мы, вы**, and **они**, and in a few other special cases. All plural case endings for nouns and adjectives will be added in Book 2.

						8.a
Машина **была** новая.	5. Задача _____ лёгкая.	10. Фильм _____ ужасный.				
1. Телефон _____ новый.	6. Задание _____ трудное.	11. Бельё _____ чистое.				
2. Окно _____ большое.	7. Музей _____ огромный.	12. Работа _____ трудная.				
3. Словарь _____ хороший.	8. Статья _____ скучная.	13. Мыло _____ дорогое.				
4. Неделя _____ трудная.	9. Книга _____ русская.	14. Ручка _____ старая.				

---

*Think back to last year for these short exchanges. As Russians say, "a lot of water has flowed away" (**много воды утекло**) since then!*

Какая у тебя была одежда?
What kind of clothes did you have?

Дорогая или дешёвая?
Expensive or cheap?

Моя одежда была дешёвая.
My clothes were cheap.

1. Какая у тебя была **комната**?	Большая или маленькая?	Моя комната _____.
2. Какое у тебя было **окно**?	Большое или маленькое?	Моё окно _____.
3. Какой у тебя был **рюкзак**?	Чистый или грязный?	Мой рюкзак _____.
4. Какой у тебя был **телефон**?	Новый или старый?	Мой телефон _____.
5. Какой у тебя был **компьютер**?	Дорогой или дешёвый?	Мой компьютер _____.
6. Какое у тебя было **расписание**?	Трудное или лёгкое?	Моё расписание _____.
7. Какой у тебя был **зонт**?	Хороший или плохой?	Мой зонт _____.
8. Какая у тебя была **ручка**?	Обычная или необычная?	Моя ручка _____.
9. Какая у тебя была **лампа**?	Дорогая или дешёвая?	Моя лампа _____.

Что было, то было. That which was, was. (i.e., there's no changing the past).

---

[1] Historically, a full set of conjugated forms existed. On very rare occasions, one may still hear the 3rd plural form **суть**: (they) are.
[2] Note how the ending "а" is stressed. A good number of verbs will follow this stress pattern in the past tense: the feminine ending is stressed, but the others aren't. This is not predictable, but it is more likely to occur with verbs whose infinitive has one syllable.

8.4 Future-tense forms of the verb быть

The Russian verb **быть** has a full set of conjugated **future-tense** forms, as shown below. In fact, it's the only Russian verb with a distinct set of future-tense forms of this kind. As we'll learn in Chapter 2, all other verbs will form their future tense either by simple conjugation, or by using the forms below as **helping verbs**.

singular		plural	
я **бу́ду**	I will be	мы **бу́дем**	we will be
ты **бу́дешь**	you will be	вы **бу́дете**	you will be
он, она́, оно́ **бу́дет**	he, she, it will be	они́ **бу́дут**	they will be

The verb endings tell us a lot about the subject — so much that the personal pronouns are often omitted, especially in casual speech. Generally, it's best for students to **include** the pronouns to avoid sounding brusque.[1]

Ты бу́дешь до́ма?	**Бу́дешь до́ма?**	**Бу́ду!**
Will you be at home?	Will (you) be at home?	Yes, I will be!

Так бы́ло... так бу́дет!
So it was... so it will be!
(Наполео́н и Ги́тлер)

8.b. Using **сего́дня**[2] (today), **вчера́** (yesterday) and **за́втра** (tomorrow), say these people were at home (**до́ма**) in the past and future.

1. **Я** (Бори́с) **до́ма сего́дня.**

   Я _____ до́ма вчера́.

   Я _____ до́ма за́втра.

2. **Я** (Ю́лия) **до́ма сего́дня.**

   Я _____ до́ма вчера́.

   Я _____ до́ма за́втра.

3. **Ты** (Михаи́л) **до́ма сего́дня.**

   Ты _____ до́ма вчера́.

   Ты _____ до́ма за́втра.

4. **Ты** (ма́ма) **до́ма сего́дня.**

   Ты _____ до́ма вчера́.

   Ты _____ до́ма за́втра.

5. **Ири́на до́ма сего́дня.**

   Она́ _____ до́ма вчера́.

   Она́ _____ до́ма за́втра.

6. **Па́вел до́ма сего́дня.**

   Он _____ до́ма вчера́.

   Он _____ до́ма за́втра.

7. **Мы до́ма сего́дня.**

   Мы _____ до́ма вчера́.

   Мы _____ до́ма за́втра.

8. **Вы до́ма сего́дня.**

   Вы _____ до́ма вчера́.

   Вы _____ до́ма за́втра.

9. **Па́вел и Ири́на до́ма сего́дня.**

   Они́ _____ до́ма вчера́.

   Они́ _____ до́ма за́втра.

8.5 Adverbs of degree

The forms we just used — **сего́дня, вчера́, за́втра** — are **adverbs**. Adverbs usually modify verbs, but they can also modify adjectives and other adverbs. Let's introduce a few useful adverbs that can modify adjectives and adverbs; we can use them to express more nuanced opinions — as in, "That car is <u>completely</u> new!"

very, really **о́чень**	completely **совсе́м**	quite **дово́льно**	relatively **сравни́тельно**
not very, not really **не о́чень**	not completely **не совсе́м**	horribly **ужа́сно**	too **сли́шком**

Note that Russian adverbs <u>**never change**</u> their form, so we don't have to worry about **agreement** with adverbs!

Э́то **дово́льно** интере́сный фильм.	Ко́мната у тебя́ **дово́льно** гря́зная!	Как дела́? **Дово́льно** хорошо́!
This is a rather interesting film.	Your room is quite filthy!	How are things? Rather good!

---

*Ты — **оптими́ст** или **пессими́ст**? Share your expectations regarding your future life. Throw in some of the **adverbs of degree** above.*

Кака́я у тебя́ бу́дет **маши́на**? Дорога́я или дешёвая?   Кака́я у тебя́ бу́дет **рабо́та**? Интере́сная или ску́чная?

Како́й у тебя́ бу́дет **телеви́зор**? Большо́й или ма́ленький?   Како́е у тебя́ бу́дет **расписа́ние**? Тру́дное или лёгкое?

[1] In time, you'll develop a feel for when to drop pronouns. Based on my experience, it's much easier, early on, to include them by default.
[2] Remember: **сего́дня** is pronounced as if written **сево́дня** (much like the genitive forms **его́** and **него́** that we learned earlier).

8.6 Three tricky conjunctions ("and" and "but" in Russian)

We've encountered several **conjunctions**, such as и (and) and **или** (or). Let's examine three: **и**, **а**, and **но**. The first one — "**и**" — simply translates as "and," and the third — "**но**" simply translates as "but." It's the one in the middle — "**а**" — that causes confusion; it can translate as "and" and "but!" Let's take some examples:

1) First off, "**и**" simply links two (or more) things together, simply **adding to a list** without any kind of comparison.

и	У меня есть ручка **и** карандаш.	Какая у тебя ручка?	Новая **и** хорошая.
	I have a pen **and** a pencil.	What kind of pen do you have?	A new **and** good one.

2) The essential meaning of "**а**" is perhaps best captured by the English "**while**" or "**whereas**." It's most often used to describe or compare **two different people or things**. So, while there may be a **distinction**, there's no **internal contradiction**: "this is a pencil, **while** that is a pen," or "this one is good, **whereas** that one is bad."

а	Это карандаш, **а** это ручка.	Карандаш новый и хороший, **а** ручка старая.
	This is a pencil, **and** that is a pen.	The pencil is new and good, **but** the pen is old.
	(Or: This is a pencil, while that is a pen.)	*(Or: The pencil is new and good, while the pen is old.)*

3) Finally, "**но**" is used to describe a real **contradiction** concerning a **single thing, person, or situation**.

но	Ручка у меня старая, **но** хорошая.	Сегодня я дома, **но** завтра я буду на работе.
	My pen is old, **but** good.	Today I'm at home, **but** tomorrow I'll be at work.

Describe, compare, and contrast several of your things. In your answer, create a construction including the requested conjunction.

1. Какой у тебя **компьютер**? use **и**: _____.

2. Какой у тебя **рюкзак**? use **но**: _____.

3. Какой у тебя **шампунь**? А какое у тебя **мыло**? use **а**: _____.

4. Какой у тебя **карандаш**? А какая у тебя **ручка**? use **а**: _____.

5. Какая у тебя **комната**? use **но**: _____.

There are two additional uses of **а**: 1) In spoken Russian, **follow-up questions** often begin with **а**.[1] 2) Also, **а** can be used following **не**, in the sense of "**but rather**." In everyday English, we'd usually leave out the "rather."

а	У тебя есть ручка?	Да, есть.	**А** карандаш есть?	Это не карандаш, **а** ручка.
	Do you have a pen?	Yes, I do.	What about a pencil?	This isn't a pencil, **but (rather)** a pen.

One more note: if we repeat **и** (**и**... **и**...), we get the Russian equivalent of "**both**... **and**..." [2]

и	У меня **и** ручка, **и** карандаш.	Ручка есть **и** у неё, **и** у меня.	Я буду дома **и** сегодня, **и** завтра.
	I have **both** a pen **and** a pencil.	**Both** she **and** I have a pen.	I'll be home **both** today **and** tomorrow.

И ЗАСУХУ ПОБЕДИМ!

и doesn't always simply mean "and"

As we saw in the poster at the start of today's lesson, **и** doesn't always mean "and." It sometimes conveys a sense of "too" or "as well," or "even." The poster to the left includes another example.

The caption means something like "We will defeat **even** drought!" (**засуха**, here in the accusative) or "We will defeat drought **as well**!"

The implication is that the U.S.S.R. has overcome many challenges in the past — and will overcome drought **as well**.

Note: **победим** is a conjugated form of **победить** (to defeat). The form **победим** means "we will defeat (completely, successfully)."

---

[1] This is extremely common in spoken Russian; listen for it, while keeping in mind that it doesn't mean much of anything!

[2] Similarly: **ни**... **ни**... (neither... nor...) and **или**... **или**... (either... or...)

day 9:   possessive pronouns

possessive pronouns and the question word **чей**;
two ways of expressing possession; two ways of saying "now"

Наш ультиматум взрослым. Our ultimatum to adults. Here, young pioneers (**пионеры**) demand that adults stop smoking in their presence!

9.1   Possessive pronouns and the question word чей

The question word **чей?** (Whose...?) is adjectival, like **какой?** So, it has a full set of adjectival endings, and must match the gender of the noun it refers to.

To answer a "**чей, чья, чьё**" question, use a **possessive pronoun** — the Russian equivalents of "my, your, our, etc." These words are referred to as pronouns because they can **stand in for a noun** (like the English "mine," as in "mine is new."), but most often they modify another noun ("my book"). In both cases, they take **adjectival endings**, and must **agree** in gender with the noun they modify.

So, both the question word **чей** and the **possessive pronouns** are **adjectival**, but in many cases their endings **differ** (often slightly) from those of ordinary adjectives. Therefore, we'll refer to such words as **special modifiers**.

	masc.	fem.	neut.	
	чей?	**чья?**	**чьё?**	Whose?
я →	**мой**	**моя**	**моё**	my
ты →	**твой**	**твоя**	**твоё**	your
мы →	**наш**	**наша**	**наше**	our
вы →	**ваш**	**ваша**	**ваше**	your
он →	**его**[1]	**его**[1]	**его**[1]	his
она →	**её**	**её**	**её**	her
оно →	**его**[1]	**его**[1]	**его**[1]	its
они →	**их**	**их**	**их**	their

Take note of the **third-person forms** in the black boxes. These **possessive** pronoun forms (his, her, its, their) **never change in any way.**[2] The same form is used to modify nouns of **all three genders**; for example:

Чей это стол? **Whose** table is this?	Это **мой** стол.	This is **my** table.	Это **его** стол.	This is **his** table.
Чья это книга? **Whose** book is this?	Это **моя** книга.	This is **my** book.	Это **его** книга.	This is **his** book.
Чьё это окно? **Whose** window is this?	Это **моё** окно.	This is **my** window.	Это **его** окно.	This is **his** window.
	Это **наш** стол.	This is **our** table.	Это **её** стол.	This is **her** table.
	Это **наша** книга.	This is **our** book.	Это **её** книга.	This is **her** book.
	Это **наше** окно.	This is **our** window.	Это **её** окно.	This is **her** window.

38   [1] Pronounced "ево"   [2] This includes not adding an initial **н**! Don't confuse these **possessive** forms (e.g. **его** in the possessive sense of "**his**"), which **never** change (У **его** мамы есть машина. = His mom has a car, "at his mom is car."), with case forms of ordinary pronouns, which do change (Это **он**. **Его** зовут Борис. У **него** есть машина. = That's him. His name is Boris. He has a car, "at him is car.")

Whose? (чей?)	use мой:	use твой:	use наш:	use ваш:	use его:	use её:	use их:
1. ____ это **ручка**?	Она ____?	Она ____?	Она ____?	Она ____?	Она ____?	Она ____?	Она ____?
2. ____ это **зонт**?	Он ____?	Он ____?	Он ____?	Он ____?	Он ____?	Он ____?	Он ____?
3. ____ это **бельё**?	Оно ____?	Оно ____?	Оно ____?	Оно ____?	Оно ____?	Оно ____?	Оно ____?
4. ____ это **рюкзак**?	Он ____?	Он ____?	Он ____?	Он ____?	Он ____?	Он ____?	Он ____?
5. ____ это **машина**?	Она ____?	Она ____?	Она ____?	Она ____?	Она ____?	Она ____?	Она ____?
6. ____ это **окно**?	Оно ____?	Оно ____?	Оно ____?	Оно ____?	Оно ____?	Оно ____?	Оно ____?
7. ____ это **идея**?	Она ____?	Она ____?	Она ____?	Она ____?	Она ____?	Она ____?	Она ____?
8. ____ это **мяч**?	Он ____?	Он ____?	Он ____?	Он ____?	Он ____?	Он ____?	Он ____?

Было ваше, стало наше. It was yours, it became ours (said when something has been shamelessly stolen).

Чей это **телефон**?	**Какой он**?		
1. ____ это **машина**?	_____ ____?	5. ____ это **ключ**?	_____ ____?
2. ____ это **мяч**?	_____ ____?	6. ____ это **мыло**?	_____ ____?
3. ____ это **полотенце**?	_____ ____?	7. ____ это **шампунь**?	_____ ____?
4. ____ это **рубашка**?	_____ ____?	8. ____ это **одеяло**?	_____ ____?
		9. ____ это **простыня**?	_____ ____?

Чей это **был** словарь вчера?
Whose dictionary **was** that yesterday?

Это **был мой новый** словарь.
That **was my new** dictionary.

Ничего[1] себе!
Wow!

1. ____ это _____ **машина** вчера?	Это _____ _____ _____ машина.	Ничего себе!
2. ____ это _____ **мяч** вчера?	Это _____ _____ _____ мяч.	Ничего себе!
3. ____ это _____ **кресло** вчера?	Это _____ _____ _____ кресло.	Ничего себе!
4. ____ это _____ **книга** вчера?	Это _____ _____ _____ книга.	Ничего себе!
5. ____ это _____ **телефон** вчера?	Это _____ _____ _____ телефон.	Ничего себе!

Two ways of expressing possession

As we know, constructions with **у** (у меня, у нас, у него, etc.) can be used to **ask about** and **establish** possession:

У тебя есть машина?
"At you is car?"

Да, есть.
"Yes, is."

У меня есть машина.
"At me is car."

Furthermore, such **у** constructions can be used interchangeably with the possessive pronouns we've just learned to express possession in a more neutral fashion:

Компьютер **у меня** плохой.
"Computer at me bad."

Мой компьютер плохой.
"My computer bad."

So, is there any difference between these two? The second example (with "мой") gives some added emphasis to the idea of **possession**, beyond simply neutrally expressing the idea of **having**: this is *my* computer. It may imply the following kind of comparison:

Мой компьютер плохой, а **твой** хороший.
My computer is bad, while yours is good.

Relying on English, many students tend to overuse possessive pronouns like "мой." [2] Generally speaking, the **у** construction often sounds more idiomatically Russian.

Наше дело правое. Враг будет разбит! Our cause is just. The enemy will be crushed! [3]

---

[1] Pronounced "ничево"   [2] Possessives are often omitted altogether, especially when speaking of family members, as we'll learn later.
[3] This phrase became famous as part of the official announcement of the Nazi invasion of the Soviet Union over Soviet radio.

9.d

Чья <u>э</u>то кн<u>и</u>га?	Тво<u>я</u>, или его?	<u>Э</u>то не **его** кн<u>и</u>га.	Он<u>а</u> мо<u>я</u>.
Whose book is this?	**Yours**, or his?	This isn't **his** book.	**It's mine.**

1. _____ <u>э</u>то **компь<u>ю</u>тер**? | _____ или его? | <u>Э</u>то не _____ компь<u>ю</u>тер. | _____ _____.

2. _____ <u>э</u>то **расп<u>и</u>сание**? | _____ или её? | <u>Э</u>то не _____ расп<u>и</u>сание. | _____ _____.

3. _____ <u>э</u>то **кошелёк**? | _____ или их? | <u>Э</u>то не _____ кошелёк. | _____ _____.

4. _____ <u>э</u>то **с<u>у</u>мка**? | _____ или её? | <u>Э</u>то не _____ с<u>у</u>мка. | _____ _____.

5. _____ <u>э</u>то **бельё**? | _____ или ег<u>о</u>? | <u>Э</u>то не _____ бельё. | _____ _____.

Чья <u>э</u>то кн<u>и</u>га?	Н<u>а</u>ша, или в<u>а</u>ша?	<u>Э</u>то не **н<u>а</u>ша** кн<u>и</u>га.	Он<u>а</u> в<u>а</u>ша.
Whose book is this?	**Ours**, or yours?	This isn't **our** book.	**It's yours.**

6. _____ <u>э</u>то **зонт**? | _____ или _____? | <u>Э</u>то не _____ зонт. | _____ _____.

7. _____ <u>э</u>то **м<u>е</u>сто**? | _____ или _____? | <u>Э</u>то не _____ м<u>е</u>сто. | _____ _____.

8. _____ <u>э</u>то **слов<u>а</u>рь**? | _____ или _____? | <u>Э</u>то не _____ слов<u>а</u>рь. | _____ _____.

9. _____ <u>э</u>то **каранд<u>а</u>ш**? | _____ или _____? | <u>Э</u>то не _____ каранд<u>а</u>ш. | _____ _____.

10. _____ <u>э</u>то **маш<u>и</u>на**? | _____ или _____? | <u>Э</u>то не _____ маш<u>и</u>на. | _____ _____.

Мо<u>я</u> х<u>а</u>та с кр<u>а</u>ю. My hut is at the edge (of the village) — i.e., I don't care, it's none of my business, other people's problems don't concern me.

9.e

У теб<u>я</u> есть кн<u>и</u>га?	Есть. Вот **мо<u>я</u>** кн<u>и</u>га.
Do you have a book?	Yes, I do. Here's **my** book.

1. У **теб<u>я</u>** есть окн<u>о</u>? | Есть. Вот _____ окн<u>о</u>.

2. У **вас** есть маш<u>и</u>на? | Есть. Вот _____ маш<u>и</u>на.

3. У **них** есть велосип<u>е</u>д? | Есть. Вот _____ велосип<u>е</u>д.

4. У **нег<u>о</u>** есть оде<u>я</u>ло? | Есть. Вот _____ оде<u>я</u>ло.

5. У **неё** есть слов<u>а</u>рь? | Есть. Вот _____ слов<u>а</u>рь.

6. У **мен<u>я</u>** есть м<u>е</u>сто? | Есть. Вот _____ м<u>е</u>сто.

The "showing word" вот

вот is a more emphatic version of **<u>э</u>то**; instead of merely pointing something out, it shows it, inviting people to look. It often expresses amazement.

Вот мо<u>я</u> н<u>о</u>вая маш<u>и</u>на.
Look, here's my new car.

Вот <u>э</u>то хор<u>о</u>шая ид<u>е</u>я!
Now there's a good idea!

Вот н<u>а</u>ша пр<u>и</u>быль![1] Here's our profit!

ВОТ НАША ПРИБЫЛЬ!

Товарищи! (Comrades!) Act out the following dialogue (let's call it... **Диалект<u>и</u>ческий материал<u>и</u>зм**), picking a new item of property each time. The dialogue is between **коммун<u>и</u>ст н<u>о</u>мер од<u>и</u>н** (Communist No. 1) and **коммун<u>и</u>ст н<u>о</u>мер два** (Communist No. 2). After a pernicious but thankfully brief flirtation with bourgeois notions of private property, you will come to the dialectically unavoidable conclusion that each item is to be owned communally (that is, it is to be communal, shared — **<u>о</u>бщий**). Substitute other nouns if you like!

		Choose a possession:
Коммун<u>и</u>ст № 1:	Чей / чья / чьё <u>э</u>то _____?	
Коммун<u>и</u>ст № 2:	<u>Э</u>то мой / мо<u>я</u> / моё _____.	**кварт<u>и</u>ра** (apartment)
Коммун<u>и</u>ст № 1:	Нет, <u>э</u>то не твой / тво<u>я</u> / твоё _____.	**туал<u>е</u>т** (bathroom)
	Он / он<u>а</u> / он<u>о</u> мой / мо<u>я</u> / моё.	**к<u>у</u>хня** (kitchen)
Коммун<u>и</u>ст № 2:	Твой / тво<u>я</u> / твоё?! Нет! Он / он<u>а</u> / он<u>о</u> мой / мо<u>я</u> / моё	**в<u>а</u>нна** (bathtub)
Коммун<u>и</u>ст № 1:	Мой / мо<u>я</u> / моё!!	**руб<u>а</u>шка** (shirt)
Коммун<u>и</u>ст № 2:	Л<u>а</u>дно, тов<u>а</u>рищ. <u>Э</u>то наш / н<u>а</u>ша / н<u>а</u>ше _____.	**метр<u>о</u>** (subway)
Коммун<u>и</u>ст № 1:	Да, тов<u>а</u>рищ, <u>э</u>то пр<u>а</u>вда. Он / он<u>а</u> / он<u>о</u> наш / н<u>а</u>ша / н<u>а</u>ше	**самолёт** (airplane)
Коммун<u>и</u>ст № 2:	Т<u>о</u>чно (exactly)! <u>Э</u>то не его _____.	**танк** (tank)
Коммун<u>и</u>ст № 1:	<u>Э</u>то не её _____.	**кор<u>о</u>ва** (cow)
Коммун<u>и</u>ст № 2:	<u>Э</u>то не их _____.	**карт<u>о</u>шка** (potatoes)
Вм<u>е</u>сте (together):	<u>Э</u>то наш / н<u>а</u>ша / н<u>а</u>ше <u>о</u>бщий / <u>о</u>бщая / <u>о</u>бщее _____!	**кн<u>и</u>га** (book)

40   [1] Some nouns ending in a **soft consonant** are actually **feminine**. We'll formally introduce such nouns on Day 56.

9.2 Two ways of saying "now"

We've seen a few temporal adverbs already: **сегодня** (today), **вчера** (yesterday), and **завтра** (tomorrow). Today we'll add **сейчас** and **теперь**, both of which can be translated as "now."

What's the difference? Think of **сейчас** as a <u>neutral</u> expression for "now," and of **теперь** as a more <u>emphatic</u> expression that **contrasts** "now" with some time in the past (**раньше**: before, previously).

For this reason, we often see the combination "**но теперь**" when comparing how something is with how it used to be.

ЦАРСКИЕ ПОЛКИ И КРАСНАЯ АРМИЯ

ЗА ЧТО СРАЖАЛИСЬ ПРЕЖДЕ

ЗА ЧТО СРАЖАЮТСЯ ТЕПЕРЬ

<u>Ц</u>арские полки и кр<u>а</u>сная <u>а</u>рмия. Tsarist Regiments and the Red Army— what soldiers are fighting for now (**теперь**) and what they fought for before (**прежде = раньше**).

Бор<u>и</u>с **сейчас** д<u>о</u>ма?	Р<u>а</u>ньше он был д<u>о</u>ма, но **теперь** нет.
Is Boris at home now?	He was home earlier, but now he's not.

Маш<u>и</u>на был<u>а</u> н<u>о</u>вая, но **теперь** он<u>а</u> ст<u>а</u>рая.
The car used to be new, but now it's old.

Компь<u>ю</u>тер у теб<u>я</u> хор<u>о</u>ший <u>и</u>ли плох<u>о</u>й?   Р<u>а</u>ньше он был плох<u>о</u>й,   но тепе́рь **он хор<u>о</u>ший**.   9.f
Is your computer good or bad?   Before it was bad,   but now it's good.[1]

1. **Расписа́ние** у теб<u>я</u> тр<u>у</u>дное <u>и</u>ли лёгкое?   Р<u>а</u>ньше _____ _____, но тепе́рь _____ _____.

2. **К<u>о</u>мната** у теб<u>я</u> больш<u>а</u>я <u>и</u>ли м<u>а</u>ленькая?   Р<u>а</u>ньше _____ _____, но тепе́рь _____ _____.

3. Твой **телеф<u>о</u>н** хор<u>о</u>ший <u>и</u>ли плох<u>о</u>й?   Р<u>а</u>ньше _____ _____, но тепе́рь _____ _____.

4. **Раб<u>о</u>та** у нас интер<u>е</u>сная <u>и</u>ли ск<u>у</u>чная?   Р<u>а</u>ньше _____ _____, но тепе́рь _____ _____.

5. **Окн<u>о</u>** у вас больш<u>о</u>е <u>и</u>ли м<u>а</u>ленькое?   Р<u>а</u>ньше _____ _____, но тепе́рь _____ _____.

6. Твой **велосип<u>е</u>д** дорог<u>о</u>й <u>и</u>ли дешёвый?   Р<u>а</u>ньше _____ _____, но тепе́рь _____ _____.

7. В<u>а</u>ша **од<u>е</u>жда** дорог<u>а</u>я <u>и</u>ли дешёвая?   Р<u>а</u>ньше _____ _____, но тепе́рь _____ _____.

---

*Choose more adjectives to compare your things with those of a partner. Since we're simply comparing two **different** objects, we'll use the conjunction **а**. Speaking of a **single** object, use **и** to add to the list of non-contradictory adjectives (or **но** to introduce a contradiction).*

М<u>о</u>я кн<u>и</u>га **н<u>о</u>вая** и **интер<u>е</u>сная**,   а **тво<u>я</u> ст<u>а</u>рая** и **неинтер<u>е</u>сная**.
My book is new and interesting,   while yours is old and uninteresting.

1. _____ **каранд<u>а</u>ш** _____ и _____,   а _____ и _____.

2. _____ **рюкз<u>а</u>к** _____ и _____,   а _____ и _____.

3. _____ **р<u>у</u>чка** _____ и _____,   а _____ и _____.

4. _____ **к<u>о</u>мната** _____ и _____,   а _____ и _____.

5. _____ **шамп<u>у</u>нь** _____ и _____,   а _____ и _____.

6. _____ **окн<u>о</u>** _____ и _____,   а _____ и _____.

7. _____ **бельё** _____ и _____,   а _____ и _____.

*Repeat, by comparing your things in the **past**, and in the **future** (speculate!). Or, report to the class, as in "**У меня..., а у него / у неё...**"*

---

[1] Let's assume that life has improved! Although you could try the exercise again under the opposite assumption!

41

day 10: demonstrative pronouns

the demonstrative pronouns **этот** and **тот**; this, that and it; the (right) one, the wrong one; the relative pronoun **который**; the same one, a different one

Новая Москва. Юрий Иванович Пименов, 1937. **Это** Москва. **Этот** город — столица России (This is Moscow. This city is the capital of Russia).

10.1 The demonstrative pronouns этот and тот

The Russian for "this" (**этот**) and "that" (**тот**) are also **special modifiers**; that is, they act as **adjectives**, but their endings differ from those of ordinary adjectives. Since they can stand in for nouns (as in "this one is good, that one is bad"), they can be classified as **pronouns**.

masculine	feminine	neuter	
этот	**эта**	**это**	this[1]
тот	**та**	**то**	that

As we'll explain in a moment, it's essential to note that these are **adjectival**; their endings must **agree** with the nouns they refer to. For example:

Этот ключ новый, а **тот** старый.	*This* key is old, while *that* one is new.
Эта книга новая, а **та** старая.	*This* book is old, while *that* one is new.
Это платье новое, а **то** старое.	*This* dress is old, while *that* one is new.

Note that the second noun is usually omitted, to avoid needless repetition; but it remains understood. Both pronouns agree with the noun they refer to.

Этот ключ новый, а **тот** [ключ] старый.

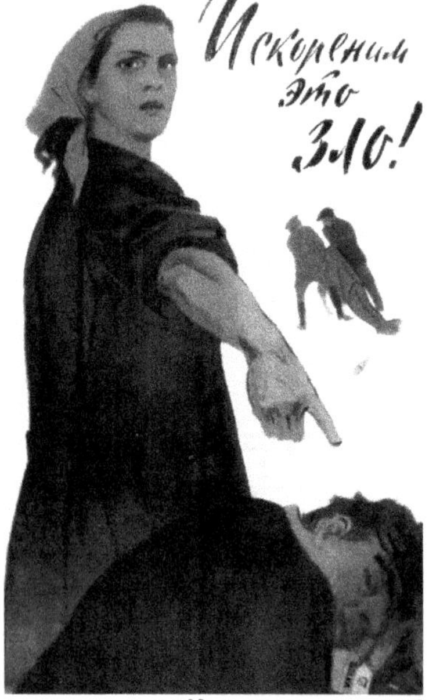

Искореним это зло!
We will eradicate this evil!
(Namely, the evil of алкоголизм)

[1] As we'll see on page 44, the "this / that" distinction is not consistent between English and Russian: "**этот**" could mean "this" or "that." In short, Russian uses "**этот**" by default, and "**тот**" only in an emphatic sense, as in "that one over there," or "that one, as opposed to this." As we'll see later in this lesson, "**тот**" can also have other meanings, like "the (right) one."

этот русский словарь

1. _____ русский музей
2. _____ русская книга
3. _____ новая ручка
4. _____ ужасный фильм
5. _____ скучная русская статья
6. _____ старая газета
7. _____ интересный журнал
8. _____ безобразная идея
9. _____ огромная комната
10. _____ необычная картина
11. _____ дорогое платье

Этот словарь большой, а **тот** маленький.

12. _____ машина дорогая, а _____ дешёвая.
13. _____ окно чистое, а _____ довольно грязное.
14. _____ фильм интересный, а _____ скучный.
15. _____ лампа обычная, а _____ очень странная.
16. _____ задание трудное, а _____ лёгкое.
17. _____ работа лёгкая, а _____ трудная.
18. _____ полотенце чистое, а _____ грязное.
19. _____ музей огромный, а _____ маленький.
20. _____ велосипед дорогой, а _____ дешёвый.

10.2 This, that and it

Three very simple words we've learned can cause a **lot** of confusion, particularly if we rely too much on their possible **English translations**:[1]

1. the "pointing word" **это**, which **never changes its form**.
2. the demonstrative pronoun **этот, эта, это**, which **agrees** with its noun.
3. the pronouns **он, она, оно**, which mean "it" when they refer to objects.

Note that the forms of the pointing word **это** (this is...) and the **neuter** demonstrative pronoun **это** (this) *do coincide*. Only context would allow us to determine which word is being used: does the **это** modify a neuter noun, or is it merely pointing at something? The poster to the right provides an example: the **это** could, in theory, modify the neuter noun **дело** (это дело), as in "**Это дело не моё!**" (This business is not mine!). But the word order and the context make clear that this **это** is the **pointing word**: the conceited young woman is **pointing out** this menial labor and saying that she wants nothing to do with it. Clearly, she disdains **труд** (labor)!

Это не моё дело!
Это не моё дело!
That (this) is none of my business!

First, let's compare the **unchanging** pointing word with the **changing** (adjectival) demonstrative **этот, эта, это**:

pointing word		demonstrative pronoun	
Это новый стол.	**This is** a new table.	**Этот стол** новый.	**This table** is new.
Это новая книга.	**This is** a new book.	**Эта книга** новая.	**This book** is new.
Это новое окно.	**This is** a new window.	**Это окно** новое.	**This window** is new.

The **pointing word это** is neither a noun or pronoun, and cannot act as the **subject** of a sentence: a grammatical subject must be in the **nominative case**, but **это** has no case. In these past-tense examples, note how the verbs **agree** with the nouns — the nouns are the subjects, not **это**! In the basic English translation, though, "it" serves as the subject (a so-called "dummy" subject). Obviously, there is no "it" present in the Russian itself.

pointing word		demonstrative pronoun	
Это был новый стол.	**It** was a new table.	**Этот стол** был новый.	**This table** was new.
Это была новая книга.	**It** was a new book.	**Эта книга** была новая.	**This book** was new.
Это было новое окно.	**It** was a new window.	**Это окно** было новое.	**This window** was new.

Compare the pointing word with the pronouns **он, она, оно**. Of course, these pronouns can serve as **subjects**.

pointing word		pronoun	
Это стол.	**This is** a table.	**Он** новый.	**It** is new.
Это книга.	**This is** a book.	**Она** новая.	**It** is new.
Это окно.	**This is** a window.	**Оно** новое.	**It** is new.

[1] Time and time again in your study of Russian, you'll likely find that the real confusion comes not so much from the Russian itself, but from the expectation that Russian idioms will match up with English idioms — and with English translations. This confusion can arise even (and especially!) with simple examples. Always try to *focus on the Russian*, not relying on translations only!

It must be said that the Russian **тот, та, то** is not used as frequently as the English "that." In English, we say "that" very often to refer to things that are (even slightly) **remote** in space or time. By default, the Russian is:

Э́то хоро́шая маши́на.	That's a nice car.	**Э́та маши́на хоро́шая.**	That car's nice.

Russians use **тот, та, то** exclusively in a more emphatic sense — that is, to emphasize something "**(way) over there**," or to emphasize a **contrast** between **this** and **that**. This is most common in comparisons:

Э́та маши́на но́вая, а **та** ста́рая.   *This* car is new, while *that* one is old.

So, think of the Russian "this" (**э́тот, э́та, э́то**) as the **default**. This will help you avoid (once again!) being misled by English translations, in which **э́тот, э́та, э́то** (as well as the pointing word **э́то**) is sometimes best translated as "that," especially in past- or future-tense sentences (since the thing referred to is temporally "remote").

Э́то хоро́шая иде́я.	**Э́то была́ хоро́шая иде́я.**	**Э́та иде́я была́ хоро́шая.**	**Э́то бу́дет хорошо́.**
That's a good idea.	That was a good idea.	That idea was a good one.	That will be good.

By the way, you can learn a lot about Russian grammar not only by paying attention to your own mistakes, but also to those made by Russian learners of English! They'll often have the same struggles, but the other way around. For example, you may notice Russian speakers overusing the English "this" in place of "that."

10.b	**Э́то** но́вая кни́га.	**Э́та** кни́га но́вая.	**Она́** но́вая.
	This is a new book.	**This** book is new.	**It** is new.
1.	_____ ста́рый стул.	_____ стул _____.	_____ ста́рый.
2.	_____ большо́й стол.	_____ стол _____.	_____ большо́й.
3.	_____ но́вая ру́чка.	_____ ру́чка _____.	_____ но́вая.
4.	_____ но́вый телефо́н.	_____ телефо́н _____.	_____ но́вый.
5.	_____ дешёвое пла́тье.	_____ пла́тье _____.	_____ дешёвое.

	Э́то была́ но́вая кни́га.	**Э́та** кни́га **была́** но́вая.	**Она́ была́** но́вая.
	It was a new book.	**That** book **was** new.	**It was** new.
6.	_____ _____ ста́рый стул.	_____ стул _____ _____.	_____ _____ ста́рый.
7.	_____ _____ большо́й стол.	_____ стол _____ _____.	_____ _____ большо́й.
8.	_____ _____ но́вая ру́чка.	_____ ру́чка _____ _____.	_____ _____ но́вая.
9.	_____ _____ но́вый телефо́н.	_____ телефо́н _____ _____.	_____ _____ но́вый.
10.	_____ _____ дешёвое пла́тье.	_____ пла́тье _____ _____.	_____ _____ дешёвое.

10.3 The (right) one, the wrong one

та, то, тот is used in a few other useful expressions: for example, "the one" ("the right one," "the one I meant," "the one I wanted," "the one I needed"). Negating it with **не** gives us "not the one" ("the wrong one").

Э́то **тот** слова́рь?	Да, **тот**.	Нет, **не тот**.
Is this **the (right)** dictionary?	Yes, that's *the one*.	No, that's *not the one* (the wrong one).
Э́то **та** газе́та?	Да, **та**.	Нет, **не та**.
Is this **the (right)** newspaper?	Yes, that's *the one*.	No, that's *not the one* (the wrong one).
Э́то **то** пла́тье?	Да, **то**.	Нет, **не то**.
Is this **the (right)** dress?	Yes, that's *the one*.	No, that's *not the one* (the wrong one).

10.4 The same one, a different one: тот же

The adjective **друг<u>о</u>й**[1] means "a different" or "another." How do we say "the same?" In the right context, the constructions we just used (**тот, та, то**) can mean "the same," as in "that" one that we had before. For example:

<u>Э</u>то **та** кн<u>и</u>га?	Да, **та**.	<u>Э</u>то **тот** словарь?	Нет, **не тот**.
Is this the (same) book?	Yes, that's the (same) one.	Is this the (same) dictionary?	No, that's not the (same) one.

To emphasize the idea of "the same," we can add the emphatic particle **же**,[2] and even the adjective **самый**, giving us the following three constructions. They mean essentially the same thing, but with increasing emphasis.

тот з<u>о</u>нт	**тот же** з<u>о</u>нт	**тот же с<u>а</u>мый** з<u>о</u>нт	the same umbrella
та кн<u>и</u>га	**та же** кн<u>и</u>га	**та же самая** кн<u>и</u>га	the same book
то м<u>е</u>сто	**то же** м<u>е</u>сто	**то же самое** м<u>е</u>сто	the same place

<u>Э</u>то **тот же** мяч?	Да, **тот же**.	Нет, <u>э</u>то **друг<u>о</u>й** мяч.
Is this the (same) ball?	Yes, it's the same.	No, this is a different ball.
<u>Э</u>то **то же с<u>а</u>мое** м<u>е</u>сто?	Да, **то же с<u>а</u>мое**.	Нет, <u>э</u>то **друг<u>о</u>е**.
Is this the same seat?	Yes, it's the same.	No, this is a different one.

<u>Э</u>то **тот** словарь?	Нет, не **тот**. <u>Э</u>то **друг<u>о</u>й**.	4. <u>Э</u>то _____ газ<u>е</u>та? Нет, не ____. <u>Э</u>то _____.	**10.c**
Is this the dictionary?	No, it's not. It's a different one.	5. <u>Э</u>то _____ ключ? Нет, не ____. <u>Э</u>то _____.	
1. <u>Э</u>то _____ кн<u>и</u>га?	Нет, не ____. <u>Э</u>то _____.	6. <u>Э</u>то _____ муз<u>е</u>й? Нет, не ____. <u>Э</u>то _____.	
2. <u>Э</u>то _____ журн<u>а</u>л?	Нет, не ____. <u>Э</u>то _____.	7. <u>Э</u>то _____ м<u>е</u>сто? Нет, не ____. <u>Э</u>то _____.	
3. <u>Э</u>то _____ м<u>ы</u>ло?	Нет, не ____. <u>Э</u>то _____.	8. <u>Э</u>то _____ зонт? Нет, не ____. <u>Э</u>то _____.	

10.5 The same kind: так<u>о</u>й же

Now we know two demonstrative pronouns (**<u>э</u>тот** and **тот**). There's another set of demonstrative forms that we'll be learning gradually. For each **question word**, there is a corresponding **demonstrative**, usually beginning with **т**, that is used not to **ask** about something, but to **show** or point something out.

For example, **Как<u>о</u>й**? asks "of what kind?" The corresponding demonstrative form is **так<u>о</u>й**, meaning "of such a kind" or "one like this."

Как<u>о</u>й у теб<u>я</u> ключ? **Так<u>о</u>й**?	Да, **так<u>о</u>й**.
What kind of key do you have? One **like this**?	Yes, one **like that**.

Just as we did above, we can add the emphatic particle **же** to **так<u>о</u>й** to get a new phrase: **так<u>о</u>й же**, meaning "of the same kind."

У мен<u>я</u> **так<u>о</u>й же** ключ.	У мен<u>я</u> **так<u>о</u>й** же ключ, **как** у теб<u>я</u>.
I have **the same** kind of key.	I have **the same** kind of key **as** you do.

А ты не так<u>о</u>й? Are you not like this?[3] (one of many posters discouraging **хулиг<u>а</u>нство**, hooliganism).

<u>Э</u>то **тот же** словарь?	Да, **тот же**.	<u>Э</u>то **так<u>о</u>й же** словарь?	Да, **так<u>о</u>й же**.	**10.d**
Is this the same dictionary?	Yes, it is.	Is this the same kind of dictionary?	Yes, it is.	
1. <u>Э</u>то _____ ____ плак<u>а</u>т?	Да, _____ ____.	4. <u>Э</u>то _____ ____ плак<u>а</u>т?	Да, _____ ____.	
2. <u>Э</u>то _____ ____ карт<u>и</u>на?	Да, _____ ____.	5. <u>Э</u>то _____ ____ карт<u>и</u>на?	Да, _____ ____.	
3. <u>Э</u>то _____ ____ пл<u>а</u>тье?	Да, _____ ____.	6. <u>Э</u>то _____ ____ пл<u>а</u>тье?	Да, _____ ____.	

Б<u>о</u>же мой, Б<u>о</u>же, пое<u>д</u>им, посп<u>и</u>м да оп<u>я</u>ть за то же. My God, my God — we'll eat a bit, sleep a bit, and then do the same (old) thing.

[1] друг<u>о</u>й is an ordinary end-stressed adjective, like больш<u>о</u>й or плох<u>о</u>й.
[2] This particle (же) can add emphasis in a number of situations. Unlike monosyllabic nouns, it is **never stressed**.
[3] See how the young hooligan cheats in school, doesn't help old ladies carry groceries, wields a slingshot, and dresses sloppily.

Nouns & pronouns

hard nouns		
masculine	**feminine**	**neuter**
сто́л table	кни́га book	де́ло matter, business
сту́л chair	ко́мната room	окно́ window
велосипе́д bicycle	оде́жда clothes	ме́сто place, seat
телефо́н phone	рабо́та work	зе́ркало mirror
компью́тер computer	карти́на picture	кре́сло easy chair
телеви́зор television	футбо́лка t-shirt	письмо́ letter
плака́т poster	этаже́рка bookshelf	одея́ло blanket
каранда́ш pencil	маши́на car	мы́ло soap
рюкза́к backpack	переда́ча TV broadcast / show	у́тро morning
ковёр carpet	оши́бка mistake	пальто́ coat
мя́ч ball	страни́ца page	кино́ cinema, movie(s)
клю́ч key	газе́та newspaper	
ве́чер evening	су́мка purse	
зо́нт umbrella	те́ма topic, theme	
сериа́л TV series	пробле́ма problem	
фи́льм film, a movie	зада́ча (math) problem, task	
журна́л magazine	ру́чка pen	
вопро́с question	ла́мпа lamp	
отве́т answer	руба́шка shirt	
кошелёк wallet	бума́га paper	
уче́бник textbook		

soft nouns		
masculine	**feminine**	**neuter**
шампу́нь shampoo	иде́я idea	пла́тье dress
слова́рь dictionary	неде́ля week	полоте́нце towel
де́нь day	простыня́ bedsheet	бельё laundry
музе́й museum	статья́ article	и́мя first name
	семья́ family	

special soft nouns		
masculine	**feminine**	**neuter**
кафете́рий cafeteria	фами́лия last name	расписа́ние schedule
	фотогра́фия photo	упражне́ние exercise (in textbook)
	исто́рия story, history	зада́ние assignment

pronouns					
singular			**plural**		
nominative	у + genitive	accusative	nominative	у + genitive	accusative
я I	у меня́ I have ("at me")	меня́ me	мы we	у нас we have ("at us")	нас us
ты you	у тебя́ you have ("at you")	тебя́ you	вы you	у вас you have ("at you")	вас you
он he	у него́[1] he has ("at him")	его́[1] him			
она́ she	у неё she has ("at her")	её her	они́ they	у них they have ("at them")	их them
оно́ it	у него́[1] it has ("at it")	его́[1] it			

[1] Recall that **его́** is pronounced as if written **ево́**, and **него́** is pronounced as if written **нево́**.

Adjectives & special modifiers

	stem	ordinary hard adjectives		
		masculine: -ый	feminine: -ая	neuter: -oe
new:	**нов-**	новый	новая	новое
old:	**стар-**	старый	старая	старое
boring:	**скучн-**	скучный	скучная	скучное
favorite ("loved"):	**любим-**	любимый	любимая	любимое
hard, difficult:	**трудн-**	трудный	трудная	трудное
strange:	**странн-**	странный	странная	странное
clean:	**чист-**	чистый	чистая	чистое
dirty:	**грязн-**	грязный	грязная	грязное
cheap:	**дешёв-**	дешёвый	дешёвая	дешёвое
awful:	**ужасн-**	ужасный	ужасная	ужасное
huge:	**огромн-**	огромный	огромная	огромное
excellent, great:	**отличн-**	отличный	отличная	отличное
hideous, awful:	**безобразн-**	безобразный	безобразная	безобразное
important:	**важн-**	важный	важная	важное
(not) pretty:	**(не)красив-**	(не)красивый	(не)красивая	(не)красивое
(un)usual:	**(не)обычн-**	(не)обычный	(не)обычная	(не)обычное
(un)interesting:	**(не)интересн-**	(не)интересный	(не)интересная	(не)интересное

		affected by the 7-letter spelling rule		
		masculine: -ий	feminine: -ая	neuter: -oe
small:	**маленьк-**	маленький	маленькая	маленькое
easy, light:	**лёгк-**	лёгкий	лёгкая	лёгкое
Russian:	**русск-**	русский	русская	русское

		affected by the 5- and 7-letter spelling rules		
		masculine: -ий	feminine: -ая	neuter: -ee
good:	**хорош-**	хороший	хорошая	хорошее

		end-stressed adjectives		
		masculine: -ой	feminine: -ая	neuter: -oe
bad:	**плох-**	плохой	плохая	плохое
big:	**больш-**	большой	большая	большое
expensive:	**дорог-**	дорогой	дорогая	дорогое
funny:	**смешн-**	смешной	смешная	смешное
a different, another:	**друг-**	другой	другая	другое
of what kind?	**как-**	какой	какая	какое
of such a kind:	**так-**	такой	такая	такое

possessive pronouns

	masc.	fem.	neut.	
	чей?	чья?	чьё?	Whose?
я →	мой	моя	моё	my
ты →	твой	твоя	твоё	your
мы →	наш	наша	наше	our
вы →	ваш	ваша	ваше	your
он →	его[1]	его[1]	его[1]	his
она →	её	её	её	her
оно →	его[1]	его[1]	его[1]	its
они →	их	их	их	their

demonstrative pronouns

masculine	feminine	neuter	
этот	эта	это	this
тот	та	то	that

the "pointing word" (never changes!)

это	this is...

[1] Again, remember that **его** is pronounced as if written **ево**.

Same and different

тот зонт	**тот же** зонт	**тот же самый** зонт	the same umbrella	**другой** зонт	another / a different umbrella
та книга	**та же** книга	**та же самая** книга	the same book	**другая** книга	another / a different book
то место	**то же** место	**то же самое** место	the same place	**другое** место	another / a different place

Adverbs

adverbs					
очень	very, really	**совсем**	completely	**сегодня**	today
не очень	not very, not really	**не совсем**	not completely	**вчера**	yesterday
довольно	quite	**ужасно**	horribly	**завтра**	tomorrow
слишком	too	**сейчас**	now	**раньше**	before, previously
сравнительно	relatively	**теперь**	now (contrasted with past)	**тоже**	also

The verb "to be"

быть (to be): present tense	
есть	is, are (one form only; often omitted unless emphasized)

быть (to be): future tense			
singular		**plural**	
я **буду**	I will be	мы **будем**	we will be
ты **будешь**	you will be	вы **будете**	you will be
он, она, оно **будет**	he, she, it will be	они **будут**	they will be

быть (to be): past tense			
singular		**plural**	
был	he was (masc.)		
была	she was (fem.)	**были**	they were
было	it was (neut.)		

Other words and expressions

Здравствуй! / Здравствуйте!	Hello! (pronounced "здраствуй")		**Добрый день!**	Good day!
До свидания!	Goodbye!		**Добрый вечер!**	Good evening!
Привет!	Hi! (informal)		**Доброе утро!**	Good morning!
Здорово!	Good to see you! (informal)			
Пока!	Bye! (informal)		**Будь здоров / здорова!**	Bless you! (informal)
Счастливо!	Take it easy! (informal)		**Будьте здоровы!**	Bless you! (formal)
Давайте перейдём на "ты".	Let's "cross over" to ты.		**и**	and (adding to a list)
Хорошо!	OK!		**а**	while (comparing)
Пожалуйста	Please (pronounced "пожалста")		**но**	but (stark contrast)
Спасибо	Thank you		**или**	or
Извини! / Извините!	Excuse me! Sorry! (informal / formal)			
Как вы сказали?	What? What did you say?		**Что?**	What?
Повторите, пожалуйста.	Repeat, please. (formal)		**Сколько?**	How many / how much?
Можно?	May I? ("is it possible?")		**Чей? Чья? Чьё?**	Whose?
Как (у вас / у тебя) дела?	How are things going?		**Какой? Какая? Какое?**	What kind of?
Давайте познакомимся.	Let's get acquainted.			
Меня зовут...	My name is...			
Как вас / тебя зовут?	What's your name?			
к сожалению	unfortunately[1]			
по-русски / по-английски	in Russian / in English			
Вот...	Here is... / Here are... (showing)			

---

[1] Pronounce this preposition phrase as though it were a single word — that is, exactly like **ксожалению**.

БАНКОВСКИЕ БИЛЕТЫ ОБЕСПЕЧИВАЮТСЯ ЗОЛ
МЕТАЛЛАМИ И ПРОЧИМИ АКТИВАМИ ГОСУ
100
ЗЗ 069539
СТО КАРБОВАНЦІВ · СТО РУБЛЕ
SIMTAS RUBLIŲ · SIMTS RUBL
1947

II

people and activities

verbs, the genitive, and the accusative

In this chapter, we'll learn both the genitive and accusative cases, and how to express possession and non-existence. We'll learn the basics of verb conjugation, discuss all three verb tenses, and begin our discussion of a very tricky topic in Russian grammar: verbal aspect.

day 11:   the genitive case

animate nouns; genitive endings; mobile vowels;
uses of the genitive case; adjectives that can stand
alone as nouns; end-stressed masculine nouns

Пла́ны па́ртии — пла́ны наро́да! The Party's plans are the people's plans! This guy's big Soviet hair didn't fit into the frame.

11.1 Animate nouns

Animate nouns answer the question **Кто?** (Who?), and refer to **people** — or **animals** (but not plants!).

hard nouns					
masculine				**feminine**	
враг	enemy	студе́нт	student (male)	студе́нтка	student (female)
а́втор	author	аспира́нт	grad student (male)	аспира́нтка	grad student (fem.)
поэ́т	poet	друг	friend (male)	подру́га	friend (female)
сосе́д	neighbor/roommate	профе́ссор	professor	сестра́	sister
ма́льчик	boy	оте́ц	father	ма́ма	mom
сын	son	челове́к	human being	же́нщина	woman
кот	cat (male)	брат	brother	де́вушка	young woman
котёнок	kitten	ро́дственник	relative	де́вочка	girl
щено́к	puppy	това́рищ	comrade; buddy	соба́ка	dog
президе́нт	president	нача́льник	boss	ко́шка	cat (female)
знако́мый[1]	male acquaintance	**masculine (with feminine endings!)**		знако́мая[1]	fem. acquaintance
внук	grandson	па́па	dad	ба́бушка	grandmother
муж	husband	де́душка	grandfather	вну́чка	granddaughter
жени́х	groom, fiancé	колле́га	colleague	до́чка	daughter
ребёнок	child	зану́да	boring person, killjoy	жена́	wife
игро́к	a player / gambler	мужчи́на	man	неве́ста	bride, fiancée
солда́т	soldier	пья́ница	drunkard	сосе́дка	neighbor/roommate
soft nouns					
masculine				**feminine**	
па́рень	guy	писа́тель	writer	тётя	aunt
геро́й	hero	**masculine (but feminine endings!)**			
прия́тель	pal, buddy	дя́дя	uncle		

52   [1] these are **adjectives** that can **stand alone as nouns**, but will always take **adjectival endings**! Note the masculine and feminine variants: знако́мый is a male acquaintance, while знако́мая is a female acquaintance.

11.2 Genitive case endings

So far, we've used nouns in the **nominative** case. There are five more cases to learn! Today we'll add the **genitive** case, which expresses possession. Note the new endings in bold below, in both hard and soft variants: for example, **hard** masculines end in -a, while **soft** ones end in -я (the "soft version" of the very same ending). Adjectives **agree** with the nouns they modify in terms of both **gender** and **case**.

masculine				
	hard	**soft**		**special soft**[1]
nom.	новый	стол	словарь	музей	кафетерий
gen.	нов**ого**	стол**а**	словар**я**	музе**я**	кафетери**я**

feminine			
	hard	**soft**	**special soft**[1]
nom.	новая	газета	неделя	фамилия
gen.	нов**ой**	газет**ы**	недел**и**	фамили**и**

neuter			
	hard	**soft**	**special soft**[1]
nom.	новое	окно	море	бельё	задание
gen.	нов**ого**	окн**а**	мор**я**	бель**я**	задани**я**

Воин красной армии, спаси!
Warrior of the Red Army, save (us)!

Effects of the spelling rules on genitive endings

	4 "hushings"	3 "velars"	1	
	ж ч ш щ	г к х	ц	
7-letter rule: after these 7 letters...	ж ч ш щ	г к х	_	...write: **и** ...not: **ы**
5-letter rule: after these 5 letters...	ж ч ш щ	_____	ц	...write: **е** ...not: unstressed **о**

The two rules we've learned are **universally applicable.** Look in the black boxes to see how they affect the genitive.

The 7-letter rule can affect feminine nouns:	газета → **газеты**	*but:* книга → **книги**, водка → **водки**, дача → **дачи**
The 5-letter rule can affect adjectives:	новый → **нового**	русский → **русского** *but:* хороший → **хорошего**
	новая → **новой**	русская → **русской** *but:* хорошая → **хорошей**

When the ending **-ой** is **unstressed**, it sounds like "uh"+**й**, **not** like the "oy" in "boy." The failure to reduce this ending properly is very noticeable. The same is true of the **o** in the ending **-ого**, when unstressed: say "uh-vuh."

reduced (unstressed) -ой	reduced (unstressed) -ого	but: stressed "o" is never reduced!
словарь нов**ой** студентки	начало русск**ого** романа	начало плох**ой** книги
книга русск**ой** поэзии	конец эт**ого** ужасн**ого** фильма	фотография Больш**ого** театра
конец интересн**ой** статьи	словарь нов**ого** студента	

новый студент:	книга нов**ого** студент**а** the book **of the new student**		5. хороший поэт:	книга хорош_____ поэт____ **11.a**
1. новая студентка:	комната нов_____ студентк____		6. хорошая кошка:	фотография хорош_____ кошк____
2. русский друг:	сестра русск_____ друг____		7. русский писатель:	статья русск_____ писател____
3. русская подруга:	отец русск_____ подруг____		8. большая собака:	фотография больш_____ собак___
4. старый фильм:	начало стар_____ фильм____		9. новый сосед:	ключ нов_____ сосед____
			10. новая соседка:	окно нов_____ соседк____

Повторение — мать учения. Repetition is the mother of learning (учение, here in the genitive).

[1] Note that, for now, the **special soft** adjectives are still behaving exactly like ordinary soft nouns.

11.3 The mobile vowel

An **o**, **e** or **ё** in the final syllable of a masculine noun that is stuck between two consonants is (in many cases[1]) a **mobile vowel**, and is "squeezed out" whenever any **ending** (including a genitive ending) is added.

				but:				
щен(о)к →	**щенка**	ребён(о)к →	**ребёнка**		человек →	**человека**	вопрос →	**вопроса**
кон(е)ц →	**конца**	от(е)ц →	**отца**		игрок →	**игрока**	ответ →	**ответа**
ков(ё)р →	**ковра**	пар(е)нь →	**парня**		кот →	**кота**	вечер →	**вечера**

Note how from now on we'll use parentheses to indicate the presence of a mobile vowel in the vocabulary.[1]

11.4 Uses of the genitive case

The genitive is used to express **possession** or some other **close relationship** between two nouns. If we translate a Russian word that is in the genitive case using "**of**," we will usually get a good sense of the meaning — but in everyday English we'd often prefer a form with "apostrophe s."

комната **нового студента**	the room **of the new student** (the s.'s room)
друг **Ивана**	a friend **of Ivan** (Ivan's friend)
окно **кухни**	the window **of the kitchen** (kitchen window)
карта **России**	a map **of Russia**
конец **фильма**	the end **of the movie**
поэзия **Пушкина**	the poetry **of Pushkin**

....

It's not uncommon to see chains of two or more genitive nouns!

резиденция **президента России**
the residence of the president of Russia

начало **конца блокады Ленинграда**
the beginning of the end of the siege of Leningrad.

ИЗУЧАЙТЕ ВЕЛИКИЙ ПУТЬ
ПАРТИИ ЛЕНИНА-СТАЛИНА!

Изучайте великий путь партии
Ленина-Сталина! Study the great path of
the party of Lenin and Stalin!

11.5 Prepositions that take the genitive

Whenever we add a new cases, we'll also learn some common prepositions that are followed by that case. The prepositions (including the final phrase) below are **always** followed by objects in the **genitive** case.

у	"at"	**У мамы** есть новая машина.
		Mom has a new car. (possession)
		Я была **у мамы** вчера.
		I was at mom's place yesterday.
без	without	Комната у меня **без окна!**
		I have a room without a window!
от	from	У меня письмо **от друга.**
		I have a letter from (my) friend.[2]
для	for	Это подарок **для отца.**
		This is a present for (my) father.
против	against	Ты **против коммунизма?**
		Are you against Communism?
во время	during	**Во время блокады** Ленинграда не было еды.
		During the siege of Leningrad there was no food.

Болтун — находка для врага!
A blabbermouth is a
find for the enemy!

[1] Any good dictionary should give the nominative and genitive singular forms; comparing them will tell you whether a mobile vowel is present.
[2] Again, Russian tends to omit possessives like "my" when it is clear the person is speaking of their own things, relatives, etc.

11.6 Remaining genitive forms

For each case, we'll also have to learn new forms for the so-called **special modifiers** — words that take **adjectival endings** that may differ slightly from those of **ordinary adjectives**. Furthermore, the question words **что** and **кто** also have special forms for each case.

	что (what?)	кто (who?)
nom.	что	кто
gen.	**чего**	**кого**

этот (тот)[1]	masc.	fem.	neut.
nom.	этот	эта	это
gen.	этого	этой	этого

мой (твой)	masc.	fem.	neut.
nom.	мой	моя	моё
gen.	моего	моей	моего

наш (ваш)	masc.	fem.	neut.
nom.	наш	наша	наш
gen.	нашего	нашей	нашего

Finally, here are the genitive forms for the **personal pronouns** (we've seen them already with the preposition **у**).

Notice the forms in the **black boxes**. As we've seen, **third-person** pronouns have special forms that are used **following prepositions** — namely, they add an **н**.

Meanwhile, the third-person **possessive** forms from 9.1 (**его, её, их** — his, her, their) **never change** in any way. These examples illustrate this tricky point:[2]

pronouns						
singular			plural			
nom.	gen.	preposition + gen.	nom.	gen.	preposition + gen.	
я	меня	→ у меня	мы	нас	→ у нас
ты	тебя	→ у тебя	вы	вас	→ у вас
он	его	→ у него	они	их	→ у них
она	её	→ у неё			
оно	его	→ у него			

у + **он**	⇒	У **него** новая машина.		у + **его** друг	⇒	У **его** друга новая машина.
at + *he*		**He** has a new car. (**н** added)		at + *his* friend		**His friend** has a new car. (no **н**!)

Без **чего** ты не можешь жить?
"Without **what** can you not live?"

Я не могу жить без **хорошей машины**!
I can't live without **a good car**.

1. русская литература: Без русск_____ литератур___.
2. русский словарь: Без русск_____ словар___.
3. мой новый телефон: Без мо___ нов_____ телефон___.
4. моя любимая книга: Без мо____ любим____ книг___.
5. наше большое окно: Без наш____ больш____ окн___.
6. их компьютер: Без ____ компьютер___.
7. фотография кошки: Без фотографи____ кошки.
8. хороший друг: Без хорош_____ друг____.
9. его старая собака Без ____ стар____ собак___.

11.b

Для **кого** это подарок?
For **whom** is this present?

Это подарок для **нашего старого друга**.
This is a present for **our old friend**.

10. этот новый студент: Для эт___ нов___ студент___.
11. наш профессор: Для наш_____ профессор___.
12. его от(е)ц: Для ____ от_____.
13. ваша мама: Для ваш_____ мам___.
14. её бабушка: Для ____ бабушк___.
15. их сын: Для ____ сын____.
16. наш старый друг: Для наш____ стар____ друг___.
17. любимый писатель: Для любим_____ писател___.
18. твоя подруга: Для тво____ подруг____.

Пиво без водки — деньги на ветер. (Drinking) beer without vodka is (throwing) money to the wind.

---

*Ask whether your partner can live **without** the following things, or think of your own examples — be sure to put them into the genitive case following* **без***! We'll learn more about the verb forms soon; for now, just practice them.*

Ты можешь жить без _____?
Can you live without _____?

Нет, я не могу жить без _____. **Да, я могу жить без _____.**
No, I can't live without _____. Yes, I can live without ____.

классическая музыка	кошка / собака
русская литература	русская поэзия
дорогое вино (wine)	философия
чистая вода (clean water)	икра (caviar)
большое окно	красивый ковёр

---

[1] **тот** declines exactly like **этот** — minus the "э"
[2] This is an enduring source of confusion for students, which we've mentioned already... take another careful look at it!

11.7 Adjectives that can stand alone as nouns

Some Russian adjectives, including many that describe a personal quality, can often stand alone, without an accompanying noun. For example, the adjective **знакомый** means "known" or "familiar," and the phrase **знакомый человек** would refer to a "familiar person" — that is, an "acquaintance." Russians typically drop the noun and use the adjective by itself. However, in terms of endings, "**once an adjective, always an adjective.**" That is, if a word is by definition an **adjective**, it will always take **adjectival endings**, regardless of its role.

Of course, these endings reflect the grammatical **gender** of the noun referred to. So, a **знакомый** is a male acquaintance, and a **знакомая** is a female acquaintance. Secondly, if these terms are used in the **genitive** case, they must take the appropriate adjectival genitive endings. For example:

знакомый male acquaintance → Это машина моего нового **знакомого**.　That's my new acquaintance's car.

знакомая female acquaintance → Это машина моей новой **знакомой**.　That's my new acquaintance's car.

Other examples include **пьяный** (a drunken person, a drunk) and **больной** (a sick person, a patient).

11.c Чей это телевизор?　мой отец:　　Это телевизор **моего отца**.
Whose television is this?　　　　　　This is the television **of my father** ("my father's…").

1. _____ это машина?　моя мама:　　Это машина мо_____ мам_____.

2. _____ это фотография?　мой брат:　　Это фотография мо_____ брат_____.

3. _____ это окно?　его сестра:　　Это окно _____ сестр_____.

4. _____ это бабушка?　наш русский друг:　　Это бабушка наш_____ русск_____ друг_____.

5. _____ это дедушка?　наша русская подруга:　　Это дедушка наш_____ русск_____ подруг_____.

6. _____ это брат?　наш знакомый:　　Это брат наш_____ знаком_____.

7. _____ это сестра?　наша знакомая:　　Это сестра наш_____ знаком_____.

11.8 End-stressed masculine nouns

Stress is very important in Russian, and is a very difficult part of learning the language.[1] We must simply "know" where the stress falls in a given word. Knowing this is almost as important as knowing a word's spelling! Furthermore, stress will often **shift** to other syllables when we change a word's endings. When it comes to such patterns, the best we can often do is to provide general **guidelines** — alas, there are almost always **exceptions**!

Generally, when we **change the case** of a noun, the stress remains where it was in the **nominative** form:

мама → **мамы**　сестра → **сестры**　девушка → **девушки**　окно → **окна**　mobile vowel: отец → **отца**

As we know, masculine nouns have **no ending** in the **nominative singular**. Some masculine nouns are **end-stressed**, meaning that whenever we **add** <u>any</u> case ending to them, that ending will **always be stressed**; we can say that the stress **shifts** to the ending. Here are all such nouns we've seen thus far:

кот → **кота**	царь → **царя**	словарь → **словаря**	карандаш → **карандаша**
стол → **стола**	враг → **врага**	рюкзак → **рюкзака**	
мяч → **мяча**	ключ → **ключа**	жених → **жениха**	

This is one reason why good **dictionaries** (and this textbook) typically give the nominative singular, followed by the genitive singular (the ending, or the entire form), which helps to indicate any unusual stress patterns or mobile vowels. Compare: **брат**, -a and **кот**, -а (the latter is end-stressed!); or **от(е)ц**, отца (look, a mobile vowel!).

Generally, masculine nouns not stressed on the **final syllable** in the nominative can never be end-stressed:

автор → **автора**　писатель → **писателя**　родственник → **родственника**

---

[1] Noun stress will be dealt with more comprehensively on Day 161. Generally, one can assume that noun stress does *not* shift when endings change, while taking care to learn those special cases when it *does*. Note that the **adjective** forms we've seen thus far do **not** shift stress.

day 12: existence and non-existence

existence with the nominative; non-existence with the genitive; masculine nouns ending in -**а** or -**я**

Человек страны советов в космосе. A person of the country of the Soviets in space (a stamp celebrating **Юрий Гагарин**).

12.1 Existence with the nominative

On Day 6, we learned how to say that something "is," or that we "have" it. Russian expresses **existence** using the **nominative** case, which marks the **grammatical subject** of a sentence. We might call such existence statements "**subject constructions**," in the sense that they include a subject — in the nominative. If a **verb** is present, it **agrees** with the subject. The fact that the verb **есть** is sometimes omitted does not affect the grammar.

Есть **машина**?	Да, есть. **Машина** есть.	У тебя есть **машина**?	Да, у меня есть **машина**.[1]
Is there a car?	Yes, there is. There is a car.	Do you have a car?	Yes, I have a car.

To say the same things in various **tenses**, we'd just change the **verb** form, which must always agree with its subject. Since all our subjects are singular (for now), these changes are most noticeable in the **past** tense, whose forms also reflect the gender of the subject. Pay careful attention to **subject-verb agreement** in these examples:

			masculine:	feminine:	neuter:
present:	Что у тебя (**есть**)?	➡	У меня (**есть**) стол.	У меня (**есть**) книга.	У меня (**есть**) окно.
	What do you have?		I have a table.	I have a book.	I have a window.
past:	Что у тебя **было**?	➡	У меня **был** стол.	У меня **была** книга.	У меня **было** окно.
	What did you have?		I had a table.	I had a book.	I had a window.
future:	Что у тебя **будет**?	➡	У меня **будет** стол.	У меня **будет** книга.	У меня **будет** окно.
	What will you have?		I will have a table.	I will have a book.	I will have a window.

Note: the question word **что** is always **neuter** singular for purposes of agreement (**кто** is **masculine** singular).[2]

---

[1] Remember, the Russian literally says something like "A **car** is at me." So the noun is the **subject**, not the direct object, as it would be in the English idiom "I have a **car**."

[2] For example: "**Кто это был?**" (Who was that?). No matter who we're asking about, the "who" is treated as masculine singular.

57

12.2 Non-existence with the genitive

So, how do we say that something "is not," or that we "don't have" it? Well, it's surprisingly tricky! Russian expresses non-existence with the construction **нет + the genitive**. This is another Russian **idiom** that cannot be translated word for word into English, so it's essential that we use our imagination to become comfortable with this very important construction!

This construction is strange for English speakers because of what it's missing: it has **no subject**. That is to say: it has no noun in the **nominative** case. We'll refer to such Russian constructions as **subjectless**.

This strikes us as strange because English typically **insists on a subject**, if only a so-called "dummy subject," as in "**It** is raining," or "**There** is a tree." English has no truly subjectless constructions of the kind Russian does.

If a subjectless construction has **no grammatical subject**, then what does its **verb** agree with? A **subjectless verb** is always in the **neuter singular**, regardless of the gender of the thing that "isn't." This means that any subjectless construction has **only three** possible verb forms — one for each tense. In all three tenses, the thing that "isn't" must remain in the **genitive**!

Бога нет! There is no God!

A believer might claim that "**Бог есть!**"
To which a Marxist might respond:
"**Религия — опиум для народа!**"

		masculine:	feminine:	neuter:
present:	**нет** + genitive there is no…	⇒ Нет **стола**. There is no table.[1]	Нет **книги**. There is no book.	Нет **окна**. There is no window.
past:	**не было**[2] + genitive there was no…	⇒ Не было **стола**. There was no table.	Не было **книги**. There was no book.	Не было **окна**. There was no window.
future:	**не будет** + genitive there will be no…	⇒ Не будет **стола**. There will be no table.	Не будет **книги**. There will be no book.	Не будет **окна**. There will be no window.

12.a	щен(о)к	кошка	мыло
I have…	У меня _____ _____.	У меня _____ _____.	У меня _____ _____.
I had…	У меня _____ _____.	У меня _____ _____.	У меня _____ _____.
I will have…	У меня _____ _____.	У меня _____ _____.	У меня _____ _____.
I don't have…	У меня _____ _____.	У меня _____ _____.	У меня _____ _____.
I didn't have…	У меня ___ _____ _____.	У меня ___ _____ _____.	У меня ___ _____ _____.
I won't have…	У меня ___ _____ _____.	У меня ___ _____ _____.	У меня ___ _____ _____.

На нет и суда нет. There's no judgment for "no" — that is to say, "a no is a no".[3] Note the genitive form of the end-stressed **суд, а**: judgment, court.

Polite wishes using the genitive

Many polite wishes in Russian are expressed using the genitive. The full expression involves the verb **желать**, "to wish" and a dative pronoun, followed by an object (what you're wishing) in the genitive: "**[Я желаю тебе] приятного аппетита!**" In everyday speech, the verb and pronoun are usually **left out**, but they remain **understood** — so the object is still in the genitive! Here are a few such common wishes. Some involve genitive forms of noun types we haven't studied yet. For now, simply learn them as set phrases:

Приятного аппетита!	Bon appetit!	**Удачи!**	Good luck!
Счастливого пути!	Bon voyage!	**Спокойной ночи!**	Good night!
Хорошего отдыха!	"Good relaxation!"	**Всего доброго!**	All the best!
Хороших выходных!	Nice weekend! (literally, "days off" — in the genitive plural)		

58 [1] Here too, it may help to use some "bad English" by translating the Russian as literally as we can: "There is not *of table*."
[2] In this construction, the stress is on the **не**. There is no stress on the **было**; pronounce the **не было** as if it were a single word: **не́было**.
[3] Can be said when someone refuses to do something, or simply has nothing to give: there's no judging them, no point in getting upset!

*Put these statements of **existence** into the past and future based on the model. The verb must **change** to agree with the **subject**.*   **12.b**

У меня есть **новая машина**. I have a new car.	**(Раньше)** у меня **была** новая машина. (Previously) I had a new car.	**(Скоро)** у меня **будет** новая машина. (Soon) I'll have a new car.
1. У нег<u>о</u> есть **новый ключ**.	У нег<u>о</u> _____ н<u>о</u>вый ключ.	У нег<u>о</u> _____ н<u>о</u>вый ключ.
2. У не<u>ё</u> есть **новая кошка**.	У не<u>ё</u> _____ новая кошка.	У не<u>ё</u> _____ новая кошка.
3. У них есть **чистое бельё**.	У них _____ ч<u>и</u>стое бельё.	У них _____ ч<u>и</u>стое бельё.
4. У вас есть **странная идея**.	У вас _____ стр<u>а</u>нная ид<u>е</u>я.	У вас _____ стр<u>а</u>нная ид<u>е</u>я.
5. У теб<u>я</u> есть **словарь**.	У теб<u>я</u> _____ слов<u>а</u>рь.	У теб<u>я</u> _____ слов<u>а</u>рь.
6. У нас есть **большая проблема**.	У нас _____ пробл<u>е</u>ма.	У нас _____ пробл<u>е</u>ма.

---

*Put these statements of **non-existence** into the past and future. The verb of these **subjectless** constructions must be **neuter**!*   **12.c**

У мен<u>я</u> нет **машины**. I don't have a car.	**(Р<u>а</u>ньше)** у мен<u>я</u> **не было** машины. (Previously) I didn't have a car.	**(Скоро)** у мен<u>я</u> **не будет** машины. (Soon) I won't have a car.
1. У него нет **н<u>о</u>в____ ключ___**.	У нег<u>о</u> _____ н<u>о</u>в____ ключ__.	У нег<u>о</u> _____ н<u>о</u>в_____ ключ__.
2. У неё нет **н<u>о</u>в___ кошк___**.	У не<u>ё</u> _____ н<u>о</u>в____ к<u>о</u>шк__.	У не<u>ё</u> _____ н<u>о</u>в_____ к<u>о</u>шк__.
3. У них нет **ч<u>и</u>ст___ бель___**.	У них _____ ч<u>и</u>ст____ бель___.	У них _____ ч<u>и</u>ст_____ бель__.
4. У вас нет **странн____ иде___**.	У вас _____ странн___ иде___.	У вас _____ странн_____ иде__.
5. У теб<u>я</u> нет **словар___**.	У теб<u>я</u> _____ словар___.	У теб<u>я</u> _____ словар___.
6. У нас нет **проблем___**.	У нас _____ проблем___.	У нас _____ проблем___.

....
Нет д<u>ы</u>ма без огн<u>я</u>. There is no smoke (**дым**) without fire (**ог(о)нь** — note the mobile vowel, indicated by the parentheses!).

---

*Answer these existence questions both positively and negatively. Watch **tense** very carefully!*[1]   **12.d**

Есть **машина**? Is there a car?	Да, **машина** есть. Yes, there is a car.	Нет, **машины** нет. No, there is no car.
1. **Ключ** б<u>у</u>дет?	_____.	_____.
2. **Телев<u>и</u>зор** у вас был?	_____.	_____.
3. **М<u>ы</u>ло** у них есть?	_____.	_____.
4. **Зад<u>а</u>ние** у нас было?	_____.	_____.
5. **Компь<u>ю</u>тер** б<u>у</u>дет?	_____.	_____.
6. **Ош<u>и</u>бка** был<u>а</u>?	_____.	_____.

У твоег<u>о</u> **брата** нет **машины**, правда? Your **brother** doesn't have a **car**, right?	Что ты! **Машина** у **него** есть, кон<u>е</u>чно! What are you talking about? **He** has a **car**, of course!	**12.e**
1. У тво<u>е</u>й **сестры** нет **словаря**, правда?	Что ты! _____ у _____ есть, кон<u>е</u>чно!	
2. У твоег<u>о</u> **отца** нет **телевизора**, правда?	Что ты! _____ у _____ есть, кон<u>е</u>чно!	
3. У **них** нет **ребёнка**, правда?	Что ты! _____ у _____ есть, кон<u>е</u>чно!	
4. У **нас** сег<u>о</u>дня нет **задания**, правда?	Что ты! _____ у _____ есть, кон<u>е</u>чно!	
5. У **профессора** нет **ручки**, правда?	Что ты! _____ у _____ есть, кон<u>е</u>чно!	
6. У **тебя** нет **ключа**, правда?	Что ты! _____ у _____ есть, кон<u>е</u>чно!	

....
Крест<u>а</u> на теб<u>е</u> нет! There's no cross (**крест**) on you! (said to an evil, shameless person; Orthodox Russians typically wear a necklace with a cross).

[1] Students frequently ignore **tense**. When analyzing any Russian sentence, be sure to note whether it is present, past or future!

Take turns asking a partner whether or not they have these things. Feel free to substitute other nouns and adjectives!

У теб**я** есть **новый компь**ю**тер?**	Да, есть. У мен**я** есть **новый компь**ю**тер.**	хор**о**шая к**о**мната
Do you have a new computer?	Yes, I do. I have a new computer.	больш**о**е окн**о**
	Нет. У мен**я** нет **нового компь**ю**тера.**	дорог**о**й ков(ё)р
	No. I don't have a new computer.	хор**о**шее мыло

*Let's try the **past** tense. What about when you were twelve years old. Did you have these things?*

р**у**сский слов**а**рь, -**я**

У теб**я был новый компь**ю**тер?**	Да, **был**. У мен**я был новый компь**ю**тер.**	р**у**сский друг
Did you have a new computer?	Yes, I did. I had a new computer.	р**у**сская подр**у**га
	Нет. У мен**я не было нового компь**ю**тера.**	н**о**вая маш**и**на
	No. I didn't have a new computer.	больш**о**й телев**и**зор

*Finally, the **future** tense. Speculate about what you'll have this time next year.*

н**о**вый телеф**о**н

У теб**я будет новый компь**ю**тер?**	Да, **будет**. У мен**я будет новый компь**ю**тер.**	хор**о**ший велосип**е**д
Will you have a new computer?	Yes, I will. I will have a new computer.	дорог**а**я од**е**жда
	Нет. У мен**я не будет нового компь**ю**тера.**	тр**у**дное распис**а**ние
	No. I won't have a new computer.	

*To say, for example, that you don't have a computer at all, nevermind a new one, use **вообще** (generally).*

У теб**я** есть н**о**вый компь**ю**тер?	Нет. У мен**я** нет компь**ю**тера **вообще**.
Do you have a new computer?	No. I don't have a computer **at all** (of any kind).

12.3 Masculine nouns that take feminine endings

Our animate nouns in this unit include several **masculine** nouns that have **feminine endings:**

па**па** dad	**д**е**душка** grandfather	**колл**е**га** colleague[1]	**пь**я**ница** drunkard
мужчи**на** man	**д**я**дя** uncle	**зан**у**да** a bore, killjoy	

Such nouns take **feminine endings** by definition. In all cases, we will treat them just as we would any feminine noun. *But,* these nouns are **masculine** for purposes of **agreement**. So, any adjectives that modify them, and any verbs for which they are the subject, will have **masculine** forms. Look at the adjectives and verbs below:

мой д**е**душка →	Мой д**е**душка **был** у мен**я**.[2]	У мо**е**г**о** д**е**душки нет телев**и**зора.
наш но**вый** колл**е**га →	Наш н**о**вый колл**е**га **был** у нас.	У **нашего нового колл**е**ги** был**а** пробл**е**ма.
этот мужч**и**на →	**Э**тот стр**а**нный мужч**и**на **был** здесь.	У **этого стр**а**нного мужч**и**ны** есть ид**е**я.
наш д**я**дя →	Наш люб**и**мый д**я**дя **был** у нас.	У **нашего люб**и**мого д**я**ди** есть н**о**вая жен**а**.
compare: мо**я** м**а**ма →	Мо**я** м**а**ма **был**а** у мен**я** сег**о**дня.	У **мо**е**й м**а**мы** хор**о**шая н**о**вая маш**и**на.

12.f тво**й** д**е**душка: У **тво**е**г**о** д**е**душки** есть велосип**е**д?   *Try asking and answering these questions in conversation.*
Does your granddad have a bicycle?

1. тво**й** п**а**па:	У тво_____ пап___ есть маш**и**на?	4. тво**я** б**а**бушка	У тво_____ бабушк_____ есть к**о**шка?
2. тво**я** м**а**ма:	У тво_____ мам___ есть маш**и**на?	5. тво**й** д**я**дя:	У тво_____ дяд___ есть **я**хта (yacht)?
3. тво**й** д**е**душка:	У тво_____ дедушк___ есть соб**а**ка?	6. тво**я** т**ё**тя:	У тво_____ тёт___ есть мотоц**и**кл?

---

1. У теб**я** есть люб**и**мый **рестор**а**н**? Как**о**й?	3. У теб**я** есть люб**и**мая **кн**и**га**? Как**а**я?	*Take turns asking about your favorites.*
2. У теб**я** есть люб**и**мый **сери**а**л**? Как**о**й?	4. У теб**я** есть люб**и**мый **фильм**? Как**о**й?	

---

60   [1] If this noun refers to a female colleague, then it would act as a feminine noun, e.g. **мо**я** н**о**вая колл**е**га**.
     [2] As we'll practice more later, the "y + genitive" idiom can also express visiting people — being "at" them, at their places.

day 13: verb conjugation: verb types with ё endings

introduction to verb types; the **ё** endings; verb structure; stress patterns in conjugated verbs; introduction to imperative forms; **АЙ** verbs; **А** verbs

Мы говорим — Ленин, подразумеваем — партия. (When) we say Lenin, we mean the party. From Mayakovsky's poem **Владимир Ильич Ленин**.

13.1 Introduction to Russian verb types

An infinitive like **быть** (to be) simply names an action. To link it to a subject, we must change the verb's forms to agree with that subject (as in: to be → I am, you are, she is, etc.). This process is called **conjugation**. In Russian, this involves removing the **infinitive ending** (usually -**ть**) and adding **personal endings** to the verb's **stem**:

читать (to read) →	я чита**ю**	I read	мы чита**ем**	we read
	ты чита**ешь**	you read	вы чита**ете**	you read
	он, она, оно чита**ет**	he, she, it reads	они чита**ют**	they read

Russian verbs conjugate according to roughly 25 patterns, or **verb types**.[1] For now, we'll only learn some of the most common types. Alas! — we often can't determine verb type simply by looking at a Russian **infinitive**.

While some infinitive forms allow us to **guess the verb type** with great accuracy, some forms will allow, at best, an educated guess, based purely on frequency. This is particularly true of infinitives ending in -**ать**, which could belong to multiple verb types. For example, the infinitives **читать** (to read) and **писать** (to write) look similar, but these verbs are conjugated very differently. We must simply **know** the type to which each belongs!

For each **new verb type** that we introduce, we'll provide a **head verb** that will serve as our model for conjugation. All other verbs in the given type will follow its pattern. Then, as we add **new verbs**, we'll **tag** each infinitive by verb type — for example, **читать** АЙ: to read. This tells us that **читать** is a so-called "**АЙ verb.**"

13.2 What features define a given verb type?

Generally, a given verb type is defined by two important features: 1) what **set of endings** does it take? and, 2) does its **stem change** in any conjugated forms (for example: does its **final stem consonant ever mutate**)?

As for the first feature, there are **only two sets** of endings to choose from. Each verb type will, by definition, take either **ё endings** or **и endings**. Today's and tomorrow's lessons will focus on verb types that take **ё endings**.

[1] This sounds daunting, but many types behave similarly. See the back of the book for a full list; we will not see all types in Book 1! Keep in mind that although the "types" we'll use do capture meaningful features of Russian verbs, they are ultimately mere conventions, for learning purposes. Native speakers do not classify verbs in this manner — they "simply know" the conjugated forms!

What about the second feature — stem change, and, more specifically, **consonant mutation**? In certain situations, some Russian consonants are said to **mutate** — that is, to change into another consonant. Mutation is quite **predictable** in Russian, in the sense that each consonant that *can* mutate has **only one** possible mutation.[1] For example, when **д** mutates, it always mutates to **ж**. We could write up this mutation as: **д → ж**.

13.3 The ё endings

Today, we'll focus on verb types that take the **first** of two sets of endings: the **ё endings**.

singular	plural
я **-у** (ю)	мы **-ём**
ты **-ёшь**	вы **-ёте**
он, он<u>а</u>, он<u>о</u> **-ёт**	он<u>и</u> **-ут** (ют)

All of the verb types we learn today will take this set of endings.

IMPORTANT: as we know, the letter "ё" can only occur in **stressed** syllables. So, if the verb endings above happen to be **unstressed** (more on this soon!), we will write and pronounce "**e**" instead of "**ё**."

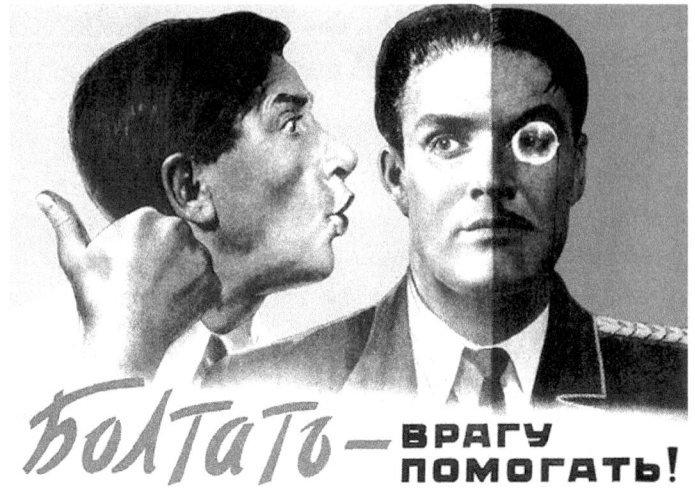

Болтать — врагу помогать! To babble is to help the enemy!

The two infinitives here, **болтать** and **помогать**, are both **АЙ** verbs. When conjugated, **АЙ** verbs take ё endings, as in: **болт<u>а</u>ю, болт<u>а</u>ешь, болт<u>а</u>ет, болт<u>а</u>ем, болт<u>а</u>ете, болт<u>а</u>ют** — I babble, you babble, etc.

13.4 General introduction to the structure of Russian verb forms

Russian verbs may include the following parts:

1) A basic <u>root</u>, to which most verb types add a <u>suffix</u> (or simply a **stem vowel**) to form the verb **stem**. We will **tag** many verb types using the given type's suffix or stem vowel.

2) To the stem, <u>endings</u> are added, such as **infinitive** endings or **personal** endings.

3) Some verbs will have <u>prefixes</u> as well.

The third example to the right includes **no suffix**. It adds endings directly to its root (stem). We'll call such verb types **non-suffixed**, and **tag** them with their **final stem consonant**.

We tag many verb types by their **suffix**, as in: **прочитать АЙ**: to read:[2]

про - чит - ай - ут ➡ **прочитают**
prefix | root | suffix | ending — "they will read"
stem

Other verb types are tagged by **stem vowel**, as in: **написать А**: to write:

на - пис - а - ть ➡ **написать**
prefix | root | stem vowel | ending — "to write"
stem

Non-suffixed verbs are tagged by **final stem consonant**: **жить В**: to live:

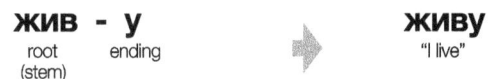

жив - у ➡ **живу**
root (stem) | ending — "I live"

13.5 Stress patterns in conjugated verbs

We've mentioned how stressful Russian **stress** can be for students. It can **shift** about in ways that seem hopelessly unpredictable at first. All the more important, then, to take careful note of any reliable **stress patterns.**

Fortunately, the conjugated forms of **all regular verbs** obey **one** of the following **THREE** patterns: 1) the stress is always on the personal <u>ending</u>; 2) the stress is always on the <u>stem</u>; or 3) the stress <u>shifts</u>.[3]

For regular verbs with shifting stress, note that there is <u>only one</u> shifting stress pattern. If we say a verb has <u>shifting</u> stress, we always mean that it is <u>end</u>-stressed in the **я** form, and <u>stem</u>-stressed **everywhere else**.

Below are examples of each stress pattern, using verbs that take ё endings. The <u>arrows</u> tell the whole story! Remember, these patterns apply to **regular** verbs. Fortunately, Russian has very **few** truly **irregular** verbs!

[1] The only exceptions involve "Church Slavonic" mutations which occur for historical reasons. These are covered in Books 3 and 4.
[2] This form (**прочитать**) is the perfective equivalent of the imperfective verb **читать**. We'll learn what this means on Day 17.
[3] For infinitives whose stress pattern can't be guessed, we'll indicate it in superscript following the verb type tag.

	stem stress			end stress			shifting stress	
	чит<u>а</u>ть	to read		**жить**	to live		**пис<u>а</u>ть**	to write
я	чит<u>а</u>ю	I read		жив<u>у</u>	I live		пиш<u>у</u>	I write
ты	чит<u>а</u>ешь	you read		жив<u>ё</u>шь	you live		п<u>и</u>шешь	you write
он, он<u>а</u>, он<u>о</u>	чит<u>а</u>ет	he, she, it reads		жив<u>ё</u>т	he, she, it lives		п<u>и</u>шет	he, she, it writes
мы	чит<u>а</u>ем	we read		жив<u>ё</u>м	we live		п<u>и</u>шем	we write
вы	чит<u>а</u>ете	you read		жив<u>ё</u>те	you live		п<u>и</u>шете	you write
он<u>и</u>	чит<u>а</u>ют	they read		жив<u>у</u>т	they live		п<u>и</u>шут	they write
ты	чит<u>а</u>й![1]	read!		жив<u>и</u>!	live!		пиш<u>и</u>!	write!

The third and final spelling rule

Our final rule, the **8-letter** rule, often accounts for the spelling of certain **verb endings**. After all eight letters, we can't write the soft vowels **я** or **ю**; instead, we must write **a** or **y**.

		4 "hushings"	3 "velars"	1 "odd man out"			
		ж ч ш щ	г к х	ц			
7-letter rule: after these 7 letters...		ж ч ш щ	г к х	_	...write: **и**	...not:	**ы**
5-letter rule: after these 5 letters...		ж ч ш щ		ц	...write: **e**	...not:	unstressed **o**
8-letter rule: after these 8 letters...		ж ч ш щ	г к х	ц	...write: **a/y**	...not:	**я/ю**

For example, in the conjugation of **пис<u>а</u>ть** shown above, the 8-letter rule reminds us that we cannot write **я пиш<u>ю</u>** or **он<u>и</u> пиш<u>ют</u>**.

13.6 Introduction to imperative forms

Look again at the verb tables above: at the top, we have the infinitive of each verb, followed by its conjugated forms, and, at the bottom, its basic **imperative** form, which is used for giving **commands** — as in, **чит<u>а</u>й!** (read!).

This basic form provided in the table is the **ты** imperative. You would use this to give informal commands to a single person you are addressing using **ты**. To give commands to multiple people, or to give polite commands to a single person you are addressing using **вы**, you would use the **вы** imperative. This is very easy to form: simply add **-те** to the basic **ты** imperative:

чит<u>а</u>й! → чит<u>а</u>й**те**!   пиш<u>и</u>! → пиш<u>и</u>**те**!   жив<u>и</u>! → жив<u>и</u>**те**!

We will discuss imperatives in detail on Days 29 and 30, but we will be including the **ты** imperative form in our verb tables from the very start. For now, just develop a passive feel for them. For some verb types, you'll notice that the imperative form corrresponds to the bare stem, as is the case for **чит<u>а</u>ть** АЙ → **чит<u>а</u>й!**

БУДЬ НА ЧЕКУ.
В ТАКИЕ ДНИ
ПОДСЛУШИВАЮТ СТЕНЫ.
НЕДАЛЕКО ОТ БОЛТОВНИ
И СПЛЕТНИ
ДО ИЗМЕНЫ.

НЕ БОЛТАЙ!

Не болт<u>а</u>й! Don't babble!

13.7 How to drill Russian verb conjugations

With all of this background information under our belt, we're finally ready to begin learning some major **verb types**. For each new type, we'll give a brief **definition** (noting which **set of endings** the verb type takes, and whether any **mutations** occur), then give a **head verb** as a model of the conjugation pattern.

In practice, mastering a verb type begins with simply **memorizing** the conjugation pattern in the head verb. For example, the head verb for the **АЙ** type is **чит<u>а</u>ть** АЙ. Recite this pattern over and over until you've memorized it, then practice conjugating other verbs in this type — remember, any new verb we tag with **АЙ** will be conjugated exactly like the head verb **чит<u>а</u>ть** АЙ. The only difference, of course, is the stem!

Develop "muscle memory" by reciting the head verb first, then other verbs of that type. Drill, drill, drill!

[1] The form below the second black line is the verb's **ты** imperative, as discussed in 13.6. Along with the conjugated forms, this imperative form may be considered an important basic form of the verb.

This is *the* most common verb type. We'll call them **АЙ** verbs (like English "eye") because their stems end in the suffix **ай**. So, when we add an ending in **-у** to this suffix, we end up with **-ю** (чита**й** + **у** = чита**ю**). The **ты** imperative of this verb type is identical to the verb stem (**читай**). The stress is **always on the stem** (on the same syllable as in the **infinitive**).

If you see an infinitive in **-ать**, chances are it's an **АЙ** verb. But **it may not be**, as we'll soon see! On a practical level, you may think of АЙ verbs as the **default** for infinitives in **-ать**, while carefully noting which verbs belong to **other types**.

читать АЙ: to read		**думать** АЙ: to think	**терять** АЙ: to lose	**знать** АЙ: to know	**работать** АЙ: to work
чита**ю**	I read	дума**ю**	теря**ю**	зна**ю**	работа**ю**
чита**ешь**	you read	дума**ешь**	теря**ешь**	зна**ешь**	работа**ешь**
чита**ет**	he, she, it reads	дума**ет**	теря**ет**	зна**ет**	работа**ет**
чита**ем**	we read	дума**ем**	теря**ем**	зна**ем**	работа**ем**
чита**ете**	you read	дума**ете**	теря**ете**	зна**ете**	работа**ете**
чита**ют**	they read	дума**ют**	теря**ют**	зна**ют**	работа**ют**
чита**й**!	read!	думай!	теряй!	знай!	работай!

делать АЙ: to do	**спрашивать** АЙ: to ask	**отдыхать** АЙ: to relax	**слушать** АЙ: to listen	**понимать** АЙ: to understand
дела**ю**	спрашива**ю**	отдыха**ю**	слуша**ю**	понима**ю**
дела**ешь**	спрашива**ешь**	отдыха**ешь**	слуша**ешь**	понима**ешь**
дела**ет**	спрашива**ет**	отдыха**ет**	слуша**ет**	понима**ет**
дела**ем**	спрашива**ем**	отдыха**ем**	слуша**ем**	понима**ем**
дела**ете**	спрашива**ете**	отдыха**ете**	слуша**ете**	понима**ете**
дела**ют**	спрашива**ют**	отдыха**ют**	слуша**ют**	понима**ют**
дела**й**!	спрашивай!	отдыхай!	слушай!	понимай!

13.a Что ты **делаешь**?   Я **работаю** и **слушаю** музыку.   Я **читаю** книгу, но плохо **понимаю**.
What are you doing?   I'm working and listening to music.   I'm reading a book, but I understand poorly.

1. Что **он** дела_____?   Он работа_____ и слуша_____ музыку.   Он чита_____ книгу, но плохо понима_____.

2. Что **мы** дела_____?   Вы работа_____ и слуша_____ музыку.   Вы чита_____ книгу, но плохо понима_____.

3. Что **она** дела_____?   Она работа_____ и слуша_____ музыку.   Она чита_____ книгу, но плохо понима_____.

4. Что **они** дела_____?   Они работа_____ и слуша_____ музыку.   Они чита_____ книгу, но плохо понима_____.

5 Что **вы** дела_____?   Мы работа_____ и слуша_____ музыку.   Мы чита_____ книгу, но плохо понима_____.

6. Что дела_____ **все**?[1]   Все работа_____ и слуша_____ музыку.   Все чита_____ книгу, но плохо понима_____.

7. Что **ты** дела_____?   Я работа_____ и слуша_____ музыку.   Я чита_____ книгу, но плохо понима_____.

Глаза боятся, а руки делают. The eyes fear, while the hands do (i.e. I can't believe I'm actually doing this).

13.b Вы **работаете** сейчас?   Нет, я **отдыхаю** наконец.   Я ничего не **делаю**.
Are you working right now?   No, I'm finally relaxing.   I'm not doing anything.

1. **Она** работа_____ сейчас?   Нет, она отдыха_____ наконец.   Она ничего не дела_____.

2. **Он** работа_____ сейчас?   Нет, он отдыха_____ наконец.   Он ничего не дела_____.

3. **Они** работа_____ сейчас?   Нет, они отдыха_____ наконец.   Они ничего не дела_____.

4. **Ты** работа_____ сейчас?   Нет, **я** отдыха_____ наконец.   Я ничего не дела_____.

---

1. Что ты **делаешь** сегодня? **Работаешь**, или **отдыхаешь**?   3. Ты много (a lot) **работаешь**? Очень много?

2. Ты **слушаешь** музыку, когда (when/while) **работаешь**?   4. Ты часто **теряешь** зонт? А телефон?[2] А рюкзак?

[1] The form "**все**" means "everyone," and requires **plural** verbs. We'll discuss it further at a later point.
[2] Again, note how "**а**" typically starts a follow-up question in Russian. One might translate it as "What about...?"

Drilling new verbs

For practice, here are a few verbs that we won't learn actively for a while. *But*, since we've tagged them as **АЙ** verbs, can you conjugate them? Drill yourself!

Remember, only ONE STRESSED SYLLABLE per word!

чих<u>а</u>ть АЙ	to sneeze	**ик<u>а</u>ть** АЙ	to hiccup
пл<u>а</u>вать АЙ	to swim	**оп<u>а</u>здывать** АЙ	to be running late
гул<u>я</u>ть АЙ	to stroll	**расск<u>а</u>зывать** АЙ	to tell, narrate

---

A verbs like **пис<u>а</u>ть** . . . . take ё endings, and mutate in all forms

We'll call these verbs as "**A**" verbs (that's **Russian** "a" — as in, open up and say "ah") because they are formed using the **stem vowel** "a." In conjugated forms, the stem vowel is discarded, and the final stem consonant **mutates in all forms.**

Generally, when we say a verb **mutates** in certain forms, we mean that a mutation occurs in that form **whenever a mutation is possible**. Not all Russian consonants can mutate. But those that **can** mutate do so quite predictably. For example, the consonant <u>с can only mutate to ш</u>. Likewise, **з** can only mutate to **ж**. To repeat — in this particular verb type, we have mutations in **all** conjugated forms. So, here, consonants that **can** mutate **do** mutate, in **all forms.**

In the verbs below, we see **three** consonant mutations (for **с, к, з**). We'll continue adding more as we encounter them.

С → Ш	С → Ш	К → Ч	З → Ж	З → Ж
пис<u>а</u>ть A^{shift}: to write[1]	**напис<u>а</u>ть** A^{shift}: to write[1]	**пл<u>а</u>кать** A: to cry	**сказ<u>а</u>ть** A^{shift}: to say	**показ<u>а</u>ть** A^{shift}: to show
пиш<u>у</u> I write	напиш<u>у</u>	пл<u>а</u>чу	скаж<u>у</u>	покаж<u>у</u>
п<u>и</u>шешь you write	нап<u>и</u>шешь	пл<u>а</u>чешь	ск<u>а</u>жешь	пок<u>а</u>жешь
п<u>и</u>шет he, she, it writes	нап<u>и</u>шет	пл<u>а</u>чет	ск<u>а</u>жет	пок<u>а</u>жет
п<u>и</u>шем we write	нап<u>и</u>шем	пл<u>а</u>чем	ск<u>а</u>жем	пок<u>а</u>жем
п<u>и</u>шете you write	нап<u>и</u>шете	пл<u>а</u>чете	ск<u>а</u>жете	пок<u>а</u>жете
п<u>и</u>шут they write	нап<u>и</u>шут	пл<u>а</u>чут	ск<u>а</u>жут	пок<u>а</u>жут
пиш<u>и</u>! write!	напиш<u>и</u>!	пл<u>а</u>чь!	скаж<u>и</u>!	покаж<u>и</u>!

Take a moment to look at the **stress** patterns above. For **A verbs**, we can make a useful generalization: if the infinitive is **end**-stressed (that is, stressed on -ать), then its conjugated forms will show **shifting** stress. But one verb here is different: the **A** verb **пл<u>а</u>кать** is stem-stressed in the infinitive — in such cases, the stress will **remain on the stem.**

<u>**IMPORTANT**</u>: The observation we just made yields a **universally valid** and extremely useful rule regarding stress in Russian verbs: if the **infinitive** is stem-stressed (that is, not stressed on its final syllable), we know **for certain** that it will show **stem** stress in all conjugated forms. Otherwise, as we'll discuss later, things can be less predictable!

You'll notice that the imperative forms for **A** verbs do not match their stems, as they did with **АЙ** verbs. Here, we see two different endings: **stressed и** (пиш<u>и</u>! скаж<u>и</u>! покаж<u>и</u>!), and a **soft sign** (пл<u>а</u>чь!). Stress patterns affect these forms as well: the stress in these **imperatives** corresponds to the stress in the conjugated **я form**.[2] So, for example:

я пиш<u>у</u> → пиш<u>и</u>!   я скаж<u>у</u> → скаж<u>и</u>!   я покаж<u>у</u>! → покаж<u>и</u>!   *but:* я пл<u>а</u>чу → пл<u>а</u>чь!

One more important point: if we compare the verbs **пис<u>а</u>ть** and **напис<u>а</u>ть**, we see only one difference: the second form has added a **prefix**, **на-**. As we'll discuss on Day 17, this prefix marks **напис<u>а</u>ть** as being **perfective** in terms of aspect; **пис<u>а</u>ть** is its **imperfective** counterpart. For now, the important point is more simple: adding a prefix has not affected the conjugation at all. This is universal rule: **prefixed** forms of a given verb will be conjugated just like the **unprefixed** form.

Что ты **дел<u>а</u>ешь**? What are you doing?	Я **пиш<u>у</u>** письм<u>о</u> и **пл<u>а</u>чу**. I'm writing a letter and crying.	Почем<u>у</u> ты **пл<u>а</u>чешь**? Why are you crying?	Не **скаж<u>у</u>**! И письм<u>о</u> не **покаж<u>у</u>**! I won't say! And I won't show the letter!	**13.c**
Что **он** дел<u>а</u>____?	Он пиш____ письм<u>о</u> и плач____.	Почем<u>у</u> он плач____?	Не скаж____! И письм<u>о</u> не покаж____!	
Что **они** дел<u>а</u>____?	Он<u>и</u> пиш____ письм<u>о</u> и плач____.	Почем<u>у</u> он<u>и</u> плач____?	Не скаж____! И письм<u>о</u> не покаж____!	
Что **вы** дел<u>а</u>____?	Мы пиш____ письм<u>о</u> и плач____.	Почем<u>у</u> вы плач____?	Не скаж____! И письм<u>о</u> не покаж____!	

---

[1] Yes, both **пис<u>а</u>ть** and **напис<u>а</u>ть** both mean "to write." The first is an "imperfective" form, while the latter is "perfective." Conjugated perfective forms are actually **future-tense in meaning** (I will write, you will write, etc.). We'll learn why on Day 17.

[2] Again, wait for Days 29 and 30 for a detailed discussion of imperatives.

day 14: more verb types with ё endings

the verb types **ОВА**, **НУ**, **ЕЙ**; introduction to non-suffixed
verb types; **всё** (everything) and **все** (everyone)

Товарищ Ленин митингует. The verb **митинговать** is an OBA verb built from a foreign word: **митинг**, which in Russian means "political rally."

14.1 More verb types with ё endings

Today's lesson introduces some remaining important verb types that take **ё endings**, just like yesterday's types.

OBA verbs like **рисовать** . . . . take ё endings; the suffix **ова** collapses to **у**

We'll tag this type as "**OBA**" (say: "oh-vah") based on its stem suffix, which __collapses to "у"__ in all conjugated forms. Note that this verb type, like the **АЙ** type, is **extremely** common, in large part because Russian often uses the **OBA** suffix to create Russian verbs from foreign words (see Day 175). This means that you can often grasp the meaning of **OBA** verbs you've never seen before, such as: **эмигрировать**, **планировать**, **арестовать**, **реставрировать**... the list goes on and on! Best of all: if we do see an infinitive ending in -**овать**, we can be **certain** that it belongs to this type.

In keeping with the 5-letter spelling rule, **OBA** becomes **ЕВА** if the stem ends in **ж**, **ч**, **ш**, **щ**, or **ц** (see **танцевать** below).

рисовать OBA: to draw		**нарисовать** OBA: to draw	**танцевать** OBA: to dance	**потанцевать** OBA: to dance
рисую	I draw	нарисую	танцую	потанцую
рисуешь	you draw	нарисуешь	танцуешь	потанцуешь
рисует	he, she, it draws	нарисует	танцует	потанцует
рисуем	we draw	нарисуем	танцуем	потанцуем
рисуете	you draw	нарисуете	танцуете	потанцуете
рисуют	they draw	нарисуют	танцуют	потанцуют
рисуй!	draw!	нарисуй!	танцуй!	потанцуй!

Drilling new verbs

Again, try drilling a few random **OBA** verbs. First, repeat the conjugation of the head verb **рисовать**.

протестовать OBA to protest

организовать OBA to organize

психовать OBA to be a **псих**[1]

зомбировать OBA to zombify[2]

---

66 [1] That is, to be a psycho; to be bonkers or act in a crazy way.
[2] Something a **зомбоящик**, a "zombie box" (a TV!) does to its viewers. Such words are often used to discuss more recent propaganda!

*Let's practice all three of the types we've learned. Begin by drilling each of the verbs below. Remember, **ова** collapses to **у**.*

делать АЙ	**работать** АЙ	**читать** АЙ	**писать** А	**рисовать** ОВА	**танцевать** ОВА
to do	to work	to read	to write	to draw	to dance
1. Что **ты** дела____?	**Я** работа____.	Я чита____.	Я пиш____.	Я рису____.	Я танцу____.
2. Что **он** дела____?	Он работа____.	Он чита____.	Он пиш____.	Он рису____.	Он танцу____.
3. Что **вы** дела____?	**Мы** работа____.	Мы чита____.	Мы пиш____.	Мы рису____.	Мы танцу____.
4. Что **они** дела____?	Они работа____.	Они чита____.	Они пиш____.	Они рису____.	Они танцу____.
5. Что **она** дела____?	Она работа____.	Она чита____.	Она пиш____.	Она рису____.	Она танцу____.
6. Что дела____ **все**?	Все работа____.	Все чита____.	Все пиш____.	Все рису____.	Все танцу____.
7. Что **мы** дела____?	**Вы** работа____.	Вы чита____.	Вы пиш____.	Вы рису____.	Вы танцу____.
8. Что **я** дела____?	**Ты** работа____.	Ты чита____.	Ты пиш____.	Ты рису____.	Ты танцу____.

Что ты **делаешь?**	работать АЙ:	Почему ты всегда **работаешь?**	Почему ты никогда не **отдыхаешь?** 14.b
What are you doing?		Why are you always working?	Why do you never relax?
1. Что **они** дела____?	работать АЙ:	Почему они всегда _____?	Почему они никогда не отдыха____?
2. Что **вы** дела____?	читать АЙ:	Почему вы всегда _____?	Почему вы никогда не отдыха____?
3. Что **он** дела____?	писать А:	Почему он всегда _____?	Почему он никогда не отдыха____?
4. Что **мы** дела____?	рисовать ОВА:	Почему мы всегда _____?	Почему мы никогда не отдыха____?
5. Что **она** дела____?	думать АЙ:	Почему она всегда _____?	Почему она никогда не отдыха____?
6. Что **ты** дела____?	танцевать ОВА:	Почему ты всегда _____?	Почему ты никогда не отдыха____?
7. Что дела____ **Иван?**	работать АЙ:	Почему он всегда _____?	Почему он никогда не отдыха____?
8. Что дела____ **Ира?**	писать А:	Почему она всегда _____?	Почему она никогда не отдыха____?

НУ verbs like **отдохнуть** . . . . take ё endings; the н in the suffix remains

This verb type is called **НУ** (read: "noo") based on its stem suffix. To conjugate, just keep the **н** and add the **ё** endings. The **stress** will remain where it is in the **infinitive**. Like **ОВА** verbs, these verbs are easy to spot and conjugate.

We will tag *some* of these verbs as **(НУ)** — with parentheses — and call them "**disappearing** НУ verbs." We'll learn why when we study the **past** tense. For this reason, there are **two head verbs** listed below — one for each kind of НУ verb.

отдохнуть НУ[end]: to relax[1]		**привыкнуть** (НУ): to get used (to)[1]		**мёрзнуть** (НУ): to freeze[2]	**замёрзнуть** (НУ): to freeze[1]
отдохну	I will relax	привыкну	I will get used	мёрзну	замёрзну
отдохн**ёшь**	you will relax	привык**нешь**	you will get used	мёрз**нешь**	замёрз**нешь**
отдохн**ёт**	he, she, it will relax	привык**нет**	he, she, it will get used	мёрз**нет**	замёрз**нет**
отдохн**ём**	we will relax	привык**нем**	we will get used	мёрз**нем**	замёрз**нем**
отдохн**ёте**	you will relax	привык**нете**	you will get used	мёрз**нете**	замёрз**нете**
отдохн**ут**	they will relax	привык**нут**	they will get used	мёрз**нут**	замёрз**нут**
отдохн**и!**	relax!	привык**ни!**	get used!	мёрз**ни!**	замёрз**ни!**

Мы **мёрзнем.**	Ничего, **привыкнете.**	2. **Они** мёрзн_____.	Ничего, **они** привыкн_____14.c
We're freezing.	It's nothing, you'll get used to it.	3. **Ты** мёрзн_____?	Ничего, **я** привыкн_____.
1. **Я** мёрзн_____.	Ничего, **ты** привыкн_____.	4. **Вы** мёрзн_____?	Ничего, **мы** привыкн_____.

[1] Again, when we conjugate a **perfective** verb, the resulting forms are **future** tense. We'll discuss this in detail on Day 17.
[2] A very useful verb if you're planning to visit Russia during the winter; it is intransitive, as in "I'm freezing out here!"

This verb type is called "**ЕЙ**" (like English "yay!") based on its stem suffix (similarly to **АЙ** verbs). Common **ЕЙ** verbs include **уметь** and **иметь**. There are also many **ЕЙ** verbs formed from adjectives, meaning "to become" that adjective. For example: **глупеть** (to become **глупый**, stupid), **богатеть** (to become **богатый**, rich), **краснеть** (to become **красный**, red; to blush). As with **АЙ** verbs, stress will always be in the **stem**, in the same place as in the infinitive.

уметь ЕЙ: to know how		иметь ЕЙ: to have, possess	успеть ЕЙ: to manage in time	стареть ЕЙ: to become old
умею	I know how	имею	успею	старею
умеешь	you know how	имеешь	успеешь	стареешь
умеет	he, she, it knows how	имеет	успеет	стареет
умеем	we know how	имеем	успеем	стареем
умеете	you know how	имеете	успеете	стареете
умеют	they know how	имеют	успеют	стареют
умей!	know how!	имей!	успей!	старей!

14.d Ты **умеешь** читать по-русски?
Do you know how to read in Russian?

Ты **успеешь** прочитать этот русский текст?
Will you manage to read this Russian text in time?

1. **Он** уме_____ читать эту книгу?[1]
Он успе_____ прочитать эту книгу?

2. **Они** уме_____ всё[2] делать?
Они успе_____ всё сделать?

3. **Вы** уме_____ писать статью[2]?
Вы успе_____ написать статью?

4. **Она** уме_____ это делать?
Она успе_____ это сделать?

5. **Михаил** уме_____ писать письмо?
Он успе_____ написать письмо?

6. **Юлия** уме_____ рисовать?
Она успе_____ нарисовать эту кошку?

Толстеть — значит стареть! Питайтесь разнообразно, регулярно, умеренно.
To grow fat means to grow old. Nourish yourself in a varied, regular, and moderate way.

14.2 Some useful phrases with иметь (to have)

As we know, Russian does not usually express **possession** using a verb "to have." Instead, it uses **у + gen**. (У меня есть машина, etc.). However, there **is** a verb meaning "to have."

The verb "to have" (**иметь**) is used in a more formal or figurative sense. Here are three examples of some common phrases that *do* use this verb (two have a direct object in the **genitive** due to the **negated verb**).[3] For now, simply learn the phrases.

иметь в виду
to have in mind, to mean

иметь значение (не иметь значения[3])
(not) to "have significance," to matter (or not)

не иметь понятия[3]
to "have no understanding," have no idea

Что ты имеешь в виду?
What do you mean?

Это не имеет значения.
That doesn't matter.

— Почему он это делает?
— Why is he doing that?

—Понятия не имею!
— I have no idea!

14.e Почему они **краснеют**?
Why are they blushing?
Я понятия не имею!
I have no idea!

1. Какое **это** име_____ значение? Я понятия не имею!

2. **Мы** успе_____ всё сделать? Я понятия не имею!

3. **Он** уме_____ танцевать? Я понятия не имею!

4. Что **она** име_____ в виду? Я понятия не имею!

5. Что **мы** здесь дела_____? Я понятия не имею!

6. Почему **мы** чита__ этот текст? Я понятия не имею!

7. **Кто** слуша_____ такую музыку? Я понятия не имею!

8. **Ребёнок** уме_____ читать? Я понятия не имею!

9. Что **он** рису_____? Я понятия не имею!

10. **Они** хорошо танцу_____? Я понятия не имею!

68   [1] As we'll soon learn, direct objects are in the **accusative** case.
[2] As we'll see in 14.4, **всё** means "everything," while "**все**" means "everyone."
[3] While no longer a "rule," modern Russian retains a tendency to put the **direct objects of negated verbs** into the **genitive** case.

14.3 Introduction to non-suffixed verb types

There are many ё verb types that have one thing in common: unlike the types we've seen so far, they are not built using any **verbal suffixes** or **stem vowels**. Instead, ё endings are added **directly to the stem**. We can refer to these types collectively as **non-suffixed** verb types.

In one sense, these verbs are easy: simply add the ё endings to the stem. But there's one big problem: the **final consonant** in the stem is rarely seen in the infinitive form: historically, the consonant has been "**swallowed**" (so to speak) by the infinitive ending.

Look at the verb meaning "to live": **жить** B: живу, живёшь, живёт, etc. From the conjugated forms, the stem is clearly visible: **жив**. But in the infinitive, we have not **живть**, but **жить**. So, for most non-suffixed verbs, we must simply know the **stem** in addition to the **infinitive**.

Since these **non-suffixed** verbs don't add a stem vowel or other verbal suffix to their root, it stands to reason that their infinitives are typically **monosyllabic** (like **жить**), whereas the infinitives of **suffixed** verbs are almost always **multisyllabic** (**читать, писать, танцевать**, etc.).[1] This is even true of **понять**: if we ignore the **по-**, which is a prefix, we are left with a basic infinitive that is monosyllabic: **-нять**.[2]

This leads to a useful rule of thumb, as we move forward: if we see a new infinitive that is **one syllable** only (**ignoring any prefixes!**), we can guess that it's likely a non-suffixed verb, and that we'll need to consult a dictionary to learn the stem before we can conjugate the verb.

"Жить стало лучше, товарищи, жить стало веселее, а когда весело живётся, работа спорится."

— Сталин

A notorious quote from Stalin. Roughly: "To live has become better, comrades; to live has become happier, and when one lives happily, one works successfully."

В verbs like **жить** . . . . take ё endings, and never mutate

жить B^{end}: to live	
живу	I live
живёшь	you live
живёт	he, she, it lives
живём	we live
живёте	you live
живут	they live
живи!	live!

Most non-suffixed verb types will look something like this. They'll be tagged according to the final element in their stem — in this case, the **final consonant**. Again, this is the crucial bit of information that cannot be gleaned from the **infinitive** itself.

Here, the tag **В** lets us know that, once we remove the infinitive ending **-ть** and are left with **жи-**, we need to add the final consonant **в**. So, our stem is **жив-**. To this, we simply add the ё endings. The vast majority of non-suffixed verbs have **no mutations**.

To give another example: **стать** H^{stem} (to become) → стану, станешь, станет, etc.

Г verbs like **мочь** . . . . take ё endings, and mutate in the "inner forms"

мочь Г^{shift}: to be able to, "can"[3]	
могу	I can
можешь	you can
может	he, she, it can
можем	we can
можете	you can
могут	they can

not used

As non-suffixed verbs go, this type is tricky: it's one of only two that does have **mutations** — namely, in the so-called "inner forms" (as opposed to the "outer forms," **могу** and **могут**, which do not mutate). Here, the mutation is **г → ж**.

Most beginner's textbooks would simply present this very common verb as an "irregular" verb. Of course, no matter how we label it, we simply have to memorize its pattern. But even now it's worth tagging this verb by type. The other type that works in this way is **К**. For example: **печь** K^{end} (to bake) : пеку, печёшь, печёт... пекут. But generally we won't see many verbs of these types in Books 1 and 2.

Он хорошо **живёт**?
Is he living well?

1. Ты хорошо жив_____?

2. Мы хорошо жив_____?

3. Они хорошо жив_____?

4. Вы хорошо жив_____?

Она **может** работать?
Is she able to work?

5. Ты мож_____ работать?

6. Они мог_____ работать? **14.f**

7. Вы мож_____ работать?

8. Я мог_____ работать?

---

[1] There are few exceptions: one is **знать** АЙ: to know.
[2] On prefixes, see Day 77. Common ones include **по-, на-, про-, вы-, в(о)-, у-, при-, пере-, за-, под-, с(о)-, до-**, and **от-**.
[3] Note the alternate infinitive ending here: **-чь**. Only a very few Russian infinitives have this ending.

понять Й/М[end]: to understand	
пойм**у**	I will understand
пойм**ёшь**	you will understand
пойм**ёт**	he, she, it will understand
пойм**ём**	we will understand
пойм**ёте**	you will understand
пойм**ут**	they will understand
пойм**и**!	understand!

This is another tricky — but frequently used — verb that many textbooks would present as irregular. But, again, we will go ahead and tag it by type: **й/м.**

Whenever we see a **forward slash** (/) within a verb type tag, it means that we are dealing with a **non-syllabic** stem, or root. For this type, the root is **й/м**, which has to do with "grasping." Unlike, for example, **пис** (writing), this root includes no vowel of its own; without a vowel, it doesn't constitute a syllable. That is, it is **non-syllabic.**

In fact, this particular root (**й/м**) is perhaps the trickiest in Russian, since it appears in three guises: it has a syllabic variant (**ним**), and in infinitives it often appears as **нять**. As we'll soon discuss further, if we look at the full aspectual pair[1] for the verb "to understand," we can spot all three of the guises that this particular root may assume:

по**ним**ать АЙ (по**ним**аю, по**ним**аешь...) / по**ня**ть Й/М[end] (пойм**у**, пойм**ё**шь...)

14.g Скажи **ему**, почему бельё у тебя такое грязное.
Tell him (dative case!), why your laundry is so dirty.

Он не **поймёт**.
He won't understand.

Он ничего не **понимает**.
He doesn't understand anything.

1. Скажи **нам**, какая у тебя новая идея.

Вы не пойм_____.

Вы ничего не понима_____.

2. Скажи **ей**, почему у тебя нет русского словаря.

Она не пойм_____.

Она ничего не понима_____.

3. Скажи **им**, почему одежда у тебя такая странная.

Они не пойм_____.

Они ничего не понима_____.

4. Скажи **мне**, почему телефон у тебя такой старый.

Ты не пойм_____.

Ты ничего не понима_____.

5. Скажите **мне**, что вы имеете в виду.

Вы не пойм_____.

Вы ничего не понима_____.

6. Скажи **ему**, почему у твоего дедушки нет компьютера.

Он не пойм_____.

Он ничего не понима_____.

7. Я скажу **тебе**, какая у меня проблема.

Я не пойм_____.

Я ничего не понима_____.

14.4 Всё (everything) and все (everyone)

In today's exercises, we've seen two similar words: **всё** (everything) and **все** (everyone).[2] By the way, since the dots above the letter **ё** are not usually included in real Russian texts, the reader must often distinguish between these two words based entirely on context! In these textbooks, however, we'll try to always include the dots.

Note carefully that **всё** is **neuter singular** (and takes singular verbs), while **все** is **plural** and takes plural verbs:

Всё было хорошо.
Everything was good.

Всё работает.
Everything is working.

Все работают.
Everyone is working.

Все были дома.
Everyone was at home.

14.h *Let's practice all of the types we've learned so far. Begin by drilling each of the verbs below. Remember, **ова** collapses to **у**.*

	читать АЙ to read	**писать** А to write	**рисовать** ОВА to draw	**мёрзнуть** НУ to freeze	**стареть** ЕЙ to get old	**жить** В to live	**мочь** Г to be able	**понять** Й/М to understand
1. **он**:	чита____	пиш____	рису____	мёрзн____	старе____	жив___	мож____	пойм____
2. **мы**:	чита____	пиш____	рису____	мёрзн____	старе____	жив___	мож____	пойм____
3. **я**:	чита____	пиш____	рису____	мёрзн____	старе____	жив___	мог____	пойм____
4. **они**:	чита____	пиш____	рису____	мёрзн____	старе____	жив___	мог____	пойм____
5. **вы**:	чита____	пиш____	рису____	мёрзн____	старе____	жив___	мож____	пойм____
6. **ты**:	чита____	пиш____	рису____	мёрзн____	старе____	жив___	мож____	пойм____
7. **она**:	чита____	пиш____	рису____	мёрзн____	старе____	жив___	мож____	пойм____
8. **все**	чита____	пиш____	рису____	мёрзн____	старе____	жив___	мог____	пойм____

---

[1] As we'll learn on Day 17, most Russian verbs come in "pairs" of infinitives. For now, simply have a look at the forms of this particular pair.
[2] Actually, **все** means "all..." — as in "all the people." This helps explain why it's a plural form — not singular like the English "everyone."

day 15: verb types with и endings

stress patterns in verbs, revisited; the **и** endings;
И verbs and **Е** verbs

Кур<u>и</u>! Smoke! (from **кур<u>и</u>ть** И: to smoke) Fragment of an advertisement for cigarettes for sale at **Моссельпр<u>о</u>м**. What is this guy smoking?!

15.1 Stress patterns in verbs, revisited

As we learned on Day 13, there are only **three** possible **stress patterns** for regular verbs. Here are three more examples, chosen from the verb types we'll introduce today, which take the **second** set of endings — **и endings**, which we haven't used so far. The stress patterns are especially hard to predict for these new verb types.

As always, if the **infinitive** itself is **stem**-stressed, we know **for certain** that all forms will remain **stem**-stressed. But if the infinitive is stressed on the **final syllable**, all we know for sure is that the **я form** will be end-stressed; we can't guess whether the remaining forms will show **end**-stress or **shifting**-stress![1] For this reason, such **ambiguous** verbs will have to add either "**end**" or "**shift**" to their tags, as in: **говор<u>и</u>ть** И[end] or **получ<u>и</u>ть** И[shift].

	stem stress		end stress		shifting stress	
	отв<u>е</u>тить И [2]	to answer	**говор<u>и</u>ть** И[end]	to say, speak	**получ<u>и</u>ть** И[shift]	to receive
я	отв<u>е</u>чу	I will answer	говор<u>ю</u>	I say	получ<u>у</u>	I will receive
ты	отв<u>е</u>тишь	you will answer	говор<u>и</u>шь	you say	получ<u>и</u>шь	you will receive
он	отв<u>е</u>тит	he, she, it will a.	говор<u>и</u>т	he, she, it says	получ<u>и</u>т	he, she, it will r.
мы	отв<u>е</u>тим	we will answer	говор<u>и</u>м	we say	получ<u>и</u>м	we will receive
вы	отв<u>е</u>тите	you will answer	говор<u>и</u>те	you say	получ<u>и</u>те	you will receive
они	отв<u>е</u>тят	they will answer	говор<u>я</u>т	they say	получ<u>а</u>т	they will receive
ты	отв<u>е</u>ть!	answer!	говор<u>и</u>!	say! speak!	получ<u>и</u>!	receive!

[1] Remember — the stress of the **imperative** forms (at the bottom) corresponds to that in the **я** form.
[2] Note carefully why it would be superfluous to mark this as "stem" stressed; we can see this immediately from the infinitive!

71

плат<u>и</u>ть И	**прос<u>и</u>ть** И	**гот<u>о</u>вить** И	**получ<u>и</u>ть** И	**отв<u>е</u>тить** И	**п<u>о</u>мнить** И	**куп<u>и</u>ть** И
to pay	to ask, request	to prepare	to receive	to answer	to remember	to buy

*What if we considered the **first two conjugated forms**? As the following examples show, knowing the **я** and **ты** forms is enough to allow us to establish the stress pattern for any regular verb! Give the stress pattern for these forms by writing **stem**, **end**, or **shift**.*

1. **плат<u>и</u>ть**:   плач<u>у</u>, пл<u>а</u>тишь   _____

4. **уч<u>и</u>ть**:   уч<u>у</u>, <u>у</u>чишь   _____

2. **говор<u>и</u>ть**:   говор<u>ю</u>, говор<u>и</u>шь   _____

5. **сид<u>е</u>ть**:   сиж<u>у</u>, сид<u>и</u>шь   _____

3. **куп<u>и</u>ть**:   купл<u>ю</u>, к<u>у</u>пишь   _____

6. **смотр<u>е</u>ть**:   смотр<u>ю</u>, см<u>о</u>тришь   _____

15.2 The и endings

Remember: **by definition**, a given verb type takes **either ё** endings (the endings we've seen thus far) **or и** endings. Today, we'll see two major types that take **и** endings. Be sure to distinguish them from the **ё** endings — particularly in the 3rd plural, which students often confuse: **и** endings include **ят / ат** (not **ют / ут**!).

и endings				ё endings		
singular		**plural**		**singular**		**plural**
я **-ю** (у)		мы **-им**		я **-у** (ю)		мы **-ём**
ты **-ишь**		вы **-ите**		ты **-ёшь**		вы **-ёте**
он, он<u>а</u>, он<u>о</u> **-ит**		они **-ят** (ат)		он, он<u>а</u>, он<u>о</u> **-ёт**		он<u>и</u> **-ут** (ют)

In the table of **и** endings, look at the **я** and **они** endings. How do we **choose** between them? As a rule, we will try to write the **soft** variants (**ю, ят**), unless the 8-letter spelling rule prevents this — in which case we'll have to write the **hard** variants (**у, ат**) instead. For example: говор<u>ю</u>, купл<u>ю</u>, смотр<u>ю</u>... *but*: сиж<u>у</u>, пл<u>а</u>чу.

И verbs like **отв<u>е</u>тить** .... take и endings, and mutate in the я form only

The largest group of Russian verbs taking **и** endings are called **И** verbs (say "ee," as in "see"), because of their stem vowel **и**. This is the second most common verb type, and it's quite easy to spot. If we see an infinitive in -**ить** that is **more than one syllable** (ignoring prefixes), we can bet that it's an **И** verb. As we learned, a **monosyllabic** infinitive, including those ending in -**ить** (like **жить**) suggests a **non-suffixed** verb, and will conjugate very differently. For example:

We can tell these **are** И verbs: **плат<u>и</u>ть, прос<u>и</u>ть, отв<u>е</u>тить, люб<u>и</u>ть**, and **заплат<u>и</u>ть** (the prefix за + **плат<u>и</u>ть**)

We can tell that these are **not**:   **пить, бить, шить, стричь, жить**, and **прож<u>и</u>ть** (the prefix про + **жить**)

If we spot an **И** verb, we will be able (with rare exceptions[1]) to conjugate it, if we know the rules! Just remember that these verbs mutate in the **я form only** (whenever a mutation is possible). To better illustrate this, we can divide **И verbs** into **three subgroups** based on their final stem consonants — namely, *whether* they can mutate, and, if so, *how*.

In the **first group**, show below, the final stem consonant **can mutate** — and so it does, in the **я form only**.

| **Т → Ч** | **Т → Ч** | **С → Ш** | **С → Ш** |

отв<u>е</u>тить И: to answer		**плат<u>и</u>ть** И^{shift}: to pay	**прос<u>и</u>ть** И^{shift}: to ask, request	**спрос<u>и</u>ть** И^{shift}: to ask, inquire
отв<u>е</u>чу	I will answer	плач<u>у</u>	прош<u>у</u>	спрош<u>у</u>
отв<u>е</u>тишь	you will answer	плат<u>и</u>шь	прос<u>и</u>шь	спрос<u>и</u>шь
отв<u>е</u>тит	he, she, it will a.	плат<u>и</u>т	прос<u>и</u>т	спрос<u>и</u>т
отв<u>е</u>тим	we will answer	плат<u>и</u>м	прос<u>и</u>м	спрос<u>и</u>м
отв<u>е</u>тите	you will answer	плат<u>и</u>те	прос<u>и</u>те	спрос<u>и</u>те
отв<u>е</u>тят	they will answer	плат<u>я</u>т	прос<u>я</u>т	спрос<u>я</u>т
отв<u>е</u>ть!	answer!	плат<u>и</u>!	прос<u>и</u>!	спрос<u>и</u>!

[1] Namely, if a given verb shows Church Slavonic mutations; see Day 126. These are relatively rare, although still very important.

The **second group** of **И verbs**, show below, also involve mutations. Their stems end in a **labial** consonant (a consonant we form using our **lips**).

When in doubt, simply make the sound, and notice whether you're using your lips. If you are, then the sound is a labial and will mutate in this fashion.

All such consonants **mutate** by adding a **soft л**, as in б → **бль**. Of course, when we add the vowel -**у**, we end up with the spelling: -**блю** (я **люблю**).

ЛЮБИТЕ РОДИНУ!

Любите родину! Love your homeland!

б → бль

любить И[shift]: to love	
люблю	I love
любишь	you love
любит	he, she, it loves
любим	we love
любите	you love
любят	they love
люби!	love!

в → вль

готовить И: to prepare	
готовлю	
готовишь	
готовит	
готовим	
готовите	
готовят	
готовь!	

п → пль

купить И[shift]: to buy	
куплю	
купишь	
купит	
купим	
купите	
купят	
купи!	

15.b

Кто платит сегодня?
Who is paying today?

1. **Я** _____ сегодня.
2. **Мы** _____ сегодня.
3. **Она** _____ сегодня.
4. **Они** _____ сегодня.

Кто ответит на вопрос?
Who will answer the question?

5. **Он** _____ на вопрос.
6. **Все** _____ на вопрос.
7. **Я** _____ на вопрос.
8. **Ты** _____ на вопрос.

Кто любит русскую литературу?
Who loves Russian literature?

9. **Мы** _____ русскую литературу.
10. **Вы** _____ русскую литературу.
11. **Все** _____ русскую литературу.
12. **Я** _____ русскую литературу.

The **third group** of **И verbs**, shown below, involve **no mutations**. Simply put, their final stem consonants **cannot mutate**, so they don't! For example, "hushing" consonants like **ч**, **ж**, and **ш** cannot mutate, so they remain unchanged.

Remember: as a rule of thumb, in the **я** and **они** forms, write the **soft** endings (**ю, ят**) by default, unless the **8-letter spelling rule** prevents this. Namely, after the hushings **ж, ч, ш,** and **щ**, we must write the hard endings (**у, ат**) instead.

говорить И[end]: to say, speak	
говорю	I say
говоришь	you say
говорит	he, she, it says
говорим	we say
говорите	you say
говорят	they say
говори!	say! speak!

помнить И: to remember	
помню	
помнишь	
помнит	
помним	
помните	
помнят	
помни!	

учить И[shift]: to teach	
учу	
учишь	
учит	
учим	
учите	
учат	
учи!	

получить И[shift]: to receive	
получу	
получишь	
получит	
получим	
получите	
получат	
получи!	

15.c

Кто получит письмо?
Who will receive a letter?

1. **Я** _____ письмо.
2. **Мы** _____ письмо.
3. **Вы** _____ письмо.
4. **Все** _____ письмо.

Кто помнит ответ?
Who remembers the answer?

5. **Она** _____ ответ.
6. **Мы** _____ ответ.
7. **Ты** _____ ответ.
8. **Я** _____ ответ.

Кто хорошо говорит по-русски?
Who speaks Russian well?

9. **Мы** хорошо _____ по-русски.
10. **Ты** хорошо _____ по-русски.
11. **Я** хорошо _____ по-русски.
12. **Все** хорошо _____ по-русски.

The **only difference** between **И verbs** and **E verbs** is the **stem vowel**: **и** versus **е**. In conjugated forms, the stem vowel is discarded, and the **и** endings added. And, just like **И verbs**, **E verbs** mutate in the **я form only**, whenever possible! So, in effect, these two types are identical in the present tense. Avoid the **common mistake** of trying to preserve the "е" (as in: сижу, сидешь, сидет, etc.). Remember, we need the **и** endings here as well: сиж<u>у</u>, сид<u>и</u>шь, сид<u>и</u>т, etc.

д → ж	д → ж	д → ж	**no mutation**
сид<u>е</u>ть E^{end}: to sit	**в<u>и</u>деть** E: to see	**ненав<u>и</u>деть** E: to hate	**смотр<u>е</u>ть** E^{shift}: to look, watch
сиж<u>у</u> I sit	виж<u>у</u>	ненавиж<u>у</u>	смотр<u>ю</u>
сид<u>и</u>шь you sit	вид<u>и</u>шь	ненавид<u>и</u>шь	смотр<u>и</u>шь
сид<u>и</u>т he, she, it sits	вид<u>и</u>т	ненавид<u>и</u>т	смотр<u>и</u>т
сид<u>и</u>м we sit	вид<u>и</u>м	ненавид<u>и</u>м	смотр<u>и</u>м
сид<u>и</u>те you sit	вид<u>и</u>те	ненавид<u>и</u>те	смотр<u>и</u>те
сид<u>я</u>т they sit	вид<u>я</u>т	ненавид<u>я</u>т	смотр<u>я</u>т
сид<u>и</u>! sit!	*not used*	*not used*	смотр<u>и</u>!

You may also have noticed that this is our second verb type with an infinitive in -**еть**. Recall that **ЕЙ** verbs like **им<u>е</u>ть**, **ум<u>е</u>ть**, **стар<u>е</u>ть** followed a very different pattern, taking **ё** endings (**им<u>е</u>ю**, **им<u>е</u>ешь**, etc.). So, this is another instance in which the infinitive doesn't tell us much about a verb — the verb type must be learned in addition to the infinitive.

15.d Поч<u>е</u>му он всё вр<u>е</u>мя[1] **сид<u>и</u>т** и **смотр<u>и</u>т** телев<u>и</u>зор?   Потом<u>у</u> что он **ненав<u>и</u>дит** общ<u>е</u>ние.
Why does he **sit** and **watch** television all the time?   Because he **hates** socializing.

1. Поч<u>е</u>му **он<u>и</u>** всё вр<u>е</u>мя _____ и _____ телев<u>и</u>зор?   Потом<u>у</u> что **он<u>и</u>** _____ общ<u>е</u>ние.

2. Поч<u>е</u>му **Серг<u>е</u>й** всё вр<u>е</u>мя _____ и _____ телев<u>и</u>зор?   Потом<u>у</u> что **он** _____ общ<u>е</u>ние.

3. Поч<u>е</u>му **Мар<u>и</u>на** всё вр<u>е</u>мя _____ и _____ телев<u>и</u>зор?   Потом<u>у</u> что **он<u>а</u>** _____ общ<u>е</u>ние.

4. Поч<u>е</u>му **все** всё вр<u>е</u>мя _____ и _____ телев<u>и</u>зор?   Потом<u>у</u> что **все** _____ общ<u>е</u>ние.

5. Поч<u>е</u>му **я** всё вр<u>е</u>мя _____ и _____ телев<u>и</u>зор?   Потом<u>у</u> что **ты** _____ общ<u>е</u>ние.

6. Поч<u>е</u>му **вы** всё вр<u>е</u>мя _____ и _____ телев<u>и</u>зор?   Потом<u>у</u> что **мы** _____ общ<u>е</u>ние.

Рыб<u>а</u>к рыбак<u>а</u> в<u>и</u>дит издалек<u>а</u>. One fisherman sees another from far away (i.e., birds of a feather flock together).

15.e   All of the verb types below <u>may</u> involve a **mutation**. Show which ones do by providing the conjugated forms requested.

Look very closely at the verb type! Remember: if we say that a given type mutates, then it will mutate in the relevant forms only when a **mutation is possible** *— that is, when its final stem consonant* **can** *mutate. <u>One</u> example below can't mutate!*

1. **плат<u>и</u>ть** И^{shift}   я _____   ты _____   ... он<u>и</u> _____

2. **смотр<u>е</u>ть** E^{shift}   я _____   ты _____   ... он<u>и</u> _____

3. **пл<u>а</u>кать** A   я _____   ты _____   ... он<u>и</u> _____

4. **мочь** Г^{shift}   я _____   ты _____   ... он<u>и</u> _____

5. **люб<u>и</u>ть** И^{shift}   я _____   ты _____   ... он<u>и</u> _____

6. **спрос<u>и</u>ть** И^{shift}   я _____   ты _____   ... он<u>и</u> _____

7. **показ<u>а</u>ть** A^{shift}   я _____   ты _____   ... он<u>и</u> _____

8. **куп<u>и</u>ть** И^{shift}   я _____   ты _____   ... он<u>и</u> _____

9. **сказ<u>а</u>ть** A^{shift}   я _____   ты _____   ... он<u>и</u> _____

---

[1] The adverbial phrase **всё вр<u>е</u>мя** means "all the time," and is a more casual synonym for **всегд<u>а</u>** (always).

Good news: we've now covered the **most common verb types**. And most of the types that remain are varieties of non-suffixed verbs—we'll learn many of them in later chapters of Books 1 and 2. For now, let's review the types we know so far. Drill, drill, drill!

The table below lists all of our **head verbs**. First, give their conjugations to review the basic pattern. Then, try orally conjugating some other verbs in the given type. You should continue practicing this drill with all the new verbs we encounter. As this "muscle memory" continues to improve, so will your ability to spontaneously produce these forms in conversation. It does take some time!

ё endings

	чит**а**ть АЙ	пис**а**ть А^{shift}	рис**ова**ть ОВА	им**е**ть ЕЙ	отдохн**у**ть НУ^{end}
я	_____	_____	_____	_____	_____
ты	_____	_____	_____	_____	_____
он, он**а**	_____	_____	_____	_____	_____
мы	_____	_____	_____	_____	_____
вы	_____	_____	_____	_____	_____
он**и**	_____	_____	_____	_____	_____

думать АЙ
раб**о**тать АЙ
сл**у**шать АЙ
отдых**а**ть АЙ
покуп**а**ть АЙ
получ**а**ть АЙ
тер**я**ть АЙ
потер**я**ть АЙ
поним**а**ть АЙ
забыв**а**ть АЙ

напис**а**ть А^{shift}
пл**а**кать А
запл**а**кать А
сказ**а**ть А^{shift}
показ**а**ть А^{shift}

нарис**ова**ть ОВА
танцев**а**ть ОВА
потанцев**а**ть ОВА

ум**е**ть ЕЙ
сум**е**ть ЕЙ
усп**е**ть ЕЙ
стар**е**ть ЕЙ

м**ё**рзнуть (НУ)
зам**ё**рзнуть (НУ)
прив**ы**кнуть (НУ)

ё endings (non-suffixed types)

	жить В^{and}	мочь Г^{shift}	пон**я**ть Й/М^{end}
я	_____	_____	_____
ты	_____	_____	_____
он, он**а**	_____	_____	_____
мы	_____	_____	_____
вы	_____	_____	_____
он**и**	_____	_____	_____

и endings

	говор**и**ть И^{end}	отв**е**тить И	люб**и**ть И^{shift}	сид**е**ть Е^{end}
я	_____	_____	_____	_____
ты	_____	_____	_____	_____
он, он**а**	_____	_____	_____	_____
мы	_____	_____	_____	_____
вы	_____	_____	_____	_____
он**и**	_____	_____	_____	_____

п**о**мнить И
получ**и**ть И^{shift}
уч**и**ть И^{shift}

плат**и**ть И^{shift}
заплат**и**ть И^{shift}
прос**и**ть И^{shift}
спрос**и**ть И^{shift}

куп**и**ть И^{shift}
гот**о**вить И
пригот**о**вить И

в**и**деть Е
ненав**и**деть Е
смотр**е**ть Е^{shift}

1. Как (how) ч**а**сто ты **см**о**тришь** телев**и**зор? К**а**ждый день? Иногд**а**? М**о**жет быть, ты не **см**о**тришь** ег**о** вообщ**е**?

2. Как хорош**о** ты **говор**и**шь** по-р**у**сски? **О**чень хорош**о**? Не **о**чень хорош**о**? Пл**о**хо? А по-англ**и**йски?

day 16: the accusative case and animacy

the accusative, direct objects, and animacy; verbs followed by prepositions; prepositions that take the accusative; pronouns in the accusative

За ро́дину, за Ста́лина! For the homeland, for Stalin! (the preposition **за** takes the **accusative** case)

16.1 The accusative case, direct objects, and animacy

A **direct object** is a person or thing **directly affected** by the action of a verb. We might say that the direct object
"absorbs" the force of the given action. As a rule, direct objects appear in the **accusative** case. Only two types
of nouns (**feminine** nouns, and **masculine** *animate* nouns) differ from the nominative in the accusative:

subject (nominative):	Это **но́вый компью́тер**. This is a new computer.	Это **но́вая кни́га**. This is a new book.	Это **но́вый студе́нт**. This is a new student.
direct object (accusative):	Я покупа́ю **но́вый компью́тер**. I am buying a new computer.	Я чита́ю **но́вую кни́гу**. I am reading a new book.	Я ви́жу **но́вого студе́нта**. I see a new student.

The noun **студе́нт** is **animate** (since it refers to a person or animal). As we can see, **masculine animates** take
the **same** noun and adjectival endings in the **accusative** as in the **genitive**. So these endings are not really new![1]

subject (nominative):	Это **но́вый студе́нт.** This is a new student.	Это **ру́сский писа́тель**. This is a Russian writer.	Это **наш оте́ц**. This is our father.
possession (genitive):	Это ме́сто **но́вого студе́нта**. This is the new student's seat.	Это кни́га **ру́сского писа́теля**. This is the Russian writer's book.	Это маши́на **на́шего отца́**. This is our father's car.
direct object (accusative):	Я зна́ю **но́вого студе́нта**. I know the new student.	Я чита́ю **ру́сского писа́теля**. I am reading the Russian writer.	Мы лю́бим **на́шего отца́**. We love our father.

76

[1] We will see other cases where various case endings happen to be the same. In such cases, context will usually make clear
which case you're actually dealing with.

In fact, we only have one **entirely new** ending to learn for today's lesson. In the accusative, **all feminine nouns** (whether animate or inanimate!) take **-y** (or its soft variant **-ю**), while feminine adjectives take **-ую**. We could sum this up as follows: in the **feminine accusative, а → у**, and **я → ю**.[1]

So, note how the feminine accusatives and genitives below are **distinct**, and that when it comes to feminine nouns, we do not need to differentiate between animates and inanimates in the accusative.[2]

subject (nominative):	Это **русская передача.** This is a Russian broadcast.	Это **новая студентка.** This is a new (female) student.	Это **ваша статья.** This is your article.
possession (genitive):	Это начало **русской передачи.** This is the start of a Russian broadcast.	Это место **новой студентки.** This is the new student's seat.	Это конец **вашей статьи.** This is the end of your article.
direct object (accusative):	Я смотрю **русскую передачу.** I'm watching a Russian broadcast.	Я знаю **новую студентку.** I know the new student.	Они читают **вашу статью.** They're reading your article.

---

*Fill in the blanks with these **feminine** accusative forms. Remember: **а → у**, and **я → ю**.*　　　　**16.a**

1. Это **наша новая кошка.**　　　Мы так любим _____ _____ _____!

2. Это фотография **моей любимой тёти.**　　　Я очень редко вижу _____ _____ _____.

3. Это **сестра** нашего друга.　　　Мы хорошо знаем его _____.

4. **Эта новая студентка** говорит по-русски.　　　Ты знаешь _____ _____ _____?

5. Это **её новая статья.**　　　Все читают _____ _____ _____.

6. У тебя есть **бабушка**?　　　Ты часто видишь _____? Есть фотография бабушки?

7. У него была очень **странная идея.**　　　Я совсем не понимаю его _____ _____.

8. **Эта работа** такая скучная!　　　Я ненавижу _____ _____.

9. Это **Маша**, а это **Таня.**　　　Вы знаете _____ и _____?

....
Рука руку моет. One hand washes the other (or, in Latin: Manus manum lavat)

---

*Now try some **masculine** and **neuter** forms. Remember, all accusatives look like the nominative, except for **masculine animates**!*　　**16.b**

Бей фашистского гада!
Crush the fascist vermin!
(**гад** is masculine animate)

1. **русский словарь**:　　　Мы сегодня покупаем _____ _____.

　　новый щен(о)к:　　　Мы сегодня покупаем _____ _____.

2. **наше общежитие** (dorm):　　　Мой сосед так ненавидит _____ _____.

　　наш профессор:　　　Мой сосед так ненавидит _____ _____.

3. **этот писатель**:　　　Моя соседка хорошо понимает _____ _____.

　　этот вопрос:　　　Моя соседка хорошо понимает _____ _____.

4. **старый начальник** (boss):　　　Я плохо помню _____ _____.

　　старый ков(ё)р:　　　Я плохо помню _____ _____.

5. **большой дом**:　　　Ребёнок рисует _____ _____.

　　большой кот:　　　Ребёнок рисует _____ _____.

6. **твой друг**:　　　Я вижу _____ _____.

　　тот же фильм:　　　Мы смотрим _____ _____ _____.

....
Делать из мухи слона. To make an elephant (**слон**) out of a fly (**муха**); to make a mountain out of a molehill. The preposition **из** takes the genitive.

---

1. Ты каждый день читаешь **газету** (или онлайн-газету)?　　　3. Ты любишь читать **русскую поэзию**?

2. Кто читает **русского писателя** сейчас? **Кого**?　　　4. **Какого русского поэта** ты любишь читать?

---

[1] In the future, we'll see feminine nouns that end in a consonant (e.g. **тетрадь**). These remain the same in the accusative.
[2] We will need to distinguish between animate and inanimate in the feminine accusative **plural** (see Day 64).

16.2 Masculine nouns with feminine endings and stand-alone adjectives

As we've seen, some **adjectives**, like **знак<u>о</u>мый**, can stand alone as nouns (see 11.7), and some **masculine nouns**, like **п<u>а</u>па** and **д<u>я</u>дя,** take feminine endings (12.3), despite being masculine for purposes of agreement with adjectives and verbs. This remains true, of course, in the accusative case as well.

Look at these examples, noting the agreement arrows. Note in particular the adjectives modifying **animate** masculine nouns.

Я в<u>и</u>жу **н<u>а</u>шего люб<u>и</u>мого д<u>я</u>дю.**
I see our favorite uncle.

Я зн<u>а</u>ю **<u>э</u>того стр<u>а</u>нного мужч<u>и</u>ну.**
I know that strange man.

Я в<u>и</u>жу **ст<u>а</u>рого знак<u>о</u>мого.**
I see an old (male) acquaintance.

Я в<u>и</u>жу **ст<u>а</u>рую знак<u>о</u>мую.**
I see an old (female) acquaintance.

16.3 Verbs followed by prepositions

An important part of using verbs correctly is knowing what preposition(s) can follow them. For example, in English we pay *for* something. The Russian equivalent is **плат<u>и</u>ть за** + the accusative. Dictionaries often use case forms of **что** and **кто** to convey this information concisely, as in: **плат<u>и</u>ть за что-либо / за ког<u>о</u>-либо**: to pay for something / for someone.[1] Some dictionaries, including this book's vocabulary lists, will shorten this to the question word itself, as in: **плат<u>и</u>ть за <u>что</u> / за <u>кого</u>.** This is enough to show that we need the accusative.

So, when studying verbs, take careful note of any information concerning what cases and prepositions can follow each verb. By default, we assume that **all direct objects** will be in the **accusative**. But certain verbs take objects in other cases — or, as we've just seen, must connect to their object via a certain preposition. We'll speak more about these issues later. For now, here are a few examples from our vocabulary thus far:

плат<u>и</u>ть И[shift] за что / кого   **отвеч<u>а</u>ть** АЙ на вопр<u>о</u>с   **смотр<u>е</u>ть** Е[shift] на что / ког<u>о</u>   *but:* **смотр<u>е</u>ть** Е фильм
to pay for   to answer a question   to look at   to watch a movie

As always, it's dangerous to assume that the **Russian idiom** will mirror the English. For example, in English we "answer a question" — with no preposition needed. But in Russian we do need one: we answer "**на вопр<u>о</u>с.**"

16.4 Prepositions that take the accusative

Let's see examples using these verbs as we list some common prepositions that take the **accusative**:

за	for, in favor of (opposite of **пр<u>о</u>тив**)	Мы **за** своб<u>о</u>ду сл<u>о</u>ва. Кто же[2] пр<u>о</u>тив своб<u>о</u>ды сл<u>о</u>ва? We are **for** freedom of speech ("the word"). Who's against freedom of speech?	
	for, in exchange for	От<u>е</u>ц пл<u>а</u>тит **за** нас. Он пл<u>а</u>тит **за** наш об<u>е</u>д. (Our) father is paying **for** us. He is paying **for** our lunch.	
на	at, onto	Почем<u>у</u> ты всегд<u>а</u> см<u>о</u>тришь **на** мен<u>я</u>? Why are you always looking **at** me?	*but:* Мы см<u>о</u>трим <u>э</u>тот фильм. We're watching this film.
	in response to	Кто зн<u>а</u>ет отв<u>е</u>т **на** <u>э</u>тот вопр<u>о</u>с? Who knows the answer **to** this question?	Кто м<u>о</u>жет отв<u>е</u>тить **на** вопр<u>о</u>с? Who can answer the question?

16.c 1. **н<u>о</u>вый студ<u>е</u>нт**:   Почем<u>у</u> ты так см<u>о</u>тришь на <u>э</u>того _____ _____?

2. **как<u>о</u>й фильм**:   _____ _____ вы см<u>о</u>трите? Р<u>у</u>сский?

3. **<u>э</u>та р<u>у</u>сская газ<u>е</u>та**:   Кто пл<u>а</u>тит за _____ _____ _____?

4. **войн<u>а</u>** (war):   — Ты пр<u>о</u>тив _____? — Кон<u>е</u>чно! Кто же за _____?

5. **<u>э</u>тот тр<u>у</u>дный вопр<u>о</u>с**:   Кто м<u>о</u>жет отв<u>е</u>тить на _____ _____ _____?

6. **фотогр<u>а</u>фия мо<u>е</u>й соб<u>а</u>ки**:   — На что вы см<u>о</u>трите? — На _____ _____ _____.

Посад<u>и</u> свинь<u>ю</u> за[2] стол, он<u>а</u> и н<u>о</u>ги на[3] стол. Seat a pig at your table, and it (will put) its feet onto the table (Give an inch and they'll take a mile).

[1] The **либо** here is a rather formal way of marking an indefinite; hence, **что-либо** means "something." We'll learn ordinary indefinites later.
[1] The emphatic particle **же** simply adds emphasis to the preceding word — here lending an air of incredulity to the question.
[2] In certain set expressions, you may occasionally notice the stress in a prepositional phrase falling on the **preposition**.

*Discuss whether you're "for" (**за** + accusative) or "against" (**против** + genitive) the following things or political figures.*

коммун<u>и</u>зм Communism   **капитал<u>и</u>зм** Capitalism   **<u>я</u>дерное ор<u>у</u>жие** nuclear weapons   **царь**, <u>я</u> the tsar
демокр<u>а</u>тия Democracy   **свob<u>о</u>да сл<u>о</u>ва** free speech   **взят<u>о</u>чничество** bribe-taking   **Л<u>е</u>нин** Lenin

Уничт<u>о</u>жим кулак<u>а</u> как класс.
"We will destroy the kulak as a class."

A reference to the brutal "dekulakization" (**раскул<u>а</u>чивание**) efforts (1929-32) to eradicate relatively wealthy peasants who supposedly exploited the true peasantry. Even such meager "riches" as an extra cow could result in execution or imprisonment. Both **кул<u>а</u>к** and **класс** are in the accusative here (**класс** is in apposition to **кул<u>а</u>к** — that is, it renames or defines it).

16.5 Pronouns in the accusative

Accusative pronoun forms are exactly the same as the **genitive** forms. Remember, 3rd-person forms add an **н** when following prepositions!

pronouns								
singular					**plural**			
nom.	gen.	acc.	*with preposition:*		nom.	gen.	acc.	*with preposition:*
я	мен<u>я</u>	мен<u>я</u>	→ на мен<u>я</u>		мы	нас	нас	→ на нас
ты	теб<u>я</u>	теб<u>я</u>	→ на теб<u>я</u>		вы	вас	вас	→ на вас
он	ег<u>о</u>	ег<u>о</u>	→ на нег<u>о</u>		он<u>и</u>	их	их	→ на них
он<u>а</u>	её	её	→ на неё					
он<u>о</u>	ег<u>о</u>	ег<u>о</u>	→ на нег<u>о</u>					

*Supply the appropriate pronouns. The needed **case** is dictated by the **context**!*   **16.d**

1. Ты покуп<u>а</u>ешь **кн<u>и</u>гу**?   Да, я _____ покуп<u>а</u>ю. _____ интер<u>е</u>сная.
2. У вас есть н<u>о</u>вый **фильм**?   Да, сейч<u>а</u>с _____ см<u>о</u>трим. _____ хор<u>о</u>ший.
3. Я не в<u>и</u>жу **Бор<u>и</u>са**. Где _____?   Я т<u>о</u>же _____ не в<u>и</u>жу. _____ здесь нет.
4. Кто **он<u>и</u>**? Ты _____ зн<u>а</u>ешь?   Я был у _____ вчер<u>а</u>, но я _____ пл<u>о</u>хо зн<u>а</u>ю.
5. Ты чит<u>а</u>ешь <u>э</u>ту **газ<u>е</u>ту**?   Нет, я _____ ненав<u>и</u>жу. _____ так<u>а</u>я ск<u>у</u>чная!
6. В<u>и</u>дишь **Нат<u>а</u>шу**? Где _____?   Я _____ не в<u>и</u>жу. _____ здесь нет.
7. Ты л<u>ю</u>бишь <u>э</u>того **щенк<u>а</u>**?   Да! Я вообщ<u>е</u> не мог<u>у</u> жить без _____!

Люб<u>и</u>те кн<u>и</u>гу — ист<u>о</u>чник зн<u>а</u>ния:
Love "the book" — the source (**ист<u>о</u>чник**) of knowledge (**зн<u>а</u>ние**).

Both **кн<u>и</u>гу** and **ист<u>о</u>чник** are in the accusative (**ист<u>о</u>чник**, because it is in apposition to **кн<u>и</u>гу**).

Don't rely on word order when reading Russian!

English relies largely on word order to convey the role played by nouns in a sentence. The typical order is **subject—verb—object** (SVO):

The man is buying a newspaper.

Here, **man** is the subject, and **newspaper** is the direct object. Of course, this is the only reading of this sentence that makes sense, since a newspaper can't buy a man. But in some cases, we must rely entirely on word order to distinguish between subject and object:

The man loves the woman.

Russian's basic sentence structure is also **subject—verb—object**, but since it is richly **inflected** (changing word endings to convey information), it can vary this order for effect. As we know, Russian often prefers to **save new information**, or the "most interesting" element of the sentence, for the **end of the sentence**. Quite often, this is the subject:

Это **н<u>о</u>вая кн<u>и</u>га.**   Кн<u>и</u>гу напис<u>а</u>л **изв<u>е</u>стный р<u>у</u>сский пис<u>а</u>тель.**
This is a new book.   A famous Russian writer wrote the book.

Hence, a general principle that is **ESSENTIAL** for understanding Russian:

*When reading Russian, you'll often find that the **subject** of a sentence comes **at the very end**! So, don't expect the first word in a sentence to be the subject. Always be prepared to "wait" for a word in the **nominative** case — that's the subject!*

[1] Generally speaking, Russian may also be classified as an "SVO" language, by default — but because its word order is so flexible, this is of little practical help, if not simply misleading! Insisting on reading the first noun in a given sentence as the subject is one of the most common mistakes made by students when reading. Remember: making sense of a Russian sentence means paying attention to **endings!**

day 17: verbal aspect and tense

introduction to aspect; aspect and tense; forming the present.
past, and future tenses; a summary of all verb forms

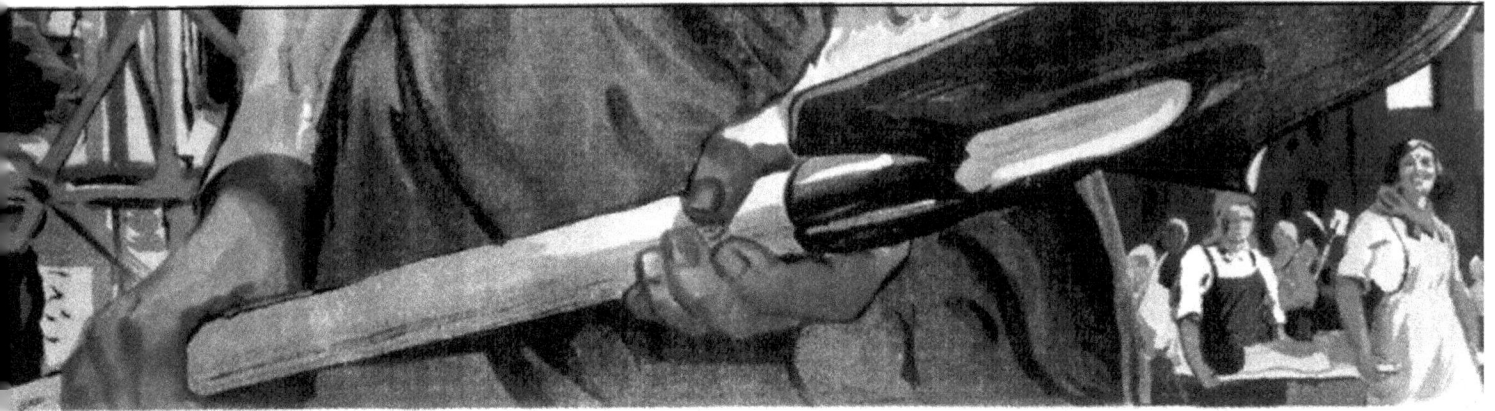

ВИКТОР ИВАНОВ-45.

ОТСТРОИМ НА СЛАВУ!

Отстроим на славу! We'll rebuild gloriously!
(The pair is: **отстраивать** АЙ / **отстроить** И: to rebuild)

17.1 Introduction to aspect

Almost all Russian verbs come in **aspectual pairs**: two infinitives, one **imperfective** and one **perfective**. What's the difference in their meaning? The answer is not a simple one! Let's begin exploring with a few examples:

ОТСТОИМ МОСКВУ!

Отстоим Москву:
We _will defend_ Moscow.

Perfective aspect emphasizes completion, success, result. The pair for this verb is **отстаивать** АЙ / **отстоять** ЖА. When conjugated, a perfective verb is _future_ tense in meaning.

Ты будешь жить счастливо!
You _will live_ happily.

Imperfective aspect emphasizes the action itself, including extended duration. Imperfective verbs use a compound form in the _future_ tense.

ТЫ БУДЕШЬ ЖИТЬ СЧАСТЛИВО!

ЗАЩИТИМ ГОРОД ЛЕНИНА

Защитим город Ленина: We _will defend_ the city of Lenin.

Perfective aspect emphasizes completion, success, result. The aspectual pair for this verb is **защищать** АЙ / **защитить** И

Мы победили!
We _have won!_

Perfective aspect emphaszes completion, success, result: the war is over, and the result is victory! The pair for this verb is **побеждать** АЙ / **победить** И. The _past_ tense is used in this example.

80

Verbal aspect is one of the most pervasive features of Russian grammar — and one of the **most difficult** for learners who are not native speakers of a Slavic language, in much the same way that the use of **articles** is hard for Slavic learners of English, since Slavic lacks articles altogether.[1] Only when you try to explain to a Russian friend how articles work will you realize how many subtleties influence your choice between definite articles, indefinite articles, and no articles at all! Using aspect in Russian can be similarly complex and context-driven. And since English lacks aspect as a regular grammatical feature, aspect is difficult to present succinctly to students.

Every time a Russian describes an action, he or she must **choose between two infinitives**: one **imperfective**, and one **perfective**.[2] If we are asked "How do you say '**to read**' in Russian?" we should really answer with **two** infinitives: "**читать / прочитать**." This pair of infinitives is called an **aspectual pair**. We will discuss how these pairs are formed in tomorrow's lesson. For now, we'll work with a few simple pairs and focus on a more basic question: when we want to use the verb "to read" in Russian, **how do we choose** between these two infinitives?

Aspect is a daunting topic, and will take time to master. In Books 1 and 2, we will limit ourselves to "**Basic Aspect**," which is restricted to **three basic criteria** that can rather clearly determine our choice of aspect in a majority of everyday situations. In Book 3 (Day 109), we'll move on to "**Advanced Aspect**," and introduce more complex distinctions that rely more heavily on **context** and a speaker's choice of **emphasis within that context**.

17.2 Aspect and tense

The table below presents the aspectual pair, **читать** АЙ / **прочитать** АЙ. This is how we will write up these pairs in our vocabulary: first the **imperfective** infinitive, then a **foward slash**, then the **perfective** infinitive.

Next, the table shows which of the three Russian verb tenses (**present, past, future**) can be formed from each infinitive. We've noted (Day 6) that Russian has only **three grammatical tenses**: present, past, and future. While Russian is relatively "poor" in **tenses** (with 3), its rich, highly descriptive use of **aspect** more than compensates.

When **translating** a Russian verb in a given tense (past tense, for example), we have **multiple English tenses** at our disposal: we could use the **simple past** (I read), the **past progressive** (I was reading), or a **perfect tense** (I had read). Some of these **suggested translations** are given below — but in practice, our actual choice will often depend on **context**. Your fluency with English tense usage will typically inspire you to make the best choice!

IMPORTANT: there is **no direct correspondence whatsoever between "perfect" tense forms in English and "perfective" aspect in Russian**. Remember: **tense** and **aspect** are separate categories!

In the table, note how the basic meanings inherent to each aspect carry over across the three tenses.

	imperfective	perfective
basic aspectual criteria:	1. **Ongoing** action (no mention of result). 2. **Repeated** or habitual action. 3. Emphasis on **attempt** or effort.[3]	1. **Completed** action (emphasis on result). 2. **One-time** action. 3. Emphasis on **success** or accomplishment.[3]

читать АЙ   /   прочитать АЙ

present tense:	мы чит**а**ем 1. **We are reading** (in the process of reading) 2. **We read** (repeatedly, habitually) 3. **We are reading** (trying to read)	— — —
past tense:	мы чит**а**ли 1. **We were reading** (in the process of reading) 2. **We would read** (repeatedly, habitually) 3. **We were reading** (trying to read)	мы прочит**а**ли 1. **We read, have read, had read** (completely) 2. **We read, have read, had read** (once) 3. **We read, have read, had read** (successfully)
future tense:	мы б**у**дем чит**а**ть 1. **We will be reading** (in the process of reading) 2. **We will read** (repeatedly, habitually) 3. **We will be reading** (trying to read)	мы прочит**а**ем 1. **We will read** (completely) 2. **We will read** (once) 3. **We will read** (successfully)

---

[1] Bulgarian is an exception!   [2] Certain verbs only have a single, imperfective form.
[3] Criterion 3 follows logically from Criterion 1, but it is still worth distinguishing, particularly with certain pairs, such as **реш**а**ть** АЙ / **реш**и**ть** И: to solve — which could be understood as: "to try to solve" / "to solve (successfully)"

17.3 Forming the present tense

Only imperfective verbs can be used in the **present** tense. Why? Quite logically, if an action is in the present, it is by definition **ongoing**; it is still unfolding. Only an imperfective verb can describe this kind of action. So, to speak about present actions, we simply **conjugate** an **imperfective** infinitive: **мы читаем**: we are reading.

So, what happens if we **conjugate** a **perfective** verb? The conjugated forms will automatically be **future tense** in meaning: **прочитаем**: we will read (completely).

In this sense, we must simply **know** the **aspect** of a given verb form in order know what **tense** it describes: present or future. Clearly, learning verbs **as aspectual pairs** is essential for making sense of Russian!

17.4 Forming the past tense

As we've already seen with **быть**, forming the **past tense** is generally **extremely simple**. For almost all verbs, we simply begin with the infinitive, remove the infinitive ending, add the past tense marker **л**, and then any gender/number endings. Note that verbs of **both aspects** form their past tense in exactly the same way.

It's worth emphasizing how **easy** the past tense usually is. In the present tense, the many different verb types all conjugate differently, and can take time to learn well. But these difficulties rarely carry over into the past tense. The past tense comes directly from the infinitive — and that usually includes the **stress**.

А как ты сегодня работал?
And how did you work today?

But two verbs we've seen have unusual stress in the past tense:[1]

ПОНЯ́ТЬ:	он по́нял	она́ поняла́	оно́ по́няло	они́ по́няли
ЖИ́ТЬ:	он жил	она́ жила́	оно́ жи́ло	они́ жи́ли

	imperfective	perfective
basic aspectual criteria:	1. **Ongoing** action (no mention of result). 2. **Repeated** or habitual action. 3. Emphasis on **attempt** or effort.	1. **Completed** action (emphasis on result). 2. **One-time** action. 3. Emphasis on **success** or accomplishment.

чита́ть АЙ / прочита́ть АЙ

past tense:	чита́ть →	он **чита́л** она́ **чита́ла** оно́ **чита́ло** они́ **чита́ли**		прочита́ть →	он **прочита́л** она́ **прочита́ла** оно́ **прочита́ло** они́ **прочита́ли**	

17.a *Give the requested **past**-tense forms. Note that 1st and 2nd person singular pronouns (**я** and **ты**) can be **masculine** or **feminine**.*

1. **гото́вить** И: он _____   она́ _____   они́ _____

2. **сде́лать** АЙ: ты (f.) _____   ты (m.) _____   вы _____

3. **уме́ть** ЕЙ: я (m.) _____   я (f.) _____   мы _____

4. **написа́ть** А: они́ _____   вы _____   мы _____

5. **смотре́ть** Е^shift: все _____   он _____   она́ _____

6. **нарисова́ть** ОВА: я (f.) _____   ты (f.) _____   она́ _____

7. **жи́ть** В^end: я (m.) _____   я (f.) _____   мы _____

8. **поня́ть** Й/М^end: он _____   она́ _____   они́ _____

Ба́бушка на́двое сказа́ла. Grandma said two things (spoke ambiguously) — i.e. nothing is known yet for certain, the jury is still out.

[1] Our vocab sections will provide past-tense forms for verbs that are unusual in any way in the past (including in terms of stress). The most common stress irregularity (see **жи́ть**) is simply to have the stress jump to the **feminine** ending (-a) only, remaining on the stem elsewhere.

делать АЙ	/ **сделать** АЙ	*Give some past-tense forms, and use them in past-tense sentences (watch **aspect**).* **17.b**
он: _____	_____	1. What was he doing yesterday?[1] _____
он<u>а</u>: _____	_____	2. What did she get done yesterday? _____
он<u>и</u>: _____	_____	3. What did they usually (об<u>ы</u>чно) do? _____
гот<u>о</u>вить И	/ **пригот<u>о</u>вить** И	
он: _____	_____	4. He cooked dinner (<u>у</u>жин) yesterday. _____
он<u>а</u>: _____	_____	5. She was cooking dinner yesterday. _____
он<u>и</u>: _____	_____	6. They rarely (р<u>е</u>дко) cooked dinner. _____

17.5 Forming the future tense

As we've seen, only imperfective verbs can be used in the present tense, since they describe ongoing actions. If we simply conjugate a **perfective** verb, the resulting forms automatically describe actions in the **future.**

To form the future tense of **imperfective** verbs, combine the **infinitive** with a **helping verb** — the future-tense forms of **быть** that we learned on Day 6. Only **быть** is conjugated (e.g. not **я б<u>у</u>ду чит<u>а</u>ю**, but **я б<u>у</u>ду чит<u>а</u>ть**).

	imperfective	perfective
basic aspectual criteria:	1. **Ongoing** action (no mention of result). 2. **Repeated** or habitual action. 3. Emphasis on **attempt** or effort.	1. **Completed** action (emphasis on result). 2. **One-time** action. 3. Emphasis on **success** or accomplishment.

чит<u>а</u>ть АЙ   /   прочит<u>а</u>ть АЙ

future tense:	я **б<u>у</u>ду** чит<u>а</u>ть		я **прочит<u>а</u>ю**
	ты **б<u>у</u>дешь** чит<u>а</u>ть		ты **прочит<u>а</u>ешь**
	он, он<u>а</u>, он<u>о</u> **б<u>у</u>дет** чит<u>а</u>ть		он, он<u>а</u>, он<u>о</u> **прочит<u>а</u>ет**
	мы **б<u>у</u>дем** чит<u>а</u>ть		мы **прочит<u>а</u>ем**
	вы **б<u>у</u>дете** чит<u>а</u>ть		вы **прочит<u>а</u>ете**
	он<u>и</u> **б<u>у</u>дут** чит<u>а</u>ть		он<u>и</u> **прочит<u>а</u>ют**

делать АЙ	/ **сделать** АЙ	*Give **future**-tense forms for both aspects, then use them to translate the English. Choose **aspect** carefully!* **17.c**
вы: _____	_____	

1. What will you be doing tomorrow?	Что вы _____ з<u>а</u>втра?
2. What will you get done tomorrow?	Что вы _____ з<u>а</u>втра?

пис<u>а</u>ть А[shift]	/ **напис<u>а</u>ть** А	
он: _____	_____	

3. He'll write a letter tomorrow.	З<u>а</u>втра он _____ письм<u>о</u>.
4. He'll write a letter every day.	Он _____ к<u>а</u>ждый день письм<u>о</u> _____.

рисов<u>а</u>ть ОВА	/ **нарисов<u>а</u>ть** ОВА	
он<u>а</u>: _____	_____	

5. She'll be drawing a poster (плак<u>а</u>т).	Он<u>а</u> _____ плак<u>а</u>т.
6. She'll get it drawn tomorrow.	Он<u>а</u> его з<u>а</u>втра _____.

[1] In all such examples, convey the **gist** of the English through your **choice of aspect**; certainly don't translate word for word!!

17.5 A summary of verb forms, for both aspects and all three tenses

We can now present a **table of all forms** for the aspectual pair "to read," in all three tenses. Keep in mind how much we've learned — there are **no other tenses** in Russian! The only verbal forms left to learn include deverbals (verbal adjectives, adverbs, and nouns), which will be covered in Book 3, and, of course, imperatives.

	imperfective	perfective
basic aspectual criteria:	1. **Ongoing** action (no mention of result). 2. **Repeated** or habitual action. 3. Emphasis on **attempt** or effort.	1. **Completed** action (emphasis on result). 2. **One-time** action. 3. Emphasis on **success** or accomplishment.

чит**а**ть АЙ / прочит**а**ть АЙ

	imperfective	perfective
present tense:	я чит**а**ю ты чит**а**ешь он, он**а**, он**о** чит**а**ет мы чит**а**ем вы чит**а**ете он**и** чит**а**ют	
past tense:	он чит**а**л он**а** чит**а**ла он**о** чит**а**ло он**и** чит**а**ли	он прочит**а**л он**а** прочит**а**ла он**о** прочит**а**ло он**и** прочит**а**ли
future tense:	я **буду** чит**а**ть ты **будешь** чит**а**ть он, он**а**, он**о** **будет** чит**а**ть мы **будем** чит**а**ть вы **будете** чит**а**ть он**и** **будут** чит**а**ть	я прочит**а**ю ты прочит**а**ешь он, он**а**, он**о** прочит**а**ет мы прочит**а**ем вы прочит**а**ете он**и** прочит**а**ют

17.d *Now, given the following aspectual pairs, capture the **gist** of the English in Russian through your choice of **aspect** and tense.*

писа**ть** A[shift] / **напис**а**ть** A[shift]:
1. I'm writing an interesting article.   Я _____ интер**е**сную стать**ю**.
2. Have you (ты, f.) written the letter?   Ты уж**е** _____ письм**о**?
3. I'll get it written tomorrow.   Я ег**о** з**а**втра _____ .

гото**вить** И / **пригот**о**вить** И:
4. My mom used to cook dinner (**у**жин).   Р**а**ньше м**а**ма _____ **у**жин.
5. But now (теп**е**рь) I cook it.   Но теп**е**рь я ег**о** _____ .
6. I'll be cooking every evening (в**е**чер)!   Я к**а**ждый в**е**чер _____ _____ !

плати**ть** И[shift] / **заплат**и**ть** И[shift]:
7. Who paid[1] for lunch (об**е**д) yesterday?   Кто _____ за об**е**д вчер**а**?
8. My father. He always pays.   Мой от**е**ц. Он всегд**а** _____ .
9. He always paid, and he always will.   Он всегд**а** _____ , и всегд**а** _____ _____ .

говори**ть** И[end] / **сказ**а**ть** A[shift]:
10. She used to talk a lot (мн**о**го).   Р**а**ньше он**а** мн**о**го _____ .
11. What did she say?   Что он**а** _____ ?
12. What will she say?   Что он**а** _____ ?

---

[1] As a rule of thumb, the **simple past** (paid) and the **simple future** (will pay) are typically best translated using **perfective** verbs, as long as they refer to a specific, one-time action.

day 18:   aspectual pairs and aspectual "red flags"

aspectual pairs; basic pairs with prefixed perfectives; pairs with
derived imperfectives; other special aspectual forms;
imperfective and perfective "red flags"

Все на праздник ударного труда! Everyone (come) to a holiday of shock work!
Они будут работать и в субботу (They'll work even on Saturday)! This was called a "**субботник.**"

18.1 Aspectual pairs

Now that we know the basics of how aspect works, we'll be learning Russian verbs as **aspectual pairs** from
now on. Learning these pairs and developing an ability to switch between aspects is a difficult process, and will
take a lot of time and practice, and plenty of **drilling**.[1] But it is absolutely essential for mastering Russian.

So, how are aspectual pairs formed? Unfortunately, there's no simple answer, so at first we'll simply have to
memorize the pairs. Having memorized the pair, we will simply "know," when confronted with a given form,
whether it is imperfective or perfective. That being said, we can point out a few general patterns now — and,
in the process, provide an overview of most of the aspectual pairs in this chapter's vocabulary. We'll also get a
sense of special nuances of meaning in certain aspectual forms.

Think of this as an introduction. Eventually, you'll develop a more intuitive sense of how pairs are formed, and
memorizing the pairs will become **much** easier. We will revisit this topic in detail later (e.g. Days 108 & 173).

18.2 Basic pairs with prefixed perfectives

Many basic imperfective verbs form their perfective by simply **adding a prefix**. As we'll see later, prefixes often
lend the verb a new meaning, but in the examples below, they simply **mark the perfective**. The most common
prefix used to mark the perfective is **по-**, but others can be used as well. Can you "drill" these conjugations?

читать АЙ / **про**читать АЙ	писать А^{shift} / **на**писать А^{shift}	делать АЙ / **с**делать АЙ
to read	to write	to do, make
просить И^{shift} / **по**просить И^{shift}	готовить И / **при**готовить И	рисовать ОВА / **на**рисовать ОВА
to ask, request	to prepare, cook	to draw
смотреть Е^{shift} / **по**смотреть Е^{shift}	слушать АЙ / **по**слушать АЙ	учить И^{shift} / **на**учить И^{shift}
to watch, look	to listen	to teach

[1] Bear in mind that these are the only two "principle parts" of Russian verbs you'll have to learn, and that there are no additional subjunctive forms to learn, etc. All things considered, Russian verbs may be less difficult than they are made out to be!

NOTE: the **prefixed** form of a basic verb will conjugate exactly like the **unprefixed** verb. This is a universally valid rule in Russian, and a very useful one. For example, **написать** will conjugate exactly like **писать**. The same will be true of other prefixed forms we'll see later, like **описать** (to describe) or **подписать** (to sign, to "write under").

18.3 Pairs with derived imperfectives

Based on what we've just learned, we know that the **prefixed** verb **спрос<u>и</u>ть** will conjugate exactly like the basic verb **прос<u>и</u>ть** (to ask, to request). But the aspectual pair for the latter is **прос<u>и</u>ть / попрос<u>и</u>ть**. So in this case, the prefix **с-** is not simply **marking the perfective** — it is creating an **entirely new** prefixed perfective verb with a new meaning, namely "to ask" (as in, to ask a question). To have a full **aspectual pair** for this new verb, we need to create an **imperfective** form to go with it.

In such instances, Russian generates a **derived imperfective**:

спр<u>а</u>шивать АЙ / спрос<u>и</u>ть И

Fortunately, these derived imperfectives are created according to very **reliable rules**, which we'll explore in detail on Days 108 & 173. At the intermediate level, familiarity with these patterns will make memorizing aspectual pairs much easier. Best of all: all derived imperfectives are **АЙ verbs**, making them very easy to conjugate, despite their length!

Below are the pairs from this chapter with derived imperfectives:

Как раб<u>о</u>тал, так и зараб<u>о</u>тал!
As you worked, so have you earned!

The verb **зараб<u>о</u>тать** means "to earn" and is conjugated just like **раб<u>о</u>тать**. Russian derives an imperfective form to go with it, giving us: **зараб<u>а</u>тывать АЙ / зараб<u>о</u>тать АЙ** (to earn).

Here, the form **раб<u>о</u>тал** (imperfective) can be thought of as emphasizing the **process** of work, **repetition** (every day!) and **effort**. The perfective **зараб<u>о</u>тать** emphasizes the **result** — the size of your paycheck!

спр<u>а</u>шивать АЙ / **спрос<u>и</u>ть** И[shift]
to ask, inquire

показ<u>ы</u>вать АЙ / **показ<u>а</u>ть** А[shift]
to show

получ<u>а</u>ть АЙ / **получ<u>и</u>ть** И[shift]
to receive

рассказ<u>ы</u>вать АЙ / **рассказ<u>а</u>ть** А
to tell (a story)

отвеч<u>а</u>ть АЙ / **отв<u>е</u>тить** И
to answer

успев<u>а</u>ть АЙ / **усп<u>е</u>ть** ЕЙ
to manage (in time)

отдых<u>а</u>ть АЙ / **отдохн<u>у</u>ть** НУ[end]
to relax

поним<u>а</u>ть АЙ / **пон<u>я</u>ть** Й/М[end]
to understand

реш<u>а</u>ть АЙ / **реш<u>и</u>ть** И[end]
to solve (a problem)

18.4 Perfectives with по- meaning "for a bit"

Many verbs describing **activities** have perfectives that don't necessarily imply **completion**, but, rather, describe doing the activity "for a bit" (and then stopping). Such perfectives begin with **по-**.

In fact, we can create "**alternate**" perfectives in **по-** for almost any activity verb, apart from its usual perfective forms. For example, the usual perfective of **читать**, **прочитать**, implies "to read **completely**," while the alternate perfective **почитать** implies "to read **for a bit**."

Below are the pairs from this chapter's vocabulary whose usual perfective form actually falls under this somewhat special category:

раб<u>о</u>тать АЙ / **по**раб<u>о</u>тать АЙ
to work / work for a bit

думать АЙ / **по**думать АЙ
to think / think for a bit

танцев<u>а</u>ть ОВА / **по**танцев<u>а</u>ть ОВА
to dance / dance for a bit

Ещё пораб<u>о</u>таем!
We'll work a bit more still!

[1] Note that we can't use this verb to say "**спрос<u>и</u>ть вопрос**" in the sense of "to ask a question." The verb **спрос<u>и</u>ть** can only be used with a person as its object, e.g. "**спрос<u>и</u>ть профессора**" (to ask the professor). As we'll learn later, the verb for "to ask a question" is **задав<u>а</u>ть** АВАЙ / **зад<u>а</u>ть вопрос** кому (the "кому" indicates that this expression is used with the dative case).

18.5 Perfectives of inception

We tend to say that perfective verbs describe **completion**, as opposed to an **ongoing process**. But some perfective verbs — often due to the kind of action they describe — emphasize **inception**.

Consider the verb **плакать**. Its perfective, **заплакать**, doesn't mean "to **finish** crying," but "to **begin** crying" — or, as we might say, to "burst out crying." Or, take **любить** (to love): we might say that the perfective **полюбить** means to **begin** loving, or "to **come** to love."

The alternate **по-** perfective **поплакать** would mean "to cry for a bit."

плакать А / **за**плакать А
to cry / to begin crying

видеть Е / **у**видеть Е
to see / catch sight of

любить И[shift] / **по**любить И[shift]
to love / to come to love

ненавидеть Е / **воз**ненавидеть Е
to hate / to come to hate

18.6 Suppletive pairs

A few aspectual pairs in modern Russian clearly consist of verbs that have completely **different roots**, but that have historically come together (in a process known as **suppletion**) to constitute a "single" verb, a single aspectual pair. For now, we have only one example.

говорить И[end] / **сказать** А[shift]
to say

18.7 Imperfective only

Some verbs only have an **imperfective** form. In many cases, this is due to the fact that the action they descirbe is, by definition, an **ongoing process** or activity — as with, for example, **сидеть** (to *be in* a sitting position[1]). Do note that for some, we could create an alternate perfective such as **посидеть** (to sit for a bit).

сидеть Е[end]	**иметь** ЕЙ	**знать** АЙ	**значить** И	**жить** В[end]
to be sitting[1]	to have	to know	to mean	to live

Finally, a few imperfective Russian verbs give special emphasize to **frequency**, describing actions that happen from time to time, or with regularity. Here is the most common example, and the only one we'll use this year:

бывать АЙ[2]
to be (or happen) repeatedly, regularly, often

— **Я опять потерял ключ!**
— I've forgotten my key again!

— **Это бывает!**
— That happens!

---

*Let's review the aspect and tense material from yesterday's lesson. Convey the **gist** of the English by choosing the right aspect!* **18.a**

показывать АЙ / **показать** А[shift]:	1. They were showing a photograph.	Они _____ фотографию.
	2. I showed the new puppy yesterday.	Вчера я _____ нового щенка.
	3. She'll show our new cat tomorrow.	Завтра она _____ нашу новую кошку.
получать АЙ / **получить** И[shift]:	4. I receive a letter from him every day.	Я каждый день _____ от него письмо.
	5. Before, we'd receive a letter every week.	Раньше мы _____ письмо каждую неделю.
	6. I'll receive yet another letter tomorrow.	Завтра я _____ ещё одно письмо.
работать АЙ / **поработать** АЙ:	7. My neighbor (m.) was working.	Мой сосед _____.
	8. He'll work a bit more tomorrow.	Завтра он ещё _____.
	9. I'll be working a lot (много) tomorrow.	Я _____ много _____ завтра.
видеть Е / **увидеть** Е:	10. I'll see you tomorrow.	Я тебя _____ завтра.
	11. I'll see you every day.	Я _____ тебя _____ каждый день.
	12. I (f.) caught sight of an old friend (f.).	Я _____ старую подругу.

---

[1] Note that the only meaning of this form is "to be in a sitting position." It does not mean "to sit down" (see Days 151-153).
[2] The perfective **побывать** (in the special sense of, "to spend a bit of time somewhere") does exist, but we won't be using it for now. Verbs like **бывать** that emphasize frequency are referred to as **iteratives** (from the Latin verb iterāre, "to repeat").

18.8 Imperfective "red flags"

On the level of **Basic Aspect**, the criteria by which we choose aspect are quite straightforward. Often, a "**red flag**" will make very clear which aspect we need, such that using the other would be a glaring mistake.

For example, if we use an adverb or phrase that expresses **frequency** or repetition (or "**always**"), we must use an imperfective verb. Only the imperfective can describe repeated actions, so our choice here is crystal-clear. This is also generally the case with "**never**" (никогда).[1]

This includes many frequency phrases in the accusative, as in "every day" (with **каждый**: each, every). We can call this use of the accusative the **accusative of time**. Note that only **неделя** (f.) actually changes!

всегда always			
часто often	утро	**каждое утро** every morning	
иногда sometimes	день	**каждый день** every day	
редко rarely	вечер	**каждый вечер** every evening	
	неделя	**каждую неделю** every week	
никогда не never	месяц	**каждый месяц** every month	
	год	**каждый год** every year	

Каждый день — ударный!
Every day is a shock-work day!

Here are some examples, in all three tenses. We could substitute any of the phrases above for **каждый день**:

Я **читаю** газету каждый день.
I read the paper every day.[2]

Я **читала** газету каждый день.
I would read the paper every day.

Я **буду читать** газету каждый день.
I will read the paper every day.

---

*Tell **how often** you do these things, being sure to use the **imperfective** verb. Try asking about the **past** or **future** as well!*

Как часто ты...

читаешь роман (novel)?

читаешь русскую поэзию (poetry)?

читаешь газету?

читаешь статью?

смотришь телевизор?

слушаешь музыку?

видишь маму и папу?

видишь брата или сестру?

просто (simply) **сидишь** и **отдыхаешь**?

пишешь сочинение (a paper / composition)?

получаешь письмо?

отвечаешь на письмо?

знаешь ответ на вопрос профессора?

забываешь (forget) русское слово (word)?

говоришь по-русски?

готовишь обед или ужин?

Furthermore, only **imperfective** verbs can describe an **extended process**, as opposed to completion and result. So, any adverbs or adverbial phrases that express **duration** (an extended period of time) serve as **imperfective red flags**: we must use an imperfective verb in these situations!

We can also use the **accusative of time** with the time increments below in the sense of "for" an hour, a day, etc. Again, only the feminine forms — **неделя** and **минута** — change in the accusative.

To the far right, note the forms following the **numbers**. The numbers 2, 3, and 4 are followed by nouns in the **genitive singular**; numbers 5 and above are followed by the **genitive plural**. We will learn and discuss numbers in detail in Book 2 (Days 58, 59, 66). For now, simply memorize these examples.

долго for a long time	**минуту** for a minute	(один) **час** for 1 hour
недолго not for long	**день** for a day	**два часа** for 2 hours
	неделю for a week	**три часа** for 3 hours
ещё still (ongoing action)	**месяц** for a month	**четыре часа** for 4 hours
уже не not anymore	**год** for a year	**пять часов** for 5 hours

целый + acc. all, entire — e.g. **целый день** (a whole day), **целую неделю** (all week), etc.

[1] Never (**никогда**) does sometimes pair with perfective verbs in the future, for example: **Я тебя никогда не забуду** (I'll never forget you).
[2] Remember, if we're using the **present** tense, we absolutely must use the **imperfective** — regardless of whether we have repetition!

Again, here are a few examples. Note that many such phrases of duration are best translated using "spent."

Он три час**а** гот**о**вил об**е**д!	Я нед**е**лю чит**а**л **э**ту кн**и**гу.	Мы б**у**дем раб**о**тать д**о**лго з**а**втра.
He spent 3 hours making dinner!	I spent a week reading this book.	We'll work for a long time tomorrow.

---

*Now, tell **for how long** you do (did, will do) the following things. Since we're speaking of an extended activity, we need the **imperfective**.*

Как д**о**лго ты...	раб**о**тал(а) вчер**а**?	б**у**дешь раб**о**тать сег**о**дня в**е**чером (this evening)?
	смотр**е**л(а) телев**и**зор вчер**а**?	б**у**дешь смотр**е**ть телев**и**зор сег**о**дня в**е**чером?
	чит**а**л(а) **э**тот уч**е**бник вчер**а**?	б**у**дешь чит**а**ть **э**тот уч**е**бник сег**о**дня в**е**чером?

18.9 Perfective "red flags"

Perfective red flags are somewhat less reliable than imperfective flags. Still, they're well worth considering.

Whereas imperfective flags imply frequency or duration, **perfective** flags all imply completion (like уж**е**: already), instantaneous action (like ср**а**зу: right away, or вдруг: suddenly), or something done "once more, again" (in past or future). When we use any of these adverbs, there's a **good chance** we'll need the **perfective.**

This is especially true in the past or future tenses, as in "I've already read the paper" (and finished it!). But many of the adverbs below can be used with **present**-tense verbs, and in this case — as always! — we absolutely must use the **imperfective**! Less frequently, they can also refer to an **ongoing** or **repeating** process, in which case we'd also need the **imperfective**, for example: "I was already reading the paper."

<u>IMPORTANT</u>: many guidelines we give regarding use of the **perfective** are trumped whenever we begin talking about **repetition** or **process**. In such cases — quite obviously! — the **imperfective** takes over!

ср**а**зу right away	Реб**ё**нок вдруг **запл**а**кал**, не зн**а**ю поч**е**му.[1]
вдруг suddenly	The child suddenly began to cry; I don't know why.
након**е**ц finally	
уж**е** already	Я **проч**и**т**а**ю письм**о** и ср**а**зу отв**е**чу на нег**о**.
ещ**ё** не not yet	I will read the letter and answer it right away.
оп**я**ть again	— Ты уж**е** **пригот**о**вил** об**е**д? — Нет, ещ**ё** не **пригот**о**вил**.
ещ**ё** раз again, one more time	— Have you already made dinner? — No, I haven't made it yet.

смотр**е**ть E^shift / посмотр**е**ть E фильм:	— Ты (m.) уж**е** **посмотр**е**л** фильм?	— Нет, я ещ**ё** **смотр**ю**!	**18.b**
1. смотр**е**ть E^shift / посмотр**е**ть E сери**а**л:	— Ты (f.) уж**е** _____?	— Нет, я ещ**ё** _____.	
2. чит**а**ть АЙ / проч**и**т**а**ть АЙ стать**ю**:	— Ты (m.) уж**е** _____?	— Нет, я ещ**ё** _____.	
3. отвеч**а**ть АЙ / отв**е**тить И на письм**о**:	— Вы уж**е** _____?	— Нет, мы ещ**ё** _____.	

смотр**е**ть E / посмотр**е**ть E фильм:	— Я (m.) уж**е** **посмотр**е**л** фильм.	Я его уж**е** не **смотр**ю**.	**18.c**
1. гот**о**вить И / пригот**о**вить И **у**жин:	— Я (f.) уж**е** _____.	Я его уж**е** не _____.	
2. пис**а**ть А / напис**а**ть А соч**и**н**е**ние:	— Я (m.) уж**е** _____.	Я его уж**е** не _____.	
3. сл**у**шать АЙ / посл**у**шать АЙ м**у**зыку:	— Мы уж**е** _____.	Мы её уж**е** не _____.	

---

*Add verbs to contrast what you usually do (**imperfective**!) with what you'll do once (**perfective**!) today.*   **18.d**

1. пок**а**зывать АЙ / показ**а**ть А: I usually (об**ы**чно) show a photo of my dog, but today I'll show a photo of my cat.

Я об**ы**чно _____ фотогр**а**фию соб**а**ки, но сег**о**дня я _____ фотогр**а**фию к**о**шки.

2. чит**а**ть АЙ / проч**и**т**а**ть АЙ: I usually don't read the Russian newspaper, but today I'll read one article.

Я об**ы**чно не _____ р**у**сскую газ**е**ту, но сег**о**дня я _____ одн**у** стать**ю**.

---

[1] As this example shows, Russian (like French) is much more tolerant of "comma splices" (joining two "complete" sentences with a comma) than English. This helps explain why semicolons are far less common in Russian texts than in English.

89

day 19: using multiple verbs and infinitives

aspect with multiple verbs; verbs followed by an infinitive; the irregular verb **хот<u>е</u>ть**; choosing aspect with infinitives; using the verb **мочь**

Накоп<u>и</u>л и маш<u>и</u>ну куп<u>и</u>л! I saved up and bought a car! (encouraging people to save money at the **Сберк<u>а</u>сса**, the Soviet equivalent of a savings bank). The aspectual pair for "to save" is **коп<u>и</u>ть** И / **накоп<u>и</u>ть** И.

19.1 Using aspect with multiple verbs

What if we use multiple verbs in a sentence? Quite logically, there are three possible combinations of aspect!

1. Multiple imperfective verbs:

Multiple **imperfective** verbs describe overlapping, simultaneous, extended (and possibly repeating) actions.

Мы **сид<u>е</u>ли** и **смотр<u>е</u>ли** телев<u>и</u>зор.
We were sitting and watching television.

Когд<u>а</u> мы **смотр<u>е</u>ли** телев<u>и</u>зор, реб<u>ё</u>нок **чит<u>а</u>л**.
While we were sitting and watching television, the child was reading.

2. Multiple perfective verbs:

Multiple **perfective** verbs describe a **sequence** of actions. Sequences are often expressed using the adverbs **снач<u>а</u>ла** (first...), **пот<u>о</u>м** (then...), **након<u>е</u>ц** (finally...).

Снач<u>а</u>ла я **прочит<u>а</u>ла** газ<u>е</u>ту, пот<u>о</u>м **написа<u>а</u>ла** письм<u>о</u>, и наконе<u>е</u>ц **посмотр<u>е</u>ла** люб<u>и</u>мый сери<u>а</u>л.
First I read the newspaper, then I wrote a letter, and finally I watched my favorite TV series.

The verbs in such sequences can also include perfective verbs that focus on **inception**. For example:

Он **прочит<u>а</u>л** письм<u>о</u> и **запл<u>а</u>кал.**
He read the letter and began to cry.

Когд<u>а</u> я ег<u>о</u> **ув<u>и</u>дела**, я ср<u>а</u>зу **полюб<u>и</u>ла** его.
When I caught sight of him, I fell in love with him right away.

Finally, sequences can also include perfectives with **по-** that mean "to do something for a bit." For example:

П<u>о</u>сле зан<u>я</u>тия мы **посид<u>е</u>ли** и **поговор<u>и</u>ли**.
After class we sat around for a bit and had a chat.

Снач<u>а</u>ла **поч<u>и</u>таю**, пот<u>о</u>м **напиш<u>у</u>** письм<u>о</u>.
First I'll read for a bit, then I'll write a letter.

3. A combination of imperfective and perfective verbs:

In such a combination, an **imperfective** verb describes a kind of **extended** "backdrop" action that is interrupted by a **sudden** action. Imperfective verbs "set the scene," and perfective verbs "advance the narrative."

Когда я **сидела** и **читала** книгу, он меня **спросил**, какую книгу я читаю.
While I was sitting and reading a book, he asked me what kind of book I was reading (note the tense of читаю).

Complete the translation of these English sentences by choosing the proper aspect of the Russian verbs. **19.a**

1. While his girlfriend **was dancing**, he **was** just **sitting** and **listening** to music.
Когда его подруга (танцевала / потанцевала), он просто (сидел / посидел) и (слушал / послушал) музыку.

2. We **were dancing** when she suddenly **asked** what my name was.
Мы (танцевали / потанцевали), когда она вдруг (спрашивала / спросила), как меня зовут.

3. When he **had read** his brother's letter, he suddenly began to **cry**.
Когда он (читал / прочитал) письмо брата, он вдруг (плакал / заплакал).

4. They **sat** around and **watched** television all evening.
Они целый вечер (сидели / посидели) и (смотрели / посмотрели) телевизор.

5. I'd **been reading** this Russian novel for an entire semester, and finally I **finished** reading it.
Я целый семестр (читал / прочитал) этот русский роман, и наконец его (читал / прочитал)!

6. What **were** you all **doing** today while I **was working**?
Что вы (делали / сделали) сегодня, когда я (работала / поработала)?

7. What did you all **get done** today while I **was working**?
Что вы (делали / сделали) сегодня, когда я (работала / поработала)?

---

*Tell what you did yesterday evening in two ways: 1) in the form of overlapping activities (imperfective), and 2) as sequence (perfective). Choose from the actions below or supply your own. In a sequence, use **сначала** (first) and **потом** (then, next).*

читать АЙ / **прочитать** АЙ текст, книгу, статью
слушать АЙ / **послушать** АЙ музыку

смотреть E[shift] / **посмотреть** E телевизор, сериал, фильм
писать A[shift] / **написать** A сочинение, письмо, статью, эсэмэску[1]

19.2 Verbs followed by the infinitive

A number of useful verbs can be followed by an infinitive. This generally mirrors uses of the infinitive in English:

хотеть / захотеть to want / to get the urge	Я хочу **читать** Достоевского. I want **to read** Dostoevsky.	Он захотел **танцевать**. He got the urge **to dance**.
мочь Г / **смочь** Г to be able ("can")	Я не могу **читать** Толстого по-русски. I'm not able **to read** Tolstoy in Russian.	Я не смогу всё **прочитать**. I won't be able **to read** everything.
уметь ЕЙ / **суметь** ЕЙ to know how, manage	Мы не умеем **танцевать**. We don't know how **to dance**.	Он не сумел **ответить** на вопрос. He couldn't **answer** the question.
любить И[shift] to love (to...)	Мы любим **слушать** музыку. We love **to listen** to music.	Он любил **читать** газету каждое утро. He loved **to read** the paper every morning.
успевать АЙ / **успеть** ЕЙ to manage (in time)	Я не успеваю всё **делать**. I'm not managing **to do** everything.	Я не успел всё **сделать**. I didn't manage **to do** everything.
забывать АЙ / **забыть** to forget	Он часто забывал **купить** хлеб. He would often forget **to buy** bread.	Она забыла **прочитать** статью. She forgot **to read** the article.
просить И[shift] / **попросить** И to ask, request	Она меня попросила **купить** хлеб. She asked me **to buy** bread.	Я хотел **попросить** тебя **прочитать** статью. I wanted **to ask** you **to read** the article.
решать АЙ[2] / **решить** И[end] to decide to, resolve to...	Она решила **купить** новую машину. She decided **to buy** a new car.	Она решила **не покупать** новую машину. She decided **not to buy** a new car (at all).

---

[1] эсэмэска is a colloquial term for an SMS-message, which could also be called an эсэмэс-сообщение or текст-сообщение.
[2] This verb also means "to solve" (a problem, etc.). In the sense of "to decide," it would rarely be seen in the imperfective.

19.3 The irregular verb хот<u>е</u>ть

Why isn't the verb **хот<u>е</u>ть / захот<u>е</u>ть** tagged with a verb type? Because it doesn't belong to a type; it's **irregular**! Notice how it has two different **stems**, mixes **ё** and **и** endings, and even has an irregular **stress** pattern.

From now on, any verb you encounter in the vocabulary **without a tag** can be considered irregular. There aren't very many in the entire language. For now, we have one more: **заб<u>ы</u>ть**, which conjugates using the future-tense forms of быть: я **заб<u>у</u>ду**, ты **заб<u>у</u>дешь**, он **заб<u>у</u>дет**, etc.

Let's review these and other conjugations of verbs that can be followed by an infinitive:

Если хоч<u>е</u>шь быть здоров — закаляйся!

Если х<u>о</u>чешь быть здор<u>о</u>в — закал<u>я</u>йся!
If you want to be healthy, take a bracing cold shower!

(The verb **закал<u>я</u>ться** АЙ suggests tempering steel).

хот<u>е</u>ть / захот<u>е</u>ть		забыв<u>а</u>ть АЙ / заб<u>ы</u>ть		успев<u>а</u>ть АЙ / усп<u>е</u>ть ЕЙ		ум<u>е</u>ть ЕЙ / сум<u>е</u>ть ЕЙ		люб<u>и</u>ть И
to want / to get the urge		to forget		to manage (in time)		to know how / manage		to love (to...)
хоч<u>у</u>	захоч<u>у</u>	забыв<u>а</u>ю	заб<u>у</u>ду	успев<u>а</u>ю	усп<u>е</u>ю	ум<u>е</u>ю	сум<u>е</u>ю	любл<u>ю</u>
х<u>о</u>чешь	зах<u>о</u>чешь	забыв<u>а</u>ешь	заб<u>у</u>дешь	успев<u>а</u>ешь	усп<u>е</u>ешь	ум<u>е</u>ешь	сум<u>е</u>ешь	л<u>ю</u>бишь
х<u>о</u>чет	зах<u>о</u>чет	забыв<u>а</u>ет	заб<u>у</u>дет	успев<u>а</u>ет	усп<u>е</u>ет	ум<u>е</u>ет	сум<u>е</u>ет	л<u>ю</u>бит
хот<u>и</u>м	захот<u>и</u>м	забыв<u>а</u>ем	заб<u>у</u>дем	успев<u>а</u>ем	усп<u>е</u>ем	ум<u>е</u>ем	сум<u>е</u>ем	л<u>ю</u>бим
хот<u>и</u>те	захот<u>и</u>те	забыв<u>а</u>ете	заб<u>у</u>дете	успев<u>а</u>ете	усп<u>е</u>ете	ум<u>е</u>ете	сум<u>е</u>ете	л<u>ю</u>бите
хот<u>я</u>т	захот<u>я</u>т	забыв<u>а</u>ют	заб<u>у</u>дут	успев<u>а</u>ют	усп<u>е</u>ют	ум<u>е</u>ют	сум<u>е</u>ют	л<u>ю</u>бят
		забыв<u>а</u>й!	заб<u>у</u>дь!	успев<u>а</u>й!	усп<u>е</u>й!	ум<u>е</u>й!	сум<u>е</u>й!	люб<u>и</u>!
— — —	— — —							

19.b *use conjugated (present-tense) forms of* **хот<u>е</u>ть**: | *use conjugated (future-tense!) forms of* **заб<u>ы</u>ть**:

1. Я _____ смотр<u>е</u>ть фильм, а он<u>а</u> не _____ .

4. Ты не _____ сделать задание?

2. Он<u>и</u> _____ потанцев<u>а</u>ть, а мы не _____ .

5. Я д<u>у</u>маю, что он<u>и</u> _____ куп<u>и</u>ть газ<u>е</u>ту.

3. Вы не _____ посид<u>е</u>ть и поговор<u>и</u>ть?

6. Мы вас не _____ . И вы нас не _____ !

19.4 Choosing aspect with infinitives

Of course, Russian infinitives are not conjugated and have no tense, but they do have **aspect**! Here too, we usually have a choice to make — between the two infinitives in a given aspectual pair.

When choosing an infinitive, keep the same old **aspectual criteria** in mind. If we are emphasizing the activity itself, or describing repeated actions or effort, then we need the **imperfective**. If we're describing specific one-time actions or emphasizing completion or success, then we need the **perfective**. For example:

imperf.: Я хоч<u>у</u> **чит<u>а</u>ть** <u>э</u>тот ром<u>а</u>н.
I want **to read** this novel.[1]

perf.: Я хоч<u>у</u> **прочит<u>а</u>ть** <u>э</u>тот ром<u>а</u>н.
I want **to read** this novel (and finish it).

Since **ум<u>е</u>ть** and **люб<u>и</u>ть** speak to general abilities and loves, they're usually followed by the **imperfective**:

imperf.: Я ум<u>е</u>ю **танцев<u>а</u>ть**.
I know how **to dance**.

imperf.: Я любл<u>ю</u> **смотр<u>е</u>ть** кин<u>о</u>.
I love **to watch** movies.

But the perfective **сум<u>е</u>ть** speaks to a specific accomplishment, and so is followed by the **perfective**:

perf.: Студ<u>е</u>нт не сум<u>е</u>л **отв<u>е</u>тить** на вопр<u>о</u>с.
The student wasn't able **to answer** the question.

perf.: Я не сум<u>е</u>ю **нарисов<u>а</u>ть** её портр<u>е</u>т.
I won't be able **to draw** her portrait.

Similarly, **забыв<u>а</u>ть** АЙ / **заб<u>ы</u>ть** and **успев<u>а</u>ть** АЙ / **усп<u>е</u>ть** ЕЙ focus on success or completion — as in, "I meant to do something, but I forgot to actually get it done." They are typically followed by **perfective** verbs:

perf.: Я заб<u>ы</u>ла **сд<u>е</u>лать** зад<u>а</u>ние.
I forgot **to do** the assignment.

perf.: Я не усп<u>е</u>л **прочит<u>а</u>ть** газ<u>е</u>ту вчер<u>а</u>.
I didn't manage **to read** the paper yesterday.

92

[1] Note that the imperfective doesn't necessarily imply non-completion — it simply doesn't mention it. If one wanted to talk specifically about completion or non-completion, one would use the perfective. The imperfective simply names the activity (here, the general intention).

There's one final point to make. If we **negate** the verb "to want" (**не хочу**...), we will need an **imperfective** infinitive. Why? Because if we say that we don't want to do something, we probably mean that we don't want to do it "**at all**," or "**in the first place**" — much less to go ahead and do it **completely**. For this reason, the imperfective usually makes sense here. We will delve into this issue in much greater detail on Day 109.

imperf.: Я не хочу **смотреть** этот фильм.
I don't want to watch this film.

imperf.: Они не хотят **отвечать** на этот вопрос.
They don't want to answer this question.

---

*Circle the most appropriate **infinitive**, based on aspectual distinctions. Can you explain your choice? Watch for "red flags!"*   **19.c**

1. Я люблю (**читать / прочитать**) русскую поэзию.

2. Она не успела (**делать / сделать**) задание.

3. Наш друг не умел (**танцевать / потанцевать**).

4. Мы никогда не успеваем всё (**читать / прочитать**).

5. Как (how) ты успеешь всё это (**делать / сделать**)?!

6. Мы не сумели (**отвечать / ответить**) на вопрос.

7. Он любил каждый день (**смотреть / посмотреть**) кино.

8. Я вдруг захотел (**спрашивать / спросить**), как её зовут.

9. Ты умеешь (**говорить / сказать**) по-русски?

10. Наш отец забыл (**готовить / приготовить**) ужин.

11. Твоя мама любит (**слушать / послушать**) музыку?

12. Я не хочу (**смотреть / посмотреть**) этот сериал.

19.5 Using "to be able" (мочь)

Let's review a final verb that can be followed by an infinitive. We introduced this verb on Day 14. Although it does belong to a regular type (**Г** verbs), it is so unusual that, for now, we could almost regard it as an irregular verb.

In the present tense, remember that this verb mutates (**г → ж**) in the "inner forms" (**можешь**, etc.), but retains the **г** in the "outer forms" (**могу**, **могут**).

This verb is also unusual in the **past tense**. In fact, it's our **first example** of a verb whose past tense cannot be formed directly from the **infinitive**. Instead, its past tense forms are based on its actual root, **мог**. The past-tense marker (**л**) has vanished from the masculine form (**могл → мог**), but it has remained in front of an ending (**могла**, **могло**, **могли**).

мочь ⌐shift / смочь ⌐shift	
to be able ("can")	
могу	смогу
можешь	сможешь
может	сможет
можем	сможем
можете	сможете
могут	смогут
— — —	— — —
мог	смог
могла	смогла
могло	смогло
могли	смогли

Мой друг **хочет** танцевать, но не **может** сегодня.
My friend **wants** to dance, but **can't** today.

➡ Мой друг **хотел** танцевать вчера, но не **мог**.   **19.d**
My friend **wanted** to dance yesterday, but **couldn't**.

1. Мы _____ слушать музыку, но не _____ .

2. Она _____ работать, но не _____ .

3. Я _____ купить книгу, но не _____ .

4. Я _____ решить задачу, но не _____ .

5. Они _____ посмотреть фильм, но не _____ .

6. Ты _____ всё сделать, но не _____ .

7. Вы _____ понять вопрос, но не _____ .

Мы _____ слушать музыку, но не _____ .

Она _____ работать, но не _____ .

Я (m.) _____ купить книгу, но не _____ .

Я (f.) _____ решить задачу, но не _____ .

Они _____ посмотреть фильм, но не _____ .

Ты (m.) _____ всё сделать, но не _____ .

Вы _____ понять вопрос, но не _____ .

Tell about a few things you want to do, but can't yet (ещё). As in: *Я хочу свободно говорить по-русски, но ещё не могу.*

свободно говорить по-русски	**купить новую машину**	**написать симфонию**
хорошо танцевать	**читать "Войну и мир"**	**написать великий роман**
хорошо готовить	**получить Нобелевскую премию**	**отдохнуть**

day 20: subordinate clauses

question words in direct questions; forming indirect questions;
why and because; the relative pronoun **кот<u>о</u>рый**

Я друг<u>о</u>й так<u>о</u>й стран<u>ы</u> не зн<u>а</u>ю, где так в<u>о</u>льно д<u>ы</u>шит челов<u>е</u>к! I know of no other such country where a human being breathes so freely!

20.1 Question words in direct questions

Let's review all of the question words we've seen so far:

что? what?		**как**? how?	
кто? who? (nom.)		**почем<u>у</u>**? why?	
ког<u>о</u>? whom? (acc./gen.)		**как<u>о</u>й**, -<u>ая</u>, -<u>ое</u>? what kind of?	
где? where?		**чей**, чья, чьё? whose?	
когд<u>а</u>? when?		**кот<u>о</u>рый**, -<u>ая</u>, -ое? which?	

Note that the final three words are **adjectival**!

Что ты д<u>е</u>лаешь?[1]	**What** are you doing?
Кто <u>э</u>то? **Кто** <u>э</u>то был?	**Who** is that? **Who** was that?
Ког<u>о</u> вы в<u>и</u>дите?	**Whom** do you see?
От **ког<u>о</u>** письм<u>о</u>?	From **whom** is the letter?
Где вы жив<u>ё</u>те?	**Where** do you live?
Когд<u>а</u> и **как** ты отдых<u>а</u>ешь?	**When** and **how** do you relax?
Почем<u>у</u> ты не л<u>ю</u>бишь чит<u>а</u>ть?	**Why** don't you like to read?
Как<u>а</u>я у теб<u>я</u> к<u>о</u>мната?	**What kind of** room do you have?
Чь<u>ё</u> <u>э</u>то окн<u>о</u>?	**Whose** window is that?

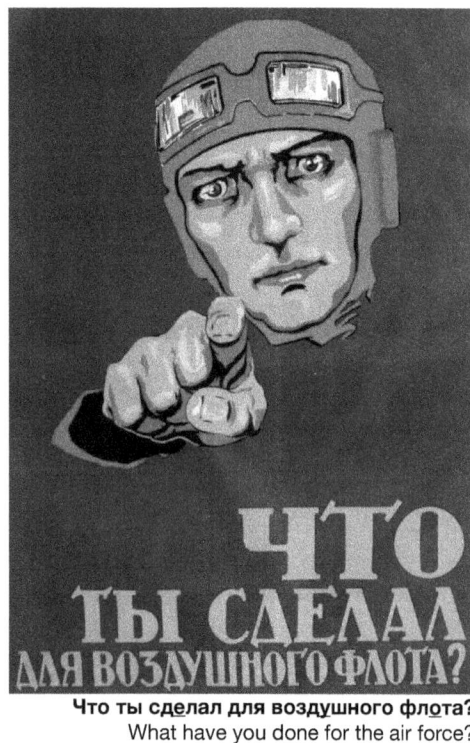

Что ты сделал для воздушного флота?
What have you done for the air force?

94   [1] As is often the case, we could omit the **pronoun** (Что делаешь?), but this can sound brusque, especially in questions!

The question word **Что?** is always **neuter singular** for purposes of agreement, while **Кто?** is always **masculine singular**, even if we are asking about a female person, or multiple people. Remember, **это** is not the subject!

Что это было?	**Кто это был?**
What was that?	Who was that?
Кто читает Толстого?	**Кто написал статью?**
Who's reading Tolstoy?	Who wrote the article?

Note that three question words are adjectival: **какой, который,** *and* **чей.** *Make sure they always agree with the noun they modify.*

1. Как_____ это книга? Интересная или скучная?

2. Как_____ книгу ты купил? Дорогую или дешёвую?

3. Чь___ это фотография? Павла или Татьяны?

4. На чь____ фотографию вы смотрите?

Complete the blanks with forms of **кто** *and* **что.**   **20.a**
Remember, the accusative and genitive of **кто** *is* **кого.**

5. К_____ это? На к_____ вы смотрите?

6. Ч_____ ты получила? Письмо? От к_____?

7. Для к_____ этот подарок (gift)? К_____ его получит?

8. К_____ спросил тебя, как тебя зовут?

Try asking and answering these (and other) questions with a partner.

1. **Что** ты делал(а) вчера вечером?

2. **Кого** ты видел(а) вчера?

3. От **кого** ты получил(а) эсэмэску вчера?

4. **Какая** у тебя комната? А **какой** у тебя компьютер?

5. **Как** ты отдыхаешь? Ты смотришь телевизор или слушаешь музыку?

6. **Когда** ты работаешь? Утром (in the morning) или вечером (evening)?

— **А когда досуг-то будет?** — **А когда нас не будет.** — When will there be time off from work (**досуг**: leisure time)? — When we no longer exist.

20.2 Forming indirect questions

Today we'll provide an overview of simple **subordinate clauses**. The first kind, an **indirect question** or **reported question**, is very simple. It begins with a **question word**, and is identical to the corresponding **direct question**. We can simply rewrite the direct question as a subordinate clause, being sure to set it off with a **comma**.

"Что он делает?"
"What is he doing?" *(direct question)*

Я хочу знать, **что он делает.**
I want to know what he is doing.

Я спросил, **что он делает.**
I asked what he **was** doing.

In the **black box**, notice the difference in **tense**: when the verb in the main clause is past-tense, Russian preserves the tense of the original direct question, while English **changes it to past**. The English "**was** doing" is past, while the Russian "**делает**" is present.[1]

Translate these sentences involving simple indirect questions — but pay very close attention to **tense** *in the Russian!*   **20.b**

1. He's asking **where** I live now.
Он спрашивает, _____.

2. He asked me **where** I live now.
Он меня спросил, _____.

3. He asked me **where** I used to live. *(use past!)*
Он меня спросил, _____.

4. I don't know **what** they're doing today.
Я не знаю, _____.

5. They don't understand **why** we don't watch television.
Они не понимают, _____.

6. We wanted to know **what kind of** room he has.
Мы хотели знать, _____.

What do your parents and friends always want to know about you? Pick from among the indirect questions below, or make up your own!

1. Мой папа / моя мама всегда спрашивает, ...

2. Мой друг / подруга хочет знать, ...

3. Мой сосед / соседка не понимает, ...

...**что** я делаю.   ...**почему** я никогда не работаю.

...**где** я был(а).   ...**какое** у меня расписание.

...**когда** я буду дома.   ...**как** я живу.

---

[1] The verb would only be in the past if the direct question would have also been in the past, as in: **Я спросил, что он делал.** (I asked what he'd been doing.) This would correspond to the direct question: **Что ты делал?** (What have you been doing? What were you doing?).

20.3 "That" clauses beginning with что

The question word **что** can also begin subordinate clauses, just like the English "that." In this usage, **что** is **unstressed**; when beginning a reported question clause, it is **stressed**. In Russian, don't forget the comma!

Я знаю, **что** он читает.   I know **what** he is reading.   (indirect question clause: **что** is **stressed**)

Я знаю, **что** он читает.   I know **that** he is reading.[1]   (subordinate clause with "that": **что** is **unstressed**)

Of course, "that" clauses with **unstressed что** are extremely common in Russian. Here are a few examples:

Я понимаю, **что** говорить по-русски очень трудно.
I understand **that** it's very hard to speak Russian.

Я думаю, **что** Толстой — хороший писатель.
I think **that** Tolstoy is a good writer.

Я слышала, **что** у нас будет новый профессор.
I heard **that** we're going to have a new professor.

Я вижу, **что** ты сейчас работаешь.
I see **that** you're working right now.

---

*Tell what you think using an unstressed-**что** clause. Begin your answer with, "**Да, я думаю, что...**" or "**Нет, я не думаю, что...**"*

1. Ты думаешь, что русский — интересный язык?

2. Ты думаешь, что русская грамматика трудная?

3. Ты думаешь, что трудно говорить по-русски?

4. Как ты думаешь[2] — Толстой хороший писатель или нет?

5. Как ты думаешь — читать по-русски трудно, или нет?

6. Как ты думаешь — жить в России (in Russia) интересно или нет?

20.4 Clauses with why (почему) and because (потому что)

To answer the question **Почему**? (Why?), we can use "**Потому что...**" (Because...). Just as in English, **потому что** can also begin a subordinate clause explaining why — but don't forget to set off the clause with a **comma**!

Почему ты не смотришь телевизор?
Why don't you watch television?

Я не смотрю телевизор, **потому что** я всегда работаю!
I don't watch television, **because** I'm always working!

20.c   *Translate into Russian. Remember to use the genitive with **non-existence** statements, and set off all clauses with a **comma**.*

1. I don't have a car, because I don't want to buy a car.

   У меня нет машины, _____.

2. I don't have an umbrella, because I (f.) forgot it.

   У меня нет зонта, _____.

3. I can't read this article because I don't have a Russian dictionary (русский словарь).

   Я не могу читать эту статью, _____.

4. I couldn't do my assignment (задание) because I didn't have a pen (ручка).

   Я не смог сделать задание, _____.

5. I m.) haven't watched the TV series (сериал) yet, because I don't have a TV (телевизор).

   Я ещё не смотрел сериал, _____.

Answer a few "Why?" questions using some basic "because" answers. Try making up your own questions and answers too.

1. **Почему** ты не танцуешь?   Я не танцую, ...**потому что** я не хочу!

2. **Почему** ты не пишешь роман?   Я не пишу роман, ...**потому что** я не могу!

3. **Почему** ты не сидишь дома и не отдыхаешь?   Я не сижу дома и не отдыхаю, ...**потому что** я не умею!

4. **Почему** ты не работаешь всё время?   Я не работаю всё время, ...**потому что** не люблю!

[1] Everyday English often drops the "that" (as in, "I know he is reading"). Russians may sometimes drop **что**, but students are advised not to!
[2] "**Как ты думаешь**" (literally, "**How** do you think?") is a very common phrase, equivalent to the English "What do you think?"

20.5 The relative pronoun котОрый

The adjective **котОрый** can act as a relative pronoun; that is, it introduces a "**who**" or "**which**" clause (although in everyday English we usually say "**that**" instead of "which"). As an **adjective**, it agrees with the **noun** in the main clause to which it refers in terms of **gender**, but its **case** depends on the role it plays **within its clause**. It has nothing to do with the **case** of the noun it refers to!

So, if **котОрый** is the **subject** of its clause, it is in the **nominative**:

ПисАтель, [**котОрый** написАл Эту статьЮ], рУсский.
The writer **who** wrote this article is Russian.

Я знАю студЕнтку, [**котОрая** ужЕ читАет ТолстОго].
I know a student **who** is already reading Tolstoy.

....

But if it is the **direct object** of its clause, it is in the **accusative**:

ПисАтель, [**котОрого** мы сейчАс читАем], рУсский.
The writer (**whom**) we are reading right now is Russian.

КнИга, [**котОрую** мы читАем], Очень интерЕсная.
The book (**that**) we are reading is very interesting.

....

If it expresses **possession**, we need the **genitive**:

Автор, [кнИгу **котОрого** мы читАем], рУсский.[1]
The author whose book ("the book of whom") we are reading, is Russian.

....

Its case can also be determined by a preposition:

Мой друг, [от **котОрого** я вчерА получИл письмО], студЕнт.
My friend, from whom I received a letter yesterday, is a student.

Note that in English we often omit the relative **pronoun** (the "who" or "that"), as in: "The dictionary he bought is good" — as well as the **comma**. In Russian, both are **required**!

НЕТ ТАКОЙ СИЛЫ, КОТОРАЯ ПОРАБОТИЛА БЫ НАС.
КузьмА МИнин.

Нет такОй сИлы, котОрая поработИла бы нас.
No power (**сИла**) exists that might enslave us.

Since the relative pronoun refers to **сИла**, it has a feminine ending: **котОрая**. Since **котОрая** is the subject of its clause ("that might enslave"), it is in the nominative.

The verb here is in a **hypothetical** form — such forms refer not to facts, but to possibilities, desires, fears, etc. — things that **could** happen.

In Russian, these forms are extremely simple: we add the particle **бы** and use the **past tense form** of the verb (note, however that hypothetical expressions don't actually have tense). We'll study these forms in depth on Days 119 & 120.

The verb pair for "to enslave" is **порабощАть АЙ / поработИть И**, meaning to make someone a **раб**, a slave, to subject them to **рАбство**, slavery.

Supply the correct form of **котОрый**. *Be sure to choose the right case, based on the role of* **котОрый** *within its clause.*   **20.d**

1. **СтудЕнт**, _____ здесь живЁт, рУсский. **КнИга**, _____ он читАет, рУсская.

2. РУсский **студЕнт**, _____ мы знАем, хорошО говорИт по-англИйски.

3. **СестрА**, от _____ я вчерА получИл письмО, пИшет, что у неЁ всЁ хорошО.

4. **ВопрОс**, на _____ онА отвЕтила, был Очень трУдный.

5. Все говорЯт, что **мУзыка**, _____ мы слУшаем, Очень стрАнная, а я дУмаю, что онА интерЕсная.

6. РУсский **писАтель**, ромАн _____ мы сейчАс читАем, довОльно извЕстный.

7. **ЧеловЕк**, машИну _____ я купИл, сказАл, что онА стАрая и грЯзная, но хорОшая.

8. Я дУмаю, что тот **фильм**, _____ мы вчерА посмотрЕли, Очень хорОший. А как ты дУмаешь?

9. У той рУсской **семьИ**, у _____ я жил, былА **собАка**, _____ менЯ срАзу полюбИла.

10. Я забЫл ту **кнИгу**, _____ ты хотЕл читАть. А у тебЯ есть **зонт**, _____ я у тебЯ забЫл?

---

[1] Somewhat more formally, we can use **чей** (whose) in this fashion: "Автор, **чью** кнИгу мы читАем, рУсский."

case endings

	special modifiers					adjectives	masculine nouns			
							hard	soft		special soft
nom.	э́тот	оди́н	чей	мой	наш	но́вый	стол	слова́рь	музе́й	кафете́рий
gen.	э́того	одного́	чьего́	моего́	на́шего	но́вого	стола́	словаря́	музе́я	кафете́рия
acc.	э́тот	оди́н	чей	мой	наш	но́вый	стол	слова́рь	музе́й	кафете́рий
animate:	э́того	одного́	чьего́	моего́	на́шего	но́вого	студе́нта	писа́теля		ге́ния

	special modifiers					adjectives	feminine nouns			
							hard	soft		special soft
nom.	э́та	одна́	чья	моя́	на́ша	но́вая	газе́та	неде́ля		фами́лия
gen.	э́той	одно́й	чьей	мое́й	на́шей	но́вой	газе́ты	неде́ли		фами́лии
acc.	э́ту	одну́	чью	мою́	на́шу	но́вую	газе́ту	неде́лю		фами́лию

	special modifiers					adjectives	neuter nouns			
							hard	soft		special soft
nom.	э́то	одно́	чьё	моё	на́ше	но́вое	окно́	мо́ре	бельё	зада́ние
gen.	э́того	одного́	чьего́	моего́	на́шего	но́вого	окна́	мо́ря	белья́	зада́ния
acc.	э́то	одно́	чьё	моё	на́ше	но́вое	окно́	мо́ре	бельё	зада́ние

Only the accusative forms in the black boxes above differ from the nominative!

nouns

hard nouns

masculine		feminine
враг, -а́ enemy	студе́нт, -а student (male)	студе́нтка, -и student (female)
а́втор, -а author	аспира́нт, -а grad student (male)	аспира́нтка, -и grad student (fem.)
поэ́т, -а poet	друг, -а friend (male)	подру́га, -и friend (female)
сосе́д, -а neighbor/roommate	профе́ссор, -а professor	сестра́, -ы́ sister
ма́льчик, -а boy	оте́ц, отца́ father	ма́ма, -ы mom
сын, -а son	челове́к, -а human being	же́нщина, -ы woman
кот, -а́ cat (male)	брат, -а brother	де́вушка, -и young woman
котён(о)к, -нка kitten	ро́дственник, -а relative	де́вочка, -и girl
щен(о)к, -нка puppy	това́рищ, -а comrade; buddy	соба́ка, -и dog
президе́нт, -а president	нача́льник, -а boss	ко́шка, -и cat (female)
знако́мый, -ого male acquaintance	masculine (with feminine endings!)	знако́мая, -ой fem. acquaintance
внук, -а grandson	па́па, -ы dad	ба́бушка, -и grandmother
муж, -а husband	де́душка, -и grandfather	вну́чка, -и granddaughter
жени́х, -а́ groom, fiancé	колле́га, -и colleague	до́чка, -и daughter[1]
ребён(о)к, -нка child	зану́да, -ы boring person, killjoy	жена́, -ы́ wife
игро́к, -а́ a player / gambler	мужчи́на, -ы man	неве́ста, -ы bride, fiancée
солда́т, -а soldier	пья́ница, -ы drunkard	сосе́дка, -и neighbor/roommate

soft nouns

masculine		feminine
пар(е)нь, па́рня guy	писа́тель, -я writer	тётя, -и aunt
геро́й, геро́я hero	masculine (with feminine endings!)	
прия́тель, -я pal, buddy	дя́дя, -и uncle	

[1] This is actually a diminutive form of **дочь**, an irregular noun that we will learn on Day 57.

adverbs, question words, conjunctions

adverbs (imperfective flags)	
всегда	always
часто	often
иногда	sometimes
редко	rarely
никогда не	never
долго	for a long time
недолго	for a short time
ещё	still
уже не	not anymore
(один) год	for a year
два года	for two years
пять лет	for five years
(один) час	for an hour
два часа	for two hours
пять часов	for five hours
два раза	two times
пять раз	five times
целый день	for an entire day
целую неделю	for an entire week

adverbs (perfective flags)	
ещё не	not yet
опять	again
ещё раз	one more time
уже	already
вдруг	suddenly
сразу	right away
сначала...	at first...
потом...	then / next...
наконец...	finally...
(один) раз	once

question words	
что?	what? (nom./acc.)
чего?	what? (gen.)
кто?	who? (nom.)
кого?	whom? (gen./acc.)
ли	whether
где?	where?
когда?	when?
почему?	why?
чей / чья / чьё?	whose?
как?	how?
так	thus, in such a way
какой / ая / ое?	what kind of?
такой / ая / ое	such, of such a kind

conjunctions	
потому что	because
который	who / which
когда	when
что	that

prepositions followed by the genitive

у	"at"	**У мамы** есть новая машина. Mom has a new car. (possession)
	at someone's place, visiting someone	Я была **у мамы** вчера. I was at mom's place yesterday.
без	without	Комната у меня **без окна!** My room is without a window!
от	from	У меня письмо **от друга.** I have a letter from (my) friend.
для	for	Это подарок **для отца.** This is a present for (my) father.
против	against	Ты **против коммунизма?** Are you against Communism?
во время	during	**Во время блокады** Ленинграда не было еды. During the siege of Leningrad there was no food.

prepositions followed by the accusative

за	for, in favor of (opposite of **против**)	Мы **за** свободу слова. Кто же против свободы слова? We are **for** freedom of speech. Who's against freedom of speech?	
	for, in exchange for	Отец платит **за** нас. Он платит **за** наш обед. (Our) father is paying **for** us. He is paying **for** our lunch.	
на	at, onto	Почему ты всегда смотришь **на** меня? Why are you always looking **at** me?	*but:* Мы смотрим этот фильм. We're watching this film.
	in response to	Кто знает ответ **на** этот вопрос? Who knows the answer to this question?	Кто может ответить **на** вопрос? Who can answer the question?

Verbs: aspectual pairs with prefixed perfective forms

читать АЙ / прочитать АЙ	
to read	
читаю	прочитаю
читаешь	прочитаешь
читает	прочитает
читаем	прочитаем
читаете	прочитаете
читают	прочитают
читай!	прочитай!

делать АЙ / сделать АЙ	
to do, make	
делаю	сделаю
делаешь	сделаешь
делает	сделает
делаем	сделаем
делаете	сделаете
делают	сделают
делай!	сделай!

работать АЙ / поработать АЙ	
to work / to work for a bit	
работаю	поработаю
работаешь	поработаешь
работает	поработает
работаем	поработаем
работаете	поработаете
работают	поработают
работай!	поработай!

думать АЙ / подумать АЙ	
to think / to think for a bit	
думаю	подумаю
думаешь	подумаешь
думает	подумает
думаем	подумаем
думаете	подумаете
думают	подумают
думай!	подумай!

слушать АЙ / послушать АЙ что / кого	
to listen (to)	
слушаю	послушаю
слушаешь	послушаешь
слушает	послушает
слушаем	послушаем
слушаете	послушаете
слушают	послушают
слушай!	послушай!

плакать А / заплакать А	
to cry / to start crying	
плачу	заплачу
плачешь	заплачешь
плачет	заплачет
плачем	заплачем
плачете	заплачете
плачут	заплачут
плачь!	заплачь!

писать А^{shift} / написать А^{shift}	
to write	
пишу	напишу
пишешь	напишешь
пишет	напишет
пишем	напишем
пишете	напишете
пишут	напишут
пиши!	напиши!

рисовать ОВА / нарисовать ОВА	
to draw	
рисую	нарисую
рисуешь	нарисуешь
рисует	нарисует
рисуем	нарисуем
рисуете	нарисуете
рисуют	нарисуют
рисуй!	нарисуй!

танцевать ОВА / потанцевать ОВА	
to dance / to dance for a bit	
танцую	потанцую
танцуешь	потанцуешь
танцует	потанцует
танцуем	потанцуем
танцуете	потанцуете
танцуют	потанцуют
танцуй!	потанцуй!

готовить И / приготовить И	
to prepare, cook	
готовлю	приготовлю
готовишь	приготовишь
готовит	приготовит
готовим	приготовим
готовите	приготовите
готовят	приготовят
готовь!	приготовь!

любить И^{shift} / полюбить И^{shift}	
to love / to come to love	
люблю	полюблю
любишь	полюбишь
любит	полюбит
любим	полюбим
любите	полюбите
любят	полюбят
люби!	полюби!

платить И^{shift} / заплатить И^{shift} за что	
to pay (for)	
плачу	заплачу
платишь	заплатишь
платит	заплатит
платим	заплатим
платите	заплатите
платят	заплатят
плати!	заплати!

просить И^{shift} / попросить И кого + inf.	
to request, ask (someone to...)	
прошу	попрошу
просишь	попросишь
просит	попросит
просим	попросим
просите	попросите
просят	попросят
проси!	попроси!

видеть Е / увидеть Е	
to see / catch sight of	
вижу	увижу
видишь	увидишь
видит	увидит
видим	увидим
видите	увидите
видят	увидят
—	—

смотреть Е^{shift} / посмотреть Е на что[1]	
to watch, look (at)	
смотрю	посмотрю
смотришь	посмотришь
смотрит	посмотрит
смотрим	посмотрим
смотрите	посмотрите
смотрят	посмотрят
смотри!	посмотри!

[1] For example, смотреть **на** фотографию, but: смотреть фильм: to watch a movie

ненавидеть Е / возненавидеть Е to hate / to come to hate		уметь ЕЙ / суметь ЕЙ + inf. to know how to / to manage to		помнить И / вспомнить И to remember	
ненави**жу**	возненави**жу**	ум**ею**	сум**ею**	п**о**мню	всп**о**мню
ненави**дишь**	возненави**дишь**	ум**е**ешь	сум**е**ешь	п**о**мнишь	всп**о**мнишь
ненави**дит**	возненави**дит**	ум**е**ет	сум**е**ет	п**о**мнит	всп**о**мнит
ненави**дим**	возненави**дим**	ум**е**ем	сум**е**ем	п**о**мним	всп**о**мним
ненави**дите**	возненави**дите**	ум**е**ете	сум**е**ете	п**о**мните	всп**о**мните
ненави**дят**	возненави**дят**	ум**е**ют	сум**е**ют	п**о**мнят	всп**о**мнят
—	—	ум**ей**!	сум**ей**!	п**о**мни!	всп**о**мни!

учить И^shift / научить И кого + inf. to teach		мёрзнуть (НУ) / замёрзнуть (НУ)[1] to freeze	
уч**у**	науч**у**	м**ё**рзну	зам**ё**рзну
уч**ишь**	науч**ишь**	м**ё**рзнешь	зам**ё**рзнешь
уч**ит**	науч**ит**	м**ё**рзнет	зам**ё**рзнет
уч**им**	науч**им**	м**ё**рзнем	зам**ё**рзнем
уч**ите**	науч**ите**	м**ё**рзнете	зам**ё**рзнете
уч**ат**	науч**ат**	м**ё**рзнут	зам**ё**рзнут
уч**и**!	науч**и**!	м**ё**рзни!	зам**ё**рзни!

Verbs: aspectual pairs with derived imperfectives

получать АЙ / получить И^shift to receive		понимать АЙ / понять Й/М^end to understand		отдыхать АЙ / отдохнуть НУ^end to relax / relax a bit	
получ**аю**	получ**у**	поним**аю**	пойм**у**	отдых**аю**	отдохн**у**
получ**аешь**	получ**ишь**	поним**аешь**	пойм**ёшь**	отдых**аешь**	отдохн**ёшь**
получ**ает**	получ**ит**	поним**ает**	пойм**ёт**	отдых**ает**	отдохн**ёт**
получ**аем**	получ**им**	поним**аем**	пойм**ём**	отдых**аем**	отдохн**ём**
получ**аете**	получ**ите**	поним**аете**	пойм**ёте**	отдых**аете**	отдохн**ёте**
получ**ают**	получ**ат**	поним**ают**	пойм**ут**	отдых**ают**	отдохн**ут**
получ**ай**!	получ**и**!	поним**ай**!	пойм**и**!	отдых**ай**!	отдохн**и**!

успевать АЙ / успеть ЕЙ + inf. to manage (in time) to...		забывать АЙ / забыть что / + inf. to forget, to forget to...		спрашивать АЙ / спросить И^shift кого to ask, inquire[2]	
успев**аю**	усп**ею**	забыв**аю**	забуд**у**	спрашив**аю**	спрош**у**
успев**аешь**	усп**еешь**	забыв**аешь**	забуд**ешь**	спрашив**аешь**	спр**о**сишь
успев**ает**	усп**еет**	забыв**ает**	забуд**ет**	спрашив**ает**	спр**о**сит
успев**аем**	усп**еем**	забыв**аем**	забуд**ем**	спрашив**аем**	спр**о**сим
успев**аете**	усп**еете**	забыв**аете**	забуд**ете**	спрашив**аете**	спр**о**сите
успев**ают**	усп**еют**	забыв**ают**	забуд**ут**	спрашив**ают**	спр**о**сят
успев**ай**!	усп**ей**!	забыв**ай**!	забудь!	спрашив**ай**!	спрос**и**!

показывать АЙ / показать А^shift to show		рассказывать АЙ / рассказать А^shift to tell, narrate		решать АЙ / решить И^end to solve; to decide to (usually perf.)	
показыв**аю**	покаж**у**	рассказыв**аю**	расскаж**у**	реш**аю**	реш**у**
показыв**аешь**	покаж**ешь**	рассказыв**аешь**	расскаж**ешь**	реш**аешь**	реш**ишь**
показыв**ает**	покаж**ет**	рассказыв**ает**	расскаж**ет**	реш**ает**	реш**ит**
показыв**аем**	покаж**ем**	рассказыв**аем**	расскаж**ем**	реш**аем**	реш**им**
показыв**аете**	покаж**ете**	рассказыв**аете**	расскаж**ете**	реш**аете**	реш**ите**
показыв**ают**	покаж**ут**	рассказыв**ают**	расскаж**ут**	реш**ают**	реш**ат**
показыв**ай**!	покаж**и**!	рассказыв**ай**!	расскаж**и**!	реш**ай**!	реш**и**!

[1] The flag (НУ) marks a "disappearing НУ" verb in which the НУ vanishes in past-tense forms, e.g. он мёрз, она мёрзла, они мёрзли.
2 Remember: we can't use this verb to say "to ask a question," only "to ask a person..." (that is, спрос**и**ть вопрос is incorrect).

A suppletive pair (two historically unrelated verbs that came to form a single pair)

говорить И^{end} / сказать А^{shift}	
to speak, say	
говор**ю**	скаж**у**
говор**ишь**	скаж**ешь**
говор**ит**	скаж**ет**
говор**им**	скаж**ем**
говор**ите**	скаж**ете**
говор**ят**	скаж**ут**
говор**и**!	скаж**и**!

Verbs used in the imperfective only

сидеть Е^{end}	иметь ЕЙ	знать АЙ	значить И	жить В^{end ↑}
to be sitting	to have	to know	to mean	to live
сиж**у**	им**е**ю	зн**а**ю	знач**у**	жив**у**
сид**ишь**	им**е**ешь	зн**а**ешь	знач**ишь**	жив**ёшь**
сид**ит**	им**е**ет	зн**а**ет	знач**ит**	жив**ёт**
сид**им**	им**е**ем	зн**а**ем	знач**им**	жив**ём**
сид**ите**	им**е**ете	зн**а**ете	знач**ите**	жив**ёте**
сид**ят**	им**е**ют	зн**а**ют	знач**ат**	жив**ут**
сид**и**!	им**е**й!	зна**й**!	—	жив**и**!

Two irregular verbs

мочь Г^{shift} / смочь Г^{shift} + inf.		хотеть / захотеть + inf.	
to be able to… ("can")		to want / to get the urge to…	
мог**у**	смог**у**	хоч**у**	захоч**у**
мо**ж**ешь	смо**ж**ешь	хо**ч**ешь	захо**ч**ешь
мо**ж**ет	смо**ж**ет	хо**ч**ет	захо**ч**ет
мо**ж**ем	смо**ж**ем	хот**им**	захот**им**
мо**ж**ете	смо**ж**ете	хот**ите**	захот**ите**
мог**ут**	смо**г**ут	хот**ят**	захот**ят**
– – –	– – –	– – –	– – –
мог	смог		
мог**ла**	смог**ла**		
мог**ло**	смог**ло**		
мог**ли**	смог**ли**		

¹ There is a perfective form **прожить** В (to live "through" a specific period of time), and of course **пожить** В (to live for a bit).

Бннэт Государственного

СТО РУ

ВАНКОВСКИЕ БИЛЕТЫ ОБЕСПЕЧИВАЮТСЯ ЗОЛ
МЕТАЛЛАМИ И ПРОЧИМИ АКТИВАМИ ГОСУ

100

33 069539

СТО КАРБОВАНЦІВ · СТО РУБЛЕ
ЙУЗ МАНАТ · ЯЬЛ ВАБОØΟ · ΖΠΙΒΘΗΓ ΠΟΗΡ
ЮЗ СŸМ · САД ОŸМ · ЖУЗ СОМ · ЖУЗ СОМ
О СУТЗ РУБЛЕ · SIMTAS RUBLIŲ · SIMTS RUBLI

1947

III

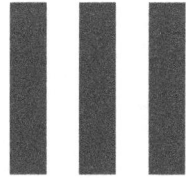

food & feelings

the dative case and reflexive verbs

In this chapter, we'll add the dative case, and learn a variety of constructions in which the dative is used, including some new subjectless constructions of "feeling." We'll also look in detail at the various meanings of reflexive verbs, and learn how to give commands using imperative forms of verbs.

day 21: the dative case and indirect objects

indirect objects; dative case endings; pronouns in the dative;
subjectless constructions with the dative; predicate and
modal adverbs used with infinitives

Хлеб — родине! Bread — to (for) the homeland! (**родина** is in the dative case here).

21.1 Indirect objects

Direct objects are directly affected by the action of a verb; in Russian, direct objects typically apper in the **accusative** case. **Indirect objects** are indirectly affected by the action of a verb, and in Russian appear in the **dative** case. In English, we typically express indirect objects using **prepositions**, or simply through **word order**:

I fed the **fish** to my **cat**. = I fed my **cat** the **fish**.   (in both, **fish** is the **direct** object, **cat** the **indirect** object)

In these examples, the **subject** is "I," and the verb "fed" is a **transitive verb** (that is, it can take a direct object). The direct object (here, "fish") is **directly** affected by the action of the verb. The indirect object (here, "cat") is **indirectly** affected by that action. We might say that the cat "benefits" from the action you directed at the fish.

Most of our examples with indirect objects will involve "benefit" — for example, **giving** things to people. But, looking forward, we should remember that indirect objects can be "indirectly affected" both **positively and negatively**. In some cases, we will have cause to speak of a "dative of disadvantage" or "dative of deprivation!"

106

Since English lacks case endings, it depends heavily on prepositions and word order to convey the roles words play in sentences. Note how drastically a simple change in word order can affect the meaning in English!

I fed my **cat** the **fish**. ➡ I fed the **fish** my **cat**. = I fed my cat to the fish!

With its rich assortment of case endings, Russian word order is much more flexible, allowing for subtleties of emphasis. By the same token, Russian word order tells us very little about the roles of words in a sentence (as we noted on Day 16). In short, the **endings tell us everything**!

21.2 Dative case endings

The dative answers the questions **Кому**? and **Чему**? Here are the endings:

	adjective:	noun:
MASCULINE & NEUTER:	**-ому** (-ему)	**-у** (-ю)
FEMININE:	**-ой** (-ей)	**-е**

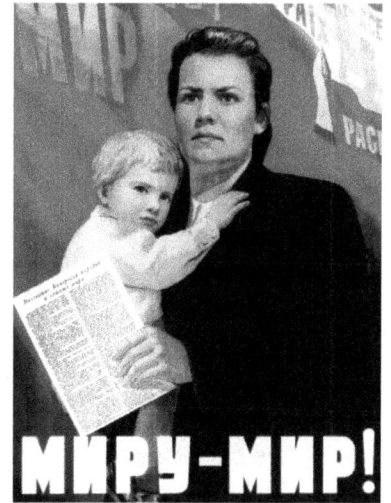

Миру — мир! "To the world, peace!" or "For the world, peace!"

(a play on two meanings of the word **мир**: world and peace).

Study the more detailed table below; pay attention to the special modifiers!

	special modifiers					adjectives	masculine nouns hard	soft		special soft
nom.	э́т**от**	оди́н	чей	мой	наш	но́в**ый**	стол	слова́рь	музе́й	кафете́рий
dat.	э́т**ому**	одн**ому́**	чь**ему́**	мо**ему́**	на́ш**ему**	но́в**ому**	стол**у́**	словар**ю́**	музе́**ю**	кафете́ри**ю**

	special modifiers					adjectives	feminine nouns hard	soft	special soft
nom.	э́т**а**	одн**а́**	чь**я**	мо**я́**	на́ш**а**	но́в**ая**	газе́та	неде́ля	фами́ли**я**
dat.	э́т**ой**	одн**о́й**	чь**ей**	мо**е́й**	на́ш**ей**	но́в**ой**	газе́т**е**	неде́л**е**	фами́ли**и**[1]

	special modifiers					adjectives	neuter nouns hard	soft		special soft
nom.	э́т**о**	одн**о́**	чь**ё**	мо**ё**	на́ш**е**	но́в**ое**	окн**о́**	мо́ре	бель**ё**	зада́ни**е**
dat.	э́т**ому**	одн**ому́**	чь**ему́**	мо**ему́**	на́ш**ему**	но́в**ому**	окн**у́**	мо́р**ю**	бель**ю́**	зада́ни**ю**

First, create a direct object using the accusative, then an indirect object using the dative.   **21.a**

икра́: | Кому́ ты даёшь **икру́**? | ➡ | ма́ма: | Даю́ икру́ **ма́ме.**
To whom are you giving the caviar? | | | *I'm giving the caviar to mom.*

1. **хлеб**: Кому́ ты даёшь _____? **брат**: Даю́ _____ _____.

2. **чай**: Кому́ ты даёшь _____? **сестра́**: Даю́ _____ _____.

3. **ры́ба**: Кому́ ты даёшь _____? **сосе́д**: Даю́ _____ _____.

4. **борщ**: Кому́ ты даёшь _____? **сосе́дка**: Даю́ _____ _____.

5. **вино́**: Кому́ ты даёшь _____? **от(е́)ц**: Даю́ _____ _____.

6. **сыр**: Кому́ ты даёшь _____? **друг**: Даю́ _____ _____.

7. **квас**: Кому́ ты даёшь _____? **подру́га**: Даю́ _____ _____.

8. **смета́на**: Кому́ ты даёшь _____? **знако́мый**: Даю́ _____ _____.

9. **пи́во**: Кому́ ты даёшь _____? **дя́дя**: Даю́ _____ _____.

10. **мя́со**: Кому́ ты даёшь _____? **тётя**: Даю́ _____ _____.

Сове́тской нау́ке — сла́ва! Сла́ва сове́тскому челове́ку — пе́рвому космона́вту!
Glory to Soviet science! Glory to Soviet man — the first cosmonaut!

[1] This is the first case in which a **special soft** ending differs from that of a normal soft noun — hence the need to keep them separate!

21.b новый студент: Что ты даёшь **новому студенту**?

1. этот писатель: Что ты даёшь _____ _____?
2. эта женщина: Что ты даёшь _____ _____?
3. новая подруга: Что ты даёшь _____ _____?
4. старый друг: Что ты даёшь _____ _____?
5. новый сосед: Что ты даёшь _____ _____?
6. твой отец: Что ты даёшь _____ _____?
7. ваша мама: Что вы даёте _____ _____?
8. наш дядя: Что мы даём _____ _____?
9. его друг: Что ты даёшь _____ _____?
10. бабушка: Что ты даёшь _____ _____?
11. дедушка: Что ты даёшь _____ _____?

Ни к селу ни к городу. Neither toward the village (**село**) nor the city (**город**); i.e. neither here nor there — said of something pointless or irrelevant.

21.3 Pronouns in the dative

We can also add the dative forms to our table of pronouns.

As always, the third-person forms beginning with a vowel will **add н** whenever used following a **preposition**.

pronouns						
singular				**plural**		
nom.	gen./acc.	dative		nom.	gen./acc.	dative
я	меня	мне		мы	нас	нам
ты	тебя	тебе		вы	вас	вам
он	его	ему	→ к нему	они	их	им	→ к ним
она	её	ей	→ к ней			
оно	его	ему	→ к нему			

21.c **Я** дал русский **словарь** новому **студенту**.
I gave the Russian dictionary to the new student.
➡ **Я** дал(а) **его ему**.
I gave it to him.
Потом **он** вернул **его мне**.
Later he returned it to me.

1. **Ты** дал новую **ручку** твоей **соседке**.
_____ дал(а) _____ _____. Потом _____ вернула _____ _____.

2. **Мы** дали **ложку и вилку** нашей **маме**.
_____ дали _____ _____. Потом _____ вернула _____ _____.

3. **Профессор** дал **студентке бумагу**.
_____ дал _____ _____. Потом _____ вернула _____ _____.

4. **Моя подруга** дала нашему **соседу нож**.
_____ дала _____ _____. Потом _____ вернул _____ _____.

21.4 Forming adverbs from adjectives

Adverbs can answer the question **Как?** (How?) Unlike adjectives, adverbs **never change their endings**. We've seen a few adverbs of time already, like **часто** or **сегодня**.

Many adverbs are formed from adjectives; just replace the adjectival ending with **-о**. One important exception are adjectives ending in **-ский**; to form their adverb, just shorten the ending to **-ски**. The examples below also adds **по-**.[1]

хороший →	**хорошо**	well
плохой →	**плохо**	badly, poorly
свободный →	**свободно**	freely, fluently
интересный →	**интересно**	interestingly
русский →	**по-русски**	in Russian[2]
английский →	**по-английски**	in English[2]

Строить быстро, дёшево, хорошо!
Build quickly, inexpensively, and well!

As the saying goes, **Работе время, а досугу час.**
"There's time for work, and (just) an hour for leisure."

Such adverbs are most commonly used to modify verbs, as in the following examples:

Мы уже говорим **по-русски**.
We're already speaking in Russian.

Я говорю **плохо**, а он говорит **хорошо**.
I speak poorly, while he speaks well.

Она **интересно** рассказывает.
She "tells (stories) interestingly."

---

*Use the adverbs we've just learned (**хорошо, плохо, свободно**) to answer the questions. Try using other adverbs to qualify them, such as: **очень** (very), **не очень** (not very), and **довольно** (quite, rather).*

1. Как хорошо ты говоришь по-русски?

2. Как хорошо ты будешь говорить через год (in a year)? Как ты думаешь?

---

[1] The **по-** is characteristic of language and nationality adverbs in **-ски** such as **по-русски**. We'll learn many more on Day 71.
[2] More literally, these mean something like "in the Russian way" or "in the English way." To speak Russian is to "speak in the Russian way."

21.5 Subjectless constructions[1] with the dative

We can use such adverbs in another way as well — as **predicate adverbs**. As we'll see in 24.3, predicate **adjectives** follow a linking verb like "is." We use predicate adjectives in some very simple English expressions, such as "That's good," or "Things are good." Note that both of these English constructions have **subjects**.

Russian, however, uses **adverbs** in many constructions of this type — constructions that describe "how things feel," or "how things are going," or even the current "vibe" or mood. As in, "Things are going **well**." Or, very simply: "**Well**." A Russian adverb of this kind can constitute an entire sentence! Furthermore, such constructions have no subject; they are **subjectless**, since they include no word in the **nominative** case. As we learned on Day 12, the verbs in subjectless constructions are always **neuter singular** (since they have no subject to agree with!).

So, what if we want to pin down these general feelings to a person who feels them? We tell "**for whom**" things are going "well," using the **dative** case. Still, there is no grammatical subject! Compare, in all three tenses — noting, as always, that the English approximation does not convey the actual grammar of the Russian **idiom**:

Хорошо.	Things are good.	**Мне** хорошо.	I feel good / Things are going well for me.
Было **хорошо.**	Things were good.	**Мне** было хорошо.	I felt good / Things were going well for me.
Будет **хорошо.**	Things will be good.	**Мне** будет хорошо.	I will feel good / Things will go well for me.

Here are some common **adjectives** (many of which we have seen) and their corresponding **adverbs**, all of which are often combined with the **dative** to express feelings:

хороший	good	мне **хорошо**	I feel good
плохой	bad	мне **плохо**	I feel bad
интересный	interesting	мне **интересно**	I'm interested
весёлый	happy	мне **весело**	I'm happy
невесёлый	unhappy	мне **невесело**	I'm unhappy
грустный	sad	мне **грустно**	I'm sad
больной	sick, painful	мне **больно**	I feel pain
стыдный	shameful	мне **стыдно**	I'm ashamed
неловкий	awkward	мне **неловко**	I feel awkward
страшный	horrible	мне **страшно**	I'm afraid
лёгкий	easy	мне **легко**	It's easy for me
трудный	difficult	мне **трудно**	It's hard for me
скучный	boring	мне **скучно**	I'm bored
холодный	cold	мне **холодно**	I'm cold

Стыдно! Shameful! **Ему стыдно!** He is ashamed! Why? "**Напился** (he got drunk), **ругался** (went around cursing), **сломал деревцо** (broke a little tree)—**стыдно смотреть людям в лицо!** (it's shameful to look people in the face)."

In the past tense, we could say: **Ему было стыдно!**

And, in the future: **Ему будет стыдно!**

мой брат:	**Моему брату** хорошо.	6. **я**:	_____ будет очень интересно в России. **21.d**
1. **твоя сестра**:	Тво_____ сестр_____ невесело.	7. **ты**:	_____ было так стыдно вчера!
2. **новый профессор**:	Нов_____ профессор_____ трудно.	8. **он**:	_____ очень неловко сейчас.
3. **наш от(е)ц**:	Наш_____ отц____ было плохо.	9. **она**:	_____ будет легко говорить по-русски.
4. **их новый сосед**:	Их нов_____ сосед____ скучно.	10. **вы**:	_____ было трудно читать Достоевского.
5. **её новая соседка**:	Её нов_____ соседк_____ грустно.	11. **они**:	_____ хорошо и весело сегодня.

наш друг:	**Нашему другу** хорошо. Our friend feels good.	**Нашему другу было** хорошо. Our friend felt good.	**Нашему другу будет** хорошо. Our friend will feel good. **21.e**
1. **наша подруга**:	_____ _____ плохо.	_____ _____ _____ плохо.	_____ _____ _____ плохо.
2. **мой сын**:	_____ _____ скучно.	_____ _____ _____ скучно.	_____ _____ _____ скучно.
3. **моя дочка**:	_____ _____ грустно.	_____ _____ _____ грустно.	_____ _____ _____ грустно.
4. **его жена**:	_____ _____ стыдно.	_____ _____ _____ стыдно.	_____ _____ _____ стыдно.
5. **её муж**:	_____ _____ весело.	_____ _____ _____ весело.	_____ _____ _____ весело.

---

[1] Recall that we've already seen one kind of **subjectless** construction (non-existence) — see 12.2 to review.

21.6 Predicate and modal adverbs used with infinitives

Many adverbial constructions with the dative case, like the ones we've just seen, can combine with **infinitives**. These include the new "**modal adverbs**" listed below, which have to do with ability, necessity, etc.

надо	it is necessary (to...)	**нельзя**	it is not allowed (to...)
можно	it is possible (to...)	**пора**	it is time (to...)
невозможно	it is impossible (to...)	**лень**[1]	(I'm) too lazy (to...)

Most of the adverbs we just learned can also be followed by infinitives:

трудно	it is difficult (to...)	**интересно**	it is interesting (to...)
легко	it is easy (to...)	**страшно**	it is scary (to...)
скучно	it is boring (to...)	**стыдно**	it is shameful (to...)
весело	it is fun (to...)	**грустно**	it is sad (to...)

All such adverbial constructions are **subjectless**! Note the neuter verbs!

Мне **надо** работать.	I have to work.
Мне **надо** было работать.	I had to work.
Мне **надо** будет работать.	I will have to work.
Мне **трудно** говорить по-русски.	It's hard for me to speak Russian.
Мне **трудно** было говорить по-русски.	It was hard for me to speak Russian.
Мне **трудно** будет говорить по-русски.	It will be hard for me to speak Russian.

Remember to choose infinitives based on **aspectual** distinctions. Are we talking about a general, repeated action, or a specific, one-time action?[2]

It's worth noting that **можно** is quite possibly the most useful single word in Russian. You can get a lot done in Russia (while being polite!) by simply gesturing and asking, "**Можно**?" Add an infinitive, and it'll be even better!

ПАРТИЯ СКАЗАЛА: НАДО, КОМСОМОЛ ОТВЕТИЛ: ЕСТЬ!

НА ПОЛЯ, НА СТРОЙКИ!

Партия сказала: надо, комсомол ответил: есть!
На поля, на стройки!

"The Party said: it must be done, and the *komsomol* answered: understood! To the fields, to the construction sites!"

Here, **есть!** is used as the standard response to an order (in the military, for example).

21.f *Circle the appropriate infinitive below, in terms of **aspect**. As always, watch out for any "red flags."*

1. Мне надо каждый день (**читать** / **прочитать**) газету.
2. Мне надо сегодня (**читать** / **прочитать**) эту статью.
3. Ему вообще можно (**смотреть** / **посмотреть**) телевизор?
4. Пора (**работать** / **поработать**)! Завтра у нас экзамен!
5. Он русский. Ему легко (**читать** / **прочитать**) по-русски.
6. Надо всегда (**говорить** / **сказать**) правду.
7. Надо сейчас (**платить** / **заплатить**) за ужин.
8. Мне лень было (**писать** / **написать**).
9. Здесь (here) нельзя (**танцевать** / **потанцевать**)!
10. Нам было трудно (**решать** / **решить**) эту задачу.

21.g *Supply an adverb. Remember that all of these adverbial constructions are **subjectless**! As always, don't forget about tense!*

1. He wants to watch TV, but he **isn't allowed**! — Он хочет смотреть телевизор, но ему _____!
2. He wanted to watch TV, but he **wasn't allowed**! — Он хотел смотреть телевизор, но ему _____ _____!
3. **May** we sit here (здесь)? — Нам _____ здесь сидеть?
4. We**'ll have to** ask them when the exam is. — Нам _____ _____ спросить их, когда у нас экзамен.
5. It **was** very **interesting** for us to watch the Russian film. — Нам _____ очень _____ смотреть русский фильм.
6. It**'s** so **difficult** for me to read this Russian book! — Мне так _____ читать эту русскую книгу!

Ask and answer the following questions involving subjectless adverbial constructions. Try adding a few of your own.

1. Что тебе **надо** сделать?
2. Что тебе **надо** купить?
3. Тебе **трудно** говорить по-русски?
4. Тебе интересно смотреть телевизор?
5. Тебе **лень** работать сегодня?
6. Тебе **надо** приготовить ужин сегодня?

---

[1] Expressions with **лень** are more colloquial than the others, but are quite common. **лень** is also a noun, meaning "laziness."
[2] In practice, **пора** is almost always followed by the **imperfective**, and **лень** always is. The remaining forms can be followed by either.

day 22: focus on non-suffixed verb types

in-depth description of non-suffixed verbs; the types
ОЙ, **Ь**, **/Н**, and **n/sA**; overview of irregular verbs

Ждём тебя на стройку, товарищ! We're waiting for you to join us at the construction site, comrade!

22.1 Non-suffixed verbs

In 14.3, we briefly introduced non-suffixed verbs, like **жить** and **понять**. We mentioned that these tricky verbs are fairly easy to spot: their infinitives are usually **monosyllabic** (one syllable only), once we ignore any prefixes.[1] The infinitives of such verbs are typically monosyllabic because the verbs are not built by adding suffixes (like **ай**, **ей**, **ова**, or **ну**) or even stem vowels (like **и**, **е** or **а**) to their root.

жить Bᵉⁿᵉ: to live	**начать** /Hᵉⁿᵉ: to begin	**ждать** n/sA: to wait
жив**у**	начн**у**	жд**у**
жив**ёшь**	начн**ёшь**	жд**ёшь**
жив**ёт**	начн**ёт**	жд**ёт**
жив**ём**	начн**ём**	жд**ём**
жив**ёте**	начн**ёте**	жд**ёте**
жив**ут**	начн**ут**	жд**ут**
жив**и**!	начн**и**!	жд**и**!

For example, **жить** is clearly monosyllabic — and so is **понять**, if we ignore the prefix **по-**. Down the road, if we see prefixed forms such as **выжить** or **прожить**, we'll know we are dealing with the same underlying verb — that is, the monosyllabic infinitive **жить**. Another example we've seen is the verb **мочь** (to be able), to which we will add the prefixed verb **помочь** ("to help," perfective) later in this chapter. It will conjugate just like **мочь.**

Non-suffixed verbs are easy in one sense: they **all** take the **ё** endings. The main difficulty with non-suffixed verbs is that some final portion of their **stem** (usually, its final consonant) is usually not present in the infinitive (compare the three examples above!). So, we have no choice but to learn the **stem** in addition to the **infinitive** for all non-suffixed verbs. Once we have the stem, however, things are usually very simple: we just add the **ё** endings directly to the stem.[2]

We will **tag** non-suffixed verbs based on their **final stem consonant** (sometimes, a pair of letters) — that is, by the piece of information we usually can't get from the infinitive. So, **жить** is a "**В** verb," (say "veh") and **мочь** is a "**Г** verb" (say "geh" — that is, we're simply naming the letter, as on page 15.

---

[1] Again, common prefixes include **по-**, **на-**, **про-**, **вы-**, **в(о)-**, **у-**, **при-**, **пере-**, **за-**, **под-**, **с(о)-**, **до-**, and **от-**.
[2] **Г** verbs like **мочь** add one additional complication: they mutate in their "inner" forms: **могу, можешь, может... могут.**

What if the **tag** contains a **forward slash** (/)? This means that the verb's root (stem) is **non-syllabic**. As we've seen, most Russian roots consist of at least two consonants and a vowel in between, such as **пис** (writing). But some roots have **no vowel**, and therefore **do not constitute a syllable**. For example, the root of **начать** /Н is **ч/н** (where the slash occupies the position normally filled by a vowel). So, the verb type /Н includes all such non-syllabic vowels whose stem ends in -**н**. Note again how this final consonant is **not present in the infinitive**!

There are quite a variety of non-suffixed types (like: **Н, Й, Д, Т, С, З, ОЙ, Ь, /Н, /Р, Й/М**, etc.) — and this variety can seem overwhelming at first glance.[1] But keep in mind how similarly they conjugate, and remember — we'll only see some of them in Book 1. The only trick here is **knowing the stem**, then adding the **ё** endings.

ОЙ verbs like **мыть** . . . . have stems ending in **ой**, and take **ё** endings

For this type, the tag provides the **final two letters** in the stem (-**ой**), both of which are absent from the infinitive form. Note the spellings that result when we add the **ё** endings to this stem: the **й** disappears (мой + у → **мою**). The past tense, as usual, is formed from the infinitive: он **мыл**, она **мыла**, они **мыли** (likewise, он **пел**, она **пела**, они **пели**).

мыть ОЙstem: to wash		петь ОЙend: to sing		закрыть ОЙstem: to close		открыть ОЙstem: to open	
мою	I wash	пою		закрою		открою	
моешь	you wash	поёшь		закроешь		откроешь	
моет	he, she, it washes	поёт		закроет		откроет	
моем	we wash	поём		закроем		откроем	
моете	you wash	поёте		закроете		откроете	
моют	they wash	поют		закроют		откроют	
мой!	wash!	пой!		закрой!		открой!	
мыл	he washed	пел		закрыл		открыл	
мыла	she washed	пела		закрыла		открыла	
мыло	it washed	пело		закрыло		открыло	
мыли	they washed	пели		закрыли		открыли	

Below are the full aspectual pairs that include these **ОЙ** verbs. The first two verbs form **prefixed perfectives** that conjugate just like the non-prefixed forms. Meanwhile, the second two are already prefixed perfectives — so, they **derive imperfectives** (see 18.3). As always, these derived imperfectives are **АЙ** verbs — very easy to conjugate!

мыть ОЙstem / помыть ОЙ	петь ОЙend / спеть ОЙ	закрывать АЙ / закрыть ОЙstem	открывать АЙ / открыть ОЙstem
to wash	to sing	to close	to open

22.a 1. She'll wash the car. Она _____ машину.

2. He washed the dishes. Он _____ посуду.

3. Won't you wash them? Не _____ посуду?

4. I already washed them.[2] Я её[2] уже _____.

5. She sings very well. Она очень хорошо _____.

6. We'll sing him a song. Мы _____ ему песню.

7. He sang the child a song. Он _____ ребёнку песню.

8. She loves to sing. Она любит _____.

9. They were washing dishes. Они _____ посуду.

10. I won't sing at all. Не буду _____ вообще.

22.b 1. Who opened the window? I'm cold! Кто _____ окно? Мне холодно!

2. They're always opening the window. Они всегда _____ окно.

3. I'll close it. I'll always close it. Я его _____. Я всегда буду его _____.

4. They opened a new restaurant (**ресторан**). Они _____ новый ресторан.

5. She forgot to close the fridge (**холодильник**). Она забыла _____ холодильник.

6. Her husband (**муж**) closed it. Её муж его _____.

7. He would open the window every day. Он каждый день _____ окно.

8. She was opening her umbrella. Она _____ зонт.

[1] For an overview, consult the complete table of verb types in the back of the book.
[2] "Dishes" is plural in English, but is **singular only** in Russian: **посуда**. Be on the lookout for such "singular only" and "plural only" nouns.

1. Кто у вас до́ма обы́чно **мо́ет** посу́ду? Или, мо́жет быть, у вас есть посудомо́ечная маши́на (dishwasher)?

2. Ты лю́бишь петь? Ты хорошо́ поёшь? Не споёшь нам сейча́с пе́сню? (**пе́сня**: song)

ь (soft sign) verbs like ПИТЬ . . . . have stems ending in ь, and take ё endings

The root of these verbs actually ends in -**ий**, but this combination never actually appears in written Russian. In conjugated forms, it "collapses" to -**ь**. Note that in **perfective** forms (in вы́пить, for example), the prefix вы- is **always stressed**. Note how this stress rule affects the perfective forms below (even the past tense forms!).

пить Ь: to drink		вы́пить Ь: to drink (perfective)	бить Ь: to beat, strike	разби́ть Ь: to break, shatter
пью	I drink	вы́пью	бью	разобью́[1]
пьёшь	you drink	вы́пьешь	бьёшь	разобьёшь
пьёт	he, she, it drinks	вы́пьет	бьёт	разобьёт
пьём	we drink	вы́пьем	бьём	разобьём
пьёте	you drink	вы́пьете	бьёте	разобьёте
пьют	they drink	вы́пьют	бьют	разобью́т
пей!	drink!	вы́пей!	бей!	разбе́й!
пил	he drank	вы́пил	бил	разби́л
пила́	she drank	вы́пила	била́	разби́ла
пи́ло	it drank	вы́пило	би́ло	разби́ло
пи́ли	they drank	вы́пили	би́ли	разби́ли

Also note that the perfective **вы́пить** can mean "to drink completely" (e.g. to finish one's drink), or simply "to have a drink." Truth be told, the latter often implies having **several** drinks (that is, a drinking session)!

Он вы́пил буты́лку вина́.
He drank a bottle of wine (completely).

Не хо́чешь вы́пить?
Would you like to "grab a drink"?

Он вы́пил во́дку и съел огуре́ц.
He downed the vodka and ate a pickle.

Here are two aspectual pairs for the verbs above.
Note how **разби́ть derives** an **АЙ** imperfective:

пить Ь / вы́пить Ь	разбива́ть АЙ / разби́ть Ь
to drink	to break, shatter

1. He doesn't drink wine.   Он не _____ вино́.
2. I like to drink juice.   Люблю́ _____ сок.
3. We were drinking vodka.   Мы _____ во́дку.
4. We drank the vodka.   Мы _____ во́дку.
5. I'll drink the tea.   Я _____ чай.

6. What was she drinking?   Что она́ _____ ? **22.c**
7. Who drank up the milk?   Кто _____ молоко́?
8. He drank a bottle of beer.   Он _____ буты́лку пи́ва.
9. They rarely drink alcohol.   Они́ ре́дко _____ алкого́ль.
10. They were drinking coffee.   Они́ _____ ко́фе.

1. Did he break the plate? He's always breaking dishes!   Он _____ таре́лку? Он всегда́ _____ посу́ду! **22.d**
2. Careful, or you'll break my new vase!   Осторо́жно, а то _____ мою́ но́вую ва́зу!
3. Oh my God! The child is beating the cat!   Бо́же мой! Ребёнок _____ ко́шку!

Some Russian sayings involving the dative case:

Что ру́сскому хорошо́, то не́мцу смерть.   That which is good for the Russian is death for the German.
Как коро́ве седло́.   Like a saddle for a cow (said of something useless)
За э́то по голо́вке не погла́дят.   They won't stroke one on the head for that (i.e. they won't like it!).
Чему́ быть, того́ не минова́ть.   That which is to be cannot be avoided.
Ни Бо́гу свеча́, ни чёрту кочерга́.   Neither a little candle for God, nor a fire rake for the devil (neither good nor bad).
Челове́к челове́ку волк.   Man is wolf to man (in Latin, *Homō hominī lupus*.)
Любопы́тной Варва́ре на база́ре нос оторва́ли.   They tore curious Barbara's nose off at the fair. (i.e. curiosity killed the cat!)[2]

---

[1] Note the mobile vowel "о" inserted in conjugated forms following the prefix. This is not a universal feature of prefixed verbs.
[2] Our first example of a "dative of disadvantage" (also called a "dative of deprivation"). Barbara has been deprived of her nose.

начать /H^{end}: to begin¹	
начн**у**	I will begin
начн**ёшь**	you will begin
начн**ёт**	he, she, it will begin
начн**ём**	we will begin
начн**ёте**	you will begin
начн**ут**	they will begin
начн**и**!	begin!
начал	he began
начал**а**	she began
начал**о**	it began
начал**и**	they began

We will see only one example of this type in Book 1, but it's an important one: **to begin** (perfective). Its root is **ч/н**; as usual, the tag **/H** provides the final element of the stem that can't be gleaned from the infinitive.

To the right is the full aspectual pair for "to begin." Its imperfective is a derived imperfective — again, an **АЙ** verb. Many non-syllabic verb types derive their imperfective by inserting a vowel (**и**) into their otherwise non-syllabic root.

In this case, **ч/н → чин**. So, from the perfective **начать** /H we get the imperfective **начинать**.

начинать АЙ / **начать** /H^{end} + inf.	
to begin	
начина**ю**	начн**у**
начина**ешь**	начн**ёшь**
начина**ет**	начн**ёт**
начина**ем**	начн**ём**
начина**ете**	начн**ёте**
начина**ют**	начн**ут**
начина**й**!	начн**и**!
начинал	начал
начинал**а**	начал**а**
начинал**о**	начал**о**
начинал**и**	начал**и**

Just as in English, this verb can be followed by a **direct object** (e.g. to begin work) or by an **infinitive** (e.g. to begin to work). In this chapter, we can make a quick addendum to our criteria for choosing **aspect**: following verbs of **starting** or **stopping**, we can only use **imperfective** infinitives, since we are speaking of the start or end of an extended **process**.

Моя сосе́дка начала́ рабо́ту.
My neighbor began (her) work.

Она́ начала́ рабо́тать.
She began to work.

Она́ начнёт писа́ть статью́.
She'll begin to write (start writing) an article.

22.e 1. She starts working every day at 8.

Она́ _____ рабо́тать ка́ждый день в во́семь.

2. My colleague would start working at 8.

Мой колле́га _____ рабо́тать в во́семь.

3. The child will soon start talking.

Ребёнок ско́ро _____ говори́ть.

4. Our new neighbor began to cook dinner.

Наш но́вый сосе́д _____ гото́вить у́жин.

5. The grad student (f.) began reading a new book.

Аспира́нтка _____ чита́ть но́вую кни́гу.

6. They began to call us every day.

Они́ _____ нам звони́ть ка́ждый день.

7. She began to get used to Russia.

Она́ _____ привыка́ть к Росси́и.

8. OK, I'll begin telling you this story.

Хорошо́, я _____ расска́зывать тебе́ э́ту исто́рию.

---

n/sA verbs like ждать .... have non-syllabic roots + A, and take ё endings

Technically, these verbs are **not** non-suffixed verbs, since their infinitives are created by adding the **stem vowel** "a" to a **non-syllabic stem** (hence the flag, **n/sA** — say "in es ah"). This detail aside, they work much like non-suffixed verbs: just add ё endings to the stem. For example, the verb **ждать** is built as follows: **ж/д + а + ть**.

In some **n/sA** verbs, a mobile vowel (either "o" or "e") appears in all conjugated forms to "**fill in**" the non-syllabic root. For this reason, our table will include three head verbs: **ждать** n/sA (which adds no mobile vowel), **звать** n/sA (which adds the mobile vowel "o"), and **брать** n/sA (which adds the mobile vowel "e").

no inserted mobile vowel

ждать n/sA^{end}: to wait	
жд**у**	I wait
жд**ёшь**	you wait
жд**ёт**	he, she, it waits
жд**ём**	we wait
жд**ёте**	you wait
жд**ут**	they wait
жд**и**!	wait!

inserted mobile vowel "o"

звать n/sA^{end}: to name, call	
зов**у**	I call
зов**ёшь**	you call
зов**ёт**	he, she, it calls
зов**ём**	we call
зов**ёте**	you call
зов**ут**	they call
зов**и**!	call!

inserted mobile vowel "e"

брать n/sA^{end}: to take	
бер**у**	I take
бер**ёшь**	you take
бер**ёт**	he, she, it takes
бер**ём**	we take
бер**ёте**	you take
бер**ут**	they take
бер**и**!	take!

Here are the aspectual pairs for these three verbs:

ждать n/sA / **подожда́ть** n/sA кого́
to wait (on)

звать n/sA / **назва́ть** n/sA
to name, call

брать n/sA / **взять**
to take

---

114 ¹ This is "to begin" in the transitive sense, as in "to begin work" (or, with an infinitive, "to begin to work" or "to start working"). We will learn the intransitive form (as in "work is beginning" or "work is starting") in 27.3.

Как зов**у**т...	Ко**г**о ты ждёшь?	Что ты бер**ё**шь с соб**о**й?[1]
1. _____ (ваш друг)	4. _____ (друг мо**е**г**о** бр**а**та)	7. _____ (зонт)
2. _____ (тво**я** сестра)	5. _____ (н**а**ша подр**у**га)	8. _____ (кн**и**га)
3. _____ (твой брат)	6. _____ (проф**е**ссор)	9. _____ (пальт**о**)

22.2 Overview of irregular verbs

With these new verb types under our belt, we can give a quick summary of important aspectual pairs that include at least one entirely irregular form. We know one already — **хот**е**ть** (to want).

Again, note the irregularities, from changing stems to mixed endings to multiple shifts in stress! And remember — if a given infinitive in our vocabulary is **not tagged** by verb type, then we should assume that it is **irregular**.

Keep in mind that no matter how strange (or downright irregular!) a verb's conjugated forms may be, its **past** tense is almost always formed directly from the **infinitive**. The only exception we have seen so far is **мочь** (мог, могл**а**, etc.).

А н**у**-ка, вз**я**ли!
"Come on, let's grab it / take it" (Let's get started!). This past-tense verb acts here as an urgent command, in the sense of "let's do this already!"

хот**е**ть / захот**е**ть + inf.		дав**а**ть АВ**А**Й[2] / дать		есть / съесть		брать n/sA[end] / взять	
to want / to get the urge		to give		to eat		to take	
хоч**у**	захоч**у**	да**ю**	дам	ем	съем	бер**у**	возьм**у**
х**о**чешь	зах**о**чешь	да**ё**шь	дашь	ешь	съешь	берёшь	возьм**ё**шь
х**о**чет	зах**о**чет	да**ё**т	даст	ест	съест	берёт	возьм**ё**т
хот**и**м	захот**и**м	да**ё**м	дад**и**м	ед**и**м	съед**и**м	берём	возьм**ё**м
хот**и**те	захот**и**те	да**ё**те	дад**и**те	ед**и**те	съед**и**те	берёте	возьм**ё**те
хот**я**т	захот**я**т	да**ю**т	дад**у**т	ед**я**т	съед**я**т	бер**у**т	возьм**у**т
— — —	— — —	дав**а**й!	дай!	ешь!	съешь!	бер**и**!	возьм**и**!
хот**е**л	захот**е**л	дав**а**л	дал	ел	съел	брал	взял
хот**е**ла	захот**е**ла	дав**а**ла	дал**а**	**е**ла	съ**е**ла	брал**а**	взял**а**
хот**е**ло	захот**е**ло	дав**а**ло	д**а**ло	**е**ло	съ**е**ло	бр**а**ло	вз**я**ло
хот**е**ли	захот**е**ли	дав**а**ли	д**а**ли	**е**ли	съ**е**ли	бр**а**ли	вз**я**ли

1. She took the backpack.	Она _____ рюкз**а**к.	7. They gave me a pen.	Он**и** _____ мне р**у**чку. **22.g**
2. I'll take the umbrella.	Я _____ зонт.	8. We'll give you food.	Мы _____ теб**е** ед**у**.
3. We always take the umbrella.	Мы всегд**а** _____ зонт.	9. We always give you food.	Мы всегд**а** _____ теб**е** ед**у**.
4. They eat so much!	Он**и** _____ так мн**о**го!	10. I want to speak Russian.	Я _____ говор**и**ть по-р**у**сски.
5. They ate all the caviar!	Он**и** _____ всю икр**у**!	11. We want to relax.	Мы _____ отдохн**у**ть.
6. I don't eat meat.	Я не _____ м**я**со.	12. They want to eat.	Он**и** _____ есть.

1. Ты уж**е** н**а**чал / начал**а** в**и**деть сны[3] (dreams) по-р**у**сски?

2. Ты х**о**чешь жить в Росс**и**и? А что ты там (there) б**у**дешь есть?

3. Что ты берёшь с соб**о**й к**а**ждый день?

4. Ты ешь м**я**со, или нет? А р**ы**бу? А икр**у**?

[1] The phrase "с соб**о**й" literally means "with oneself." The phrase **брать с соб**о**й** is much like the English "to take along."
[2] We will look at this new verb type in detail in tomorrow's lesson.   [3] **сон** can mean "sleep" or "dream" in Russian.

day 23:   verbs with the dative

verbs with indirect objects in the dative; **АВАЙ** verbs like **дава́ть**; verbs of giving; helping and believing; advising and recommending; making phonecalls

Спаси́бо люби́мому Ста́лину — за счастли́вое де́тство! Thanks to our beloved Stalin for a happy childhood!

23.1 Verbs with indirect objects in the dative

As we know, indirect objects appear in the dative case in Russian. It may sometimes be tricky to spot indirect objects if we rely on English. Take the phrase, "to thank **someone**." Is the "someone" a direct object or an indirect object? If we rephrase this a bit — "to say 'thank you' **to** someone" — then we come closer to the Russian **idiom**: "thanking" requires an **indirect object** in the dative. In Russian, the "someone" we say thanks to is in the dative, and we say thanks "for" something using **за + the accusative**.

На́до сказа́ть **профе́ссору** спаси́бо за кни́гу.	Я сказа́л **ему́** спаси́бо за кни́гу.	Спаси́бо за но́вую кни́гу!
I need to thank the professor for the book.	I thanked him for the book.	Thanks for the new book!

We can use the **dative** generally for indirect objects following the verb "to speak, to say," and with most any other Russian verb of **giving, telling, or showing** that in English could be followed by "to" or "for."

Here is a list of common verbs whose use of the dative for indirect objects closely mirrors such English constructions:

говори́ть И^end / **сказа́ть** А^shift to speak, tell, say (to...)	**расска́зывать** АЙ / **рассказа́ть** А^shift to tell a story (to...)
покупа́ть АЙ / **купи́ть** И^shift to buy (for...)	**дари́ть** И^shift / **подари́ть** И^shift to give a gift (to...)
пока́зывать АЙ / **показа́ть** А^shift to show (to...)	**отвеча́ть** АЙ / **отве́тить** И to answer (to...)
плати́ть И^shift / **заплати́ть** И^shift за что to pay (to...)	**писа́ть** А^shift / **написа́ть** А^shift to write (to...)
чита́ть АЙ / **прочита́ть** АЙ to read (to...)	**петь** ОЙ^end / **спеть** ОЙ^end to sing (to...)

Recall that our two verbs for **"asking"** are followed by direct objects in the **accusative**, not indirect objects in the dative.

спра́шивать И / **спроси́ть** И^shift кого to ask, inquire	**проси́ть** И^shift / **попроси́ть** И кого + inf. to ask (someone to...), ask for, request

Note that **спра́шивать / спроси́ть** has to do with "making an inquiry," while **проси́ть / попроси́ть** has to do with "making a request."

Мы **спроси́ли** профе́ссора, когда́ у нас бу́дет экза́мен.
We asked the professor when our exam would be.

У нас нет ключа́. На́до ключ **попроси́ть**.
We don't have a key. We need to request a key.

Мы **попроси́ли** профе́ссора отве́тить на вопро́с.
We asked the professor to answer a question.

Мо́жно **попроси́ть** ключ **у нача́льника**.
We can ask the boss for a key (note the idiom with **у**).

ЧТО ДА́ЛА ОКТЯ́БРЬСКАЯ РЕВОЛЮ́ЦИЯ РАБО́ТНИЦЕ и КРЕСТЬЯ́НКЕ

Что да́ла октя́брьская револю́ция рабо́тнице и крестья́нке.

What the October Revolution has given to the (female) worker and peasant.

---

*Fill in the blanks with either the **accusative** or **dative**, as needed.* **23.a**

1. Мы _____ (**он**) спроси́ли, где он живёт, но он _____ (**мы**) не отве́тил.

2. — _____ (**кто**) пи́шешь? — Пишу́ _____ (**ста́рый друг**), кото́рый живёт в Росси́и.

3. Ма́ма спроси́ла _____ (**сын**), что он де́лал вчера́, и он _____ (**она́**) всё рассказа́л.

4. Ва́ша сестра́ попроси́ла _____ (**я**) показа́ть _____ (**вы**) фотогра́фию мое́й семьи́.

5. Как ты _____ (**они́**) отве́тил? Ты написа́л _____ (**они́**) эсэмэ́ску и́ли позвони́л по телефо́ну?

6. Студе́нт написа́л _____ (**оте́ц**) письмо́, и попроси́л _____ (**он**) сказа́ть _____ (**ма́ма**), что всё хорошо́.

7. _____ (**что**) ты пода́ришь _____ (**брат**) на день рожде́ния (birthday)? А что ты _____ (**он**) обы́чно да́ришь?

8. Почему́ ты _____ (**но́вый колле́га**) спра́шиваешь? На́до _____ (**нача́льник**) спроси́ть!

9. — Что он _____ (**вы**) говори́л? — Он _____ (**мы**) расска́зывал, что он де́лает в Росси́и.

10. Мы вчера́ купи́ли _____ (**но́вый щено́к**)! Мы хоти́м _____ (**он**) _____ (**ты**) показа́ть!

11. Ма́ма прочита́ла _____ (**до́чка**) ру́сскую ска́зку, а пото́м спе́ла _____ (**она́**) _____ (**пе́сня**).

12. Я попроси́л _____ (**подру́га**) сказа́ть _____ (**я**) всю _____ (**пра́вда**).

---

*Translate these "ask" sentences, choosing carefully between **спра́шивать / спроси́ть** and **проси́ть / попроси́ть**.* **23.b**

1. My mom asked when I would be (literally, "will be"[1]) home.

Ма́ма меня́ _____, когда́ я бу́ду до́ма.

2. She would always ask what I had been doing.

Она́ всегда́ меня́ _____, что я де́лал(а).

3. She asked me to always take an umbrella.

Она́ меня́ _____ взять зонт.

4. I'll ask my brother for an umbrella.

Я _____ зонт у бра́та.

---

[1] Again, note how the Russian indirect question preserves the tense of the original, direct question: "When **will** you be home?"

We will tag this verb type as **АВАЙ** based on its stem suffix, which **collapses** to "a" in all conjugated forms. Note how the suffix remains in the imperative form — and, of course, in past-tense forms, which are formed directly from the infinitive. There are really <u>only three</u> basic **АВАЙ** verbs in all of Russian: 1) **дав<u>а</u>ть**: to give; 2) **-став<u>а</u>ть**: to stand; 3) **-знав<u>а</u>ть**: to know. However, only the first form can stand alone. The other two are only seen **with prefixes** (such as **встав<u>а</u>ть**: to get up, **узнав<u>а</u>ть**: to find out). The verb **дав<u>а</u>ть** also occurs in many prefixed forms (such as **передав<u>а</u>ть**: to hand over or deliver). So, these verbs are quite common in Russian — easy to spot, and easy to conjugate!

дав<u>а</u>ть АВАЙ: to give		**продав<u>а</u>ть** АВАЙ: to sell	**встав<u>а</u>ть** АВАЙ: to get up	**узнав<u>а</u>ть** АВАЙ: to find out
да**ю**	I give	прода**ю**	вста**ю**	узна**ю**
да**ёшь**	you give	прода**ёшь**	вста**ёшь**	узна**ёшь**
да**ёт**	he, she, it gives	прода**ёт**	вста**ёт**	узна**ёт**
да**ём**	we give	прода**ём**	вста**ём**	узна**ём**
да**ёте**	you give	прода**ёте**	вста**ёте**	узна**ёте**
да**ют**	they give	прода**ют**	вста**ют**	узна**ют**
дав<u>а</u>й!	give!	продав<u>а</u>й!	встав<u>а</u>й!	узнав<u>а</u>й!

Here are the aspectual pairs for the verbs shown above. Note the variety of verb types among their perfective forms:

дав<u>а</u>ть АВАЙ / **дать**	**продав<u>а</u>ть** АВАЙ / **прод<u>а</u>ть**	**встав<u>а</u>ть** АВАЙ / **встать** Hstem	**узнав<u>а</u>ть** АВАЙ / **узн<u>а</u>ть** АЙ
to give	to sell	to get up	to find out, recognize

Finally, we'll know how to say "ask a question." The Russian idiom is **задав<u>а</u>ть вопр<u>о</u>с** — much like the English "to pose" a question. It can take the dative, as in: **Мы зада<u>ё</u>м вопр<u>о</u>с профессору** (We're "posing a question to the professor.")

задав<u>а</u>ть АВАЙ / **зад<u>а</u>ть** вопрос
to ask (pose) a question

23.2 Verbs of giving

Now that we've seen the verb type **АВАЙ**, we can learn the pairs for the verb "to give," as well as a prefixed form meaning "to sell." The Russian "to give" is tricky for a number of reasons, and deserves plenty of attention, since it's so common. First, its perfective form **дать** (and all prefixed forms thereof!) is completely **irregular**, and features the "stressed a" in the **past** tense.

дав<u>а</u>ть АВАЙ / **дать**		**продав<u>а</u>ть** АВАЙ / **прод<u>а</u>ть**		**задав<u>а</u>ть** АВАЙ / **зад<u>а</u>ть**	
to give		to sell		to pose (a question)	
да**ю**	дам	прода**ю**	продам	зада**ю**	задам
да**ёшь**	дашь	прода**ёшь**	продашь	зада**ёшь**	задашь
да**ёт**	даст	прода**ёт**	продаст	зада**ёт**	задаст
да**ём**	дадим	прода**ём**	продадим	зада**ём**	зададим
да**ёте**	дадите	прода**ёте**	продадите	зада**ёте**	зададите
да**ют**	дад<u>у</u>т	прода**ют**	продад<u>у</u>т	зада**ют**	задад<u>у</u>т
дав<u>а</u>й!	дай!	продав<u>а</u>й!	прод<u>а</u>й!	задав<u>а</u>й!	зад<u>а</u>й!
дав<u>а</u>л	дал	продав<u>а</u>л	прод<u>а</u>л[1]	задав<u>а</u>л	зад<u>а</u>л[1]
дав<u>а</u>ла	дал<u>а</u>	продав<u>а</u>ла	прода<u>л</u>а	задав<u>а</u>ла	задал<u>а</u>
дав<u>а</u>ло	дал<u>о</u>	продав<u>а</u>ло	прод<u>а</u>ло	задав<u>а</u>ло	зад<u>а</u>ло
дав<u>а</u>ли	дали	продав<u>а</u>ли	прод<u>а</u>ли	задав<u>а</u>ли	зад<u>а</u>ли

Долой кухонное рабство! Даёшь новый быт! "Down with kitchen slavery! Give us (literally, 'you give') a new daily way of life." Soviet women are being saved from their kitchen drudgery by the "**столовая**" (cafeteria).

23.c *Form sentences using the verbs above. Remember* — *place the direct object in the* **accusative***, and the indirect object in the* **dative***!*

1. Д<u>е</u>душка и б<u>а</u>бушка д<u>а</u>ли _____ (люб<u>и</u>мый внук) _____ (конф<u>е</u>та).

2. Наш от<u>е</u>ц пр<u>о</u>дал _____ (ст<u>а</u>рая маш<u>и</u>на) _____ (сос<u>е</u>д).

3. Студ<u>е</u>нтка задал<u>а</u> _____ (интер<u>е</u>сный вопр<u>о</u>с) _____ (проф<u>е</u>ссор).

Жизнь даёт од<u>и</u>н т<u>о</u>лько Бог, а отним<u>а</u>ет вс<u>я</u>кая г<u>а</u>дина. God alone gives life, while all kinds of vermin (**гад, г<u>а</u>дина**) take it away.

---

[1] Note also how these prefixed perfectives (like **прод<u>а</u>л** and **зад<u>а</u>ли**) stress the **prefix** in the past forms (aside from the "stressed-a" feminine form. Stress can sometimes jump onto a prefix in this fashion; watch out for it in our tables.

23.3 Helping and believing

To summarize, it's no surprise to English speakers that most of the Russian verbs we've seen so far today (giving, telling, showing, etc.) are used with the dative, since this usage closely mirrors English "to" phrases. However, there are other Russian verbs whose use of the dative may seem rather arbitrary to us. We could simply say that they "**take the dative**," and leave it at that. As we'll see, certain Russian verbs are followed by a particular case, simply by definition.

Some verbs that take the dative involve the idea of helping or believing. In English, "to help" is usually followed by a direct object, but we could rephrase it a bit: "to give help **to** someone." The latter phrasing is more in keeping with the Russian. It's harder to think of such a phrasing for "believe" — perhaps, "to lend credence **to** someone."

Note that the perfective **помочь** is a prefixed form of **мочь**, and so is conjugated exactly like **мочь**, including in the **past** tense.

Я всегда помогаю **соседу**, а он **мне** всегда помогает.
I always help (my) neighbor, and he always helps me.

Вчера моя жена помогла **сыну** сделать задание.
Yesterday my wife helped (our) son do an assignment.

Я помогу **тебе** приготовить ужин.   Правда? Я **тебе** не верю!
I'll help you cook dinner.   Really? I don't believe you!

помогать АЙ / помочь Гshift кому + inf.	
to help (+ dative!)	
помога́ю	помогу́
помога́ешь	помо́жешь
помога́ет	помо́жет
помога́ем	помо́жем
помога́ете	помо́жете
помога́ют	помо́гут
помога́й!	помоги́!
помога́л	помо́г
помога́ла	помогла́
помога́ло	помогло́
помога́ли	помогли́

верить И / поверить И кому	
to believe (+ dative!)	
ве́рю	пове́рю
ве́ришь	пове́ришь
ве́рит	пове́рит
ве́рим	пове́рим
ве́рите	пове́рите
ве́рят	пове́рят
верь!	поверь!

Ты ча́сто помога́ешь...

1. _____ (сосе́д / сосе́дка)   ...реша́ть зада́чу по фи́зике?
2. _____ (друг / подру́га)   ...чита́ть тру́дный ру́сский текст?
3. _____ (ма́ма / па́па)   ...мыть посу́ду?
4. _____ (брат / сестра́)   ...покупа́ть но́вую оде́жду?

Не помо́жешь...

5. _____ (ребёнок)   ...реши́ть зада́чу по матема́тике?
6. _____ (знако́мый / знако́мая)   ...написа́ть письмо́ па́рню / де́вушке?[1]
7. _____ (профе́ссор)   ...нарисова́ть ка́рту (map) Росси́и?
8. _____ (ба́бушка / де́душка)   ...купи́ть но́вый компью́тер?

---

1. She helped me yesterday. _____ **23.d**

2. We always helped him. _____

3. He'll always help you (ты). _____

4. I'll help you (вы) tomorrow. _____

5. I (masc.) helped them. _____

Case endings and knowing the nominative singular

The importance of case endings in Russian can't be emphasized enough — especially since, as English speakers, we are used to making sense of a sentence based largely on word order. Relying on English expectations regarding word order is one of the most common mistakes students make, and it's understandably difficult to overcome this deep-seated habit. The only way to escape it is to pay close, close attention to **endings**!

Often, however, even the endings are of little help without knowing the **nominative singular** of a given word. Look at this simple example: **Сыну партии — слава!** Is "**сыну**" a masculine noun in the dative? Or is it a feminine noun in the accusative? To decide, we must **simply know** the nominative singular (that is, the gender) of the noun: **сын** (masculine). The slogan means "Glory (**слава**) to a son (**сын**) of the party (**партия**)!"

---

* The terms **пар(е)нь** (guy) and **девушка** (girl) can be used in the sense of "boyfriend" and "girlfriend."

23.4 Advising and recommending

These two synonyms (one a native Russian verb, one borrowed), meaning "to advise" or "to recommend," can also be followed by the **dative**.

But first — they can take a direct object in the **accusative**, as in "I recommend French wine."

Как**о́е вино́** ты сове́туешь?   Я сове́тую францу́зское **вино́**.
What wine do you recommend?   I recommend French wine.

If we also specify "to whom" or "for whom" we are making the recommendation, we need an indirect object in the **dative**:

Я **вам** рекоменду́ю францу́зское вино́.
I "recommend to you" French wine.

Or, we can add an infinitive, as in "I advise you to..."

Я сове́тую вам **пить** то́лько францу́зское вино́.
I advise you **to drink** French wine only!

сове́товать ОВА / посове́товать ОВА	
to advise, recommend	
сове́тую	посове́тую
сове́туешь	посове́туешь
сове́тует	посове́тует
сове́туем	посове́туем
сове́туете	посове́туете
сове́туют	посове́туют
сове́туй!	посове́туй!

рекомендова́ть ОВА / порекомендова́ть ОВА	
to advise, recommend	
рекоменду́ю	порекоменду́ю
рекоменду́ешь	порекоменду́ешь
рекоменду́ет	порекоменду́ет
рекоменду́ем	порекоменду́ем
рекоменду́ете	порекоменду́ете
рекоменду́ют	порекоменду́ют
рекоменду́й!	порекоменду́й!

---

1. Како́й **фильм** ты сове́туешь дру́гу / подру́ге? А како́й фильм он / она́ тебе́ сове́тует?

2. А каку́ю **кни́гу** ты ему́ / ей сове́туешь прочита́ть? Есть у тебя́ люби́мая кни́га? Кака́я?

3. Како́й **язы́к** ты сове́туешь изуча́ть (study)? Ру́сский? Или ты ду́маешь, что он сли́шком (too) тру́дный?

4. Како́й **сериа́л** ты нам сове́туешь смотре́ть по телеви́зору? Этот сериа́л смо́трят в Росси́и?

5. Ты не мо́жешь нам посове́товать **музыка́льную гру́ппу** (band)? А э́ту гру́ппу зна́ют в Росси́и?

6. Како́го **писа́теля** ты нам сове́туешь чита́ть? А кто твой люби́мый ру́сский писа́тель?

23.5 Making phonecalls

In English, we use the verb "to call" with a direct object, as in "I called my friend." In Russian, we need the **dative** case. of it as "making a call **to** someone," and this use of the dative seems much easier to understand. To specify "by telephone," we can say "**по телефо́ну**" (or: **по Ска́йпу**, etc.).

In Russian, this verb literally means "to ring."

звони́ть И^end / позвони́ть И^end кому́[1]	
to call ("to make a call to...")	
звоню́	позвоню́
звони́шь	позвони́шь
звони́т	позвони́т
звони́м	позвони́м
звони́те	позвони́те
звоня́т	позвоня́т
звони́!	позвони́!

---

1. Ты ча́сто звони́шь па́пе или ма́ме? А они́ ка́ждый день тебе́ звоня́т? А что они́ спра́шивают, когда́ звоня́т?

2. Кому́ ты звони́л(а) вчера́? А кто тебе́ звони́л? Друг и́ли подру́га? Ма́ма и́ли па́па? Президе́нт?

3. А кому́ ты позвони́шь за́втра? Кто тебе́ наве́рно (probably) позвони́т? Друг и́ли подру́га? Ма́ма и́ли па́па?

A note on the dative case versus possessive forms

The Soviet anthem (which we'll learn on Day 71!) contains the phrase: **Ле́нин вели́кий нам путь озари́л!** The simplest translation would probably be: Great Lenin illuminated **our** path. But note that in situations where English often uses **possessive** forms (here: our), Russian often prefers a **dative** (here: **нам**, instead of **наш путь**, though either would be grammatically correct; the meanings are essentially the same).

Such uses of the dative are extremely common in Russian. Watch for them, and remember that they are often best translated using an English possessive — as in, "Lenin illuminated our path" instead of "Lenin illuminated the path for us."

ЛЕНИН ВЕЛИКИЙ НАМ ПУТЬ ОЗАРИЛ!

[1] You may hear this verb treated as a shifting-stress verb by some Russian speakers.

day 24:   everything & everyone; short-form adjectives

saying "all" and "entire" with **весь** and **целый**; **всё** and **все**;
telling how you feel with short-form adjectives;
saying you need something with **нужен**

И э͟то всё из к͟ильки! And all of this is (made) from anchovies! (Note the absence of the dots above the ё on the actual poster!)

24.1 Saying "all" and "entire"

In 14.4, we introduced the words **всё** (everything) and **все** (everyone). These are actually the neuter singular and plural forms of a **special modifier**, **весь**. Compare its unusual adjectival endings with that of an ordinary adjective that is close in meaning — **целый**. We can often translate **весь** as "all" or "whole," and **целый** as "whole" or "entire."

Весь мир бу͟дет наш!
The whole world will be ours!

For the love of God, someone stop this child!

	masculine		feminine		neuter	
nom.	весь[1]	торт	вся	икр**а**	всё	молок**о**
gen.	вс**его**	то͟рт**а**	вс**ей**	икр**ы**	вс**его**	молок**а**
acc.	весь	торт	вс**ю**	икр**у**	всё	молок**о**
dat.	вс**ему**	то͟рт**у**	вс**ей**	икр**е**	вс**ему**	молок**у**

	masculine		feminine		neuter	
nom.	це͟л**ый**	стак**а͟н**	це͟л**ая**	буты͟лк**а**	це͟л**ое**	я͟блок**о**
gen.	це͟л**ого**	стак**а͟на**	це͟л**ой**	буты͟лк**и**	це͟л**ого**	я͟блок**а**
acc.	це͟л**ый**	стак**а͟н**	це͟л**ую**	буты͟лк**у**	це͟л**ое**	я͟блок**о**
dat.	це͟л**ому**	стак**а͟ну**	це͟л**ой**	буты͟лк**е**	це͟л**ому**	я͟блок**у**

[1] Note that the "**е**" in this form is a **mobile vowel**, which drops out when any ending is added — that is, in all remaining forms.   121

Here are some examples. While these words are almost synonymous, there can be a slight difference in meaning: **весь** usually refers to something known and concrete, in situations where we would use a definite article (the) in English; **целый** often works best in situations where we'd use an indefinite article (a, an). Compare:

Ребёнок съел **весь торт**.	The child ate all the cake.	Он съел **целый торт**.	He ate an entire cake.
Он съел **всю нашу икру**.	He ate all of our caviar.	Он съел **целую пиццу**.	He ate an entire pizza.
Он выпил **всё молоко**.	He drank all the milk.	Он съел **целое яблоко**.	He ate an entire apple.

24.a Give the forms of **весь**. Many examples express disbelief with "**неужели**," meaning "Can it really be that..." or simply "really?"

1. Я тебе не верю! Неужели ты выпил _____ водку?

2. Неужели _____ французское вино такое хорошее?

3. Они сказали, что прочитали _____ статью, но я им не поверил.

4. Неужели ты посмотрел _____ этот скучный фильм?

5. Я хочу помогать _____ человечеству (humanity, neuter)!

6. Неужели твоя кошка съела _____ рыбу?

7. Неужели мальчик съест _____ бутерброд?

8. Сосед помогает _____ нашей семье.

9. Неужели ребёнок выпьет _____ молоко?

10. Я работал _____ день. Хочу отдохнуть!

24.b Fill in the correct forms of **целый**. Try translating it with an indefinite article, as in "an entire..."

1. Вчера я прочитала _____ книгу. Она была такая интересная!

2. Мой друг жил _____ год (year) в России. Ему было так интересно!

3. _____ бутылка вина стоит только сто двадцать два (122) рубля!

4. Неужели такой маленький ребёнок сможет съесть _____ порцию борща?

5. — Вы только одно яблоко хотите? — Нет, я хочу _____ килограмм.

6. — Вы хотите _____ курицу (chicken), или только половину (half)?

Я, ты, он, она — вместе целая страна. I, you, he, she — together, the entire country.

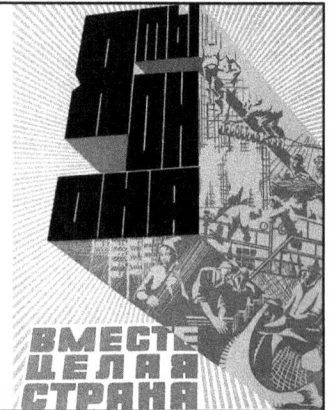

---

1. Ты можешь выпить целую бутылку шампанского?

2. Ты можешь съесть целую банку (tin, jar) икры?

3. Ты можешь прочитать целый русский роман?

4. Ты можешь написать целую статью сегодня?

24.2 Distinguishing всё and все

As we know, **всё** (the neuter singular) and **все** (the plural) can stand alone, in the sense of "everything" and "everyone." As we'll see later when we add plural forms, **все** can also mean "all" with regard to multiple things, as in "all the..."

Я люблю **всё**. **Всё** здесь так хорошо.
I love everything. Everything here is so good.

Неужели ты не пьёшь квас? **Все** любят квас!
Do you really not drink kvas? Everyone loves kvas!

Не знаю, какую машину купить. Я люблю **все**!
I don't know which car to buy. I love them all!

Again, actual Russian texts — like the posters to the right — will typically not include the "dots" above the **всё**. We'll have to decide based on context whether to read "**всё**" or "**все**."

ВСЕ НА ВЫБОРЫ!

Все на выборы! Everyone to the elections (that is, go vote!).

"Everyone" (**все**) is the only word that makes sense here, so we read it with a "**е**."

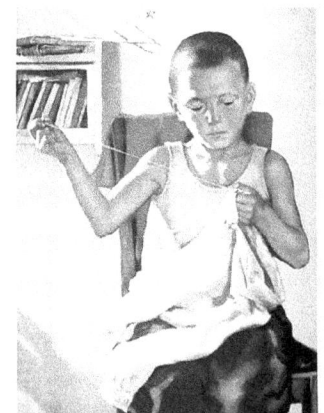

УЧИСЬ ВСЕ ДЕЛАТЬ САМ!

Учись всё делать сам! Learn to do everything yourself!

Here, **всё** is the only word that makes sense, so we read it with a "**ё**."

Would we use **всё** *or* **все** *in these examples? Look for contextual and grammatical clues. Verb endings are often a big help!*

1. _____ говорят, что этот новый фильм интересный.

2. Я хочу помочь тебе. Я сделаю _____ для тебя.

3. _____ знают, что в России часто пьют чай.

4. _____ они хотели жить целый год в России.

5. — Какой у тебя любимый плакат? — Я люблю их _____!

6. _____ мы уже можем читать _____.

7. Она умеет _____ — готовить, танцевать, рисовать.

8. Как у тебя дела? _____ у тебя хорошо?

24.3 Telling how you feel with short-form predicate adjectives

In 21.5, we learned how to express feelings using **predicate adverbs** in subjectless constructions with the dative, as in "**Мне хорошо.**" We made the very important point that any verb form appearing in a subjectless construction must always be in the **neuter singular**, since there is **no subject** for the verb to agree with. So, the past and future forms of "**Мне хорошо**" would be "**Мне было хорошо**" and "**Мне будет хорошо.**"

Many other phrases for telling how one feels involve not predicate adverbs, but **predicate adjectives**. A predicate adjectives is joined to the subject with a **linking verb**, as in "I am hungry" or "I was hungry." In this predicate position, Russian typically prefers adjectives in special **short forms** whose endings resemble the various noun endings we've seen — "zero ending" for masculine, "a" for feminine, and "o" for neuter.

While in theory many long-form Russian adjectives have short forms, in practice just a short list are used with great frequency in these constructions — namely, as **short-form predicate adjectives**. They're listed below.

By the way, if you see a vocab item with two stress marks (e.g. трезвы), it means that either stress is acceptable.

	long form	short form			
certain, sure	уверенный →	уверен	уверена	уверено	уверены
drunk	пьяный →	пьян	пьяна	пьяно	пьяны
sober	трезвый →	трезв	трезва	трезво	трезвы
healthy	здоровый →	здоров	здорова	здорово	здоровы
ready, finished	готовый →	готов	готова	готово	готовы
happy	счастливый →	счастлив	счастлива	счастливо	счастливы
busy, occupied	занятый[1] →	занят	занята	занято	заняты
sated, full	сытый →	сыт	сыта	сыто	сыты
alive	живой →	жив	жива	живо	живы
dead	мёртвый →	мёртв	мертва	мертво	мертвы
satisfied	довольный →	доволен	довольна	довольно	довольны
free, available	свободный →	свободен	свободна	свободно	свободны
hungry	голодный →	голоден	голодна	голодно	голодны
sick, ill	больной →	болен	больна	больно	больны
needed, necessary	нужный →	нужен	нужна	нужно	нужны

The second group above includes adjectives whose masculine short-forms (in the black box) include a **mobile vowel** (e). Note how the л remains soft in all forms (e.g. **больной** → **болен, больна**).

Short-forms are preferred in the **predicate position only**; otherwise, long forms must be used. For example:

Этот студент **голоден**. | Это **голодный** студент. | Эта студентка **голодна**. | **Голодная** студентка читает.
This student is hungry. | This is a hungry student. | This student is hungry. | The hungry student is reading.

Can **long-form** adjectives be used in the predicate? Yes — in fact, we used many in Chapter 1. If an adjective (like **русский**) has no short form, then of course we have no choice but to use the long form. For adjectives that do have both long and short forms, the **short** forms are typically preferred in the predicate when speaking of **temporary** states (feelings), whereas **long** forms imply **permanent** qualities. Here are two examples:

Этот человек **болен**. | Этот человек **больной**. | Эта студентка **занята**. | Это очень **занятая** студентка.
This person is sick. | This is a sick person. | This student is busy. | This is a very busy student.

For now, our use of short-form adjectives will be largely confined to those in the table above, since they are used extremely often in their short forms to describe temporary feelings. We'll revisit this topic in the future.

[1] The long-form used to describe people specifically (i.e. a "busy" person) is end-stressed: **занятой**. NOTE: one cannot use this adjective to describe a "busy" schedule, as in "**занятое расписание.**" Instead, one could say "**насыщенное расписание.**"

24.d *Give the correct short forms of these adjectives. Check the table on the previous page for stress, especially in feminine forms.*

1. готовый → **готов**: Они _____ есть! Он _____, и она _____.

2. занятой → **занят**: Студент сегодня очень _____. Его подруга тоже очень _____.

3. счастливый → **счастлив**: Ты (m.) _____, или нет? Ты (f.) _____, или нет?

4. пьяный → **пьян**: Он _____. Он всю водку выпил. Они _____. Они всё пиво выпили.

5. трезвый → **трезв**: Она _____. Она водку не пила. Мы _____. Мы пиво не пили.

6. здоровый → **здоров**: Слава Богу![1] Я (m.) жив и _____! Слава Богу! Все живы и _____!

7. сытый → **сыт**: Они съели весь торт. Они _____. Собака съела всё мясо. Она _____.

....

*The adjectives below involve a mobile vowel (e) in the masculine form. Be sure to keep the **л** soft in all other forms as well.*

8. довольный → **доволен**: Как у неё дела? Она _____? Как у них дела? Они _____?

9. свободный → **свободен**: Это место _____? Этот стол _____?

10. голодный → **голоден**: Брат и сестра ужасно _____. Я думаю, что кошка _____.

11. больной →: **болен**: Бабушке плохо. Она опять _____. Дедушке плохо. Он опять _____.

---

1. Ты очень **занят** / **занята** сегодня? Расписание у тебя насыщенное?

2. Ты **свободен** / **свободна** сегодня вечером (this evening)?

3. Ты **голоден** / **голодна** сейчас? Все сейчас **голодны**?

4. Что ты обычно ешь, когда ты **голоден** / **голодна**?
   бутерброд? шоколад? мороженое? яблоко? банан? конфету?

5. Что ты обычно пьёшь, когда ты **хочешь пить**? (see note to right!)
   воду? лимонад? (soda, not limonade!) молоко? кофе? чай? пиво?

6. Тебе хорошо сегодня? Ты **болен** / **больна**, или **здоров** / **здорова**?

7. Твоё задание на сегодня **готово** или нет?

There is no adjective in Russian for "thirsty." To say "I'm thirsty," say "Я хочу пить."[2]

The classic Soviet film **Белое солнце пустыни** (The White Sun of the Desert - пустыня) begins with our hero, **товарищ Сухов**, giving water to a man buried up to his head in sand

Этот человек ужасно хочет пить. Наш герой (hero), товарищ Сухов, даёт ему пить, слава Богу (thank God!).

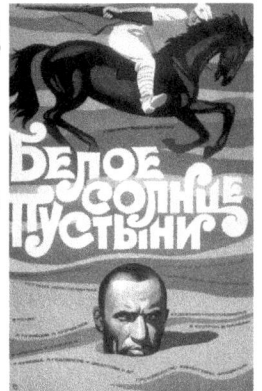

24.4 Saying you need something with нужен

The short-form adjective **нужен, нужна, нужно, нужны** can be translated as "needed" or "necessary," and can be combined with the **dative**. This use of the dative is quite clear, if we think of the Russian literally: for example, "this dictionary is necessary **for** me" or "**to** me." Of course, it is more natural to translate such phrases into English using the verb "to need," as in "I need this dictionary" — but, again, be careful not to rely on this translation, since it obscures the Russian **idiom**. In the Russian, "dictionary" is the **subject**!

Мне **нужен** словарь.
I need a dictionary.
"A dictionary is necessary for me."

Мне **нужна** ручка.
I need a pen.
"A pen is necessary for me."

Каждому студенту **нужны** словарь и ручка.
Every student needs a dictionary and pen.
"A dictionary and pen are necessary for every student."

24.e мама + хлеб: **Маме нужен хлеб.**
Mom needs bread.

1. от(е)ц + пиво: Отцу _____ _____.

2. моя сестра + чай: Моей сестре _____ _____.

3. студент + ответ: Студенту _____ _____.

4. кошка + молоко: Кошке _____ _____.

5. мой друг + пальто: Моему другу _____ _____.

6. я + кофе (masc!): _____

7. ты + вилка и нож: _____

8. он + ложка: _____

9. она + кефир: _____

10. они + сахар: _____

11. вы + масло: _____

12. мы + шоколад: _____

[1] Literally, "Glory to God" (like the English "thank God!")   [2] Or, in a construction we'll learn in 27.6, "**Пить хочется.**"

day 25: prepositions with the dative

prepositions with the dative; opinions with **по**; verbs followed
by dative prepositions; predicate adjectives and adverbs;
obligation with **должен**

Вперёд, к победе коммунизма! Onward, toward the victory of Communism!

25.1 Prepositions that take the dative

Today we'll learn two prepositions that take the **dative** case. The first, **к**, literally means "toward" (including "to" someone's place), and is also used following certain verbs. The second, **по**, has a variety of meanings.

к	to, toward; to visit (a person)	Надо привыкнуть **к русскому менталитету.** One has to get used to the Russian mentality.	Мы едем[1] **к бабушке.** We're going to see grandma.
по	along (a path); around (an area)	Мы гуляем **по улице.** We're strolling down the street.	Мы гуляем **по городу.** We're strolling around the city.
	by (means of), via	Я позвонил отцу **по телефону.** I called my father on the telephone.	Я пишу маме **по электронной почте.** I write mom by e-mail ("electronic mail").
	according to	**По расписанию** у нас сегодня нет урока русского языка. According to the schedule we don't have Russian class today.	
		По моему мнению это не так! In ("according to") my opinion that isn't so!	
	in (a subject)	У нас сегодня лекция **по русской истории.** Today we have a lecture in Russian history.	
		Это новый учебник **по русскому языку.** This is a new Russian language textbook.	

[1] We'll learn about verbs meaning "to go" in Chapter 4.

25.a *Supply the dative form following* **по** *to talk about these academic subjects.*

1. Это учебник по... _____ (русский язык) _____ (философия)

2. У нас лекция по... _____ (русская история) _____ (русская литература)

3. Решаю задачу по... _____ (математика) _____ (физика)

4. Читаю учебник по... _____ (химия) _____ (история литературы)

. . . .

Supply the dative form following **по** *in a few other of its meanings.*

5. Я пишу папе по... _____ (почта) _____ (электронная почта)

6. Я звоню маме по... _____ (телефон) _____ (Скайп)

7. Я люблю гулять по... _____ (улица - street) _____ (город)

_____ (берег - shore) _____ (парк)

25.2 Expressing opinions with по

Using **по** (according to) with the noun **мнение** (opinion) gives us some very useful phrases: "in my opinion," "in your opinion," etc. Some of these phrases have abbreviated (in bold) forms that are extremely common:

по моему мнению →	**по-моему**	in my opinion	по его мнению	in his opinion
по твоему мнению →	**по-твоему**	in your opinion (ты)	по её мнению	in her opinion
по вашему мнению →	**по-вашему**	in your opinion (вы)	по их мнению	in their opinion

1. Русская литература хорошая или нет, по-твоему? Она интересная, или нет? Она обычно смешная, или грустная?

2. Русская кухня (cuisine) по-твоему интересная, или нет? Она вкусная (tasty)? Странная? Острая (spicy)?

3. Кто, по-твоему, самый лучший (the best) русский писатель? Может быть, Толстой? Пушкин? Достоевский?

25.3 Pronouncing single-consonant prepositions

Russian has several prepositions (like **к**) that are single consonants. They must be pronounced **together** with the word that follows, just as if the two formed **a single word**. That is, **к победе** (toward victory) should be read as though it were written **кпобеде**, without the slightest pause or vowel sound inserted between the **к** and **п**.

Нам надо привыкнуть...	**к русской еде**	**к такой погоде**	**к грамматике**	**к произношению**
We need to get used...	to Russian food	to such weather	to grammar	to pronunciation

25.4 Verbs followed by dative prepositions

The prepositions we just learned can appear after certain verbs. For example, **привыкать** means "to get used" or "become accustomed." But what comes next? How do we say "to get used **to** something." In Russian, we use the preposition **к** + the dative. Since this is such an important feature of this verb, it's included in our vocab entry.

Another verb, **скучать** (to miss) is followed by **по** + the dative.

Мы **привыкнем к** русской еде.   Я **скучаю по** маме и папе.
We'll get used to Russian food.   I miss mom and dad.

Note that the perfective **привыкнуть** is tagged not as **НУ**, but as **(НУ)** — with parentheses. This marks it as a "**disappearing НУ**" verb, meaning that the suffix -**ну** simply "disappears" in past-tense forms. Compare the forms here with those of a regular **НУ** verb like **отдохнуть** (отдохнул, отдохнула, отдохнуло, отдохнули).

привыкать АЙ / привыкнуть (НУ) к чему	
to get used to	
привыка́ю	привы́кну
↓	↓
привыка́ешь	привы́кнешь
привыка́ет	привы́кнет
привыка́ем	привы́кнем
привыка́ете	привы́кнете
привыка́ют	привы́кнут
привыка́й!	привы́кни!
привыка́л	привы́к
привыка́ла	привы́кла
привыка́ло	привы́кло
привыка́ли	привы́кли

скучать АЙ / соскучиться[1] И по кому
to miss / to come to miss

[1] The perfective form of this verb includes a reflexive particle, -**ся**. We'll learn more about this in tomorrow's lesson.

Наше будущее — коммунизм! "Our future is Communism!" Remember that — **по Марксу** — Socialism was only a temporary stage. The goal was to build Communism, a kind of utopia whose guiding principal was to be: **От каждого по способностям, каждому по потребностям.** "From each (person) according to his abilities (dative plural!), to each according to his needs."

Ты привыкнешь... 1. к _____ (русская кухня)? **25.b**

2. к _____ (русский менталитет)?

3. к _____ (русская погода)?

Ты привык(ла)... 4. к _____ (русский язык)?

5. к _____ (русский алфавит)?

6. к _____ (русская грамматика)?

Ты скучаешь... 7. по _____ (собака / кошка)?

8. по _____ (дом)?

9. по _____ (семья)?

10. по _____ (брат / сестра)?

11. по _____ (старый друг)?

12. по _____ (старая подруга)?

---

1. По кому (или чему) ты **скучаешь** сейчас? По семье? По собаке или кошке? Или по дому вообще?

2. Ты **соскучишься** по дому, когда ты будешь в России? А ты **будешь скучать** по России, когда ты будешь дома?

3. К чему ты **привыкнешь** в России, а к чему ты никогда **не привыкнешь**? Почему?

25.5 A comparison of predicate adverbs and predicate adjectives

Having introduced short-form predicate adjectives yesterday, we can summarize two extremely common constructions in Russian. They are both very simple, but they differ greatly in terms of grammar. This difference is often hard for English speakers to grasp, since the English translations are often grammatically identical.

The tables below present an example of each construction, in all three tenses. The **English** translations are the same grammatically: "My brother is hungry" and "My brother is cold." That is, both include a **subject**, a linking verb, and a **predicate adjective**. Notice how in the first table the Russian construction is the same as that of the English: it features a **subject**, and a verb and adjective that **change** to agree with that subject. Any construction in Russian that has a subject (in the **nominative** case!) can be called a "**subject construction.**"

The second table features "**subjectless constructions.**" How do we know these sentences are **subjectless**? Because they contain no word in the **nominative** case. That which is the subject of the English translation (my brother) appears in the **dative** in Russian. So, the **idiom** in the two languages is completely different.

As we learned in 21.5, many basic feelings are expressed using predicate adverbs like **холодно**. Like all adverbs, they never change their form, and are used with the dative ("it is cold **for** someone"). Most importantly, as in all subjectless constructions, the **verb can only appear in the neuter singular**; since there is no subject, the verb can't change form to agree with it. This is most apparent in the past tense (in the black box below).

subject constructions				subjectless constructions		
nominative	linking verb	predicate adj.		dative	linking verb	predicate adv.
Мой брат		голоден.		**Моему брату**		холодно.
Моя сестра		голодна.		**Моей сестре**		холодно.
My brother / sister	is	hungry.		My brother / sister	is	cold.
Мой брат	был	голоден.		**Моему брату**	было	холодно.
Моя сестра	была	голодна.		**Моей сестре**	было	холодно.
My brother / sister	was	hungry.		My brother / sister	was	cold.
Мой брат	будет	голоден.		**Моему брату**	будет	холодно.
Моя сестра	будет	голодна.		**Моей сестре**	будет	холодно.
My brother / sister	will be	hungry.		My brother / sister	will be	cold.

25.c *Use the following short-form predicate **adjectives** in **subject** constructions. The verb and adjective must **agree** with the subject.*

1. **гот_о_в**: He is ready. _____. He was ready. _____.

2. **пьян**: They are drunk. _____. They were drunk. _____.

3. **з_а_нят**: She is busy. _____. She will be busy. _____.

4. **ув_е_рен**: She was sure. _____. He was sure. _____.

5. **б_о_лен**: They were sick. _____. They will be sick. _____.

....

*Use the following predicate **adverbs** in **subjectless** constructions. Remember, the verb must always appear in the **neuter singular**.*

6. **гр_у_стно**: He feels sad. _____. He felt sad. _____.

7. **в_е_село**: They are happy. _____. They were happy. _____.

8. **хорош_о_**: She feels good. _____. She will feel good. _____.

9. **ск_у_чно**: She was bored. _____. He was bored. _____.

10. **пл_о_хо**: They felt bad. _____. They will feel bad. _____.

25.6 Expressing obligation with the short-form adjective до́лжен

In 21.6, we introduced modal adverbs like **надо** (it is necessary), **нельзя** (one may not) and **можно** (it is possible, one may), which are used like predicate adverbs and followed by an infinitive, as in "Мне **надо** раб_о_тать."

There is also one short-form **predicate adjective** that can be followed by an infinitive in this manner: **должен, должна, должно_, должны**. It expresses obligation[1]; we can often best translate it using "should" or "supposed" or "ought," as in: "**Я до́лжен раб_о_тать**" (I ought, I should, I am supposed to work).

Let's underscore the difference in these constructions once more. Since **до́лжен** is a predicate **adjective**, it is used in **subject** constructions and changes to agree with its subject. Compare it to the **adverb надо**, which is used in **subjectless** constructions with the dative; it never changes form, and is used with neuter singular verbs.

subject constructions with ДОЛЖЕН			subjectless constructions with НАДО		
nominative	adj. + verb	infinitive	dative	adv. + verb	infinitive
Мой брат	**до́лжен**	**раб_о_тать.**	**Моему́ бра́ту**	**надо**	**раб_о_тать.**
Мо_я_ сестра	**должна**	**раб_о_тать.**	**Мо_е_й сестре**	**надо**	**раб_о_тать.**
My brother / sister	is supposed to	work.	My brother / sister	has to	work.
Мой брат	**до́лжен был**	**раб_о_тать.**	**Моему́ бра́ту**	надо б_ы_ло	**раб_о_тать.**
Мо_я_ сестра	**должна была**	**раб_о_тать.**	**Мо_е_й сестре**	надо б_ы_ло	**раб_о_тать.**
My brother / sister	was supposed to	work.	My brother / sister	had to	work.
Мой брат	**до́лжен будет**	**раб_о_тать.**	**Моему́ бра́ту**	**надо будет**	**раб_о_тать.**
Мо_я_ сестра	**должна будет**	**раб_о_тать.**	**Мо_е_й сестре**	**надо будет**	**раб_о_тать.**
My brother / sister	will be supposed to	work.	My brother / sister	will have to	work.

25.d *Rewrite the sentences with **надо** using **должен** — and vice versa! Watch the nominative and dative forms, and verb forms!*

1. Нам **надо** заплат_и_ть за к_о_фе. _____.

2. Мо_я_ сестра **должна** куп_и_ть подарок. _____.

3. Мой брат **до́лжен был** позвон_и_ть м_а_ме. _____.

4. Н_а_шему др_у_гу **надо б_ы_ло** пом_о_чь нам. _____.

5. Профе́ссору **надо будет** пом_о_чь нам. _____.

128 [1] This form is derived from **долг**, a noun meaning duty or debt — hence, obligation.

day 26: reflexive verbs

the reflexive particle **ся**; overview of the meanings of reflexive verbs;
reflexive and passive meanings; saying "to study for";
focus on passive meanings

Учи́ться, учи́ться и учи́ться. Study, study, and study.

26.1 The reflexive particle -ся

This chapter includes several reflexive verbs. We will use the term **reflexive verb** to refer to any verb that includes the **reflexive particle**: -ся (-сь). The next few lessons will look at several different meanings of reflexive verbs.

First, let's simply learn how to use the reflexive particle. It's quite simple: just **add** it to **any ordinary verb form**. If the given verb form ends in a **consonant**, add -ся. If it ends in a **vowel**, add -сь.

учи́ть И / научи́ть И кого + inf.	
to teach	
учу́	научу́
учи́шь	научи́шь
учи́т	научи́т
учи́м	научи́м
учи́те	научи́те
у́чат	нау́чат
учи́!	научи́!
учи́л	научи́л
учи́ла	научи́ла
учи́ло	научи́ло
учи́ли	научи́ли

учи́ться И / научи́ться И + inf.	
to learn; to study (in college)	
учу́сь	научу́сь
учи́шься	научи́шься
учи́тся	научи́тся
учи́мся	научи́мся
учи́тесь	научи́тесь
у́чатся	нау́чатся
учи́сь!	научи́сь!
учи́лся	научи́лся
учи́лась	научи́лась
учи́лось	научи́лось
учи́лись	научи́лись

26.2 Pronouncing the reflexive particle

The reflexive particle -ся is very common, and Russians have grown slightly "lazy" in pronouncing it clearly in the third-person and infinitive forms (that is, **following а т**). Be sure to practice pronouncing these forms as follows:

write:	**учи́ться**	*write:*	**учится**	*write:*	**учатся**
but say:	**учица**	*but say:*	**учица**	*but say:*	**учаца**

Note that **all remaining forms** are pronounced **as written** — including, for example, **учимся** and **учи́лся**.

26.a *Practice using **present-tense** forms of **учи́ться**, with the reflexive particle. Here we'll use it in the sense of "studying in college."*

1. Где ты _____?

2. Ты хо́чешь _____ в Росси́и?

3. Мой друг о́чень хорошо́ _____.

4. Где вы _____?

5. Твой брат и сестра́ хорошо́ _____?

6. Я _____ в Росси́и. Она́ то́же _____ в Росси́и.

*Try some **past-tense** forms of **учи́ться**.*

7. Где ты (m.) _____?

8. Где ты (f.) _____?

9. Где вы _____?

10. Они́ _____ в Росси́и и́ли нет?

26.3 The meanings of reflexive verbs: an overview

So, when we add a reflexive ending to a verb, how does the meaning change? We can break down the various meanings of reflexive verbs into the following four categories. Today, we'll focus on the first two.

1) **reflexivity** (not all reflexive forms are "reflexive" in terms of meaning!)
2) **passivity**
3) **reciprocity**
4) **spontaneity**

26.4 Reflexivity and passivity

Some verbs with the reflexive particle have **reflexive meaning** in the strict sense. That is, their action is **reflected back** onto their **subject**. For example, in English, one can teach someone, or one can teach **one- self**. The second meaning is reflexive. If "I" am the subject, my action (teaching) is directed back at the subject — at myself.

Бу́дем учи́ться, труди́ться, расти́. К звёздам далёким проло́жим пути́!
We will learn, labor, and grow. We will blaze trails to the distant stars!

Let's begin with the Russian verb **учи́ть / научи́ть** (to teach) — **without** the reflexive particle. This is a **transitive** verb — that is, it **can take a direct object**: we can teach someone or something. Look at the Russian examples below. Note the direct objects (the people we're teaching) in the **accusative**. We can add an **infinitive**, as in English: to teach someone **to speak**. Or, we can add a noun (a subject or skill) in the **dative**.[1]

Ма́ма **научи́ла** меня́ чита́ть.	Он **учит** нас говори́ть по-ру́сски.	Они́ **учат** нас ру́сскому языку́.[1] (!)
Mom taught me to read.	He's teaching us to speak Russian.	They're teaching us Russian.

What if we add the reflexive particle: **учи́ться / научи́ться**. The reflexive particle (**ся / сь**) essentially means "oneself." It can lend reflexive meaning to a transitive verb: instead of teaching **someone else**, the subject can now teach him- or herself to do something. This is **reflexive meaning** in a strict sense: "**to teach oneself**."

But, depending on the context, we might understand this same verb in a slightly different way. Instead of teaching **someone else**, the subject is **being taught**. This is the **passive** meaning: "**to be taught**."

учи́ть И / научи́ть И	учи́ться И / научи́ться И	
Профе́ссор нас **учит** чита́ть.	*reflexive:* Я **научи́лся** чита́ть.	*passive:* Я **научи́лся** чита́ть.
The professor is teaching us to read.	I taught myself how to read.	I was taught how to read.

[1] This is an extremely unusual and counter-intuitive use of the dative, since we would likely expect the opposite: to teach a subject (**accusa- tive**) to a person (**direct object**). To translate literally, "They're teaching us to Russian."

Of course, we could translate either of these sentences more loosely, as "**I learned how to read.**" But, as always, note how the most natural English translation may obscure the literal sense of the Russian construction.

Let's look at one more example. The verb **мыть / помыть** (to wash) is **transitive** — that is, we can wash **something** (dishes, for example). We can add the reflexive particle to create a new verb, **мыться / помыться**. Again, depending on the context, this reflexive verb could have a strictly **reflexive** sense (to wash oneself), or a **passive** sense (to be washed). But in either sense the reflexive verb is **intransitive**: we cannot add a direct object.

мыть ОЙ / **помыть** ОЙ	**мыться** ОЙ / **помыться** ОЙ	
Я **мою** посуду.[1]	*reflexive:* Я **моюсь** каждый день.	*passive:* Посуда **моется** каждый день.
I am washing the dishes.	I bathe ("wash myself") every day.	The dishes are washed every day.

---

*Try creating **new aspectual pairs** by adding the reflexive particle. Can you explain their possible meanings, and conjugate them?* **26.b**

1. **учить** И / **научить** И: to teach _____ / _____

2. **мыть** ОЙ / **помыть** ОЙ: to wash _____ / _____

3. **делать** АЙ / **сделать** АЙ: to do _____ / _____

4. **писать** А / **написать** А: to write _____ / _____

5. **продавать** АВАЙ / **продать**: to sell _____ / _____

---

*Use the correct form of **учить / научить** and **мыть / помыть** to translate — be sure to add the reflexive particle if necessary!* **26.c**

1. Are you working or studying? Ты рабо́таешь или _____?

2. My brother learned to dance. Мой брат _____ танцева́ть.

3. My sister is learning to draw. Моя́ сестра́ _____ рисова́ть.

4. Dad is teaching us to cook (гото́вить). Па́па _____ нас гото́вить.

5. The professor is teaching us Russian. Профе́ссор _____ нас ру́сскому языку́.

6. We are learning Russian. Мы _____ ру́сскому языку́.

7. We were washing the car. Мы _____ маши́ну.

8. The car gets washed very rarely (ре́дко). Маши́на о́чень ре́дко _____.

9. One should bathe every day! На́до _____ ка́ждый день!

10. I'll bathe first, then wash the dishes. Я снача́ла _____, а пото́м _____ посу́ду.

Не сра́зу Москва́ стро́илась. Moscow wasn't built overnight (right away, in an instant). Compare the transitive "to build": стро́ить И / постро́ить И

26.5 Saying "to study for"

To say that we're studying for a test (or preparing for some other event), we can use a reflexive verb with a strictly **reflexive** meaning: literally, "**to prepare oneself**" for something. This verb is followed by **к + the dative**. Note that if we are speaking specifically of getting ready for a test (that is, **studying**), the perfective must have the prefix **под**.

гото́вить И / пригото́вить И
to prepare, cook

гото́виться И / пригото́виться И к чему
to prepare oneself, get ready for

гото́виться И / подгото́виться И к чему
to study for (an exam, etc.)

---

*Fill in the blanks with 1) the correct form of **гото́виться / подгото́виться** (to study for) and 2) the dative form of the nouns.* **26.d**

1. Я не могу́ смотре́ть телеви́зор. Я сего́дня _____ к _____ (экза́мен).

2. Мы вчера́ о́чень до́лго _____ к _____ (экза́мен) по _____ (фи́зика).

3. Контро́льная по _____ (ру́сский язы́к) о́чень тру́дная. На́до хорошо́ _____!

4. К _____ (како́й экза́мен) ты сейча́с _____? К _____ (хи́мия)?

---

[1] As we've noted, the Russian word for "dishes" is **singular** only.
[2] In fact, one could also say "**Мы у́чим ру́сский язы́к**"(!), but don't let this somewhat exceptional example confuse you!

26.6 Focus on passive meanings of reflexive verbs

Let's focus on verbs that can add a reflexive particle to produce a new verb that is **passive** in meaning (that is, not reflexive in a strict sense). Almost any verb can be made passive in this way, assuming its passive form makes sense! Try translating the examples for each verb below, both with and without the reflexive particle.

продав<u>а</u>ть АВ<u>А</u>Й / **прод<u>а</u>ть**	to sell	Он<u>и</u> продаю<u>т</u> п<u>и</u>во здесь?
продав<u>а</u>ться АВ<u>А</u>Й / **прод<u>а</u>ться**	to be sold	П<u>и</u>во здесь продаётся?
пис<u>а</u>ть A^{shift} / **напис<u>а</u>ть** A	to write	Я напиш<u>у</u> теб<u>е</u> письм<u>о</u>.
пис<u>а</u>ться A / **напис<u>а</u>ться** A	to be written	Как <u>э</u>то сл<u>о</u>во п<u>и</u>шется?
д<u>е</u>лать АЙ / **сд<u>е</u>лать** АЙ	to do	Я всё сд<u>е</u>лаю з<u>а</u>втра.
д<u>е</u>латься АЙ / **сд<u>е</u>латься** АЙ	to be done	Почем<u>у</u> <u>э</u>то д<u>е</u>лается?
гот<u>о</u>вить И / **пригот<u>о</u>вить** И	to cook	М<u>а</u>ма ч<u>а</u>сто гот<u>о</u>вит борщ.
гот<u>о</u>виться И / **пригот<u>о</u>виться** И	to be cooked	Борщ д<u>о</u>лго гот<u>о</u>вится.
фотограф<u>и</u>ровать ОВА / **сфотограф<u>и</u>ровать** ОВА	to photograph	Х<u>о</u>чешь, я теб<u>я</u> сфотограф<u>и</u>рую?
фотограф<u>и</u>роваться ОВА / **сфотограф<u>и</u>роваться** ОВА	to be photographed	Х<u>о</u>чешь сфотограф<u>и</u>роваться?

26.e *Supply the verb. Think very carefully — do you need the reflexive particle or not? As always, watch aspect and tense!*

1. I want to get my picture taken.

   Я хоч<u>у</u> _____.

   OK, I'll take your picture ("photograph you").

   Хорош<u>о</u>, я теб<u>я</u> _____.

2. How is this word spelled? ("how is it written?")

   Как это сл<u>о</u>во _____?

   I can write it for you.

   Я мог<u>у</u> его _____ для теб<u>я</u>.

3. We cooked borshch yesterday.

   Мы вчер<u>а</u> _____ борщ.

   It "was cooked" for a really long time.

   Он _____ <u>о</u>чень д<u>о</u>лго.

4. Is milk sold here?

   Молок<u>о</u> здесь _____?

   Yes, but we've already sold all (of it).

   Да, но (мы) всё уж<u>е</u> _____.

5. Will you show me how this is done?

   Ты мне пок<u>а</u>жешь, как <u>э</u>то _____?

   No. I'll just simply do it.

   Нет, я <u>э</u>то пр<u>о</u>сто _____.

---

1. Ты л<u>ю</u>бишь фотограф<u>и</u>ровать? Ты хор<u>о</u>ший фот<u>о</u>граф (photographer)? Что <u>и</u>ли ког<u>о</u> ты об<u>ы</u>чно фотограф<u>и</u>руешь?

2. Ты л<u>ю</u>бишь фотограф<u>и</u>роваться, <u>и</u>ли нет? Почем<u>у</u> ты иногд<u>а</u> (sometimes) не х<u>о</u>чешь фотограф<u>и</u>роваться?

3. Ты д<u>о</u>лго б<u>у</u>дешь гот<u>о</u>виться к контр<u>о</u>льной по р<u>у</u>сскому язык<u>у</u>? Ты хорош<u>о</u> подгот<u>о</u>вишься?

4. Ты л<u>ю</u>бишь гот<u>о</u>вить? Что у теб<u>я</u> д<u>о</u>лго (for a long time) гот<u>о</u>вится, а что б<u>ы</u>стро (quickly)?

Уваж<u>а</u>емые пассаж<u>и</u>ры! Esteemed passengers!

Announcements and signs in the subway are a part of one's daily life in Moscow or Petersburg. Here are two examples with **-ся**:

Осор<u>о</u>жно, дв<u>е</u>ри закрыв<u>а</u>ются!
Careful, the doors are closing, "being closed!" (said over the loudspeaker)

Не прислон<u>я</u>ться!
Don't lean ("lean yourself")! (printed on subway doors)

By the way, don't forget: **Б<u>у</u>дьте вза<u>и</u>мно в<u>е</u>жливы!** Be mutually polite!

day 27: notes on transitivity

reflexive verbs and transitivity; beginning and ending; reciprocity and spontaneity with reflexive verbs; the subjectless verb **хоте́ться**

Они́ верну́лись! They have returned! The sign atop the traincar reads "**Мы из Берли́на**" — "We're (returning) from Berlin."

27.1 Notes on reflexive verbs and transitivity

We've mentioned that a verb is **transitive** if it can take a direct object. This seems clear enough. But the concept of transitivity can be tricky for English speakers, largely because English verbs are often highly ambiguous in this regard. Compare these two "dictionary entries":

возвраща́ть АЙ / **верну́ть** НУ	to return
возвраща́ться АЙ / **верну́ться** НУ	to return

What's the difference in these verbs, if the translation is the same?! Notice how the English verb "to return" can be used in a **transitive** sense, as in "to return a book," and in an **intransitive** sense, as in "he returned home." This important distinction is actually much more apparent in the Russian: in verbs of this kind, the pair **without** the reflexive particle is typically **transitive**, while the pair **with** the particle is **intransitive**. Compare these examples:

Мне на́до **верну́ть** кни́гу.	I need to return the book.
Мне на́до **верну́ться** домо́й.	I need to return home.

It may sometimes help to think of a reflexive verb more literally to underscore its meaning — as in, "he **returned himself** home."

ОНИ ВЕРНУЛИ СВОЁ СЧАСТЬЕ!

Они́ верну́ли своё сча́стье! They have regained ("returned") their happiness! We might also say: "Он верну́лся домо́й по́сле войны́" (He returned home after the war.)

27.2 A look at verbs whose transitivity is ambiguous in English

In short, transitivity in English verbs is often vague: where Russian typically draws a clear distinction with two separate forms — one transitive, one intransitive — English often uses the same form for both. As a result, English speakers are often "lazy" when it comes to making this all-important distinction in Russian.

Let's take two more verbs — compare the English and Russian, and note the clear distinction in the Russian.

ломать АЙ / **сломать** АЙ	to break (transitive!)	Я опять **сломал** телефон. I broke my phone again.
ломаться АЙ / **сломаться** АЙ	to break (intransitive!)	Телефон опять **сломался**. The phone broke again.

начинать АЙ / **начать** /Н[end]	to begin (transitive!)	Она **начала** новую работу. She began a new job.
начинаться АЙ / **начаться** /Н	to begin (intransitive!)	Балет скоро **начнётся**. The ballet will begin soon.

As you continue to study Russian, you'll notice a great many such examples.

27.a Use **past-tense** forms of reflexive verbs. Follow the same rules as always — just add the **reflexive** particle! Use the **perfective**.

ломаться АЙ / **сломаться** АЙ to break (said of appliances, etc.)	телевизор... _____	холодильник... _____
	машина... _____	радио... _____
разбиваться АЙ / **разбиться** Ь to break, shatter (e.g. a window)	окно... _____	стакан... _____
	лампа... _____	зеркало... _____
начинаться АЙ / **начаться** /Н to begin	фильм... _____	балет... _____
	опера... _____	экзамен... _____

27.b This exercise lists all of the verbs we've seen with ambiguous transitivity in English. Choose verb forms carefully when translating.

возвращать АЙ / **вернуть** НУ
возвращаться АЙ / **вернуться** НУ
to return

1. I think that your dog will return home (домой) soon.

   Я думаю, что твоя собака скоро _____ домой.

2. The student returned the book to the professor.

   Студент _____ книгу профессору.

ломать АЙ / **сломать** АЙ
ломаться АЙ / **сломаться** АЙ
to break (appliances, etc.)

3. Our son broke our computer.

   Наш сын _____ наш компьютер.

4. The computer is always breaking.

   Компьютер постоянно (всегда) _____.

разбивать АЙ / **разбить** Ь
разбиваться АЙ / **разбиться** Ь
to break (to shatter)

5. The child accidentally broke the plate (тарелка).

   Ребёнок нечаянно _____ тарелку.

6. The plate broke.

   Тарелка _____.

открывать АЙ / **открыть** ОЙ[stem]
открываться АЙ / **открыться** ОЙ
to open

7. My uncle opened a new restaurant (ресторан).

   Мой дядя _____ новый ресторан.

8. The restaurant opens every morning (утро).

   Ресторан _____ каждое утро.

закрывать АЙ / **закрыть** ОЙ[stem]
закрываться АЙ / **закрыться** ОЙ
to close

9. Who closed the window?

   Кто _____ окно?

10. When does the store (магазин) close?

    Когда магазин _____?

1. У тебя телефон часто **ломается**? Он недавно (recently) **сломался**? А кто его **сломал**?

2. Ты часто **разбивал**(а) посуду, когда ты был(а) ребёнком[1]? А мама была довольна, когда посуда **разбивалась**?

27.3 Beginning and ending

As we've seen, the verb "to begin" (**начинать / начать**) should also be included in our list of verbs with ambiguous transitivity in English, along with "to end" or "to finish" (**заканчивать / закончить**).

To this group of useful verbs, we should add another verb meaning "to stop" (**переставать / перестать**). But note that this verb can never appear with the reflexive particle.

Review the somewhat tricky conjugations for the pairs to the right.

переставать АВАЙ / перестать H[stem] + inf.		начинать АЙ / начать /H[end] + inf.		
to stop		to begin, start		
перестаю	перестану	начинаю	начну	
перестаёшь	перестанешь	начинаешь	начнёшь	
перестаёт	перестанет	начинает	начнёт	
перестаём	перестанем	начинаем	начнём	
перестаёте	перестанете	начинаете	начнёте	
перестают	перестанут	начинают	начнут	
перестав**ай**!	перестан**ь**!	начин**ай**!	начн**и**!	
переставал	перестал	начинал	начал	начался[2]
переставала	перестала	начинала	начала	началась
переставало	перестало	начинало	начало	началось
переставали	перестали	начинали	начали	начались

Here are some examples with all three pairs. All can be followed by an **infinitive**, but it must be **imperfective**!

начинать АЙ / начать /H[end] + inf.	заканчивать АЙ / закончить И	переставать АВАЙ / перестать H[stem]
начинаться АЙ / начаться /H	заканчиваться АЙ / закончиться И	
to begin, start	to end, finish	to stop
Я **начала** читать роман.	Я **закончила читать** роман.	Я **перестала** читать роман.
I began to read a novel.	I finished reading a novel.	I stopped reading the novel.
Я **начала** роман.	Я **закончила** роман.	
I began the novel.	I finished the novel.	
Балет **начался**.	Балет **закончился**.	
The ballet began.	The ballet ended.	

начинать АЙ / начать /H[end] + inf.	
начинаться АЙ / начаться /H	
to begin, start	

1. When does the opera (опера) start?

Когда опера _____?

2. My sister is starting a new job (работа).

Моя сестра _____ новую работу.

3. I'll start preparing dinner soon (скоро).

Я скоро _____ готовить ужин.

заканчивать АЙ / закончить И
заканчиваться АЙ / закончиться И
to end, finish

4. Have you finished the article?

Ты уже _____ статью?

5. I (f.) finally (наконец) finished writing the article.

Я наконец _____ писать статью.

6. When will the ballet (балет) end?

Когда балет _____?

переставать АВАЙ / перестать H[stem]
to stop

7. He would often stop working when he felt sad.

Он часто _____ работать, когда ему было грустно.

8. I'll stop working soon.

Я скоро _____ работать.

Всё хорошо, что хорошо кончается. All's well that ends well. **кончаться АЙ / кончиться** И also means "to end" (or, "to run out").

[1] Here **ребёнок** is in the **instrumental** case, often used for predicate nouns. We'll cover this in detail in Chapter 5.
[2] Note the unusual stress pattern in the reflexive.

135

27.4 Reciprocity with reflexive verbs

As the examples thus far suggest, most verbs with reflexive particles can be understood as either **reflexive** in meaning (again, in the strict sense of the subject directing action back upon itself), or **passive** in meaning.

Less frequently, reflexive verbs may be understood as **reciprocal** in meaning, when two or more subjects are doing something reciprocally (that is, **to each other**). For now, we'll look at only two very common examples:

видеть Е / увидеть Е	to see	Я **увижу** тебя завтра.	I'll see you tomorrow.
видеться Е / увидеться Е	to see each other	Мы скоро **увидимся**.	We'll see each other soon.
встречать АЙ / встретить И	to meet	Я **встречу** тебя завтра.	I'll meet you tomorrow.
встречаться АЙ / встретиться И	to meet up	Мы скоро **встретимся**.	We'll meet up soon.

One **word of warning**: whenever we learn a new verb form (like the reciprocal forms above), it can be tempting to want to create such a form for any Russian verb we know. Unfortunately, this doesn't always work. Many (in fact, most!) verbs simply don't form **reciprocal** reflexive verbs of the kind shown above.[1]

For example, knowing that "**любить**" means "to love," one might be tempted to create a verb "**любиться**," meaning "to love one another," as in "**Они любятся**." Alas, this simply isn't said. Instead, most verbs will employ a **reciprocal pronoun** construction that we'll learn on Day 49: "**Они любят друг друга**."

27.d

видеть Е / увидеть Е
видеться Е / увидеться Е
to see / to see each other

1. They see each other very rarely.

   Они очень редко _____.

2. When we were in college (учились) we would see each other every day.

   Когда мы учились, мы _____ каждый день.

3. I saw him yesterday (use the imperfective — i.e., "saw," not "caught sight of").

   Я его _____ вчера.

4. Goodbye! We'll see each other tomorrow.

   До свидания! Завтра _____.

встречать АЙ / встретить И
встречаться АЙ / встретиться И
to meet / to meet up

5. They met me at the train station.

   Они меня _____ на вокзале.

6. We often run into each other.

   Мы часто _____.

7. Where do you want to meet up?

   Где ты хочешь _____?

8. We used to meet up quite often.

   Мы _____ довольно часто.

Как встретишь Новой год, так его и проведёшь. As you (will) meet the New Year, so too will you spend it (i.e., party well on New Year's Eve!).

27.5 Spontaneity with reflexive verbs

Finally, let's look at a fourth and final possible meaning of reflexive verbs: they can convey a sense of **spontaneity**. There's no doubt that this fourth meaning is considerably more nebulous than the other three, but sometimes this is the best way to attempt to understand why a verb includes the reflexive particle.

Take the verb **улыбаться** АЙ (to smile). In what sense can we interpret the reflexive particle? It's not **reflexive** in a strict sense (to smile oneself?); it's not **passive** (to be smiled?); and it's not **reciprocal** (to "smile at each other" would be "**друг другу улыбаться**"). Only the fourth option — **spontaneity** — remains. And, on reflection, it seems to make sense: one can think of smiling as something that tends to happen spontaneously. Similar examples include **смеяться** А (to laugh) and **бояться** ЖА (to be afraid). We'll study these verbs in depth later.

In fact, many such verbs **cannot** be used at all **without** the reflexive particle. That is, the forms **улыбать**, **смеять**, and **боять** simply don't exist! Tomorrow, we'll see more verbs that **always have the reflexive particle**.

[1] The best tip for avoiding such mistakes is to refrain, for now at least, from "inventing" any verb forms that aren't presented in our vocabulary. In time, you'll develop a much better sense for which verbs can be used in which ways, and what simply "isn't said" in Russian.

27.6 The subjectless verb хоте́ться

Now, let's introduce a very peculiar type of verb. From the verb **хоте́ть / захоте́ть** (to want), we can form the reflexive verb **хоте́ться / захоте́ться**. In a sense, we might think of it too as conveying **spontaneity**.

But what exactly does this verb mean? It's hard to explain — because English has no such verbs: this is our first example of a **subjectless** verb. We've seen several important subjectless expressions (12.2, 21.5), and discussed how any verbs in such expressions can only appear in the **neuter singular**, since they have no subject to agree with. Now, we have a **verb** that is **itself** always "subjectless." It can only appear in the **neuter singular.**

If we use **хоте́ть**, we include a subject, and such phrases translate easily into English: **Я хочу́ танцева́ть** (I want to dance). But the subjectless **Хо́чется танцева́ть** cannot be translated directly into English. The verb **хо́чется** means something like "there is a wanting" or "an urge is being felt," and suggests spontaneity, as opposed to the deliberate action of a subject. If we want to "tie down" this urge to the person feeling it, we must use the **dative**: **Мне хо́чется танцева́ть**. Note carefully: **no nominative** case — thus, no grammatical **subject** in the Russian!

In one sense, we can convey the meaning of the Russian reasonably well: "I feel like dancing," as opposed to "I want to dance." But note how, in any attempted translation of a subjectless expression, English inevitably **introduces a subject**: "I" feel like dancing. This may seem like a minor point. But, as we'll see in time, English's insistence on a grammatical subject can hamper its ability to capture spontaneous actions with the directness that Russian can; English subtly suggests that some subject is somehow always "in control" of the situation.[1]

A particularly vivid example is the verb "to vomit" (!). In English, we sovereignly declare, "**I vomited**." But Russian uses a subjectless verb, with "me" as a direct object: "**Меня́ вы́рвало**." (The basic verb here, рвать, means "to tear" or "jerk"). Let's attempt to unpack this: "Some impersonal force, some 'it' that I cannot even concretize with a pronoun, tore at my gut. I would like to claim that I was, so to speak, 'driving the porcelain bus,' but in truth I must admit: I was merely along for the ride." Does this not better capture the experience of vomiting?

In short, subjectless constructions can convey a sense of being the passive object of obscure impersonal forces in a way that English can't. This can be deployed to powerful effect in literature.

Let's look at a complete set of examples of **хоте́ться** in all three tenses.

imperfective		perfective	
Мне **хо́чется** танцева́ть.	I feel like dancing.		
Мне **хоте́лось** танцева́ть.	I felt like dancing.	Мне **захоте́лось** танцева́ть.	I got the urge to dance.
Мне **бу́дет хоте́ться** танцева́ть.	I will feel like dancing.	Мне **захо́чется** танцева́ть.	I'll get the urge to dance.

Compare these forms with those of the subject verb **хоте́ть**: since the latter has a subject, its forms will change to agree with that subject. Look at the past tense, for example:

subject construction		subjectless construction	
Он **хоте́л** танцева́ть.	He wanted to dance.	Ему́ **хоте́лось** танцева́ть.	He felt like dancing.
Она́ **хоте́ла** танцева́ть.	She wanted to dance.	Ей **хоте́лось** танцева́ть.	She felt like dancing.
Они́ **хоте́ли** танцева́ть.	They wanted to dance.	Им **хоте́лось** танцева́ть.	They felt like dancing.

---

*Use the subjectless verb **хоте́ться / захоте́ться**. All forms must be **neuter singular!** Don't let the English idiom mislead you!*   **27.e**

1. Do you feel like speaking Russian?   Тебе́ _____ говори́ть по-ру́сски?

2. Maybe (мо́жет быть) you'll get the urge tomorrow.   Мо́жет быть тебе́ за́втра _____.

3. Did they often (ча́сто) feel like dancing?   Им ча́сто _____ танцева́ть?

4. We suddenly (вдруг) got the urge to watch television.   Нам вдруг _____ смотре́ть телеви́зор.

5. When I watch TV, I feel the urge to read.   Когда́ я смотрю́ телеви́зор, мне _____ чита́ть.

---

1. Тебе́ ча́сто хо́чется говори́ть по-ру́сски?   3. Тебе́ ча́сто хо́чется звони́ть дру́гу по телефо́ну?

2. Тебе́ ча́сто хо́чется есть, когда́ ты слу́шаешь ле́кцию?   4. Тебе́ неда́вно (recently) захоте́лось есть икру́?

---

[1] By the way, Nietzsche warned against letting such "prejudices of grammar" distort our view of the world. Descartes famously declared, "I think, therefore I am." But how does the fact that "thinking is going on" prove the existence of a thinking subject?

day 28: passive constructions; saying "to like"

the third-plural "passive"; verbs that always include the reflexive particle; liking with **нр<u>а</u>виться** / **понр<u>а</u>виться**; saying "I like you"; verbs for "trying"

Нигд<u>е</u> кр<u>о</u>ме, как в Моссельпр<u>о</u>ме! Nowhere but at Mosselprom! (note the rhyme!)

28.1 The third-plural "passive"

In theory — provided the result makes sense! — one can take almost any active, transitive Russian verb and make it passive by adding the reflexive particle. As we saw in 26.6, for example, we can take **продав<u>а</u>ть** / **прод<u>а</u>ть** (to sell) and create the passive **продав<u>а</u>ться** / **прод<u>а</u>ться** (to be sold).

However, such truly passive verbs often sound far too formal in everyday speech; while rarely "wrong," they are more at home in formal, written Russian. Instead, Russians typically substitute a **third-plural active** form. For example:

true passive verb		third-plural "passive"
Здесь **прода<u>ё</u>тся** икр<u>а</u>.	→	Здесь **продаю́т** икр<u>у</u>.
Caviar is sold here.		(They) sell caviar here.

To **point out the obvious**, the second example is **not actually passive** in terms of its grammar, but it is effectively equivalent to a passive construction in terms of its emphasis. Since its subject is an anonymous, understood "**they**," it shifts focus from the subject to the action itself and its object. So, we'll insist on calling these constructions **"passive"** (in quotation marks!) — all the more so since they are often easily translated into English using passive verbs ("Caviar is sold here" versus "They sell caviar here").

Such sentences often speak of customs, habits, etc. — "What one does."

В Росс<u>и</u>и **говор<u>я</u>т** по-р<u>у</u>сски.
In Russia they speak Russian.

В Росс<u>и</u>и **пьют** чай и **ед<u>я</u>т** икр<u>у</u>.
In Russia they drink tea and eat caviar.

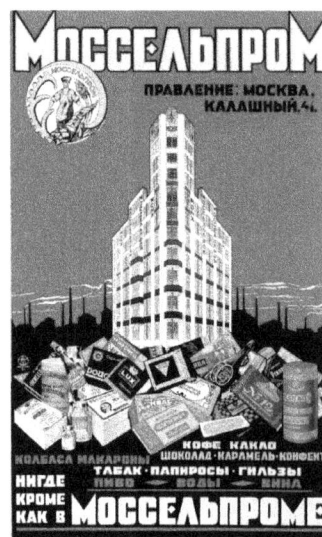

Что продаю́т? Что прода<u>ё</u>тся?
What is sold at Mosselprom?

К<u>о</u>фе (coffee), как<u>а</u>о (cocao), колбас<u>а</u> (sausage), макар<u>о</u>ны (macaroni), шокол<u>а</u>д (chocolate), кар<u>а</u>мель (caramel), конф<u>е</u>ты (candy), таб<u>а</u>к (tobacco), папир<u>о</u>сы (cigarettes), п<u>и</u>во (beer), в<u>о</u>ды (waters), в<u>и</u>на (wines).

What is a "форточка"?

Что **делают** в России, когда душно (stuffy) или жарко (hot)? Форточку **открывают**! Что такое форточка? Форточка — это небольшое окно, которое **открывается**, когда душно. Открыть форточку очень просто и легко. Можно, конечно, и всё окно открыть, если очень душно! Но так обычно **не делают**.

By the same token, when it's cold outside, be sure to avoid the dreaded **сквозняк** — a draft of air sneaking through an opening (the adverb **сквозь** means "through"). Many Russians have an almost superstitious dread of such drafts. Beyond matters of personal comfort, it is often thought that simply being cold can cause one to become ill.

Что делают в России? *Make a few generalizations about what Russians do. Put all objects in the accusative and verbs in the 3rd plural!*

Что едят в России?   В России едят...

_____	икра (caviar)	_____	рыба (fish)
_____	шоколад (chocolate)	_____	мясо (meat)
_____	колбаса (sausage)	_____	картошка (potatoes)

Что пьют в России?   В России пьют...

_____	вода (water)	_____	чай (tea)
_____	водка (vodka)	_____	кофе (coffee)
_____	квас (kvas)	_____	пиво (beer)
_____	вино (wine)	_____	шампанское

Как отдыхают в России?   В России...

готовить + шашлык (shish-kebabs):   _____

смотреть Eshift + футбол или хоккей: _____

читать АЙ + классическая литература: _____

гулять АЙ + по + город: _____

Кого читают в России?   В России читают...

(since all people are animate, treat these last names as *animate nouns* — or adjectives, if they have adjectival endings, as many Russian names do!)

_____	Пушкин	_____	Цветаева
_____	Ахматова	_____	Маяковский (adj.!)
_____	Достоевский (adj.!)	_____	Чехов
_____	Толстой (adj.!)	_____	Булгаков
_____	Толстая (adj.!)	_____	Платонов

Как говорится... / Как говорят...

The phrases just above are often used to **introduce** a folk saying (**поговорка**) or proverb (**пословица**) like those scattered throughout this book — in the sense of "as it is said..." or "as they say..." or, "as the saying goes..." Use it to introduce these sayings:

Нет худа без добра.	There's no bad without good (i.e. every cloud has a silver lining).
Кого люблю, того и бью.	He whom I love, I beat (i.e. tough love is better than indifference).
Бог дал, Бог и взял.	God gave, and God took (i.e. the Lord giveth, the Lord taketh away)
Ни рыба, ни мясо.	Neither fish nor meat (i.e., neither fish nor fowl).
Попытка не пытка.	An attempt isn't torture (i.e. doesn't hurt to try).
Спасибо не булькает.	Thank-you doesn't make bubbling sounds (like a liquid being poured).

The final saying implies that a simple "thank you" isn't enough; you expect to be thanked with vodka as well.

28.a *Give the questions and answers in Russian, using the third-plural "passive" construction — all verbs should be in the **third plural**!*

1. What do they do in Russia when it's stuffy?	Что _____ в России, когда душно?
They open the vent window (форточка)!	_____ форточку!
2. What do they do when it's hot?	А что _____, когда жарко?
They drink water or kvas!	_____ воду или квас!
3. What do they drink in Russia when it's cold?	Что _____ в России, когда холодно?
(They drink) tea or vodka!	(_____) чай или водку!
4. What do they eat when they drink vodka?	А что _____, когда _____ водку?
(They eat) black bread, pickles, and other snacks!	(_____) чёрный хлеб, огурцы, и другие закуски!
5. What do they do in Russia when they want to dance?	Что _____ в России, когда хочется танцевать?
They dance, of course!	_____, конечно!

28.2 Verbs that always include the reflexive particle

We can conclude our discussion of the meanings of reflexive particles with one final category: verbs that **always** include the reflexive particle, and for **no apparent reason**! That is to say, the **-ся** is present for, say, historical reasons, but it is impractical to try to "understand" it in terms of any of the four meanings we detailed earlier. For such verbs, simply memorize the pair, and remember never to leave off the **-ся**!

One such verb is **нравиться** И / **понравиться** И ("to be pleasing to..."), whose use we'll now examine.

28.3 Telling what you like with нравиться

Saying "I like" can seem tricky in Russian. In English, we begin with the subject ("I"); the thing we like is a direct object ("I like kvass.")

But the Russian **idiom** is very different. We use the verb **нравиться / понравиться** with the **dative**, and the thing we like is the **subject** of this verb. The correct Russian construction may be clearer if we rephrase the English a bit: not "**I like kvas**," but "**Kvas is pleasing to me**."

I like kvas. ➡ Kvas is pleasing to me. ➡ **Мне нравится квас.**

We can also use an **infinitive** as a subject, with the verb in neuter singular:

I like to read. ➡ To read is pleasing to me. ➡ **Мне нравится читать.**

This verb is often used to tell about "likes" or passing impressions. If you really **love** something in an intense or sustained way, use **любить**, just as in English — as in, "I love kvas" or "I love to read."

Я **люблю** квас.
I love kvas.

Я (очень) **люблю** читать.
I (really) love to read.

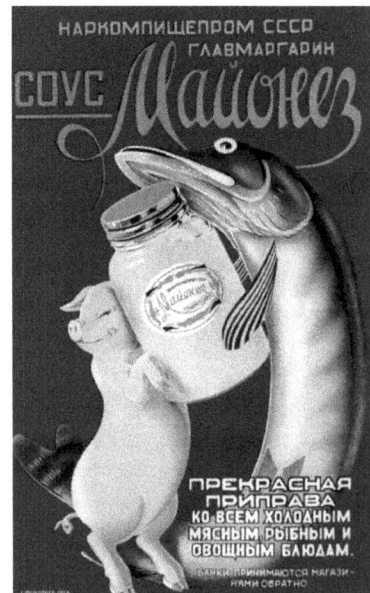

Тебе нравится майонез? Тогда (then, in that case) тебе понравится жить в России! Там очень любят майонез.

*Practing using **нравится** by asking whether your partner likes the following things and activities. Feel free to add your own!*

Тебе нравится...	литература?	майонез?	футбол?		читать поэзию?	танцевать?
	балет?	кетчуп?	хоккей?		петь?	работать?
	опера?	шоколад?	баскетбол?		учиться?	смотреть телевизор?
	кино?	борщ?	пинг-понг?		готовить?	говорить по телефону?

140

28.4 Sharing impressions with понр**а**виться

The imperfective verb **нр**а**виться** speaks to general, "ongoing" likes and dislikes, while the perfective **понр**а**виться** speaks to one-time impressions:

Мне всегд**а** **нр**а**вился** квас.	Мне **о**чень **понр**а**вился** квас вчер**а**.
I've always liked kvas.	I really liked the kvas yesterday.

Here are more examples with **понр**а**виться**:

Эта кн**и**га мне так **понр**а**вилась**!	Твой **н**о**вый** друг мне ср**а**зу **понр**а**вился**.
I liked this book so (much)!	I took an instant liking to your new friend.
Попр**о**буй квас! Теб**е** **понр**а**вится**!	Б**о**ря и Л**е**на теб**е** **понр**а**вятся**.
Try the kvas! You'll like it.	You're going to like Borya and Lena.

Use the **imperfective** to inquire whether someone has "ever" done something:

Ты **смотр**е**л** этот фильм?	Да, смотр**е**л. Мне **о**чень **понр**а**вился**.
Have you ever watched this film?	Yes, I have. I really liked it.

By the way, be careful when pronouncing "**мне**" in such sentences: if you don't enunciate the "**м**" sound clearly, then "**мне понр**а**вилось**" (etc.) can easily sound like its opposite (!) — "**не понр**а**вилось**."

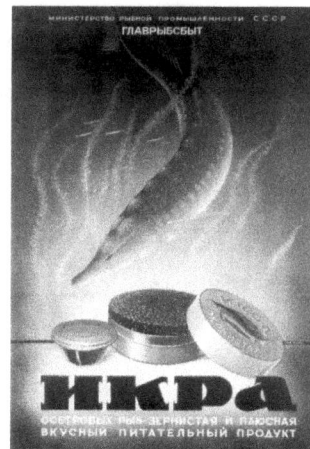

Ты пр**о**бовал(а) икр**у**? (Have you tried caviar?) Он**а** теб**е** понр**а**вилась, или нет?

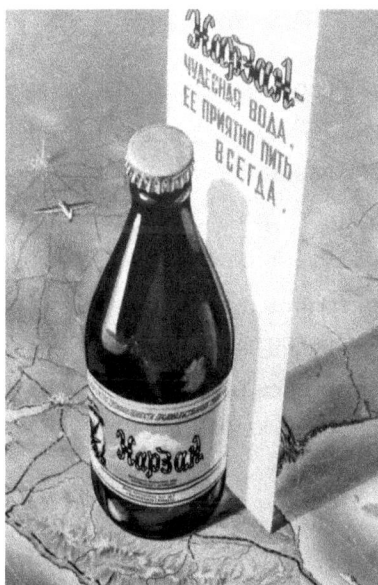

Нарз**а**н — чуд**е**сная вод**а**.
Её при**я**тно пить всегд**а**.

Narzan is wondrous water. It's always pleasant to drink it. (note the rhyme!)

Нарз**а**н — минер**а**льная вод**а**.

28.b

1. My friend (m.) likes Russian cinema.

   Мо**е**м**у** др**у**гу _____ р**у**сское кин**о**.

2. He really liked the Russian movie that we watched yesterday.

   Ем**у** **о**чень _____ р**у**сский фильм,

   кот**о**рый мы вчера посмотр**е**ли.

3. My sister always liked to read Russian literature.

   Мо**е**й сестр**е** всегд**а** _____ чит**а**ть р**у**сскую литерат**у**ру.

4. You'll like the borshch that I made for you.

   Теб**е** _____ борщ, кот**о**рый я теб**е** приготовил.

5. Our friend (f.) likes everything. She even (д**а**же) liked your pasta (п**а**ста).

   Н**а**шей подр**у**ге _____ всё.

   Ей _____ д**а**же тво**я** п**а**ста.

6. They like everyone. They even liked your mother-in-law (тёща).

   Им все _____.

   Им _____ д**а**же тво**я** тёща.

28.5 Saying "I like you"

What if we want to say things like "I like you" (that is, "You are pleasing to me.")? Then **ты** (or **вы**) would be our subject, and we'd need the **ты** form of **нр**а**виться**. Review the full set of conjugated forms to the right. They're a bit tricky — we have an **И verb** with a labial mutation in the **я** form, and, of course, the **reflexive particle** in all forms!

Ты мне **нр**а**вишься**!	Я теб**е** **нр**а**влюсь**?
I like you!	Do you like me?
Я ей не **понр**а**влюсь**.	Я ей не **понр**а**вился**.
She won't like me.	She didn't like me.

нр**а**виться И / понр**а**виться И кому	
to be pleasing to, "to like"	
нр**а**влюсь	понр**а**влюсь
↓	↓
нр**а**вишься	понр**а**вишься
нр**а**вится	понр**а**вится
нр**а**вимся	понр**а**вимся
нр**а**витесь	понр**а**витесь
нр**а**вятся	понр**а**вятся
нр**а**вься!	понр**а**вься!

28.c   1. I don't think that he'll like me.

     Я не ду́маю, что я ему́ _____.

2. They never liked us.

     Мы им никогда́ не _____.

3. Do you like me? I like you!

     Я тебе́ _____? Ты мне _____!

4. You'll like them, and they'll like you.

     Они́ тебе́ _____, и ты им _____.

5. It seems to me that they didn't like us.

     Мне ка́жется, что мы им не _____.

6. My sister will really like you. She likes everyone.

     Ты о́чень _____ мое́й сестре́.

     Ей все _____.

Зимо́й и ле́том вку́сно и поле́зно.
Ice cream (моро́женое): Tasty and
healthy in winter and summer.
Тебе́ нра́вится моро́женое?

28.6 Verbs for "trying"

There are three common verbs for "to try." Only the first can be used for trying new things, like food:

пробовать OVA / попробовать OVA	Ты не хо́чешь квас **попро́бовать**?	Да! Я никогда́ его́ не **про́бовала**!
to try (to "give a try")	Don't you want to try the kvas?	Sure! I've never tried it.

The other two can be followed by **infinitives**; the first suggests simply "**making an attempt**," while the second suggests serious or sustained **effort**. Both are examples of verbs that must **always** include the reflexive particle!

пытаться AЙ / попытаться AЙ	Я попыта́юсь ему́ **позвони́ть**.[1]	Мы **пыта́лись** откры́ть окно́.
to try, make an attempt	I'll try calling him.	We were trying to open the window.
стараться AЙ / постараться AЙ	Я ви́жу, что ты о́чень **стара́ешься**!	Я **постара́юсь** всё сде́лать.
to try to... ("to strive" to...)	I see you're really making an effort.	I'll do my best to get everything done.

28.d   1. Have you (вы) ever tried caviar? Do you want to try it?

     Вы _____ икру́? Хо́чешь её _____?

2. We really tried, but we didn't manage to solve the problem.

     Мы о́чень _____, но не суме́ли реши́ть зада́чу.

3. I'll try to make borshch tomorrow.

     Я _____ пригото́вить борщ за́втра.

4. I always strive to do everything on time (во́время).

     Я всегда́ _____ сде́лать всё во́время.

5. — Will you be able to help me?   — I don't know, but I'll do my best!

     — Ты смо́жешь мне помо́чь?

     — Не зна́ю, но я _____!

Моско́вский хле́бный квас.

Квас — традицио́нный ру́сский напи́ток (beverage). Его́ де́лают из хле́ба. Ты про́бовал(а) квас? Хо́чешь его́ попро́бовать? Тебе́ понра́вится.

As whether a partner has ever tried these things, and whether or not they want to try them.

Ты про́бовал(а)...	квас	кефи́р	творо́г	чёрный хлеб
Ты хо́чешь попро́бовать...	икра́	борщ	конья́к	шампа́нское

   [1] **пробовать / попробовать** can also be followed by an infinitive in this same meaning, as in: "**Я попро́бую ему́ позвони́ть.**"

day 29: giving commands with the imperative

forming the imperative using the "step-by-step" method; exceptions that can't be formed this way

Рабочий ударник, вступай в ряды авторов технической литературы! Shock-worker, join the ranks of authors of technical literature!

29.1 How to form the imperative

We've been providing imperative forms along with the conjugated forms of our verbs, and we've had a brief introduction to the imperative already. Now, in today's and tomorrow's lessons, we'll look at it in detail. While it's useful to practice imperative forms in terms of verb types (as in, **делать** АЙ → **делай**!, and so on for all АЙ verbs), there's also a **step-by-step** method for forming the imperative. It **almost always** works, for either aspect.

Just remove the ending (ют, ут, ят, ат) from the **они** form of the verb. If you're left with a **vowel**, things are easy:

infinitive	они form	remove the ending		add	ты	вы: add -те[1]
дел**а**ть	**дел**ают	**дел**а- (vowel)		й	**дел**ай!	**дел**айте!
					не **дел**ай!	не **дел**айте!

But, if you're left with a consonant when you remove the ending from the **они** form, there's an **extra step** to take: we have to consider the **stress** on the **я** form of the verb. The stress in the imperative will mirror that in the **я** form: if the **я** form shows **end-stress**, we add a **stressed -и**; if it shows **stem-stress**, we add -ь instead.

infinitive	они form	remove the ending	look at я-form stress	add	ты	вы: add -те
пис**а**ть	**пиш**ут	**пиш**- (consonant)	пиш**у** (end-stress)	и	**пиш**и!	**пиш**ите!
					не **пиш**и!	не **пиш**ите!
отв**е**тить	**отв**етят	**отв**ет- (consonant)	**отв**ечу (stem-stress)	ь	**отв**еть!	**отв**етьте!
					не **отв**еть!	не **отв**етьте!

[1] Remember: the **вы** imperative can be used with multiple people (whether formally or informallyl), or formally to a single person. The **вы** imperative is *always* formed by simply adding -**те** to the **ты** form — no exceptions whatsoever!

29.a
Follow the guidelines to create **ты** *imperatives. These verbs don't require the "extra step."*

infinitive	они form	remove the ending	add	ты	вы: add -те
де́лать АЙ	де́лают	де́ла- (vowel)	й	де́лай!	де́лайте!
сде́лать АЙ	ОНИ: _____			ТЫ: _____!	
отвеча́ть АЙ	ОНИ: _____			ТЫ: _____!	
танцева́ть ОВА	ОНИ: _____			ТЫ: _____!	
попро́бовать ОВА	ОНИ: _____			ТЫ: _____!	
име́ть ЕЙ	ОНИ: _____			ТЫ: _____!	
петь ОЙ^end	ОНИ: _____			ТЫ: _____!	
помы́ть ОЙ^stem	ОНИ: _____			ТЫ: _____!	
откры́ть ОЙ^stem	ОНИ: _____			ТЫ: _____!	
закры́ть ОЙ^stem	ОНИ: _____			ТЫ: _____!	
закрыва́ть АЙ	ОНИ: _____			ТЫ: _____!	

НЕ ОТДЫХАЙ НА РЕЛЬСАХ

Не отдыха́й на ре́льсах.

Don't relax on train tracks.

О́чень хоро́ший сове́т!

29.b
If the stem ends in a **consonant***, then an* **extra step** *is required: what is the stress in the* **я** *form? Recall that if the verb's infinitive is more than two syllables, and is end-stressed, then we know the* **я** *form will be too.*

infinitive	они form	remove the ending	look at я-form stress	add	ты	вы: add -те
писа́ть А	пи́шут	пиш- (consonant)	пишу́ (end-stress)	и	пиши́!	пиши́те!
отве́тить И	отве́тят	отве́т- (consonant)	отве́чу (stem-stress)	ь	отве́ть!	отве́тьте!
сказа́ть А^shift	ОНИ: _____		Я: _____		ТЫ: _____!	
спроси́ть И^shift	ОНИ: _____		Я: _____		ТЫ: _____!	
пригото́вить И	ОНИ: _____		Я: _____		ТЫ: _____!	
сиде́ть Е^end	ОНИ: _____		Я: _____		ТЫ: _____!	
отдохну́ть НУ^end	ОНИ: _____		Я: _____		ТЫ: _____!	
нача́ть /Н^end	ОНИ: _____		Я: _____		ТЫ: _____!	
переста́ть Н^stem	ОНИ: _____		Я: _____		ТЫ: _____!	
поня́ть Й/М^end	ОНИ: _____		Я: _____		ТЫ: _____!	
жить В^end	ОНИ: _____		Я: _____		ТЫ: _____!	
звать n/sА^end	ОНИ: _____		Я: _____		ТЫ: _____!	
брать n/sА^end	ОНИ: _____		Я: _____		ТЫ: _____!	
взять^end	ОНИ: _____		Я: _____		ТЫ: _____!	

Скажи́ мне, кто твой друг, и я скажу́, кто ты. Tell me who your friend is, and I'll tell who you are.

29.c
We'll now look at imperative forms **by verb type***. First,* **АЙ** *and* **ЕЙ** *verbs like* **де́лать** *and* **име́ть***.*

infinitive	они form	remove the ending	add	ты	вы: add -те
де́лать АЙ	де́лают	де́ла- (vowel)	й	де́лай!	де́лайте!
име́ть ЕЙ	име́ют	име́- (vowel)	й	име́й!	име́йте!
чита́ть АЙ	ОНИ: _____			ТЫ: _____!	
прочита́ть АЙ	ОНИ: _____			ТЫ: _____!	
открыва́ть АЙ	ОНИ: _____			ТЫ: _____!	
уме́ть ЕЙ	ОНИ: _____			ТЫ: _____!	

Не име́й сто рубле́й, а име́й сто друзе́й. Don't have a hundred roubles; have a hundred friends.[1]

РАБОТАЙ ПО-КОММУНИСТИЧЕСКИ!

Раб́отай по-коммунисти́чески!
Work like a Communist!

144

[1] To which the cynical response is: "Не име́й сто рубле́й, а име́й ты́сячу (a thousand) рубле́й."

Путешествуйте по горам Кавказа! Travel through the mountains of the Caucasus!

ОВА *verbs like* **рисовать**.   **29.d**

infinitive	они form	remove the ending	add	ты	вы: add -те
рисовать ОВА	**рисуют**	**рису-** (vowel)	**й**	**рисуй!**	**рисуйте!**
попробовать ОВА	они: _____			ты: _____!	
планировать ОВА	они: _____			ты: _____!	
советовать ОВА	они: _____			ты: _____!	
танцевать ОВА	они: _____			ты: _____!	
потанцевать ОВА	они: _____			ты: _____!	
игнорировать ОВА	они: _____			ты: _____!	

Не просят, не советуй. Don't give advice if no one's asking for it.

Мой руки! Wash hands!

ОЙ *verbs like* **мыть**.   **29.e**

infinitive	они form	remove the ending	add	ты	вы: add -те
мыть ОЙ[stem]	**моют**	**мо-** (vowel)	**й**	**мой!**	**мойте!**
помыть ОЙ[stem]	они: _____			ты: _____!	
петь ОЙ[end]	они: _____			ты: _____!	
спеть ОЙ[end]	они: _____			ты: _____!	
закрыть ОЙ[stem]	они: _____			ты: _____!	
открыть ОЙ[stem]	они: _____			ты: _____!	

Мной хоть полы мой, да не называй мочалкой. Clean the floors with me, but don't call me a washcloth.

А *verbs like* **писать**. *Remember, these mutate in all forms. We'll always need the extra step here: consider the stress in the **я** form!*   **29.f**

infinitive	они form	remove the ending	look at я-form stress	add	ты	вы: add -те
писать А	**пишут**	**пиш-** (consonant)	**пишу** (end-stress)	**и**	**пиши!**	**пишите!**
плакать А	**плачут**	**плач-** (consonant)	**плачу** (stem-stress)	**ь**	**плачь!**	**плачьте!**
показать А[shift]	они: _____		я: _____		ты: _____!	
написать А[shift]	они: _____		я: _____		ты: _____!	
сказать А[shift]	они: _____		я: _____		ты: _____!	
рассказать А[shift]	они: _____		я: _____		ты: _____!	

Плачь не плачь, а есть-пить надо. Cry if you want (literally, "cry, don't cry"), but you've got to eat and drink.

Курите сигареты! Smoke cigarettes! (курить: to smoke)

И *and* **Е** *verbs require the extra step. Try writing down the **я** form first,[1] then jump to the imperative!*   **29.g**

infinitive	look at я-form stress	add	ты	вы: add -те
говорить И	**говорю** (end-stress)	**и**	**говори!**	**говорите!**
готовить И	**готовлю** (stem-stress)	**ь**	**готовь!**	**готовьте!**
верить И	я: _____		ты: _____!	
получить И[shift]	я: _____		ты: _____!	
купить И[shift]	я: _____		ты: _____!	
сидеть Е[end]	я: _____		ты: _____!	

Сиди высоко да плюй далеко! Sit high and spit far! (плевать ОВА / плюнуть НУ: to spit)

[1] Again — with suffixed verbs, it is usually enough to look at the stress of the infinitive itself, since the **я** form follows it.

145

29.h

More **И** and **E** verbs. Again, try writing down the **я** form first, then jumping to the imperative!

заплат<u>и</u>ть И[shift]	я: _____	ты: _____ !
люб<u>и</u>ть И[shift]	я: _____	ты: _____ !
попрос<u>и</u>ть И[shift]	я: _____	ты: _____ !
позвон<u>и</u>ть И[end]	я: _____	ты: _____ !
пригот<u>о</u>вить И	я: _____	ты: _____ !
реш<u>и</u>ть И[end]	я: _____	ты: _____ !
посмотр<u>е</u>ть E[shift]	я: _____	ты: _____ !

Гот<u>о</u>вь с<u>а</u>ни л<u>е</u>том, а тел<u>е</u>гу зим<u>о</u>й. Ready your sleigh in summer, and your wagon in winter.

Раст<u>и</u>, богат<u>ы</u>рь![1]
Grow, hero!

to grow: **раст<u>и</u>** (раст<u>у</u>, раст<u>ё</u>шь) / **в<u>ы</u>расти**

29.2 Exceptions

Thankfully, there are very few verbs whose imperative forms cannot be derived using the step-by-step method we've just learned. These imperative can simply be thought of as irregular, in one way or another, and memorized. As the tables show, if we follow the usual steps, we won't successfully arrive at the correct form.

1) **Ь** verbs like **пить**, **бить**, and **лить** have imperatives ending in -**ей**:

пить Ь	➡ **пьют**	➡ **пь-**	*but:* **пей!**	**пейте!**

2) **АВАЙ** verbs, such as **дав<u>а</u>ть**, retain the -**авай** in the imperative:

дав<u>а</u>ть АВАЙ	➡ **да<u>ю</u>т**	➡ **да-**	*but:* **давай!**	**давайте!**

3) verbs that would otherwise take an imperative in -**ь**, but whose stems end in a **consonant cluster**, take an **unstressed -и** instead:

п<u>о</u>мнить И	➡ **п<u>о</u>мнят**	➡ **я п<u>о</u>мню**	*but:* **п<u>о</u>мни!**	**п<u>о</u>мните!**
прив<u>ы</u>кнуть НУ	➡ **прив<u>ы</u>кнут**	➡ **я прив<u>ы</u>кну**	*but:* **прив<u>ы</u>кни!**	**прив<u>ы</u>кните!**

Бей! по враг<u>у</u> культ<u>у</u>рной револ<u>ю</u>ции.

Strike at the enemy of the cultural revolution! (то есть, бей по алког<u>о</u>лю!)

4) here are the irregular imperatives of a few common irregular verbs:

дать	➡ **дад<u>у</u>т**	➡ **дад-**	*but:* **дай!**	**дайте!**
есть	➡ **ед<u>я</u>т**	➡ **ед-**	*but:* **ешь!**	**ешьте!**
быть	➡ **б<u>у</u>дут** (fut.!)	➡ **буд-**	*but:* **будь!**	**будьте!**

5) some verbs, like **в<u>и</u>деть** and **хот<u>е</u>ть**, simply do not form imperatives in modern Russian. Others may theoretically form imperatives, but, due to their meaning, they would almost never be used in everyday speech.[2]

29.i

Give the **irregular** imperative forms for these verbs.

пить Ь	ты: _____	вы: _____ !
в<u>ы</u>пить Ь	ты: _____	вы: _____ !
разб<u>и</u>ть Ь	ты: _____	вы: _____ !
заб<u>ы</u>ть	ты: _____	вы: _____ !
м<u>ё</u>рзнуть НУ	ты: _____	вы: _____ !

Give the **ты** imperatives only for these aspectual pairs that include one **АВАЙ**-type verb.

давать АВАЙ / дать: _____ / _____

продав<u>а</u>ть АВАЙ / прод<u>а</u>ть: _____ / _____

перестав<u>а</u>ть АВАЙ / перест<u>а</u>ть H[stem]: _____ / _____

Будь друг, да не вдруг. Be a friend, but not all of a sudden (notice that да doesn't always simply mean "yes").

Дай к<u>а</u>чество! Give (us) quality! The poster plays on the meaning of "**во**," a colloquial form of **вот**, meaning something like, "cool, great, that's what I wanted!"

[1] A **богат<u>ы</u>рь** is the hero of a Slavic legend, a **был<u>и</u>на**. The more general term for "hero" is **гер<u>о</u>й** ("heroine" is **гер<u>о</u>иня**).
[2] In such cases, our verb conjugation tables may simply leave the imperative boxes blank.

day 30: more on the imperative

aspect with the imperative; forming the imperative of reflexive verbs; first-person suggestions with **давай(те)**; third-person suggestions with **пусть**

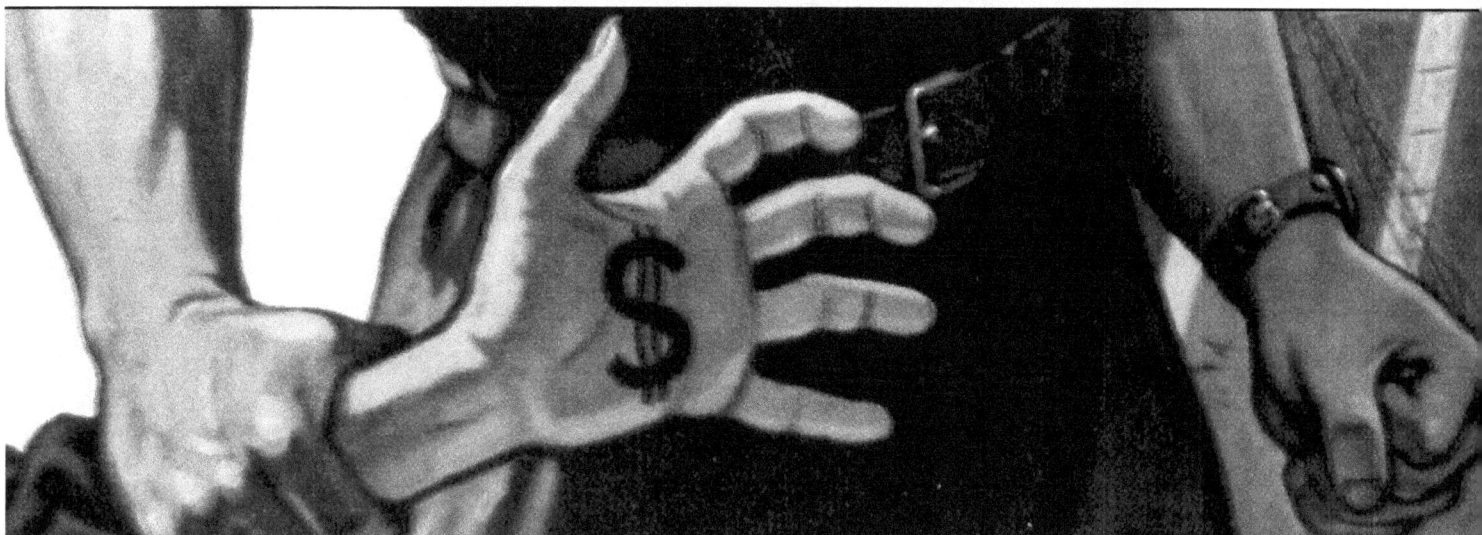

Бдительность — наше оружие! Vigilance is our weapon! Calls of "**Будь бдительным![1]**" (Be vigilant!) are common in propaganda posters.

30.1 Aspect with the imperative

So far, we've focused on simply forming the imperative. But how do we choose aspect when issuing commands? As we know, aspect is always a complex topic. For now, we'll provide some general guidelines.

Context is often key: are we issuing a generally valid command — as in, "always" do this, or "never" do that? Or, are we issuing a very specific command — as in, do this "right here, right now?" The more general the context, the more likely we are to need the imperfective; the more specific, the more likely we are to need the perfective. We will discuss these contextual issues in greater detail when **Advanced Aspect** is introduced in Book 3.

30.2 General commands with the imperfective

If a **positive** command is generally valid (meant to be fulfilled always, habitually, or repeatedly), then we should use the **imperfective**. If a **negative** command is a **general prohibition** (don't **ever** do something), then it too should be imperfective.

Examples may include "red flags" (such as **никогда**), but even if they are left understood (not explicit), the need for the imperfective remains.

Не лги никогда! Never, ever lie! (or, "Don't lie — ever!). The verb "**лгать / солгать**" has a tricky conjugation:

я лгу	мы лжём
ты лжёшь	вы лжёте
он лжёт	они лгут

Не **делай** этого[2] (никогда)!
Don't (ever) do that!

Делай задание (каждый день)!
Do the assignment (every day)!

Читай эту газету!
Read this paper!
(i.e. it's good; read it regularly!)

Не **читай** эту газету!
Don't read this paper!
(i.e. it's bad, don't ever read it!)

---

[1] The adjective appears in the instrumental here; we'll learn why in Chapter 5.
[2] An example of a direct object of a negated verb appearing in the genitive.

30.3 Specific commands with the perfective

On the other hand, if our command is very specific, of the "do this, do that — right here, right now" variety, we will almost always use a perfective form.

This means that most **simple, everyday requests** are in the perfective.

Дайте, пожалуйста, чашку кофе.
Give me a cup of coffee, please.

Возьми зонт, пожалуйста!
Take the umbrella, please!

Позвони ему завтра, хорошо?
Give him a call tomorrow, OK?

Помоги мне, пожалуйста!
Give me a hand, please!

30.4 Negative commands in the perfective

It is rare to use the perfective in negative commands. Obviously, such commands are not **general** prohibitions (if they were, we'd use the imperfective). Instead, they tend to focus on **specific**, here-and-now contexts (whoah, hey, wait, don't do that!) or warn someone against doing something by accident (something that, generally, they'd never want to do in the first place).

Не **забывайте** зонт!
Don't ever forget your umbrella!

Не **разбивайте** посуду!
Don't break dishes — ever!

Не **забудь** зонт!
Don't go and forget the umbrella!

Смотри, не **разбей** тарелку!
Look out, don't break that plate!

Папа, не пей! Papa, *please* don't drink!

Even in specific, here-and-now contexts, the imperfective may be used in an exhortative sense — if you're pleading, begging, urging someone on, etc.

30.a *Give the following commands, using* **ты**. *Don't translate word for word —capture the* **gist** *through your choice of* **aspect**!

покупать АЙ / **купить** И^shift:

1. Buy me a bottle of vodka. _____ мне бутылку водки.

2. Don't (ever) buy that vodka. Не _____ эту водку.

3. Don't go and forget the vodka! Не забудь _____ водку!

писать А^shift / **написать** А:

4. Write to him tomorrow. _____ ему завтра.

5. Do write me! (i.e. keep in touch!) _____ (мне)!

6. Don't write that person. Не _____ этому человеку.

звонить И^end / **позвонить** И:

7. Call me (I'm begging you!) _____ (мне)!

8. Don't call my fiancée (невеста). Не _____ моей невесте.

9. Give your dad a call tomorrow. _____ отцу завтра.

10. Call your mom (regularly!). _____ маме!

показывать АЙ / **показать** А^shift:

11. Show me the photo. _____ мне фотографию.

12. Don't ever show that photo! Никогда не _____ эту фотографию!

13. Whoah, don't show that photo! Не _____ эту фотографию!

мыть ОЙ^stem / **помыть** ОЙ:

14. Wash the dishes every evening. _____ посуду каждый вечер.

15. Wash the dishes, please. _____ посуду, пожалуйста:

помогать АЙ / **помочь** Г^shift:

16. Help me. _____ мне.

17. Don't help him. Не _____ ему.

Богу молись, а к берегу гребись. Pray to God, but row toward the shore. (**молиться** И: to pray; **грести**(сь) Б: to row)

Учись на ПЯТЬ!

Учись на пять! Get an A! (literally, study to earn a 5). Numbers are used instead of letters for a grade (**оценка** or **отметка**) in Russia.

A =	5	пятёрка
B =	4	четвёрка
C =	3	тройка
D =	2	двойка
F =	1	единица (кол)

Пионер! Учись сражаться за дело рабочего класса!
Pioneer! Learn to fight for the cause of the working class!

30.5 Forming the imperatives of reflexive verbs

Remember that the forms of reflexive verbs are no different from ordinary verbs — in each case, we just need to add the **reflexive particle** at the end. The same is true of imperatives: form them just as we practiced yesterday, then add -**ся** after consonants and -**сь** after vowels.

infinitive		ТЫ		ВЫ
стара́ть**ся** АЙ	➡ стара́й →	стара́й**ся**!	➡ стара́йте →	стара́йте**сь**!
учи́ть**ся** И^shift	➡ учи́ →	учи́**сь**!	➡ учи́те →	учи́те**сь**!
гото́вить**ся** И	➡ гото́вь→	гото́вь**ся**!	➡ гото́вьте →	гото́вьте**сь**!

---

*Give the imperative forms. As a first step, you can give the non-reflexive forms, just as we learned yesterday — but then be sure to add the -**ся** or -**сь**!*   **30.b**

	without the particle:	with the particle:
1. верну́ться НУ^end:	ТЫ: _____ →	_____!
	ВЫ: _____ →	_____!
2. мы́ться ОЙ^stem:	ТЫ: _____ →	_____!
	ВЫ: _____ →	_____!
3. подгото́виться И:	ТЫ: _____ →	_____!
	ВЫ: _____ →	_____!
4. попыта́ться АЙ:	ТЫ: (_____) →	_____!
	ВЫ: (_____) →	_____!
5. фотографи́роваться ОВА:	ТЫ: _____ →	_____!
	ВЫ: _____ →	_____!
6. научи́ться И^shift:	ТЫ: _____ →	_____!
	ВЫ: _____ →	_____!
7. стара́ться АЙ:	ТЫ: (_____) →	_____!
	ВЫ: (_____) →	_____!

Век живи́ — век учи́сь. Live for a century (lifetime), learn for a century (lifetime).

ОПОМНИСЬ!

Скажи́ тост по-ру́сски!

Even at informal gatherings, not to mention formal events such as weddings, you're likely to hear toasts made before each round of drinking. There is a wide range of toasts: from humorous, to philosophical, to heartfelt, to perfunctory. Giving simple toasts in Russian is easy: just use the preposition **за** plus the accusative:

(Дава́йте вы́пьем) за...	**здоро́вье!**[1]	health
(Let's drink) to...	**дру́жбу!**	friendship
	иску́сство!	art
	Фёдора Миха́йловича!	(a man)
	А́нну Андре́евну!	(a woman)

Опо́мнись!
Come to your senses!

---

[1] It's a popular misconception that the standard Russian toast is **На здоро́вье!** This is almost never said as a toast; rather, it is said when giving food or drink to a guest. Compare also: **Будь здоро́в(а)! / Бу́дьте здоро́вы!** (be healthy!), said when someone sneezes.

30.6 First-person suggestions with давай(те)

НЕТ!

The imperative forms of дав**а**ть (**дав**а**й! дав**а**йте!**) can be used in a special construction meaning "Let's..." that is extremely common and useful.

Дава**й(те)** is followed by <u>the **мы** form of a verb</u> **in the future tense.**[1] Of course, the future tense of **imperfective** verbs is the compound future (here, using **будем**). As we might expect, **positive** suggestions ("Let's...") are **perfective**, while **negative** suggestions ("Let's not...") are **imperfective.** Here is a summary of these constructions for two aspectual pairs:

смотр**е**ть E^shift / посмотр**е**ть E ➡ **Дав**а**й(те) посм**о**трим** фильм!
Let's watch a movie!

Дава**й(те) не б**у**дем смотр**е**ть** фильм!
Let's not watch a movie!

гот**о**вить И / пригот**о**вить И ➡ **Дав**а**й(те) пригот**о**вим** борщ!
Let's make borshch!

Дава**й(те) не б**у**дем гот**о**вить** борщ!
Let's not make borshch!

— Сл**у**шай, дав**а**й в**ы**пьем!

— Нет! Дав**а**й не б**у**дем пить!
Не н**а**до так мн**о**го пить!

— Л**а**дно, не п**е**йте.

We can use the **я form** of the verb — also **in the future tense** — in the sense of "Let me..." or "Why don't I..."

помог**а**ть АЙ / пом**о**чь Г^shift ➡ **Дав**а**й** я теб**е** **помог**у**.
Let me help you. (using ты)

Дава**йте** я вам **помог**у**.
Let me help you. (using вы)

делать АЙ / сд**е**лать АЙ ➡ **Дав**а**й** я это **сд**е**лаю.
Let me do it. Why don't I do it. (ты)

Дава**йте** я это **сд**е**лаю.
Let me do it. Why don't I do it. (вы)

Finally, **Дав**а**й!** and **Дав**а**йте!** are often used alone, in the sense of "Great! Let's do it! Come on!"

30.c **мыть** ОЙ^stem / **пом**ы**ть** ОЙ: 1. Let's wash the dishes.   _____

2. Let's not wash the dishes.   _____

3. Let me wash the dishes.   _____

чита**ть** АЙ / **прочит**а**ть** АЙ: 4. Let's read this article.   _____

5. Let's not read this article.   _____

6. Why don't I read this article.   _____

звони**ть** И / **позвон**и**ть** И: 7. Let's call mom.   _____

8. Let's not call mom.   _____

9. Why don't I call mom.   _____

Some additional imperative forms

Infinitives can carry the force of an imperative, but this is one of the most impolite ways to give commands in Russian — it's the kind of form one might expect to hear from a drill sergeant. But it's also seen in authoritative warnings, like on street signs: "**М**а**шины не парков**а**ть!**" (No parking!). Or, in the subway: "**Не прислон**я**ться!**" — "Don't lean (on the door)!" Or, as on the poster to the right: **Не кур**и**ть!** "Don't smoke!" (No smoking!). Also watch for the adjective **запрещ**ё**нный** (prohibited).

Perfective verbs of motion are commonly used in the **past tense** in emphatic suggestions, such as **Пошл**и**!** (Let's get going already!) — or, by vehicle, **Поех**а**ли!** (Let's roll!). We'll study verbs of motion in depth in the following chapter, but these two forms are well worth learning on their own.

НЕ КУРИТЬ

[1] It can also be followed by an infinitive, but students are strongly encouraged to learn the **мы** forms shown here (they're very common!).

30.7 Third-person suggestions with пусть

Somewhat less common are third-person suggestions with the word **пусть**, in the sense of "let..." or "may..." We use these constructions to suggest that someone **else** (he, she, they, etc.) do something.

Пусть must be followed by a **third-person** verb, singular or plural, in either the present or future. Either aspect can be used, based on general guidelines for aspectual choice.

<u>де</u>лать АЙ / <u>сде</u>лать АЙ ➡ **Пусть де<u>л</u>ает, что х<u>о</u>чет.**
Let him/her do what he/she wants.

Пусть де<u>л</u>ают, что хот<u>я</u>т.
Let them do what they want.

Пусть он <u>э</u>то сд<u>е</u>лает.
Let him do it.

The word **пусть** can be used by itself, in a general sense of "fine, let it be that way, I don't care" — often in the set phrase, **ну и пусть!** (fine then!)

Он<u>а</u> не б<u>у</u>дет теб<u>е</u> звон<u>и</u>ть. | **Ну и пусть. Мне всё равн<u>о</u>.**
She's not going to call you. | Fine, whatever. I don't care.

An alternate form of пусть, **пуск<u>а</u>й**, may be encountered in literary texts.

Пусть всегд<u>а</u> б<u>у</u>дет н<u>е</u>бо! Пусть всегд<u>а</u> б<u>у</u>дет с<u>о</u>лнце! Пусть всегд<u>а</u> б<u>у</u>дет м<u>а</u>ма! Пусть всегд<u>а</u> б<u>у</u>ду я!

From a popular Soviet children's song: "May there always be sky! May there always be sun! May there always be mom! May there always be me!"

The Soviets failed to abolish mortality.

Review all of the imperative constructions we've studied with the following examples. Assume **ты** *forms for basic imperatives.* **30.d**

гот<u>о</u>вить И / пригот<u>о</u>вить И:	1. Cook dinner!	_____
	2. Let's not cook dinner.	_____
	3. Let dad cook dinner.	_____
пис<u>а</u>ть А[shift] / напис<u>а</u>ть А:	4. Why don't I write to them.	_____
	5. Don't write to them!	_____
	6. Let them write to us.	_____
звон<u>и</u>ть И[end] / позвон<u>и</u>ть И:	7. Give her a call.	_____
	8. No, let's not call her.	_____
	9. Let her call us.	_____

A few everyday imperatives

Here are some imperative forms you're likely to use on a daily basis:

говор<u>и</u>ть И[end] / сказ<u>а</u>ть А[shift] ➡ **Скаж<u>и</u>те, пож<u>а</u>луйста... где здесь туал<u>е</u>т?**
Tell me, please... where is the restroom?

дав<u>а</u>ть АВАЙ / дать ➡ **Д<u>а</u>йте, пож<u>а</u>луйста... квас, в<u>о</u>ду, п<u>и</u>во.**
Give me, please... kvass, water, beer (when ordering food).

извин<u>я</u>ть АЙ / извин<u>и</u>ть И[end] ➡ **Извин<u>и</u>те! Извин<u>и</u>!**
Excuse me!

быть ➡ **Будь здор<u>о</u>в! Будь здор<u>о</u>ва! Будьте здор<u>о</u>вы!**
Be healthy! (said when someone sneezes)[1]

ПУСТЬ ЗДРАВСТВУЕТ И ПРОЦВЕТАЕТ НАША РОДИНА!

Пусть здр<u>а</u>вствует и процвет<u>а</u>ет н<u>а</u>ша р<u>о</u>дина! May our homeland be healthy and prosper!

---

[1] By the way, when someone sneezes in Russia, it proves that whatever was said just before the sneeze was true.

Case endings

			special modifiers				adjectives	masculine nouns hard	soft		special soft
nom.	этот	весь	один	чей	мой	наш	новый	стол	словарь	музей	кафетерий
gen.	этого	всего	одного	чьего	моего	нашего	нового	стола	словаря	музея	кафетерия
acc.	этот	весь	один	чей	мой	наш	новый	стол	словарь	музей	кафетерий
animate:	этого	всего	одного	чьего	моего	нашего	нового	студента	писателя		гения
dat.	этому	всему	одному	чьему	моему	нашему	новому	столу	словарю	музею	кафетерию

			special modifiers				adjectives	feminine nouns hard	soft	special soft
nom.	эта	вся	одна	чья	моя	наша	новая	газета	неделя	фамилия
gen.	этой	всей	одной	чьей	моей	нашей	новой	газеты	недели	фамилии
acc.	эту	всю	одну	чью	мою	нашу	новую	газету	неделю	фамилию
dat.	этой	всей	одной	чьей	моей	нашей	новой	газете	неделе	фамилии

			special modifiers				adjectives	neuter nouns hard	soft		special soft
nom.	это	всё	одно	чьё	моё	наше	новое	окно	море	бельё	задание
gen.	этого	всего	одного	чьего	моего	нашего	нового	окна	моря	белья	задания
acc.	это	всё	одно	чьё	моё	наше	новое	окно	море	бельё	задание
dat.	этому	всему	одному	чьему	моему	нашему	новому	окну	морю	белью	заданию

Nouns

hard nouns			
masculine			**feminine**

masculine

прибор, -а — set of utensils
нож, -а — knife
стакан, -а — cup
холодильник, -а — refrigerator
сахар, -а — sugar
квас, -а — kvas
лимонад, -а — soda (not limonade!)
напит(о)к, -тка — beverage
кофе — coffee (indeclinable)
подар(о)к, -рка — present, gift
хлеб, -а — bread
десерт, -а — dessert
торт, -а — cake
пирог, -а — pie
пирож(о)к, -жка — stuffed roll
бутерброд, -а — open-faced sandwich
борщ, -а — borshch
кус(о)к, куска — a piece
гарнир, -а — a side dish
сюрприз, -а — surprise
чайник, -а — teapot
кефир, -а — a yogurt drink
соус, -а — sauce

шоколад, -а — chocolate
коньяк, -а — brandy
тост, -а — a toast
сыр, -а — cheese
суп, -а — soup
творог, -а — cottage cheese[1]
салат, -а — salad
рис, -а — rice

neuter

молоко, -а — milk
мясо, -а — meat
блюдо, -а — a dish
масло, -а — butter
яблоко, -а — apple
лекарство, -а — medicine
шампанское, -ого — champagne (adj)
мороженое, -ого — ice cream (adj)
вино, -а — wine
пиво, -а — beer

feminine

еда, -ы — food
тарелка, -и — plate
миска, -и — bowl
ложка, -и — spoon
вилка, -и — fork
салфетка, -и — napkin
чаша, чашка, -и — (tea)cup
бутылка, -и — bottle
кружка, -и — mug
рюмка, -и — a shot (glass)
минералка, -и — mineral water[2]
икра, -ы — caviar
рыба, -ы — fish
сметана, -ы — sour cream
свинина, -ы — pork
говядина, -ы — beef
курица, -ы — chicken
добавка, -и — a second helping
открывалка, -и — bottle opener
колбаса, -ы — sausage
булка, -и — roll
конфета, -ы — piece of candy
посуда, -ы — dishes

[1] Two stress marks means that either stress is acceptable. [2] The full term for "mineral water" is **минеральная вода**

soft nouns		
masculine	**feminine**	**neuter**
ча**й**, ча**я** tea	пе**сня**, -**и** song	пе**ченье** cookies ново**селье** moving-in party

special soft nouns		
masculine	**feminine**	**neuter**
	по**рция**, -**ии** portion	мне**ние**, -**ия** opinion

Short-form predicate adjectives and predicate adverbs

	short-form adjectives				predicate adverbs (with dative)	
certain, sure	уверен	уверен**а**	уверен**о**	уверен**ы**	мне **хорошо**	I feel good
drunk	пьян	пьян**а**	пьян**о**	пьян**ы**	мне **плохо**	I feel bad
sober	трезв	трезв**а**	трезв**о**	трезв**ы**	мне **интересно**	I'm interested
healthy	здоров	здоров**а**	здоров**о**	здоров**ы**	мне **весело**	I'm happy
ready, finished	готов	готов**а**	готов**о**	готов**ы**	мне **невесело**	I'm unhappy
happy	счастлив	счастлив**а**	счастлив**о**	счастлив**ы**	мне **грустно**	I'm sad
busy, occupied	занят	занят**а**	занят**о**	занят**ы**	мне **больно**	I feel pain
sated, full	сыт	сыт**а**	сыт**о**	сыт**ы**	мне **стыдно**	I'm ashamed
alive	жив	жив**а**	жив**о**	жив**ы**	мне **неловко**	I feel awkward
dead	мёртв	мертв**а**	мертв**о**	мертв**ы**	мне **страшно**	I'm afraid
					мне **легко**	It's easy for me
satisfied	доволен	доволь**на**	доволь**но**	доволь**ны**	мне **трудно**	It's hard for me
free, available	свободен	свобод**на**	свобод**но**	свобод**ны**	мне **скучно**	I'm bored
hungry	голоден	голод**на**	голод**но**	голод**ны**	мне **холодно**	I'm cold
sick, ill	болен	боль**на**	боль**но**	боль**ны**		
needed, necessary	нужен	нуж**на**	нуж**но**	нуж**ны**		
obligated ("should"	должен + inf.	долж**на** + inf.	долж**но** + inf.	долж**ны** + inf.		

modal adverbs + inf.	
мне **нельзя**	I am not allowed
мне **можно**	I can, I may
мне **пора**	it is time for me to
мне **лень**	I'm too lazy to
мне **надо**	I have to

Prepositions followed by the dative

к	to, toward	Надо привыкнуть **к русскому менталитету.** One has to get used to the Russian mentality.	
по	along (a path), around (an area)	Мы гуляем **по улице.** We're strolling down the street.	Мы гуляем **по городу.** We're strolling around the city.
	by (means of), via	Я позвонил отцу **по телефону.** I called my father on the telephone.	Я пишу маме **по электронной почте.** I write mom by e-mail ("electronic mail").
	according to	**По расписанию** у нас сегодня нет урока русского языка. According to the schedule we don't have Russian class today.	
		По моему мнению (по-моему) это не так! In (according to) my opinion that isn't so!	
	in (a subject)	У нас сегодня лекция **по русской истории.** Today we have a lecture in Russian history.	
		Это новый учебник **по русскому языку.** This is a new Russian language textbook.	

Verbs used with the dative

давать АВАЙ / дать кому что		продавать АВАЙ / продать кому что		задавать АВАЙ / задать кому вопрос	
to give		to sell		to pose (a question)	
даю	дам	продаю	продам	задаю	задам
даёшь	дашь	продаёшь	продашь	задаёшь	задашь
даёт	даст	продаёт	продаст	задаёт	задаст
даём	дадим	продаём	продадим	задаём	зададим
даёте	дадите	продаёте	продадите	задаёте	зададите
дают	дадут	продают	продадут	задают	зададут
давай!	дай!	продавай!	продай!	задавай!	задай!
давал	дал	продавал	продал	задавал	задал
давала	дала	продавала	продала	задавала	задала
давало	дало	продавало	продало	задавало	задало
давали	дали	продавали	продали	задавали	задали

звонить И end / позвонить И end кому		нравиться И / понравиться И кому		посылать АЙ / послать A end кому что	
to call		to be pleasing to ("to like")		to send	
звоню	позвоню	нравлюсь	понравлюсь	посылаю	пошлю[1]
звонишь	позвонишь	нравишься	понравишься	посылаешь	пошлёшь
звонит	позвонит	нравится	понравится	посылает	пошлёт
звоним	позвоним	нравимся	понравимся	посылаем	пошлём
звоните	позвоните	нравитесь	понравитесь	посылаете	пошлёте
звонят	позвонят	нравятся	понравятся	посылают	пошлют
звони!	позвони!	нравься!	понравься!	посылай!	пошли!

желать АЙ / пожелать АЙ кому чего		показывать АЙ / показать A shift кому		рассказывать АЙ / рассказать A shift кому	
to wish (someone something)		to show		to tell (a story)	
желаю	пожелаю	показываю	покажу	рассказываю	расскажу
желаешь	пожелаешь	показываешь	покажешь	рассказываешь	расскажешь
желает	пожелает	показывает	покажет	рассказывает	расскажет
желаем	пожелаем	показываем	покажем	рассказываем	расскажем
желаете	пожелаете	показываете	покажете	рассказываете	расскажете
желают	пожелают	показывают	покажут	рассказывают	расскажут
желай!	пожелай!	показывай!	покажи!	рассказывай!	расскажи!

советовать ОВА / посоветовать ОВА кому		верить И / поверить И кому		рекомендовать ОВА / порекомендовать кому	
to advise, recommend		to believe		to advise, recommend	
советую	посоветую	верю	поверю	рекомендую	порекомендую
советуешь	посоветуешь	веришь	поверишь	рекомендуешь	порекомендуешь
советует	посоветует	верит	поверит	рекомендует	порекомендует
советуем	посоветуем	верим	поверим	рекомендуем	порекомендуем
советуете	посоветуете	верите	поверите	рекомендуете	порекомендуете
советуют	посоветуют	верят	поверят	рекомендуют	порекомендуют
советуй!	посоветуй!	верь!	поверь!	рекомендуй!	порекомендуй!

[1] Note the very unusual cluster mutation here: сл mutates to шль

объясня́ть АЙ / объясни́ть И^{end} кому́	
to explain	
объясня́**ю**	объясн**ю́**
объясня́**ешь**	объясни́**шь**
объясня́**ет**	объясни́**т**
объясня́**ем**	объясни́**м**
объясня́**ете**	объясни́**те**
объясня́**ют**	объясн**я́т**
объясня́**й**!	объясни́!

помога́ть АЙ / помо́чь Г кому́ + inf.	
to help ("give help to…")	
помога́**ю**	помог**у́**
помога́**ешь**	помо́ж**ешь**
помога́**ет**	помо́ж**ет**
помога́**ем**	помо́ж**ем**
помога́**ете**	помо́ж**ете**
помога́**ют**	помо́г**ут**
помога́**й**!	помоги́!
помога́л	помо́г
помога́л**а**	помогл**а́**
помога́л**о**	помогл**о́**
помога́л**и**	помогл**и́**

привыка́ть АЙ / привы́кнуть (НУ) к чему́	
to work / to work for a bit	
привыка́**ю**	привы́кн**у**
привыка́**ешь**	привы́кн**ешь**
привыка́**ет**	привы́кн**ет**
привыка́**ем**	привы́кн**ем**
привыка́**ете**	привы́кн**ете**
привыка́**ют**	привы́кн**ут**
привыка́**й**!	привы́кни!
привыка́л	привы́к
привыка́л**а**	привы́кл**а**
привыка́л**о**	привы́кл**о**
привыка́л**и**	привы́кл**и**

хоте́ться / захоте́ться + кому́ + inf.	
to feel like / to get the urge to	
хо́чется	захо́чется
хоте́лось	захоте́лось

скуча́ть АЙ / соску́читься И по кому́, чему́	
to miss / to begin missing, come to miss	
скуча́**ю**	соску́ч**у**(сь)
скуча́**ешь**	соску́ч**ишь**(ся)
скуча́**ет**	соску́ч**ит**(ся)
скуча́**ем**	соску́ч**им**(ся)
скуча́**ете**	соску́ч**ите**(сь)
скуча́**ют**	соску́ч**ат**(ся)
скуча́**й**!	соску́чь(ся)!

Verbs that can be used with reflexive particles

учи́ть И^{shift} / научи́ть И^{shift} кого́ + inf.	
to teach (someone to)	
учи́ться И^{shift} / научи́ться И^{shift} + inf.	
to study (in college); to learn	
уч**у́**(сь)	науч**у́**(сь)
у́ч**ишь**(ся)	нау́ч**ишь**(ся)
у́ч**ит**(ся)	нау́ч**ит**(ся)
у́ч**им**(ся)	нау́ч**им**(ся)
у́ч**ите**(сь)	нау́ч**ите**(сь)
у́ч**ат**(ся)	нау́ч**ат**(ся)
учи́(сь)!	научи́(сь)!

мыть ОЙ^{stem} / помы́ть ОЙ что	
to wash	
мы́ться ОЙ / помы́ться ОЙ	
to wash up	
мо́**ю**(сь)	помо́**ю**(сь)
мо́**ешь**(ся)	помо́**ешь**(ся)
мо́**ет**(ся)	помо́**ет**(ся)
мо́**ем**(ся)	помо́**ем**(ся)
мо́**ете**(сь)	помо́**ете**(сь)
мо́**ют**(ся)	помо́**ют**(ся)
мо́**й**(ся)!	помо́й(ся)!

закрыва́ть АЙ / закры́ть ОЙ^{stem}	
to close	
закрыва́ться АЙ / закры́ться ОЙ	
to be closed (to close)	
закрыва́**ю**(сь)	закро́**ю**(сь)
закрыва́**ешь**(ся)	закро́**ешь**(ся)
закрыва́**ет**(ся)	закро́**ет**(ся)
закрыва́**ем**(ся)	закро́**ем**(ся)
закрыва́**ете**(сь)	закро́**ете**(сь)
закрыва́**ют**(ся)	закро́**ют**(ся)
закрыва́**й**(ся)!	закро́й(ся)!

гото́вить И / пригото́вить И	
to prepare, cook	
гото́виться И / подгото́виться[1] к чему́	
to get ready (study for)	
гото́вл**ю**(сь)	подгото́вл**ю**(сь)
гото́в**ишь**(ся)	подгото́в**ишь**(ся)
гото́в**ит**(ся)	подгото́в**ит**(ся)
гото́в**им**(ся)	подгото́в**им**(ся)
гото́в**ите**(сь)	подгото́в**ите**(сь)
гото́в**ят**(ся)	подгото́в**ят**(ся)
гото́вь(ся)!	подгото́вь(ся)!

возвраща́ть АЙ / верну́ть НУ^{end} что	
to return, give back	
возвраща́ться АЙ / верну́ться НУ	
to return, go back	
возвраща́**ю**(сь)	верн**у́**(сь)
возвраща́**ешь**(ся)	верн**ёшь**(ся)
возвраща́**ет**(ся)	верн**ёт**(ся)
возвраща́**ем**(ся)	верн**ём**(ся)
возвраща́**ете**(сь)	верн**ёте**(сь)
возвраща́**ют**(ся)	верн**у́т**(ся)
возвраща́**й**(ся)!	верни́(сь)!

фотографи́ровать ОВА / сфотографи́ровать	
to photograph	
фотографи́роваться / сфотографи́роваться	
to be photographed	
фотографи́ру**ю**(сь)	сфотографи́ру**ю**(сь)
фотографи́ру**ешь**(ся)	сфотографи́ру**ешь**(ся)
фотографи́ру**ет**(ся)	сфотографи́ру**ет**(ся)
фотографи́ру**ем**(ся)	сфотографи́ру**ем**(ся)
фотографи́ру**ете**(сь)	сфотографи́ру**ете**(сь)
фотографи́ру**ют**(ся)	сфотографи́ру**ют**(ся)
фотографи́ру**й**(ся)!	сфотографи́ру**й**(ся)!

[1] Note that the prefix **под-** (not **при-**) is used with the reflexive form in the specific sense of "preparing oneself" (studying) for an **exam**, etc. The reflexive form **пригото́виться** (that is, with **при-**) is used for getting ready for other things, in a general sense.

разбива́ть АЙ / разби́ть Ь		лома́ть АЙ / слома́ть АЙ	
to break, shatter		to break	
разбива́ться АЙ / разби́ться Ь		лома́ться АЙ / слома́ться АЙ	
to be broken, shattered		to break down, be broken	
разбива́ю(сь)	разобью́(сь)	лома́ю(сь)	слома́ю(сь)
разбива́ешь(ся)	разобьёшь(ся)	лома́ешь(ся)	слома́ешь(ся)
разбива́ет(ся)	разобьёт(ся)	лома́ет(ся)	слома́ет(ся)
разбива́ем(ся)	разобьём(ся)	лома́ем(ся)	слома́ем(ся)
разбива́ете(сь)	разобьёте(сь)	лома́ете(сь)	слома́ете(сь)
разбива́ют(ся)	разобью́т(ся)	лома́ют(ся)	слома́ют(ся)
разбива́й(ся)!	разбе́й(ся)!	лома́й(ся)!	слома́й(ся)!

Verbs that can be used with the reflexive particle to express reciprocity

ви́деть Е / уви́деть Е		встреча́ть АЙ / встре́тить И кого	
to see / catch sight of		to meet	
ви́деться Е / уви́деться Е [1]		встреча́ться АЙ / встре́титься И	
to see each other		to meet each other, meet up	
ви́жу(сь)	уви́жу(сь)	встреча́ю(сь)	встре́чу(сь)
ви́дишь(ся)	уви́дишь(ся)	встреча́ешь(ся)	встре́тишь(ся)
ви́дит(ся)	уви́дит(ся)	встреча́ет(ся)	встре́тит(ся)
ви́дим(ся)	уви́дим(ся)	встреча́ем(ся)	встре́тим(ся)
ви́дите(сь)	уви́дите(сь)	встреча́ете(сь)	встре́тите(сь)
ви́дят(ся)	уви́дят(ся)	встреча́ют(ся)	встре́тят(ся)
—	—	встреча́й(ся)!	встре́ть(ся)!

Starting and stopping (always followed by imperfective verbs!)

начина́ть АЙ / нача́ть /Н end		перестава́ть АВАЙ / переста́ть Н stem		зака́нчивать АЙ / зако́нчить И	
to start, begin		to stop, cease		to end	
начина́ться АЙ / нача́ться /Н end				зака́нчиваться АЙ / зако́нчиться И	
to be started, begun (to start)				to be ended (to end)	
начина́ю(сь)	начну́(сь)	перестаю́	переста́ну	зака́нчиваю(сь)	зако́нчу(сь)
начина́ешь(ся)	начнёшь(ся)	перестаёшь	переста́нешь	зака́нчиваешь(ся)	зако́нчишь(ся)
начина́ет(ся)	начнёт(ся)	перестаёт	переста́нет	зака́нчивает(ся)	зако́нчит(ся)
начина́ем(ся)	начнём(ся)	перестаём	переста́нем	зака́нчиваем(ся)	зако́нчим(ся)
начина́ете(сь)	начнёте(сь)	перестаёте	переста́нете	зака́нчиваете(сь)	зако́нчите(сь)
начина́ют(ся)	начну́т(ся)	перестаю́т	переста́нут	зака́нчивают(ся)	зако́нчат(ся)
начина́й(ся)!	начни́(сь)!	переставай!	переста́нь!	зака́нчивай(ся)!	зако́нчи(сь)!
начина́л(ся)	на́чал, начался́				
начина́ла(сь)	начала́(сь)				
начина́ло(сь)	на́чало, начало́сь				
начина́ли(сь)	на́чали, начали́сь				

[1] For the time being, we've only used this reflexive verb in the plural, as in "**Мы ре́дко ви́димся.**" Using it in the singular would require the instrumental case, which we'll learn in Chapter 5, as in: "**Я ре́дко с ним ви́жусь.**" The same is true of the following verb, **встреча́ться**.

Verbs for trying

пытаться АЙ / попытаться АЙ + inf.	
to try, make an attempt	
пытаюсь	попытаюсь
пытаешься	попытаешься
пытается	попытается
пытаемся	попытаемся
пытаетесь	попытаетесь
пытаются	попытаются
пытайся!	попытайся!

пробовать ОВА / попробовать ОВА	
to try, to give a try (food, etc.)	
пробую	попробую
пробуешь	попробуешь
пробует	попробует
пробуем	попробуем
пробуете	попробуете
пробуют	попробуют
пробуй!	попробуй!

стараться АЙ / постараться АЙ + inf.	
to try, to strive to (with real effort)	
стараюсь	постараюсь
стараешься	постараешься
старается	постарается
стараемся	постараемся
стараетесь	постараетесь
стараются	постараются
старайся!	постарайся!

Other verbs, including some common irregular verbs

хотеть / захотеть + inf.		давать АВАЙ / дать		есть / съесть		пить Ь / выпить Ь		брать n/sA / взять	
to want / to get the urge		to give		to eat		to drink		to take	
хочу	захочу	даю	дам	ем	съем	пью	выпью	беру	возьму
хочешь	захочешь	даёшь	дашь	ешь	съешь	пьёшь	выпьешь	берёшь	возьмёшь
хочет	захочет	даёт	даст	ест	съест	пьёт	выпьет	берёт	возьмёт
хотим	захотим	даём	дадим	едим	съедим	пьём	выпьем	берём	возьмём
хотите	захотите	даёте	дадите	едите	съедите	пьёте	выпьете	берёте	возьмёте
хотят	захотят	дают	дадут	едят	съедят	пьют	выпьют	берут	возьмут
— — —	— — —	давай!	дай!	ешь!	съешь!	пей!	выпей!	бери!	возьми!
хотел	захотел	давал	дал	ел	съел	пил	выпил	брал	взял
хотела	захотела	давала	дала	ела	съела	пила	выпила	брала	взяла
хотело	захотело	давало	дало	ело	съело	пило	выпило	брало	взяло
хотели	захотели	давали	дали	ели	съели	пили	выпили	брали	взяли

ждать n/sA / подождать кого		петь ОЙend / спеть ОЙ		звать n/sA / назвать	
to wait (for)		to sing		to call (by name)	
жду	подожду	пою	спою	зову	назову
ждёшь	подождёшь	поёшь	споёшь	зовёшь	назовёшь
ждёт	подождёт	поёт	споёт	зовёт	назовёт
ждём	подождём	поём	споём	зовём	назовём
ждёте	подождёте	поёте	споёте	зовёте	назовёте
ждут	подождут	поют	споют	зовут	назовут
жди!	подожди!	пой!	спой!	зови!	назови!
ждал	подождал	пел	спел	звал	назвал
ждала	подождала	пела	спела	звала	назвала
ждало	подождало	пело	спело	звало	назвало
ждали	подождали	пели	спели	звали	назвали

Билет Государственного

Сто ру

БАНКОВСКИЕ БИЛЕТЫ ОБЕСПЕЧИВАЮТСЯ ЗОЛ
МЕТАЛЛАМИ И ПРОЧИМИ АКТИВАМИ ГОСУ

100

33 069539

СТО КАРБОВАНЦІВ · СТО РУБЛЕ
ЙУЗ МАНАТ · ՃԱՐ ՌՈՒԲԼԻ · ЗӦРВОЛР ПОЬР
ЮЗ СЎМ · САД СҮМ · ЖҮЗ СОМ · ЖУЗ СОМ
О СУТЭ РУБЛЕ · ŠIMTAS RUBLIŲ · SIMTS RUBL

1947

IV

going places

motion verbs and the prepositional case

In this chapter, we'll add the prepositional case, and learn how to talk about being in locations and going to and from locations. After reviewing time expressions, we'll turn to a challenging topic: verbs of motion. We'll also learn some "ordinary" verbs that are often used with locations.

day 31: the prepositional case

location with the prepositional case; prepositional endings; reminders concerning pronunciation; choosing between **в** and **на**

Нет на св_е_те прекр_а_сней од_ё_жи, чем бр_о_нза м_у_скулов и св_е_жесть к_о_жи. — В. Маяк_о_вский
There are no more beautiful raiments in the world than the bronze of muscles and freshness of skin. (note the rhyme!)

31.1 Describing location with the prepositional case

The **prepositional** case is used most often to describe **location** (for this reason, it is sometimes referred to as the **locative** case[1]). For example, it follows the prepositions **в** (in) and **на** (on) to describe **where** something is. Note that such phrases may not always translate into English as "in" or "on," but rather simply as "at" ("at" an event, "at" school, etc.). In Russian, such phrases answer the question **где** (where).

в к_о_мнат**е**	в те_а_тр**е**	в окн**е**	в муз_е_**е**	на стол**е**	на ст_у_л**е**	на л_е_кц**ии**	на ур_о_к**е**
in the room	in the theater	in the window	at the museum	on the table	on the chair	at the lecture	in class

31.2 Other prepositions that take the prepositional case

Perhaps the best answer to the question, "When do we use the prepositional?" is simply: **after certain prepositions**. Not all prepositions that take the prepositional case describe **location** — take, for example, **о(б)** (about):

о язык**е**	о ед**е**	о словар**е**	о Росс_ии_	об ист_о_р_ии_	о р_у_сск**ой** литерат_у_р**е**
about language	about food	about the dictionary	about Russia	about history	about Russian literature

160 [1] As we'll see, some nouns have alternate prepositional endings used specifically for **location**; we'll refer to those endings as **locative**.

Some prepositions followed by the prepositional may have a basic location-related meaning that can extend to more figurative relationships. For example, the preposition **при** literally means "near" or "at," but is rarely used in that literal sense. It can also mean something like "in the presence of," in either a spatial or temporal sense. It is often best translated using "under" (for political regimes and rulers) or even "(up)on":

при коммуни́зм**е**	при Ста́лин**е**	при вы́ход**е**[1]	при себ**е́**
under Communism	under Stalin	upon exiting	on one's person

31.3 The prepositional case must follow a preposition!

As we've seen, most cases can be used **following** certain prepositions, or on their own, **without** a preposition. Take the genitive, for example:

У моег<u>о</u> дру́га есть маши́на.	Это маши́на **моег<u>о</u> дру́га**.
My friend has a car.	This is my friend's car.

The prepositional is the sole exception: it can **never** appear without a preposition. That is, **теа́тре** alone makes **no sense**.[2] We need to add a preposition: **в теа́тре** (at the theater), **о теа́тре** (about the theater), etc.

31.4 Prepositional endings

The prepositional case answers questions such as: **О чём?** (about what?) and **О ком?** (about whom?). It can also answer **Где?** (where?) questions, including **В чём?** (in what?) or **На чём?** (on what?)

	adjective:	noun:
MASCULINE & NEUTER:	**-ом** (-ем)	**-е**

	adjective:	noun:
FEMININE:	**-ой** (-ей)	**-е**

Note, again, the **black boxes** below: **special soft nouns** in all genders take **-ии**, instead of the expected **-е**!

	special modifiers						adjectives	masculine nouns hard	soft		special soft
nom.	э́т**от**	весь	оди́н	чей	мой	наш	но́в**ый**	стол	слова́рь	музе́й	кафете́рий
prep.	э́т**ом**	вс**ём**	одн**о́м**	чь**ём**	мо**ём**	на́ш**ем**	но́в**ом**	стол**е́**	словар**е́**	музе́**е**	кафете́ри**и**

	special modifiers						adjectives	feminine nouns hard	soft		special soft
nom.	э́т**а**	вс**я**	одн**а́**	чь**я**	мо**я́**	на́ш**а**	но́в**ая**	газе́т**а**	неде́л**я**		фами́ли**я**
prep.	э́т**ой**	вс**ей**	одн**о́й**	чь**ей**	мо**е́й**	на́ш**ей**	но́в**ой**	газе́т**е**	неде́л**е**		фами́ли**и**

	special modifiers						adjectives	neuter nouns hard	soft		special soft
nom.	э́т**о**	вс**ё**	одн**о́**	чь**ё**	мо**ё**	на́ш**е**	но́в**ое**	окн**о́**	мо́р**е**	бель**ё́**	зада́ни**е**
prep.	э́т**ом**	вс**ём**	одн**о́м**	чь**ём**	мо**ём**	на́ш**ем**	но́в**ом**	окн**е́**	мо́р**е**	бель**е́**	зада́ни**и**

---

*O чём? Answer "About what?" using the **prepositional**. Write **об** before words beginning with vowels (but not before **soft** vowels!)* **31.a**

1. ру́сская му́зыка: о _____
2. но́вый слова́рь: о _____
3. ста́рый профе́ссор: о _____
4. Ру́сский музе́й: о _____
5. Эрмита́ж   об _____
6. на́ше общежи́тие: о _____
7. твоя́ иде́я: о _____
8. вся ва́ша рабо́та   о _____
9. э́то зада́ние: об _____
10. твой ру́сский друг о _____

Что у кого́ боли́т, тот о том и говори́т. Everyone talks about what is hurting them. (**боле́ть** E: to hurt)

[1] E.g. in the subway: **При вы́ходе из по́езда, не забыва́йте сво<u>и</u> ве́щи.** When exiting the train, don't forget your things.
[2] It is true that such prepositions were once left out when writing telegrams (!), to save space, as in: "**Бу́ду за́втра Москв<u>е́</u>.**"

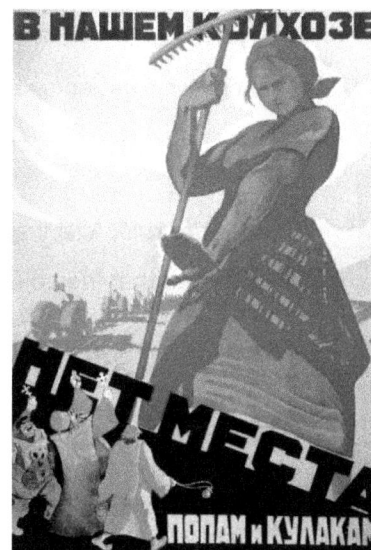

В нашем колхозе нет места попам и кулакам. There is no place in our collective farm for priests and kulaks.

Колхо́з — э́то коллекти́вное хозя́йство. Проце́сс коллективиза́ции шёл при Ста́лине. Что вы зна́ете об исто́рии коллективиза́ции?

31.5 Adjectives affected by spelling rules in the prepositional

Remember, Russian spelling rules apply universally. The 5-letter rule can affect prepositional endings with **-o**.

	4 "hushings"				3 "velars"			1
	Ж	Ч	Ш	Щ	Г	К	Х	Ц

5-letter rule: After these 5 letters: **Ж Ч Ш Щ** _____ **Ц** ...write: **е** ...not: unstressed **o**

This means that the adjectival endings **-ом** and **-ой** can only appear after these 5 letters **when stressed**. If the ending is unstressed, then we must write **-ем** and **-ей** instead. So far, our only such adjective is **хоро́ший**. By definition, the 5-letter rule does not affect end-stressed adjectives, such as **большо́й**. Compare:

большо́й музе́й	➡	в большо́м музе́е		больша́я ко́мната	➡	в большо́й ко́мнате
хоро́ший музе́й	➡	**в хоро́шем музе́е**		хоро́шая ко́мната	➡	**в хоро́шей ко́мнате**

31.6 Reminders concerning pronunciation

Vowel reduction rules also apply universally. If an adjectival ending with "o" is **unstressed**, then the "oh" is reduced to "uh." Of course, this never occurs in end-stressed adjectives: stressed vowels are never reduced!

reduced (unstressed) -ой	reduced (unstressed) -ом		but: stressed "o" is never reduced!
в но́вой ко́мнате	в но́вом па́рке		в большо́й ко́мнате / в большо́м па́рке

As we've seen with **к**, Russian has several single-consonant prepositions — including **в**. Pronounce it **as if it were part of the word that follows.** One might even imagine the two words written **as one**. Resist the temptation to **insert a vowel** sound, or a pause — even the slightest one — between the **в** and the word that follows.

If the word that follows also begins with **в**, the result is a double consonant, **"вв"** (held longer than a single **в**[1]):

в магази́не	➡ say: **вмагази́не**	**в ба́ре**	➡ say: **вба́ре**	**в не́бе**	➡ say: **вне́бе**
in the store		in the bar		in the sky	
в Москве́	➡ say: **вмоскве́**	**в Росси́и**	➡ say: **вросси́и**	**в Вашингто́не**	➡ say: **ввашингто́не**
in Moscow		in Russia		in Washington	

Since these combinations are read as a single unit, rules for devoicing in **consonant clusters** apply. Namely, if the **в** is followed by an **unvoiced consonant**, it assimilates, and becomes **devoiced** itself, to **ф**.

в ко́мнате	➡ say: **фко́мнате**	**в теа́тре**	➡ say: **фтеа́тре**	**в Петербу́рге**	➡ say: **фпетербу́рге**
in the room		in the theater		in Petersburg	

Reading phrases as a single unit also affects vowel reduction in **o** (about): unstressed "oh" reduces to "ah."

о кни́ге	➡ say: **ah-knigyeh**	**о войне́**	➡ say: **ah-vaynyeh**[2]	**обо мне́**	➡ say: **ah-bah-mnyeh**
about the book		about the war		about me	

31.b *Try writing the preposition and the word following it as a single word, changing **в** to **ф** if necessary to reflect devoicing before any unvoiced consonant; then, say the entire phrase. This is an important principle of Russian pronunciation — don't insert a vowel, or pause, after the **в**!*

1. **в э́той** кварти́ре: _____

2. **в хоро́шем** общежи́тии: _____

3. **в го́роде**: _____

4. **в це́нтре** го́рода: _____

5. **в э́том** до́ме: _____

6. **в торго́вом** це́нтре: _____

7. **в па́рке**: _____

А ещё говоря́т: в Москве́ кур доя́т. And next they'll say that people are milking chickens in Moscow.

MOSCOW

Мавзоле́й Ле́нина, у стены́ Кремля́, в це́нтре Москвы́.

---

[1] Of course, in rapid speech a "double **в**" may be all but indistinguishable from a single one.
[2] We'd expect the first "o" to reduce to "uh" (based on the rules in 2.4), but this degree of reduction is not heard in prepositions.

31.7 Choosing between в and на

Think of **в** as the default preposition for telling "where" (**где**). Although it literally means "in" or "inside," it can also describe location more broadly, much like the English "at."

в комнате	в рюкзаке	в библиотеке	в окне
in the room	in the backpack	at (in) the library	in the window

When do we use **на**? **На** literally means "on"— on a flat surface, like a table or a wall. But **на** is also used in some less obvious situations. Use **на**...

1) For **flat surfaces**, both horizontal and vertical:

на столе	на земле	на стене	на доске
on the table	on the ground	on the wall	on the blackboard

2) For **events** — parties, performances, meetings, etc.:[1]

на вечеринке	на лекции	на встрече	на балете
at the party	at the lecture	at the meeting	at the ballet

3) Going "by" vehicles (unless emphasizing being literally "inside" a vehicle):

на поезде	на машине	на велосипеде	на метро
by train	by car	by bike	by subway

4) For **points of the compass** (N: **север**, S: **юг**, E: **восток**, W: **запад**):

на севере	на юге	на востоке	на западе
in the north	in the south	in the east	in the west

5) For **certain locations**, vaguely conceived of as open, sprawling, or complex. This category is unpredictable, so we'll specify in our vocabulary which nouns take **на** for some reason other than those enumerated above:

на вокзале	на станции	на остановке	на стадионе	на почте	на работе
at the train station	at the station	at the (bus) stop	at the stadium	at the post office	at work

Seemingly odd exceptions include **в парке** (in the park) or **в саду** (in the garden). Aren't these open, sprawling spaces? Yes, but they simply don't take **на** in Russian — likely because they are thought of as enclosed (walled-off) spaces. The same is true of **в городе** (in the city), as cities were historically walled. Hence: **в Москве**.

В НЕБЕСАХ

НА ЗЕМЛЕ И НА МОРЕ

В небесах, на земле и на море. In the skies (**небеса**, plural of **небо**), on the ground (**земля**), and on the sea (**море**). "Ground" and "sea" are thought of as flat, open spaces, and thus take "**на**." In fact, one can also say "**на небе**" (in the sky).

Some nouns can take both prepositions — if something were *in* the sea, we would say "**в море**."

---

*Describe being "at" these locations and events. Choose **в** or **на**, and use the prepositional case.*   **31.c**

1. ресторан: _____   4. концерт: _____

2. остров (island): _____   5. тротуар (sidewalk): _____

3. спальня (bedroom): _____   6. запад (west): _____

Кто в Москве не бывал, красоты не видал. He who has never been in Moscow has never seen beauty (**видать** = видеть).

---

*Some nouns can follow **в** or **на**, depending on what we mean. Give both variants, using these nouns in the prepositional case.*   **31.d**

1. река:	in the river:	в _____		4. дерево:	in the tree:	в _____
	on the river:	на _____			on the tree:	на _____
2. земля:	in the ground:	в _____		5. море:	in the sea:	в _____
	on the ground:	на _____			on the sea:	на _____
3. трава:	in the grass:	в _____		6. автобус:	inside the bus:	в _____
	on the grass:	на _____			on the bus:	на _____

Когда рак на горе свистнет. When a crayfish whistles on a mountain (i.e. when pigs fly). **гора**: mountain; **свистеть** Е / **свистнуть** НУ: to whistle.

---

[1] Students sometimes think of "the theater" as an event, but it is a place — so, **в театре**, *but* **на спектакле**, **на балете**, **на опере**, etc. We would say "**в опере**," etc., to speak of being in the production ourselves — or what happened in it.

day 32:   more on the prepositional

the mobile vowel and **во**; adjectival place names;
declining foreign place names; the alternate "locative"
prepositional ending

Советский человек в космосе! Величайшая победа нашего строя, нашей науки, нашей техники, нашего мужества.
Soviet man in space! The greatest victory of our political system (строй), our science (наука), our technology (техника), our courage (мужество).

32.1 The mobile vowel: в and во

As we've seen, a mobile vowel (**о**, **е**, or **ё**) **disappears** from the
final syllable of a masculine noun when any ending is added:

Облетев землю в корабле-спутнике, я увидел, как прекрасна наша планета. Люди, будем хранить и приумножать эту красоту, а не разрушать её! — Юрий Гагарин.

Having orbited the earth in the satellite, I have
seen how beautiful our planet is. People, let us
preserve and multiply this beauty, not destroy it!

— Yuri Gagarin

щен(о)к

щенка	of the puppy
щенку	to the puppy
о щенке	about the puppy

от(е)ц

отца	of the father
отцу	to the father
об отце	about the father

ков(ё)р

ковра	of the carpet
к ковру	toward the carpet
о ковре	about the carpet

д(е)нь

дня	of the day
к дню	by the day
о дне	about the day

In certain situations, Russian can also **insert** a mobile vowel to
break up tricky **consonant clusters**. So, mobile vowels "come
and go" depending on the letters (and sounds) around them.

For example, the mobile vowel **о** is added after single-consonant
prepositions like **в** when the following word begins with:

1) the **same consonant** (or its devoiced/devoiced equivalent),
2) **PLUS** any another consonant.

Владивосток (в + л)	➡	**во Владивостоке**	in Vladivostok
Франция (ф + р)	➡	**во Франции**	in France
Флорида (ф + л)	➡	**во Флориде**	in Florida
Вашингтон (в only!)	➡	**в Вашингтоне**	in Washington

164

All of the following places require **в**. *Give the prepositional form, being careful to write* **во** *where necessary.*

1. стран**а**	country	_____ _____	8. дере**в**ня	village[1]	_____ _____
2. к**о**смос	space	_____ _____	9. больн**и**ца	hospital	_____ _____
3. ресто**ра**н	restaurant	_____ _____	10. Фр**а**нция	France	_____ _____
4. Москв**а**	Moscow	_____ _____	11. рюкз**а**к	backpack	_____ _____
5. г**о**род	city	_____ _____	12. слов**а**рь	dictionary	_____ _____
6. Петерб**у**рг	Petersburg	_____ _____	13. гост**и**ная[2]	living room	_____ _____
7. общеж**и**тие	dormitory	_____ _____	14. корид**о**р	hallway	_____ _____

В семье **не без ур**о**да.** There's a freak in every family. (**ур**о**д**: a misborn freak)

As we learned yesterday, some nouns require **на** *instead of* **в**. *Many such nouns are sprawling, open spaces; but in many cases, it is not entirely clear why* **на** *is required; we must simply use it as a rule. This exercise summarizes all such nouns in our chapter vocabulary. Keep in mind that any* **event** *will require* **на**. *How might you explain the use of* **на** *with these spaces — if at all?*

1. трот**уа**р	sidewalk	_____ _____	13. двор	court(yard)	_____ _____
2. пляж	beach	_____ _____	14. ур**о**к	lesson	_____ _____
3. д**а**ча	dacha	_____ _____	15. ков(**ё**)р	carpet	_____ _____
4. к**у**хня	kitchen	_____ _____	16. стади**о**н	stadium	_____ _____
5. земл**я**	ground	_____ _____	17. стран**и**ца	page	_____ _____
6. зан**я**тие	class	_____ _____	18. доск**а**	blackboard	_____ _____
7. л**е**кция	lecture	_____ _____	19. стен**а**	wall	_____ _____
8. п**о**чта	post office	_____ _____	20. л**е**стница	staircase	_____ _____
9. **о**стров	island	_____ _____	21. эскал**а**тор	escalator	_____ _____
10. **у**лица	street	_____ _____	22. сторон**а**	side	_____ _____
11. вечер**и**нка	party	_____ _____	23. н**а**бережная	embankment	_____ _____
12. вокз**а**л	train station	_____ _____	24. рын(о)к	market	_____ _____

ПРИ СОЦИАЛИЗМЕ НЕТ МЕСТА БЕЗРАБОТИЦЕ! **ПРИ КАПИТАЛИЗМЕ МИЛЛИОНЫ БЕЗРАБОТНЫХ РУК!**

При социали**зме нет м**е**ста безраб**о**тице! При капитал**и**зме милли**о**ны безраб**о**тных рук!** Under socialism there is no place (**м**е**сто**) for unemployment (**безраб**о**тица**, here in the dative), but under capitalism there are millions of jobless (workless) hands!

1. Ты жив**ё**шь в общеж**и**тии **и**ли в кварт**и**ре?

   В как**о**м общеж**и**тии, **и**ли в как**о**й кварт**и**ре?

2. Ты был(**а**) на ур**о**ке р**у**сского язык**а** вчер**а**?

3. Ты п**и**шешь иногд**а** эсэм**э**с-сообщ**е**ния на зан**я**тии?

4. Где теб**е** нр**а**вится жить — в г**о**роде или в дер**е**вне?

5. Ты был(**а**) нед**а**вно (recently) на вечер**и**нке?

   А где был**а** вечер**и**нка? В общеж**и**тии? В кл**у**бе?

6. Что у теб**я** в рюкз**а**ке?

7. Есть у теб**я** д**о**ма плак**а**т на стен**е**? Как**о**й он?

8. Что у теб**я** есть д**о**ма на п**и**сьменном стол**е** (desk)?

9. Ты был(**а**) уж**е** в Росс**и**и? А во Фр**а**нции? А в **А**нглии?

[1] This word can refer to a single village, or to "the countryside" in general (as opposed to the city).
[2] Note that this is a stand-alone adjective! It is understood to modify "room," as in **гост**и**ная к**о**мната** (see 32.2).

32.2 Adjectival place names

We've seen (11.7) how adjectives can sometimes **stand alone as nouns**. This is true of many "place" (and even time!) nouns in Russian, such as the feminine adjective **ванная** (bathroom). Why feminine? Because it is understood to modify **комната** (ванная комната): it is the room with a **ванна** (bath, bathtub). Remember: once an adjective, always an adjective — these "nouns" must always take **adjectival endings**!

ванная	bathroom	➡ **в ванной**	in the bathroom
гостиная	living room	➡ **в гостиной**	in the living room
набережная	embankment	➡ **на набережной**	on the embankment
прошлое	the past (n.)[1]	➡ **в прошлом**	in the past
будущее	the future (n.)[1]	➡ **в будущем**	in the future

32.3 Declining foreign place names

How do we deal with foreign nouns (including names of cities and states) in Russian? We can give a few basic guidelines:

1) If the noun happens to end in a consonant, it is easily treated like any Russian **masculine** noun: **Берлин** → в Берлине.

2) If the noun happens to end in an "a," then it is easily treated like any Russian **feminine** noun: **Америка** → в Америке.

3) If, however, the foreign noun happens to end in the vowels **о, е, и,** or **у**, then it is treated as **indeclinable** — that is, its **endings never change**. Here are some examples of some indeclinable place nouns:

кино ➡ **в кино**   кафе ➡ **в кафе**   Сочи ➡ **в Сочи**   Чикаго ➡ **в Чикаго**   Баку ➡ **в Баку**

When using a foreign noun in Russian, be sure to "Russify" its pronunciation; to make sure you're doing this correctly, look up its official Russian spelling (Wikipedia is a good resource for this[2]) and pronounce it accordingly.

Трудящимся — здоровый отдых!
Healthy relaxation (vacation)
to those who labor!

В Советском Союзе любили отдыхать на юге, на Чёрном море — в Сочи или в Крыму, например.

32.c   *Give the prepositional. Watch for adjectival forms, and for foreign nouns that may not decline!*

1. Лондон: в _____
2. метро: в _____
3. Бостон: в _____
4. Торонто: в _____
5. гостиная: в _____
6. Вашингтон: в _____

7. Париж: в _____
8. Токио: в _____
9. такси: в _____
10. шоссе: на _____
11. Рим: в _____
12. Пекин: в _____

13. Филадельфия: в _____
14. Гонолулу: в _____
15. Дублин: в _____
16. Монреаль: в _____
17. прошлое: в _____
18. будущее: в _____

32.d   *We can tell what city or country we're **from** using **из** + the genitive. Try it with a few more foreign place names:*

1. Мюнхен: из _____
2. Хельсинки: из _____
3. Барселона: из _____

4. Осло: из _____
5. Сиэтл: из _____
6. Прага: из _____

7 Копенгаген: из _____
8. Флоренция: из _____
9. Варшава: из _____

Can you tell what city you're from, and what city you live in now? Refer to Wikipedia [2] to make sure the Russian spelling is correct.

— Откуда ты? Из какого города? **— Я из _____.** — А в каком городе ты живёшь сейчас? **— В _____.**

---

[1] Literally, "that which was (that which has gone past)" and "that which will be."
[2] Often, the easiest method is to look up your city in English, then simply switch to the Russian (**русский**) version of the page.

Here's the Russian for the American state names (and Puerto Rico). Practice pronouncing them as a Russian would. The rules for declining these foreign names are the same as those in 32.3. Practice saying "in" each state (в...). Which state names are indeclinable nouns?

Айдахо	Idaho	**Калифорния**	California	**Нью-Джерси**	New Jersey
Айова	Iowa	**Канзас**	Kansas	**Нью-Йорк**	New York
Алабама	Alabama	**Кентукки**	Kentucky	**Нью-Мексико**	New Mexico
Аляска	Alaska	**Колорадо**	Colorado	**Огайо**	Ohio
Аризона	Arizona	**Коннектикут**	Connecticut	**Оклахома**	Oklahoma
Арканзас	Arkansas	**Луизиана**	Louisiana	**Орегон**	Oregon
Вайоминг	Wyoming	**Массачусетс**	Massachusetts	**Пенсильвания**	Pennsylvania
Вашингтон	Washington	**Миннесота**	Minnesota	**Пуэрто-Рико**	Puerto Rico
Вермонт	Vermont	**Миссисипи**	Mississippi	**Род-Айленд**	Rhode Island
Вирджиния	Virginia	**Миссури**	Missouri	**Северная Дакота**	North Dakota
Висконсин	Wisconsin	**Мичиган**	Michigan	**Северная Каролина**	North Carolina
Гавайи[1]	Hawaii[1]	**Монтана**	Montana	**Теннесси**	Tennessee
Делавэр	Delaware	**Мэн**	Maine	**Техас**	Texas
Джорджия	Georgia	**Мэриленд**	Maryland	**Флорида**	Florida
Западная Вирджиния	West Virginia	**Небраска**	Nebraska	**Южная Дакота**	South Dakota
Иллинойс	Illinois	**Невада**	Nevada	**Южная Каролина**	South Carolina
Индиана	Indiana	**Нью-Гэмпшир**	New Hampshire	**Юта**	Utah

Give the prepositional case forms for these state names: **32.e**

1. Техас: в _____   3. Колорадо: в _____   5. Флорида: во _____

2. Нью-Йорк: в _____   4. Нью-Джерси: в _____   6. Вирджиния: в _____

Tell what state you're from, and what state you live in now.[2]

— Откуда ты? Из какого штата? **— Я из _____.** — А в каком штате ты живёшь сейчас? **— В _____.**

32.4 The alternate "locative" ending: stressed у

The prepositional case involves an important "alternate" noun ending: **stressed "у"** (instead of the expected "е"). Certain words take this ending when the prepositional case is used in its **locative** sense only — that is, to describe **location** specifically. Otherwise (for example, following the preposition "о" — "about"), they take the regular prepositional ending, "е."

These exceptions will be marked in the vocabulary. Here are a few:

шкаф	wardrobe	➡ **в шкафу**	*but:*	о шкафе
аэропорт	airport	➡ **в аэропорту**		об аэропорте
сад	garden	➡ **в саду**		о саде
лес	forest	➡ **в лесу**		о лесе
берег	shore	➡ **на берегу**		о береге
Крым	Crimea	➡ **в Крыму**		о Крыме
край	edge	➡ **на краю**		о крае

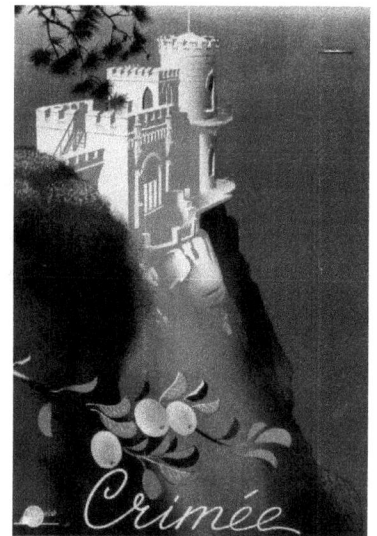

Дворец «Ласточкино гнездо» в Крыму, на берегу Чёрного моря.
The Swallow's Nest castle in Crimea, on the shore of the Black Sea.

---

*All of these nouns take the alternate "**stressed-у**" ending when describing location. Try it:*   **32.f**

1. сад (garden): в _____   3. снег (snow): в _____   5. берег (shore): на _____

2. пол (floor): на _____   4. мост (bridge): на _____   6. аэропорт: в _____

---

[1] This is a *plural* form —and, like **остров** (island), takes **на**; to say "in Hawaii," say на **Гаваях**; "from" is: с **Гаваев**
[2] If you're not from the U.S., be patient for now — we'll cover names of countries in Book Two. Or, consult Wikipedia!

day 33: time expressions

time expressions with the accusative; time expressions with the genitive; days of the week; this, last and next

Все на коммунистический суббо́тник! A "суббо́тник" (from суббо́та) was a "voluntary" work day. The related term for Sunday was "воскре́сник."

33.1 An introduction to time expressions in Russian

When we learned the accusative case, we saw several uses of what we called the "accusative of time." However, not all time expressions use the accusative. As we'll see today, many involve the **prepositional**. In short, to talk about time, we'll eventually need to learn a variety of constructions with a **variety of cases**.

In today's and tomorrow's lessons, we'll review and introduce several useful time constructions, before providing a more comprehensive overview of time expressions on Day 68. Start by reviewing the units of time to the right:

секу́нда	second
мину́та	minute
час	hour
день	day
неде́ля	week
ме́сяц	month
семе́стр	semester
год	year

33.2 Time expressions with the accusative

Here is a summary of the sorts of accusative-case time expressions we've seen:

день day ⇒	день for a day	неде́ля week ⇒	неде́лю for a week	год year ⇒	год for a year
	ка́ждый день every day		**ка́ждую неде́лю** every week		**ка́ждый год** every year
	весь день the whole day		**всю неде́лю** the whole week		**весь год** the whole year
	це́лый день an entire day		**це́лую неде́лю** an entire week		**це́лый год** an entire year

168

Since these phrases describe **duration** or **repetition**, they should be used with **imperfective** verbs:

Он**а** **год** ж**и**ла в Москв**е**.
She lived **for a year** in Moscow.

Он**а** **всю нед**елю п**и**сала стать**ю**.
She spent the whole week writing an article.

Он**а** **к**аждую нед**е**лю звон**и**ла м**а**ме.
She used to call her mom **every week**.

Он**а** **ц**елую нед**е**лю п**и**сала стать**ю**.
She spent an entire week writing an article.

Let's learn three other constructions with the accusative. The first, **за + accusative**, means "in" (within), in the sense of the time it took to accomplish something, as in: "I read this book in a week."

Since this phrase emphasizes **accomplishment**, it should be used with **perfective** verbs (absent repetition!).

| **за** | (with)in | Я прочит**а**л всю кн**и**гу **за нед**елю. | Я напиш**у** письм**о** **за час**. |
| | | I read the whole book in a week. | I'll write the letter (with)in an hour. |

To specify when something will happen in the **future**, as in "I'll to go Russia in a year (from now)," use **через + the accusative**. To specify time in the **past**, use **назад + the accusative** — but note that **назад** comes after its noun; for this reason, we might call it a **postposition** instead of a preposition. This is quite unusual for Russian.

через	in... (from now)	Я б**у**ду в Росс**и**и **через год**.	Конц**е**рт б**у**дет **через нед**елю.
		I will be in Russia in a year (from now).	The concert will be in a week.
назад	ago	**Год назад** я был в Росс**и**и.	Конц**е**рт был **нед**елю **назад**.
		A year ago I was in Russia.	The concert was a week ago.

33.3 Time expressions with the genitive

Here are two prepositions of time that are followed by the **genitive** case.

| **до** | before | **До войн**ы они ж**и**ли в Ленингр**а**де.[1] | **п**осле | after | **П**осле войн**ы** они верн**у**лись. |
| | | Before the war they lived in Leningrad. | | | After the war they returned. |

Вперёд! На запад! Onward! Westward!

назад is also an adverb, meaning "backwards" — the opposite of **вперёд**.

By the way, if one had to choose a single word to express the essence of all Soviet propaganda, it would probably be **Вперёд!** (Onward! Foreward!).

				33.a
1. Мы ж**и**ли в Росс**и**и...	for a year		for a week	
	_____		_____	
	for an entire month		for an entire year	
	_____		_____	
2. Мы верн**у**лись дом**о**й...	a week ago		a month ago	
	_____		_____	
3. Мы б**у**дем сн**о**ва (again) в Росс**и**и...	in a week from now		in a year from now	
	_____		_____	
4. Я теб**е** позвон**ю**...	in a minute from now		in an hour from now	
	_____		_____	
5. Я звон**ю** дом**о**й....	every week		every month	
	_____		_____	
6. Мы ув**и**димся...	before class (зан**я**тие)		after the lecture (л**е**кция)	
	_____		_____	
7. Мы прочит**а**ли "Войн**у** и мир"...	(with)in a year		(with)in a month	
	_____		_____	
8. Мы реш**и**ли зад**а**чу по матем**а**тике...	(with)in an hour		(with)in a minute	
	_____		_____	

[1] Note that **до** means "at any point prior to." When we learn the instrumental case (in chapter 5), we'll learn another preposition, **перед**, which suggests "just before," immediately before.

1. Как часто (often) ты звонишь домой? Каждый день?   3. Где ты был(а) час назад?   5. Где ты был(а) год назад?

2. Ты всегда делаешь задание до занятия?   4. Где ты будешь через час?   6. Где ты будешь через год?

33.4 Days of the week

The days of the week can be used with a number of cases. Let's take **пятница** (Friday). If someone asks, "What day is it?" then we simply state the day in the **nominative** case. But if we want to say that something happens **on** Friday, when we use **в + the accusative**.

— **Какой** сегодня день?   — **В какой день** у нас контрольная?
— What day is it today?   — On what day do we have a test?

— (Сегодня) **пятница.**   — (У нас контрольная) **в пятницу.**
— (Today is) Friday.   — (We have a test) on Friday.

To tell "from" and "until" with days of the week (and other time units), use these prepositions with the **genitive**:

— **Как долго ты будешь в Москве?**   **с** + gen. — **С понедельника...**   **до** + gen.   **... до пятницы.**
— How long will you be in Moscow?   from   — From Monday...   until   until Friday.

                                                  or: **по** + acc.   **... по пятницу.**
                                                         until   until Friday.

To be absolutely clear that you'll be staying **through** Friday, you could add the adverb **включительно** (literally, "inclusive"). Below are all the days of the week, along with the forms we've just learned.

		on... (в + acc.)	from... (с + gen.)[1]	until... (до + gen.)
понедельник	Monday	в понедельник	с понедельника	до понедельника
вторник	Tuesday	во вторник	со вторника	до вторника
среда	Wednesday	в среду *(note stress!)*	со среды	до среды
четверг	Thursday	в четверг	с четверга	до четверга
пятница	Friday	в пятницу	с пятницы	до пятницы
суббота	Saturday	в субботу	с субботы	до субботы
воскресенье	Sunday	в воскресенье	с воскресенья	до воскресенья

You can also use the days of the week with **каждый** + acc.: **Каждую пятницу мы смотрим новый фильм.**

33.b   1. Сегодня **понедельник**. On Monday I work all day.   **В понедельник** _____

2. Сегодня _____.   On Tuesday I read in the library.   _____

3. Сегодня _____.   On Wednesday I sit at home.   _____

4. Сегодня _____.   On Thursday I call my mom.   _____

5. Сегодня _____.   On Friday I drink wine at a bar.   _____

6. Сегодня _____.   On Saturday I dance at a party.   _____

7. Сегодня _____.   On Sunday I relax all day.   _____

33.c   1. Я буду занят с понедельник_____ до сред_____.   4. Моя подруга свободна до четверг_____.

2. Мой друг будет у нас до воскресень_____.   5. Они будут в Москве до пятниц_____, включительно.

3. Мы будем снова (once again) на работе со вторник_____.   6. С суббот_____ будет новый спектакль в этом театре.

---

1. Что ты делаешь в понедельник, во вторник, и т. д.?[2]   3. Какой день недели твой любимый день?

2. Какой день недели у тебя самый трудный (the hardest)?   4. В какой день у нас контрольная по русскому языку?

---

[1] Can also be used in the sense of "starting on," as in **с понедельника** (starting on Monday; as of Monday)   [2] = **и так далее** = etc.

33.5 This, last, and next

We can specify "this," "last," and "next" Monday by adding an adjective to the accusative phrases we just learned. These adjectives are: **этот** (this), **прошлый** (last), and **следующий** (next, following). The adjective agrees with its noun — in the accusative case. We can add a similar accusative phrase with **раз** (time).

on... (в + асс.)	this	last	next
в понедельник	в **этот** понедельник	в **прошлый** понедельник	в **следующий** понедельник
во вторник	в **этот** вторник	в **прошлый** вторник	в **следующий** вторник
в среду	в **эту** среду	в **прошлую** среду	в **следующую** среду
в четверг	в **этот** четверг	в **прошлый** четверг	в **следующий** четверг
в пятницу	в **эту** пятницу	в **прошлую** пятницу	в **следующую** пятницу
в субботу	в **эту** субботу	в **прошлую** субботу	в **следующую** субботу
в воскресенье	в **это** воскресенье	в **прошлое** воскресенье	в **следующее** воскресенье
	в **этот** раз this time	в **прошлый** раз last time	в **следующий** раз next time

1. This Saturday we have to work. _____ нам надо работать.   **33.d**

2. Last Saturday we were free. _____ мы были свободны.

3. Next Monday I'll make dinner. _____ я приготовлю ужин.

4. I make dinner every Monday. Я готовлю ужин _____.

5. Last time I made borshch. _____ я приготовил борщ.

6. This time I'll make soup. _____ я приготовлю суп.

7. Next time I'll make potatoes. _____ я приготовлю картошку.

Никогда не делай сегодня то, что можно отложить на завтра. Never do today what you can postpone until tomorrow.

33.6 Specifying which day, week, month, semester, year

When telling "when" in terms of week, month, semester, or year, use the prepositions **в** and **на** with the **prepositional** case. To specify "which," we can use the same adjectives as above: **этот** (this), **прошлый** (last), and **следующий** (next) — but since the nouns here are in the **prepositional**, the adjectives will be too.

<u>IMPORTANT</u>: **неделя** is a **на** noun. All of the remaining time units we've learned are **в** nouns.

	this	last	next
день	сегодня	вчера	завтра
неделя	на **этой** неделе	на **прошлой** неделе	на **следующей** неделе
месяц	в **этом** месяце	в **прошлом** месяце	в **следующем** месяце
семестр	в **этом** семестре	в **прошлом** семестре	в **следующем** семестре
год	в **этом** году[1]	в **прошлом** году	в **следующем** году

1. This week I'm (m.) busy, but next week I'll be free.   **33.e**

_____ я занят, но _____ я буду свободен.

2. Last month I didn't cook, but next month I'll cook every evening.

_____ и не готовила, но _____ я буду готовить каждый вечер.

3. This year we don't watch TV, but last year we watched every day.

_____ мы не смотрим телевизор, но _____ мы смотрели каждый день.

1. Что ты делаешь на этой неделе?   2. Что ты делал(а) на прошлой неделе?   3. Что ты будешь делать на следующей неделе?

[1] Note that **год** — like the nouns in 32.5 — takes the alternate prepositional ending, stressed **-у**

day 34: more time expressions; saying "for"

months; asking questions about time; summary of
useful adverbs; prepositions meaning "for"

Да здравствует пе́рвое ма́я! Long live the first of May! **Пе́рвое ма́я — День Труда́.** (труд: labor)

34.1 Months

The Russian names for months resemble
their English counterparts.[1] To say "in" a
certain month, use **в + prepositional**.

Note that all months are **masculine** — some
hard, some **soft**.

The months with soft endings are generally
end-stressed, following the same pattern
we've seen with **слова́рь**: any case ending we add will be stressed, for example:
янва́рь → в январе́ / до января́.

The only exception is **апре́ль → в апре́ле /
до апре́ля**.

	in	from (as of)	until
янва́рь	в январе́	с января́	до января́
февра́ль	в феврале́	с февраля́	до февраля́
март	в ма́рте	с ма́рта	до ма́рта
апре́ль	в апре́ле	с апре́ля	до апре́ля
май	в ма́е	с ма́я	до ма́я
ию́нь	в ию́не	с ию́ня	до ию́ня
ию́ль	в ию́ле	с ию́ля	до ию́ля
а́вгуст	в а́вгусте	с а́вгуста	до а́вгуста
сентя́брь	в сентябре́	с сентября́	до сентября́
октя́брь	в октябре́	с октября́	до октября́
ноя́брь	в ноябре́	с ноября́	до ноября́
дека́брь	в декабре́	с декабря́	до декабря́

Just as we did yesterday, we can specify "which" month by adding the adjectives **э́тот** (this), **про́шлый** (last),
and **сле́дующий** (next). The adjectives goes into the prepositional case, to agree with its noun. For example:

в э́том ме́сяце this month	**в про́шлом ме́сяце** last month	**в сле́дующем ме́сяце** next month
в э́том январе́ this January	**в про́шлом январе́** last January	**в сле́дующем январе́** next January

[1] This is *very* good news, since some Slavic languages (like Czech, Polish, and Ukrainian) have entirely different, Slavic names for months!

1. В _____ (январь) у меня экзамен по истории.

2. Ты будешь у нас в Москве в _____ (октябрь)?

3. Я буду в Питере с _____ (июнь) до _____ (ноябрь).

4. — С какого месяца ты будешь здесь? — С _____ (апрель).

5. — А до какого месяца? — До _____ (декабрь).

6. — В каком месяце у нас экзамен? — В _____ (май).

7. Я была в России в _____ (прошлый февраль).

8. В _____ (июль) я буду работать в ресторане.

9. А в _____ (август) я буду снова в университете.

10. Я буду свободна с _____ (май) до _____ (июнь).

11. С _____ (декабрь) я буду во Владивостоке.

12. Моя семья будет жить там до _____ (март).

13. В _____ (ноябрь) у них будет концерт.

14. В _____ (апрель) я буду в США (say: "в сэ-шэ-а").

"Октябрь" — известный фильм Сергея Эйзенштейна об Октябрьской революции.

В каком месяце...

Экзамен по русскому языку?	Конец следующего семестра?
Начало этого семестра?	Весенние каникулы?[1] (Spring Break)
Конец этого семестра?	Осенние каникулы? (Fall Break)
Начало следующего семестра?	Летние каникулы? (Summer Break)

34.2 Asking questions about time

Let's summarize the various questions we can ask so far about time, and sample answers to those questions:

Когда?	**В какой день?**	**На какой неделе?**	**В каком месяце?**	**В каком году?**
When?	On what day?	In what week?	In what month?	In what year?
В пятницу.		**На этой неделе.**	**В следующем месяце.**	**В прошлом году.**
On Friday.		This week.	Next month.	Last year.
	С какого дня?	**С какого месяца?**	**До какого дня?**	**До какого месяца?**
	From what day?	From what month?	Until what day?	Until what month?
	С понедельника.	**С января.**	**До воскресенья.**	**До июня.**
	Starting on Monday.	Starting in January.	Until Sunday.	Until June.
Как долго?	**Совсем недолго.**	**Час.**	**Целую неделю.**	**Весь день.**
For how long?	Not long at all.	For an hour.	For an entire week.	All day.
Как часто?	**Очень редко.**	**Каждый день.**	**Каждую неделю.**	**Каждый год.**
How often?	Very rarely.	Every day.	Every week.	Every day.

---

1. Как часто ты смотришь телевизор?

2. Как долго ты обычно смотришь телевизор?

3. Как долго ты работаешь каждый день?

4. В каком году ты начал (начала) изучать (study) русский язык?

5. В каком месяце у тебя день рождения (birthday)?

6. Когда ты будешь в России? С какого месяца? До какого месяца?

---

[1] These terms for breaks (from the French *canicule*: a hot period) are plural in Russian, so we haven't studied these forms yet.

34.3 Summary of useful adverbs

With so much to say about noun declensions and verb conjugations, it's easy to let Russian adverbs slip through the cracks. But they're among the most common and most useful words in the language. Let's summarize some of the most common, many of which have to do with time. Some we've seen, and some are new.

often with imperfective verbs:		often with perfective verbs:[1]		qualifying:	
всегда	always	опять	again	очень	very
часто	often	ещё раз	once more time	довольно	quite, rather
обычно	usually	снова	once again	слишком	too
регулярно	regularly	скоро	soon	совсем	completely, fully
иногда	sometimes	вдруг	suddenly	ужасно	terribly
редко	rarely	только что	just now	сравнительно	relatively
никогда не	never	со временем	eventually	много	a lot, much
долго	for a long time	недавно	recently	мало	a little, not much
недолго	not for long	заранее	ahead of time		
давно уже	for a long time now	впервые	for the first time	**other:**	
ещё	still	сначала	at first	только	only
уже не	not anymore	потом	then, next	тоже	also
сейчас	now	наконец	finally	быстро	quickly
теперь	(but) now	ещё не	not yet	медленно	slowly
раньше	previously, before	уже	already	почти	almost
		вовремя	on time	давно	a long time ago

34.b

1. You work too much! — Ты _____ _____ работаешь!

2. I'm almost always working. — Я _____ _____ работаю!

3. I never relax anymore. — Я _____ _____ не отдыхаю.

4. I (f.) would relax before, but now I can't. — _____ я отдыхал, но _____ не могу.

5. Soon I'll be in Russia once again. — _____ я буду _____ в России.

6. We finally saw each other recently. — Мы _____ увиделись _____.

7. We haven't seen each other in a long time. — Мы _____ не виделись.

8. We used to see each other quite often. — Раньше мы _____ _____ виделись.

9. Eventually I (m.) got used to Russian food. — ___ _____ я привык к русской еде.

10. I (f.) bought a train ticket ahead of time. — Я купила билет на поезд _____.

11. He did everything very quickly. — Он всё делал _____ _____.

Шоссе — не космос!
The highway is not outer space.
Это слишком быстро (too fast)!

34.4 Prepositions meaning "for"

The preposition "for" is extremely common in English. Unfortunately, it has a number of meanings — some of which are time-related, and some not. This makes it tricky to translate into Russian. Let's start by reviewing a few common Russian equivalents, before looking at the various "for" uses of the preposition **на**.

для + gen.	for (a person or purpose)	У меня **для тебя** огромный сюрприз. I have a huge surprise **for you**.	Нам надо купить гель **для душа**. We need to buy "gel for shower."
за + acc.	for (exchange)	Кто сегодня заплатит **за пиво**? Who will pay **for the beer** today?	Огромное спасибо **за подарок**! "Huge" thanks **for the present**!
	for (in favor)	Они **за войну**, а я против войны. They're for the war, but I'm against war.	Солдат воевал **за родину**. The soldier fought for his homeland.
от + gen.	for (with medicines)	Мне нужно лекарство **от кашля**. I need medicine for coughing.	Это таблетка **от простуды**. This is a pill for a cold (a cold pill).

[1] These adverbs tend to be used with the perfective because they suggest one-time or sudden past or future actions; but, as is usually the case, they may be seen with the imperfective when describing a **present-tense** (ongoing) situation, or **repetition**.

34.5 Saying "for" with the preposition на

We can use **на** + acc. in the sense of "for" when **looking ahead** to future time periods (speaking of plans, trips, assignments "for" a certain time) or purposes (money "for" a purchase, tickets "for" a concert, etc.). For these examples, we'll resort to two **plural** nouns: **планы** (plans — the plural of **план**) and **деньги** (money). These plurals are the same in the nominative and the accusative. We'll formally introduce plural forms in Book 2.

на + acc.			
for (plans, assignments)	У вас есть планы **на следующий год**? Do you have plans **for next year**?	У нас есть работа **на пятницу**? Do we have any work **for Friday**?
for (tickets, reservations)	Я купила тебе билет **на концерт**. I bought you a ticket **for the concert**.	Я заказал[1] стол **на завтра**. I booked a table **for tomorrow**.
for (a purchase)	У тебя есть деньги **на билет**? Do you have money **for a ticket**?	Дай мне деньги **на метро**. Give me money **for the subway**.
for (a period of time)	Я еду в Россию **на месяц**. I'm going to Russia for a month.	Мне нужна комната **на три ночи**. I need a room **for three nights**.
for (an occasion)	Что ты купишь ей **на день рождения**? What will you buy her **for her birthday**?	**На Новый год** нам подарили икру. They gave us caviar **for New Year's**.

Note that if someone asks about your plans "for" a certain day (using **на** + acc.), you would respond by telling what you will do "on" that day (using **в** + acc.) — or a corresponding "when" construction for a week, year, etc.

У тебя есть планы **на субботу**?
 Do you have plans **for Saturday**?

В субботу я буду отдыхать.
 On Saturday I'm going to relax.

Какие у тебя планы **на следующую неделю**?
 What plans do you have **for next week**?

На следующей неделе я должен буду работать.
 Next week I'll have to work.

Навсегда! Forever! (Февраль 1917)

The February Revolution led Nicholas II to abdicate, giving way to a Provisional Government (**Временное правительство**), which in turn was overthrown by the Bolsheviks.

Pick the right preposition from among those meaning "for" listed above. **34.c**

1. Моя мама делает всё _____ нас. Мы должны купить ей подарок.

2. Ты должен сказать бабушке спасибо _____ торт.

3. Я еду в Москву _____ неделю, потом вернусь домой.

4. У нас есть задание по русскому языку _____ завтра?

5. У нас есть деньги _____ билет _____ поезд?

6. Ты не можешь сегодня заплатить _____ кофе? А я завтра заплачу.

7. Давайте закажем стол _____ пятницу.

8. Какие у тебя планы _____ эту субботу? А _____ следующую?

9. Это хороший план _____ завтра. Я _____ (I'm in favor).

10. Мы попросили у соседа деньги _____ билет _____ поезд.

11. Какое у нас задание по русскому языку _____ понедельник?

12. Очень рекомендую это лекарство _____ гриппа (грипп: flu).

13. _____ кого ты купил этот шоколад? _____ новой подруги?

14. Моя сестра больна. Я _____ неё купила лекарство _____ кашля (cough).

15. Что ты обычно покупаешь отцу _____ день рождения?

---

1. Что тебе обычно дарят на день рождения?

2. Что ты обычно покупаешь маме и папе на день рождения?

3. Какие у тебя планы на следующую субботу?

4. Какие у тебя планы на следующий год?

5. Тебе надо купить билет? А на что именно?

6. У нас есть задание по русскому языку на завтра?

---

[1] The verb **заказывать** АЙ / **заказать** A generally means "to order," but can also mean "to book" or "reserve."

day 35: prepositions and locations

where, where to, and where from; **где** / **куда** / **откуда**
with **в** nouns; introducing verbs of motion;
где / **куда** / **откуда** with **на** nouns

Наш триумф в космосе — гимн Стране Советов! Our triumph in space is a hymn to the Country of the Soviets!

35.1 Where, where to, and where from

The word "where" in English is slightly vague. Compare "Where are you?" and "Where are you going?" The first "where" asks about **location**, while the second asks about a **destination**. We could distinguish a third question as well: "where from."[1] Russian asks and answers each of these three questions in very different ways:

	где? = where?		куда? = where to?		откуда? = where from?	
библиотека *(a "в" noun)*	в + prep.	**в библиотеке** at / in the library	в + acc.	**в библиотеку** to the library	из + gen.	**из библиотеки** from the library
вокзал *(a "на" noun)*	на + prep.	**на вокзале** at the station	на + acc.	**на вокзал** to the station	с + gen.	**с вокзала** from the station
лекция *(an event)*	на + prep.	**на лекции** at the lecture	на + acc.	**на лекцию** to the lecture	с + gen.	**с лекции** from the lecture

176 [1] Once upon a time, English had distinct terms for each question — "where," "whence," and "whither" — but these are rarely heard today!

Whenever we speak of a location in Russian, we'll be careful to distinguish between **где** phrases, **куда** phrases, and **откуда** phrases. Note that nouns which take **на** when telling "where" and "where to" take **с** when telling "where from." Thus, we can speak of two "**sets**" of prepositions: one for **в** nouns, and one for **на** nouns.

35.2 где / куда / откуда with "в nouns"

As we know, most nouns use **в** to describe location with the prepositional. These so-called **в nouns** use the following **set** of prepositions to tell "where to" and "where from." Think of this as a distinct "set" for **в** nouns

That is, if we use **в** to tell **где** for a particular noun, then we will use **в** to tell **куда** and **из** to tell **откуда**.

	где	куда	откуда
	в + prep.	**в** + acc.	**из** + gen.
комната ➡	в комнат**е** in the room	в комнат**у** into the room	из комнат**ы** from the room
бар ➡	в бар**е**	в бар	из бар**а**
рюкзак ➡	в рюкзак**е**	в рюкзак	из рюкзак**а**
ресторан ➡	в ресторан**е**	в ресторан	из ресторан**а**
общежитие ➡	в общежити**и**	в общежити**е**	из общежити**я**
Москва ➡	в Москв**е**	в Москв**у**	из Москв**ы**
Россия ➡	в Росси**и**	в Росси**ю**	из Росси**и**

Since the preposition **в** is used in both **где** and **куда** expressions, we need to pay special attention to the case that follows it.[1]

в + prepositional = **где**, "where"	**в** + accusative = **куда**, "where to"

Even without a verb or further context, **в + accusative** clearly conveys motion *to a destination*, while **в + prepositional** clearly conveys being *in a location*.

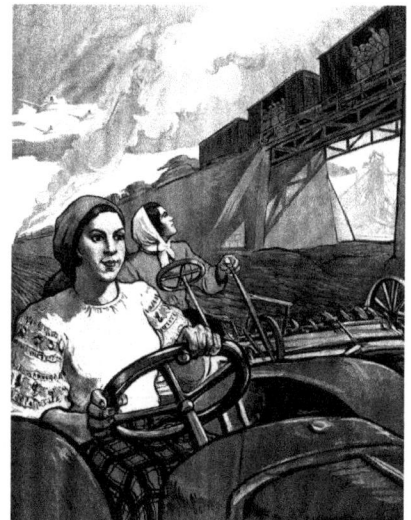

ТРАКТОР В ПОЛЕ— ЧТО ТАНК В БОЮ!

Трактор в поле — что танк в бою!
A tractor in the field is like a tank in battle!
(or: a tractor in the field is as good as a tank in battle).

The word **бой** (battle) takes the alternate "locative" prepositional ending, stressed **у** — since the ending is soft, we write **в бою**. This is a **где** phrase, as is **в поле**.

В сберкассе деньги накопила, путёвку на курорт купила! I saved up (my) money at a *sberkassa*, and bought a trip (**путёвка**) to a resort (**курорт**)!

A **сберкасса** was a kind of Soviet savings bank. The phrase **в сберкассе** — with the **prepositional** case — tells us **где** (where) she saved her money.

В СБЕРКАССЕ ДЕНЬГИ НАКОПИЛА, ПУТЕВКУ НА КУРОРТ КУПИЛА

КТО-КУДА А Я В СБЕРКАССУ!

Кто — куда, а я — в сберкассу! Posters often use pithy and elliptical, even verbless, language. Literally: "Who to where, but I to the *sberkassa*!" The idea is something like "People go all kinds of places, as they wish, but *I'm* going to the *sberkassa*!" The phrase **в сберкассу** — with the **accusative** case—tells us **куда** (where to) this guy is going.

---

[1] Students who have studied other inflected European languages may recall a similar case distinction, e.g. German "im Zimmer" versus "ins Zimmer," or Latin "in cubiculō" versus "in cubiculum."

35.a   *Fill in the correct case forms. Practice listening to questions from your instructor or partner, and answer with the right construction. Always think in terms of где / куда / откуда!*

где	куда	откуда
в + prep.	**в** + acc.	**из** + gen.

1. стран<u>а</u>   _____   _____   _____

2. к<u>о</u>смос   _____   _____   _____

3. рестор<u>а</u>н   _____   _____   _____

4. Москв<u>а</u>   _____   _____   _____

5. Петерб<u>у</u>рг   _____   _____   _____

6. общеж<u>и</u>тие   _____   _____   _____

7. Росс<u>и</u>я   _____   _____   _____

8. Фр<u>а</u>нция   _____   _____   _____

9. кварт<u>и</u>ра   _____   _____   _____

10. те<u>а</u>тр   _____   _____   _____

11. магаз<u>и</u>н   _____   _____   _____

12. гост<u>и</u>ная   _____   _____   _____

13. м<u>о</u>ре   _____   _____   _____

Не пуск<u>а</u>й козл<u>а</u> в огор<u>о</u>д. Don't let a goat (**козёл**) into the garden (i.e., a bull into a china shop).

Молодёжь, в бой за р<u>о</u>дину!
Youth (here, young men), into battle for the homeland!

In this poster, we have **бой** (battle) in the accusative: **в бой** (to battle, into battle) is a **куда** phrase.

Compare **в бой** (куда) with **в бою** (где) in the poster on the previous page.

В к<u>о</u>смос! Into space!

A poster supporting the Soviet space program. Note how clearly — even without a verb — this phrase implies motion *into* space. We might translate it as "To space!" or "Into outer space!" This is a **куда** phrase.

Compare this to the **где** phrase, **в к<u>о</u>смосе**. Как мы уж<u>е</u> зн<u>а</u>ем, сов<u>е</u>тский космон<u>а</u>вт Ю́рий Гаг<u>а</u>рин был п<u>е</u>рвый челов<u>е</u>к в к<u>о</u>смосе.

35.3 Introducing verbs of motion

To begin using **куда** and **откуда** phrases, we'll introduce two simple motion verbs. Don't worry — we'll spend the next several lessons discussing motion verbs in great detail.

ты ид<u>ё</u>шь	you're going (on foot)
ты <u>е</u>дешь	you're going (by vehicle)

Since these verbs describe **motion** to or from a location, they're often used with **куда** and **откуда** phrases:

Куда ты ид<u>ё</u>шь?   **В библиот<u>е</u>ку.**
Where are you going?   To the library.

Откуда ты ид<u>ё</u>шь?   **Из библиот<u>е</u>ки.**
Where are you coming from?   From the library.

Куда ты <u>е</u>дешь?   **В Росс<u>и</u>ю.**
Where are you going?   To Russia.

Откуда ты <u>е</u>дешь?   **Из Росс<u>и</u>и.**
Where are you coming from?   From Russia.

We can combine **куда** and **откуда** phrases:

Я <u>е</u>ду **из Москв<u>ы</u> в Петерб<u>у</u>рг**.
I'm going **from Moscow to Petersburg**.

Я ид<u>у</u> **из библиот<u>е</u>ки в общеж<u>и</u>тие**.
I'm going **from the library to the dorm**.

We can combine multiple **где** phrases, multiple **куда** phrases, etc.

Я <u>е</u>ду **в г<u>о</u>род, в те<u>а</u>тр**.
I'm going **to town, to the theater**.

Я возвращ<u>а</u>юсь **из г<u>о</u>рода, из те<u>а</u>тра**.
I'm returning **from the city, from the theater**.

Я был **в г<u>о</u>роде, в те<u>а</u>тре**.
I was in town, at the theater.

35.4 где / куда / откуда with "на nouns"

When we introduced the prepositional case, we saw that certain nouns use **на** to tell **где** — including: flat, open spaces; events; and the four cardinal directions (east, west, north, south). Such **на nouns** use a different "set" of prepositions to talk about location. Most importantly, they use **с** (**never из!**) to tell **откуда**.[1] Here are several sets of examples:

	где **на** + prep.	куда **на** + acc.	откуда **с** + gen.
стол	на стол**е** on the table	на стол onto the table	со стол**а** from the table
вокзал	на вокз**а**ле	на вокз**а**л	с вокз**а**ла
стадио**н**	на стади**о**не	на стади**о**н	со стади**о**на
бе**рег**	на берег**у**	на **б**ерег	с **б**ерега
концерт	на конц**е**рте	на конц**е**рт	с конц**е**рта
рабо**та**	на раб**о**те	на раб**о**ту	с раб**о**ты
лекция	на лекц**ии**	на лекц**ию**	с лекц**ии**
за**пад**	на з**а**паде	на з**а**пад	с з**а**пада**

На запад! Westward! "In the West" is **на з**а**паде** (a **где** phrase). So, if we are moving *to* the West, we need a **куда** phrase: **на** + the accusative. The Soviet soldier is tearing down a sign reading "nach Osten," the German for **На восток!** — "To the East! Eastward!"

Женщина, на парово**з!** А **паров**о**з** is a locomotive (something that transports using steam, **п**а**ра**).

Since **паров**о**з** is in the accusative here, it's telling **куда**. So the poster is inviting women "onto the locomotive," to work as conductors.

*These are all **на** nouns. Ask and answer где / куда / откуда questions about them.* **35.b**

	где **на** + prep.	куда **на** + acc.	откуда **с** + gen.
1. ур**о**к	_____	_____	_____
2. зан**я**тие	_____	_____	_____
3. рын(о)к	_____	_____	_____
4. л**е**стница	_____	_____	_____
5. спект**а**кль	_____	_____	_____
6. вечер**и**нка	_____	_____	_____
7. двор	_____	_____	_____
8. д**а**ча	_____	_____	_____
9. пляж	_____	_____	_____
10. бал**е**т	_____	_____	_____
11. **о**стров	_____	_____	_____
12. п**о**чта	_____	_____	_____

Ры**ба гни**ё**т с голов**ы**.** A fish rots from the head.   **С кораб**л**я на бал.** From the ship to the ball.

*Куд**а** ты ид**ё**шь сег**о**дня? Что ты там (there) б**у**дешь д**е**лать? Что теб**е** там н**у**жно?*

examples with в nouns

1. Ты ид**ё**шь сег**о**дня **в библиот**е**ку**?
2. Ты ид**ё**шь сег**о**дня **в магаз**и**н**?
3. Ты ид**ё**шь сег**о**дня **в стол**о**вую**?
4. Ты ид**ё**шь сег**о**дня **в коф**е**йню**?
5. Ты ид**ё**шь сег**о**дня **в рестор**а**н**?
6. Ты **е**дешь **в Росс**и**ю** в **э**том год**у**?

examples with на nouns

7. Ты ид**ё**шь сег**о**дня **на л**е**кцию**?
8. Ты ид**ё**шь сег**о**дня **на спект**а**кль**?
9. Ты ид**ё**шь сег**о**дня **на пляж**?

[1] Understood most literally, **с** means "(down) from off of" a flat surface — as in **со стол**а or **со ст**е**ны**, as opposed to "from out of" an enclosed surface.   [2] The "**с**" assimilates here: say "ззапада" (or, said quickly, simply **з**а**пада**)

day 36: introduction to verbs of motion

verbs with three infinitives; translating versus "unpacking"; indeterminate, determinate and perfective verbs of motion; conjugating motion verbs; "breakdowns"

Лично (personally) **Гитлеру** (to Hitler) **в Берлин** (to Berlin). Addressing bombs during World War II (while smoking!?).

36.1 Russian verbs of motion: verbs with three infinitives!

As we know, the vast majority of Russian verbs come in aspectual pairs — that is, **two infinitives**: the first **imperfective** (ongoing or repeated action), and the second **perfective** (completed or one-time action).

But a few verbs come in sets of **three infinitives** — they have **two imperfective infinitives**. We'll write them up as follows, to make clear that the first two infinitives (to the left of the forward slash) are **both imperfective**:

ordinary verbs: 2 infinitives		verbs of motion: 3 infinitives (2 imperfective!)	
читать АЙ / **прочитать** АЙ	to read	**ходить** И^{shift} - **идти** / **пойти**	to go (by foot)
писать А^{shift} / **написать** А	to write	**ездить** И - **ехать** / **поехать**	to go (by vehicle)

Such verbs are referred to as **verbs of motion** (in Russian, **глаголы движения**). Note that not every Russian verb that **describes** motion is a "verb of motion" in this sense.[1] There are only about 18 of these special verbs in the entire language; today, we'll look at the two most common — for motion by foot, and motion by vehicle.

36.2 Aspect and determinacy

So, if motion verbs have **two imperfective infinitives**, what's the difference between them? To answer this question, we must introduce an additional category: **determinacy**. A motion verb's first imperfective infinitive (like **ходить** or **ездить** above) is **indeterminate**, while the second infinitive (like **идти** or **ехать**) is **determinate**.

180   [1] An example is **гулять** АЙ / **погулять** АЙ: to stroll. We will use the term "verbs of motion" strictly to refer to verbs with **three infinitives**.

It's essential to remember that **both** of these infinitives are **imperfective** — so, by definition, they can **both** describe 1) **ongoing** action; and 2) **repeated** action. Resist the common mistake of vaguely imagining that **ходить**, for example, is somehow "more imperfective" than **идти**!

So, what's the difference in meaning between an **indeterminate** form and a **determinate** form? We will try to capture this distinction using both **keywords** and **pictograms**. In essence, **indeterminate** verbs describe going "**around**" (visualize: ↻), while **determinate** verbs describe being "**underway**" (visualize: →).

36.3 Translating verbs of motion versus "unpacking" verbs of motion

When describing motion, English speakers often use some form of "**go**." But with respect to the range of Russian motion verb forms, the verb "to go" is hopelessly vague. If we simply **translate** Russian verbs of motion into everyday English, a lot of crucial information will be lost, and we'll fail to pick up on important distinctions.

So, for learning purposes, it's often useful to "**unpack**" all of the nuanced information a Russian verb of motion conveys. This ensures that we are fully understanding the Russian verb's meaning. The keywords (and pictograms) we just learned are very helpful in nailing down these nuances. Compare:

	translated	"unpacked"	
ходи́ть:	to go	to go **around** on foot	↻
е́здить:	to go	to go **around** by vehicle	↻

	translated	"unpacked"	
идти́:	to go	to be **underway** by foot	→
е́хать:	to go	to be **underway** by vehicle	→

36.4 Indeterminate motion verbs

Let's begin today's overview of motion verbs by focusing on **imperfective** forms, to the right.

The keyword **around** (and the pictogram ↻) captures the basic meanings of **indeterminate** verbs like **ходи́ть** and **е́здить**:

1. going **around** in circles
2. going **around** aimlessly
3. making **round** trips, there and back again

36.5 Determinate motion verbs

The keyword **underway** (and the pictogram →) captures the basic meaning of **determinate** verbs like **идти́** and **е́хать**.

1. to be underway — going with some sense of destination or purpose, however vague!

imperfective
1. **Ongoing** action (no mention of result).
2. **Repeated** or habitual action.
3. Emphasis on **attempt** or effort.

ходи́ть И - **идти́** /
е́здить И - **е́хать** /

indeterminate	determinate
↻ keyword: **around**	→ keyword: **underway**

These imperfective verb can describe **ongoing** action...

| ↻ to be going **around**; to make a **round** trip | → to be **underway**, be making a one-way trip |

...or, **repeated** action, as in:

| ↻↻ to make multiple **round** trips | ⇒ to be **underway** on multiple one-way trips |

---

*Can you choose the Russian infinitive that would best capture these kinds of motion? Rely on our **keywords** and **pictograms**![1]* **36.a**

1. you're heading to class right now _____

2. you go to class every day _____

3. you used to go to Russia once per year _____

4. you used to go to class every day _____

5. where were you walking to yesterday? _____

6. you'd like to go to Russia frequently _____

7. you were on a train to Moscow _____

8. the child knows how to walk _____

9. we're walking around in the park _____

10. I'm on my way to New York _____

11. your friend never goes to class _____

12. I'll go to class every day next semester! _____

[1] Consult the key for this excercise; some answers may surprise you! We'll delve into each situation in the coming lessons.

36.6 Perfective verbs of motion

Let's complete our table by adding the **perfective** infinitives, giving us a total of **three infinitives** for each type of motion. As we'd expect, these perfective forms share important features with any other perfective verb:

1) if we simply conjugate these verbs, we get **future** tense. For example: **я пойду** means "I *will* go..."
2) these verbs emphasize one-time, specific actions; they can never describe **repeated** motion.

Compare these motion verbs (3 infinitives) with an **ordinary** verb (2 infinitives) like **читать** / **прочитать**.

imperfective	perfective
1. **Ongoing** action (no mention of result).	1. **Completed** action (emphasis on result).
2. **Repeated** or habitual action.	2. **One-time** action.
3. Emphasis on **attempt** or effort.	3. Emphasis on **success** or accomplishment.
# чит**а**ть АЙ	/ # прочит**а**ть АЙ

Now look at verbs of motion, with their **two imperfective forms**, and various basic meanings.

imperfective		perfective
indeterminate	**determinate**	
1. **Ongoing** action (no mention of result).		1. **Completed** action (emphasis on result).
2. **Repeated** or habitual action.		2. **One-time** action.
3. Emphasis on **attempt** or effort.		3. Emphasis on **success** or accomplishment.
# ход**и**ть И - идт**и**		# пойт**и**
# **е**здить И - **е**хать		# по**е**хать
↺ keyword: **around**	→ keyword: **underway**	⇉ keyword: **setting out** (and assumed arrival)
↺ to be going **around**; to make a **round** trip	→ to be **underway**, be making a one-way trip	↦ to **set out** ↦ to **make it** somewhere (a one-way trip)
↻ to make multiple **round** trips	⇒ to be **underway** on multiple one-way trips	these perfective verbs cannot describe ongoing or repeated action, and can never be present-tense!

In our discussion of aspect (18.5), we learned that while most perfective verbs describe **completion** of a one-time action, some are best thought of as describing the **inception** of a one-time action. An example we've seen is **заплакать** (to begin crying, to burst out crying).

Perfective verbs of motion like **пойти** and **поехать** are also essentially **inceptive** in meaning. Let's take two examples — one past-tense, one future-tense (remember, perfective verbs can never be present-tense!).

			translated	"unpacked"
пойти:	⇨	Он **пошёл** в библиот**е**ку.	He went to the library.	He **set out** on foot for the libary. ↦
пое**хать**:	⇨	Он**а** по**е**дет в Росс**и**ю.	She will go to Russia.	She will **set out** by vehicle for Russia. ↦

It's very important to note that, strictly speaking, a perfective verb of motion only conveys **inception**: someone "set out" for a destination. Absent additional information, we don't know whether they reached their destination.

In everyday speech, however, we usually assume that the person not only "set out," but also "got there." That is, perfective motion verbs are used to describe one-way, one-time trips whose completion is assumed.

Let's unpack the same examples again, with regard to what they literally state, and what we often assume:

			literally stated:	typically assumed:
пойти:	⇨	Он **пошёл** в библиот**е**ку.	He set off on foot for the library.	He **made it** to the library. ↠
пое**хать**:	⇨	Он**а** по**е**дет в Росс**и**ю.	She will set off by vehicle for Russia.	She will **make it** to Russia. ↠

36.7 Conjugating verbs of motion

Here is a first look at the conjugated forms for motion on foot and by vehicle. Treat **идти** and **ехать** as irregular verbs that must simply be memorized, while noting that **ходить** and **ездить** are **И verbs** and follow the same patterns that we've seen before. Finally, perfective forms are essentially determinate forms prefixed with **по-**.

	imperfective		perfective
	indeterminate	determinate	
	↻ around	→ underway	⇥ setting out (and making it)

ходить И - идти / пойти

present tense:	хожу ходишь ходит ходим ходите ходят	иду идёшь идёт идём идёте идут	✕
past tense:	ходил ходила ходило ходили	шёл[1] шла шло шли	пошёл[1] пошла пошло пошли
future tense:	буду ходить будешь ходить будет ходить будем ходить будете ходить будут ходить	буду идти будешь идти будет идти будем идти будете идти будут идти	пойду пойдёшь пойдёт пойдём пойдёте пойдут

ездить И - ехать / поехать

present tense:	езжу ездишь ездит ездим ездите ездят	еду едешь едет едем едете едут	✕
past tense:	ездил ездила ездило ездили	ехал ехала ехало ехали	поехал поехала поехало поехали
future tense:	буду ездить будешь ездить будет ездить будем ездить будете ездить будут ездить	буду ехать будешь ехать будет ехать будем ехать будете ехать будут ехать	поеду поедешь поедет поедем поедете поедут

[1] The verb **идти** (and, in turn, **пойти**) is one of the few Russian verbs that is **irregular in the past tense**. All other past tense forms here are formed from the infinitive, for example: ходил, ездила, ехали, поехал, etc.

36.8 "Breakdowns" in the system of motion verbs

We've looked at the essential meanings of each infinitive and learned some keywords and mental pictures for envisioning these essential meanings. Of course, when we conjugate the infinitives across the three tenses (past, present, future), they will generally preserve those basic meanings. Here are some simple examples, "unpacked":

Он **идёт**.	He is underway by foot.	Он **ходит** в школу.	He makes round trips to school.
Он **шёл**.	He was underway by foot.	Он **ходил** в школу.	He made round trips to school.
Он **будет идти**.	He will be underway by foot.	Он **будет ходить** в школу.	He will make round trips to school.

So, generally, the Russian motion verb system is highly descriptive and largely consistent: each infinitive has a distinct inherent meaning, and that same meaning is carried over across the various tenses.

However, as we look at these verbs in depth, we'll see a few specific instances (we'll call them **breakdowns**) in which this system breaks down a bit, in ways that may seem inconsistent, but which are perfectly clear and accepted in everyday usage. Here is a simplified table of our two verbs of motion to refer to in the exercises below.

	imperfective		perfective
	indeterminate	determinate	
by foot:	**ходить** И	- **идти** /	**пойти**
by vehicle:	**ездить** И	- **ехать** /	**поехать**
	↻ around	→ underway	⟼ setting out (assumed arrival ⟼ᵢ)

36.b *What infinitive would best capture this motion? Think carefully in terms of our **keywords**: 1) around, 2) underway, 3) setting out.*

	keyword:	pictogram:	infinitive:
1. you'll attend class every day next semester	_____	_____	_____
2. you never go to classes	_____	_____	_____
3. you were walking to class	_____	_____	_____
4. your friend left for class	_____	_____	_____
5. "Where's Jane?" "She went off to class."	_____	_____	_____
6. Jane went to class this morning. Now she's home.	_____	_____	_____
7. "Where's Bob?" "He's gone to Russia."	_____	_____	_____
8. Bob went to Russia last year. Now he's back home.	_____	_____	_____
9. Bob used to go to Russia often.	_____	_____	_____
10. Jane has never been to Russia. (think carefully!)	_____	_____	_____

36.c *Try "unpacking" these verbs of motion using our **keywords** and specifying the **type of motion** (by foot or by vehicle).*

1. Моя подруга всегда **ходит** на урок. _____

2. Куда ты **шёл** вчера, когда я тебя увидел в коридоре? _____

3. Вчера я **ходила** в театр на балет. _____

4. Завтра они **поедут** в Россию на два месяца. _____

5. "Куда она **пошла**?" "Не знаю. На лекцию, может быть?" _____

6. Я долго **ходила** в парке и думала о русской литературе. _____

day 37: indeterminate verbs of motion

going "around"; five basic kinds of motion; taking vehicles and going by foot; round trips; moving within a space

Он любит лет**а**ть. Куд**а** он лет**и**т сейч**а**с? (**лет**а**ть** АЙ: to fly **around**, indeterminate; **лет**е**ть** Е: to be **underway** by flight, determinate)

37.1 Going "around" ↻

Today we're looking in detail at **indeterminate** verbs of motion. Remember, these forms are "indeterminate" in the sense that they imply no sense of directionality or purpose. This essential meaning is best captured by the keyword "**around**." We'd use these forms to:

1) Describe the activity itself.	Реб**ё**нок уж**е** ум**е**ет **ход**и**ть**. The child already knows how to walk. Я любл**ю** **б**е**гать** в п**а**рке. I love to run (jog) in the park.
2) Describe going in circles, or back and forth.	Он два час**а** **ход**и**л** по к**о**мнате. He paced the room for two hours. Скаж**и**те, авт**о**бус здесь **х**о**дит**?[1] Tell me, does the bus run (circulate) here?
3) Going or wandering around "aimlessly."	Мы д**о**лго **ход**и**ли** по г**о**роду. We walked around the city for a long time. Я ц**е**лый м**е**сяц **е**здила по Росс**и**и. I traveled around Russia for an entire month.

Учи**тесь пл**а**вать!** Learn to swim!

When speaking of the activity itself (swimming, running, walking, etc.), Russian uses the indeterminate form, since no determinacy or directionality is implied, but simply swimming **вообщ**е (generally, in all directions!).

А вы уме**ете пл**а**вать?**

Try visualizing the motion in these sentences. Do you see why the *indeterminate* (↻) is most appropriate here? Why would a *determinate* form (keyword: "underway") make less sense?

[1] To learn why a "motion by foot" verb is used here, turn the page and see Breakdown No. 1.

185

37.2 Five basic kinds of motion

As we examine verbs of motion, we'll fill in the forms for all five basic types of motion. For each **type of motion**, there is a full set of **three infinitives**, which are given below. For now, we'll only use the indeterminate forms.

General definitions are given here; each verb may have multiple meanings: going by water could mean "swimming," "sailing," "floating," "drifting," etc.!

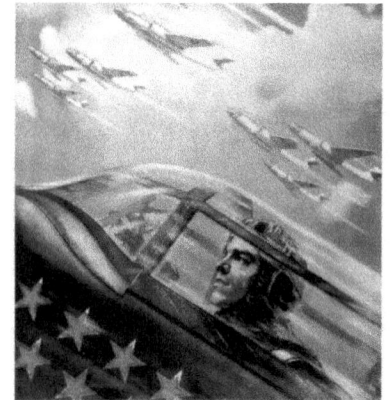

ходить И^{shift} - **идти** / **пойти**	**ездить** И - **ехать** / **поехать**
to go by foot	to go by vehicle

↻ ⦷	→ ⇶	↦ ⇥	↻ ⦷	→ ⇶	↦ ⇥

хожу

ходишь
ходит
ходим
ходите
ходят

ходи!

езжу

ездишь
ездит
ездим
ездите
ездят

езди!

ЛЕТАТЬ ВЫШЕ ВСЕХ, ДАЛЬШЕ ВСЕХ, БЫСТРЕЕ ВСЕХ.

Летать выше всех, дальше всех, быстрее всех. Fly higher, further, and faster than everyone. An indeterminate verb is used to describe the activity itself— "flying" **вообще**.

летать АЙ - **лететь** Е^{end} / **полететь** Е	**плавать** АЙ - **плыть** В / **поплыть** В	**бегать** АЙ - **бежать** / **побежать**
to go by air	to go by water	to go by running

летаю

летаешь
летает
летаем
летаете
летают

летай!

плаваю

плаваешь
плавает
плаваем
плаваете
плавают

плавай!

бегаю

бегаешь
бегает
бегаем
бегаете
бегают

бегай!

37.a *Think about what type of motion you're describing, then use the appropriate conjugated form to describe the following situations in Russian.*

1. She loves to swim in the pool (бассейн),

   Она любит _____ в бассейне.

2. The plane (самолёт) flew around in the sky (небо) for a long time.

   Самолёт долго _____ на небе.

3. — Where have you (pl.) been? — We've been traveling around Russia.

   — Где вы были?   — Мы _____ по России.

4. What's that floating around in my beer (пиво)?!

   Что это _____ в моём пиве?

5. The dog runs around in the park every morning.

   Собака каждое утро _____ в парке.

6. Every evening I (f.) would walk around in the city center (центр).

   Я каждый вечер _____ в центре.

7. A human being (человек) cannot fly.

   Человек не может _____.

Волка бояться — в лес не ходить. If you fear the wolf (**волк**), don't go into the forest.

Ленин на субботнике.
Lenin at a "voluntary Saturday work day."

Ленин ходил на работу даже в субботу!

Breakdown No. 1: Vehicles

If we ourselves are going by vehicle, we use "motion by vehicle" verbs like **ездить**. But what if we're referring to the motion of a wheeled vehicle itself? In this case, Russian generally prefers "motion by foot" verbs like **ходить**, especially for public transport (trains, buses, etc.).

Meanwhile, note that "motion by vehicle" verbs are indeed used for smaller vehicles, like cars.)

Why? Perhaps because these vehicles aren't "riding" anything; they're going under their own power! Here are two common examples:

Автобусы здесь **ходят**?	Смотри, наш поезд **идёт**!
Do buses run (circulate) here?	Look, our train is on its way!

But, whenever describing passengers on a bus or train, we'd use "motion by vehicle" verbs:

Мы **ездим** на автобусе.	Мы **едем** на поезде.

This old Soviet movie is called **Поезд идёт на восток** (The train is going — "is underway!"— eastward).

In the image: ПОЕЗД ИДЁТ НА ВОСТОК

37.3 Taking vehicles and going by foot

To describe your means of transport, use **ездить** (motion by vehicle), along with a **где** construction specifying the kind of vehicle.

Typically, we use **на** with vehicles (e.g. on the bus, by bus), unless we are specifically describing something that happened "in / inside" (**в**) the vehicle.

Я обычно езжу на работу **на автобусе**.	Я обычно читаю, когда я сижу **в автобусе**.
I usually go to work by bus (on the bus).	I usually read while I'm sitting in the bus.

If you're going on foot, you should, obviously, use motion-by-foot verbs. To be clear, you can add the adverb **пешком** (by foot, on foot). We'll see on the next page why it may be important to emphasize "on foot."

Я никогда не езжу **на автобусе**.	Я всегда **хожу пешком**.
I never take the bus.	I always go on foot.

---

1. **Я обычно езжу...**

на _____	(**машина**: car)	на _____	(**электричка**[1])	**37.b**
на _____	(**автобус**: bus)	на _____	(**велосипед**: bicycle)	
на _____	(**поезд**: train)	на _____	(**метро**: subway)	
на _____	(**трамвай**: streetcar)	на _____	(**такси**: taxi)	

2. **Я редко летаю..**

на _____	(**самолёт**: airplane)	на _____	(**вертолёт**: helicopter)

3. **Я часто плаваю...**

на _____	(**катер**: tour boat)	на _____	(**корабль**: ship)
на _____	(**яхта**: yacht)	на _____	(**лодка**: boat)

На чём ты обычно **ездишь** (или летаешь, или плаваешь!)...? (Или, может быть, ты просто **ходишь пешком**?)

в университет?	_____.	на остров?	_____.
на работу?	_____.	в кинотеатр?	_____.
на занятие?	_____.	в общежитие?	_____.
в Нью-Йорк?	_____.	на вечеринку?	_____.
домой?	_____.	в любимый ресторан?	_____.

---

[1] A suburban train, often featuring a colorful cohort of ice-cream peddlers, amateur musicians, etc. Never a dull moment here!

Out-of-town trips

It's important to note that "motion by vehicle" verbs are **absolutely** necessary when describing a trip outside the city. In such cases, using "motion by foot" verbs implies that you are **literally** making a voyage **on foot**! This can often strike the listener as quite comical.

Since all of the destinations in these examples (including the dacha!) are outside the city center, a real trip by vehicle is clearly implied.

not: Я **ходил** в Росси́ю.	I walked to Russia (!).
but: Я **е́здил** в Росси́ю.	I went to Russia.
not: Я **ходил** в Москву́.	I walked to Moscow (!).
but: Я **е́здил** в Москву́.	I went to Moscow.
not: Я **ходил** на да́чу.	I walked to the dacha (!).
but: Я **е́здил** на да́чу.	I went to the dacha.

Breakdown No. 2: In-town outings

So, generally, it's important to distinguish clearly between **motion by vehicle** and **motion by foot**. However, this guideline breaks down in one very important way: when describing **in-town** outings (going to the theater, the store, the park, etc.), Russians use motion-by-**foot** verbs <u>by default</u>, even when these trips actually involve vehicles. For in-town outings, motion-by-**vehicle** verbs would only be used if the **mode of transport** were being **emphasized** — if the point weren't simply "going," but "going by vehicle."

This is much like English, where we would normally say "I'm **going** to the movies" by default. We would only say "I'm **driving** to the movies" if we were emphasizing "how we're getting there," not the simple fact that we're going at all.

Я **иду́** в теа́тр.	Я ча́сто **хожу́** в теа́тр. И сего́дня **пойду́**.	Я **е́ду** в теа́тр.
I'm **going** to the theater. (default)	I often **go** to the theater. I'm **going** today too.	I'm **taking transport** to the theater.

If we specify a vehicle, then we absolutely must use motion-by-vehicle verbs:

Я **е́ду** в теа́тр на авто́бусе.
I'm **taking the bus** to the theater.

37.4 Single round trips: ↻

So, the basic meaning of **indeterminate** verbs like **ходи́ть** and **е́здить** is to go **around** — in circles, or back and forth, with no real sense of destination. But they can also describe a **round trip** (there and back again) to a destination. Look at these past-tense examples:

	translated	"unpacked"	
Я **ходи́л** в теа́тр.	I went to the theater.	I took a **round** trip to the theater.	↻
Я **е́здил** в Росси́ю.	I went to Russia.	I took a **round** trip by vehicle to Russia.	↻

It's very important to think of such completed trips as **round trips** — you went somewhere, then came home again. As we'll see, other motion-verb forms mean very different things. Here's a preview:

Я **шёл** в теа́тр.	I was going to the theater.	I was **underway** (on foot) to the theater.	⟶
Я **пошёл** в теа́тр.	I went to the theater.	I **set out** (on foot) for the theater.	⊢⟶

37.5 Multiple round trips: ↻↻↻

Remember: indeterminate verbs like **ходи́ть** and **е́здить** are **imperfective** in terms of aspect. This means that they, like any other imperfective verb, can describe both **ongoing** and **repeated** actions.

Я **хожу́** в теа́тр.	I go to the theater.	I take **round** trips to the theater.	↻↻↻
Я **е́зжу** в Росси́ю.	I go to Russia.	I take **round** trips by vehicle to Russia.	↻↻↻

37.6 Round trips in the past

In the **present** tense, an indeterminate form like **ходи́ть** and **е́здить** necessarily implies **repeated** round trips (since the action of going there and back again is ongoing, in the present). In the past, though, they can refer to both 1) a **single**, completed round trip, and 2) **multiple** round trips.

Я **ходи́л** в теа́тр.	I went to the theater.	I took one **round** trip to the theater.	↻
	or: I used to go to the theater.	I took multiple **round** trips to the theater.	↻↻↻

Я **е́здила** в Росси́ю.	I went to Russia.
or:	I used to go to Russia.

I took one **round** trip to Russia by vehicle. ↺
I made multiple **round** trips to Russia by vehicle. ⟲⟲⟲

Context usually helps us interpret these verb forms properly (is it **one** trip or **multiple** trips?):

Я **ходи́л** в теа́тр вчера́.	I went to the theater yesterday.
Я ча́сто **е́здила** в Росси́ю.	I would often go to Russia.

I took one **round** trip to the theater yesterday. ↺
I often made **round** trips to Russia by vehicle. ⟲⟲⟲

Students are often bothered at first by the fact that these imperfective verbs can describe a **single completed** trip. Doesn't that sound like something a **perfective** verb would do? Yes — but remember, we're talking specifically about verbs of motion, and they do some strange things. If **ходи́ть** essentially means "to make a **round** trip," then, when we make it past-tense, it can describe a **completed** round trip.[1]

Remember as well that the perfective equivalent (**пойти́**) only describes "setting out" and, often, "assumed arrival" — but only for a **one-way** trip. It describes going "there" only, not "there and back again."

Breakdown No. 3: Future round trips

What about the future tense? Based on all we've just said about indeterminate verbs like **ходи́ть** in the past tense (namely, that they can describe both **single** round trips and **multiple** round trips), we'd expect the same things to be true in the future. But this is not the case. In the **future** tense, a verb like **ходи́ть** is automatically understood to describe **multiple** trips. As we'll soon discuss, if we are describing a **single** trip in the **future**, we have **no choice** but to use a perfective like **пойти́**.

Я **бу́ду ходи́ть** в теа́тр.	I'll go (repeatedly) to the theater.		Я **пойду́** в теа́тр.	I'll go (once) to the theater.
Я **бу́ду е́здить** в Росси́ю.	I'll go (repeatedly) to Russia.		Я **пое́ду** в Росси́ю.	I'll go (once) to Russia.

37.7 Moving within a space

Remember, to specify a **destination**, use a **куда́** phrase, with **в** or **на** + accusative. Of course, such destinations are very common with motion verbs. Can we ever use a **где** phrase (**в** or **на** + prepositional) with such verbs? Yes, to describe **location** — that is, when we're "going around" **within** a space. Compare:

куда́:	Я бе́гаю **в парк** ка́ждый день.	I run **to the park** every day (round trips).
где:	Я бе́гаю **в па́рке** ка́ждый день.	I run (around) **in the park** every day.[2]

**НЕ ХОДИ́
ПО НЕИСПРА́ВНЫМ
МО́СТКАМ**

Не ходи́ по неиспра́вным мостка́м!
Don't walk on defective footbridges!

1. **Росси́я**:	Я е́здил(а) в Росси́ю.	Я был(а́) в Росси́и.	**37.с**
2. **ко́мната**:	Я ходи́л(а) в ко́мнат____.	Я был(а́) в ко́мнат____.	
3. **столо́вая**:	Я ходи́л(а) в столо́в_____.	Я был(а́) в столо́в_____.	
4. **конце́рт**:	Я ходи́л(а) на конце́рт____.	Я был(а́) на конце́рт____.	
5. **Евро́па**:	Я е́здил(а) в Евро́п____.	Я был(а́) в Евро́п____.	
6. **Петербу́рг**:	Я е́здил(а) в Петербу́рг___.	Я был(а́) в Петербу́рг___.	
7. **вечери́нка**:	Я ходи́л(а) на вечери́нк___.	Я был(а́) на вечери́нк___.	

---

*Combine these words to say that these people took (**past tense**!) round trips to these places "on" these vehicles.*

1. мой друг + лета́ть + Москва́ + самолёт

2. моя́ сестра́ + е́здить + Нью-Йо́рк + электри́чка

3. мой знако́мый + лета́ть + Росси́я + самолёт

4. моя́ знако́мая + пла́вать + Хе́льсинки + кора́бль

5. мой оте́ц + лета́ть + Москва́ + самолёт

6. мой профе́ссор + лета́ть + Евро́па + самолёт

7. его́ подру́га + е́здить + го́род + тролле́йбус

8. её ма́ма + е́здить + торго́вый центр + авто́бус

9. их сосе́дка + е́здить + дере́вня + маши́на

10. мы + е́здить + центр + метро́

---

[1] On Day 116, we'll introduce prefixed perfective forms for making "quick round trips," such as **сходи́ть** and **съе́здить**.
[2] In this instance, **по па́рку** doesn't quite work, as it suggests aimlessness (as in **Мы гуля́ем по го́роду**).

day 38: determinate verbs of motion

being underway; being underway along a path; conjugating
determinate verbs; an ongoing one-way trip;
repeated determinate motion

"Летят журавли" (The Cranes are Flying, 1957) — это старый и очень грустный советский фильм о Великой Отечественной войне.

38.1 Being underway: →

Our next set of motion verbs are **determinate**. Instead of going **around**, in circles, aimlessly, or with no clear sense of destination, these verbs describe being **underway**, going along a path with some sense of purpose or destination (however vague it might be!)

Our keyword (**underway**) and pictogram (→) are especially useful for these *determinate* verbs, which often cause students the most confusion. If we "unpack" them using "**underway**," or — better yet — visualize the kind of motion they're describing, then the distinction between these verbs and verbs like **ходить** is usually clear (→ versus ↻). And the same basic "**underway**" meaning carries over across all three tenses:

Я **иду** в театр.	I am underway to the theater.
Я **шёл** в театр.	I was underway to the theater.
Я **буду идти** в театр.	I will be underway to the theater.
Я **еду** в Москву.	I am underway to Moscow (by vehicle!).
Я **ехала** в Москву.	I was underway to Moscow.
Я **буду ехать** в Москву.	I will be underway to Moscow.

In each case, we should visualize someone on an unfolding one-way trip... walking down the street, riding in a train, **on their way**.

38.2 Being underway along a path

It's no surprise that we often see **determinate** verbs of motion used with the preposition **по** + dative, in the sense of going **along** (or down) a path.[1]

Keep in mind: a path may be **winding**, but it still **leads** somewhere. Determinate verbs don't necessarily mean that you're going in a straight line!

As migratory birds, cranes are associated in Russia with voyages, and returning home. So, the determinate verb **летят** (from **лететь**) is very important here — it describes birds "on their way," flying across the sky. If we used an indeterminate verb, the picture painted would be very different:

Летят журавли.
Cranes are flying past, across the sky, clearly going somewhere (like, home).

Летают журавли.
Cranes are flying around (or even in circles!) with no sense of direction.

[1] Recall that with **indeterminate** verbs **по** + the dative describes movement *around* a space: Я хожу по городу (I'm walking around the city).

идти:	Она **идёт** по тротуару.	She is walking down the sidewalk.
ехать:	Мы **едем** по улице.	We're driving down the street.
плыть B^end:	Корабль **плывёт** по реке.	The ship is sailing down the river.
бежа́ть:	Он **бежал** по лестнице.	He was running up/down the stairs.
лете́ть E^end:	Самолёт **летел** по небу.	The plane was flying across the sky.

Here are examples of **по** + dative with each of the determinate verbs we'll be focusing on today. Note that three are **irregular**!

38.3 Conjugating determinate verbs

Now, we can add determinate forms to our table of motion verbs. Note that **идти, ехать,** and **бежа́ть** are all irregular, so take care to memorize them. Furthermore, the imperative form of **ехать** is irregular: **езжай! езжайте!** Finally, remember that **идти** is one of a very few verbs with an irregular past. All others are regular in the past, but note that **плыть** is end-stressed in the feminine:

past tense of **идти**: он **шёл**, она **шла**, оно **шло**, они **шли**
past tense of **плыть**: он **плыл**, она **плыла**, оно **плыло**, они **плыли**

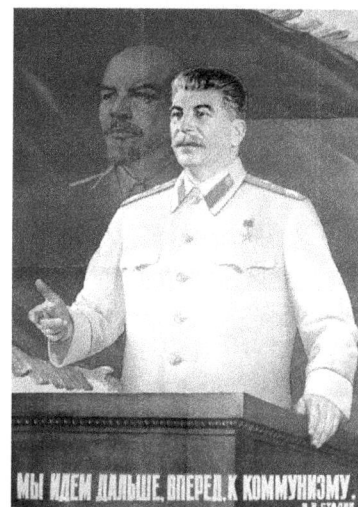

Мы идём дальше, вперёд, к коммунизму. We are going further, onward, toward Communism.

It's very revealing to note how common determinate verbs like **идти** are in Soviet propaganda (we're *underway!*) — while indeterminate verbs like **ходить** (conveying aimlessness) are nowhere to be found.[1]

ходить И^shift - **идти** / **пойти**				**ездить** И - **ехать** / **поехать**			
to go by foot				to go by vehicle			
↺ 🌀	→ ⇛	↦ ⇥		↺ 🌀	→ ⇛	↦ ⇥	
хож**у́**	ид**у́**			езж**у**	ед**у**		
ход**ишь**	ид**ёшь**			езд**ишь**	ед**ешь**		
ход**ит**	ид**ёт**			езд**ит**	ед**ет**		
ход**им**	ид**ём**			езд**им**	ед**ем**		
ход**ите**	ид**ёте**			езд**ите**	ед**ете**		
хо́д**ят**	ид**у́т**			езд**ят**	ед**ут**		
ход**и**!	ид**и**!			езд**и**!	езж**ай**!		

летать АЙ - **лете́ть** E^end / **полете́ть** E			**плавать** АЙ - **плыть** B^end / **поплы́ть** B			**бе́гать** АЙ - **бежа́ть** / **побежа́ть**		
to go by air			to go by water			to go by running		
↺ 🌀	→ ⇛	↦ ⇥	↺ 🌀	→ ⇛	↦ ⇥	↺ 🌀	→ ⇛	↦ ⇥
лета́ю	леч**у́**		пла́ваю	плыв**у́**		бе́гаю	бег**у́**	
лета́ешь	лет**ишь**		пла́ваешь	плыв**ёшь**		бе́гаешь	беж**ишь**	
лета́ет	лет**ит**		пла́вает	плыв**ёт**		бе́гает	беж**ит**	
лета́ем	лет**им**		пла́ваем	плыв**ём**		бе́гаем	беж**им**	
лета́ете	лет**ите**		пла́ваете	плыв**ёте**		бе́гаете	беж**ите**	
лета́ют	лет**ят**		пла́вают	плыв**у́т**		бе́гают	бег**у́т**	
лета́й!	лет**и**!		пла́вай!	плыв**и**!		бе́гай!	бег**и**!	

---

*Which **infinitive** would you choose to use in these situations? (Try giving the full sentence too, if you like). Remember to use your imagination, while thinking in terms of Russian categories: does the English suggest motion **around** or being **underway**?* **38.a**

1. Where do you go every day? _____
2. Where are you going right now? _____
3. You never go to Russia. _____
4. Where was he traveling to? _____
5. I often fly to Petersburg. _____
6. The swan was swimming around. _____

7. The dog was running around. _____
8. I'm flying to Moscow now. _____
9. Our plane was going in circles. _____
10. She was running down the street. _____
11. The swan swam along the canal. _____
12. Where was he walking? _____

Лес ру́бят — ще́пки летя́т. When they're chopping down a forest, woodchips fly (i.e. you can't make an omelette without breaking a few eggs).

[1] Indeed, the form **идём** (like **вперёд!**) is a good one-word summary of Soviet propaganda: **we** (the collective) are **underway**. Meanwhile, many late-Soviet rock songs (like those of Victor Tsoi) prominently feature motifs of aimless, idle wandering.

38.4 An ongoing one-way trip →

Since determinate verbs like **идти** describe "being underway," we can often combine them with **куда** and/or **откуда** phrases: "where to" are you underway? And "where from?"

As you can imagine, these determinate verbs are very useful for describing a single leg of an ongoing trip. Remember our prepositions:

	где	куда	откуда
в nouns:	**в** + prepositional	**в** + accusative	**из** + genitive
на nouns:	**на** + prepositional	**на** + accusative	**с** + genitive

идти to go by foot	ехать to go by vehicle	лететь E^{end} to go by air	плыть B to go by water	бежать to go by running
→ ⇛	→ ⇛	→ ⇛	→ ⇛	→ ⇛
иду	еду	лечу	плыву	бегу
идёшь	едешь	летишь	плывёшь	бежишь
идёт	едет	летит	плывёт	бежит
идём	едем	летим	плывём	бежим
идёте	едете	летите	плывёте	бежите
идут	едут	летят	плывут	бегут
иди!	езжай!	лети!	плыви!	беги!
шёл	ехал	летел	плыл	бежал
шла	ехала	летела	плыла	бежала
шло	ехало	летело	плыло	бежало
шли	ехали	летели	плыли	бежали

38.b *Fill in the correct form of the **determinate** verbs above, based on context.*

идти:
1. Они едут в театр, а мы _____ туда пешком.

2. Я сейчас _____ в столовую. А куда ты _____?

3. Куда вы _____ вчера, когда мы вас видели?

ехать:
4. Откуда ты _____ сейчас? Я _____ из Петербурга.

5. Мы _____ в Москву, когда наша машина сломалась.

лететь:
6. Я _____ в Нью-Йорк, а они _____ в Лондон.

плыть:
7. Мы с берега смотрели, как катер _____ по реке.[1]

бежать:
8. Почему все _____ по улице? В чём дело?

38.c *Supply a **куда** or **откуда** clause, using the proper prepositions and cases.*

1. Куда она едет? (Москва) _____

2. Куда ты шла вчера? (вечеринка) _____

3. Куда они бегут? (клуб, концерт) _____

4. Куда он бежал вчера? (столовая) _____

5. Откуда ты идёшь? (общежитие) _____

6. Откуда вы бежали? (скучная лекция) _____

7. Куда плывёт катер? (Васильевский остров) _____

8. Откуда он летит? (Петербург) _____

"Я шагаю по Москве" "I walk through Moscow" (official English title: *Walking the Streets of Moscow*).

This extremely popular film from the post-Stalin "Thaw" (**Оттепель**) in the 60's features a song in which a young man sings: "**А я иду, шагаю по Москве**..." The second verb, **шагать**, means to "stride" or "march," to take steps (**шаг**: step).

Based on the poster above, he might also have sung: "Я **еду** (на велосипеде)..."

This example shows how in some cases the verb choice depends on how a speaker perceives motion — and how, strictly speaking, the existence of a "destination" is irrelevant. The singer seems to be going nowhere in particular, yet he sings: "**Я иду**..." He's "underway," walking through Moscow. Also, subsequent lyrics make clear that he's walking *along* a Moscow street, flirting with the girls who walk past. Он **идёт**.

In fact, the song contains another determinate verb: he speaks fancifully of looking into the eyes of the girls who walk past him; in their eyes, he says, "**бежит Садовое кольцо**" — the Garden Ring (a street in Moscow) is "running" or "racing past" (determinate!). So, the entire scene is full of determinate motion: he's underway on foot, the girls are underway as they walk past, and the street itself runs past, as reflected in their eyes.

So, this example points out that while determinate verbs often imply a clear destination, **in essence** they don't have to. The difference ultimately boils down to the ideas of "around" versus "underway." Even where "underway" is understood vaguely, it's still very different from "around."

Sometimes the speaker must simply choose: what kind of motion are we dealing with? Is it indeterminate (↻), or determinate (→)?

---

[1] Use the present tense. Much as with indirect questions, Russian will preserve the "original" tense in this clause: literally, "We were watching, how the tour boat **is sailing** down river." The English equivalent would be simply: "We watched the boat sail..."

38.5 Repeated determinate motion ⇶

Both **indeterminate** forms like **ходить** and **determinate** forms like **идти** are *imperfective* in aspect. This means that they can describe **ongoing** action (including in the present tense!) and **repeated action.**

We've seen how indeterminate verbs like **ходить** can describe multiple **round trips**: ⟳

Determinate verbs like **идти** describe being **underway**, and typically describe an **ongoing one-way trip** (I'm "on my way" right now, from one place to another). Our pictogram for this kind of motion is: ➡

If this motion is repeated, we might draw it like this: ⇶ In practice, this usually means **multiple one-way trips**.

ongoing:	Я **иду** на лекцию.	*repeated:*	Каждое утро я **иду** на лекцию.
	I'm on my way to a lecture. ➡		Every morning I go to a lecture. ⇶

Note that if we break up recurring round trips into particular "legs," we end up with this kind of picture: ⇶ ⇶ ⇶

round trip:	Каждый день я **хожу** в университет.
	Every day I go to the university (that is, everyday I make a round trip to the university). ⟳
repeating legs:	Каждое утро я **иду** в университет, а каждый вечер я **иду** домой в общежитие.
	Every morning I go to the university, and every evening I go home to the dorm. ⇶ ⇶

Breakdown No. 4: Strongly implied "round trips"

Both **indeterminate** and **determinate** forms are **imperfective** in terms of aspect; this means that they can both describe **repeated** action. Strictly speaking, then, **indeterminate** verbs would refer specifically to **repeated round trips** (⟳), while **determinate** verbs would refer specifically to **repeated one-way trips** (⇶).

This is all true — yet in everyday Russian, the strongly implied idea of repeated **round trips** can trump the technically more accurate idea of repeated **one-way** trips. Why? Say we go to class at 8 every morning. Strictly speaking, then, at 8 every morning we are **underway**. But if we "zoom out," from the point of view of our daily routine, we are going to class and coming back again at some later time — we are making repeated **round** trips. This latter idea tends to predominate. Luckily, either variant is acceptable.

Каждое утро в восемь часов я **иду** на занятие.[1]		Каждое утро в восемь часов я **хожу** на занятие.	
Every morning at 8 o'clock I go to class. ⇶		Every morning at 8 o'clock I go to class. ⟳	

In the event of repeated sequences, the **final "leg"** (which is clearly one-way, not round-trip!) *must* be determinate!

Каждый день я **хожу** на лекцию, потом (я **хожу**) в библиотеку, потом (я **хожу**) в столовую, и наконец я **иду** домой.
Every day I go to a lecture, then I go to the library, then I go to the dining hall, and finally I go home. ⟳ ⟳ ⟳ ⇶

ПОЕЗД ИДЕТ
ОТ ст. СОЦИАЛИЗМ
ДО ст. КОММУНИЗМ

Поезд идёт от станции социализм до станции коммунизм. The train is underway from Socialism Station to Communism Station.

Use pictograms to depict either repeated round-trip or repeated one-way motion. **38.d**
Give the technically accurate picture, then discuss why the "round trip" idea may take over.

1. Куда ты ходишь каждый день? _____

2. Куда ты идёшь каждое утро в восемь часов? _____

3. Когда она жила в Москве, она каждый вечер ходила в театр. _____

4. Она шла туда пешком, а ехала домой на маршрутке. _____

5. Я надеюсь, что в следующем году буду часто ездить в Россию. _____

6. Этот самолёт летает в Сочи каждое утро. _____

7. Этот корабль плавает в Хельсинки каждый день. _____

Describe your daily routine. **Indeterminate** *verbs are more likely,* **except for the final "leg!"**

Сначала я иду / хожу _____ (куда?)

... потом я иду / хожу _____ (куда?)

... и наконец я иду _____ (куда?).

---

[1] Choosing this variant can also serve to emphasize the *process* of getting somewhere — the "slog," the "schlep," etc.

ходить - идти	ездить И - ехать	летать АЙ - лететь Е	плавать АЙ - плыть В	бегать АЙ - бежать
to go by foot	to go by vehicle	to go by air	to go by water	to go by running

38.e *Referring to the indeterminate and determinate forms above, give a pictogram.*

1. Я тебя видел вчера в центре. Куда ты так бежала? _____

2. Ты ездишь на машине в университет, или ходишь пешком? _____

3. Мы часто ездим в Петербург. Там каждый день ходим в театр. _____

4. Наша собака очень любит бегать в парке. _____

5. Когда я летел в Москву, я читал роман Толстого на русском. _____

6. Что тебе больше (more) нравится — бегать или плавать? _____

7. Корабль плывёт сегодня из Петербурга в Хельсинки. _____

8. Чтобы (in order to) научиться плавать, надо ходить в бассейн. _____

9. Эта маршрутка едет на вокзал? _____

10. Автобусы уже не ходят. Надо будет идти пешком. _____

11. Когда я возвращаюсь домой, моя собака всегда бежит ко мне. _____

12. Я думаю, что этот самолёт летел на юг. В Сочи, наверное. _____

13. Странная птица летала весь день у нас на дворе. _____

14. Каждый день в восемь часов я иду на урок русского языка. _____

38.f *Now, pick the infinitive (from those above) you'd use here. First, give a pictogram.*

1. I go to Russia once per year. _____ _____

2. — Where are you going?   — To Russia. _____ _____

3. She goes to the gym five times per week. _____ _____

4. She's going to the gym right now. _____ _____

5. My flight from the US to Russia took nine hours. _____ _____

6. They were walking down the sidewalk. _____ _____

7. They were walking around the city. _____ _____

8. He was running along the embankment (набережная). _____ _____

9. He was jogging in the park. _____ _____

10. She goes home every evening at six o'clock.[1] _____ _____

1. Что ты обычно делаешь, когда едешь на поезде?

2. А что ты будешь делать, когда ты будешь лететь в Россию?

3. Ты ездил(а) в Россию? (то есть: ты был(а) уже в России?)

4. Тебе нравится летать на самолёте? Тебе не страшно (scary)?

5. Ты ходишь пешком в университет, или ездишь на машине или велосипеде?

6. Куда ты ходил(а) вчера? На занятие, в магазин, в столовую или кафе?

7. Ты любишь бегать? А где ты обычно бегаешь? В парке, например?

Future tense of determinates

Verbs like **идти**, **ехать** and **лететь** can certainly be used in the future tense, although such situations are rare, and won't be the focus of our exercises. If we use the keyword, the meaning is clear enough: someone **"will be underway."** Here are a few examples, unpacked:

Когда я **буду лететь** в Москву, я буду читать русский роман.

When I will be underway by air to Moscow, I'll read a Russian novel.

Когда вы **будете ехать** из аэропорта в центр Петербурга, вы сможете увидеть огромный памятник Ленину.

When you will be underway by vehicle from the airport to the center of Petersburg, you may see a huge monument to Lenin.

Если ты **будешь идти** мимо аптеки, купи мне, пожалуйста, аспирин.

If you will be underway by foot past a pharmacy, please buy me some aspirin. (that is, "if you happen to pass a pharmacy...")

How long does it take?

If you're talking about how long a trip takes, then you're really asking about a **process** — how long did that process take? That is, "for how long were you underway?"

In such cases, Russian quite logically uses **determinate** verbs. Take a look at these examples:

— Сколько **ехать** из Москвы в Петербург на поезде?
— Часа четыре (4) минимум!

— Наконец я в Москве!
— А сколько ты **летела**?
— Девять (9) часов!

— Завтра я вернусь в США.
— А сколько **будешь лететь**?

— Сколько ты **идёшь** на работу?
— Двадцать (20) минут.

[1] Because this is the repeating **final** leg of her daily routine (we assume), we must use a determinate form here.

day 39: perfective verbs of motion

conjugating perfective verbs; setting out; assumed arrival
and one-way trips; describing single future trips;
perfective sequences; summary

Слава первому космонавту, Ю. А. Гагарину! Glory to the first cosmonaut, Yu. A. Gagarin!

39.1 Conjugating perfective verbs

The third and final verb of motion form to examine is the **perfective**. These forms are made by prefixing the **determinate** forms with **по-**. And, like all such prefixed forms, these verbs conjugate just like their non-prefixed forms.

The only exception is **пойти**: its infinitive is *not* **поидти**, and its conjugated forms have an **й** where we might expect an **и** (e.g. **пойду**, *not* **поиду**).

идти	⇨	пойти	я **пойду**, ты **пойдёшь**...	они **пойдут**
ехать	⇨	поехать	я **поеду**, ты **поедешь**...	они **поедут**
лететь Е	⇨	полететь Е	я **полечу**, ты **полетишь**...	они **полетят**
плыть В	⇨	поплыть В	я **поплыву**, ты **поплывёшь**...	они **поплывут**
бежать	⇨	побежать	я **побегу**, ты **побежишь**...	они **побегут**

Past-tense forms also mirror those of the determinate verbs, including:

| идти | ⇨ | пойти | он **пошёл**, она **пошла**, оно **пошло**, они **пошли** |

Motion verbs with **по-** are **perfective**: their conjugated forms are future-tense:

	translated	"unpacked"
я **пойду**	I will go	I will **set off** on foot
он **поедет**	he will go	he will **set off** by vehicle
ты **побежишь**	you will run	you will **set off** running, run off

**ТАК ПОЙДЕМ ЖЕ СМЕЛО ВПЕРЕД.
ПО ПУТИ. ВЕДУЩЕМУ К КОММУНИЗМУ !**
Л.И. БРЕЖНЕВ

**Так пойдём же смело вперёд, по
пути, ведущему к коммунизму!**
So, let's go forward boldly, along the
path leading to Communism!

Remember, since verbs like **пойти**
are **perfective**, their conjugated
forms are **future** in meaning. So the
verb "**пойдём**" would normally be
translated as "we will go," or unpacked as "we will set off on foot."

Here, this form is used more as a
proposal, a call to action: "Let's go!"

39.2 The meaning of perfective verbs of motion: setting out

Since perfective motion verbs are... **perfective**... they can't describe **ongoing** or **repeated** action, and they can never be **present**-tense. So, they can only describe **one-time** actions in the **past** or **future**.

As we reviewed in 36.6, perfective verbs of motion are best thought of as describing not completion, but **inception**. So, our keyword for them is **setting out** (or, heading off): someone is stationary, and then sets off moving.

39.a   *Try "unpacking" these sentences in order to convey the full meaning of the verbs.*

1. Он сказал "До свидания" и **пошёл**.

2. Мы **поплыли** по каналу на катере.

3. Где она? Куда она **пошла**?

4. Я не знаю, куда они **поехали**.

5. Самолёт **полетел** на юг.

6. Моя собака **побежала** в парк.

7. Через час **пойдём** на лекцию.

8. Всё готово. Катер скоро **поплывёт**.

39.3 Assumed arrival and one-way trips

So, at a bare minimum, perfective verbs of motion with **по-** describe **inception:** setting out — whether by foot, by vehicle, by air, etc. In everyday usage, however, such verbs also typically imply **completion** of a one-way trip. That is, we typically assume that the person successfully reached their destination, unless we are told otherwise. Consider this exchange:

СОВЕТСКИЙ ЧЕЛОВЕК В КОСМОСЕ

Just before lift-off, Yuri Gagarin famously said "**Поехали!**" In colloquial Russian, this past-tense form means something like "Let's go already!" or "Let's get going!" — by vehicle! If you're going somewhere on foot, friends might say, "**Пошли!**" — "**Пошли в кино!**" This usage is somewhat more informal and emphatic than "**Пойдём!**" All three expressions are extremely common.

— Где Павел?		— Он **пошёл** в библиотеку.
— Where's Pavel?	*translated:*	— He went to the library.
	unpacked:	— He **set off** on foot for the library.
	we assume:	(He's at the library now.)[1]

So, in practical terms, perfective motion verbs are used for **completed one-way** trips. Remember that completed **round trips** would require indeterminate verbs. Note the follow-up questions and answers!

Он **ходил** в библиотеку.	*translated:* He went to the library.	— Где он теперь?	— Дома.
	unpacked: He made a **round** trip to the library.		

Он **пошёл** в библиотеку.	*translated:* He went to the library.	— Где он теперь?	— В библиотеке.
	unpacked: He **set out** for the library.		

In the **first** example, if were to ask, "Where is he now?" then the typical answer would be "Back at home." That is, he completed the round trip to the library, and is back. In the **second** example, the typical answer would be "At the library." He's definitely not back home, and we can only assume he's made it to the library by now.

39.b   *Read the examples carefully, then tell where — in all likelihood — the person is **now**.*

Моя подруга живёт в общежитии...	1. Она **пошла** в тренажёрный зал.	Теперь она _____.
Юрий Гагарин живёт на Земле...	2. Он **летал** в космос.	Теперь он _____.
Джон живёт в Америке...	3. Он **поехал** в Россию.	Теперь он _____.
	4. Он **ездил** в Россию.	Теперь он _____.
Наташа живёт в квартире...	5. Она **побежала** в магазин.	Теперь она _____.
	6. Она **бегала** в магазин.	Теперь она _____.
*What if we used a **determinate** verb:*	7. Она **бежит** в магазин.	*Then she's still "on her way!" (= она ещё в пути)*

---

[1] To be absolutely clear: we do **not** know this for a fact! The verb **пошёл** does not "get him to the library." All we know for sure is that he left. We can only assume arrival. On Day 77, we will learn forms that will allow us to say unambiguously that he "arrived at the library."

196

39.4 Describing single future trips

As we learned on Day 37 (Breakdown No. 3),an **indeterminate** verb like **ходить** can describe both **single** and **repeated** round trips in the **past** tense. More context would make clear which is the case.

	translated	"unpacked"
Он **ездил** в Россию.	He went to Russia.	He made **one** round trip to Russia by vehicle.
or:	He would go to Russia.	He made **multiple** round trips to Russia.

Meanwhile, in the **future** tense, an indeterminate verb *automatically* describes **repeated round trips**.

Он **будет ездить** в Россию.	He will go (repeatedly) to Russia.	He will make **multiple** round trips to Russia.

By the way, if we use a **determinate** verb in the future tense, we don't complete the trip; we're still "**underway**."

Он **будет ехать** в Россию.	He'll be traveling to Russia.	He will be **underway** by vehicle to Russia.

This brings us to a very important rule: The **only** kind of motion verb that we can use to describe a **complete, single future trip** in Russian is with a **perfective** motion verb with **по-**.[1] Once again: all the verb really tells us is that someone will **set out** for Russia, and we assume that they'll **get there**. Hence — a completed future trip.

Он **поедет** в Россию.	He'll go to Russia.	He'll make **one** trip to Russia by vehicle.

Even if the motion verb is used as an **infinitive** (after **хочу** or **надо**, for example), the same distinctions apply:

Он х<u>о</u>чет **поехать** в Россию.	He wants to go to Russia.	He wants to make **one** trip to Russia.
Он х<u>о</u>чет **ездить** в Россию.	He wants to go to Russia.	He wants to make **multiple** trips to Russia.
Он х<u>о</u>чет **ехать** в Россию.	He wants to be traveling to Russia.	He wants to be **underway** to Russia (!).

Obviously, the third example is rare — this is a somewhat unusual thing to say!

39.5 I don't want to go!

What if we negate the final three examples above? What if we ***don't*** want to go? This situation generally calls for an **imperfective** infinitive — it's not that we don't want to "go and do" something once (by accident), but that we don't want to do it "at all," "in the first place." When it comes to motion verbs, such one-time accidents make little sense. Simply put, we can never say "Я не х<u>о</u>чу **поехать**" or "Я не х<u>о</u>чу **пойти**." This leaves us with:

Он не х<u>о</u>чет **ездить** в Россию.	He doesn't want to go to Russia.	He doesn't want to make **multiple** trips to Russia.
Он не х<u>о</u>чет **ехать** в Россию.	He doesn't want to go to Russia.	He doesn't want to make (this) **one** trip to Russia.
Он не х<u>о</u>чет **ходить** на раб<u>о</u>ту.	He doesn't want to go to work.	He doesn't want to make **multiple** trips to work.
Он не х<u>о</u>чет **идти** на раб<u>о</u>ту.	He doesn't want to go to work.	He doesn't want to make (this) **one** trip to work.

Breakdown No. 5: Trips in the "near future"

We've reached our final "breakdown." Fortunately, this one mirrors English usage exactly!

If we're describing a future-tense trip, then logically, of course, we'd expect to use the future tense. As we know, to describe a **single trip in the future**, we use perfective verbs in **по-**, since using an indeterminate verb in the future automatically implies **repeated trips.**

Я сег<u>о</u>дня **пойду** в те<u>а</u>тр.	I **will go** to the theater today (once).

But, actually, we rarely use the **future** tense ("I will go") in such instances in English. Instead, if we vaguely regard this future point in time as the "near future," we tend to use the **present** tense: "I'm going to the theater today," or "I'm going to Russia next month." Russians do the same thing — and since this is a single trip, they use the present tense of the **determinate** verb:

Я сег<u>о</u>дня **пойду** в те<u>а</u>тр.	=	Я сег<u>о</u>дня **иду** в те<u>а</u>тр.	I'm going to the theater today.
В и<u>ю</u>не я **поеду** в Россию.	=	В и<u>ю</u>не я **еду** в Россию.	I'm going to Russia in June.

Both variants are perfectly acceptable and virtually synonymous — although, as in English, the **present** tense is probably more likely.

---

[1] There is one other way, with special prefixed perfective forms such as **сходить**, **съездить**, **сбегать**, etc., but that topic is separate from the present dicussion of **unprefixed** motion verbs, and will be covered in Book 3.

39.c   *Pick an infinitive to describe these future-tense trips. Give a pictogram or keyword first!*

1. I'm going to Russia in a month.   _____ _____ _____

2. I want to go to Russia this summer.   _____ _____ _____

3. I'll be traveling to Russia once per year.   _____ _____ _____

4. I want to go to Russia often.   _____ _____ _____

5. As I flew to Moscow I watched a movie.   _____ _____ _____

6. We're going to the store in twenty minutes.   _____ _____ _____

7. We'll be going to the store every evening.   _____ _____ _____

8. It'll take us ten minutes on foot.   _____ _____ _____

Добро пожаловать в Москву! Welcome to Moscow! A poster for the 1980 Olympics, which the United States boycotted due to the Soviet Union's war in Afghanistan.

39.6   Perfective sequences →⊢ →⊢ →⊢

Since motion verbs with **по-** are **perfective**, they can be used to describe one-time **sequences**, as we've seen (19.1). Multiple verbs with **по-** can describe various legs of a one-time trip, in the sense of "First I went here, then I went there, and then I went there." This can be useful for describing the course of your day, moving from point A to point B to point C. The verb needn't be repeated each time — a **куда** phrase will suffice!

Since each particular stop on the trip could be thought of as a **round** trip, there are two possibilities here:

Сначала я **пошла** на лекцию, потом (я **пошла**) в библиотеку, потом в столовую, и наконец (**пошла**) домой.

Сначала я **ходила** на лекцию, потом (я **ходила**) в библиотеку, потом в столовую, и наконец (**пошла**) домой.
First I went to a lecture, then I went to the library, then to the cafeteria, and finally (I went) home.

....

For ongoing (present-tense) sequences, we can use determinate or indeterminate verbs (see Breakdown No. 4!):

Сначала я **иду** на лекцию, потом (я **иду**) в библиотеку, потом в столовую, и наконец (я **иду**) домой.

Сначала я **хожу** на лекцию, потом (я **хожу**) в библиотеку, потом в столовую, и наконец (я **иду**[1]) домой.
First I go to a lecture, then I go to the library, then to the cafeteria, and finally home.

....

Finally, if you're telling "where you've been" during the course of the day — not as a narrative sequence but as a completed round trip with multiple stops — use the indeterminate.

— Куда ты **ходила** сегодня?   — (Я ходила) на лекцию, в библиотеку, и в столовую.
— Where did you go today?   — (I went) to a lecture, to the library, and to the cafeteria.

39.d   *Use **сначала**, **потом**, and **наконец** in your sequences. As shown above, multiple variants may be possible.*

1. First I go to a lecture, then to a cafe, and finally home.

_____

2. Yesterday we went to the store, then to the theater, then to a restaurant.

_____

3. Tomorrow I'll go to class, then to the library, and finally home to the dorm.

_____

4. In a month I'll first fly to France, then to Russia.

_____

А куда ты ходишь каждый день? Куда ты ходил(а) вчера? Расскажи!

[1] Again, the final leg of this trip requires a determinate verb — repeated one-way motion.

39.7 Summary of forms

Motion verbs are difficult![1] When using them, resort to the **key-words** ("around," "underway," "setting out") as necessary, and, as with any Russian verb, think carefully about **tense** and **aspect**. Motion verbs are generally quite "systematic" — but always watch out for those special situations we've called "breakdowns." Past-tense forms are given for convenience; only forms of **идти** and **пойти** are irregular!

ходить И[shift] - идти / пойти			ездить И - ехать / поехать		
to go by foot			to go by vehicle		
↺ ⦾	→ ⇶	↦ →|	↺ ⦾	→ ⇶	↦ →|
хож**у**	ид**у**	пойд**у**	езж**у**	ед**у**	поед**у**
ход**ишь**	ид**ёшь**	пойд**ёшь**	езд**ишь**	ед**ешь**	поед**ешь**
ход**ит**	ид**ёт**	пойд**ёт**	езд**ит**	ед**ет**	поед**ет**
ход**им**	ид**ём**	пойд**ём**	езд**им**	ед**ем**	поед**ем**
ход**ите**	ид**ёте**	пойд**ёте**	езд**ите**	ед**ете**	поед**ете**
ход**ят**	ид**ут**	пойд**ут**	езд**ят**	ед**ут**	поед**ут**
ход**и**!	ид**и**!	пойд**и**!	езд**и**!	езж**ай**!	поезж**ай**!
ходил	шёл	пошёл	ездил	ехал	поехал
ходила	шла	пошл**а**	ездила	ехала	поехала
ходило	шло	пошл**о**	ездило	ехало	поехало
ходили	шли	пошл**и**	ездили	ехали	поехали

лет**а**ть АЙ - лет**е**ть Е[end] / полет**е**ть Е			пл**а**вать АЙ - плы**ть** В / попл**ы**ть В			б**е**гать АЙ - беж**а**ть / побеж**а**ть		
to go by air			to go by water			to go by running		
↺ ⦾	→ ⇶	↦ →|	↺ ⦾	→ ⇶	↦ →|	↺ ⦾	→ ⇶	↦ →|
лет**аю**	леч**у**	полеч**у**	плав**аю**	плыв**у**	поплыв**у**	бег**аю**	бег**у**	побег**у**
лет**аешь**	лет**ишь**	полет**ишь**	плав**аешь**	плыв**ёшь**	поплыв**ёшь**	бег**аешь**	беж**ишь**	побеж**ишь**
лет**ает**	лет**ит**	полет**ит**	плав**ает**	плыв**ёт**	поплыв**ёт**	бег**ает**	беж**ит**	побеж**ит**
лет**аем**	лет**им**	полет**им**	плав**аем**	плыв**ём**	поплыв**ём**	бег**аем**	беж**им**	побеж**им**
лет**аете**	лет**ите**	полет**ите**	плав**аете**	плыв**ёте**	поплыв**ёте**	бег**аете**	беж**ите**	побеж**ите**
лет**ают**	лет**ят**	полет**ят**	плав**ают**	плыв**ут**	поплыв**ут**	бег**ают**	бег**ут**	побег**ут**
лет**ай**!	лет**и**!	полет**и**!	плав**ай**!	плыв**и**!	поплыв**и**!	бег**ай**!	бег**и**!	побег**и**!
летал	летел	полетел	плавал	плыл	поплыл	бегал	бежал	побежал
летала	летела	полетела	плавала	плыл**а**	поплыл**а**	бегала	бежала	побежала
летало	летело	полетело	плавало	плыл**о**	поплыл**о**	бегало	бежало	побежало
летали	летели	полетели	плавали	плыл**и**	поплыл**и**	бегали	бежали	побежали

Give a keyword and/or pictogram to help clarify your choice of verb, then translate the Russian. Watch tense and aspect! **39.e**

1. Did you (pl.) go to the lecture today?
   Вы _____ на лекцию сегодня?

2. I go to a lecture every morning.
   Каждое утро я _____ на лекцию. *(2 possibilities)*

3. First I (m.) went to the lecture,
   Сначала я _____ на лекцию, *(2 possibilities)*
   then I went home.
   а потом я _____ домой.

4. I'm flying to Moscow next week.
   Я _____ в Москву на следующей неделе. *(2 possibilities)*

5. I want to go to Moscow in a week.
   Я хочу _____ в Москву на следующей неделе.

6. I'm going to fly to Moscow often.
   Я _____ часто _____ в Москву.

7. Where was he running to yesterday?
   Куда он _____ вчера?

8. Where did he run off to?
   Куда он _____?

9. She loves to run in the park.
   Она любит _____ в парке.

10. I usually go to the theater on foot,
    Я обычно _____ в театр пешком,
    but I take the subway home.
    а _____ домой пешком.

11. I went to New York yesterday.
    Вчера я _____ в Нью-Йорк.

12. Where is that boat going to?
    Куда _____ этот корабль?

---

[1] The good news is that, for all practical purposes, this chapter has exhausted the usage of so-called **unprefixed** verbs of motion. We will introduce **prefixed** verbs of motion (which are much simpler!) on Day 77 and look at them in great depth in Book 3.

other verbs describing motion; other verbs used with **где** / **куда** / **откуда** phrases; adverbs of place; imperative forms of motion verbs

Мужеством, ловкостью, силой горды — множим советских спортсменов ряды!
Proud of our courage, lightness, and strength, we multiply the ranks of Soviet athletes!

Эти спортсмены **идут**. Можно ещё сказать, что они **шагают**.

40.1 Not all verbs describing motion are "verbs of motion"

We've now looked at the five most common verbs of motion in great detail; there are only 18 such verbs in the entire language, and we'll learn the remaining ones in Book 3. There, we'll also learn how to add prefixes to these basic, unprefixed verbs of motion to create countless new verbs describing more specific kinds of motion.

Keep in mind that when we say "verb of motion," we are referring to a verb **with three infinitives**. This is what makes verbs of motion so unusual, and so difficult. If, at this point, you feel reasonably comfortable with verbs of motion, you should pat yourself on the back: this is one of the most difficult topics in Russian grammar!

Meanwhile, note that not every Russian verb that describes motion is a "verb of motion" in this sense. Most, in fact — like the vast majority of Russian verbs — have only **two infinitives**. With any such aspectual **pair** of 2 infinitives, our choice of infinitive depends entirely on **aspect** — imperfective or perfective. The entire category of **determinacy** — indeterminate or determinate — **does not apply**!

Here are a few examples of aspectual pairs that describe movement, yet are not "verbs of motion."

гулять АЙ / **погулять** АЙ to stroll / to stroll for a bit	Давай **погуляем** по набережной. Let's stroll along the embankment.
прыгать АЙ / **прыгнуть** НУ to jump	Собака бегает и **прыгает**. The dog is running around and jumping.
шагать АЙ / **шагнуть** НУ[end] to step, stride, march	"А я иду, **шагаю** по Москве…" "I'm walking, striding around Moscow…"
ступать АЙ / **ступить** И to step, stride, march	Астронавт впервые **ступил** на Луну. An astronaut first stepped onto the Moon.
падать АЙ / **упасть** Д[end] to fall	Ваза упала на **пол**[1] и разбилась. The vase fell onto the floor and broke.
двигаться АЙ or А / **двинуться** НУ to move	Мне больно! Не могу **двинуться**. I'm hurting! I can't move.

What's going on with the final verb? Is its imperfective an **АЙ** verb or an **А** verb? In modern Russian, it can be treated as either. That is, it can be conjugated as **двигаюсь, двигаешься** or as **движусь, движешься**. This is very unusual in Russian.

СМОТРИ

КУДА СТУПАЕШЬ

Смотри куда ступаешь.
Watch where you're stepping (to!).

Он не смотрел, и упал!

Try some examples with the verb pairs above. If it isn't a "verb of motion," then the category of determinacy no longer applies! **40.a**

1. I love to stroll through the city. Я люблю _____ по городу.

2. We strolled for a bit, then set off for the cafe. Мы _____ немножко, а потом пошли в кафе.

3. The child jumped into the pool (бассейн). Ребёнок _____ в бассейн.

4. Don't jump around in the living room! Не _____ в гостиной!

5. The lock (замок) broke. It's not moving. Замок сломался. Он не _____.

Ступай домой — и Бог с тобой. Go home (get out of here), and God be with you.

40.2 Other verbs used with где / куда / откуда phrases

Many verbs — not just "verbs of motion" — can be used with **где / куда / откуда** phrases. Here are some of the most useful, many of which we have seen already. These are often used with **куда** and **откуда** phrases:

возвращаться АЙ / **вернуться** НУ[end] to return, go back	**приглашать** АЙ / **пригласить** И[end] to invite	**звонить** И[end] / **позвонить** И кому to call[1]
опаздывать АЙ / **опоздать** АЙ to be late	**успевать** АЙ / **успеть** ЕЙ to make it, manage (on time)	**спешить** И[end] / **поспешить** И to hurry, rush

1. I want to invite you to a party (вечеринка).	Я хочу пригласить тебя ____ _____	**40.b**
2. We returned home (домой) from the party.	Мы _____ домой с вечеринки.	
3. I need to call the police (полиция)![2]	Мне надо _____ в полицию!	
4. You're always late to class (занятие)!	Ты всегда _____ на занятие!	
5. We won't catch (make it to) the train!	Мы не _____ на поезд!	
6. One should make it to class on time.	Надо _____ на занятие.	
7. I'm rushing to work!	Я _____ на работу!	

---

1. Ты опаздываешь иногда на занятие? Часто?

2. Тебе будет грустно, когда ты вернёшься домой из России?

3. Ты часто звонишь домой? Каждый день или каждую неделю?

4. Ты успел(а) сегодня на первое (first) занятие?

5. Куда ты спешишь после урока русского языка?

6. У тебя будет вечеринка. Кого пригласишь?

---

[1] Stress can fall onto the preposition in certain set expressions.   [2] To call a person (like mom), use the dative: **Я позвонила маме**. But to call a place or organization, use a куда phrase: **Я позвонила в больницу** (I called the hospital).

40.c 1. **Москва**: Возвращаюсь _____ (откуда). Жил _____ (где) целый месяц.

2. **Питер:**[1] Она завтра полетит в _____ (куда). Она будет учиться _____ (где).

3. **вокзал**: — Мы скоро вернёмся _____ (откуда). — Что вы делаете _____ (где)?

4. **лекция**: — Через час вернусь _____ (откуда). — А Паша был сегодня _____ (где)?

5. **стадион, концерт**: — Ты идёшь сегодня _____ (куда) _____ (куда)? — Конечно!

6. **библиотека**: Я спешу _____ (куда). Я должна сегодня весь день работать _____ (где).

7. **урок**: Студент опоздал сегодня _____ (куда). Но он почти каждый день _____ (где).

8. **новоселье**: Ты не опоздаешь _____ (куда) завтра? Я буду _____ (где) весь вечер.

9. **театр**: Она очень опаздывала _____ (куда), а подруга уже час её ждала _____ (где).

These verbs are often used with **где** phrases:

оставаться АВАЙ / остаться Н	оставлять АЙ / оставить И что	забывать АЙ / забыть что
to remain, stay	to leave (something)	to forget (something)

40.d 1. I often leave my student ID at home. — Я часто _____ студенческий билет дома.

2. I (f.) "forgot my student ID at home." — Я _____ студенческий билет дома.

3. We'll leave my dog at the neighbor's. — Мы _____ собаку у соседа.

4. She'll stay at home tomorrow. — Она _____ дома завтра.

5. They decided (решить) to stay in Russia. — Они решили _____ в России.

6. Our neighbor often stays at home. — Наша соседка часто _____ дома.

---

1. Ты обычно берёшь зонт с собой, или оставляешь его дома?

2. У тебя есть собака, которая осталась дома у мамы и папы?

3. Тебе скучно, когда остаёшься дома?

4. Ты часто забываешь телефон? А где?

Гулять, так гулять... If we're going to party, then let's party!

The common verb **гулять** АЙ / **погулять** АЙ means "to stroll," but it often has further connotations in Russian: to carouse, to party. It may suggest a kind of defiant affirmation of one's freedom from the norms and strictures of everyday life (**быт**). As we'll see in Book 4, Dostoevsky (in his *Notes from the House of the Dead*) drew some of his most profound conclusions regarding human nature from his observation of Siberian convicts who would endure months and months of drudgery and misery in the mere hope of, just once a year, buying enough smuggled vodka to drink themselves senseless... that is, to **погулять**:

"...именинник[2] **напивался как стелька и... ходил по казармам... стараясь показать всем, что он пьян, что он «гуляет»... Везде в русском народе к пьяному чувствуется некоторая симпатия."**

"...the 'birthday boy' would get as soused as a boot-liner and walk around the barracks... trying to show everyone that he was drunk, that he was 'partying'... A certain sympathy toward a drunken person is felt everywhere among the Russian people."

....

The poster to the right warns that foreign agents are on the hunt for people who love to "**выпить**," and cites a well-known **пословица**:
Что у трезвого на уме, то у пьяного на языке. literally:
That which is on the mind of a sober man is on the tongue of a drunken man.

Which brings to mind another bit of folk wisdom:
Гуляй гуляй, да не загуливайся.
If you want to party, party, but don't over-party.

---

[1] **Питер** is a colloquial, often affectionate term for **Петербург**. [2] An **именинник** (fem. **именинница**) is one who is celebrating his or her **именины**, the Feast Day of the saint for whom one is named. Traditionally this day was treated much as birthdays are today.

40.3 Adverbs of place with где / куда / откуда

Modern English is somewhat vague with regard to the words "here" and "there."[1] For example, "here" can describe both location (I live here) and destination (Come here — that is, come *to* here). Russian has full sets of three adverbs for "here," "there," and "home." As always, when speaking of a location in Russian, we must clearly differentiate between **где**, **куда** and **откуда** expressions.

	где	куда	откуда
"here" ➡	здесь here	сюда to here	отсюда from here
"there" ➡	там there	туда to there	оттуда from there
"home" ➡	дома at home	домой to home	из дома from home

Here are some simple examples of all of these forms:

Мы **здесь** живём. We live here.	Иди **сюда**. Come here.	Я еду **отсюда**. I'm going from here.
Они **там** живут. They live there.	Смотри **туда**. Look there.	Он вернулся **оттуда**. He returned from there.
Я работаю **дома**. I work at home.	Я спешу **домой**. I'm going home.	Он вернулся **из дома**. He returned from home.

Где работа — идите туда:
первое мая — праздник труда.

Where there is work, go there (i. e. go where there's work); May 1st is a holiday (**праздник**) of labor.

40.e

дом: 1. Возвращаюсь _____ (куда). Я так люблю быть _____ (где).

2. Она сначала поработала _____ (где). Теперь она спешит _____ (откуда) на работу.

здесь: 3. Нам нравится _____ (где) в Москве, но мы завтра едем _____ (откуда) на юг.

4. — Где ты? Ты _____ (куда) едешь? Поспеши, все уже ждут тебя _____ (где)!

там: 5. — Я вернусь _____ (куда) через месяц. — А что ты будешь _____ (где) делать?

6. Когда мы вернулись _____ (откуда), мы сразу поняли, что мы _____ (где) забыли зонт.

40.4 Imperative forms of motion verbs

Here are **ты** imperative forms for the two most common verbs of motion. Note that the imperatives of **ехать** and **поехать** are irregular!

	indeterminate	determinate	perfective
motion by foot:	ходи!	иди!	пойди!
motion by vehicle:	езди!	езжай!	поезжай!

In everyday usage, **negative** commands use the **indeterminate** form exclusively (**Не ходи туда!**), while **positive** commands (**Иди сюда!**) tend to use the **determinate**, unless we are making a general command that suggests repeated trips (**Ходи на занятие!**).

Don't walk on fish! (**рыба**)

40.f

These examples include imperatives. Repeat, substituting an adverb of place from those in 40.3.

1. Не ходи на вечеринку. Не ходи _____.

2. Иди ко мне. Иди _____.

3. Останься здесь. Не ходи _____.

5. Не езди в Россию зимой (in winter). Не езди _____.

6. Я не хочу тебя видеть. Иди _____.

7. Ты пьян. Иди в общежитие. Иди _____.

---

[1] As with "where, whither, whence," English used to distinguish these terms with "here, hither, hence" and "there, thither, thence."

Case endings

	special modifiers						adjectives	masculine nouns			
								hard	soft		special soft
nom.	э́тот	весь	оди́н	чей	мой	наш	но́вый	стол	слова́рь	музе́й	кафете́рий
gen.	э́того	всего́	одного́	чьего́	моего́	на́шего	но́вого	стола́	словаря́	музе́я	кафете́рия
acc.	э́тот	весь	оди́н	чей	мой	наш	но́вый	стол	слова́рь	музе́й	кафете́рий
animate:	э́того	всего́	одного́	чьего́	моего́	на́шего	но́вого	студе́нта	писа́теля		ге́ния
dat.	э́тому	всему́	одному́	чьему́	моему́	на́шему	но́вому	столу́	словарю́	музе́ю	кафете́рию
prep.	э́том	всём	одно́м	чьём	моём	на́шем	но́вом	столе́	словаре́	музе́е	кафете́рии

	special modifiers						adjectives	feminine nouns			
								hard	soft		special soft
nom.	э́та	вся	одна́	чья	моя́	на́ша	но́вая	газе́та	неде́ля		фами́лия
gen.	э́той	всей	одно́й	чьей	мое́й	на́шей	но́вой	газе́ты	неде́ли		фами́лии
acc.	э́ту	всю	одну́	чью	мою́	на́шу	но́вую	газе́ту	неде́лю		фами́лию
dat.	э́той	всей	одно́й	чьей	мое́й	на́шей	но́вой	газе́те	неде́ле		фами́лии
prep.	э́той	всей	одно́й	чьей	мое́й	на́шей	но́вой	газе́те	неде́ле		фами́лии

	special modifiers						adjectives	neuter nouns			
								hard	soft		special soft
nom.	э́то	всё	одно́	чьё	моё	на́ше	но́вое	окно́	мо́ре	бельё	зада́ние
gen.	э́того	всего́	одного́	чьего́	моего́	на́шего	но́вого	окна́	мо́ря	белья́	зада́ния
acc.	э́то	всё	одно́	чьё	моё	на́ше	но́вое	окно́	мо́ре	бельё	зада́ние
dat.	э́тому	всему́	одному́	чьему́	моему́	на́шему	но́вому	окну́	мо́рю	белью́	зада́нию
prep.	э́том	всём	одно́м	чьём	моём	на́шем	но́вом	окне́	мо́ре	белье́	зада́нии

Months and days of the week

months	
янва́рь, -я́	January
февра́ль, -я́	February
март, -а	March
апре́ль, -я	April
май, ма́я	May
ию́нь, -я	June
ию́ль, -я	July
а́вгуст, -а	August
сентя́брь, -я́	September
октя́брь, -я́	October
ноя́брь, -я́	November
дека́брь, -я́	December

days of the week	
понеде́льник	Monday
вто́рник	Tuesday
среда́	Wednesday
четве́рг	Thursday
пя́тница	Friday
суббо́та	Saturday
воскресе́нье	Sunday

Nouns

hard nouns

masculine

конце́рт, -а (на)	concert
уро́к, уро́ка (на)	lesson (class)
курс, -а (на)	course, class[1]
класс, -а	grade in school[1]
теа́тр, -а	theater
аэропо́рт, -а (в -у́)	airport
авто́бус, -а	bus
велосипе́д, -а	bike
мост, -а (на -у́)	bridge
проспе́кт, -а	boulevard
вокза́л, -а (на)	train station
ры́н(о)к, -нка (на)	market
магази́н, -а	store
центр, -а	(city) center
торго́вый центр, -а	trade center, mall
бе́рег, -а (на -у́)	shore, bank
эскала́тор, -а (на)	escalator
коридо́р, -а	hallway
вход, -а (в...)	entrance
вы́ход, -а (из...)	exit
перехо́д, -а (через)	crossing (across)
пол, -а (на -у́)	floor
шкаф, -а (в -у́)	wardrobe
храм, -а	place of worship
туале́т, -а	restroom
ко́смос, -а	outer space
бассе́йн, -а	swimming pool
вид, -а (тра́нспорта)	form of transp.
кана́л, -а	canal / channel
тренажёрный зал, -а	gym

го́род, -а	city
сад, -а (в -у́)	garden
тротуа́р, -а (на)	sidewalk
по́езд, -а (на)	train
стадио́н, -а (на)	stadium
матч, -а	(sports) match
самолёт, -а	airplane
ка́тер, -а	small tour boat
о́стров, -а (на)	island
парк, -а	park
лес, -а (в -у́)	forest
двор, -а́ (на)	(court)yard
бар, -а	bar
рестора́н, -а	restaurant
биле́т, -а (куда́)	ticket (to)
лифт, -а (на)	elevator
пляж, -а (на)	beach
океа́н, -а	ocean
дом, -а	house (building)
университе́т, -а	university

neuter

кино́, -а	movie theater
метро́, *indeclinable*	subway
о́зеро, -а	lake
не́бо, -а	sky
де́рево, -а	tree
кафе́, *indecl.*	café
такси́, *indecl.*	taxi
шоссе́ (на), *indecl.*	highway

feminine

библиоте́ка, -и	library
маши́на, -ы	car
у́лица, -ы (на)	street
река́, -и́	river
да́ча, -и (на)	dacha
на́бережная, -ой (на)	embankment
электри́чка, -и	suburban train
столо́вая, -ой	cafeteria
доро́га, -и	road, way
вы́ставка, -и (на)	exhibition
пти́ца, -ы	bird
трава́, -ы́ (газо́н)	grass (lawn)
ло́дка, -и	boat
ле́стница, -ы (на)	staircase
мину́та, -ы	minute
секу́нда, -ы	second
страна́, -ы́	country
сторона́, -ы́	side
шко́ла, -ы	school
бу́лочная, -ой	pastry shop
ла́вка, -и	shop
вечери́нка, -и	party
апте́ка, -и	pharmacy
встре́ча, -и (на)	meeting
больни́ца, -ы	hospital
парикма́херская, -ой	salon
маршру́тка, -и	minibus
по́чта, -ы (на)	post office
электро́нная по́чта	e-mail

soft nouns

masculine

музе́й, -я	museum
трамва́й, -я	streetcar
край, -я (на краю́)	edge
автомоби́ль, -я	automobile
жура́вль, -я́	crane (the bird)
ле́бедь, -я	swan

спекта́кль, -я	performance
каш(е)ль, ка́шля	cough(ing)
кора́бль, -я́	ship

neuter

мо́ре, -я	sea
по́ле, -я	field

feminine

спа́льня, -и	bedroom
земля́, -и́ (на)	ground, earth
кофе́йня, -и	coffee shop
ку́хня, -и (на)	kitchen
дере́вня, -и (на)	countryside
ба́ня, -и	Russian sauna

special soft nouns

feminine

ле́кция, -ии	lecture

neuter

зда́ние, -ия	building
заня́тие, -ия (на)	class, classes

Adjectives

adjectives

regular hard adjectives

про́шлый	last, previous

affected by the 5- and 7-letter spelling rules

сле́дующий	next

---

[1] Note that **класс** refers to a year (grade) in school, while **курс** refers to a year of study in college — or a college course. Note also that **класс** can never refer to a "class" or "course" at school — instead, choose between **курс**, **уро́к**, **заня́тие**.

Verbs of motion

ходить И[shift] - идти / пойти		
to go by foot		
↺ 🌀	→ ⇉	↦ ⇥
хожу	иду	пойду
ходишь	идёшь	пойдёшь
ходит	идёт	пойдёт
ходим	идём	пойдём
ходите	идёте	пойдёте
ходят	идут	пойдут
ходи!	иди!	пойди!
ходил	шёл	пошёл
ходила	шла	пошла
ходило	шло	пошло
ходили	шли	пошли

ездить И - ехать / поехать		
to go by vehicle		
↺ 🌀	→ ⇉	↦ ⇥
езжу	еду	поеду
ездишь	едешь	поедешь
ездит	едет	поедет
ездим	едем	поедем
ездите	едете	поедете
ездят	едут	поедут
езди!	езжай!	поезжай!
ездил	ехал	поехал
ездила	ехала	поехала
ездило	ехало	поехало
ездили	ехали	поехали

летать АЙ - лететь Е[end] / полететь Е		
to go by air		
↺ 🌀	→ ⇉	↦ ⇥
летаю	лечу	полечу
летаешь	летишь	полетишь
летает	летит	полетит
летаем	летим	полетим
летаете	летите	полетите
летают	летят	полетят
летай!	лети!	полети!
летал	летел	полетел
летала	летела	полетела
летало	летело	полетело
летали	летели	полетели

плавать АЙ - плыть В[end] / поплыть В		
to go by water		
↺ 🌀	→ ⇉	↦ ⇥
плаваю	плыву	поплыву
плаваешь	плывёшь	поплывёшь
плавает	плывёт	поплывёт
плаваем	плывём	поплывём
плаваете	плывёте	поплывёте
плавают	плывут	поплывут
плавай!	плыви!	поплыви!
плавал	плыл	поплыл
плавала	плыла	поплыла
плавало	плыло	поплыло
плавали	плыли	поплыли

бегать АЙ - бежать / побежать		
to go by running		
↺ 🌀	→ ⇉	↦ ⇥
бегаю	бегу	побегу
бегаешь	бежишь	побежишь
бегает	бежит	побежит
бегаем	бежим	побежим
бегаете	бежите	побежите
бегают	бегут	побегут
бегай!	беги!	побеги!
бегал	бежал	побежал
бегала	бежала	побежала
бегало	бежало	побежало
бегали	бежали	побежали

Adverbs of place, often used with motion verbs

	где	куда	откуда
"here"	здесь	сюда	отсюда
	here	to here	from here
"there"	там	туда	оттуда
	there	to there	from here
"home"	дома	домой	из дома
	at home	to home	from home

Examples of all possible verb of motion situations, grouped by tense

present tense			

IMPERFECTIVE (ongoing / repeated)	ХОДИТЬ (around)	ongoing: in circles/aimless ↻	Она **ходит** по комнате. She is walking around her room (back and forth / in circles).
		repeated: in circles/aimless 〰	Она **ходит** по комнате (каждый день). She walks around her room (every day).
		repeated: round trips 〰	Она **ходит** в библиотеку (каждый день). She makes round trips to the library (every day).
	ИДТИ (underway)	ongoing: underway →	Она **идёт** в библиотеку. She's underway (on her way) to the library.
		ongoing: sequence → → → (the "narrative" present)	Она **идёт** на кухню, потом на улицу, а потом в библиотеку. She goes into the kitchen, then outside, then to the library.
		repeated (sequence) ⇶ (⇶⇶)	(Каждый день в 8 часов) она **идёт** в библиотеку.[1] She goes to (is underway to) the library (every day).

past tense			

IMPERFECTIVE (ongoing / repeated)	ХОДИТЬ (around)	ongoing: in circles/aimless ↻	Она **ходила** по комнате. She was walking around her room (back and forth / in circles).
		repeated: in circles/aimless 〰	Она **ходила** по комнате (каждый день). She would walk around her room (every day).
		single round trip ↻	Она **ходила** в библиотеку. She went to the library (and came back). She made a round trip to the library.
		repeated: round trips 〰	Она **ходила** в библиотеку (каждый день). She would go to the library (every day). She would make round trips to the library.
	ИДТИ (underway)	ongoing: underway →	Она **шла** в библиотеку. She was going to ("underway to") the library.
		repeated (sequence) ⇶ ⇶⇶) (relatively unusual!)	(Каждый день в 8 часов) она **шла** в библиотеку.[1] She would go (be underway to) the library everyday (repeated one-way).
PERFECTIVE (one-time)	ПОЙТИ (setting out)	setting out ↦ (assumed arrival, 1-way trip) ↦	Она **пошла** в библиотеку. She went to (set out for) the library. (We assume she's there now.)
		one-time sequence ↦ ↦ ↦	Сначала она **пошла** на лекцию, потом в библиотеку, и наконец домой.[2] First she went to (set out for) a lecture, then to the library, and finally home.

future tense			

IMPERFECTIVE (ongoing / repeated)	ХОДИТЬ (around)	ongoing: in circles/aimless ↻	Она **будет ходить** по комнате. She will be walking around her room (back and forth / in circles).
		repeated: in circles/aimless 〰	Она **будет ходить** по комнате (каждый день). She will walk around her room (every day).
		repeated: round trips 〰	Она **будет ходить** в библиотеку (каждый день). She will go to the library (every day).
	ИДТИ (underway)	ongoing: underway → (relatively unusual!)	Она **будет идти** в библиотеку. She will be going ("on her way to") the library.
		repeated (sequence) ⇶ ⇶⇶) (relatively unusual!)	(Каждый день в 8 часов) она **будет идти** в библиотеку.[1] She will go the library every day (repeated one-way).
PERFECTIVE (one-time)	ПОЙТИ (setting out)	setting out ↦ (assumed arrival, 1-way trip) ↦	Она **пойдёт** в библиотеку. She will go (set out for) the library. (We assume she'll make it there.)
		one-time sequence ↦ ↦ ↦	Сначала она **пойдёт** на лекцию, потом в библиотеку, и наконец домой. First she'll go to a lecture, then to the library, and finally home.

[1] In "repeated one-way" situations where repeated round trips are strongly implied, indeterminate verbs are often used, unless we are speaking of the repeated final leg (that is, repeated one-way) of a trip. [2] Here too, indeterminate also possible, except for the final leg.

Other verbs used with где / куда / откуда expressions

опаздывать АЙ / опоздать АЙ		возвращаться АЙ / вернуться НУ end		приглашать АЙ / пригласить И end	
to be late		to return, go back		to invite	
опаздываю	опоздаю	возвращаюсь	вернусь	приглашаю	приглашу
опаздываешь	опоздаешь	возвращаешься	вернёшься	приглашаешь	пригласишь
опаздывает	опоздает	возвращается	вернётся	приглашает	пригласит
опаздываем	опоздаем	возвращаемся	вернёмся	приглашаем	пригласим
опаздываете	опоздаете	возвращаетесь	вернётесь	приглашаете	пригласите
опаздывают	опоздают	возвращаются	вернутся	приглашают	пригласят
опаздывай!	опоздай!	возвращайся!	вернись!	приглашай!	пригласи!

успевать АЙ / успеть ЕЙ		спешить И end / поспешить И end		оставаться АВАЙ / остаться Н stem где	
to manage, make it (on time)		to hurry, rush		to remain, stay	
успеваю	успею	спешу	поспешу	остаюсь	останусь
успеваешь	успеешь	спешишь	поспешишь	остаёшься	останешься
успевает	успеет	спешит	поспешит	остаётся	останется
успеваем	успеем	спешим	поспешим	остаёмся	останемся
успеваете	успеете	спешите	поспешите	остаётесь	останетесь
успевают	успеют	спешат	поспешат	остаются	останутся
успевай!	успей!	спеши!	поспеши!	оставайся!	останься!

оставлять АЙ / оставить И что где		забывать АЙ / забыть что где		звонить И end / позвонить И end кому, куда	
to leave (something)		to forget (something)		to call (by phone)	
оставляю	оставлю	забываю	забуду	звоню	позвоню
оставляешь	оставишь	забываешь	забудешь	звонишь	позвонишь
оставляет	оставит	забывает	забудет	звонит	позвонит
оставляем	оставим	забываем	забудем	звоним	позвоним
оставляете	оставите	забываете	забудете	звоните	позвоните
оставляют	оставят	забывают	забудут	звонят	позвонят
оставляй!	оставь!	забывай!	забудь!	звони!	позвони!

гулять АЙ / погулять АЙ где		прыгать АЙ / прыгнуть НУ		шагать АЙ / шагнуть НУ end	
to stroll / to stroll for a bit		to jump		to step, stride, march	
гуляю	погуляю	прыгаю	прыгну	шагаю	шагну
гуляешь	погуляешь	прыгаешь	прыгнешь	шагаешь	шагнёшь
гуляет	погуляет	прыгает	прыгнет	шагает	шагнёт
гуляем	погуляем	прыгаем	прыгнем	шагаем	шагнём
гуляете	погуляете	прыгаете	прыгнете	шагаете	шагнёте
гуляют	погуляют	прыгают	прыгнут	шагают	шагнут
гуляй!	погуляй!	прыгай!	прыгни!	шагай!	шагни!

ступать АЙ / ступить И shift		падать АЙ / упасть Д end		двигаться А [1] / двинуться НУ	
to step, stride, march		to fall		to move	
ступаю	ступлю	падаю	упаду	движусь	двинусь
ступаешь	ступишь	падаешь	упадёшь	движешься	двинешься
ступает	ступит	падает	упадёт	движется	двинется
ступаем	ступим	падаем	упадём	движемся	двинемся
ступаете	ступите	падаете	упадёте	движетесь	двинетесь
ступают	ступят	падают	упадут	движутся	двинутся
ступай!	ступи!	падай!	упади!	двигайся!	двинься!

[1] You may also hear this verb conjugated as an АЙ verb: двигаюсь, двигаешься, etc.

Overview of adverbs to date

often with imperfective verbs:		often with perfective verbs:	
всегда	always	опять	again
часто	often	ещё раз	once more time
обычно	usually	снова	once again
регулярно	regularly	скоро	soon
иногда	sometimes	вдруг	suddenly
редко	rarely	только что	just now
никогда не	never	со временем	eventually
долго	for a long time	недавно	recently
недолго	not for long	заранее	ahead of time
давно уже	for a long time now	впервые	for the first time
ещё	still	сначала	at first
уже не	not anymore	потом	then, next
сейчас	now	наконец	finally
теперь	(but) now	ещё не	not yet
раньше	previously, before	уже	already
		вовремя	on time

qualifying:	
очень	very
довольно	quite, rather
слишком	too
совсем	completely, fully
ужасно	terribly
сравнительно	relatively
много	a lot, much
мало	a little, not much

other:	
только	only
тоже	also
быстро	quickly
медленно	slowly
почти	almost
давно	a long time ago

Prepositions that can be translated as "for"

для + gen.	for (a person or purpose)	У меня **для тебя** огромный сюрприз. I have a huge surprise **for you**.	Нам надо купить гель **для душа**. We need to buy "gel **for shower**."	
за + acc.	for (exchange)	Кто сегодня заплатит **за пиво**? Who will pay **for the beer** today?	Огромное спасибо **за подарок**! "Huge" thanks **for the present**!	
	for (favor)	Они **за войну**, а я против войны. They're **for the war,** but I'm against it.	Солдат воевал **за родину**. The soldier fought **for his homeland**.	
от + gen.	for (with medicines)	Мне нужно лекарство **от кашля**. I need medicine **for coughing**.	Это таблетка **от простуды**. This is a pill **for a cold** (a cold pill).	
на + acc.	for (plans, assignments)	У вас есть планы **на следующий год**? Do you have plans **for next year**?	У нас есть работа **на пятницу**? Do we have any work **for Friday**?	
	for (tickets, reservations)	Я купила тебе билет **на концерт**. I bought you a ticket **for the concert**.	Я заказал стол **на завтра**. I booked a table **for tomorrow**.	
	for (a purchase)	У тебя есть деньги **на билет**? Do you have money **for a ticket**?	Дай мне деньги **на метро**. Give me money **for the subway**.	
	for (a period of time)	Я еду в Россию **на месяц**. I'm going to Russia **for a month**.	Мне нужна комната **на три ночи**. I need a room **for three nights**.	
	for (an occasion)	Что ты купишь ей **на день рождения**? What will you buy her **for her birthday**?	**На Новый год** нам подарили икру. They gave us caviar **for New Year's**.	

Prepositions of time

за+ acc.	(with)in	Я прочитал целую книгу **за неделю**. I read the entire book in a week.	Я напишу письмо **за час**. I'll write the letter (with)in an hour.
через + acc.	in... (from now)	Я буду в России **через год**. I will be in Russia in a year (from now).	Концерт будет **через неделю**. The concert will be in a week.
назад + acc.	ago	**Год назад** я был в России. A year ago I was in Russia.	Концерт был **неделю назад**. The concert was a week ago.
до + gen.	before	**До войны** они жили в Ленинграде. Before the war they lived in Leningrad.	**после** + gen. after **После войны** они вернулись. After the war they returned.

Билет Государственного

СТО РУ

ВАНКОВСКИЕ БИЛЕТЫ ОБЕСПЕЧИВАЮТСЯ ЗОЛ
МЕТАЛЛАМИ И ПРОЧИМИ АКТИВАМИ ГОСУ

100

33 069539

СТО КАРБОВАНЦІВ · СТО РУБЛЕ
ЙУЗ МАНАТ · ЉЅҊ Ҋ∂Ѣ∂ѻ|Ѻ · ҊѼѬѾ∂ѰҞ ѼѢ∂ᴴᴬᵀ
ЮЗ СЎМ · САД СЎМ · ЖУЗ СОМ · ЖУЗ СОМ
П СУТЗ РУБЛЕ · SIMTAS RUBLIŲ · SIMTS RUBLI

1947

V

work, study & interests

the instrumental case and case review

Now, we'll learn our last remaining case, the instrumental, and how to use it — especially with predicate nouns and adjectives in "non-identity" situations. We'll then review all case endings in the singular. Finally, we'll learn about reflexive pronouns and review infinitives and clause types.

day 41: the instrumental case

the instrumental case; instrumental of accompaniment with **c**;
instrumental case endings; reflexive verbs with the instrumental

ЗАНИМАЙТЕСЬ СПОРТОМ!

Занимайтесь спортом! Literally: "Busy yourself with sport!" Sports (**спорт**) is always singular in Russian.

41.1 The instrumental case

At last, our final case: the instrumental. At its most basic, this case tells **with what** are we doing something: what tool, weapon, means, or method. In Russian, such instruments simply appear in the instrumental **with no preposition!** But to translate such phrases into English, we'll need to include "with."

Чем он<u>а</u> п<u>и</u>шет?	Он<u>а</u> п<u>и</u>шет **карандаш<u>о</u>м.**
With what is she writing?	She's writing **with a pencil.**
Чем ед<u>я</u>т суп?	Суп ед<u>я</u>т **л<u>о</u>жкой.**
With what does one eat soup?	One eats soup **with a spoon**.

The instrumental has one other basic meaning that will figure in future lessons. Look at this simple metaphor (simile):

П<u>о</u>езд лет<u>е</u>л **стрел<u>о</u>й.**	= П<u>о</u>езд лет<u>е</u>л **как стрел<u>а</u>.**
The train flew **like an arrow.**	The train flew **like an arrow.**

The train is not *literally* an arrow: it's **like** one. We'll use the instrumental in a variety of such "<u>**non-identity**</u>" situations.

Кл<u>и</u>ном кр<u>а</u>сным бей б<u>е</u>лых.
With a red wedge (кр<u>а</u>сный клин) strike the Whites (the anti-Bolshevik forces in the Civil War).

In this 1919 poster by **Эль Лис<u>и</u>цкий**, the phrase **кр<u>а</u>сный клин** is in the instrumental. It could be understood as meaning "with" a red wedge (using the wedge as an instrument or weapon), or "as" a red wedge (in the form of, or like, a red wedge).

ОСТОРОЖНО С ЦАПКОЙ

Осторожно с цапкой!
Careful with the hoe (цапка)!

41.2 Instrumental of accompaniment with c

Notice how English uses "with" in two very different senses. Compare these two Russian sentences and their identical English translation:

Она пишет **карандашом**. (correct)
She's writing **with a pencil**.

Она пишет **с карандашом**. (unlikely!!)
She's writing **with a pencil**.

What's the difference? In the first sentence, she's using a pencil to write (hence, Russian puts "pencil" into the instrumental, with **no prepositon**). In the second, the Russian means something like "she's writing alongside a pencil, together with a pencil." Obviously, the former sentence is far more likely to be used!

This illustrates an important point: in Russian, we use **c** (with) only in the sense of **accompaniment**: being **alongside**, doing something **along with**, etc.:

Он ходил в театр **с другом**.
He went to the theater **with a friend**.

Я возьму кофе **с молоком**.
I'll have (take) coffee **with milk**.

41.3 Instrumental case endings

The instrumental case answers questions such as: **чем**? (with what?) and **с кем**? (with whom?).

	MASCULINE & NEUTER:	adjective: **-ым** (-им)	noun: **-ом** (-ем, -ём)	FEMININE:	adjective: **-ой** (-ей)	noun: **-ой** (-ей, -ёй)

Take special note of the **soft** noun endings in e. If these endings happen to be **stressed**, then we get **ё** instead:

masculine:	музей ⟶ музе**ем**	*but:*	словарь[1] ⟶ словар**ём**	корабль[1] ⟶ корабл**ём**
neuter:	платье ⟶ плать**ем**	*but:*	бель**ё** ⟶ бель**ём**	
feminine:	тётя ⟶ с тёт**ей**	*but:*	семья ⟶ с семь**ёй**	статья ⟶ со стать**ёй**

	special modifiers						adjectives	masculine nouns			
								hard	soft		special soft
nom.	этот	весь	один	чей	мой	наш	новый	стол	словарь	музей	кафетерий
instr.	этим	всем	одним	чьим	моим	нашим	новым	столом	словарём	музеем	кафетерием

	special modifiers						adjectives	feminine nouns			
								hard	soft		special soft
nom.	эта	вся	одна	чья	моя	наша	новая	газета	неделя		фамилия
instr.	этой	всей	одной	чьей	моей	нашей	новой	газетой	неделей	семьёй	фамилией

	special modifiers						adjectives	neuter nouns			
								hard	soft		special soft
nom.	это	всё	одно	чьё	моё	наше	новое	окно	море	бельё	задание
instr.	этим	всем	одним	чьим	моим	нашим	новым	окном	морем	бельём	заданием

новая рубашка — с нов**ой** рубашк**ой**

1. большой ковёр — с _____
2. чистая кухня — с _____
3. хорошая спальня — с _____
4. огромный парк — с _____
5. новая столовая — с _____
6. вкусная (tasty) еда — со _____
7. красивое дерево — с _____

8. новое платье — с _____ **41.a**
9. грязное бельё — с _____
10. русская баня — с _____
11. колбаса — пицца с _____
12. молоко — кофе с _____
13. сахар — кофе с _____
14. сметана — борщ со _____
15. лимон — чай с _____

[1] This is an **end-stressed** masculine noun, so any ending we add to it is automatically stressed; hence the **ё**.

41.b **С кем** ты идёшь в театр?

1. старый друг	со _____		
2. новая подруга	с _____		
3. мой знакомый	с _____		
4. жена / муж	с _____ / с _____		
5. сын / дочка	с _____ / с _____		
6. брат / сестра	с _____ / с _____		
7. мама / папа	с _____ / с _____		

С кем ты едешь в Россию?

8. большая группа	с _____
9. профессор	с _____
10. другой студент	с _____
11. другая студентка	с _____
12. этот человек	с _____
13. президент США	с _____
14. дядя / тётя	с _____ / с _____

41.4 Doing something "with" feelings

The preposition **с** + instrumental is also used to describe doing something "with" a certain feeling, as in:

Русскую поэзию надо декламировать **с энтузиазмом**.
One should declaim Russian poetry **with enthusiasm**.

— Не поедешь с нами? — Да, **с удовольствием**.
— Won't you go with us? — Yes, with pleasure.

41.c *Use the instrumental to translate the English phrases. First, think carefully: do you need to include the preposition **с** or not?*

1. Он пишет... **with a sense of humor** (чувство юмора). _____

2. Она всегда писала... **with a pencil**. _____

3. В прошлом году я ездил в Россию... **with my father**. _____

4. — Не поможешь помыть посуду? — **With pleasure!** _____

5. — С кем вы были вчера? — **With my sister and brother**. _____

6. Он убил[1] (killed) муху (муха: fly)... **with a book**. _____

7. Я возьму пиццу... **with sausage and cheese**. _____

8. У него есть комната... **with a large window**. _____

9. — Чем мы моемся? — **With soap**. _____

41.5 Happy holidays!

In 12.2 we previewed some everyday wishes that involve the **genitive** case because the underlying verb (to wish) requires the genitive:

желать АЙ / **пожелать** АЙ кому чего — to wish someone something

(Желаю тебе) **удачи**!
(I wish you) luck! (удача)

(Желаю тебе) **приятного аппетита**!
(I wish you) a "pleasant appetite!"

Note that the verb itself can be left out altogether (and usually is):

Счастливого пути!
Bon voyage!

Всего доброго!
All the best!

Similarly, many phrases of congratulation involve the **instrumental**, because in Russian we congratulate someone "with" something:

поздравлять АЙ / **поздравить** И кого с чем — to congratulate s.o. "with" s.t.

(Поздравляю тебя) **с днём рождения**!
(I congratulate you) "with" your day of birth — i.e., Happy Birthday!

С победой!
(Congratulations) "with victory" (победа)

[1] The aspectual pair for "to kill" is **убивать** АЙ / **убить** Ь.

41.d

*Congratulate people "with" these occasions using the **instrumental** case.*

День Победы:	_____!	новоселье (a new place):	_____!
Новый год:	_____!	победа (win, victory):	_____!
День рождения:	_____!	праздник (any holiday):	_____!
Рождество:	_____!	покупка (a purchase):	_____!

С праздником, товарищи! Happy holiday (праздник), comrades!

41.5 Reflexive verbs with the instrumental

To revisit to our topic from 27.1, the verb **занимать** АЙ / **занять** Й/М^end is a **transitive** verb, meaning "to occupy." If we add the **reflexive particle**, the resulting verb means "to occupy **oneself** *with* something" or "to be occupied with something." Russia expresses the "*with* something" with a noun in the **instrumental** (NOTE: no **c**!).

занимать АЙ / **занять** Й/М^end что	Вы **занимаете** моё место!	Она **занимается** спортом.
to occupy, take up	You're "occupying" my seat!	She "occupies herself with sport."
заниматься АЙ / **заняться** Й/М чем		= She does sports.
to be occupied with, to "do"		

Talking about interests works much the same way. We can use **интересовать** with a direct object (e.g. "history interests him"), or use the reflexive form in a passive sense (e.g. "he is interested *by* history).

интересовать ОВА / **заинтересовать** ОВА кого	Его **интересует** история.	Он **интересуется** историей.
to interest	History interests him.	He is interested "by" history.
интересоваться ОВА / **заинтересоваться** ОВА чем	= He is interested in history.	= He is interested in history.
to be interested in ("by")		

The perfective may be thought of as expressing **inception** — to "begin to interest" or "begin to be interested":

Этот вопрос её **заинтересовал**.   Мы **заинтересовались** русской культурой.

This question/matter sparked her interest.   We took an interest in Russian culture.

What do you do? What are you into? Tell about your activities using the instrumental with **заниматься**.   41.e

— **Чем ты занимаешься?**   1. _____ (русская история) и _____ (литература).

— **Я занимаюсь...**   2. _____ (футбол) и _____ (баскетбол).

    3. _____ (математика) и _____ (лингвистика).

    4. _____ (бег: running), _____ (бокс: boxing), _____ (гребля: rowing).

Use both active and passive constructions to tell about your interests.   41.f

1. русский язык	Меня интересует **русский язык**.	Я интересуюсь **русским языком**.
2. русская поэзия	Меня интересует _____.	Я интересуюсь _____.
3. русское искусство	Меня интересует _____.	Я интересуюсь _____.
4. русская архитектура	Меня интересует _____.	Я интересуюсь _____.

---

1. They're "occupying our table!"	Они _____ наш стол!	41.g
2. It's time (пора) to "occupy my seat."	Пора _____ место!	
3. He had always been interested in Russia.	Он всегда _____ Россией.	
4. You'll take an interest in history in Petersburg.	В Петербурге ты _____ историей.	

215

more uses of the instrumental

verbs for "studying"; talking about interests, sports and instruments; professions; prepositions with the instrumental; three nouns used frequently with **за**

Гот<u>о</u>вься к съ<u>е</u>зду п<u>а</u>ртии! Prepare yourself for the Party Congress!

42.1 Verbs for "studying"

We've now seen four common verbs that can all be translated as "to study." Review the meanings below, taking careful note of what can follow each verb; note in particular that **изуч<u>а</u>ть** (to study **something**) must be followed by a **direct object**.[1]

уч<u>и</u>ться И^{shift} / **науч<u>и</u>ться** И чему / inf.	to learn; to attend college
Где ты **уч<u>и</u>шься**?	Он<u>а</u> **науч<u>и</u>лась** пл<u>а</u>вать.
What school do you go to?	She learned to swim.

заним<u>а</u>ться АЙ чем	to be studying, do homework
Мне н<u>а</u>до **занима<u>а</u>ться**.	Мы **заним<u>а</u>лись** весь в<u>е</u>чер.
I need to study (do homework, etc.).	We spent all evening studying.

изуч<u>а</u>ть АЙ что	to study a subject[1]
Что ты **изуч<u>а</u>ешь**?	Я **изуч<u>а</u>ю** х<u>и</u>мию.
What do you study?	I study chemistry.

гот<u>о</u>виться И / **подгот<u>о</u>виться** И к чему	to study (prepare o.s.) for...
К чем<u>у</u> ты **гот<u>о</u>вишься**?	К экз<u>а</u>мену по ф<u>и</u>зике.
What are you studying for?	For a physics exam.

Уч<u>и</u>сь и раб<u>о</u>тай, раб<u>о</u>тай и уч<u>и</u>сь!
Study (learn) and work, work and study!

[1] That is, it makes no sense to say simply "**Я изуч<u>а</u>ю**" without specifying **what** you're studying.

1. Where did she **go to college**?   Где она _____?

2. I can't go to the movies. I've got **to study**.   Я не могу идти в кино. Мне надо _____.

3. We **were studying** all day yesterday.   Мы вчера весь день _____.

4. She **studies** physics (физика) and Russian.   Она _____ физику и русский язык.

5. You're **in college**? What **do you study**?   Ты _____? Что ты _____?

6. I (f.) "**studied well**" for the math exam.   Я хорошо _____ к экзамену по математике.

---

1. Где ты учишься? В каком университете?[1]

2. Где ты ходил в школу? В каком городе?

3. Что ты изучаешь, кроме (besides) русского языка?

4. Ты много занимаешься вообще?

5. Как долго ты занимался / занималась вчера?

6. Почему ты решил(а) изучать русский язык?

42.2 Talking about interests, sports, and instruments

As we learned yesterday, the reflexive verb **заниматься** can combine with the instrumental, in the sense of "to occupy oneself with something." This verb can ask, in a very general sense, "what do you do?" (more literally, "with what do you occupy yourself?"). The answer depends on the type of activity.

For most **activities**, just use a noun in the instrumental case:

Чем ты занима́ешься?   Я занима́юсь **спо́ртом** (**бале́том, фехтова́нием**).
What do you do?   I do sports (ballet, fencing).

For team **sports** and **games**, we use another verb, with **в** + the accusative.

| игра́ть АЙ во что | to play (a sport, game) |

Чем ты занима́ешься?   Я игра́ю **в футбо́л** (**в по́кер, в ша́хматы**[2]).
What do you do?   I play soccer (poker, chess).

For **musical instruments**, we also use **игра́ть**, but with **на** + the prepositional.

| игра́ть АЙ на чём | to play (a musical instrument) |

Чем ты занима́ешься?   Я игра́ю **на скри́пке** (**на фле́йте, на пиани́но**[3]).
What do you do?   I play the violin (the flute, the piano).

Железнодоро́жники! Вступа́йте в о́бщество "Локомоти́в". Занима́йтесь спо́ртом! Railway workers! Join ("step into") the "Lokomotiv" organization. Do sports!

---

1. **баскетбо́л**   Я _____.

2. **гре́бля** (rowing, crew)   Я _____.

3. **би́знес**   Я _____.

4. **бале́т**   Я _____.

5. **матема́тика**   Я _____.

6. **гита́ра** (guitar)   Я _____.

7. **хокке́й**   Я _____.

8. **пе́ние** (singing)   Я _____.

9. **труба́** (trumpet)   Я _____.

10. **лёгкая атле́тика** (track & field)   Я _____.

---

[1] Once again, Wikipedia may be the best way to learn your school's "official" name and spelling in Russian.
[2] The Russian for "chess" is a plural-only noun; we'll introduce plural forms in Book 2.   [3] The Russian for "piano" is indeclinable.

1. Ты занимаешься спортом? Каким? Во что играешь?   2. Ты играешь на музыкальном инстременте? На каком?

42.3 Talking about professions

To describe professions, you can use a simple predicate noun in the nominative ("She is a doctor"), or use the instrumental case, in the sense of "She works as a doctor." Two ways to ask about profession are given here as well:

Кто ваш брат по профессии?
Who is your brother by profession?

Он **врач**.
He's a doctor.

Кем работает ваш брат?
"As whom" does your brother work?

Он работает **врачом**.
He works as a doctor.

42.c   *Say that someone works in the following professions. Can you try it both ways?*

1. наш отец + журналист: _____
2. наша мама + профессор: _____
3. мой знакомый + бизнесмен: _____
4. моя знакомая + психолог: _____
5. твой друг + писатель: _____
6. твоя подруга + врач: _____

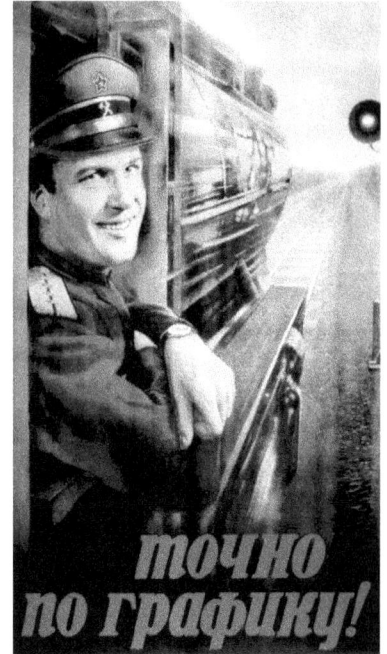

Точно по графику!
Precisely according to schedule!
Он работает машинистом.

1. Чем ты занимаешься? Ты ещё учишься или уже работаешь?   2. Если (if) ты уже работаешь, то кем?
3. Кем ты хотел(а) работать, когда ты был(а) маленьким / маленькой?   4. Кем ты хочешь работать теперь?

Работа не волк — в лес не убежит. Work isn't a wolf; it won't run off into the woods (i.e. it isn't going anywhere, it can wait!).

42.4 Prepositions of location with the instrumental

These prepositions are used with the instrumental to describe **location**:

над	above	**Над городом** летит самолёт. An airplane is flying by above the city.
под	below, under	Она сидит **под деревом** и читает. She's sitting under a tree and reading.
перед	before, in front of	**Перед нашим домом** есть небольшой парк. There's a small park in front of our building.
за	behind, beyond	**За этой стеной** есть кладбище. There's a cemetery behind (beyond) this wall.
рядом с	next to, alongside	**Рядом с магазином** есть аптека. There's a pharmacy next to the store.

Two of these prepositions have important additional meanings:

перед	just before[1] (temporally)	Надо много заниматься **перед экзаменом**. One has to study a lot (just) before an exam.
за	"after" (to go fetch...)	Мой друг пошёл в магазин **за пивом**. My friend set out for the store to get some beer.

Пьяный за рулём — преступник! A drunken man behind the wheel (руль) is a criminal!

218   [1] Compare with **до** + gen., which means **before** in the sense of "prior to" (**at any point** in time before, as opposed to **directly** before).

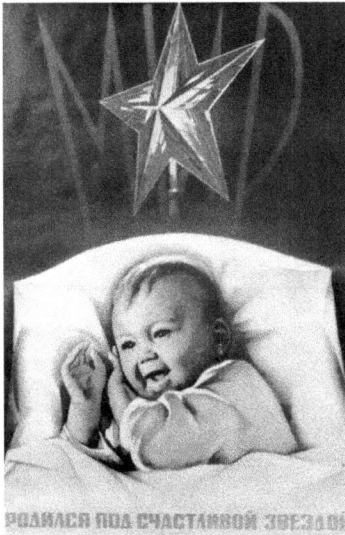

Родился под счастливой звездой. He (the ребёнок) was born beneath a lucky star (звезда).

42.d

Fill in the gaps with the correct endings. Be careful — not all are in the instrumental!

1. Кошка сидит **под** диван_____. Она обычно сидит **на** диван_____.

2. **Рядом с** торгов_____ центр_____ находится (is found) огромный кинотеатр.

3. Он сидел и читал учебник **перед** лекци____ **по** русск_____ истори___.

4. **За** эт_____ здани_____ находится большой и красивый сад **с** фонтан_____.[1]

5. **Над** мо_____ письменн_____ стол_____ есть старый советский плакат.

6. Она сидела **на** скамейк___ (bench) **перед** библиотек_____ и ждала подругу.

7. **На** лекци_____ по физик_____ я обычно сижу **рядом с** друг_____.

8. **Рядом со** станци_____ метро "Достоевская" есть большой торговый центр.

Пойдём за...	1. хлеб	_____	4. шоколад	_____	42.e
Let's go fetch...	2. молоко	_____	5. пиво	_____	
	3. колбаса	_____	6. водка	_____	

42.5 Prepositions in где and куда phrases

In Chapter 4, we learned two sets of prepositions for talking about location in terms of **где / куда / откуда**. In particular, we learned how the accusative case is associated with **куда** expressions. Similarly, two of the new prepositions we've just learned (**под** and **за**) take the **instrumental** when describing location (**где**), but take the **accusative** when telling "where to" (**куда**).

The other two, however (**перед** and **над**) take the **instrumental** in *both* instances! Since these prepositions violate the accustomed pattern of the accusative with **куда** phrases, they are presented in a black box below. Also, these two positions (above / in front) lack corresponding **откуда** forms.

This table summarizes all six sets of prepositions. Note that two (**из-под** and **из-за**) are actually compound prepositions. The first preposition determines the case; for that reason, both of these compounds require the genitive (with **из**).

It's worth noting that the **куда** and **откуда** phrases for our four new prepositions are relatively rare. For now, we'll see a limited number of such examples.

Водрузим над Берлином знамя победы!
We will hoist the banner (знамя, neuter!) of victory above Berlin!

	где	куда	откуда
in / at:	**в** + prep.	**в** + acc.	**из** + gen.
	Она живёт **в Москве**.	Она возвращается **в Москву**.	Она едет **из Москвы**.
on / at:	**на** + prep.	**на** + acc.	**с** + gen.
	Он ждёт **на вокзале**.	Он спешит **на вокзал**.	Он вернулся **с вокзала**.
beneath:	**под** + instr.	**под** + acc.	**из-под** + gen.
	Кошка сидит **под диваном**.	Кошка побежала **под диван**.	Кошка смотрит **из-под дивана**.
behind:	**за** + instr.	**за** + acc.	**из-за** + gen.
	Собака сидит **за деревом**.	Собака побежала **за дерево**.	Собака смотрит **из-за дерева**.
above:	**над** + instr.	**над** + instr.	
	Самолёт летел **над морем**.	Повесим[2] плакат **над диваном**.	
in front:	**перед** + instr.	**перед** + instr.	
	Он ждёт **перед вокзалом**.	Паркуем машину **перед театром**.	

[1] Fountain (**фонтан**) is masculine.   [2] "We will hang," from **весить** И / **повесить** И: to "put into a hanging position" (see Book 4!)

42.f *Translate the **prepositional phrase** only. Distinguish between **где** / **куда** / **откуда** situations, and choose accordingly!*

1. He placed (пост**а**вил) the empty bottle **beneath the table**.

Он пост**а**вил пуст**у**ю бут**ы**лку _____ _____.

2. The empty bottle stood **beneath the table**.

Пуст**а**я бут**ы**лка сто**я**ла _____ _____.

3. After dinner he took the bottle **from beneath the table**.

П**о**сле **у**жина он взял бут**ы**лку _____ _____.

4. The waiter walked **behind the bar** (б**а**рная ст**о**йка).

Офици**а**нт пошёл _____ _____ _____.

5. He worked for a while **behind the bar**.

Он пораб**о**тал _____ _____ _____.

6. There was a mirror **above the bar**.

З**е**ркало вис**е**ло _____ _____ _____.

7. He came out **from behind the bar** with our beer.

Он в**ы**шел[1] _____ _____ _____ с н**а**шим п**и**вом.

8. There's a huge tree **in front of our dacha**.

_____ _____ _____ есть огр**о**мное д**е**рево.

42.6 Three nouns used frequently with "за" prepositions

When Russians speak of being or going "abroad," they use prepositional phrases with **граница**, meaning "border." For example, to "go abroad" means to "go beyond the border" (**за границу**), to "be abroad" means to "be beyond the border" (**за границей**), and to return home "from abroad" means to return "from beyond the border" (**из-за границы**). Likewise, the space "outside of town" (the countryside, etc.) is conceived of as the area "beyond the city." So, to be "in the countryside" is to be "**за городом**" (note the stress on the preposition!).

Finally, being seated "at" a table is, in the Russian idiom, to be seated "behind" a table (**за столом**). Thus, the **куда** and **откуда** expressions employ the set of prepositions for "behind." Below is a complete set of examples.

	где	куда	откуда
	за + instr.	**за** + acc.	**из-за** + gen.
граница: border	Он д**о**лго жил **за границей**. He lived abroad for a long time.	Он по**е**хал **за границу**. He left on a trip abroad.	Он верн**у**лся **из-за границы**. He returned from a trip abroad.
город: city	Его д**а**ча **за городом**. His dacha is outside of town.	Он ч**а**сто **е**здит **за город**. He often travels outside town.	Он верн**у**лся **из-за города**. He returned from outside of town.
стол: table	Мы сид**е**ли **за столом**. We were sitting at the table.	Гость сел **за стол**. The guest sat down at the table.	Все вст**а**ли **из-за стола**. Everyone rose from the table.

42.g 1. We returned to America **from abroad**. _____

2. We spent a month **abroad**. _____

3. We travel **abroad** every year. _____

4. We have dinner **at the table** every night. _____

5. We sat down **at the table**. _____

6. We got up **from the table** and left the kitchen. _____

7. Our dacha is located just **outside town**. _____

8. We go **outside of town** every Saturday. _____

9. We return **from outside town** every Sunday. _____

НАХОДЯ**СЬ ЗА РУБЕЖ**О**М Р**О**ДНОЙ ЗЕМЛ**И**, Б**У**ДЬТЕ ОС**О**БЕННО БД**И**ТЕЛЬНЫ!**

Наход**я**сь за рубеж**о**м[2] родн**о**й земл**и**, б**у**дьте ос**о**бенно бд**и**тельны!

When you find yourself outside your native land, be especially vigilant!

1. Ты **е**здил(а) за гран**и**цу? Куд**а** **и**менно?

2. Ты д**о**лго был(а) за гран**и**цей?

3. Ты рад(а), когд**а** возвращ**а**ешься из-за гран**и**цы?

4. Ты ч**а**сто **е**здишь за г**о**род?

5. Где л**у**чше жить — в ц**е**нтре   или з**а** г**о**родом?

[1] An example of a (perfective) prefixed motion verb.   [2] The noun used here, **руб**е**ж**, is a less frequently used synonym for **граница**.

day 43: predicate nouns and adjectives

the instrumental with predicate nouns and adjectives; becoming; seeming; turning out to be; being; choosing between the nominative and instrumental; "you and I" phrases

Будь зо̲рким на посту! Be vigilant at your post!

43.1 The instrumental with predicate nouns & adjectives

When we introduced the imperfective, we mentioned that it is often used in simple metaphors and similes — to say that something is "like" or "as" something else. Recall our simple example:

По̲езд лете̲л **стрело̲й.** = По̲езд лете̲л **как стрела̲**.
The train flew **like an arrow.**

Such metaphoric uses of the instrumental are more likely in literary language (or proverbs) than in everyday speech. However, they point out a broader tendency: much as the **genitive** is strongly associated with **negation** (while the nominative is associated with **existence**), the **instrumental** is strongly associated with **seeming** (while the nominative is associated with **being**). In our example, the train **is** not literally an arrow. But it temporarily **acts like** or **appears like** one.

This distinction is very important when using predicate nouns or adjectives. Up to now, we have been using the **nominative** only in the predicate. But it turns out that we should only do this when we are conveying **identity** — as in, A = B (the subject *is* the predicate noun). For example:

Хо̲чешь быть таки̲м — трениру̲йся!
If you want to be like this — train!

The predicate adjective (**такой**) is in the instrumental; the boy *is* not like this now, but he hopes to **become** like this later!

subject	linking verb	predicate
Мой сын		**космона̲вт.**
My son	is	a cosmonaut.

221

This is a statement of identity: the son **is** an cosmonaut. In such cases, the predicate noun or adjective is in the **nominative**. BUT: if this claim of identity is **qualified** in any way, we will tend to use the **instrumental** instead.

subject	linking verb	predicate	
Мой сын	будет	**космон<u>а</u>втом.**	(he **will be** a cosmonaut, but he **isn't** one now)
My son	will be	a cosmonaut.	
Мой сын	был	**космон<u>а</u>втом.**	(he **was** a cosmonaut, but he **isn't** anymore)
My son	was	a cosmonaut.	
Мой сын	ст<u>а</u>нет	**космон<u>а</u>втом.**	(he **isn't** a cosmonaut, but he will **become** one)
My son	will become	a cosmonaut.	
Мой сын	х<u>о</u>чет стать	**космон<u>а</u>втом.**	(he **isn't** one, but he wants to **become** one)
My son	wants to become	a cosmonaut.	

For this reason, the instrumental often occurs following such linking verbs as "to seem" and "to become."

И я ст<u>а</u>ну механиз<u>а</u>тором!
I too will become a farm machinery operator!

43.2 Becoming

In Russian, this verb is followed by a predicate in the **instrumental**:

станов<u>и</u>ться И^{shft} / стать Н^{stem} кем, чем	
to become[1]	
становл<u>ю</u>сь	ст<u>а</u>ну
стан<u>о</u>вишься	ст<u>а</u>нешь
стан<u>о</u>вится	ст<u>а</u>нет
стан<u>о</u>вимся	ст<u>а</u>нем
стан<u>о</u>витесь	ст<u>а</u>нете
стан<u>о</u>вятся	ст<u>а</u>нут
станов<u>и</u>сь!	ст<u>а</u>нь!

Он<u>а</u> ст<u>а</u>нет **врач<u>о</u>м.**
She will become a doctor.

Он<u>а</u> ст<u>а</u>ла **врач<u>о</u>м.**
She became a doctor.

Same goes for the infinitive form:

Он<u>а</u> хот<u>е</u>ла стать **врач<u>о</u>м.**
She wanted to become a doctor.

"To become" can also be paired with predicate adverbs:

Нам ст<u>а</u>ло **легк<u>о</u>** чит<u>а</u>ть по-р<u>у</u>сски.
It has become easy for us to read in Russian.

43.a 1. Тот, кто изуч<u>а</u>ет психол<u>о</u>гию, ст<u>а</u>нет... психол<u>о</u>г: _____

2. Тот, кто изуч<u>а</u>ет философию, ст<u>а</u>нет... фил<u>о</u>соф: _____

3. Тот, кто изуч<u>а</u>ет медицину, ст<u>а</u>нет... врач: _____

4. Тот, кто изуч<u>а</u>ет пр<u>а</u>во (law), ст<u>а</u>нет... юр<u>и</u>ст: _____

5. Тот, кто изуч<u>а</u>ет ист<u>о</u>рию, ст<u>а</u>нет... ист<u>о</u>рик: _____

6. Тот, кто заним<u>а</u>ется сп<u>о</u>ртом, м<u>о</u>жет стать... спортсм<u>е</u>н: _____

7. Тот, кто изуч<u>а</u>ет журнал<u>и</u>зм, ст<u>а</u>нет... журнал<u>и</u>ст: _____

8. Тот, кто изуч<u>а</u>ет п<u>е</u>ние (singing), ст<u>а</u>нет... пев(<u>е</u>)ц[2] (m): _____

певица (f): _____

9. Тот, кто игр<u>а</u>ет в футб<u>о</u>л, м<u>о</u>жет стать... футбол<u>и</u>ст: _____

10. Тот, кто игр<u>а</u>ет в хокк<u>е</u>й, м<u>о</u>жет стать... хокке<u>и</u>ст: _____

11. Тот, кто изуч<u>а</u>ет биол<u>о</u>гию, ст<u>а</u>нет... би<u>о</u>лог: _____

Стать овц<u>о</u>ю — в<u>о</u>лки найд<u>у</u>тся. "(If you) become a sheep, wolves will be found."[3]

1. Кем ты х<u>о</u>чешь стать п<u>о</u>сле университ<u>е</u>та?

СТАНЬ УДАРНИКОМ КОММУНИСТИЧЕСКОГО ТРУДА

Стань ударником коммунисти-ческого труда! Become an *udarnik* (shock worker) of Communist labor!

An **ударник (ударница)** was a su-per-productive worker who overful-filled quotas. The term derives from **удар** (a blow, strike) and **ударить** И (to strike).

---

[1] This verb can also mean "to begin," as in: **Профессор стал говор<u>и</u>ть, и мы ст<u>а</u>ли его сл<u>у</u>шать.**   [2] Watch for the mobile vowel here.

222   [3] **-ою (-ею, -ёю)** is an alternate feminine instrumental ending. It is quite common in poetry and proverbs, but not in modern speech.

43.3 Seeming

The instrumental is also used for predicate nouns and adjectives following the verb "to seem." The verb is also used frequently with the dative, as in "it seemed **to me**."

казаться A^{shift} / показаться А кому чем	
to seem	
кажусь	покажусь
кажешься	покажешься
кажется	покажется
кажемся	покажемся
кажетесь	покажетесь
кажутся	покажутся
кажись!	покажись!

The imperfective, **казаться**, suggests a lasting or repeated impression, while the perfective, **показаться**, suggests a fleeting or one-time impression. The latter meaning can often be captured in English using "strike," as in: "He struck me as strange" (when I saw him, he seemed strange).

ВРАГ КОВАРЕН — БУДЬ НА-ЧЕКУ!

Враг коварен — будь на чеку!
The enemy is crafty — be on your guard!

Он мне всегда казался **странным**.
He always seemed strange to me.

Он мне показался **странным**.
He struck me as strange.

Note the contrast between **seeming** and **being** (with the nominative):

Эта книга кажется **интересной**, но на самом деле она **скучная**.
This book seems interesting, but in fact it's boring.

Of course, the instrumental can be used for **nouns** as well:

Он показался мне **идиотом**.
He seemed to me to be an idiot.

Снаружи (from the outside) враг кажется овцой, а внутри (on the inside) он волк!

Speaking of wolves, here's another **пословица** (proverb):

Сколько волка ни корми — он всё в лес смотрит.

However much you may feed a wolf, he'll keep looking into the forest (i.e. you can take a wolf out of the forest, but you can't take the forest out of the wolf!)

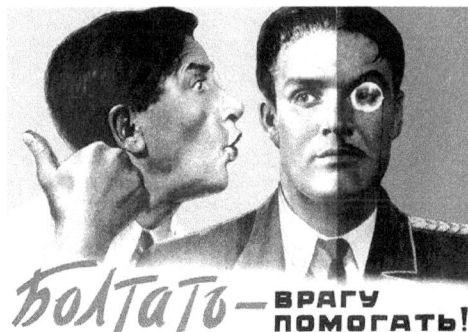

БОЛТАТЬ — ВРАГУ ПОМОГАТЬ!

Показался обычным советским человеком, но оказался немецким шпионом!

43.4 Turning out to be...

Here's a verb that can be used in conjunction with **казаться**. It means "to turn out to be," or "to prove to be," and is also followed by the **instrumental**.

Neuter singular forms can be followed by a clause with **что** (it turned out that...).

оказываться АЙ / оказаться A^{shift} чем	
to turn out to be, to prove to be	
оказываюсь	окажусь
оказываешься	окажешься
оказывается	окажется
оказываемся	окажемся
оказываетесь	окажетесь
оказываются	окажутся
оказывайся!	окажись!

Задача показалась **простой**, но оказалась очень **трудной**.
The problem seemed simple, but it turned out to be very difficult.

Оказывается, что эта задача ужасно трудная.
It turns out that this problem is terribly difficult.

---

1. Сначала моя комната показалась маленькой, но она оказалась _____ (большой).   **43.b**

2. На первый взгляд (at first glance) он может показаться _____ (странный), но на самом деле он хороший.

3. Сначала его книга показалась _____ (интересный), но на самом деле она скучная.

4. Оказалось, что он очень весёлый человек. Но сначала он казался _____ (грустный).

5. Оказывается, что русский — ужасно трудный язык. А сначала он казался таким _____ (простой[1])!

6. Кажется, что она мало занимается. Но может быть она окажется _____ (хорошая студентка).

7. Кажется, что он плохо пишет. Но кто знает! Он может стать _____ (известный писатель).

Первый блин комом. The first pancake (comes out looking) like a lump (**ком**) — try making Russian pancakes, and you'll see how true this is!

[1] **простой** means "simple" (its opposite is **сложный**: complicated).

Ты тоже будешь героем! You too will be a hero! The future of **быть** can also carry the sense of "to become" (that is, one will be something in the future). So it is often used with the instrumental, as in the poster below: **Спортсменом буду!**

43.5 Being

The verb **быть** — particularly in the future tense or imperative mood — can have much the same meaning as "to become," especially when speaking of people. For example, "I'm not an athlete now, but I'll be one — that is, I'll become one!" Or: "Be an athlete!" (you're not one right now; become one!).

Compare these almost synonymous sentences:

Она станет **врачом**.	Она будет **врачом**.[1]
She will become a doctor.	She will be a doctor.
Она хочет стать **врачом**.	Она хочет быть **врачом**.
She wants to become a doctor.	She wants to be a doctor.

The instrumental may also be used with **быть** in the past tense — for example, "I was young once, but I'm not anymore." The instrumental is used to describe a fleeting, non-essential quality of a person — something other than what they actually "are." A common example is the phrase "when I was little":

Когда я был **маленьким**, я любил бегать в парке.
When I was little (male speaker), I loved to run in the park.

Когда я была **маленькой**, я любила бегать в парке.
When I was little (female speaker), I loved to run in the park.

Similarly, we could use nouns, such as **ребён(о)к**, in the instrumental, to refer to past or future states:

Когда я был(а) **ребёнком**, я любил(а) бегать в парке.
When I was a child, I loved to run in the park.

Ты скоро будешь **отцом**. Трудно поверить!
Soon you'll be a father. Hard to believe!

Ask and answer these questions, being careful to choose between male and female endings as necessary. All words in the instrumental are in bold.

1.	male:	**Каким** ты был, когда ты был **маленьким**?
	female:	**Какой** ты была, когда ты была **маленькой**?
2.	male:	**Чем** ты интересовался, когда ты был **маленьким**?
	female:	**Чем** ты интересовалась, когда ты была **маленькой**?
3.	male:	**Кем** ты хотел стать, когда ты был **ребёнком**?
	female:	**Кем** ты хотела стать, когда ты была **ребёнком**?
4.	either:	А **кем** ты хочешь стать теперь? **Кем** хочешь работать?
5.	male:	**Каким** ты будешь через десять лет (in ten years)?
	female:	**Какой** ты будешь через десять лет?
6.	male:	**Каким** ты будешь, когда будешь **старым**? **Чем** ты будешь заниматься?
	female:	**Какой** ты будешь, когда будешь **старой**? **Чем** ты будешь заниматься?
7.	male:	Ты хочешь стать **отцом**?
	female:	Ты хочешь стать **мамой**?
8.	either:	А какой совет ты дашь сыну или дочке?

Надежда умирает последней. Hope dies last ("last" is a soft adjective in the instrumental!).

Буду химиком!
I will be a chemist!

---

[1] Here's a future-tense example with a predicate adjective: **Контрольная будет трудной** (The test will be difficult).

43.6 Choosing between the nominative and instrumental

We've looked at a number of situations when the instrumental is required. As we'll discuss more tomorrow, it can sometimes be tricky to choose between the instrumental and the nominative with predicate nouns and adjectives. Remember: the **nominative** is associated with **identity**. If we have anything less than a present-tense "**equal sign**" (namely: *seeming* or *becoming*; or *being* in the past and future), then we should choose the **instrumental**.

For example, to say, "My mom **is** a doctor," we would **never** use the instrumental: "**Моя мама — врачом.**" But to say, "My mom works **as** a doctor," we would use the instrumental. Here are the correct translations:

Моя мама — **врач**.	Моя мама работает **врачом**.
My mom is a doctor.	My mom is a doctor (literally, "works **as** a doctor").

Non-present tenses and **imperatives** also require the instrumental. Again, these imply something less than identity. Someone "was" or "will be" something, or we are telling them to "be" (become, or seem like) something:

Моя мама была **врачом**.	Моя дочка будет **врачом**.	Будь **врачом**!
My mom was a doctor.	My daughter will be a doctor.	Be a doctor!

It must be said that in everyday speech either case may sometimes be possible — for example, when describing past qualities, the instrumental is preferable in formal Russian, but the nominative may also be heard:

Finally, note that there is another, more formal way to say "to be" in Russian: the verb **являться** АЙ. It is <u>always</u> used with the instrumental.[1]

Буду машинистом!
I'll be a train conductor!

Он будет работать машинистом.

Она была **красивой**.
Она была **красивая**.
She was beautiful.

Он является **президентом**.
He is the president.

43.7 Expressions like the English "you and I"

There's one more common use of the instrumental to look at — its use in the Russian equivalent of English compound first-person plural subjects such as: "he and I," "she and I," "my brother and I," etc.

The Russian **idiom** is a slightly different take on the same idea. In Russian, we say, literally, "we with him," "we with her," "we with my brother," etc.

These phrases are used as plural subjects, with verbs in the **мы** form.

Мы с ней[2] ходили в кино.	**Мы с братом** скоро поедем в Европу.
She and I went to the movies.	**My brother and I** will soon go to Europe.

Мы с партией, с Лениным!
We are with the party, with Lenin!
Note that most male last names take **-ым** (not **-ом**) in the instrumental!

Give the Russian idiom of the "...and I" expressions, along with the verb form.   **43.c**

1. **My sister and I** went to the theater. **She and I** love opera.

   _____ ходили в театр. **Мы с ней** любим оперу.

2. **My father and I** were at the stadium. **He and I** love to watch soccer.

   _____ были на стадионе. **Мы с ним** любим смотреть футбол.

3. **My neighbor and I** were studying all evening. **He and I** study physics.

   _____ занимались весь вечер. **Мы с ним** изучаем физику.

4. **My wife and I** went to college together (вместе). **She and I** met there.

   _____ вместе учились. **Мы с ней** там познакомились.

5. **My family and I** were outside the city, at the dacha.

   _____ были за городом, на даче.

---

[1] Understood very literally, the verb means something like "to appear **as**..."   [2] Refer to p. 258 for pronoun forms.

day 44:   case usage review

the nominative and the instrumental; the nominative and the genitive;
the accusative and the genitive; the dative and the nominative

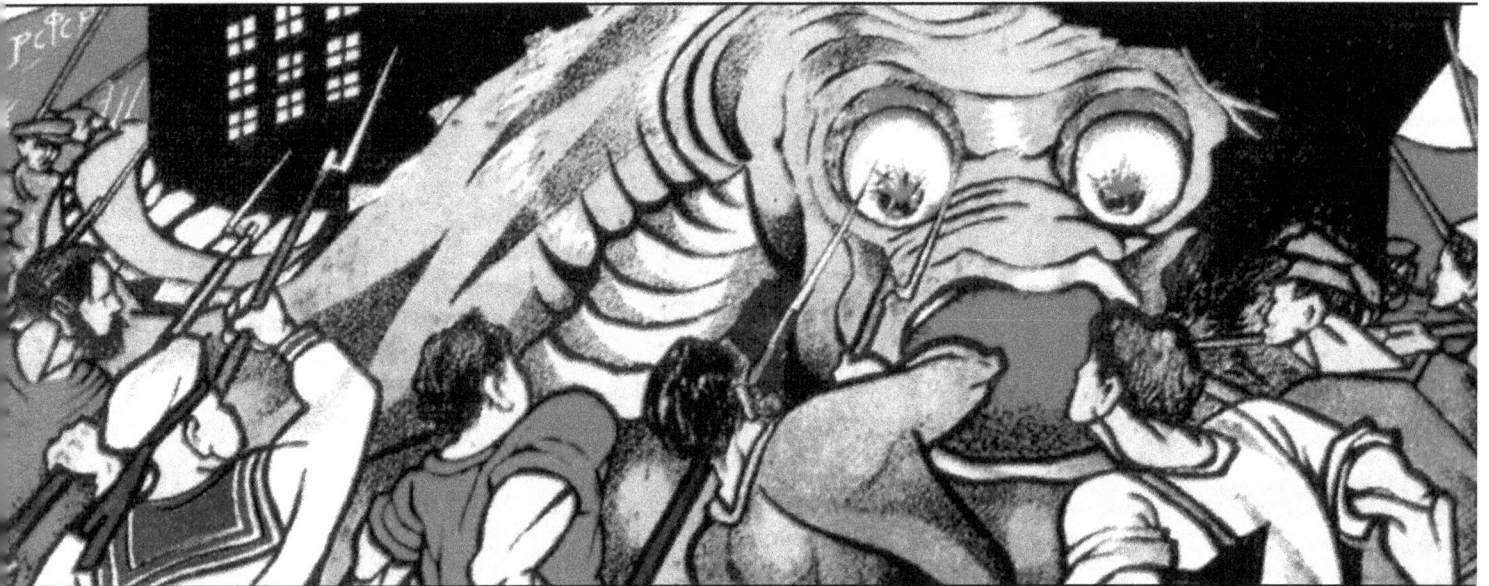

Смерть мир<u>о</u>вому империал<u>и</u>зму! Death to global imperialism!

44.1 The nominative and the instrumental

Today's lesson provides a comprehensive review of case usage **without prepositions** (we'll review prepositions tomorrow). We'll look in particular at pairs of cases that are often confusing for beginning students.

The first such pair is the one we looked at yesterday: the **nominative** and the **instrumental**. The **nominative** is used for all **subjects** and for **predicate nouns and adjectives** with a **present**-tense verb (is or are).

<u>Э</u>то мой **брат**.   **Он фил<u>о</u>соф.**   **Он интер<u>е</u>сный челов<u>е</u>к.**
This is my brother.   He is a philosopher.   He is an interesting person.

....

The **instrumental** is used for **instruments** (tools, means, methods, etc.). It can also create simple **metaphors** (something is "like" or "as" something else), and thus, as we learned yesterday, is typically used for **predicate nouns and adjectives** that express something **less than identity**: to seem, to become, or to be in the past or future. It follows these verbs:

каз<u>а</u>ться A^{shift} / показ<u>а</u>ться A кому чем	станов<u>и</u>ться И^{shift} / стать H^{stem} кем, чем
to seem	to become
ок<u>а</u>зываться АЙ / оказ<u>а</u>ться A^{shift} чем	явл<u>я</u>ться АЙ
to turn out to be, to prove to be	to be (formal)

....

Here are a few simple examples of these usages of the **instrumental**:

Он<u>а</u> п<u>и</u>шет **р<u>у</u>чкой**.   Он см<u>о</u>трит на меня **в<u>о</u>лком**.[1]   Он был **адвок<u>а</u>том**.   Он<u>а</u> ст<u>а</u>нет **журнал<u>и</u>стом**.
She writes with a pen.   He's looking at me like a wolf.   He was a lawyer.   She'll become a journalist.

НЕ БУДЬ ТАКИМ!

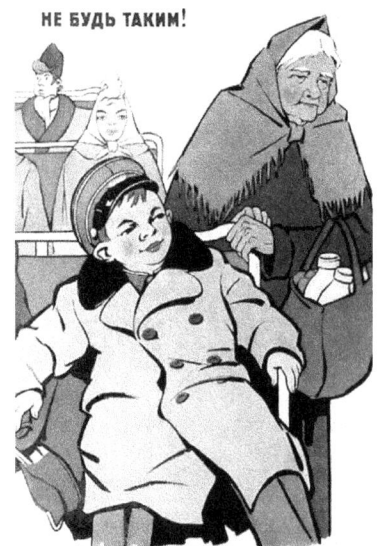

Не будь так<u>и</u>м! Don't be like this!
М<u>а</u>льчик сид<u>и</u>т и занима<u>е</u>т м<u>е</u>сто, а стар<u>у</u>шка должн<u>а</u> сто<u>я</u>ть (stand)? Как<u>о</u>й поз<u>о</u>р! (what a disgrace!)

[1] Such usage is rare in everyday speech (replaced usually with **как** + the nominative, as in "**как волк**"), but it is very common in poetry.

Он кажется **странным**.	Моя дочка скоро будет **мамой**.	Будь **вежливым**!	Он является **президентом**.
He seems strange.	My daughter will soon be a mother.	Be polite!	He is the president (formal).

Finally, the **instrumental** often appears with **reflexive verbs**, whether they are reflexive in the strict sense (like **заниматься / заняться** чем: to "occupy oneself with") or passive verbs (like **интересоваться / заинтересоваться** чем: to "be interested by"). Compare:

Меня интересует **история**.	Я интересуюсь **историей**.	Он занимается **спортом**!	Мы заняли **стол**.
History interests me.	I'm interested "by" history.	He does sports.	We "occupied" a table.

---

*Spot all words in the **nominative** and **instrumental** in this text, and explain the usage.*

Мой сосед по комнате — американец, но он занимается русским языком. Когда он был маленьким, он даже не знал, что есть такой язык, но теперь он очень интересуется русской литературой, культурой и историей. Он говорит, что он впервые (for the first time) заинтересовался русской культурой, когда прочитал роман Достоевского. Достоевский сразу (right away) стал его любимым писателем. Читать такой роман на русском языке казалось ему очень трудной задачей. Но он уже два года изучает русскую грамматику, а на прошлой неделе он прочитал рассказ Достоевского в оригинале. Слава Богу, текст оказался не таким трудным, каким он ему показался на первый взгляд (at first glance).

44.2 The nominative and the genitive

The nominative is used to express **existence**, as the **subject** of the verb "to be" (something *is*). This includes simple "pointing" statements with **это** or **вот**, and statements of possession with **у** + gen.

У вас есть **машина**?	Да, **машина** есть.	Вот наша **машина**.
Do you have a car?	Yes, we have a car.	Here's our car.

To express **non-existence** (something *isn't*, or we *don't have* something), we need to use a special idiom in Russian: **нет** + gen. This is a **subject-less** construction: the verb can only appear in the neuter singular.

present: Здесь нет **станции метро**. | У нас нет **пива**.
There is no subway station here. | We have no beer.

past: Здесь не было **станции метро**. | У нас не было **пива**.
There was no subway station here. | We had no beer.

future: Здесь не будет **станции метро**. | У нас не будет **пива**.
There will be no subway station here. | We will have no beer.

The **genitive** is also used to express **possession** (or some other close relationship). Such uses can often be translated into English using "of."

Это квартира **моего отца**.	Начало **фильма** очень страшное.
This is my father's apartment.	The beginning of the film is very scary.

Народ и армия едины! The people and the army are united (are one)!

Как говорится, один в поле не воин. A single man standing in the field is not a warrior (that is to say, people should band together, not go it alone).

Say the opposite. Watch tense carefully, and beware subjectless "non-existence" constructions.　　　　**44.a**

1. Здесь есть остановка автобуса. _____

2. В этом городе есть хороший бар. _____

3. В нашем штате (state) есть пляж. _____

4. У моего соседа был велосипед. _____

5. У него была туалетная бумага. _____

6. У нас будет машина? _____

7. Молока нет. _____

Там хорошо, где нас нет. "Things are good there, where we are not."

Завтра у нас будет вечеринка, так что (so) мы сегодня ходили на рынок и в магазин покупать еду. У нас дома пива не было вообще. Водки и вина тоже не было. Была у нас только бутылка кваса — а кто же пьёт квас на вечеринке? На рынке мы купили хлеб, колбасу, сыр, и икру. А потом мы пошли в супермаркет "Перекрёсток" (Intersection). Это любимый магазин моего друга. Там мы купили бутылку хорошего вина и ещё бутылку шампанского. Всё будет, как надо. У нас будет даже торт! Начало вечеринки — в восемь часов (at 8 o'clock). Бог знает, когда она закончится!

44.3 The accusative and the genitive

The **accusative** is our default case for **direct objects**. Do keep in mind, especially when we begin reading literature, that direct objects may appear in the **genitive** with a **negated verb.** Here are a few examples:

Я **этого** не знал.	Не пей **колы**!	Я не читал **этой книги**.
I didn't know that.	Don't drink cola!	I haven't read this book.

Remember, **accusative** forms are the same as the **nominative**, with two exceptions: **feminine** nouns and adjectives have special **accusative** endings (-**у** and -**ю** for nouns, -**ую** for adjectives). Meanwhile, the **accusative** forms of **animate masculine** nouns look exactly like their **genitive** forms.

	nominative	genitive	accusative
masc. inanim.	**новый стол**	нового стола	**новый стол**
masc. anim.	новый студент	**нового студента**	**нового студента**
fem. inanim.	новая книга	новой книги	новую книгу
fem. anim.	новая студентка	новой студентки	новую студентку
neuter.	**новое мыло**	нового мыла	**новое мыло**

ГЛАВХЛАДОПРОМ

ЛЁД

Покупайте лёд! Buy ice!
Покупайте ещё рыбу, масло, мясо, и кефир!

44.b *Complete the sentences with direct objects in the **accusative**. Watch out for animate masculine nouns!*

Мы купили...	1. новый журнал _____	2. новый щенок _____
Он часто покупает...	3. дорогое вино _____	4. банка икры _____
Они читают...	5. русская газета _____	6. Маяковский _____
Они увидели...	7. старый друг _____	8. старая подруга _____
Они съели...	9. вся икра _____	10. весь торт _____
Они выпили...	11. целая бутылка _____	12. всё молоко _____
Она хорошо знает...	13. наш город _____	14. наш профессор _____
Мы ждали...	15. наша сестра _____	16. наш отец _____
Я вижу...	17. твоя семья _____	18. их адвокат _____

*Remember, the direct object of a negated verb may appear in the **genitive**, especially in formal (or literary) Russian. Try it!*

Мы не понимаем...	19. эта теория _____	20. ваш вопрос _____

Значит, у нас вчера была вечеринка. Мы с женой купили всё, что нужно было. Даже посуду помыли. Ещё бельё постирали[1] (может быть, кто-нибудь (someone) захочет у нас остаться, чтобы не ехать домой так поздно). Были на вечеринке мой старый друг из школы, Коля, и его жена. Её зовут Аня. Мне показалось, что я её видел в прошлом году в театре, но она меня не помнила. Им очень понравился салат, который мы приготовили. Все ели и пили весь вечер. Всю икру съели, и всё шампанское выпили. В конце вечеринки я сказал тост: "За нас, ребята[2]!"

---

[1] **стирать** АЙ / **постирать** АЙ means "to wash" in the sense of "to launder," to do laundry
[2] This is a plural form used colloquially in the sense of "guys" or "kids" (both male and female). We'll discuss it further at a later time.

44.5 The dative and the nominative

The **dative** is used for **indirect objects**, and in this use can often be translated using "to" or "for." Indirect objects can follow verbs of "giving" (**дав<u>а</u>ть / дать, продав<u>а</u>ть / прод<u>а</u>ть, дар<u>и</u>ть / подар<u>и</u>ть**) and "buying" (**покуп<u>а</u>ть / куп<u>и</u>ть**), but also verbs of "telling" (**говор<u>и</u>ть / сказ<u>а</u>ть, расск<u>а</u>зывать / рассказ<u>а</u>ть**), "showing" (**пок<u>а</u>зывать / показ<u>а</u>ть**), and "seeming" (**каз<u>а</u>ться / показ<u>а</u>ться**). Verbs of helping (**помог<u>а</u>ть / пом<u>о</u>чь**) and advising (**сов<u>е</u>товать / посов<u>е</u>товать**) take objects in the dative.

Я подар<u>и</u>л **маме** телев<u>и</u>зор.	Я куп<u>и</u>ла **отцу** газ<u>е</u>ту.
I gave ("gifted") mom a television.	I bought my father a newspaper.
Он расск<u>а</u>зал **мне** анекд<u>о</u>т.	Он<u>и</u> **нам** показ<u>а</u>ли фотогр<u>а</u>фию.
He told me a funny story / joke.	They showed us a photograph.
Фильм **мне** к<u>а</u>жется хор<u>о</u>шим.	Я всегд<u>а</u> помог<u>а</u>ю **сос<u>е</u>ду**.
The film seems good to me.	I always help my neighbor.

Why might one confuse the **dative** and the **nominative**? The **dative** is used in many **subjectless** constructions in Russian (remember: by definition, any grammatical subject must be in the **nominative** — so, no nominative, no subject!). But, since English lacks subjectless constructions, such datives are often translated into English as subjects:

Смерть мировому империализму!
Death to global imperialism!

Мне хорош<u>о</u>.	**Мне** б<u>ы</u>ло хорош<u>о</u>.	**Мне** б<u>у</u>дет хорош<u>о</u>.	**Мне** х<u>о</u>чется пить.	**Мне** захот<u>е</u>лось пить.
I feel good.	I felt good.	I will feel good.	I feel like drinking.	I got the urge to drink.

Here and elsewhere, confusion often arises when we rely on English translations, instead of focusing on the Russian **idiom**! Perhaps by this stage you have grown somewhat more comfortable with many such idioms.

дав<u>а</u>ть АВАЙ / **дать**:	1. We'll give the child chocolate. _____	**44.c**
	2. They always give us wine. _____	
помог<u>а</u>ть АЙ / **пом<u>о</u>чь** Г^{shift}:	3. He really (<u>о</u>чень) helped us. _____	
	4. We'll help grandma. _____	
пок<u>а</u>зывать АЙ / **показ<u>а</u>ть** А^{shift}:	5. She showed me the dog. _____	
	6. He'll show her the cat. _____	
покуп<u>а</u>ть АЙ / **куп<u>и</u>ть** И^{shift}:	7. They bought us a cake. _____	
	8. I'll buy her expensive caviar. _____	

К<u>а</u>ждый — коллект<u>и</u>ву, коллект<u>и</u>в — к<u>а</u>ждому!
Everyone for the collective, and the collective for everyone!
(in the sense of "all for one and one for all")

Repeat these **subjectless** *constructions in the past and future.* **44.d**

1. Нам ск<u>у</u>чно на л<u>е</u>кции. _____

_____

2. Ем<u>у</u> тр<u>у</u>дно чит<u>а</u>ть. _____

_____

3. Нам есть х<u>о</u>чется. _____

_____

4. Н<u>а</u>шему др<u>у</u>гу пл<u>о</u>хо. _____

_____

Чег<u>о</u> нет, тог<u>о</u> и х<u>о</u>чется. We want what we don't have.

day 45: review of prepositions

prepositions with the prepositional, instrumental, dative, genitive, and accusative; prepositions with more than one case

О каждом из нас забо́тится Ста́лин в Кремле́. Stalin is taking care of every one of us in the Kremlin. Which cases follow the prepositions here?

45.1 The prepositional case with prepositions

You may have noticed that yesterday's lesson left out the **prepositional** case. Why? Because the prepositional case can never be used **without a preposition**. Here are the prepositions followed by the prepositional:

о (об, обо)	about	Говори́м **о литерату́ре / об иску́сстве / обо мне.** We're talking about literature / about art / about me.	
в (во)	in / at	Живём **в Москве́ / во Владивосто́ке.** We live in Moscow / in Vladivostok.	
на	on / at	Ко́шка сиде́ла **на столе́.** The cat was sitting on the table.	Мы бы́ли вчера́ **на вечери́нке.** We were at a party yesterday.
	in (a language)	Мы чита́ли тру́дный текст **на ру́сском языке́** без словаря́. We were reading a difficult text in Russian without a dictionary.	

при	in the presence of	Не говори об этом **при маме**! Don't talk about that in mom's presence!
	"upon," "when"	**При выходе** из поезда, не забывайте свои вещи. Upon (when) leaving the train, don't forget your things.
	"under" (a regime)	Дедушка жил **при Сталине** / **при коммунизме**. Grandpa lived during Stalin's rule / under Communism.

To review, the preposition **о** becomes **об** in front of vowel sounds (**и, а, э, о** — not the "soft vowels" **я, е, ё**, which begin with the sound **й**!). Meanwhile, **в** becomes **во** when followed by **в** or **ф**, <u>plus another consonant</u>. Compare these spellings of the prepositions in the examples above.

Finally, recall that some nouns take a special "locative" ending (<u>stressed</u> **у**) when describing **location**:

в шкафу	**в саду**	**в лесу**	**в году**	**на полу**	**на берегу**	**на краю**	**в аэропорту**
in the wardrobe	in the garden	in the forest	in the year	on the floor	on the shore	on the edge	at the airport

---

*Fill in the blanks with the **prepositional** case endings. Look up the word's nominative form first if you don't remember it!* **45.a**

1. Я сижу на диван____, а собака сидит на пол____.

2. Ты смотрел такой ужасный фильм при бабушк____!?

3. Он футболист. Он только о футбол____ и говорит.

4. Нет этого слова у меня в словар____.

5. Ты была сегодня на лекци____?

6. Есть известная картина в этом музе____?

7. Нельзя писать эсэмэску на заняти____.

8. У тебя есть зонт в рюкзак____?

9. Мы говорили с писателем о его стать____.

10. Он потерял билет при вход____ (entrance) в театр.

11. Она работает весь день на компьютер____.

12. Рыба плавает в рек____, а кошка сидит на берег____.

13. Наша дача находится на кра____ леса.

14. Этот поэт жил ещё при Российской импери____.

Бесплатный сыр бывает только в мышеловке. Free cheese is found only in a mousetrap (**мышеловка — мышь** = mouse, **ловить** = to catch).

45.2 The instrumental case with prepositions

Use **с** with the instrumental **only** when you mean "with" in the sense of **accompaniment.** For "with" in the sense of "with an instrument," use the instrumental case alone, **without с.**

Recall that **с** becomes **со** when followed by **с** or **з plus** another consonant.

с (со)	with	Она сидела **с подругой** и пила чай **с сахаром**. She sat with a friend and drank tea with sugar.
рядом с	next to	**Рядом с кофейней** есть ресторан. There's a restaurant next to the coffee house.
над	above, over	**Над моим письменным столом** есть лампа. There's a lamp above my desk.
под	below, under	Газета там на столе, **под журналом**. The paper is there on the table, under the magazine.
за	behind, beyond	В театре я сидела **за очень высоким человеком**. In the theater I was sitting behind a really tall person.
	chasing, "to fetch"	Они пошли в магазин **за хлебом и колбасой**. They went to the store for some bread and sausage.
перед	in front of	**Перед Русским музеем** в Петербурге есть памятник Пушкину. There's a monument to Pushkin in front of the Russian Museum in Petersburg.
	just before (temporal)	Мы приготовили всю еду **перед нашей вечеринкой**.[1] We got all the food ready before our party.

НА ЗЕМЛЕ И НАД ЗЕМЛЁЙ МЫ ЗАЖМЕМ ВРАГА ПЕТЛЕЙ!

На земле и над землёй мы зажмём врага петлёй.

On the ground (earth) and above the ground we are squeezing the enemy in a loop / noose (**петля**).

[1] Remember, **перед** suggests "directly before" or "just before," while **до** + gen. suggests "at any point prior to."

*Fill in the blanks with the **instrumental** case endings. Look up the word's nominative form first if you don't remember it!*

1. Мама сидела с пап_____ за стол_____.

2. Ты обычно пьёшь кофе с молок_____ или без?

3. В России часто едят борщ со сметан_____.

4. Все говорили перед начал_____ фильма.

5. Мальчик не хотел сидеть рядом с сестр_____.

6. Метро находится (is located) под земл_____.

7. Мы готовились весь вечер перед экзамен_____.

8. У него большая квартира с балкон_____.

За комором не с топором. You don't chase after a mosquito (**комар**) with an axe (**топор**). We'll learn more about axes in *Crime and Punishment*.

45.3 The dative case with prepositions

The preposition **к** (whose basic meaning is "to" or "toward") is used in **куда** expressions for visiting people; we'll look at this in Book 2. Note special uses of **по** with a **hyphen**: with languages (**по-русски, по-английски**), and in the phrases "in my opinion, in your opinion," etc. (**по-моему, по-твоему, по-вашему**).

к (ко)	on / at	Мы идём **к коммунизму**. We are marching towards Communism.		Мы идём **к профессору**. We're going to see the professor.
по	along, around	Мы весь день гуляли **по городу**. We strolled around the city all day.	in (a subject)	У нас лекция **по истории**. We have a lecture in history.
	via, "by"	Я поговорила с ним **по телефону**. I spoke with him by telephone.	according to	**По его мнению** это не так. In his opinion that isn't so.

As you continue with Russian, you'll see a variety of uses of **по** in the general sense of "in accordance with" or "in terms of." A simple example is **сосед по комнате**: roommate (so to speak, a "neighbor in terms of room").

*Fill in the blanks with the **dative** case endings. Look up the word's nominative form first if you don't remember it!*

1. Я часто пишу ему по электронной почт_____.

2. По моему мнени_____ это неправда.

3. По-моему ты должен пойти к врач_____.

4. Она скоро поедет в Россию к дедушк_____.

5. Это новый учебник по русскому язык_____.

6. Он шли по тротуар_____, а машина ехала по улиц_____.

7. Что показывают сегодня по телевизор_____?

8. Давайте поговорим по телефон_____.

К гадалке не ходи. Don't bother visiting the fortuneteller, **гадалка** (i.e. we know something for certain).

45.4 The genitive case with prepositions

There are a large number of prepositions taking the genitive. Here are the basic examples we've seen, plus one new one: **вместо** (instead of). Don't confuse it with the adverb **вместе** (together).

у	at, near	Она любит сидеть **у окна** и читать. She loves to sit at the window and read.
	possession	**У моего брата** есть дача под Москвой. My brother has a dacha outside Moscow.
	at some-one's place	Я был **у брата** на даче вчера. I was at my brother's dacha yesterday.
из	out of, from	Мы вернулись домой **из театра**. We returned home from the theater.
с (со)	from off of, from	Я взял книгу **со стола**. I took the book from the table.
до	before, prior to	Надо прочитать текст **до урока**.[1] We must read the text (sometime) before class.

Всё для фронта! Всё для победы!
Everything for the front! Everything for victory!

[1] Again, **перед** suggests "directly before" or "just before," while **до** + gen. suggests "at any point prior to."

После работы — в институт!
After work — to the institute!

без	without	Я всегда пью кофе **без молока и сахара**. I always drink coffee without milk and sugar.
для	for	У меня большой сюрприз **для вас**. I've got a big surprise for you all.
после	after	**После спектакля** они пошли в кафе. After the performance they set off for a cafe.
против	against	Толстой был пацифистом; он был **против войны**. Tolstoy was a pacifist; he was against war.
вместо	instead of	Сегодня я пью кофе **вместо чая**. Today I'm drinking coffee instead of tea.
от	from	Я получил письмо **от старого друга**. I received a letter from an old friend.
	from someone's place	Мы вчера вернулись из России, **от бабушки**. Yesterday we returned from Russia, from a visit to grandma.
	against (medicine)	Это лекарство **от кашля**. This is cough medicine.
	to (keys)	Это ключ **от квартиры**. This is the key to the apartment.

---

*Fill in the blanks with the **genitive** case endings. Look up the word's nominative form first if you don't remember it!*   **45.d**

1. У дедушк___ уже нет машины. Он её продал.

2. Я просто не могу жить без компьютер____.

3. Мы не могли читать этот текст без словар____.

4. После заняти____ все пошли в кафе.

5. Какой подарок ты купила для сосед____ по комнате?

6. Мы поехали на такси с вокзал____ домой.

7. Когда мы шли из кофейн____, шёл дождь (rain).

8. Где ключ от машин____? Неужели я его потерял!?

9. Вместо того фильм____ давай посмотрим вот этот.

10. Давайте пойдём в ресторан после экзамен____.

У него ни кола ни двора. He has neither a stake nor a yard (something like the English "He doesn't have a pot to piss in").

45.5 The accusative case with prepositions

в (во)	into, to	Мы сегодня идём **в театр**. We're going to the theater today.
на	onto, to	Они пошли **на стадион**. They set out for the stadium.
	for (a period)	Я еду в Россию **на неделю**. I'm going to Russia for a week.
под	under (куда)	Бутылка упала **под стол**. The bottle fell under the table.
через	in (from now)	**Через месяц** я поеду в Россию. In a month I'm going to Russia.

Октябрь открыл путь в космос! October (the October Revolution) opened the path to the cosmos! — **Вся власть советам!** All power to the soviets! — **Наука и коммунизм неотделимы!** Science and Communism are inseparable!

Recall that **назад** appears after a noun in the accusative:

назад	ago	**Год назад** я училась в России. A year ago I was studying in Russia.

The preposition **за** has a number of common meanings, including "for," as in "this for that" (exchange, etc.)

за	for (exchange)	Он заплатил **за кофе**. He paid for the coffee.	in favor of	Все мы **за свободу** слова. We're all for freedom of speech.
	behind (куда)	Кольцо упало **за шкаф**. The ring fell behind the wardrobe.	in, within (accomplishment)	Мы решили задачу **за час**. We solved the problem in an hour.

1. Кто из вас обычно платит за пив____?

2. Студентка прочитала книгу за недел____.

3. Мы едем в Россию на месяц____.

4. Через год____ я вернусь из России.

5. Месяц____ назад я купил новую квартиру.

6. Ты идёшь сегодня на вечеринк____.

7. Ты хочешь посмотреть на эту фотографи____?

8. Нам надо вернуться в общежити____.

9. — Где ручка? — Она упала. Посмотри под стол____.

10. Ты уже заплатила за квартир____ за этот месяц____?

Сегодня князь, а завтра в грязь. Today a prince, but tomorrow — into the dirt.

45.6 Prepositions that take more than one case

A number of the prepositions we've seen can take more than one case — be sure to note the difference! With motion verbs, the prepositions **в, на, за, под** take the **accusative** in **куда** ("where to") phrases. So, if we're speaking of *motion toward* a location, we need to be sure to use the accusative. Remember that **перед** and **над always take the instrumental**, regardless.

в (во)	in, at (+ prep.)	Они были опять **в театре**. They were at the theater again.	into, to (+ acc.)	Они часто ходят **в театр**. They often go to the theater.	
на	on, at (+ prep.)	Они были на матче **на стадионе**. They were at a match at the stadium.	onto, to, for (+ acc.)	Они шли **на стадион**. They were on their way to the stadium.	
под	under (+ instr.)	Мяч теперь **под диваном**. The ball is now under the sofa.	under (+ acc.)	Он только что упал **под диван**. It just now fell beneath the sofa.	
за	behind (+ instr.)	**За забором** есть сад. There's a garden behind the fence.	behind, for (+ acc.)	Собака побежала **за забор**. The dog ran off behind the fence.	
с (со)	with (+ instr.)	Я поговорил **с братом** по телефону. I spoke with my brother by phone.	from (+ gen.)	Они вернулись **со стадиона**. They returned from the stadium.	

45.f Fill in the blanks with the correct case endings. Which case do you need?

1. Мы были в Москв____ в прошлом году. Мы часто ездим в Москв____.

2. Вы не хотите пойти на концерт____? Мы давно не были на концерт____.

3. — Что есть за эт____ стен____? — Небольшой парк с фонтан____.

4. — Где мой ноутбук? — Там, под той книг____.

5. — С кем ты ездила в Петербург____? — С сестр____ и брат____.

6. Мы долго сидели на берег____ и смотрели на Нев____.

7. В Русск____ музе____ русское искусство...

8. ...а в Эрмитаж____ европейское.

9. Давай я заплачу за ед____, а ты можешь заплатить за пив____.

10. Моя соседка по комнате купила билет на балет____ на пятниц____.

11. Мы съели пиццу с сыр____, колбас____, и лук____.

12. Бабушка всегда пьёт кофе с молок____ и сахар____.

13. — Где мяч? — Не знаю. Посмотри за шкаф____. По-моему он там.

(Умереть) под забором. (To die) at the foot of the fence. In Russian, "at the foot of the fence" means something like the English "in the gutter." You can't get much lower!

ИДИ В БАНЮ
ПОСЛЕ РАБОТЫ

Иди в баню после работы.
Go to the banya (a bathhouse) after work.

А ты был(а) в русской бане?

day 46: case endings by noun type

feminine nouns; masculine nouns; neuter nouns;
special soft nouns; short-form adjectives

Слава труду! Glory to Labor! Note the classical Soviet pairing of the "worker" (**рабочий**) and the "collective farm woman" (**колхозница**).

46.1 Feminine nouns

Today we'll review all singular case endings for nouns, by **type**. Now that we've seen all of the Russian cases in the singular, it's important to consolidate our knowledge of how each noun type behaves.

Let's begin with **feminine** nouns: we can spot them in the nominative by the **a** ending for hard nouns, and **я** for soft. Looking over the table below, note how the **soft** endings are essentially the same as the **hard** endings — they're just the "**soft versions**" thereof.

It's good to distinguish **animate** and **inanimate** feminine nouns for future reference,[1] but the category of animacy doesn't affect feminine endings thus far. In the accusative singular, all of our feminine nouns take the **same ending**, regardless of animacy: **y** for hard, **ю** for soft.

Compare, for example: **Я читаю книгу** (I'm reading a book — inanimate) and **Я вижу маму** (I see mom — animate). By analogy to **masculine** animates, students sometimes mistakenly write: **Я вижу мамы**.

Слава советской женщине!
Glory to the Soviet woman!

			feminine nouns		
		long	hard	soft	short
nom.	эта	новая	газета	неделя	готова[2]
gen.	этой	новой	газеты	недели	
acc.	эту	новую	газету	неделю	
dat.	этой	новой	газете	неделе	
prep.	этой	новой	газете	неделе	
instr.	этой	новой	газетой	неделей семьёй	

Look at the soft instrumental endings, and recall that ё only occurs in a **stressed** position.

[1] Animacy will become important for feminine nouns in Book 2, when we introduce the accusative **plural**.
[2] Short-form adjectives occur in the nominative only; they can only be used in the predicate, as in: **Она готова** (She is ready).

46.a *Supply the appropriate **feminine** endings. Rely on context to determine what case you need. Is each word a noun or adjective?*

1. Мо___ сестр____ сегодня на занятии познакомилась с нов____ русск____ студентк___.

2. К сожалению у нас на кухн____ нет ни рыб___, ни куриц___. Ед___ у нас вообще нет! Значит, надо купить ед___.

3. У его семь____ есть больш____ дач____ в деревн___. Он ездит на дач____ почти кажд____ недел____.

4. Наш____ соседк____ написала стать____ карандашом, а потом переписала (rewrote) её чёрн____ ручк____.

5. Мы с подруг____ летали в Москв____ на прошл____ недел____. Мы купили тебе банк____ икр___.

6. Мы всегда стараемся помогать наш_____ тёт___, но она всегда недовольн____. Да, с тёт____ бывает трудно!

7. Через недел___ эт___ студентк___ будет читать русск____ газет___ в оригинале.

8. Они интересуются литератур___ о Втор____ миров____ войн___ и о блокад___ Ленинграда.

Собака лает, а караван идёт. The dog barks (**лаять** A: to bark), while the caravan moves on.

46.2 Masculine nouns

In the nominative singular, masculine nouns end in a **consonant** (or, to put it more precisely, they have no ending!). Note that soft masculine nouns end in a **soft consonant** (either the soft consonant й, like **музей**, or some other consonant followed by the soft sign ь, like **словарь**).

In the masculine **accusative**, we must distinguish between **animate** nouns (people and animals) and **inanimate** nouns (objects, ideas, etc.). Animate nouns take what look like **genitive** endings in the accusative.

Finally, recall that some masculine nouns referring to male people take **feminine endings**, but they are still **masculine** for purposes of agreement with adjectives and verbs. For example:

Это **мой** папа. Папа **был** на даче вчера. Папа всегда **занят**.

Слава воину-победителю!
Glory to the warrior-victor!

воин is a hard masculine noun, while **победитель** is a soft masculine noun.

	long	hard	soft		short
nom.	этот	новый	стол	словарь	музей	готов
gen.	этого	нового	стола	словаря	музея	
acc.	этот	новый	стол	словарь	музей	
animate:	этого	нового	стола	словаря	музея	
dat.	этому	новому	столу	словарю	музею	
prep.	этом	новом	столе	словаре	музее	
instr.	этим	новым	столом	словарём	музеем	

46.b *Supply the appropriate **masculine** endings. Remember that in some cases **no ending** is required!*

1. Мама купила нов____ учебник____ по физике для сын____. Он хочет стать известн____ физик____.

2. За дом____, в котор____ я жил, когда учился в Петербург____, был больш____, красив____ парк____.

3. Мы с отц____ цел____ час____ ходили по музе___, а потом долго гуляли по город____. Наконец пошли в театр___.

4. Мы хотели поехать домой из театр____ на автобус____, но не было ни одн_____ автобус____! Мы пошли пешком.

5. Почему вы заинтересовались русск____ язык____? Почему вам нравится так____ трудн____ язык?

6. Я продал щенк____ стар____ друг____ месяц____ назад. А через год____ я куплю нов____!

7. Что больше (more) нравится ваш_____ знаком_____ — ездить на автобус____ или на трамва___?

8. У нас здесь нет словар____. Мы не можем читать эт____ текст____ без словар____. А со словар____ можно!

236

*Let's focus on masculine nouns that take **feminine** endings. Any adjectives modifying them will be masculine!*

1. Это наш____ нов_____ коллег___; он из России. Давайте пригласим нов_____ коллег_____ на пиво.

2. Мы ходили в ресторан с пап____ и с наш_____ любим_____ дяд____. Мы давно не видели любим_____ дяд____!

46.3 Neuter nouns

All of the neuter nouns we've seen have been **inanimate**. Once again, note how the soft endings are simply soft "versions" of the regular hard endings. Also note where **ё** appears in place of **e** in **stressed** endings.

		long	hard	soft	short
nom.	это	новое	окно	море	бельё	готово
gen.	этого	нового	окна	моря	белья	
acc.	это	новое	окно	море	бельё	
dat.	этому	новому	окну	морю	белью	
prep.	этом	новом	окне	море	белье	
instr.	этим	новым	окном	морем	бельём	

В советском море врагу горе!
Woe to the enemy in the Soviet sea!

As one might expect, there are very few **animate** neuter nouns. One (partial) exception is the word for animal: **животное**. It is a stand-alone adjective (meaning, roughly, "a living thing").

В лесу мы сфотографировали **странное животное** ("странного животного" may also sometimes be heard).[1]
In the forest we took a photo of a strange animal.

In addition to **животное**, we've seen other stand-alone neuter adjectives, such as **мороженое** (ice cream) and **шампанское** (champagne). By definition, these words will always take neuter **adjectival** endings.

На вечеринке мы выпили целую бутылку **шампанского**.   Мы очень любим **шампанское**.
At the party we drank an entire bottle of champagne.   We really love champagne.

Remember, borrowed neuter nouns (most in -o) are **indeclinable** — their endings never change. Examples include **метро** (subway), **пианино** (piano), **пальто** (coat), **кино** (cinema), **кафе** (café), **шоссе** (highway), **такси** (taxi), **меню** (menu). Remember, by the way: **кофе** is also indeclinable, but it is *masculine*, despite its ending!

---

*Supply endings for these **neuter** nouns and adjectives.*   **46.d**

1. Ты выпил всю бутылку молок___? Что я тебе говорила о молок____? Оно для кошки! А теперь молок____ нет!

2. У нас на вечеринке не было морожен_____, но нашей подруге очень понравилось французск_____ вин____.

3. У нас есть дача на озер____, под большим дерев_____. Птица сидит в эт_____ дерев____ и поёт за мо____ окн____.

4. Мой брат интересуется искусств_____, а сестра занимается прав_____. Она сейчас изучает прав____.

5. — У ребёнка нет печень____. Давайте купим ему печень____.   — Нет, давайте купим ему яблок____.

6. Я не могу спать без хорош____ одеял____; мне бывает слишком холодно. У вас есть одеял_____?

---

*These nouns are **indeclinable** — but let's practice them anyway! This should be an easy exercise!*   **46.e**

1. Молодой человек, можно мен____ (menu)? Посмотрим, что у вас есть в мен_____.

2. Я сейчас еду на метр____. Жди меня у выхода из станции метр____ "Гостиный двор".

3. Мой знакомый любит играть на пианин____, смотреть кин____, и сидеть в каф___.

*Remember, **кофе** is a **masculine** indeclinable noun (treating it as neuter is considered sub-standard!):*

4. Наша тётя очень любит коф___. Она всегда сидит в каф___ с чашкой коф___.

---

[1] As this example shows, **животное** usually is not given genitive endings in the accusative singular, in the way that masculine animates are (though it usually is given genitive endings in the plural — "**Я люблю животных**" — as we'll learn in Book 2.)

46.4 Special soft nouns

We've been careful to distinguish a "special" set of soft nouns — one for each gender. If we look at their endings, we see that they are generally the same as the regular soft endings we've just reviewed. However, the endings in the **black boxes** are special — and that's why we have to classify these nouns separately from other soft nouns.

While masculine special softs are quite rare (for example, **гений, кафетерий, комментарий, критерий**), feminines and neuters are **extremely common.**

	special soft		
	masculine	**feminine**	**neuter**
nom.	кафетери**й**	фамили**я**	задани**е**
gen.	кафетери**я**	фамили**и**	задани**я**
acc.	кафетери**й**	фамили**ю**	задани**е**
animate:	гени**я**		
dat.	кафетери**ю**	фамили**и**	задани**ю**
prep.	кафетери**и**	фамили**и**	задани**и**
instr.	кафетери**ем**	фамили**ей**	задани**ем**

Красной армии — слава!
Glory to the Red Army!

46.f   *Supply the **special soft** endings. Remember, only those in the black boxes above differ from ordinary soft noun endings.*

1. Когда мы учились в Росси_____, мы часто занимались вместе (together) в общежити_____.

2. Мы поехали в Росси_____ год назад, а вернулись из Росси_____ неделю назад.

3. Один мальчик, с которым я ходила в школу, оказался гени_____! Теперь он изучает и биологи_____ и философи_____.

4. Я забыла фамили_____ этой студентки, но я помню, что она занимается фехтовани_____ и изучает хими_____.

5. Я не слушал профессора на лекци_____ по истори_____. Мне надо было готовиться к контрольной по хими_____!

---

1. Ты всегда слушаешь профессора на лекции?   3. Хорошо готовят в твоём кафетерии (= в твоей столовой)?

2. Тебе нравится жить в общежитии, или нет?   4. Ты бываешь голоден / голодна на занятии по русскому языку?

46.5 Short-form adjectives

Finally, let's focus on short-form adjective endings. As we mentioned, short forms occur in the **nominative** only, and can only appear in the **predicate**. If needed, take a moment to review the meanings and forms of short-form adjectives, in 24.3. Note any unusual stress patterns!

Here is a quick review of short forms, including two with a mobile vowel:

уверенный →	уверен	уверена	уверено	уверены
готовый →	готов	готова	готово	готовы
голодный →	голоден	голодна	голодно	голодны
больной →	болен	больна	больно	больны

Ленин — жил. Ленин — жив.
Ленин — будет жить.
Lenin lived. Lenin is alive.
Lenin will live.

— Владимир Маяковский

46.g   1. Словарь тебе нуж_____? А ручка нуж_____? Пальто тебе нуж_____?

2. Они были трезв_____ или пьян_____ вчера? Они жив_____ или мертв_____?

3. Этот стол занят_____? Это место занят_____? Ты (fem.) сегодня занят_____?

4. Он довол_____ и счастлив_____, а она недоволь_____ и несчастлив_____.

Голоден, как волк. Hungry as a wolf (i.e. starving!).

day 47:   declining names

Russian names; end-stressed last names; adjectival last names;
other male and female names; casual short forms of first names

Да здравствует великое, непобедимое знамя Маркса-Энгельса-Ленина-Сталина!
Long live the great, unconquerable banner of Marx-Engels-Lenin-Stalin!

47.1 Russian names

Way back in 5.1, we introduced Russian names. We learned that full names consist of a first name (**имя** —
a neuter noun, despite the **-я**!), a patronymic (**отчество**) formed from the father's name, and a last name
(**фамилия**). Now that we've learned all the cases, let's practice using Russian names in various contexts.

Predictably enough, people's names are treated as **animate**. This is especially important for male names: as
masculine animates, their **accusative** forms are identical with their **genitive** forms.

Generally, the endings below are the same as the ordinary **noun** endings we've just reviewed. This is always true
of **first names** and **patronymics** — treat them just like ordinary nouns! But be careful with **last names**: in some
instances, last names take **adjectival endings!** These instances are presented in the **black boxes** below. As you
can see, **feminine** nouns take adjectival endings everywhere but the nominative and accusative, while
masculine names do so in the instrumental only. Treat these cases as exceptional!

	female names				male names		
	имя	отчество	фамилия		имя	отчество	фамилия
nom.	Марина	Ивановна	Цветаева	nom.	Михаил	Афанасьевич	Булгаков
gen.	Марины	Ивановны	Цветаевой	gen.	Михаила	Афанасьевича	Булгакова
acc.	Марину	Ивановну	Цветаеву	acc.	Михаила	Афанасьевича	Булгакова
dat.	Марине	Ивановне	Цветаевой	dat.	Михаилу	Афанасьевичу	Булгакову
prep.	Марине	Ивановне	Цветаевой	prep.	Михаиле	Афанасьевиче	Булгакове
instr.	Мариной	Ивановной	Цветаевой	instr.	Михаилом	Афанасьевичем[1]	Булгаковым

[1] Note the effect of the 5-letter spelling rule here: we can't have an unstressed **о** following **ч**.

239

47.2 End-stressed last names

Think of the endings we've just seen as the default for Russian names. In terms of the masculine in particular, these endings apply to last names ending in **-ин** and **-ов** (that is to say, the vast majority of Russian last names!).

But certain types of names don't quite follow this pattern. The first type, shown to the right, has the same endings, but is **end-stressed**. This is typical of last names whose masculine nominative form is stressed on the **-ин**.

	male	female
nom.	Бахт**ин**[1]	Бахтин**а**
gen.	Бахтин**а**	Бахтин**ой**
acc.	Бахтин**а**	Бахтин**у**
dat.	Бахтин**у**	Бахтин**ой**
prep.	Бахтин**е**	Бахтин**ой**
instr.	Бахтин**ым**	Бахтин**ой**

So, for example, **Бородин** is end-stressed, but names like **Пушкин**, **Онегин**, **Ленин**, **Сталин**, and **Распутин** are not. As these examples suggest, end-stressed names are far less common than stem-stressed ones.

47.3 Adjectival last names

Many last names are adjectives — that is, they take adjectival endings, and decline just like any ordinary adjective. Note that since most such names end in **-ский**, the 7-letter spelling rule affects some endings, since we can't write **ы** after **к**.

Some last names, like **Толстой**, are end-stressed adjectives.[2] They decline just like **большой**.

	male	female
nom.	Маяковск**ий**	Маяковск**ая**
gen.	Маяковск**ого**	Маяковск**ой**
acc.	Маяковск**ого**	Маяковск**ую**
dat.	Маяковск**ому**	Маяковск**ой**
prep.	Маяковск**ом**	Маяковск**ой**
instr.	Маяковск**им**	Маяковск**ой**

47.a *Many subway stations are named after famous people. Whether the people are male or female, the name of the station itself will be feminine, in agreement with **станция**. Name some stations after the people below. If necessary, add the adjectival suffix **-ская**.*

1. Маяковский _____
2. Достоевский _____
3. Чехов _____
4. Пушкин _____

5. Чернышевский _____
6. Менделеев _____

*For this last one, use **-овская**:*

7. Горький _____

Станция "Арбатская" in Moscow is named after the famous street, **Арбат**.

47.4 Other male names

Some Russian names (like **Пастернак**, **Мандельштам**, and **Фет**) do not end in **-ин**, **-ов**, or **-ский**, but rather in some other **consonant**. These also include foreign names, both first and last. If a foreign male name happens to end in a consonant, then it is easily declined like any native Russian noun.

But if a foreign male name (like **Обама**) happens to end in **-а**, then it declines with feminine endings (just like папа or коллега).

nom.	Пастернак	Барак Обам**а**
gen.	Пастернак**а**	Барак**а** Обам**ы**
acc.	Пастернак**а**	Барак**а** Обам**у**
dat.	Пастернак**у**	Барак**у** Обам**е**
prep.	Пастернак**е**	Барак**е** Обам**е**
instr.	Пастернак**ом**	Барак**ом** Обам**ой**

Obama is a good example: his first name is treated as **masculine**, while his last name is treated as **feminine**.

If a foreign male name happens to end in some vowel other than **-а**, then it is treated as **indeclinable**.

Я видел Барак**а** Обам**у**.   Я читаю Эдгар**а** По.   Я люблю Пабло Пикассо.   Это фильм Фредерико Феллини.

47.5 Other female names

Finally, if a foreign female name happens to end in **-а**, then it is easily declined just like any feminine noun. In all other cases, it is treated as **indeclinable**. Note in particular that if the name happens to end in a **consonant**, it is not given female endings, nor is it declined with masculine endings.

Я видел Хиллари Клинтон.   Мы читаем Надежду Мандельштам.   Я люблю Николь Кидман.

---

[1] Mikhail Bakhtin was a brilliant Soviet-era philosopher and literary theorist — his work is not to be missed!
[2] By the way, the adjective **толстый** (stem-stress) means "fat."

Мы читаем… 47.b

Булгаков	_____	Толстая	_____	Платонов	_____
Пушкин	_____	Цветаева	_____	Набоков	_____
Бахтин	_____	Пастернак	_____	Улицкая	_____
Ахматова	_____	Горький	_____	Шекспир	_____
Маяковский	_____	Толстой	_____	Джейн Остин	_____
Гиппиус (f!)	_____	Солженицын	_____	Достоевский	_____

Анна Андреевна Ахматова _____

Владимир Владимирович Маяковский _____

Борис Леонидович Пастернак _____

Say that you're reading your favorite (non-Russian!) author. How will the name decline? Consult Wikipedia for spelling!

Я читаю... _____

---

*In Russian, we say a monument (**памятник**) is "to" someone, using the dative, as in:* **Это памятник Пушкину.** *Try it…* 47.c

1. Александр Сергеевич Пушкин _____

2. Николай Васильевич Гоголь _____

3. Анна Андреевна Ахматова _____

4. Фёдор Михайлович Достоевский _____

5. Лев Николаевич Толстой _____

6. Михаил Иванович Глинка _____

7. Владимир Ильич Ленин _____

8. императрица Екатерина Вторая _____

9. Владимир Владимирович Маяковский _____

10. Александр Пушкин и Наталья Гончарова _____

11. нос Майора Ковалёва[1] _____

12. добрая собака Гаврюша _____

[1] Look out for this strange monument in Petersburg. For more information, read Gogol's Petersburg tale entitled "The Nose" (**Нос**).

47.d With the **genitive**, say that these are the works of the given authors.

1. Толстой: "Война и мир" — роман (novel) _____.

2. Гоголь: "Нос" — рассказ (short story) _____.

3. Ахматова: "Реквием" — поэма[1] (poetic cycle) _____.

4. Достоевский: "Идиот" — роман _____.

5. Цветаева: "Двое" — стихотворение (poem) _____.

6. Замятин: "Мы" — роман-антиутопия _____.

7. Маяковский: "Послушайте!" — стихотворение _____.

8. Блок: "Коршун" (The Vulture)— стихотворение _____.

МЫ ТРЕБУЕМ МИРА, НО ЕСЛИ ТРОНЕТЕ...

Мы требуем мира, но если тронете...
We demand peace, but if you touch (us)...

— Владимир Маяковский

47.e To be polite, refer to people using the **first name** and **patronymic**. Which case do you need?

Ирина Павловна   1. Дайте этот журнал _____, пожалуйста.

Мария Сергеевна   2. Вы сегодня увидите _____?

Анна Ивановна   3. Мы завтра встретимся с _____ в ресторане.

Иван Александрович   4. Вы не поможете _____ написать эту статью?

Олег Сергеевич   5. Неужели вы не помните _____?

Сергей Михайлович   6. Мы с _____ были вчера в театре.

47.f Use the instrumental to ask was acquainted with whom.

1. — Толстой был знаком с _____ (Чехов)? — Да.

2. — Достоевский был знаком с _____ (Толстой)? — Нет.

3. — Пастернак был знаком со _____ (Цветаева)? — Да.

4. — Пушкин был знаком с _____ (Гоголь)? — Да.

5. — Лермонтов был знаком с _____ (Пушкин)? — Нет.

6. — Ахматова была знакома с _____ (Гумилёв)? — Да.

7. — Блок был знаком с _____ (Андрей Белый)? — Да.

Да, Чехов был знаком с Толстым. Они были знакомы.

47.6 Casual short forms of first names

In casual speech ("**на ты**"), Russians will typically refer to each other using special **short forms** of first names. A few common examples are shown here. We'll learn more in Book 2.

All of these short forms take **feminine endings** — even men's names. But men's names (just like **папа**) are still considered masculine, and agree with masculine adjectives and verbs.

	Михаил	Борис	Дарья	Юлия
nom.	Миша	Боря	Даша	Юля
gen.	Миши	Бори	Даши	Юли
acc.	Мишу	Борю	Дашу	Юлю
dat.	Мише	Боре	Даше	Юле
prep.	Мише	Боре	Даше	Юле
instr.	Мишей	Борей	Дашей	Юлей

47.g **Паша** (Павел): 1. Мне надо позвонить _____.

Маша (Мария): 2. Я познакомился с _____.

Серёжа (Сергей): 3. Я так давно _____ не видел!

Настя (Анастасия): 4. Что ты подарила _____?

Таня (Татьяна): 5. Ты получил письмо от _____?

Ира (Ирина): 6. Ты встречаешься с _____?

Володя (Владимир): 7. _____ позвонил мне вчера.

Коля (Николай): 8. Мы с _____ идём в кино.

Ксюша (Ксения): 9. Давайте поговорим о _____.

Лена (Елена): 10. Ты знаешь _____?

---

[1] The name **поэма** has been applied to many kinds of works by Russian authors, from long, narrative poems (like Pushkin's "The Bronze Horseman" or Blok's "The Twelve") to prose novels (like Gogol's *Dead Souls* or Yerofeyev's *Moscow-Petushki*).

day 48: pronouns & special modifiers

third-person pronouns; first- and second-person pronouns; the special modifiers **весь**, **один**, **чей**; forms of possessive pronouns

Кто — кого? Who whom? (Which "train" will beat the other — Communism, or Capitalism? Note how much is expressed without a single verb!

48.1 Third-person pronouns

Let's review the case forms for third-person pronouns (he, she, it, them) and interrogative pronouns (who, what).

	what?	who?
nom.	что	кто
gen.	чего	кого
acc.	что	кого
dat.	чему	кому
prep.	чём	ком
instr.	чем	кем

	he (masculine)		she (feminine)		it (neuter)	
nom.	он		она		оно	
gen.	его	→ него	её	→ неё	его	→ него
acc.	его	→ него	её	→ неё	его	→ него
dat.	ему	→ нему	ей	→ ней	ему	→ нему
prep.	—	→ нём	—	→ ней	—	→ нём
instr.	им	→ ним	ей	→ ней	им	→ ним

---

*You didn't quite hear what was said. Ask a simple follow-up question using an **interrogative** pronoun. Watch case!* **48.a**

1. Я видела **маму**. _____ ты видела?

2. Мы говорили об **отце**. О _____ вы говорили?

3. Мы говорили об **истории**. О _____ вы говорили?

4. Мы смотрели **фильм**. _____ вы смотрели?

5. Я верю **другу**. _____ ты веришь?

6. Мне помогал мой **брат**. _____ тебе помогал?

7. Я привык к русской **еде**. К _____ ты привык?

8. Он ездил туда с **другом**. С _____ он туда ездил?

---

*Answer these simple questions — first with the **noun**, then with the corresponding **pronoun**. Again, watch case!* **48.b**

1. Кому ты писала? отец: _____ _____
   сестра: _____ _____

2. С кем вы сидели? сосед: _____ _____
   дедушка: _____ _____

3. О чём говорили? религия: _____ _____
   кошка: _____ _____

4. На что вы смотрели? дерево: _____ _____
   река: _____ _____

48.2 First- and second-person pronouns

Below are all the forms for the first- and second-person pronouns: I, you (sing.), we, and you (pl.). The same forms are used with or without prepositions.

But do note the first-singular forms **мне** and **мной** — the initial **мн-** consonant cluster can be tricky to pronounce, especially when a preceding preposition ends in a consonant (or is one!). In such cases, a **mobile vowel** appears at the end of the preposition:

	I	you (s.)	we	you (pl.)
nom.	я	ты	мы	вы
gen.	меня	тебя	нас	вас
acc.	меня	тебя	нас	вас
dat.	мне	тебе	нам	вам
prep.	мне	тебе	нас	вас
instr.	мной	тобой	нами	вами

со мной[1]	**во мне**	**ко мне**	**надо мной**	**подо мной**	**передо мной**	*note:* **обо мне**
with me	in me	toward me	above me	below me	in front of me	about me

As we've discussed, prepositional phrases are typically pronounced **as a single unit**, almost as if they were written as a single word. The preposition itself is unstressed; the single stress within the phrase falls onto the object of the preposition, whether noun or pronoun. Practice a few examples, noting in particular vowel reduction:

со мной	**во мне**	**ко мне**	**надо мной**	**о ком?**	**в чём?**	**от него**	**к нему**
sah **mnoy**	vah **mnyeh**	kah **mnyeh**	nahdah **mnoy**	ah **kohm**?	fchyohm?	aht nyih**voh**	knyih**mu**

48.c

я:
1. Ты _____ не любишь?
2. Ты _____ не веришь?
3. Ты _____ не поможешь?
4. Позвони _____!
5. Не пойдёшь со _____?

ты:
6. Что он _____ сказал?
7. Она _____ не видит.
8. С _____ трудно жить.
9. Какая у _____ квартира?
10. Давай я _____ помогу.

мы:
11. Не поедешь с _____?
12. Что они о _____ говорят?

вы:
13. Я _____ всегда помогала.
14. Она идёт в кино с _____?
15. Машина у _____ есть?

48.3 The special modifier весь

Let's review case forms of the "special modifier" **весь, вся, всё**. Its endings resemble the soft adjectival endings we've learned. Note that the masculine includes the **mobile vowel e**, which is squeezed out when endings are added.

	masculine		feminine		neuter	
nom.	весь	торт	вся	бутылка	всё	мыло
gen.	всего	торта	всей	бутылки	всего	мыла
acc.	весь	торт	всю	бутылку	всё	мыло
anim.	всего	человека				
dat.	всему	торту	всей	бутылке	всему	мылу
prep.	всём	торте	всей	бутылке	всём	мыле
instr.	всем	тортом	всей	бутылкой	всем	мылом

ВСЯ МОСКВА СТРОИТ МЕТРО

Вся Москва строит метро! All of Moscow is building the subway. "To build" is **строить И / построить И**.

We have seen the **plural** form **все**, which can mean "all things" or, more often, "all people." So far, we have seen it used in the sense of "everyone," and contrasted it carefully with **всё** ("everything") — see 14.4 to review.

244 [1] Remember: an unstressed "o" in a preposition reduces to an "ah" sound (i.e., it sounds like Russian "a").

*Supply the correct forms of **весь**. As always, watch case!* **48.d**

1. Кто съел _____ икру?	5. Он ездил по _____ миру.	9. Спасибо за _____, что ты сделал!
2. Кошка выпила _____ молоко.	6. Я желаю мира во _____ мире.	10. _____ это знают!
3. Хочешь _____ торт, или половину?	7. И знать не хочу обо _____ этом.	11. Она сделала _____ эту работу.
4. Я люблю тебя _____ душой (soul).	8. Она помогла _____ нашей семье.	12. Во _____ городе нет воды!

48.4 Forms and uses of один

The forms of **один** generally resemble those of hard adjectives, with the exceptions of the nominative forms and the instrumental **одним**.

Besides its basic meaning of "one," **один** can also be used in several other senses. It can mean "by oneself, alone." And, although Russian has no true articles, it sometimes uses **один** where English would use the indefinite article "a /an" (we could also translate this usage as "a certain..." or "some...").

Finally, **один** can mean "the same."[1] Look at the examples and be on the lookout for these special uses of **один**.

	masc.	fem.	neut.
nom.	од**ин**	одн**а**	одн**о**
gen.	одн**ого**	одн**ой**	одн**ого**
acc.	од**ин**	одн**у**	одн**о**
anim.	одн**ого**		
dat.	одн**ому**	одн**ой**	одн**ому**
prep.	одн**ом**	одн**ой**	одн**ом**
instr.	одн**им**	одн**ой**	одн**им**

Я возьму **один кусок** пиццы.	Он (она) всегда занимается **один (одна)**.	Мы жили в **одном городе**.
I'll take **one piece** of pizza.	He (she) always studies **alone**.	We lived in **the same city**.
Я возьму **одну чашку** чая.	**Один мужчина** вас спрашивает.	"История **одного города**."
I'll take **one cup** of tea.	**Some man** (a certain man) is asking for you.	The story of **a certain city**.

*Give the correct forms of **один** and translate. Note: a **курс** is a class in college (as in, the class of 2020), and a **класс** is a grade* **48.e**
*in school. Note that **курс** is used with **на** (На каком курсе ты учишься?) and that **курс** can also refer to a "course" in college.*

1. Ты хочешь одн_____ конфету или две (two)?	4. Я вчера познакомился с одн_____ девушкой.
2. Ты возьмёшь одн_____ пиво или два (two)?	5. Мы с ней учились в одн_____ классе в школе.
3. Ты возьмёшь од_____ пирожок или два?	6. А теперь мы учимся на одн_____ курсе.

1. С кем вы учитесь в одном университете?	4. С кем вы учитесь на одном курсе (i.e. year in college)?
2. С кем вы ходили в одну школу?	5. Ты занимаешься один/одна, или с другом / с подругой?
3. С кем вы живёте в одном общежитии?	6. Тебе нравится быть один/одна, или ты любишь общаться?[2]

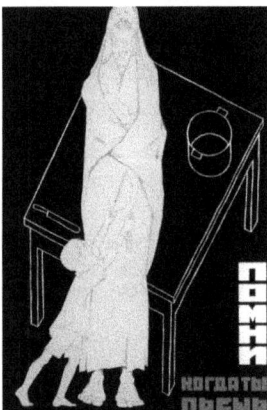

Помни! Когда ты пьёшь, твоя семья голодна! Чья это семья? О чьей семье говорит этот плакат?

48.5 Forms of чей

The question word **чей** (Whose?) also declines. Note the spelling — there is a soft sign in every form, except for the masculine **чей**. This can be important for distinguishing this word from various forms of **что**.

О **чьём** отце вы говорите?
"About **whose** father" are you talking?

	masc.	fem.	neut.
nom.	чей	чь**я**	чь**ё**
gen.	чь**его**	чь**ей**	чь**его**
acc.	чей	чь**ю**	чь**ё**
anim.	чь**его**		
dat.	чь**ему**	чь**ей**	чь**ему**
prep.	чь**ём**	чь**ей**	чь**ём**
instr.	чь**им**	чь**ей**	чь**им**

1. Ч_____ зонт ты взял? А ч_____ рубашку?	4. В ч_____ доме вы были? **48.f**
2. О ч_____ брате вы говорите? А о ч_____ сестре?	5. Ч_____ карандашом вы пишете?
3. С ч_____ собакой вы гуляли в парке?	6. С ч_____ отцом ты познакомилась?

[1] See 10.4 to review other expressions meaning "the same" (**тот же**, **тот же самый**, etc.).
[2] **общаться** АЙ is a useful verb meaning "to interact with people" or "socialize."

48.6 Forms of possessive pronouns

These possessive pronouns can also be thought of as "special modifiers." Their endings resemble the regular adjectival endings we know, but do differ somewhat, so they must be presented separately.

The first pattern, shown below, is followed by **мой** and **твой**.

	masculine		feminine		neuter	
nom.	**мой**	торт	**моя**	бутылка	**моё**	мыло
gen.	**моего**	торта	**моей**	бутылки	**моего**	мыла
acc.	**мой**	торт	**мою**	бутылку	**моё**	мыло
anim.	**моего**	друга				
dat.	**моему**	торту	**моей**	бутылке	**моему**	мылу
prep.	**моём**	торте	**моей**	бутылке	**моём**	мыле
instr.	**моим**	тортом	**моей**	бутылкой	**моим**	мылом

The second pattern is followed by **наш** and **ваш**.

	masculine		feminine		neuter	
nom.	**наш**	торт	**наша**	бутылка	**наше**	мыло
gen.	**нашего**	торта	**нашей**	бутылки	**нашего**	мыла
acc.	**наш**	торт	**нашу**	бутылку	**наше**	мыло
anim.	**нашего**	друга				
dat.	**нашему**	торту	**нашей**	бутылке	**нашему**	мылу
prep.	**нашем**	торте	**нашей**	бутылке	**нашем**	мыле
instr.	**нашим**	тортом	**нашей**	бутылкой	**нашим**	мылом

Радуюсь я — это мой труд вливается в труд моей республики.
Loosely: I'm happy to see my labor contributing to the labor of my republic (вливаться means "to be poured into").

Note the role of the "pointing word" **это** here; it's somewhat hard to translate. It's as if the speaker is looking around him, and can see how his own role fits into the collective Soviet project — even space exploration!

Finally, we have the third-person pronouns his / its, her, their (**его**, **её**, **их**), which **never change form** in any way. Here are just a few examples: note how the forms remain exactly the same, regardless of gender or case.

его торт	Я взял **его** торт.	Я видел **его** брата.	Я получил письмо от **его** брата.
его бутылка ➧	Я взял **его** бутылку.	Я видел **его** сестру.	Я получил письмо от **его** сестры.
его мыло	Я взял **его** мыло.	Я видел **его** мыло.	Я привык к **его** креслу.

Take a moment to contrast these forms with the personal pronouns in 48.1. It's true that they coincide in some cases: for example, **его** can also be the **accusative singular** of the pronouns **он** and **оно**, which have full declensions. But here, in 48.6, we are dealing with an entirely different part of speech — a **possessive** pronoun. Remember: if we are using **его**, **её**, or **их** in the **possessive** sense (**his**, **its**, **her**, **their**), they will **never change** — in particular, they will never add an **н** after a preposition, as we can notice above. Compare these examples:

Я получил письмо...	...от **него**.	*vs.*	...от **его** брата		
I received a letter...	...from him.		...from his brother.		
Я привык...	...к **нему**.	*vs.*	...к **его** креслу.		
I got used...	...to him.		...to his easy chair.		

48.g

1. **ты**: Можно попробовать тво_____ пиццу?

2. **ты**: Мы говорили о тво_____ сочинении.

3. **ты**: Ты привыкла к тво_____ общежитию?

4. **я**: Вы уже познакомились с мо_____ семьёй?

5. **я**: В мо_____ общежитии нет столовой.

6. **я**: По мо_____ мнению это совсем нехорошо!

7. **мы**: На наш_____ курсе мы будем читать Чехова.

8. **мы**: Мы поговорили с наш_____ профессором.

9. **вы**: Нам очень нравится ваш_____ квартира.

10. **вы**: Чей это ключ? Это ключ от ваш_____ комнаты?

11. **он**: Мы познакомились на _____ вечеринке.

12. **они**: В _____ квартире нет кухни, к сожалению.

13. **она**: Все говорят о _____ новой статье.

14. **он**: Мы посидели в кафе с _____ отцом.

15. **они**: Он меня попросил позвонить _____ маме.

16. **она**: Тебе понравилась _____ новая машина?

246

day 49: reflexive pronouns

the reflexive pronoun **свой**; when we can and must use **свой**; omitting possessive pronouns; reflexive pronouns; doing things "all by yourself"; reciprocity with **друг дру́га**

Мы вы́полнили но́рму, а вы? We've fulfilled our quota (**но́рма**)... what about you?
Он сде́лал **свою́** рабо́ту, а тепе́рь спра́шивает това́рища о **его́** рабо́те.

49.1 The reflexive possessive pronoun свой

Yesterday, in 48.6, we reviewed all singular forms of the possessive pronouns we've seen so far. But there's actually one more possessive pronoun to learn — the **reflexive** possessive pronoun **свой**, which declines exactly like **мой** and **твой**.

Свой is "reflexive" because it **refers back to the subject** of its sentence or clause. Generally, we can think of **свой** as meaning "one's own" (or, "his own," "her own," "my own," as the case may be). However, things aren't quite so simple. In fact, this topic can be a very confusing one!

So, when **can** we use **свой**, instead of the pronouns in 48.6?

1) When the **subject** of the clause is the **possessor** of the object modified.

Я чита́ю **свою́** кни́гу.   I'm reading my (own) book.

....

2) Hence, **свой** cannot appear in the **subject** of a sentence or clause.[1]

Свой брат чита́ет кни́гу. (incorrect!!)   "Own brother" is reading a book. (?)

....

3) Remember: these rules "**reset**" whenever a **new clause** begins

Он зна́ет, что **мы** чита́ем **его́** кни́гу.   He knows we're reading his book.

Yes, this is **his** book, but since **he** is not the subject of the second clause, we can't use **свой**. **We** is the subject of the clause, and it's not **our** book!

МЫ ЛЮБИМ СВОЙ ЯЗЫК
И СВОЮ РОДИНУ
ЛЕНИН

Мы лю́бим свой язы́к и свою́ ро́дину.
"We love our language and homeland
(**ро́дина**)" — Ле́нин.

---

[1] Truth be told, it **can**, but such situations are extremely unusual. Here are examples in proverbs: **Своя́ но́ша не тя́нет** (One's own load doesn't drag one down), and **Своя́ руба́шка бли́же к те́лу** (One's own shirt is closer to one's body).

49.2 When _may_ we use свой? In the first and second persons!

Keeping in mind the rules we just learned, we might say that **свой** is essentially interchangeable with **мой, твой, наш** and **ваш**. However, whenever **свой** can be used in such cases, it tends to be **preferred**. For example:

Я люблю **свою** кошку.	Ты любишь **свою** работу.	Мы любим **свою** машину.	_even:_ Возьми **свой** зонт!
Я люблю **мою** кошку.	Ты любишь **твою** работу.	Мы любим **нашу** машину.	Возьми **твой** зонт!

In each example, the subject is speaking of its own things, so we can use **свой**. Here, both variants are perfectly acceptable, but those with **свой** are preferred; they are more neutral in tone, whereas the examples in the lower row are more emphatic with regard to **possession**, and can imply something like "I'm reading _my_ newspaper."

49.3 When _must_ we use свой? In the third person!

However, in the **third person**, we are no longer dealing with a slight difference in tone. Our choice between **свой** and **его, её,** or **их** can result in two sentences that say completely different things! Consider these examples:

Она любит **её** мужа.	➡	She loves **her** husband.	(that is: She loves **another woman's** husband!)
Он любит **его** жену.	➡	He loves **his** wife.	(that is: He loves **another man's** wife!)

Look closely at the initial English translations. Do we **really** know whose spouses these are? Actually, no! We can only **assume** that the subjects love **their own** spouses, but the **her** could in fact mean **another woman's**, and the **his** could mean **another man's**. We typically make such assumptions without even noticing the ambiguity. But where English is ambiguous, Russian is crystal-clear: we have a scandal (**скандал**) on our hands here!

Assuming no scandal is afoot (and people love their own spouses), we should write the following:

Она любит **своего** мужа.	➡	She loves **her** husband.	(that is: She loves **her own** husband.)
Он любит **свою** жену.	➡	He loves **his** wife.	(that is: He loves **his own** wife.)

49.4 Omitting possessive pronouns

Unlike English, Russian often prefers to **omit** possessive pronouns altogether; we assume the subject is dealing with his or her own things, unless told otherwise! This is especially common with **family members**, for example:

Она покупает книгу для **сына**. She's buying a book for her son.	➡	We could include **своего** here, but usually it would go without saying that this was her **own** son. We'd be explicit only to avoid some ambiguity.
Я позвонила **маме**. I called mom.	➡	Here, the Russian could include **моей** or **своей**, but, again, we don't need to. We assume that the subject is calling her **own** mother!

49.a _Analyze these examples carefully, and determine:_ **Есть у нас здесь скандал, или нет скандала?**

1. Боря ужасно (terribly) любит свою жену.

2. Мой друг говорит, что Паша любит свою жену.

3. Игорь очень любит его молодую невесту (fiancée).

4. Я понимаю, почему он так любит свою невесту.

5. Наш приятель часто видит свою девушку.

6. Моя сестра любит своего мужа.

7. Я знаю, что их тётя часто отдыхает у её жениха (fiancé).

8. Она говорит, что её соседка очень любит своего парня.

49.b _In these examples,_ **свой** _is optional; we could use a possessive pronoun from 48.6. But_ **свой** _is preferred, so use it!_

1. I'm working in my room.   Я работаю в _____ комнате.

2. We love our city.   Мы любим _____ город.

3. Did you (f.) forget your key?   Ты забыла _____ ключ?

4. You're always talking about your dog.   Ты всегда говоришь о _____ собаке.

5. I hate my job.   Я ненавижу _____ работу.

....
В Тулу со своим самоваром не ездят. One doesn't go to Tula with one's own samovar. (Tula is famed for weapons, gingerbread, and samovars).

Vova has a girlfriend...	1. He called his girlfriend.	Он позвонил _____ подруге.
	2. His friend called his girlfriend.	Его друг позвонил _____ подруге.
Borya has a dog...	3. Borya loves his dog.	Боря любит _____ собаку.
	4. His neighbor loves his dog.	Его сосед любит _____ собаку.
They have an umbrella...	5. They took their umbrella.	Они взяли _____ зонт.
	6. Their friend took their umbrella.	Их друг взял _____ зонт.

49.5 Reflexive pronouns

The **reflexive particle** we've seen in verbs (**ся / сь**) is really nothing but a contracted form of the reflexive pronoun **себя**. Much like the reflexive possessive pronoun **свой**, the reflexive pronoun **себя** only makes sense in reference to the subject, when the action of the verb is directed **back at the subject** itself. For this reason, **себя** has no nominative form.

nom.	—
gen.	себя
acc.	себя
dat.	себе
prep.	себе
instr.	собой

ВОСПИТЫВАЙ В СЕБЕ ЛЮБОВЬ К ТРУДУ!

Depending on the gender of the subject, **себя** can be translated as "himself, herself, itself," or, more generally, as "oneself."

Мой кот увидел **себя** в зеркале.
My cat saw **itself** in the mirror.

Мой брат думает только о **себе**.
My brother thinks only of **himself**.

Возьми с **собой** зонт!
Take your umbrella with you!

У меня при **себе** нет денег.
I have no money on my person.

Воспитывай в себе любовь к труду!
Cultivate within yourself a love for labor!

Here are two very common verbs that are used with **себя**:

| **чувствовать** ОВА / **почувствовать** ОВА себя
to feel (to "feel oneself") + adverb | Как ты **себя** чувствуешь?
How do you feel? | Я чувствую **себя** хорошо!
I feel good! |
| **вести** Д^{end} / **повести** Д себя[1]
to behave oneself + adverb | Ты ведёшь **себя** нехорошо!
You're behaving badly! | Ты будешь вести **себя** хорошо?
Will you behave yourself (well)? |

1. He loves only himself.   Он любит только _____.
2. He looks at himself in the mirror.   Он смотрит на _____ в зеркале.
3. He always thinks about himself.   Он всегда думает о _____.
4. He wrote a letter to himself.   Он написал _____ письмо.
5. He behaves shamelessly (бесстыдно),   Он ведёт _____ бесстыдно,
6. but he always feels good!   но он всегда чувствует _____ хорошо!

Everyday encounters with reflexive pronouns

Here are a few phrases with reflexive pronouns you're likely to see and hear on a daily basis in Russia!

Здесь или с собой?   Is that for here or to go? (i.e., to take "with yourself")

от себя — к себе   push — pull ("away from yourself" — "toward yourself"). Printed on doors. Good to know!

Чувствуйте себя как дома!   Make yourself at home! ("feel yourself at home") — said to guests.

[1] We'll look more closely at this verb later. The forms are: **веду, ведёшь... ведут**; and, in the past, **вёл, вела, вело, вели**.

49.6 Doing things "all by yourself"

masc.	**сам**
fem.	**сама**
neut.	**само**
plural	**сами**

What about "myself, yourself, herself," etc., in the sense of "I baked this cake **myself** — all by myself"? These forms are simple short-form adjectives, and agree with the subject, but they are adverbial in terms of meaning.

— Тебе помочь? — Нет, я это **сам** сделаю!
— Want some help? — No, I'll do it myself! (m.)

Она решила задачу **сама**.
She solved the problem herself.

49.e 1. He himself doesn't understand. _____

2. They did the work themselves. _____

3. I (m.) do everything myself. _____

4. I (f.) myself don't know. _____

5. The child will do this himself. _____

Я сама! I'll do it myself! (Schoolchildren! Do your homework yourself!)

ШКОЛЬНИКИ! ДОМАШНЕЕ ЗАДАНИЕ ВЫПОЛНЯЙТЕ САМОСТОЯТЕЛЬНО!

Я сама!

ТЫ ТРУД ДРУГОГО УВАЖАЙ, САМ НАСОРИЛ, САМ УБИРАЙ !
Ты труд другого уважай, сам насорил, сам убирай! Respect another's labor; if you made a mess yourself, clean it up yourself!

49.7 Reciprocity with друг друга

В ЯДЕРНЫЙ ВЕК, ЧТОБЫ ВЫЖИТЬ, НАДО ДРУГ ДРУГА ПОНЯТЬ!

В ядерный век, чтобы выжить, надо друг друга понять! In the nuclear age, we must come to understand each other to survive!

As we've seen (27.4), reciprocity can be expressed using a reflexive verb (as in, Мы **видимся** довольно часто). But only some verbs are used in this way. Another expression of reciprocity can be used with almost any verb: we repeat **друг** twice (only the second **друг** is declined). It declines like a masculine animate noun. This term is related to the adjective **другой** — "another," or "another person."

acc.	**друг друга**	Мы хорошо знаем **друг друга**.	each other
dat.	**друг другу**	Мы всегда помогаем **друг другу**.	each other

A preposition typically falls in the middle, and, again, only the second **друг** declines:

acc.	**друг на друга**	Они смотрели **друг на друга**.	at each other
gen.	**друг без друга**	Мы не можем жить **друг без друга**.	without each other
dat.	**друг к другу**	Мы привыкли **друг к другу**.	to each other
prep.	**друг о друге**	Они часто думают **друг о друге**.	about each other
instr.	**друг с другом**	Мы ходили в театр **друг с другом**.[1]	with each other

---

49.f *Translate using the appropriate друг друга phrase.*

1. They really love each other. Они очень любят _____.

2. They always talk about each other. Они всегда говорят _____.

3. They can't live without each other. Они не могут жить _____.

4. They always help each other. Они всегда помогают _____.

5. They understand each other. Они понимают _____.

6. They believe each other. Они верят _____.

7. They've gotten used to each other. Они привыкли _____.

8. They travel to visit (к) each other. Они ездят _____.

9. They give each other money.[2] Они дают _____ деньги.

10. They tell each other the truth. Они говорят _____ правду.

11. They know everything about e. o. Они всё знают _____.

12. They often see each other. Они часто видят _____.

ТРЁХГОРНОЕ ПИВО

Трёхгорное пиво выгонит вон ханжу и самогон. (Tryokhgornoe beer drives out the hypocrite and samogon.) **Самогон** — это водка, которую "гонят сами" (то есть, делают у себя дома).[3]

---

[1] Of course, it is simpler to say **вместе** — together.   [2] Money is a plural-only noun: **деньги**, gen. **денег**.

[3] A similar term is **самиздат**. Самиздат — это литература, которую "издают сами" (то есть, публикуют сами).

250

day 50: uses of the infinitive and new clause types

more uses of the infinitive; the infinitive with **чтобы**; punctuation tips; review of clause types; result clauses with **так** and **так что**; indirect questions with **ли**; condition clauses with **если**

Чтобы стро́ить — на́до знать, что́бы знать — на́до учи́ться. In order to build, one must know; in order to know, one must study.

50.1 More uses of the infinitive

We've seen the infinitive used with certain verbs and modal adverbs, as in:

Я хочу **чита́ть**.	Мне нра́вится **чита́ть**.	Мне на́до **прочита́ть** статью́.
I want to read.	I like to read.	I need to read an article.

The infinitive is also used in simple **subjectless** constructions that are easily overlooked. Like other subjectless constructions (e.g. "Мне бы́ло хорошо́"), they can include nouns or pronouns in the dative.

Let's begin with examples that include question words:

Что **де́лать**?	Что нам **де́лать**?	Что нам бы́ло **де́лать**?
"What to do?"	"What are we to do?"	"What were we to do?"

We can try to approximate the Russian grammar with literal translations such as "What to do?" or "What is there for us to do?" — or, we can translate more loosely: "What should be done?" "What should we do?"

Here's another set of simple examples:

Как **знать**?	Мне как **знать**?	Как мне бы́ло **знать**?
"How to know?"	"How am I to know?"	"How was I to know?"

More loosely, these might translate as "Who knows?" "How am I supposed to know?" and "How was I supposed to know?"

ОТ НАРОДНОЙ МЕСТИ НЕ УЙТИ ВРАГУ!

От наро́дной ме́сти не уйти́ врагу́! The enemy will not escape the people's vengeance! (**уйти́** is an infinitive).

or, more literally: "It is not for the enemy to escape the people's vengeance!"

251

Here are several more examples that include a question word and the dative. Can you give looser translations?

Что ему **делать**?	Кого ей **спросить**?	Где мне **работать**?	Какую машину мне **купить**?
"What is he to do?"	"Whom is she to ask?"	"Where am I to work?"	"What kind of car am I to buy?"

Now let's look at examples without a question word. Again, the Russian idiom has **no subject**, making it very hard to translate literally; instead, we have little choice but to turn the Russian dative into an English subject:

Нам не **понять**, почему.	Не нам это **знать**.	Врагу не **уйти**.
"It is not for us to understand why."	"It is not for us to know this."	"It is not for the enemy to escape."
We can't understand why.	We can't know this (maybe others can).	The enemy shall not escape.

50.a   *Translate using an infinitive (with a dative pronoun, if necessary).*

1. Where are we to work?   _____

2. What should I talk about?   _____

3. What was I to think?   _____

4. To ask her, or not to ask?   _____

5. What kind of film should we watch?   _____

6. Whose article should we read?   _____

Cursed questions

It is often said that the two most burning questions in Russia are:

Что делать? (What is to be done?)   **Кто виноват**? (Who is to blame?)

The adjective **виноватый** (guilty, culpable) is used here in the short form. By the way, **Что делать**? is the title of a famous political pamphlet by Lenin (and, before that, a novel by Chernyshevsky). Note the pre-revolutionary orthography to the right, with the old letter **ѣ** (say: "**ять**").

Other popular conspiratorial questions one often hears in Russia include:

Кому это выгодно? (For whom is it profitable?)   **Кто за этим стоит**? (Who's behind it?)

Russians sometimes say: **У России две беды: дураки и дороги** (Russia has two misfortunes: its idiots and its roads). But which came first!? Quite a paradox!

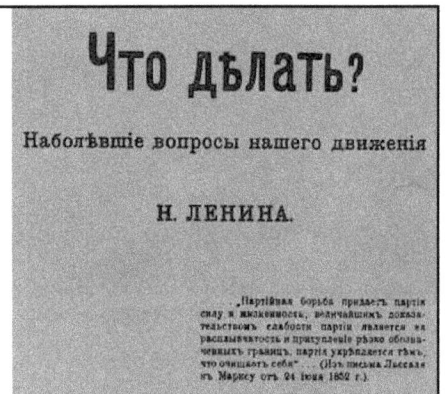

Что дѣлать?

Наболѣвшіе вопросы нашего движенія

Н. ЛЕНИНА.

50.2 The infinitive with что**бы** (in order to)

We can also use the infinitive following the conjunction **чтобы**, which, in this instance,[1] can be translated "in order to..." As always, consider aspect when choosing an infinitive — are we making a general statement, or talking about a specific task?

Чтобы готовить борщ, нужна свёкла (beets — singular only in Russian!).
In order to make borshch (generally speaking), one needs beets.

Чтобы приотовить борщ сегодня, мы должны купить свёклу.
In order to make borshch tonight (specifically), we need to buy beets.

ЧТОБЫ БОЛЬШЕ ИМЕТЬ-
НАДО БОЛЬШЕ ПРОИЗВОДИТЬ

ЧТОБЫ БОЛЬШЕ
ПРОИЗВОДИТЬ-
НАДО БОЛЬШЕ
ЗНАТЬ

Чтобы больше иметь — надо больше производить. Чтобы больше производить — надо больше знать.

In order to have more, it is necessary to make more. In order to make more, it is necessary to know more.

50.b   1. In order to live well, one must have money (деньги).

_____

2. In order to have money, one must work.

_____

3. In order to work, one must study (учиться).

_____

[1] As we'll learn in Book 3, **чтобы** can also used in what we'll refer to as hypothetical constructions, which are completely different.

50.3 Punctuation tips

Before we review some basic clause types we've seen in this book, let's talk for a moment about punctuation.[1] This is always a fraught topic in English, particularly when it comes to placement of **commas**. Fortunately, students of Russian can eliminate the vast majority of their punctuation errors by remembering two rules of thumb:

1. Russian almost **never** requires a comma after an **introductory phrase** (not to mention an introductory adverb).

2. Russian almost **always** requires a comma to **set off a subordinate clause** of any kind.

In their written Russian, students violate rule number one with astounding frequency, because they rely on English guidelines: most are told in school that an introductory phrase (such as a prepositional phrase that begins a sentence) must be set off with a comma. This isn't necessarily true in English — and it almost never is in Russian!

One more note: you've probably been warned of the dreaded **comma splice** in your English writing. We can usually fix this mistake by using a semicolon instead, or by breaking one sentence into two:

It was boring at the party, I wanted to go home. ➡ It was boring at the party; I wanted to go home.

It was boring at the party. I wanted to go home.

Good news: in Russian, such "comma splices" are, for the most part, perfectly acceptable:

На вечеринке было скучно, я хотел пойти домой.

This is one reason why **semicolons** are relatively rare in Russian. **Resist the urge to use them!**

Check puncuation! Cross out any unnecessary commas, and add commas where needed. **50.c**

1. На прошлой неделе, я отдыхала в деревне.

2. Завтра, я буду свободна. Если хочешь, можно встретиться.

3. Я пью воду потому, что пить хочется.

4. Когда я голоден, я обычно ем шоколад.

5. Они знают что я не люблю этого писателя.

6. Ты не скажешь где он живёт?

7. Мы не знаем когда он придёт.

8. В нашем городе, есть большой парк.

50.4 Review of clause types

We've seen a number of basic types of subordinate clauses so far, and we've just learned a new one. Let's review those we've seen before learning a few new ones.

"that" clauses with unstressed что:	Я знаю, **что** тебе надо работать. I know that you need to work.	Хорошо, **что** зонт есть! It's good that there's an umbrella!
indirect questions:	Я знаю, **что** ты сделал.[2] I know what you've done.	Они спросили, **где** мы живём. They asked where we lived.
"when" clauses:	**Когда** я голоден, я ем торт. When I'm hungry, I eat cake.	Мне грустно, **когда** идёт дождь. I'm sad when it rains.
"why" clauses:	Профессор спросил, **почему** я не прочитал статью. The professor asked **why** I hadn't read the article.	
"because" clauses:	Я не прочитал статью, **потому что** моя собака её съела. I hadn't read the article, **because** my dog ate it.	
"which" (that) clauses with который:	Я не прочитал статью, **которую** я должен был прочитать. I didn't read the article **that** I was supposed to read.	
"who" clauses with который:	Мой друг, **который** учится в России, скучает по своей собаке. My friend, who is studying in Russia, misses his dog.	
"in order to" clauses with чтобы:	**Чтобы** иметь деньги, надо работать. **In order to** have money, it is necessary to work ("one must work").	

Take a moment to look over these examples, and note that all of these clauses are set off with a **comma**!

---

[1] Punctuation is important. Consider this notorious example: **Казнить нельзя помиловать** (казнить means "to execute," and помиловать "to pardon"). There should be a comma. But where?! A life hangs in the balance! [2] Here, the **что** is **stressed**! 253

50.5 "So" with такой, так and так что

The demonstrative **такой** (corresponding to the question word **какой**?) translates as "so," and is often combined with other adjectives as in "That car is so expensive!" The adverbial equivalent, **так** (which corresponds to **как**?), modifies verbs and adverbs. Either word can be followed by a **result** clause with an unstressed **что**.

Эта машина **такая дорогая**!	Я **так хочу** её купить!	Она **такая** дорогая, **что** не могу её купить.
This car is so expensive!	I so want to buy it!	It's so expensive that I can't buy it.

However, if we need a result clause corresponding to the English "so" (as in, "it was raining, so..."), then in Russian we need **так что**.[1]

Шёл дождь, **так что** мы сидели дома.	Я работаю сегодня, **так что** я не могу танцевать.
It was raining, so we sat around at home.	I'm working today, **so** I can't dance.

Can you tell something about your own life with sentences based on the models above? Choose the "so" construction carefully!

50.6 Indirect questions with ли (whether)

There's another very important type of indirect question — questions that begin with "whether" (or, "whether or not"). Such questions expect a "yes" or "no" answer. In spoken English we almost always use "if" in such indirect questions, instead of "whether":

I asked **whether** she liked kvass. = I asked **if** she liked kvass.

In Russian, such "whether" clauses include the particle **ли**.[2] This particle is **never stressed**, and **cannot begin a clause**. It occupies the second **"slot" in its clause**, directly after the word that is the "point" of the question. In most instances, this is a **verb**:

Профессор её спросил, **читает ли** она Пушкина?
The professor asked her whether or not she was **reading** Pushkin.

Almost any word can precede **ли**, if it is the real "point" of the question:

Профессор её спросил, **Пушкина ли** она читает?
The professor asked her whether it was **Pushkin** she was reading.

Профессор её спросил, **она ли** читает Пушкина?
The professor asked her whether she was the one reading Pushkin?

Compare, again, the Russian examples to their English translations!

НЕ ПРОВЕРЯЙ ПАЛЬЦЕМ
ЕСТЬ ЛИ *напряжение*

Не проверяй пальцем, есть ли напряжение!

Don't check with your finger (палец) whether or not there is an electric current.

50.d   *Turn these direct questions into indirect questions. Most of these indirect questions will require a **ли**, but one won't!*

1. "Она говорит по-русски?"   Он спрашивал, ...   _____.

2. "У них будет телефон?"   Она хотела знать, ...   _____.

3. "Есть у нас лекция сегодня?"   Мы не понимаем, ...   _____.

4. "Работает он вообще?"   Я не знал, ...   _____.

5. "Где зонт?"   Как я могу знать, ...   _____.

6. "Мы будем смотреть фильм?"   Он не сказал, ...   _____.

7. "Мы должны прочитать эту статью?"   Мы забыли спросить, ...   _____.

8. "Надо заплатить за эту газету?"   Не знаю, ...   _____.

---

1. О чём спрашивает мама или папа, когда тебе звонят? (give at least one answer using **ли**)

---

[1] Writing **так** instead of **так что** in this instance is a very common mistake among students.   [2] As you continue with Russian, you'll notice (especially in literary texts) that **ли** can also act as an interrogative particle — that is, it often simply **marks a question**.

50.7 Condition clauses with <u>е</u>сли (if)

In English, "if" is used to set up **condition** clauses, in the sense of "if this, then that." The Russian equivalent is **е**сли. The clause following the "if" clause can begin with **то** (which, much like the English "then," is optional).

Если х<u>о</u>чешь говор<u>и</u>ть по-р<u>у</u>сски, (**то**) н<u>а</u>до хорош<u>о</u> знать грамм<u>а</u>тику.
If you want to speak Russian, (then) you need to know grammar well.

Н<u>а</u>до чит<u>а</u>ть П<u>у</u>шкина, **е**сли х<u>о</u>чешь хорош<u>о</u> знать р<u>у</u>сскую литерат<u>у</u>ру.
You need to read Pushkin if you want to know Russian literature well.

50.8 Tense with если

We just saw (50.6) examples of how Russian indirect questions maintain the **original** tense of the direct question they are paraphrasing, regardless of the tense in the main clause (e.g. "I asked what he *is* doing" instead of the English "I asked what he *was* doing").

Something similar occurs with "if" clauses that speak of the **future**.

Consider this English example: If it **rains** tomorrow, **we will** watch TV.

Logically, what we really mean is: If it **will rain** tomorrow, **we will** watch TV.

....

In this regard, Russian is quite "logical" in its use of tense: if it is speaking of **future conditions**, it uses **future-tense verbs**. Here's the Russian:

<u>Е</u>сли **б<u>у</u>дет** дождь, б<u>у</u>дем смотр<u>е</u>ть телев<u>и</u>зор.
literally, "If there **will be** rain, we will watch TV."

....

It can be hard to overcome rules of English tense sequence![1] Here are some more examples, translated literally:

<u>Е</u>сли не **б<u>у</u>ду** зан<u>я</u>т, мы см<u>о</u>жем посмотр<u>е</u>ть фильм.
"If I **will not** be busy, we will be able to watch a film."

Я скаж<u>у</u> ем<u>у</u> з<u>а</u>втра, <u>е</u>сли ег<u>о</u> **ув<u>и</u>жу**.
"I'll tell him tomorrow, if I **will see** him."

<u>Е</u>сли м<u>о</u>жно **б<u>у</u>дет**, я купл<u>ю</u> р<u>у</u>сскую кн<u>и</u>гу.
"If it **will be** possible, I will buy a Russian book."

<u>Е</u>сли **забуд<u>е</u>шь** <u>э</u>то сл<u>о</u>во, то спрос<u>и</u> у проф<u>е</u>ссора.
"If you will forget this word, then ask the professor."

ЕСЛИ КНИГ ЧИТАТЬ НЕ БУДЕШ

<u>Е</u>сли книг чит<u>а</u>ть не б<u>у</u>дешь, ск<u>о</u>ро гр<u>а</u>моту забуд<u>е</u>шь.

If you don't read books, you'll soon forget literacy (**гр<u>а</u>мота** — the ability to read and write).

Note that the Russian literally says, "If you **will not read** books" (future tense), unlike the English.

Books (**книг**) is in the **genitive plural** here, as the object of a negated verb. We'll learn such plural forms in Book 2.

---

*Translate these sentences involving "if" clauses referring to **present** conditions. All verbs will be present-tense.*   **50.e**

1. If you want a new car, you have to work.   _____

2. If he wants to read, he should buy a book.   _____

3. It's good if you have an umbrella.   _____

4. If you love your mom, you'll pay for her coffee.   _____

5. Buy a ticket to the theater, if you want.   _____

6. Help me, if you can.   _____

---

*Translate these sentences involving "if" clauses referring to **future** conditions. Careful! Use the **future** tense in **both** Russian clauses!*   **50.f**

1. If you ask me, I'll answer.   _____

2. It will be good if we have an umbrella..   _____

3. If we're free, we can go to a ballet tomorrow.   _____

4. I'll buy you a ticket if I can.   _____

---

1. Что ты б<u>у</u>дешь д<u>е</u>лать (<u>и</u>ли не д<u>е</u>лать!), **е**сли ты б<u>у</u>дешь бог<u>а</u>тым / бог<u>а</u>той (rich)?

---

[1] If it makes you feel better, listen for Russians making the opposite mistake when they speak English — they do so very frequently.   255

Case endings

	special modifiers						adjectives	masculine nouns hard	soft		special soft
nom.	э́тот	весь	оди́н	чей	мой	наш	но́вый	стол	слова́рь	музе́й	кафете́рий
gen.	э́того	всего́	одного́	чьего́	моего́	на́шего	но́вого	стола́	словаря́	музе́я	кафете́рия
acc.	э́тот	весь	оди́н	чей	мой	наш	но́вый	стол	слова́рь	музе́й	кафете́рий
animate:	э́того	всего́	одного́	чьего́	моего́	на́шего	но́вого	студе́нта	писа́теля		ге́ния
dat.	э́тому	всему́	одному́	чьему́	моему́	на́шему	но́вому	столу́	словарю́	музе́ю	кафете́рию
prep.	э́том	всём	одно́м	чьём	моём	на́шем	но́вом	столе́	словаре́	музе́е	кафете́рии
instr.	э́тим	всем	одни́м	чьим	мои́м	на́шим	но́вым	столо́м	словарём	музе́ем	кафете́рием

	special modifiers						adjectives	feminine nouns hard	soft		special soft
nom.	э́та	вся	одна́	чья	моя́	на́ша	но́вая	газе́та	неде́ля		фами́лия
gen.	э́той	всей	одно́й	чьей	мое́й	на́шей	но́вой	газе́ты	неде́ли		фами́лии
acc.	э́ту	всю	одну́	чью	мою́	на́шу	но́вую	газе́ту	неде́лю		фами́лию
dat.	э́той	всей	одно́й	чьей	мое́й	на́шей	но́вой	газе́те	неде́ле		фами́лии
prep.	э́той	всей	одно́й	чьей	мое́й	на́шей	но́вой	газе́те	неде́ле		фами́лии
instr.	э́той	всей	одно́й	чьей	мое́й	на́шей	но́вой	газе́той	неде́лей	семьёй	фами́лией

	special modifiers						adjectives	neuter nouns hard	soft		special soft
nom.	э́то	всё	одно́	чьё	моё	на́ше	но́вое	окно́	мо́ре	бельё	зада́ние
gen.	э́того	всего́	одного́	чьего́	моего́	на́шего	но́вого	окна́	мо́ря	белья́	зада́ния
acc.	э́то	всё	одно́	чьё	моё	на́ше	но́вое	окно́	мо́ре	бельё	зада́ние
dat.	э́тому	всему́	одному́	чьему́	моему́	на́шему	но́вому	окну́	мо́рю	белью́	зада́нию
prep.	э́том	всём	одно́м	чьём	моём	на́шем	но́вом	окне́	мо́ре	белье́	зада́нии
instr.	э́тим	всем	одни́м	чьим	мои́м	на́шим	но́вым	окно́м	мо́рем	бельём	зада́нием

Names

	female names имя	отчество	фамилия	male names имя	отчество	фамилия	short forms (m/f) Михаи́л	Да́рья
nom.	Мари́на	Ива́новна	Цвета́ева	Михаи́л	Афана́сьевич	Булга́ков	Ми́ша	Да́ша
gen.	Мари́ны	Ива́новны	Цвета́евой	Михаи́ла	Афана́сьевича	Булга́кова	Ми́ши	Да́ши
acc.	Мари́ну	Ива́новну	Цвета́еву	Михаи́ла	Афана́сьевича	Булга́кова	Ми́шу	Да́шу
dat.	Мари́не	Ива́новне	Цвета́евой	Михаи́лу	Афана́сьевичу	Булга́кову	Ми́ше	Да́ше
prep.	Мари́не	Ива́новне	Цвета́евой	Михаи́ле	Афана́сьевиче	Булга́кове	Ми́ше	Да́ше
instr.	Мари́ной	Ива́новной	Цвета́евой	Михаи́лом	Афана́сьевичем	Булга́ковым	Ми́шей	Да́шей

	male	female	male	female		
nom.	Бахти́н	Бахти́на	Маяко́вский	Маяко́вская	Пастерна́к	Бара́к Оба́ма
gen.	Бахти́на	Бахти́ной	Маяко́вского	Маяко́вской	Пастерна́ка	Бара́ка Оба́мы
acc.	Бахти́на	Бахти́ну	Маяко́вского	Маяко́вскую	Пастерна́ка	Бара́ка Оба́му
dat.	Бахти́ну	Бахти́ной	Маяко́вскому	Маяко́вской	Пастерна́ку	Бара́ку Оба́ме
prep.	Бахти́не	Бахти́ной	Маяко́вском	Маяко́вской	Пастерна́ке	Бара́ке Оба́ме
instr.	Бахти́ным	Бахти́ной	Маяко́вским	Маяко́вской	Пастерна́ком	Бара́ком Оба́мой

Nouns

hard nouns[1]

masculine		feminine
бизнесме́н, -а — businessperson	та́н(е)ц, танца́ — dance	учи́тельница, -ы — teacher
поли́тик, -а — politician[3]	спорт, -а — sports	писа́тельница, -ы[1] — (female) writer
адвока́т, -а — lawyer	би́знес, -а — business	актри́са, -ы — actress
юри́ст, -а — lawyer	журнали́зм, -а — journalism	балери́на, -ы — ballerina
полице́йский, -ого — policeman	архите́ктор, -а — architect	певи́ца, -ы — singer
журнали́ст, -а — journalist	футбо́л, -а — soccer	скри́пка, -и — violin
профе́ссор, -а — professor	волейбо́л, -а — volleyball	матема́тика, -и — mathematics
психо́лог, -а — psychologist	баскетбо́л, -а — basketball	фи́зика, -и — physics
филосо́ф, -а — philosopher	душ, -а — shower	поли́тика, -и — politics
активи́ст, -а — activist	му́сор, -а — trash	трениро́вка, -и — (sports) practice
лингви́ст, -а — linguist	за́втрак, -а — breakfast	мечта́, -ы — dream
танцо́р, -а — dancer	обе́д, -а — lunch	лингви́стика, -и — liguistics
музыка́нт, -а — musician	у́жин, -а — dinner	информа́тика, -и — computer science
пев(е́)ц, певца́ — singer	с(о)н, сна — sleep / dream	поду́шка, -и — pillow
спортсме́н, -а — athlete	кошма́р, -а — nightmare	архитекту́ра, -ы — architecture
пожа́рный, -ого — fireman	класс, -а — grade in school	лёгкая атле́тика — track and field
кри́тик, -а — critic	курс, -а (на) — college year / course	зубна́я па́ста, -ы — toothpaste
фи́зик, -а — physicist	экза́мен, -а — exam	зубна́я щётка, -и — toothbrush
матема́тик, -а — mathematician	официа́нт, -а — waiter	щётка, -и — (hair)brush
литературове́д, -а — literary scholar	актёр, -а — actor	контро́льная, -ой — test
врач, -а́ — doctor		официа́нтка, -и — waitress
буди́льник, -а — alarm clock	**neuter**	гита́ра, -ы — guitar
худо́жник, -а — artist	пра́во, -а — law	фле́йта, -ы — flute
вое́нный, -ого — military person	пиани́но — piano (indeclinable)	поли́тика, -и — politics[3]
инжене́р, -а — engineer	иску́сство, -а — art	
диплома́т, -а — diplomat		

soft nouns

masculine		feminine
учи́тель, -я — teacher	роя́ль, -я — grand piano	гре́бля, -и — crew, rowing
писа́тель, -я — writer	хокке́й, -я — hockey	
чита́тель, -я — reader	судья́, -и — judge	

special soft nouns

feminine		neuter
филосо́фия, -ии — lecture	политоло́гия, -ии — political science	пе́ние, -ия — singing
психоло́гия, -ии — psychology	социоло́гия, -ии — sociology	фехтова́ние, -ия — fencing
биоло́гия, -ии — biology	антрополо́гия, -ии — anthropology	искусствове́дение — art history
хи́мия, -ии — chemistry	репети́ция, -ии — rehearsal	программи́рование — programming
исто́рия, -ии — history	инжене́рия, -ии[2] — engineering	междунаро́дные отноше́ния — foreign relations (a plural form!)

[1] **Note on gender and professions**. Historically, most professions were the exclusive domain of men; in fact, feminine versions of the names of professions, such as **до́кторша**, did not mean "a female doctor," but "the wife of a doctor." Today, some professions do have a special feminine form (**учи́тельница** for **учи́тель**: teacher); if there is such a form, it is probably best to use it when referring to a woman. However, many words have no feminine form (for example, no **профе́ссорка**), and some forms that do exist (like **поэте́сса** for **поэ́т**, or **бизнесме́нка** for **бизнесме́н**) can easily sound condescending (e.g., "Akhmatova was a great *female* poet"). In such cases, it is best to use the **masculine** forms. This is why the vast majority of the professions given above are masculine. We will discuss this issue in much greater detail on Day 165.

[2] **Engineering**. The Russian **инжене́рия** (**инжене́рное де́ло**) is a slightly awkward term, since a Russian engineer would typically cite his or her specialty, not "engineering" in general — for example, **машинострое́ние** (mechanical engineering). If you do engineering, the best way to say this is probably simply "**Я инжене́р.**"

[3] Finally, note the gender difference in such terms as **поли́тика** (politics, fem.) and **поли́тик** (politician). Such (Greek-derived) *fields* are feminine nouns in **-a**, while the *practitioner* is a masculine noun (again, regardless of the gender of the person in question).

Pronouns

	what?	who?
nom.	что	кто
gen.	чего	кого
acc.	что	кого
dat.	чему	кому
prep.	чём	ком
instr.	чем	кем

	he (masculine)		she (feminine)		it (neuter)	
nom.	он		она		оно	
gen.	его	→ него	её	→ неё	его	→ него
acc.	его	→ него	её	→ неё	его	→ него
dat.	ему	→ нему	ей	→ ней	ему	→ нему
prep.	—	→ нём	—	→ ней	—	→ нём
instr.	им	→ ним	ей	→ ней	им	→ ним

	I	you (s.)	we	you (pl.)
nom.	я	ты	мы	вы
gen.	меня	тебя	нас	вас
acc.	меня	тебя	нас	вас
dat.	мне	тебе	нам	вам
prep.	мне	тебе	нас	вас
instr.	мной	тобой	нами	вами

	oneself
nom.	—
gen.	себя
acc.	себя
dat.	себе
prep.	себе
instr.	собой

	by oneself
masc.	сам
fem.	сама
neut.	само
plural	сами

	each other		
acc.	друг друга	Мы хорошо знаем **друг друга**.	each other
dat.	друг другу	Мы всегда помогаем **друг другу**.	each other

A preposition typically falls in the middle, and, again, only the second **друг** declines:

acc.	друг на друга	Они смотрели **друг на друга**.	at each other
gen.	друг без друга	Мы не можем жить **друг без друга**.	without each other
dat.	друг к другу	Мы привыкли **друг к другу**.	to each other
prep.	друг о друге	Они часто думают **друг о друге**.	about each other
instr.	друг с другом	Мы ходили в театр **друг с другом**.**	with each other

Possessive pronouns

мой / твой / свой

all decline according to this pattern.

	masculine		feminine		neuter	
nom.	**мой** торт		**моя** бутылка		**моё** мыло	
gen.	**моего** торта		**моей** бутылки		**моего** мыла	
acc.	**мой** торт		**мою** бутылку		**моё** мыло	
anim.	**моего** друга					
dat.	**моему** торту		**моей** бутылке		**моему** мылу	
prep.	**моём** торте		**моей** бутылке		**моём** мыле	
instr.	**моим** тортом		**моей** бутылкой		**моим** мылом	

наш / ваш

both decline according to this pattern.

	masculine		feminine		neuter	
nom.	**наш** торт		**наша** бутылка		**наше** мыло	
gen.	**нашего** торта		**нашей** бутылки		**нашего** мыла	
acc.	**наш** торт		**нашу** бутылку		**наше** мыло	
anim.	**нашего** друга					
dat.	**нашему** торту		**нашей** бутылке		**нашему** мылу	
prep.	**нашем** торте		**нашей** бутылке		**нашем** мыле	
instr.	**нашим** тортом		**нашей** бутылкой		**нашим** мылом	

Other special modifiers

	masculine		feminine		neuter	
nom.	**весь** торт		**вся** бутылка		**всё** мыло	
gen.	**всего** торта		**всей** бутылки		**всего** мыла	
acc.	**весь** торт		**всю** бутылку		**всё** мыло	
anim.	**всего** человека					
dat.	**всему** торту		**всей** бутылке		**всему** мылу	
prep.	**всём** торте		**всей** бутылке		**всём** мыле	
instr.	**всем** тортом		**всей** бутылкой		**всем** мылом	

	masc.	fem.	neut.
nom.	один	одна	одно
gen.	одного	одной	одного
acc.	один	одну	одно
anim.	одного		
dat.	одному	одной	одному
prep.	одном	одной	одном
instr.	одним	одной	одним

	masc.	fem.	neut.
nom.	чей	чья	чьё
gen.	чьего	чьей	чьего
acc.	чей	чью	чьё
anim.	чьего		
dat.	чьему	чьей	чьему
prep.	чьём	чьей	чьём
instr.	чьим	чьей	чьим

Verbs

играть АЙ / сыграть АЙ	
to play[1]	
играю	сыграю
играешь	сыграешь
играет	сыграет
играем	сыграем
играете	сыграете
играют	сыграют
играй!	сыграй!

вести Д^{end} себя / повести Д себя	
to behave, conduct oneself	
веду себя	поведу себя
ведёшь себя	поведёшь себя
ведёт себя	поведёт себя
ведём себя	поведём себя
ведёте себя	поведёте себя
ведут себя	поведут себя
веди себя!	поведи себя!
вёл себя	повёл себя
вела себя	повела себя
вело себя	повело себя
вели себя	повели себя

чувствовать ОВА себя / почувствовать себя	
to feel ("oneself")	
чувствую себя	почувствую себя
чувствуешь себя	почувствуешь себя
чувствует себя	почувствует себя
чувствуем себя	почувствуем себя
чувствуете себя	почувствуете себя
чувствуют себя	почувствуют себя
чувствуй себя!	почувствуй себя!

Verbs used with the instrumental

оказываться АЙ / оказаться А^{shift} чем	
to turn out to be / to prove to be	
оказываюсь	окажусь
оказываешься	окажешься
оказывается	окажется
оказываемся	окажемся
оказываетесь	окажетесь
оказываются	окажутся
оказывайся!	окажись!

становиться И^{shift} / стать Н^{stem} кем, чем	
to become	
становлюсь	стану
становишься	станешь
становится	станет
становимся	станем
становитесь	станете
становятся	станут
становись!	стань!

казаться А / показаться А^{shift} кому чем	
to seem	
кажусь	покажусь
кажешься	покажешься
кажется	покажется
кажемся	покажемся
кажетесь	покажетесь
кажутся	покажутся
кажись!	покажись!

интересовать ОВА / заинтересовать ОВА кого	
to interest	
интересоваться ОВА / заинтересоваться ОВА чем	
to be interested in ("by")	
интересую(сь)	заинтересую(сь)
интересуешь(ся)	заинтересуешь(ся)
интересует(ся)	заинтересует(ся)
интересуем(ся)	заинтересуем(ся)
интересуете(сь)	заинтересуете(сь)
интересуют(ся)	заинтересуют(ся)
интересуй(ся)!	заинтересуй(ся)!

занимать АЙ / занять Й/М^{end} что	
to occupy, take up	
заниматься АЙ / заняться Й/М^{end} чем	
to be occupied with, busy oneself, "do"	
занимаю(сь)	займу(сь)
занимаешь(ся)	займёшь(ся)
занимает(ся)	займёт(ся)
занимаем(ся)	займём(ся)
занимаете(сь)	займёте(сь)
занимают(ся)	займут(ся)
занимай(ся)!	займи(сь)!
занимал(ся)	занял(ся)
занимала(сь)	заняла(сь)
занимало(сь)	заняло(сь)
занимали(сь)	заняли(сь)

поздравлять АЙ / поздравить И кого с чем	
to congratulate someone on ("with") something	
поздравляю	поздравлю
поздравляешь	поздравишь
поздравляет	поздравит
поздравляем	поздравим
поздравляете	поздравите
поздравляют	поздравят
поздравляй!	поздравь!

[1] To play a sport, use **в** + accusative; to play an instrument, use **на** + prepositional.

Four verbs for "studying"

занима́ться АЙ чем	**изуча́ть** АЙ что[1]	**учи́ться** И / **научи́ться** И^shift кого чему / inf.	
to study, so homework	to study (a subject, a major)	to learn; to attend college	
занима́юсь	изуча́ю	учу́(сь)	научу́(сь)
занима́ешься	изуча́ешь	у́чишь(ся)	нау́чишь(ся)
занима́ется	изуча́ет	у́чит(ся)	нау́чит(ся)
занима́емся	изуча́ем	у́чим(ся)	нау́чим(ся)
занима́етесь	изуча́ете	у́чите(сь)	нау́чите(сь)
занима́ются	изуча́ют	у́чат(ся)	нау́чат(ся)
занима́йся!	изуча́й!	учи́(сь)!	научи́(сь)!

гото́вить И / **пригото́вить** И	
to prepare, cook	
гото́виться И / **подгото́виться** к чему	
to study for	
гото́влю(сь)	подгото́влю(сь)
гото́вишь(ся)	подгото́вишь(ся)
гото́вит(ся)	подгото́вит(ся)
гото́вим(ся)	подгото́вим(ся)
гото́вите(сь)	подгото́вите(сь)
гото́вят(ся)	подгото́вят(ся)
гото́вь(ся)!	подгото́вь(ся)!

[1] This verb *must* be used with a direct object.

Russian-English Dictionary

This learner's dictionary includes the vocabulary from Book 1 only; it will be expanded to include additional vocabulary in subsequent volumes. It does not include all vocabulary from the proverbs and poster slogans.

Most noun entries begin with the nominative singular, followed by the genitive singular ending (or the entire genitive singular form, in the case of a mobile vowel or some other irregularity).

Most verbs are listed as aspectual pairs: first the imperfective, then the perfective, along with the verb type tags. To find an aspectual pair, look up the imperfective; if you look up a perfective form, you will be referred to the imperfective form.

А

а (conjunction)	and / but (while)
а́вгуст, -а	August
авто́бус, -а	bus
автомоби́ль, -я	car
а́втор, -а	author
адвока́т, -а	lawyer
актёр, -а	actor
активи́ст, -а	activist
актри́са, -ы	actress
алкого́ль, -я	alcohol
анекдо́т, -а	anecdote, funny story
антрополо́гия, -ии	Anthropology
апре́ль, -я	April
апте́ка, -и	pharmacy
архите́ктор, -а	architect
архитекту́ра, -ы	architecture
аспира́нт, -а	graduate student (male)
аспира́нтка, -и	graduate student (female)
аэропо́рт, -а (в -у́)	airport

Б

ба́бушка, -и	grandmother
балери́на, -ы	ballerina
бале́т, -а	ballet
ба́ня, -и	Russian bathhouse, sauna
бар, -а	bar
баскетбо́л, -а	basketball
бассе́йн, -а	swimming pool
без + gen.	without
безобра́зие, -ия	something horrible, ugly
безобра́зный	horrible, ugly
бельё, -я	laundry
бе́рег, -а (на -у́)	shore
библиоте́ка, -и	library
би́знес, -а	business
бизнесме́н, -а	businessperson

биле́т, -а	ticket
биоло́гия, -ии	biology
бить Ь	to beat, strike, hit
блока́да, -ы	siege, blockade
блю́до, -а	dish
Бог, -а	God (also: **бог**: a god)
больни́ца, -ы	hospital
больно́й (бо́лен, больна́)	sick (used as noun: a patient)
большо́й	big
борщ, -а́	borshch
брат, -а	brother
брать n/sA / **взять**	to take
буди́льник, -а	alarm clock
бу́ду, бу́дешь, etc.	future tense forms of **быть**
бу́дущий	future
бу́дущее, -его	the future
бу́лка, -и	roll, bun
бу́лочная, -ой	cafe selling bread, pastries
бума́га, -и	paper
бутербро́д, -а	(open-faced) sandwich
буты́лка, -и	bottle
бы́стро	quickly, fast
быть (fut. бу́ду, бу́дешь)	to be

В

в (во)	in, into
ва́жный	important
вас	you (pl. - acc. and gen.)
ваш, ва́ша, ва́ше, ва́ши	your (pl.), yours
вдруг	suddenly
век, -а	century, lifetime
велосипе́д, -а	bicycle
ве́чер, -а	evening
вечери́нка, -и	party
ве́рить И / **пове́рить** И	to believe (кому / во что)
верну́ть НУend	perfective of **возвраща́ть**
верну́ться НУend	perfective of **возвраща́ться**
вести́ Дend / **повести́** Д себя́	to behave, act
весь, вся, всё	whole
взять	perfective of **брать**
вид, -а	view; type, kind
вид тра́нспорта	form of transportation
ви́деть Е / **уви́деть** Е	to see
ви́деться Е / **уви́деться** Е	to see each other, meet up
ви́лка, -и	fork
вино́, -а́	wine
включа́ть АЙ / **включи́ть** Иend	to include
включи́ть Иend	perfective of **включа́ть**
вме́сте	together
вме́сто + gen.	instead of
внима́ние, -ия	attention
внук, -а	grandson
вну́чка, -и	granddaughter
во́время	on time
во вре́мя + gen.	during
вода́, -ы́	water
во́дка, -и	vodka
вое́нный	military man
возвраща́ть АЙ / **верну́ть** НУend	to return (transitive)
возвраща́ться / **верну́ться**	to return, go back (instransitive)
возьму́, возьмёшь	conjugated forms of **взять**

война, -ы	war
вокзал, -а (на)	train station
волейбол, -а	volleyball
вообще	in general, at all
вопрос, -а	question
воскресенье, -я	Sunday
воспользоваться ОВА	perfective of пользоваться
вот	here, look! (showing)
впервые	for the first time
враг, -а	enemy
врач, -а	doctor
время, времени (n.)	time
все	everyone
всегда	always
всё	everything
вспомнить И	perfective of помнить
вся	see весь
вставать АВАЙ / встать Нstem	to get up, stand up
встать Нstem	perfective of вставать
встретить	perfective of встречать
встретиться	perfective of встречаться
встреча, -и	meeting
встречать АЙ / встретить И	to meet
встречаться / встретиться	to meet up
вторник, -а	Tuesday
вход, -а	entrance
вчера	yesterday
вы	you (pl. and formal)
выпить Ь	perfective of пить
выставка, -и	exhibit
выход, -а	exit

Г

газ, -а	gas
газета, -ы	newspaper
гарнир, -а	side dish
где?	where
гений, -ия	genius
герой, -я	hero
гитара, -ы	guitar
глупый	stupid, silly
говорить Иend / сказать А	to say
год, -а	year
голодный (голоден, -одна)	hungry
город, -а	city
гость, -я	guest
готовить И / приготовить И	to prepare, cook
готовиться И / подготовиться	to study for (к чему)
готовиться И / приготовиться	to be prepared, cooked
готовый (готов)	ready, prepared
грамм, -а	gramm
гребля, -и	crew, rowing
группа, -ы	group
грустный	sad
грязный	dirty
гулять АЙ / погулять АЙ	to stroll

Д

да	yes

давай(те)...	let's...
давать АВАЙ / дать	to give
давно	a long time ago
дать	perfective of давать
дарить Иshift / подарить Иshift	to give (as a gift)
дача, -и	dacha, country house
два (две before feminine nouns!)	two
двор, -а (на дворе)	courtyard
девочка, -и	girl
девушка, -и	young woman
дедушка, -и	grandfather
действительно	indeed, truly
декабрь, -я	December
делать АЙ / сделать АЙ	to do, make
дело, -а	matter, affair
день, дня	day
деревня, -и	village; countryside
дерево, -а	tree, wood
десерт, -а	dessert
дешёвый	cheap, inexpensive
дипломат, -а	diplomat
для	for + gen.
до	before, prior to + gen.
до свидания	goodbye
добавка, -и	seconds, another helping
добавить И	perfective of добавлять
добавлять АЙ / добавить И	to add
добрый	good
довольный (доволен, -льна)	satisfied
довольно	rather, quite
долг	debt
долго	for a long time
должен, должна, должны	obligated, "should" + inf.
дом, -а	house, building
дома	at home
домой	homeward, "to home"
дорога, -и	road, path, way
дорогой	expensive
до свидания	goodbye
дочка, -и	daughter (dim. of дочь)
друг, -а	friend
друг друга	one another (gen / acc.)
друг другу	one another (dat.)
друг с другом	with one another
другой	another
думать АЙ / подумать АЙ	to think
душ, -а	shower
дядя, -и	uncle

Е

его	his (never changes form!)
еда, -ы	food
еду, едешь	conjugated forms of ехать
её	her (never changes form!)
ездить И - ехать / поехать	to go by vehicle
есть / съесть	to eat
ехать	determinate of ездить

Ё

ёж	hedgehog

ёлка, -и	fir tree; Christmas tree

Ж

жаль	too bad, it's a pity
ждать n/sA / подождать n/sA	to wait
же	emphatic particle
желать АЙ / пожелать АЙ	to wish (кому чего)
жена, -ы	wife
жених, -а	fiancé, groom
женщина, -ы	woman
живой (жив, жива)	alive
жизнь, -и	life
жить В^{end}	to live (imperfective)
журавль, -я	crane
журнал, -а	magazine
журнализм, -а	journalism
журналист, -а	journalist

З

за + асс.	for, in favor of; behind (куда)
за + instr.	behind, beyond (где)
забывать АЙ / забыть	to forget
забыть	perfective of забывать
завтра	tomorrow
завтрак, -а	breakfast
задавать АВАЙ / задать вопрос	to ask a question
задание, -я	assignment
задача, -и	task, assignment, problem
заканчивать АЙ / закончить И	to finish (transitive)
заканчиваться /закончиться	to end (intransitive)
закончить И	perfective of заканчивать
закрывать АЙ / закрыть ОЙ	to close
закрываться / закрыться	to be closed
закрыть ОЙ	perfective of закрывать
закрыться (закрываться)	perfective of закрываться
закуска, -и	snack
замёрзнуть НУ	perfective of мёрзнуть
занимать АЙ / занять Й/М^{end}	to occupy, take up
заниматься / заняться	to occupy o.s. with, do; study
зануда, -ы	a boring person, killjoy
занятие, -ия	occupation; class
занятый (занят, занята)	occupied, taken
занятой	busy (of a person)
занять И/М	perfective of занимать
заняться	perfective of заниматься
запах, -а	smell
заплакать А	perfective of плакать
заранее	ahead of time
захотеть	perfective of хотеть
звать n/sA^{end} / назвать n/sA^{end}	to call someone (a name)
звонить И^{end} / позвонить И^{end}	to call, ring
здание, -ия	building
здесь	here
здорово	hi (informal)
здоровый (здоров)	healthy
здравствуй(те)!	hello
земля, -и	earth, ground, soil
зеркало, -а	mirror
знакомая, -ой	acquaintance (fem.)
знакомить И / познакомить И	to acquaint
знакомиться /познакомиться	to get acquainted
знакомый, -ого	acquaintance (masc.)
знать АЙ	to know
значить И	to mean, signify
зову, зовёшь, etc.	present tense of звать
зонт, -а	umbrella
зубная паста, -ы	toothpaste
зубная щётка, -и	toothbrush

И

и	and; even
и... и...	both... and...
играть АЙ / сыграть АЙ	to play
игрок, -а	player, gambler
идея, -и	idea
идти	determinate of ходить
идёшь, идёт	conjugated forms of идти
из	from; (made) out of + gen.
извини(те)	excuse (me)
икра, -ы	caviar
или	or
именно	namely, specifically
иметь ЕЙ	to have
имя, имени (neuter!)	first name
инженер, -а	engineer
инженерия, -ии	engineering
(инженерное дело)	engineering
иногда	sometimes
интересный	interesting
интернет, -а	Internet
информатика, -и	computer science
искусство, -а	art
искусствоведение, -ия	art history
история, -ии	history
их	their, theirs (never changes!)
июль, -я	July
июнь, -я	June

Й

йога, -и	yoga

К

к (ко) + dat.	toward
к сожалению	unfortunately
к счастью	fortunately
каждый	each
казаться А^{shift} / показаться А	to seem (кому чем)
как?	how
какой?	of what kind
канал, -а	channel (на); canal
капля, -и	drop
карандаш, -а	pencil
картина, -ы	picture
катер, -а	(tour) boat
кафе (n.)	café
кафетерий, -ия	cafeteria (столовая)
каш(е)ль, кашля	cough

квас, -а	kvas	лимонад, -а	soda
кефир, -а	kefir	лингвист, -а	linguist
килограмм, -а	kilogramm	лингвистика, -и	linguistics
кино (n.)	cinema (indeclinable)	литература, -ы	literature
кинотеатр, -а	movie theater	литературовед, -а	literary scholar
класс, -а	grade in school	литр, -а	liter
ключ, -а	key	лифт, -а	elevator
книга, -и	book	лодка, -и	(small) boat
ков(ё)р, ковра	carpet	ложка, -и	spoon
когда	when	ломать АЙ / сломать АЙ	to break
колбаса, -ы	sausage	ломаться АЙ / сломаться АЙ	to break down
коллега, -и	colleague	любимый	favorite, beloved
кольцо, -а	ring	любить И^shift / полюбить И^shift	to love / come to love
комната, -ы	room		
компьютер, -а	computer		
кон(е)ц, конца	end	**М**	
конечно	of course		
контрольная, -ой	test	магазин, -а	store
конфета, -ы	a piece of candy	май, -я	May
концерт, -а	concert	маленький	small
коньяк, -а	cognac	мало	little, not much
корабль, -я	ship	мальчик, -а	boy
коридор, -а	hallway	мама, -ы	mom
космос, -а	outer space, the cosmos	март, -а	March
кот, -а	cat (male)	маршрутка, -и	small (private) bus
котён(о)к, котёнка	kitten	масло, -а	butter
который	who, which (that)	математик, -а	mathematician
кофе (m.)	coffee (indeclinable)	математика, -и	mathematics
кофейня, -и	coffee house	матч, -а	match (in sports)
кошел(ё)к, кошелька	wallet	машина, -ы	car
кошка, -и	cat (female)	медведь, -я	bear
кошмар, -а	nightmare	медленно	slowly
край, -я	edge	международные отношения (pl.)	international relations
красивый	pretty, beautiful	место, -а	place; seat
кресло, -а	armchair	месяц, а	month
критик, -а	critic	метро (n.)	subway (indeclinable)
кружка, -и	mug (of beer)	мечта, -ы	(day)dream
кто?	who	мёрзнуть (НУ) / замёрзнуть (НУ)	to freeze (intransitive)
куда	where to, whither	мёртвый (мёртв, мертва)	dead
купить И^shift	perfective of покупать	минералка, -и	mineral water
курица, -ы	chicken (the meat)	(минеральная вода)	mineral water
курс, -а	course; year in college	минута, -ы	minute
кус(о)к, куска	piece	мир, -а	world; peace
кухня, -и (на)	kitchen; cuisine	миска, -и	bowl
		мнение, -ия	opinion
Л		много	a lot; a lot of
		мобильник, -а	mobile phone
лавка, -и	shop	(мобильный телефон)	mobile phone
ладно	OK, fine	можно	(it is) possible
лампа, -ы	lamp	мой	my, mine
лебедь, -я	swan	молоко, -а	milk
лес, -а	forest, woods	море, -я	sea
лестница, -ы	staircase	мороженое, -ого	ice cream
лет	gen. pl. of год	мост, -а	bridge
лёгкая атлетика, -и	track and field	мочь Г (могу, можешь) / смочь Г	to be able
лёгкий	light, easy	музей, -я	museum
лекарство, -а	medicine	музыка, -и	music
лекция, -ии	lecture	муж, -а	husband
летать АЙ - лететь Е / полететь	to fly, go by air	мужчина, -ы	man
лететь Е	determinate of летать	мусор, -а	trash, garbage
л(ё)д, льда	ice	мы	we
		мыло, -а	soap

мыть ОЙ^{stem} / помыть ОЙ	to clean, wash	общий	common, shared, mutual
мыться ОЙ^{stem} / помыться ОЙ	to wash up (wash o.s.)	огромный	huge, tremendous
мясо, -а	meat	одежда, -ы	clothing (sing. only)
мяч, -а	ball	одеяло, -а	cover, blanket
		один, одна, одно, одни	one; alone; the same
Н		озеро, -а	lake
		оказаться А^{shift}	perfective of оказываться
на	on (+ prep.); to; onto (+ acc.)	оказываться АЙ / оказаться А^{shift}	to turn out to be (+ instr.)
набережная, -ой	embankment	океан, -а	ocean
над	above (+ instr.)	окно, -а	window
надо	it is necessary (+ inf.)	октябрь, -я	October
назад	backward; ago	он	he
назвать n/sA	perfective of звать	она	she
наконец	finally, at last	они	they
напит(о)к, напитка	beverage	оно	it
написать А	perfective of писать	опаздывать АЙ / опоздать АЙ	to be late
нарисовать ОВА	perfective of рисовать	опоздать АЙ	perfective of опаздывать
народ, -а	people, nation	оставаться АВАЙ / остаться Н^{stem}	to remain, be left
настоящее, -его	the present	оставить И	perfective of оставлять
настоящий	real, genuine	оставлять АЙ / оставить И	to leave (behind)
научить	perfective of учить	остаться Н^{stem}	perfective of оставаться
научиться	perfective of учиться	остров, -а (на)	island
начало, -а	beginning	от	from (+ gen.)
начальник, -а	boss	ответ, -а	answer
начать /Н^{end}	perfective of начинать	ответить И	perfective of отвечать
начинать АЙ / начать /Н^{end}	to begin (transitive)	отвечать АЙ / ответить И	to answer, reply
начинаться АЙ / начаться /Н	to begin (intransitive)	отдохнуть НУ^{end}	perfective of отдыхать
наш	our, ours	отдыхать АЙ / отдохнуть НУ^{end}	to relax, vacation
небо, -а	sky	от(е)ц, отца	father
невеста, -ы	fiancée, bride	откуда	from where, whence
недавно	not long ago, recently	открывалка, -и	bottle opener
неделя, -и	week	открывать АЙ / открыть ОЙ^{stem}	to open (transitive)
недолго	not for long	открываться / открыться	to open, be opened
неловко	awkward, embarrassed	открыть ОЙ	perfective of открывать
нельзя	one shouldn't	открыться ОЙ^{stem}	perfective of открываться
ненавидеть Е / возненавидеть Е	to hate / to come to hate	отличный	excellent
необычный	unusual	отсюда	from here, hence
ни... ни...	neither... nor...	оттуда	from there, thence
никогда	never (with negated verb!)	официант, -а	waiter
но	but (stark contrast)	официантка, -и	waitress
новоселье, -я	moving-in party	оценка, -и	grade, assessment
новый	new	очень	very
нож, -а	knife	ошибка, -и	mistake, error
ноябрь, -я	November		
нравиться И / понравиться И	to be pleasing to (кому)	**П**	
нужный (нужен, нужна)	necessary, needed		
нужно = надо	it is necessary to (+ inf.)	пальто (n.)	coat (indeclinable)
		памятник, -а	monument, memorial
О		папа, -ы	dad
		пар(е)нь, парня	guy; boyfriend
о (об)	about (+ prep.)	парикмахерская, -ой	hair salon
обед, -а	lunch	парк, -а	park
обратить И^{end}	perfective of обращать	пев(е)ц, певца	singer (m.)
обратиться И	perfective of обращаться	певица, -ы	singer (f.)
обращать АЙ / обратить И^{end}	to turn, direct	пение, -ия	singing
обращаться / обратиться	to turn to, address, speak to	перед	in front of, (just) before
объяснять АЙ / объяснить И^{end}	to explain (+ dat.)	передача, -и	broadcast, program
объяснить И^{end}	perfective of объяснять	переставать АВАЙ / перестать Н	to stop, to cease (+ inf.)
обычно	usually	переход, -а	crossing
обычный	usual, ordinary	песня, -и	song
общаться АЙ / пообщаться АЙ	to interact, socialize (с кем)	петь ОЙ^{end} / спеть ОЙ^{end}	to sing
общежитие, -ия	dormitory	печенье, -я	cookies; baked goods

пиан**и**но	piano (indeclinable!)	пом**о**чь Гend	perfective of помог**а**ть
п**и**во, -а	beer	пом**ы**ть ОЙ	perfective of м**ы**ть
пир**о**ж(**о**)к, пирожк**а**	small stuffed pie	пом**ы**ться	perfective of м**ы**ться
пир**о**г, -**а**	(stuffed) pie	понед**е**льник, -а	Monday
пис**а**тель, -я	writer	понима́ть АЙ / пон**я**ть Й/Мend	to understand
пис**а**тельница, -ы	writer (fem.)	понр**а**виться И	perfective of нр**а**виться
пис**а**ть Аshift / напис**а**ть Аshift	to write	пон**я**ть Й/М	perfective of понима́ть
письм**о**, -**а**	letter	пообщ**а**ться АЙ	perfective of общ**а**ться
пить Ь / в**ы**пить Ь	to drink	попл**ы**ть В	perfective of пл**а**вать
пл**а**вать АЙ - пл**ы**ть В / попл**ы**ть	to swim, sail, go by water	попрос**и**ть И	perfective of прос**и**ть
плак**а**т, -а	poster	пор**а**	it is time + dat. + inf.
пл**а**кать А / запл**а**кать А	to cry / begin crying	пораб**о**тать АЙ	perfective of раб**о**тать
плат**и**ть Иshift / заплат**и**ть Иshift	to pay	по-р**у**сски	in Russian
пл**а**тье, -я	dress	п**о**рция, -ии	portion, helping
плох**о**й	bad	посл**а**ть А (пошл**ю**, пошлёшь)	perfective of посыл**а**ть
пл**о**хо	poorly, badly	п**о**сле	after
плыть Вend	determinate of пл**а**вать	послу́шать АЙ	perfective of сл**у**шать
пляж, -а (на)	beach	посмотр**е**ть Еshift	perfective of смотр**е**ть
по	according to;	посов**е**товать ОВА	perfective of сов**е**товать
	along, around (+ dat.)	посп**а**ть	perfective of спать
по-англ**и**йски	in English	постир**а**ть АЙ	perfective of стир**а**ть
по-р**у**сски	in Russian	пос**у**да, -ы	dishes
побеж**а**ть	perfective of б**е**гать	посыл**а**ть АЙ / посл**а**ть Аend	to send
пов**е**рить И	perfective of в**е**рить	потанцев**а**ть ОВА	perfective of танцев**а**ть
погул**я**ть АЙ	perfective of гул**я**ть	пот**о**м	next, then
под	beneath (+ instr. / acc.)	потом**у** что	because
подар**и**ть Иshift	perfective of дар**и**ть	по**у**жинать АЙ	perfective of **у**жинать
под**а**рок, под**а**рка	gift	почем**у**?	why
подгот**о**виться И	perfective of гот**о**виться	поч**и**стить з**у**бы	perfective of ч**и**стить
подожд**а**ть n/sA	perfective of ждать	п**о**чта, -ы (на)	mail; post office
подр**у**га, -и	(girl)friend	почт**и**	almost
под**у**мать АЙ	perfective of д**у**мать	по**э**зия, -ии	poetry
под**у**шка, -и	pillow	по**э**т, -а	poet
п**о**езд, -а	train	пр**а**во, -а	right; law
по**е**хать	perfective of **е**здить	презид**е**нт, -а	president
пож**а**луйста	please	при + prep.	n the presence of; while
пож**а**рный, -ого	firefighter	приб**о**р, -а	set of utensils
пожел**а**ть АЙ	perfective of жел**а**ть	прив**е**т	hi
позвон**и**ть Иend	perfective of звон**и**ть	привык**а**ть АЙ / прив**ы**кнуть (НУ)	to get used to
познак**о**мить И	perfective of знак**о**мить	прив**ы**кнуть (НУ)	perfective of привык**а**ть
познак**о**миться	perfective of знак**о**миться	priглас**и**ть Иend	perfective of приглаш**а**ть
п**о**здно	late	приглаш**а**ть АЙ / приглас**и**ть Иend	to invite
пойт**и**	perfective of ход**и**ть	пригот**о**вить И	perfective of гот**о**вить
пок**а**!	bye! (casual)	пригот**о**виться И	perfective of гот**о**виться
показ**а**ть Аshift	perfective of пок**а**зывать	при**я**тель, -я	friend, buddy
показ**а**ться	perfective of каз**а**ться	пробл**е**ма, -ы	problem
пок**а**зывать АЙ / показ**а**ть Аshift	to show (ком**у** что)	пр**о**бовать ОВА / попр**о**бовать	to try, attempt, taste
покуп**а**ть АЙ / куп**и**ть Иshift	to buy (ком**у** что)	программ**и**рование, -ия	programming
пол, -а (на пол**у**)	ground, floor	продав**а**ть АВАЙ / прод**а**ть	to sell (ком**у** что)
п**о**ле, -я	field	прод**а**ть	perfective of продав**а**ть
полет**е**ть Еend	perfective of лет**а**ть	прос**и**ть Иshift / попрос**и**ть Иshift	to ask (s.o. to do s.t.)
пол**и**тик, -а	politician	просн**у**ться НУ	perfective of просып**а**ться
пол**и**тика, -и	politics	просп**е**кт, -ы	prospekt, boulevard
политол**о**гия, -ии	political science	простын**я**, -**и**	(bed)sheet
полиц**е**йский, -ого	police officer	пр**о**тив + gen.	against
пол-л**и**тра	half-liter	проф**е**ссор, -а	professor
полот**е**нце, -а	towel	прочит**а**ть АЙ	perfective of чит**а**ть
получ**а**ть АЙ / получ**и**ть Иshift	to receive	пр**о**шлое, -ого	the past
получ**и**ть И	perfective of получ**а**ть	пр**о**шлый	past, previous, last
получ**и**ться	perfective of получ**а**ться	психол**о**г, -а	psychologist
п**о**мнить И / всп**о**мнить И	to remember	психол**о**гия, -ии	psychology
помог**а**ть АЙ / пом**о**чь Гend	to help (ком**у**)	пт**и**ца, -ы	bird

267

пусть	let...
пытаться АЙ / попытаться АЙ	to try, make attempt + inf.
пьяница, -ы	a drunkard
пьяный (пьян, пьяна)	drunk
пятница, -ы	Friday
пять	five

Р

работа, -ы	work
работать АЙ / поработать АЙ	to work
раз, -а	(a) time
разбивать АЙ / разбить Ь	to break, shatter (transitive)
разбиваться / разбиться	to be broken
разбить Ь	perfective of разбивать
разбиться	perfective of разбиваться
раздеть Н	perfective of раздевать
раздеться Н	perfective of раздеваться
раньше	earlier, before, previously
расписание, -ия	schedule
рассказать	perf. of рассказывать
рассказывать АЙ /	to tell, narrate
рассказать А^{shift}	
рассмеяться А / смеяться А^{end}	perfective of смеяться
ребён(о)к, ребёнка	child
редко	rarely
река, -и	river
репетиция, -ии	rehearsal
ресторан, -а	restaurant
решать АЙ / решить И^{end}	to (try to) solve
решить	perfective of решать
рис, -а	rice
рисовать ОВА / нарисовать	to draw
родственник, -а	relative
роман, -а	novel
рояль, -я	grand piano
ручка, -и	pen
рубашка, -и	shirt
рубль, -я	rouble
русский	Russian
рыба, -ы	fish
рын(о)к, рынка	market
рюкзак, -а	backpack
рюмка, -и	a shot, shotglass
рядом с + instr.	next to

С

с (со) + instr.	with (accompaniment)
с (со) + gen.	from (of off)
сад, -а	garden
салфетка, -и	napkin
сам	oneself (m.)
сама	oneself (f.)
самолёт, -а	airplane
сахар, -а	sugar
свет, -а	world; light
свинина, -ы	pork
свободный (свободен, -дна)	free
свой	one's own
себя (себе, собой)	oneself
сегодня	today

сейчас	now
секунда, -ы	second
семестр, -а	semester
семья, -и	family
сентябрь, -я	September
сериал, -а	TV series
сестра, -ы	sister
сидеть Е^{end}	to sit (be in a sitting position)
сказать А	perfective of говорить
сколько?	how much, how many
скоро	soon
скрипка, -и	violin
скучать АЙ / соскучиться И	to miss (по кому, чему)
скучный	boring
следующий	next
слишком	too
словарь, -я	dictionary
сломать АЙ	perfective of ломать
сломаться	perfective of ломаться
слушать АЙ / послушать АЙ	to listen
сметана, -ы	sour cream
смешной	funny
смотреть Е^{shift} / посмотреть Е^{shift}	to watch, look
смочь Г	perfective of мочь
сначала	at first
собака, -и	dog
совет, -а	advice; counsel, soviet
советовать ОВА / по-	to advise, recommend
советский	Soviet
совсем	completely, totally
сожаление (к сожалению)	regret (unfortunately)
сосед, -а	neighbor (m.)
соседка, -и	neighbor (f.)
солдат, -а	soldier
солнце, -а	sun
сон	dream
соскучиться И	perfective of скучать
соус, -а	sauce
социология, -ии	Sociology
сочинение, -ия	composition, paper
спальня, -и	bedroom
спасибо	thank you
спектакль, -я	performance, show
спеть ОЙ	perfective of петь
спорт, -а (вид спорта)	sports (a sport)
спортсмен, -а	athlete
спрашивать АЙ / спросить И^{shift}	to ask
спросить И	perfective of спрашивать
сравнительно	relatively
сразу	right away
среда, -ы	Wednesday
стадион, -а (на)	stadium
стакан, -а	glass, cup
становиться И / стать Н	to become + instr.
стараться АЙ / постараться АЙ	to try, strive + inf.
старый	old
стать Н	perfective of становиться
статья, -и	article
стирать АЙ / постирать АЙ	to launder, do laundry
стол, -а	table
столовая, -ой	cafeteria
столько	so much

268

сторон**а**, -ы	side	туд**а**	to there, thither
стран**а**, -ы	country	ты	you (s., informal)
страниц**а**, -ы	page		
стр**а**нный	strange	**У**	
стр**а**шно	awfully, frightfully		
студ**е**нт, -а	student (m.)	у (+gen.)	at (the home of)
студ**е**нтка, -и	student (f.)	убир**а**ть АЙ / убр**а**ть n/sA^end	to clean up
стул, -а	chair	убр**а**ть n/sA	perfective of **убирать**
субб**о**та, -ы	Saturday	ув**е**ренный (ув**е**рен)	certain, sure
судь**я**, -и (m.)	judge	ув**и**деть	perfective of **видеть**
сум**е**ть ЕЙ	see **уметь**	ув**и**деться	perfective of **видеться**
суп, -а	soup	узнав**а**ть АВАЙ / узн**а**ть АЙ	to find out; recognize
сфотограф**и**ровать(ся)	perfective of	узн**а**ть АЙ	perfective of **узнавать**
	фотографировать(ся)	уж**а**сно	terribly, horribly
сч**а**стливо	take it easy	уж**а**сный	terrible, horrible
сч**а**стливый (сч**а**стлив)	happy, fortunate	уж**е**	already
счёт, -а	bill, invoice, account	уж**е** не	not anymore
съесть	perfective of **есть**	**у**жин, -а	dinner
сыгр**а**ть АЙ	perfective of **играть**	**у**лица, -ы	street
сын, -а	son	ум**е**ть ЕЙ / сум**е**ть ЕЙ	to know how (+ inf.)
сыр, -а	cheese	университ**е**т, -а	university
с**ы**тый (сыт)	satisfied, sated, full	ур**о**к, -а	lesson, class
сюрпр**и**з, -а	surprise	усп**е**ть ЕЙ	perfective of **успевать**
сюд**а**	to here, hither	успев**а**ть АЙ / усп**е**ть ЕЙ	to manage (in time) + inf.
		утро, -а	morning
Т		уч**е**бник, -а	textbook
		уч**и**тель, -я	teacher (m.)
так	so, in such a way	уч**и**тельница, -ы	teacher (f.)
т**а**кже	also (as well as)	уч**и**ть И^shift / науч**и**ть И^shift	to teach + acc. + inf.
так**о**й	such, "of such a kind"	уч**и**ться И^shift / науч**и**ться И^shift	to learn, be taught + inf.
так**о**й же	the same kind of	уч**и**ться И^shift	to go to college
такс**и**	taxi	у**ю**тный	comfortable, cozy
там	there		
тан(е)ц, т**а**нца	dance	**Ф**	
танцев**а**ть ОВА /	to dance		
потанцев**а**ть ОВА		фам**и**лия, -ии	last name
танц**о**р, -а	dancer (m.)	февр**а**ль, -я	February
тар**е**лка, -и	plate	фехтов**а**ние, -ия	fencing
твой	your, yours	ф**и**зик, -а	physicist
твор**о**г, -а	similar to cottage cheese	ф**и**зика, -и	physics
те**а**тр, -а	theater	фил**о**соф, -а	philosopher
телев**и**зор, -а	television	филос**о**фия, -ии	philosophy
телеф**о**н, -а	telephone	фильм, -а	film
т**е**ма, -ы	topic, theme	фл**е**йта, -ы	flute
тётя, -и	aunt	фотогр**а**фия, -ии	photograph
тов**а**рищ, -а	comrade	фотограф**и**ровать ОВА /	to photograph
т**о**же	also, too	сфотограф**и**ровать ОВА	
т**о**лько	only	фотограф**и**роваться ОВА /	to have one's picture taken
торг**о**вый центр, -а	shopping center	сфотограф**и**роваться ОВА	
торт, -а	cake	фр**а**за, -ы	phrase
тост, -а	a toast	футб**о**л, -а	soccer
тот	that (one); the right one	футб**о**лка, -и	t-shirt
тот же (с**а**мый)	the same		
трав**а**, -ы	grass	**Х**	
трамв**а**й, -я	streetcar		
тр**е**звый (трезв)	sober	х**и**мия, -ии	chemistry
тренажёрный зал, -а	gym	хлеб, -а	bread
тренир**о**вка, -и	(sports) practice	ход**и**ть И - идт**и** / пойт**и**	to go (on foot)
три	three	хокк**е**й, -я	hockey
тротуа́р, -а	sidewalk	холод**и**льник, -а	refrigerator
тр**у**дный	difficult	хол**о**дный, х**о**лодно	cold
туал**е**т, -а	restroom	хор**о**ший	good

хоро**шо**	well
хот**е**ть / захот**е**ть	to want
хот**е**ться / захот**е**ться	to want, feel like (impersonal)
храм, -а	place of worship, cathedral
худ**о**жник, -а	artist

Ц

целый	entire
центр, -а	downtown
(торг**о**вый центр)	(mall, shopping center)

Ч

чай, -я	tea
чайник, -а	teapot
часто	often
чаша, -и, **ча**шка, -и	(tea)cup, coffee cup
чей?	whose
челов**е**к, -а	human being, person
через	in (from now) + acc.
четв**е**рг, -**а**	Thursday
чет**ы**ре	four
чистый	clean
чит**а**ть АЙ / проч**и**т**а**ть АЙ	to read
чит**а**тель, -я	reader
что	what
чт**о**бы	in order to + inf.
чувство	feeling
чувствовать ОВА себя / по-	to feel
чья, чьё, чьи	see **чей**

Ш

шамп**а**нское, -ого	champagne
шамп**у**нь, -я	shampoo
шёл	past tense of **идти**
шкаф, -а	wardrobe, closet
шк**о**ла, -ы	school
шла	past tense of **идти**
шли	past tense of **идти**
шокол**а**д, -а	chocolate
шосс**е** (n.)	highway

Щ

щен(**о**)к, щенк**а**	puppy
щётка, -и	brush

Э

экз**а**мен, -а	exam
электр**и**чка, -и	suburban train
электр**о**нная п**о**чта, -ы	e-mail
эскал**а**тор, -а	escalator
этаж**е**рка, -и	bookshelf
это	this is (pointing word)
этот	this

Ю

Я

я	I
яблоко, -а	apple
яз**ы**к, -**а**	language; tongue
янв**а**рь, -**я**	January

6.a
телефон → **он** шампунь → **он** ответ → **он** плакат → **он**
словарь → **он** идея → **она** зеркало → **оно** машина → **она**
окно → **оно** платье → **оно** задание → **оно** мяч → **он**
работа → **она** фильм → **он** история → **она** музей → **он**

6.b
1. Это книга. Это **она**. 9. Это фотография. Это **она**. 17. Это телевизор. Это **он**.
2. Это телевизор. Это **он**. 10. Это кафетерий. Это **он**. 18. Это плакат. Это **он**.
3. Это окно. Это **оно**. 11. Это ключ. Это **он**. 19. Это статья. Это **она**.
4. Это словарь. Это **он**. 12. Это картина. Это **она**. 20. Это задание. Это **оно**.
5. Это простыня. Это **она**. 13. Это музей. Это **он**. 21. Это шампунь. Это **он**.
6. Это одеяло. Это **оно**. 14. Это бельё. Это **оно**. 22. Это зонт. Это **он**.
7. Это платье. Это **оно**. 15. Это полотенце. Это **оно**. 23. Это книга. Это **она**.
8. Это расписание. Это **оно**. 16. Это этажерка. Это **она**. 24. Это имя. (!) Это **оно**.

6.c
1. Что это? Это карандаш. **Он** новый. Это **новый карандаш**.
2. Что это? Это музей. **Он** интересный. Это **интересный музей**.
3. Что это? Это платье. **Оно** новое. Это **новое платье**.
4. Что это? Это расписание. **Оно** интересное. Это **интересное расписание**.
5. Что это? Это стул. **Он** старый. Это **старый стул**.
6. Что это? Это кресло. **Оно** старое. Это **старое кресло**.
7. Что это? Это мяч. **Он** новый. Это **новый мяч**.
8. Что это? Это книга. **Она** новая. Это **новая книга**.

6.d
1. У кого есть телевизор? У **него** есть телевизор. 4. У кого есть зонт? У **тебя** есть зонт.
2. У кого есть телефон? У **неё** есть телефон. 5. У кого есть окно? У **вас** есть окно.
3. У кого есть машина? У **них** есть машина. 6. У кого есть идея? У **нас** есть идея.

7.a
1. Как **её** зовут? Как у **неё** дела? Очень хорошо. У **неё** новая лампа!
2. Как **их** зовут? Как у **них** дела? Очень хорошо. У **них** новый шампунь!
3. Как **тебя** зовут? Как у **тебя** дела? Очень хорошо. У **меня** новое одеяло!

7.b
1. **новая** книга 7. **старый** мяч 13. **интересный** вопрос
2. **новый** музей 8. **старая** комната 14. **интересный** ответ
3. **новая** рубашка 9. **старый** словарь 15. **интересная** задача
4. **новое** платье 10. **старое** одеяло 16. **интересная** история
5. **новый** рюкзак 11. **старый** плакат 17. **интересное** место
6. **новая** идея 12. **старая** машина 18. **интересная** картина

7.c
1. **русский** плакат 7. **маленькая** ошибка 13. **хороший** музей
2. **русская** книга 8. **маленький** зонт 14. **хорошая** идея
3. **русский** сериал 9. **маленькое** окно 15. **хорошее** место
4. **русская** машина 10. **маленькая** семья 16. **хорошая** работа
5. **русская** фамилия 11. **маленький** ковёр 17. **хороший** вопрос
6. **русское** имя 12. **маленький** стол 18. **хороший** словарь

7.d
1. **большой** рюкзак 5. **дорогое** мыло 9. **плохой** день
2. **большая** проблема 6. **дорогой** шампунь 10. **плохая** неделя
3. **большой** ковёр 7. **дорогая** бумага 11. **плохая** газета
4. **большое** окно 8. **дорогая** ручка 12. **плохое** мыло

7.e
1. **Какая дорогая и большая** машина! 5. **Какой ужасный и скучный** фильм!
2. **Какой старый и интересный** плакат! 6. **Какая необычная и интересная** идея!
3. **Какое красивое и необычное** платье! 7. **Какая старая и безобразная** фотография!
4. **Какое хорошее и чистое** общежитие! 8. **Какое маленькое и грязное** окно!

7.f
1. Комната у тебя большая? Нет, **она маленькая**, к сожалению. Какой ужас!
2. Телефон у тебя хороший? Нет, **он плохой**, к сожалению. Какой ужас!
3. Машина у тебя дорогая? Нет, **она дешёвая**, к сожалению. Какой ужас!
4. Рюкзак у тебя красивый? Нет, **он некрасивый**, к сожалению. Какой ужас!
5. Кафетерий у тебя хороший? Нет, **он плохой / ужасный**, к сожалению. Какой ужас!
6. Окно у тебя большое? Нет, **оно маленькое**, к сожалению. Какой ужас!
7. Задание у тебя лёгкое? Нет, **оно трудное**, к сожалению. Какой ужас!

8.a
1. Телефон **был** новый.
2. Окно **было** большое.
3. Словарь **был** хороший.
4. Неделя **была** трудная.
5. Задача **была** лёгкая.
6. Задание **было** трудное.
7. Музей **был** огромный.
8. Статья **была** скучная.
9. Книга **была** русская
10. Фильм **был** ужасный.
11. Бельё **было** чистое.
12. Работа **была** трудная.
13. Мыло **было** дорогое.
14. Ручка **была** старая.

8.b
1. Я дома сегодня.
Я **был** дома вчера.
Я **буду** дома завтра.

2. Я дома сегодня.
Я **была** дома вчера.
Я **буду** дома завтра.

3. Ты дома сегодня.
Ты **был** дома вчера.
Ты **будешь** дома завтра.

4. Ты дома сегодня.
Ты **была** дома вчера.
Ты **будешь** дома завтра.

5. Ирина дома сегодня.
Она **была** дома вчера.
Она **будет** дома завтра.

6. Павел дома сегодня.
Он **был** дома вчера.
Он **будет** дома завтра.

7. Мы дома сегодня.
Мы **были** дома вчера.
Мы **будем** дома завтра.

8. Вы дома сегодня.
Вы **были** дома вчера.
Вы **будете** дома завтра.

9. Павел и Ирина дома сегодня.
Они **были** дома вчера.
Они **будут** дома завтра.

9.a
1. **Чья** это ручка? | Она **моя**? | Она **твоя**? | Она **наша**? | Она **ваша**? | Она **его**? | Она **её**? | Она **их**?
2. **Чей** это зонт? | Он **мой**? | Он **твой**? | Он **наш**? | Он **ваш**? | Он **его**? | Он **её**? | Он **их**?
3. **Чьё** это бельё? | Оно **моё**? | Оно **твоё**? | Оно **наше**? | Оно **ваше**? | Оно **его**? | Оно **её**? | Оно **их**?
4. **Чей** это рюкзак? | Он **мой**? | Он **твой**? | Он **наш**? | Он **ваш**? | Он **его**? | Он **её**? | Он **их**?
5. **Чья** это машина? | Она **моя**? | Она **твоя**? | Она **наша**? | Она **ваша**? | Она **его**? | Она **её**? | Она **их**?
6. **Чьё** это окно? | Оно **моё**? | Оно **твоё**? | Оно **наше**? | Оно **ваше**? | Оно **его**? | Оно **её**? | Оно **их**?
7. **Чья** это идея? | Она **моя**? | Она **твоя**? | Она **наша**? | Она **ваша**? | Она **его**? | Она **её**? | Она **их**?
8. **Чей** это мяч? | Он **мой**? | Он **твой**? | Он **наш**? | Он **ваш**? | Он **его**? | Он **её**? | Он **их**?

9.b
1. **Чья** это машина? | **Какая она**?
2. **Чей** это мяч? | **Какой он**?
3. **Чьё** это полотенце? | **Какое оно**?
4. **Чья** это рубашка? | **Какая она**?
5. **Чей** это ключ? | **Какой он**?
6. **Чьё** это мыло? | **Какое оно**?
7. **Чей** это шампунь? | **Какой он**?
8. **Чьё** это одеяло? | **Какое оно**?
9. **Чья** это простыня? | **Какая она**?

9.c
1. **Чья** это **была** машина вчера? | Это **была моя новая** машина. | Ничего себе!
2. **Чей** это **был** мяч вчера? | Это **был мой новый** мяч. | Ничего себе!
3. **Чьё** это **было** кресло вчера? | Это **было моё новое** кресло. | Ничего себе!
4. **Чья** это **была** книга вчера? | Это **была моя новая** книга. | Ничего себе!
5. **Чей** это **был** телефон вчера? | Это **был мой новый** телефон. | Ничего себе!

9.d
1. **Чей** это компьютер? | **Твой** или его? | Это не **его** компьютер. | **Он мой**.
2. **Чьё** это расписание? | **Твоё** или её? | Это не **её** рюкзак. | **Оно моё**.
3. **Чей** это кошелёк? | **Твой** или их? | Это не **их** кошелёк. | **Он мой**.
4. **Чья** это сумка? | **Твоя** или её? | Это не **её** сумка. | **Она моя**.
5. **Чьё** это бельё? | **Твоё** или его? | Это не **его** бельё. | **Оно моё**.

6. **Чей** это зонт? | **Наш** или ваш? | Это не **наш** зонт. | **Он ваш**.
7. **Чьё** это место? | **Наше** или ваше? | Это не **наше** место. | **Оно ваше**.
8. **Чей** это словарь? | **Наш** или ваш? | Это не **наш** словарь. | **Он ваш**.
9. **Чей** это карандаш? | **Наш** или ваш? | Это не **наш** карандаш. | **Он ваш**.
10. **Чья** это машина? | **Наша** или ваша? | Это на **наша** машина. | **Она ваша**.

9.e
1. У тебя есть окно? | Есть. Вот **моё** окно.
2. У вас есть машина? | Есть. Вот **наша** машина.
3. У них есть велосипед? | Есть. Вот **их** велосипед.
4. У него есть одеяло? | Есть. Вот **его** одеяло.
5. У неё есть словарь? | Есть. Вот **её** словарь.
6. У меня есть место? | Есть. Вот **твоя** место.

9.f
1. Расписание у тебя трудное или лёгкое? | Раньше **оно было трудное**, но теперь **оно лёгкое**.
2. Комната у тебя большая или маленькая? | Раньше **она была маленькая**, но теперь **она большая**.
3. Твой телефон хороший или плохой? | Раньше **он был плохой**, но теперь **он хороший**.
4. Работа у нас интересная или скучная? | Раньше **она была скучная**, но теперь **она интересная**.
5. Окно у вас большое или маленькое? | Раньше **оно было маленькое**, но теперь **оно большое**.
6. Твой велосипед дорогой или дешёвый? | Раньше **он был дешёвый**, но теперь **он дорогой**.
7. Ваша одежда дорогая или дешёвая? | Раньше **она была дешёвая**, но теперь **она дорогая**.

273

Answer Key

10.a
1. **этот** русский музей
2. **эта** русская книга
3. **эта** новая ручка
4. **этот** ужасный фильм
5. **эта** скучная русская статья
6. **эта** старая газета
7. **этот** интересный журнал
8. **эта** безобразная идея
9. **эта** огромная комната
10. **эта** необычная картина
11. **это** дорогое платье

12. **Эта** машина дорогая, а **та** дешёвая.
13. **Это** окно чистое, а **то** довольно грязное.
14. **Этот** фильм интересный, а **тот** скучный.
15. **Эта** лампа обычная, а **та** очень странная.
16. **Это** задание трудное, а **то** лёгкое.
17. **Эта** работа лёгкая, а **та** трудная.
18. **Это** полотенце чистое, а **то** грязное.
19. **Этот** музей огромный, а **тот** маленький.
20. **Этот** велосипед дорогой, а **тот** дешёвый.

10.b
1. **Это** старый стул.   **Этот** стул **старый**.   **Он** старый.
2. **Это** большой стол.   **Этот** стол **большой**.   **Он** большой.
3. **Это** новая ручка.   **Эта** ручка **новая**.   **Она** новая.
4. **Это** новый телефон.   **Этот** телефон **новый**.   **Он** новый.
5. **Это** дешёвое платье.   **Это** платье **дешёвое**.   **Оно** дешёвое.

6. **Это был** старый стул.   **Этот** стул **был** старый.   **Он был** старый.
7. **Это был** большой стол.   **Этот** стол **был большой**.   **Он был** большой.
8. **Это была** новая ручка.   **Эта** ручка **была новая**.   **Она была** новая.
9. **Это был** новый телефон.   **Этот** телефон **был новый**.   **Он был** новый.
10. **Это было** дешёвое платье.   **Это** платье **было дешёвое**.   **Оно было** дешёвое.

10.c
1. Это **та** книга?   Нет, не **та**. Это **другая**.
2. Это **тот** журнал?   Нет, не **тот**. Это **другой**.
3. Это **то** мыло?   Нет, не **то**. Это **другое**.
4. Это **та** газета?   Нет, не **та**. Это **другая**.
5. Это **тот** ключ?   Нет, не **тот**. Это **другой**.
6. Это **тот** музей?   Нет, не **тот**. Это **другой**.
7. Это **то** место?   Нет, не **то**. Это **другое**.
8. Это **тот** зонт?   Нет, не **тот**. Это **другой**.

10.d
1. Это **тот же** плакат?   Да, **тот же**.
2. Это **та же** картина?   Да, **та же**.
3. Это **то же** платье?   Да, **то же**.
4. Это **такой же** плакат?   Да, **такой же**.
5. Это **такая же** картина?   Да, **такая же**.
6. Это **такое же** платье?   Да, **такое же**.

11.a
1. новая студентка: комната нов**ой** студентк**и**
2. русский друг: сестра русск**ого** друг**а**
3. русская подруга: отец русск**ой** подруг**и**
4. старый фильм: начало стар**ого** фильм**а**
5. хороший поэт: книга хорош**его** поэт**а**
6. хорошая кошка: фотография хорош**ей** кошк**и**
7. русский писатель: статья русск**ого** писател**я**
8. большая собака: фотография больш**ой** собак**и**
9. новый сосед: ключ нов**ого** сосед**а**
10. новая соседка: окно нов**ой** соседк**и**

11.b
1. русская литература: Без русск**ой** литерату**ры**.
2. русский словарь: Без русск**ого** словар**я**.
3. мой новый телефон: Без мо**его** нов**ого** телефон**а**.
4. моя любимая книга: Без мо**ей** любим**ой** книг**и**.
5. наше большое окно: Без наш**его** больш**ого** окн**а**.
6. их компьютер: Без их компьютер**а**.
7. фотография кошки: Без фотографи**и** кошк**и**.
8. хороший друг: Без хорош**его** друг**а**.
9. его старая собака   Без его стар**ой** собак**и**.
10. этот новый студент: Для эт**ого** нов**ого** студент**а**.
11. наш профессор: Для наш**его** профессор**а**.
12. его отец: Для его отц**а**.
13. ваша мама: Для ваш**ей** мам**ы**.
14. её бабушка: Для её бабушк**и**.
15. их сын: Для их сын**а**.
16. наш старый друг: Для наш**его** стар**ого** друг**а**.
17. любимый писатель: Для любим**ого** писател**я**.
18. твоя подруга: Для тво**ей** подруг**и**.

11.c
1. **Чья** это машина?   моя мама: Это машина мо**ей** мам**ы**.
2. **Чья** это фотография?   мой брат: Это фотография мо**его** брат**а**.
3. **Чьё** это окно?   его сестра: Это окно его сестр**ы**.
4. **Чья** это бабушка?   наш русский друг: Это бабушка наш**его** русск**ого** друг**а**.
5. **Чей** это дедушка?   наша русская подруга: Это дедушка наш**ей** русск**ой** подруг**и**.
6. **Чей** это брат?   наш знакомый: Это брат наш**его** знаком**ого**.
7. **Чья** это сестра?   наша знакомая: Это сестра наш**ей** знаком**ой**.

12.a
У меня **есть щенок**.   У меня **есть кошка**.   У меня **есть мыло**.
У меня **был щенок**.   У меня **была кошка**.   У меня **было мыло**.
У меня **будет щенок**.   У меня **будет кошка**.   У меня **будет мыло**.

У меня **нет щенка**.   У меня **нет кошки**.   У меня **нет мыла**.
У меня **не было щенка**.   У меня **не было кошки**.   У меня **не было мыла**.
У меня **не будет щенка**.   У меня **не будет кошки**.   У меня **не будет мыла**.

12.b

1. У него́ есть но́вый ключ.	У него́ **был** но́вый ключ.	У него́ **бу́дет** но́вый ключ.
2. У неё есть но́вая ко́шка.	У неё **была́** но́вая ко́шка.	У неё **бу́дет** но́вая ко́шка.
3. У них есть чи́стое бельё.	У них **бы́ло** чи́стое бельё.	У них **бу́дет** чи́стое бельё.
4. У вас есть стра́нная иде́я.	У вас **была́** стра́нная иде́я.	У вас **бу́дет** стра́нная иде́я.
5. У тебя́ есть слова́рь.	У тебя́ **был** слова́рь.	У тебя́ **бу́дет** слова́рь.
6. У нас есть больша́я пробле́ма.	У нас **была́** пробле́ма.	У нас **бу́дет** пробле́ма.

12.c

1. У него́ нет но́вого ключа́.	У него́ **не́ было** но́вого ключа́.	У него́ **не бу́дет** но́вого ключа́.
2. У неё нет но́вой ко́шки.	У неё **не́ было** но́вой ко́шки.	У неё **не бу́дет** но́вой ко́шки.
3. У них нет чи́стого белья́.	У них **не́ было** чи́стого белья́.	У них **не бу́дет** чи́стого белья́.
4. У вас нет стра́нной иде́и.	У вас **не́ было** стра́нной иде́и.	У вас **не бу́дет** стра́нной иде́и.
5. У тебя́ нет словаря́.	У тебя́ **не́ было** словаря́.	У тебя́ **не бу́дет** словаря́.
6. У нас нет пробле́мы.	У нас **не́ было** пробле́мы.	У нас **не бу́дет** пробле́мы.

12.d

1. Ключ бу́дет?	**Да, ключ бу́дет.**	Нет, ключа́ не бу́дет.
2. Телеви́зор у вас был?	**Да, телеви́зор был.**	Нет, телеви́зора не́ было.
3. Мы́ло у них есть?	**Да, мы́ло есть.**	Нет, мы́ла нет.
4. Зада́ние у нас бы́ло?	**Да, зада́ние бы́ло.**	Нет, зада́ния не́ было.
5. Компью́тер бу́дет?	**Да, компью́тер бу́дет.**	Нет, компью́тера не бу́дет.
6. Оши́бка была́?	**Да, оши́бка была́.**	Нет, оши́бки не́ было.

12.e

1. У твое́й сестры́ нет словаря́, пра́вда?	Что ты! **Слова́рь** у неё есть, коне́чно!
2. У твоего́ отца́ нет телеви́зора, пра́вда?	Что ты! **Телеви́зор** у него́ есть, коне́чно!
3. У них нет ребёнка, пра́вда?	Что ты! **Ребёнок** у них есть, коне́чно!
4. У нас сего́дня нет зада́ния, пра́вда?	Что ты! **Зада́ние** у нас есть, коне́чно!
5. У профе́ссора нет ру́чки, пра́вда?	Что ты! **Ру́чка** у него́ есть, коне́чно!
6. У тебя́ нет ключа́, пра́вда?	Что ты! **Ключ** у меня́ есть, коне́чно!

12.f

1. У тво**его́** па́п**ы** есть маши́на?	4. У тво**е́й** ба́бушк**и** есть ко́шка?
2. У тво**е́й** ма́м**ы** есть маши́на?	5. У тво**его́** дя́д**и** есть я́хта?
3. У тво**его́** де́душк**и** есть соба́ка?	6. У тво**е́й** тёт**и** есть мотоци́кл?

13.a

1. Что он де́лает?	Он рабо́тает и слу́шает му́зыку.	Он чита́ет кни́гу, но пло́хо понима́ет.
2. Что мы де́лаем?	Вы рабо́таете и слу́шаете му́зыку.	Вы чита́ете кни́гу, но пло́хо понима́ете.
3. Что она́ де́лает?	Она́ рабо́тает и слу́шает му́зыку.	Она́ чита́ет кни́гу, но пло́хо понима́ет.
4. Что они́ де́лают?	Они́ рабо́тают и слу́шают му́зыку.	Они́ чита́ют кни́гу, но пло́хо понима́ют.
5. Что вы де́лаете?	Мы рабо́таем и слу́шаем му́зыку.	Мы чита́ем кни́гу, но пло́хо понима́ем.
6. Что де́лают все?	Все рабо́тают и слу́шают му́зыку.	Все чита́ют кни́гу, но пло́хо понима́ют.
7. Что ты де́лаешь?	Я рабо́таю и слу́шаю му́зыку.	Я чита́ю кни́гу, но пло́хо понима́ю.

13.b

1. Она́ рабо́тает сейча́с?	Нет, она́ отдыха́ет наконе́ц.	Она́ ничего́ не де́лает.
2. Он рабо́тает сейча́с?	Нет, он отдыха́ет наконе́ц.	Он ничего́ не де́лает.
3. Они́ рабо́тают сейча́с?	Нет, они́ отдыха́ют наконе́ц	Они́ ничего́ не де́лают.
4. Ты рабо́таешь сейча́с?	Нет, я отдыха́ю наконе́ц.	Я ничего́ не де́лаю.

13.c

1. Что он де́лает?	Он пи́шет письмо́ и пла́чет.	Почему́ он пла́чет?	Не ска́жет! И письмо́ не пока́жет!
2. Что они́ де́лают?	Они́ пи́шут письмо́ и пла́чут.	Почему́ они́ пла́чут?	Не ска́жут! И письмо́ не пока́жут!
3. Что вы де́лаете?	Мы пи́шем письмо́ и пла́чем.	Почему́ вы пла́чете?	Не ска́жем! И письмо́ не пока́жем!

14.a

1. Что ты де́лаешь?	Я рабо́таю.	Я пишу́.	Я чита́ю.	Я рису́ю.	Я танцу́ю.
2. Что он де́лает?	Он рабо́тает.	Он пи́шет.	Он чита́ет.	Он рису́ет.	Он танцу́ет.
3. Что вы де́лаете?	Мы рабо́таем.	Мы пи́шем.	Мы чита́ем.	Мы рису́ем.	Мы танцу́ем.
4. Что они́ де́лают?	Они́ рабо́тают.	Они́ пи́шут.	Они́ чита́ют.	Они́ рису́ют.	Они́ танцу́ют.
5. Что она́ де́лает?	Она́ рабо́тает.	Она́ пи́шет.	Она́ чита́ет.	Она́ рису́ет.	Она́ танцу́ет.
6. Что все де́лают?	Все рабо́тают.	Все пи́шут.	Все чита́ют.	Все рису́ют.	Все танцу́ют.
7. Что мы де́лаем?	Вы рабо́таете.	Вы пи́шете.	Вы чита́ете.	Вы рису́ете.	Вы танцу́ете.
8. Что я де́лаю?	Ты рабо́таешь.	Ты пи́шешь.	Ты чита́ешь.	Ты рису́ешь.	Ты танцу́ешь.

14.b

1. Что он**и** дела**ют**?	Почему он**и** всегда **работают**?	Почему он**и** никогда не отдыха**ют**?
2. Что вы дела**ете**?	Почему вы всегда **читаете**?	Почему вы никогда не отдыха**ете**?
3. Что он дела**ет**?	Почему он всегда **пишет**?	Почему он никогда не отдыха**ет**?
4. Что мы дела**ем**?	Почему мы всегда **рисуем**?	Почему мы никогда не отдыха**ем**?
5. Что он**а** дела**ет**?	Почему он**а** всегда **думает**?	Почему он**а** никогда не отдыха**ет**?
6. Что ты дела**ешь**?	Почему ты всегда **танцуешь**?	Почему ты никогда не отдыха**ешь**?
7. Что дела**ет** Ив**а**н?	Почему он всегда **работает**?	Почему он никогда не отдыха**ет**?
8. Что дела**ет** Ира?	Почему он**а** всегда **пишет**?	Почему он**а** никогда не отдыха**ет**?

14.c

1. Я мёрзн**у**.	Нич**е**го, ты привыкн**ешь**.
2. Они мёрзн**ут**.	Нич**е**го, они привыкн**ут**.
3. Ты мёрзн**ешь**?	Нич**е**го, я привыкн**у**.
4. Вы мёрзн**ете**?	Нич**е**го, мы привыкн**ем**.

14.d

1. Он ум**е**ет чит**а**ть эту кн**и**гу*?	Он усп**е**ет прочит**а**ть эту кн**и**гу?
2. Они ум**е**ют всё д**е**лать?	Он**и** усп**е**ют всё сд**е**лать?
3. Вы ум**е**ете пис**а**ть статью?	Вы усп**е**ете написать статью?
4. Она ум**е**ет это д**е**лать?	Он**а** усп**е**ет это сд**е**лать?
5. Миха**и**л ум**е**ет пис**а**ть письм**о**?	Он усп**е**ет написать письм**о**?
6. Юлия ум**е**ет рис**о**вать?	Она усп**е**ет нарис**о**вать эту к**о**шку?

14.e

1. Как**о**е это им**е**ет знач**е**ние?	Я пон**я**тия не им**е**ю!	6. Почем**у** мы чита**ем** этот текст?	Я пон**я**тия не им**е**ю!
2. Мы усп**е**ем всё сд**е**лать?	Я пон**я**тия не им**е**ю!	7. Кто слуша**ет** так**у**ю м**у**зыку?	Я пон**я**тия не им**е**ю!
3. Он ум**е**ет танцев**а**ть?	Я пон**я**тия не им**е**ю!	8. Ребёнок ум**е**ет чит**а**ть?	Я пон**я**тия не им**е**ю!
4. Что он**а** им**е**ет в вид**у**?	Я пон**я**тия не им**е**ю!	9. Что он рис**у**ет?	Я пон**я**тия не им**е**ю!
5. Что мы здесь дела**ем**?	Я пон**я**тия не им**е**ю!	10. Он**и** хорош**о** танцу**ют**?	Я пон**я**тия не им**е**ю!

14.f

1. Ты хорош**о** жив**ёшь**?	5. Ты м**о**ж**ешь** раб**о**тать?
2. Мы хорош**о** жив**ём**?	6. Он**и** м**о**г**ут** раб**о**тать?
3. Он**и** хорош**о** жив**ут**?	7. Вы м**о**ж**ете** раб**о**тать?
4. Вы хорош**о** жив**ёте**?	8. Я мог**у** раб**о**тать?

14.g

1. Скаж**и** нам, как**а**я у теб**я** н**о**вая ид**е**я.	Вы не пойм**ёте**.	Вы нич**е**го не понима**ете**.
2. Скаж**и** ей, почем**у** у теб**я** нет русского словар**я**.	Она не пойм**ёт**.	Она нич**е**го не понима**ет**.
3. Скаж**и** им, почем**у** од**е**жда у теб**я** так**а**я стр**а**нная.	Они не пойм**ут**.	Они нич**е**го не понима**ют**.
4. Скаж**и** мне, почем**у** телеф**о**н у теб**я** так**о**й ст**а**рый.	Ты не пойм**ёшь**.	Ты нич**е**го не понима**ешь**.
5. Скаж**и** мне, что ты им**е**ешь в вид**у**.	Вы не пойм**ёте**.	Вы нич**е**го не понима**ете**.
6. Скаж**и** ем**у**, почем**у** у твоег**о** д**е**душки нет компь**ю**тера.	Он не пойм**ёт**.	Он нич**е**го не понима**ет**.
7. Я скаж**у** теб**е**, как**а**я у мен**я** пробл**е**ма.	Я не пойм**у**.	Я нич**е**го не понима**ю**.

14.h

1. он:	чита**ет**	пиш**ет**	рис**у**ет	мёрзн**ет**	старе**ет**	жив**ёт**	м**о**ж**ет**	пойм**ёт**
2. мы:	чита**ем**	пиш**ем**	рис**у**ем	мёрзн**ем**	старе**ем**	жив**ём**	м**о**ж**ем**	пойм**ём**
3. я:	чита**ю**	пиш**у**	рис**у**ю	мёрзн**у**	старе**ю**	жив**у**	мог**у**	пойм**у**
4. они:	чита**ют**	пиш**ут**	рис**у**ют	мёрзн**ут**	старе**ют**	жив**ут**	м**о**г**ут**	пойм**ут**
5. вы:	чита**ете**	пиш**ете**	рис**у**ете	мёрзн**ете**	старе**ете**	жив**ёте**	м**о**ж**ете**	пойм**ёте**
6. ты:	чита**ешь**	пиш**ешь**	рис**у**ешь	мёрзн**ешь**	старе**ешь**	жив**ёшь**	м**о**ж**ешь**	пойм**ёшь**
7. он**а**:	чита**ет**	пиш**ет**	рис**у**ет	мёрзн**ет**	старе**ет**	жив**ёт**	м**о**ж**ет**	пойм**ёт**
8. все	чита**ют**	пиш**ут**	рис**у**ют	мёрзн**ут**	старе**ют**	жив**ут**	м**о**г**ут**	пойм**ут**

15.a

1. shift	4. shift
2. end	5. end
3. shift	6. shift

15.b

1. Я **плачу** сег**о**дня.	5. Он **ответит** на вопр**о**с.	9. Мы **любим** русскую литерат**у**ру.
2. Мы **платим** сег**о**дня.	6. Все **ответят** на вопр**о**с.	10. Вы **любите** русскую литерат**у**ру.
3. Она **платит** сег**о**дня.	7. Я **отвечу** на вопр**о**с.	11. Все **любят** русскую литерат**у**ру.
4. Он**и** **платят** сег**о**дня.	8. Ты **ответишь** на вопр**о**с.	12. Я **люблю** русскую литерат**у**ру.

15.c

1. Я **получу** письмо.
2. Мы **получим** письмо.
3. Вы **получите** письмо.
4. Все **получат** письмо.

5. Она **помнит** ответ.
6. Мы **помним** ответ.
7. Ты **помнишь** ответ.
8. Я **помню** ответ.

9. Мы хорошо **говорим** по-русски.
10. Ты хорошо **говоришь** по-русски.
11. Я хорошо **говорю** по-русски.
12. Все хорошо **говорят** по-русски.

15.d

1. Почему они всё время **сидят** и **смотрят** телевизор?
2. Почему Сергей всё время **сидит** и **смотрит** телевизор?
3. Почему Марина всё время **сидит** и **смотрит** телевизор?
4. Почему все всё время **сидят** и **смотрят** телевизор?
5. Почему я всё время **сижу** и **смотрю** телевизор?
6. Почему вы всё время **сидите** и **смотрите** телевизор?

Потому что они **ненавидят** общение.
Потому что он **ненавидит** общение.
Потому что она **ненавидит** общение.
Потому что все **ненавидят** общение.
Потому что ты **ненавидишь** общение.
Потому что мы **ненавидим** общение.

15.e

1. **плачу, платишь... платят**
2. **смотрю, смотришь... смотрят**
3. **плачу, плачешь... плачут**

4. **могу, можешь... могут**
5. **люблю, любишь... любят**
6. **спрошу, спросишь... спросят**

7. **покажу, покажешь... покажут**
8. **куплю, купишь... купят**
9. **скажу, скажешь... скажут**

16.a

1. Мы так любим **нашу новую кошку**.
2. Я очень редко вижу **мою любимую тётю**.
3. Мы хорошо знаем его **сестру**.
4. Ты знаешь **эту новую студентку**?
5. Все читают **её новую статью**.

6. Ты часто видишь **бабушку**? Есть фотография бабушки?
7. Я совсем не понимаю его **странную идею**.
8. Я ненавижу **эту работу**.
9. Вы знаете **Машу** и **Таню**?

16.b

1. Мы сегодня покупаем **русский словарь**.
   Мы сегодня покупаем **нового щенка**.
2. Мой сосед так ненавидит **наше общежитие**.
   Мой сосед так ненавидит **нашего профессора**.
3. Моя соседка хорошо понимает **этого писателя**.
   Моя соседка хорошо понимает **этот вопрос**.

4. Я плохо помню **старого начальника**.
   Я плохо помню **старый ковёр**.
5. Ребёнок рисует **большой дом**.
   Ребёнок рисует **большого кота**.
6. Я вижу **твоего друга**.
   Мы смотрим **тот же фильм**.

16.c

1. Почему ты так смотришь на **нового студента**?
2. **Какой фильм** вы смотрите? Русский?
3. Кто платит за **эту русскую газету**?

4. — Ты против **войны**? — Конечно! Кто же за **войну**?
5. Кто может ответить на **этот трудный вопрос**?
6. — На что вы смотрите? — На **фотографию моей собаки**.

16.d

1. Да, я **её** покупаю. **Она** интересная.
2. Да, сейчас **его** смотрим. **Он** хороший.
3. Где **он**? Нет, я **его** не вижу. **Его** здесь нет.
4. Ты **их** знаешь? Я был у **них** вчера, но я **их** плохо знаю.

5. Нет, я **её** ненавижу. **Она** такая скучная!
6. Где **она**? Я **её** не вижу. **Её** здесь нет.
7. Да! Я вообще не могу жить без **него**!

17.a

		он		она		они	
1. готовить И:		**готовил**		**готовила**		**готовили**	
2. сделать АЙ:	ты (f.)	**сделала**	ты (m.)	**сделал**	вы	**сделали**	
3. уметь ЕЙ:	я (m.)	**умел**	я (f.)	**умела**	мы	**умели**	
4. написать А:	они	**написали**	вы	**написали**	мы	**написали**	
5. смотреть Eshift:	все	**смотрели**	он	**смотрел**	она	**смотрела**	
6. нарисовать ОВА:	я (f.)	**нарисовала**	ты (f.)	**нарисовала**	она	**нарисовала**	
7. жить В (watch stress!):	я (m.)	**жил**	я (f.)	**жила**	мы	**жили**	
8. понять Й/М (watch stress!):	он	**понял**	она	**поняла**	они	**поняли**	

17.b

он: **делал** **сделал**
она: **делала** **сделала**
они: **делали** **сделали**

он: **готовил** **приготовил**
она: **готовила** **приготовила**
они: **готовили** **приготовили**

1. What was he doing yesterday?
2. What did she get done yesterday?
3. What did they usually (обычно) do?

4. He cooked dinner (ужин) yesterday.
5. She was cooking dinner yesterday.
6. They rarely (редко) cooked dinner.

Что он делал вчера?
Что она сделала вчера?
Что они обычно делали?

Он приготовил ужин вчера.
Она готовила ужин вчера.
Они редко готовили ужин.

17.c вы: **будете делать / сделаете**

1. What will you be doing tomorrow? Что вы **будете делать** завтра?
2. What will you get done tomorrow? Что вы **сделаете** завтра?

он: **будет писать / напишет**

3. He'll write a letter tomorrow. Он **напишет** письмо завтра.
4. He'll write a letter every day. Он **будет писать** письмо **каждый день**.

она: **будет рисовать / нарисует**

5. She'll be drawing a poster (плакат). Она **будет рисовать** плакат.
6. She'll get it drawn tomorrow. Она его **нарисует** завтра.

17.d
1. Я **пишу** интересную статью.
2. Ты уже **написала** письмо?
3. Я его завтра **напишу**.
4. Раньше мама **готовила** ужин.
5. Но теперь я его **готовлю**.
6. Я каждый вечер **буду готовить**!
7. Кто **заплатил** за обед вчера?
8. Мой отец. Он всегда **платит**.
9. Он всегда **платил**, и всегда **будет платить**.
10. Она много **говорила**.
11. Что она **сказала**?
12. Что она **скажет**?

18.a
1. Они **показывали** фотографию.
2. Вчера я **показал** нового щенка.
3. Завтра она **покажет** нашу новую кошку.
4. Я каждый день **получаю** письмо.
5. Раньше мы **получали** письмо каждую неделю.
6. Завтра я **получу** ещё одно письмо.
7. Мой сосед **работал**.
8. Завтра он ещё **поработает**.
9. Я **буду** много **работать** завтра.
10. Я тебя **увижу** завтра.
11. Я **буду** тебя **видеть** каждый день.
12. Я **увидела** старую подругу.

18.b
1. Ты уже **посмотрела** фильм? Нет, я ещё **смотрю**.
2. Ты уже **прочитала** статью? Нет, я ещё **читаю**.
3. Вы уже **ответили** на письмо? Нет, мы ещё **отвечаем**.

18.c
1. Я уже **приготовил** ужин. Я его уже не **готовлю**.
2. Я уже **написал** сочинение. Я его уже не **пишу**.
3. Мы уже **послушали** музыку. Мы её уже не **слушаем**.

18.d
1. Я обычно **показываю** фотографию собаки, но сегодня я **покажу** фотографию кошки.
2. Я обычно не **читаю** русскую газету, но сегодня я **прочитаю** одну статью.

19.a
1. Когда его подруга **танцевала**, он просто **сидел** и **слушал** музыку.
2. Мы **танцевали**, когда она вдруг **спросила**, как меня зовут.
3. Когда он **прочитал** письмо брата, он вдруг **заплакал**.
4. Они целый вечер **сидели** и **смотрели** телевизор.
5. Я целый семестр **читал** этот русский роман, и наконец его **прочитал**!
6. Что вы **делали** сегодня, когда я **работала**?
7. Что вы **сделали** сегодня, когда я **работала**?

19.b
1. Я **хочу** смотреть фильм, а она не **хочет**.
2. Они **хотят** потанцевать, а мы не **хотим**.
3. Вы не **хотите** посидеть и поговорить?
4. Ты не **забудешь** сделать задание?
5. Я думаю, что они **забудут** купить газету.
6. Мы вас не **забудем**. И вы нас не **забудете**!

19.c
1. Я люблю **читать** русскую поэзию.
2. Она не успела **сделать** задание.
3. Наш друг не умел **танцевать**.
4. Мы никогда не успеваем всё **прочитать**.
5. Как ты успеешь всё это **сделать**?!
6. Мы не сумели **ответить** на вопрос.
7. Он любил каждый день **смотреть** кино.
8. Я вдруг захотел **спросить**, как её зовут.
9. Ты умеешь **говорить** по-русски?
10. Наш отец забыл **приготовить** ужин.
11. Твоя мама любит **слушать** музыку?
12. Я не хочу **смотреть** этот сериал.

19.d
1. Мы **хотим** слушать музыку, но не **можем**.
2. Она **хочет** работать, но не **может**.
3. Я **хочу** купить книгу, но не **могу**.
4. Я **хочу** решать задачу, но не **могу**.
5. Они **хотят** посмотреть фильм, но не **могут**.
6. Ты **хочешь** всё сделать, но не **можешь**.
7. Вы **хотите** понять вопрос, но не **можете**.

Мы **хотели** слушать музыку, но не **могли**.
Она **хотела** работать, но не **могла**.
Я (m.) **хотел** купить книгу, но не **мог**.
Я (f.) **хотела** решать задачу, но не **могла**.
Они **хотели** посмотреть фильм, но не **могли**.
Ты (m.) **хотел** всё сделать, но не **мог**.
Вы **хотели** понять вопрос, но не **могли**.

20.a
1. **Какая** это книга? Интересная или скучная?
2. **Какую** книгу ты купил? Дорогую или дешёвую?
3. **Чья** это фотография? Павла или Татьяны?
4. На **чью** фотографию вы смотрите?
5. **Кто** это? На **кого** вы смотрите?
6. **Что** ты получила? Письмо? От **кого**?
7. Для **кого** этот подарок (gift)? **Кто** его получит?
8. **Кто** спросил тебя, как тебя зовут?

20.b
1. Он спрашивает, **где я сейчас живу**.
2. Он меня спросил, **где я сейчас живу**.
3. Он меня спросил, **где я (раньше) жил**.
4. Я не знаю, **что они делают сегодня**.
5. Они не понимают, **почему мы не смотрим телевизор**.
6. Мы хотели знать, **какая у него комната**.

20.c
1. У меня нет машины, **потому что я не хочу покупать машину**.
2. У меня нет зонта, **потому что я его забыла**.
3. Я не могу читать эту статью, **потому что у меня нет русского словаря**.
4. Я не мог сделать (моё) задание, **потому что у меня не было ручки**.
5. Я ещё не смотрел сериал, **потому что у меня нет телевизора**.

20.c
1. Студент, **который** здесь живёт, русский. Книга, **которую** он читает, русская.
2. Русский студент, **которого** мы знаем, хорошо говорит по-английски.
3. Сестра, от **которой** я вчера получил письмо, пишет, что у неё всё хорошо.
4. Вопрос, на **который** она ответила, был очень трудный.
5. Все говорят, что музыка, **которую** мы слушаем, очень странная, а я думаю, что она интересная.
6. Русский писатель, роман **которого** мы сейчас читаем, довольно известный.
7. Человек, машину **которого** я купил, сказал, что она старая и грязная, но хорошая.
8. Я думаю, что тот фильм, **который** мы вчера посмотрели, очень хороший. А как ты думаешь?
9. У той русской семьи, у **которой** я жил, была собака, **которая** меня сразу полюбила.
10. Я забыл ту книгу, **которую** ты хотел читать. А у тебя есть зонт, **который** я у тебя забыл?

21.a
1. Кому ты даёшь **хлеб**? — Даю **хлеб маме**.
2. Кому ты даёшь **чай**? — Даю **чай сестре**.
3. Кому ты даёшь **рыбу**? — Даю **рыбу соседу**.
4. Кому ты даёшь **борщ**? — Даю **борщ соседке**.
5. Кому ты даёшь **вино**? — Даю **вино отцу**.
6. Кому ты даёшь **сыр**? — Даю **сыр другу**.
7. Кому ты даёшь **квас**? — Даю **квас подруге**.
8. Кому ты даёшь **сметану**? — Даю **сметану знакомому**.
9. Кому ты даёшь **пиво**? — Даю **пиво дяде**.
10. Кому ты даёшь **мясо**? — Даю **мясо тёте**.

21.b
1. **этому писателю**
2. **этой женщине**
3. **новой подруге**
4. **старому другу**
5. **новому соседу**
6. **твоему отцу**
7. **вашей маме**
8. **нашему дяде**
9. **его другу**
10. **бабушке**
11. **дедушке**

21.c
1. **Я** дал(а) **её ей**. — Потом **она** вернула **её мне**.
2. **Мы** дали **их ей**. — Потом **она** вернула **их нам**.
3. **Он** дал **её ей**. — Потом **она** вернула **её ему**.
4. **Она** дала **его ему**. — Потом **он** вернул **его ей**.

21.d
1. Тво**ей** сестр**е** невесело.
2. Нов**ому** профессор**у** трудно.
3. Наш**ему** отц**у** было плохо.
4. Их нов**ому** сосед**у** скучно.
5. Её нов**ой** соседк**е** грустно.
6. **Мне** будет очень интересно в России.
7. **Тебе** было так стыдно вчера!
8. **Ему** очень неловко сейчас!
9. **Ей** будет легко говорить по-русски.
10. **Вам** было трудно читать Достоевского.
11. **Им** хорошо и весело сегодня.

Answer Key

21.e
1. **Нашей подруге** плохо.
2. **Моему сыну** скучно.
3. **Моей дочке** грустно.
4. **Его жене** стыдно.
5. **Её мужу** весело.

Нашей подруге было плохо.
Моему сыну было скучно.
Моей дочке было грустно.
Его жене было стыдно.
Её мужу было весело.

Нашей подруге будет плохо.
Моему сыну будет скучно.
Моей дочке будет грустно.
Его жене будет стыдно.
Её мужу будет весело.

21.f
1. Мне надо каждый день **читать** газету.
2. Мне надо сегодня **прочитать** эту статью.
3. Ему можно **смотреть** телевизор вообще?
4. Пора **работать**! Завтра у нас экзамен!
5. Он русский. Ему легко **читать** по-русски.
6. Надо всегда **говорить** правду.
7. Надо сейчас **заплатить** за ужин.
8. Мне лень было **писать**.
9. Здесь нельзя **танцевать**!
10. Нам было трудно **решить** эту задачу.

21.g
1. Он хочет смотреть телевизор, но ему **нельзя**!
2. Он хотел смотреть телевизор, но ему **было нельзя**!
3. (Нам) **можно** здесь сидеть?
4. Нам **надо будет** спросить профессора, когда будет экзамен.
5. Нам **было** очень **интересно** смотреть русский фильм.
6. Мне так **трудно** читать эту русскую книгу!

22.a
1. She'll wash the car.
2. He washed the dishes.
3. Won't you wash them?
4. I already washed them.
5. She sings very well.

Она **помоет** машину.
Он **помыл** посуду.
Не **помоешь** посуду?
Я её уже **помыл(а)**.
Она очень хорошо **поёт**.

6. We'll sing him a song.
7. He sang the child a song.
8. She loves to sing.
9. They were washing dishes.
10. I won't sing at all.

Мы **споём** ему песню.
Он **спел** ребёнку песню.
Она любит **петь**.
Они **мыли** посуду.
Не буду **петь** вообще.

22.b
1. Кто **открыл** окно? Мне холодно!
2. Они всегда **открывают** окно.
3. Я его **закрою**. Я всегда буду его **закрывать**.
4. Они **открыли** новый ресторан.
5. Она забыла **закрыть** холодильник.
6. Её муж **закрыл** его.
7. Он **открывал** окно каждый день.
8. Она **открывала** зонт.

22.c
1. He doesn't drink wine.
2. I like to drink juice.
3. We were drinking vodka.
4. We drank the vodka.
5. I'll drink up the tea.

Он не **пьёт** вино.
Люблю **пить** сок.
Мы **пили** водку.
Мы **выпили** водку.
Я **выпью** чай.

6. What was she drinking?
7. Who drank up the milk?
8. He drank a bottle of beer.
9. They rarely drink alcohol.
10. They were drinking coffee.

Что она **пила**?
Кто **выпил** молоко?
Он **выпил** бутылку пива.
Они редко **пьют** алкоголь.
Они **пили** кофе.

22.d
1. Он **разбил** тарелку? Он всегда **разбивает** посуду!
2. Осторожно, а то **разобьёшь** мою новую вазу!
3. Боже мой! Ребёнок **бьёт** кошку!

22.e
1. Она **начинает** работать каждый день в восемь.
2. Мой коллега **начинал** работать в восемь.
3. Ребёнок скоро **начнёт** говорить.
4. Наш новый сосед **начал** готовить ужин.
5. Аспирантка **начала** читать новую книгу.
6. Они **начали** нам звонить каждый день.
7. Она **начала** привыкать к России.
8. Хорошо, я **начну** рассказывать тебе эту историю.

22.f
1. **вашего друга**
2. **твою сестру**
3. **твоего брата**
4. **друга моего брата**
5. **нашу подругу**
6. **профессора**
7. **зонт**
8. **книгу**
9. **пальто**

22.g
1. **взяла**
2. **возьму**
3. **берём**
4. **едят**
5. **съели**
6. **ем**
7. **дали**
8. **дадим**
9. **даём**
10. **хочу**
11. **хотим**
12. **хотят**

23.a
1. **его, нам**
2. **кому, старому другу**
3. **сына, ей**
4. **меня, вам**
5. **им, им**
6. **отцу, его, маме**
7. **что, брату, ему**
8. **нового коллегу, начальника**
9. **вам, нам**
10. **нового щенка, его, тебе**
11. **дочке, ей, песню**
12. **подругу, мне, правду**

23.b   1. М<u>а</u>ма меня **спрос<u>и</u>ла**, когда я б<u>у</u>ду <u>д</u>ома.
          2. Она всегда **спр<u>а</u>шивала**, что я <u>д</u>елал.
          3. Она меня **попрос<u>и</u>ла** всегда брать зонт.
          4. Я **попрош<u>у</u>** зонт у бр<u>а</u>та.

23.c   1. <u>Д</u>едушка и <u>б</u>абушка <u>д</u>али **люб<u>и</u>мому вн<u>у</u>ку конф<u>е</u>ту**.
          2. Наш от<u>е</u>ц продал **ст<u>а</u>рую маш<u>и</u>ну сос<u>е</u>ду**.
          3. Студ<u>е</u>нтка задала **интер<u>е</u>сный вопр<u>о</u>с профессору**.

23.d   1. **Она мне помогл<u>а</u> вчер<u>а</u>.**
          2. **Мы ем<u>у</u> всегда помог<u>а</u>ли.**
          3. **Он всегда б<u>у</u>дет помог<u>а</u>ть теб<u>е</u>.**
          4. **Я вам помог<u>у</u> з<u>а</u>втра.**
          5. **Я им пом<u>о</u>г.**

24.a   1. **всю**   4. **весь**   7. **весь**   10. **весь**
          2. **всё**   5. **всему**   8. **всей**
          3. **всю**   6. **всю**   9. **всё**

24.b   1. **ц<u>е</u>лую**   4. **ц<u>е</u>лую**
          2. **ц<u>е</u>лый**   5. **ц<u>е</u>лый**
          3. **ц<u>е</u>лая**   6. **ц<u>е</u>лую**

24.c   1. **все**   4. **все**   7. **всё**
          2. **всё**   5. **все** (= "them all," all the posters)   8. **всё**
          3. **все**   6. **все, всё**

24.d   1. **гот<u>о</u>вы, гот<u>о</u>в, гот<u>о</u>ва**   4. **пьян, пь<u>я</u>ны**   7. **с<u>ы</u>ты, сыт<u>а</u>**   10. **гол<u>о</u>дны, голодн<u>а</u>**
          2. **з<u>а</u>няты, занят<u>а</u>**   5. **трезв<u>а</u>, тр<u>е</u>звы**   8. **дов<u>о</u>льна, дов<u>о</u>льны**   11. **больн<u>а</u>, б<u>о</u>лен**
          3. **сч<u>а</u>стлив, сч<u>а</u>стлива**   6. **здор<u>о</u>в, здор<u>о</u>вы**   9. **своб<u>о</u>дно, своб<u>о</u>ден**

24.e   1. Отц<u>у</u> **н<u>у</u>жно п<u>и</u>во.**   4. К<u>о</u>шке **н<u>у</u>жно молок<u>о</u>.**   7. Тебе **н<u>у</u>жны в<u>и</u>лка и нож.**   10. Им **н<u>у</u>жен с<u>а</u>хар.**
          2. Мо<u>е</u>й сестре **н<u>у</u>жен чай.**   5. Мо<u>е</u>му др<u>у</u>гу **н<u>у</u>жно пальт<u>о</u>.**   8. Ему **нужн<u>а</u> л<u>о</u>жка.**   11. Вам **н<u>у</u>жно м<u>а</u>сло.**
          3. Студ<u>е</u>нту **н<u>у</u>жен отв<u>е</u>т.**   6. Мне **н<u>у</u>жен к<u>о</u>фе.**   9. Ей **н<u>у</u>жен кеф<u>и</u>р.**   12. Нам **н<u>у</u>жен шокол<u>а</u>д.**

25.a   1. **р<u>у</u>сскому язык<u>у</u>, филос<u>о</u>фии**   5. **п<u>о</u>чте, электр<u>о</u>нной п<u>о</u>чте**
          2. **р<u>у</u>сской ист<u>о</u>рии, р<u>у</u>сской литерат<u>у</u>ре**   6. **телеф<u>о</u>ну, Ск<u>а</u>йпу**
          3. **матем<u>а</u>тике, ф<u>и</u>зике**   7. **<u>у</u>лице, г<u>о</u>роду**
          4. **х<u>и</u>мии, ист<u>о</u>рии литерат<u>у</u>ры**   8. **б<u>е</u>регу, п<u>а</u>рку**

25.b   1. к **р<u>у</u>сской к<u>у</u>хне**   5. к **р<u>у</u>сскому алфав<u>и</u>ту**   9. по **семь<u>е</u>**
          2. к **р<u>у</u>сскому менталит<u>е</u>ту**   6. к **р<u>у</u>сской гр<u>а</u>мматике**   10. по **бр<u>а</u>ту / сестр<u>е</u>**
          3. к **р<u>у</u>сской пог<u>о</u>де**   7. по **соб<u>а</u>ке / к<u>о</u>шке**   11. по **ст<u>а</u>рому др<u>у</u>гу**
          4. к **р<u>у</u>сскому язык<u>у</u>**   8. по **д<u>о</u>му**   12. по **ст<u>а</u>рой подр<u>у</u>ге**

25.c   1. **Он гот<u>о</u>в.**   **Он был гот<u>о</u>в.**   6. **Ему гр<u>у</u>стно.**   **Ему б<u>ы</u>ло гр<u>у</u>стно.**
          2. **Они пь<u>я</u>ны.**   **Они б<u>ы</u>ли пь<u>я</u>ны.**   7. **Им в<u>е</u>село.**   **Им б<u>ы</u>ло в<u>е</u>село.**
          3. **Она зан<u>я</u>та.**   **Она б<u>у</u>дет зан<u>я</u>та.**   8. **Ей хорош<u>о</u>.**   **Ей б<u>у</u>дет хорош<u>о</u>.**
          4. **Она был<u>а</u> ув<u>е</u>рена.**   **Он был ув<u>е</u>рен.**   9. **Ей б<u>ы</u>ло ск<u>у</u>чно.**   **Ему б<u>ы</u>ло ск<u>у</u>чно.**
          5. **Они б<u>ы</u>ли больн<u>ы</u>.**   **Они б<u>у</u>дут больн<u>ы</u>.**   10. **Им б<u>ы</u>ло пл<u>о</u>хо.**   **Им б<u>у</u>дет пл<u>о</u>хо.**

25.d   1. **Мы должн<u>ы</u> заплат<u>и</u>ть за к<u>о</u>фе.**   4. **Наш друг д<u>о</u>лжен был пом<u>о</u>чь нам.**
          2. **Мо<u>е</u>й сестр<u>е</u> н<u>а</u>до куп<u>и</u>ть под<u>а</u>рок.**   5. **Проф<u>е</u>ссор д<u>о</u>лжен б<u>у</u>дет пом<u>о</u>чь нам.**
          3. **Мо<u>е</u>му бр<u>а</u>ту н<u>а</u>до б<u>ы</u>ло позвон<u>и</u>ть м<u>а</u>ме.**

26.a   1. **<u>у</u>чишься**   4. **уч<u>и</u>тесь**   7. **уч<u>и</u>лся**   10. **уч<u>и</u>лись**
          2. **уч<u>и</u>ться**   5. **<u>у</u>чатся**   8. **уч<u>и</u>лась**
          3. **<u>у</u>чится**   6. **уч<u>у</u>сь, <u>у</u>чится**   9. **уч<u>и</u>лись**

26.b
1. уч<u>и</u>ться / нау<u>ч</u>иться
2. м<u>ы</u>ться / пом<u>ы</u>ться
3. д<u>е</u>латься / сд<u>е</u>латься
4. пис<u>а</u>ться / напис<u>а</u>ться
5. продав<u>а</u>ться / прод<u>а</u>ться

26.c
1. Ты раб<u>о</u>таешь или уч<u>и</u>шься?
2. Мой брат нау<u>ч</u>ился танцев<u>а</u>ть.
3. М<u>о</u>я сестр<u>а</u> у<u>ч</u>ится рисов<u>а</u>ть.
4. Папа учит нас гот<u>о</u>вить.
5. Проф<u>е</u>ссор учит нас р<u>у</u>сскому языку.
6. Мы учимся р<u>у</u>сскому языку.
7. Мы мыли маш<u>и</u>ну.
8. Машина моется очень р<u>е</u>дко.
9. Надо мыться каждый день!
10. Пом<u>о</u>юсь, пот<u>о</u>м пом<u>о</u>ю пос<u>у</u>ду.

26.d
1. Я не мог<u>у</u> смотр<u>е</u>ть телев<u>и</u>зор. Я сег<u>о</u>дня гот<u>о</u>влюсь к экз<u>а</u>мену.
2. Мы вчер<u>а</u> <u>о</u>чень д<u>о</u>лго гот<u>о</u>вились к экз<u>а</u>мену по физике.
3. Контр<u>о</u>льная по р<u>у</u>сскому языку <u>о</u>чень трудная. Надо хорош<u>о</u> подгот<u>о</u>виться!
4. К как<u>о</u>му экз<u>а</u>мену ты сейч<u>а</u>с гот<u>о</u>вишься? К химии?

26.e
1. Я хоч<u>у</u> сфотограф<u>и</u>роваться.
2. Как это сл<u>о</u>во пишется?
3. Мы вчер<u>а</u> пригот<u>о</u>вили борщ.
4. Молок<u>о</u> здесь прод<u>а</u>ётся?
5. Ты мне пок<u>а</u>жешь, как это делается?
Хорош<u>о</u>, я тебя сфотограф<u>и</u>рую.
Я мог<u>у</u> его напис<u>а</u>ть для тебя.
Он <u>о</u>чень д<u>о</u>лго гот<u>о</u>вился.
Да, но мы всё уж<u>е</u> прод<u>а</u>ли.
Нет. Я это пр<u>о</u>сто сд<u>е</u>лаю.

27.a
телев<u>и</u>зор слом<u>а</u>лся
маш<u>и</u>на слом<u>а</u>лась
холод<u>и</u>льник слом<u>а</u>лся
р<u>а</u>дио слом<u>а</u>лось
окн<u>о</u> разб<u>и</u>лось
л<u>а</u>мпа разб<u>и</u>лась
стак<u>а</u>н разб<u>и</u>лся
з<u>е</u>ркало разб<u>и</u>лось
фильм нач<u>а</u>лся
<u>о</u>пера начал<u>а</u>сь
бал<u>е</u>т нач<u>а</u>лся
экз<u>а</u>мен нач<u>а</u>лся

27.b
1. Я д<u>у</u>маю, что тво<u>я</u> соб<u>а</u>ка ск<u>о</u>ро верн<u>ё</u>тся дом<u>о</u>й.
2. Студ<u>е</u>нт верн<u>у</u>л кн<u>и</u>гу проф<u>е</u>ссору.
3. Наш сын слом<u>а</u>л компь<u>ю</u>тер.
4. Компь<u>ю</u>тер всегд<u>а</u> лом<u>а</u>ется.
5. Реб<u>ё</u>нок неч<u>а</u>янно разб<u>и</u>л тар<u>е</u>лку.
6. Тар<u>е</u>лка разб<u>и</u>лась.
7. Мой д<u>я</u>дя откр<u>ы</u>л н<u>о</u>вый рестор<u>а</u>н.
8. Рестор<u>а</u>н открыв<u>а</u>ется к<u>а</u>ждое <u>у</u>тро.
9. Кто закр<u>ы</u>л окн<u>о</u>?
10. Когд<u>а</u> магаз<u>и</u>н закрыв<u>а</u>ется?

27.c
1. Когд<u>а</u> начин<u>а</u>ется <u>о</u>пера?
2. Мо<u>я</u> сестр<u>а</u> начин<u>а</u>ет н<u>о</u>вую раб<u>о</u>ту.
3. Я ск<u>о</u>ро начн<u>у</u> гот<u>о</u>вить <u>у</u>жин.
4. Ты зак<u>о</u>нчил стать<u>ю</u>?
5. Након<u>е</u>ц я зак<u>о</u>нчила пис<u>а</u>ть стать<u>ю</u>.
6. Когд<u>а</u> зак<u>о</u>нчится бал<u>е</u>т?
7. Он ч<u>а</u>сто перестав<u>а</u>л раб<u>о</u>тать, когд<u>а</u> ему б<u>ы</u>ло гр<u>у</u>стно.
8. Я ск<u>о</u>ро перест<u>а</u>ну раб<u>о</u>тать.

27.d
1. Он<u>и</u> <u>о</u>чень р<u>е</u>дко в<u>и</u>дятся.
2. Когд<u>а</u> мы уч<u>и</u>лись мы в<u>и</u>делись к<u>а</u>ждый день.
3. Я в<u>и</u>дел(а) его вчер<u>а</u>.
4. До свид<u>а</u>ния! Мы ув<u>и</u>димся з<u>а</u>втра.
5. Ты м<u>о</u>жешь меня встр<u>е</u>тить з<u>а</u>втра?
6. Мы ч<u>а</u>сто встреч<u>а</u>емся.
7. Где ты х<u>о</u>чешь встр<u>е</u>титься?
8. Мы встреч<u>а</u>лись дов<u>о</u>льно ч<u>а</u>сто.

27.e
1. Теб<u>е</u> х<u>о</u>чется говор<u>и</u>ть по-р<u>у</u>сски?
2. М<u>о</u>жет быть теб<u>е</u> зах<u>о</u>чется з<u>а</u>втра.
3. Им ч<u>а</u>сто хот<u>е</u>лось танцев<u>а</u>ть?
4. Нам вдруг захот<u>е</u>лось смотр<u>е</u>ть телев<u>и</u>зор.
5. Когд<u>а</u> я смотр<u>ю</u> телев<u>и</u>зор, мне х<u>о</u>чется чит<u>а</u>ть литерат<u>у</u>ру.

28.a
1. Что д<u>е</u>лают в Росс<u>и</u>и, когд<u>а</u> д<u>у</u>шно?
2. Что д<u>е</u>лают, когд<u>а</u> ж<u>а</u>рко?
3. Что пьют в Росс<u>и</u>и, когд<u>а</u> х<u>о</u>лодно?
4. Что ед<u>я</u>т, когд<u>а</u> пьют в<u>о</u>дку?
5. Что д<u>е</u>лают в Росс<u>и</u>и, когд<u>а</u> хот<u>я</u>т танцев<u>а</u>ть?
Открыв<u>а</u>ют ф<u>о</u>рточку!
Пьют в<u>о</u>ду или квас!
(Пьют) чай или в<u>о</u>дку!
(Ед<u>я</u>т) ч<u>ё</u>рный хлеб и огурц<u>ы</u>!
Танц<u>у</u>ют, кон<u>е</u>чно!

28.b
1. Мо<u>е</u>му др<u>у</u>гу нр<u>а</u>вится р<u>у</u>сское кин<u>о</u>.
2. Ем<u>у</u> понр<u>а</u>вился фильм, кот<u>о</u>рый мы вчер<u>а</u> посмотр<u>е</u>ли.
3. Мо<u>е</u>й сестр<u>е</u> всегд<u>а</u> нр<u>а</u>вилось чит<u>а</u>ть р<u>у</u>сскую литерат<u>у</u>ру.
4. Теб<u>е</u> понр<u>а</u>вится борщ, кот<u>о</u>рый я для теб<u>я</u> пригот<u>о</u>вил.
6. Н<u>а</u>шей подр<u>у</u>ге всё нр<u>а</u>вится. Ей д<u>а</u>же понр<u>а</u>вилась тво<u>я</u> п<u>а</u>ста.
7. Им все нр<u>а</u>вятся. Им д<u>а</u>же понр<u>а</u>вилась тво<u>я</u> т<u>ё</u>ща.

28.c
1. Я не ду́маю, что я ему́ **понра́влюсь**.
2. Мы им никогда́ не **нра́вились**.
3. Я тебе́ **нра́влюсь**? Ты мне **нра́вишься**.
4. Они́ тебе́ **понра́вятся**, и ты им **понра́вишься**.
5. Я ду́маю, что мы им не **понра́вились**.
6. Ты о́чень **понра́вишься** мое́й сестре́. Ей все **нра́вятся**.

28.d
1. Вы **про́бовали** икру́? Ты хо́чешь её **попро́бовать**?
2. Мы о́чень **стара́лись**, но не суме́ли реши́ть зада́чу.
3. Я **попыта́юсь** пригото́вить борщ за́втра.
4. Я всегда́ **стара́юсь** де́лать всё во́время.
5. Ты смо́жешь мне помо́чь? Не зна́ю, но я бу́ду **стара́ться**!

29.a

сде́лать	**сде́лают**	**сде́лай!**	петь	**пою́т**	**пой!**
отвеча́ть	**отвеча́ют**	**отвеча́й!**	помы́ть	**помо́ют**	**помо́й!**
танцева́ть	**танцу́ют**	**танцу́й!**	откры́ть	**откро́ют**	**откро́й!**
попро́бовать	**попро́буют**	**попро́буй!**	закры́ть	**закро́ют**	**закро́й!**
име́ть	**име́ют**	**име́й!**	закрыва́ть	**закрыва́ют**	**закрыва́й!**

29.b

сказа́ть	**ска́жут**	**скажу́**	**скажи́!**
спроси́ть	**спро́сят**	**спрошу́**	**спроси́!**
пригото́вить	**пригото́вят**	**пригото́влю**	**пригото́вь!**
сиде́ть	**сидя́т**	**сижу́**	**сиди́!**
отдохну́ть	**отдохну́т**	**отдохну́**	**отдохни́!**
нача́ть	**начну́т**	**начну́**	**начни́!**
переста́ть	**переста́нут**	**переста́ну**	**переста́нь!**
поня́ть	**пойму́т**	**пойму́**	**пойми́!**
жить	**живу́т**	**живу́**	**живи́!**
звать	**зову́т**	**зову́**	**зови́!**
брать	**беру́т**	**беру́**	**бери́!**
взять	**возьму́т**	**возьму́**	**возьми́!**

29.c

чита́ть	**чита́ют**	**чита́й!**
прочита́ть	**прочита́ют**	**прочита́й!**
открыва́ть	**открыва́ют**	**открыва́й!**
уме́ть	**уме́ют**	**уме́й!**

29.d

попро́бовать	**попро́буют**	**попро́буй!**	танцева́ть	**танцу́ют**	**танцу́й!**
плани́ровать	**плани́руют**	**плани́руй!**	потанцева́ть	**потанцу́ют**	**потанцу́й!**
сове́товать	**сове́туют**	**сове́туй!**	игнори́ровать	**игнори́руют**	**игнори́руй!**

29.e

помы́ть	**помо́ют**	**помо́ешь!**	закры́ть	**закро́ют**	**закро́й!**
петь	**пою́т**	**пой!**	откры́ть	**откро́ют**	**откро́й!**
спеть	**спою́т**	**спой!**			

29.f

показа́ть	**пока́жут**	**покажу́**	**покажи́!**
написа́ть	**напи́шут**	**напишу́**	**напиши́!**
сказа́ть	**ска́жут**	**скажу́**	**скажи́!**
рассказа́ть	**расска́жут**	**расскажу́**	**расскжи́!**

29.g

ве́рить	**ве́рят**	**ве́рю**	**верь!**
получи́ть	**полу́чат**	**получу́**	**получи́!**
купи́ть	**ку́пят**	**куплю́**	**купи́!**
сиде́ть	**сидя́т**	**сижу́**	**сиди́!**

29.h

заплати́ть	**запла́тят**	**заплачу́**	**заплати́!**
люби́ть	**лю́бят**	**люблю́**	**люби́!**
попроси́ть	**попро́сят**	**попрошу́**	**попроси́!**
позвони́ть	**позвоня́т**	**позвоню́**	**позвони́!**
пригото́вить	**пригото́вят**	**пригото́влю**	**пригото́вь!**
реши́ть	**реша́т**	**решу́**	**реши́!**
посмотре́ть	**посмо́трят**	**посмотрю́**	**посмотри́!**

29.i

пить	пей!	пейте!	давай! / дай!
выпить	выпей!	выпейте!	продавай! / продай!
разбить	разбей!	разбейте!	переставай! / перестань!
забыть	забудь!	забудьте!	
мёрзнуть	мёрзни!	мёрзните!	

30.a

1. **Купи** мне бутылку водки.
2. Не **покупай** эту водку.
3. Не забудь **купить** водку!
4. **Напиши** ему завтра.
5. **Пиши** (мне!)
6. Не **пиши** этому человеку.

7. **Звони** мне!
8. Не **звони** моей невесте.
9. **Позвони** отцу завтра.
10. **Звони** маме!
11. **Покажи** мне фотографию.
12. Никогда не **показывай** эту фотографию!

13. Не **покажи** эту фотографию!
14. **Мой** посуду каждый вечер.
15. **Помой** посуду, пожалуйста.
16. **Помоги** мне.
17. Не **помогай** ему.

30.b

1. верни!
   верните!
2. мой!
   мойте!
3. подготовь!
   подготовьте!
4. (попытай!)
   (попытайте!)

вернись!
вернитесь!
мойся!
мойтесь!
подготовься!
подготовьтесь!
попытайся!
попытайтесь!

5. фотографируй!
   фотографируйте!
6. научи!
   научите!
7. (старай!)
   (старайте!)

фотографируйся!
фотографируйтесь!
научись!
научитесь!
старайся!
старайтесь!

30.c

1. **Давай помоем посуду.**
2. **Давай не будем мыть посуду.**
3. **Давай я помою посуду.**

4. **Давай прочитаем эту статью.**
5. **Давай не будем читать эту статью.**
6. **Давай я прочитаю эту статью.**

7. **Давай позвоним маме.**
8. **Давай не будем звонить маме.**
9. **Давай я позвоню маме.**

30.b

1. **Приготовь ужин!**
2. **Давай не будем готовить ужин.**
3. **Пусть папа приготовит ужин.**

4. **Давай я им напишу.**
5. **Не пиши им!**
6. **Пусть они нам напишут.**

7. **Позвони ей.**
8. **Нет, давай не будем ей звонить.**
9. **Пусть она нам позвонит.**

31.a

1. о **русской музыке**
2. о **новом словаре**
3. о **старом профессоре**

4. о **Русском музее**
5. об **Эрмитаже**
6. о **нашем общежитии**

7. о **твоей идее**
8. о **всей вашей работе**
9. об **этом задании**

10. о **твоём русском друге**

31.b

1. вэтой
2. фхорошем
3. вгороде

4. фцентре
5. вэтом
6. фторговом

7. фпарке

31.c

1. в ресторане
2. на острове
3. в спальне

4. на концерте
5. на тротуаре
6. на западе

31.d

1. в реке
   на реке
2. в земле
   на земле

3. в траве
   на траве
4. в дереве
   на дереве

5. в море
   на море
6. в автобусе
   на автоубсе

32.a

1. в стране
2. в космосе
3. в ресторане
4. в Москве
5. в городе

6. в Петербурге
7. в общежитии
8. в деревне
9. в больнице
10. во Франции

11. в рюкзаке
12. в словаре
13. в гостиной
14. в коридоре

32.b
1. на тротуаре
2. на пляже
3. на даче
4. на кухне
5. на земле
6. на занятии
7. на лекции
8. на почте
9. на острове
10. на улице
11. на вечеринке
12. на вокзале
13. на дворе
14. на уроке
15. на ковре
16. на стадионе
17. на странице
18. на доске
19. на стене
20. на лестнице
21. на эскалаторе
22. на стороне
23. на набережной
24. на рынке

32.c
1. в Лондоне
2. в метро
3. в Бостоне
4. в Торонто
5. в гостиной
6. в Вашингтоне
7. в Париже
8. в Токио
9. на такси
10. на шоссе
11. в Риме
12. в Пекине
13. в Филадельфии
14. в Гонолулу
15. в Дублине
16. в Монреале
17. в прошлом
18. в будущем

32.d
1. из Мюнхена
2. из Хельсинки
3. из Барселоны
4. из Осло
5. из Сиэтла
6. из Праги
7. из Копенгагена
8. из Флоренции
9. из Варшавы

32.e
1. в Техасе
2. в Нью-Йорке
3. в Колорадо
4. в Нью-Джерси
5. во Флориде
6. в Вирджинии

32.f
1. в саду
2. на полу
3. в снегу
4. на мосту
5. на берегу
6. в аэропорту

33.a
1. год / неделю / целый месяц / целый год
2. неделю назад / месяц назад
3. через неделю / через год
4. через минуту / через час
5. каждую неделю / каждый месяц
6. до занятия / после лекции
7. за год / за месяц
8. за час / за минуту

33.b
1. понедельник / в понедельник
2. вторник / во вторник
3. среда / в среду
4. четверг / в четверг
5. пятница / в пятницу
6. суббота / в субботу
7. воскресенье / в воскресенье

33.c
1. с понедельника до среды
2. до воскресенья
3. со вторника
4. до четверга
5. до пятницы
6. с субботы

33.d
1. **В эту субботу** нам надо работать.
2. **В прошлую субботу** мы были свободны.
3. **В следующий понедельник** я приготовлю ужин.
4. Я готовлю ужин **каждый понедельник**.
5. **В прошлый раз** я приготовил борщ.
6. **В этот раз** я приготовлю суп.
7. **В следующий раз** я приготовлю картошку.

33.e
1. **На этой неделе** я занят, но **на следующей (неделе)** я буду свободен.
2. **В прошлом месяце** я не готовил, но **в следующем (месяце)** я буду готовить каждый вечер.
3. **В этом году** мы не смотрим телевизор, но **в прошлом (году)** мы его смотрели каждый день.

34.a
1. в январе
2. в октябре
3. с июня до ноября
4. с апреля
5. до декабря
6. в мае
7. в прошлом феврале
8. в июле
9. в августе
10. с мая до июня
11. с декабря
12. до марта
13. в ноябре
14. в апреле

Answer Key

34.b
1. Ты **слишком много** работаешь!
2. Я **почти всегда** работаю.
3. Я **уже никогда** не отдыхаю.
4. **Раньше** я отдыхала, но **теперь** я не могу.
5. **Скоро** я буду **опять** в России.
6. Мы **наконец** увиделись **недавно**.
7. Мы **давно** не виделись.
8. (Раньше) мы **довольно часто** виделись.
9. **Со временем** я привык к русской еде.
10. Я купил билет **заранее**.
11. Он сделал всё **очень быстро**.

34.c
1. **для**	4. **на**	7. **на**	10. **на / на**	13. **для / для**
2. **за**	5. **за / на**	8. **на / на**	11. **на**	14. **для / от**
3. **на**	6. **за**	9. **на / за**	12. **от**	15. **на**

35.a
1. в стране — в страну — из страны
2. в космосе — в космос — из космоса
3. в ресторане — в ресторан — из ресторана
4. в Москве — в Москву — из Москвы
5. в Петербурге — в Петербург — из Петербурга
6. в общежитии — в общежитие — из общежития
7. в России — в Россию — из России
8. во Франции — во Францию — из Франции
9. в квартире — в квартиру — из квартиры
10. в театре — в театр — из театра
11. в магазине — в магазин — из магазина
12. в гостиной — в гостиную — из гостиной
13. в море — в море — из моря

35.b
1. на уроке — на урок — с урока
2. на занятии — на занятие — с занятия
3. на рынке — на рынок — с рынка
4. на лестнице — на лестницу — с лестницы
5. на спектакле — на спектакль — со спектакля
6. на вечеринке — на вечеринку — с вечеринки
7. на дворе — на двор — со двора
8. на даче — на дачу — с дачи
9. на пляже — на пляж — с пляжа
10. на балете — на балет — с балета
11. на острове — на остров — с острова
12. на почте — на почту — с почты

36.a
1. идти →
2. ходить (round trip)
3. ездить (round trip)
4. ходить (round trip)
5. идти →
6. ездить (round trip)
7. ехать →
8. ходить (single round trip)
9. ходить (single round trip)
10. ехать →
11. ходить (round trip)
12. ходить (round trip)

36.b
1. round trip (round trip) ходить
2. round trip (round trip) ходить
3. underway → идти
4. set out (single) пойти
5. set out (single) пойти
6. round trip (single) ходить
7. set out (single) поехать
8. round trip (single) ездить
9. round trip (single) ездить
10. round trip (single) ездить

36.c
1. makes round trips on foot
2. were underway on foot
3. (single) round trip on foot
4. set out by vehicle
5. set out on foot
6. went around on foot

37.a
1. Она любит **плавать** в бассейне.
2. Самолёт долго **летал** в небе.
3. — Где вы были? — Мы **ездили** по России.
4. Что это **плавает** в моём пиве?!
5. Собака **бегает** в парке каждый день.
6. Каждый день я **ходила** по центру (города).
7. Человек не может **летать**.

37.b
1. на **машине** / на **автобусе** / на **поезде** / на **трамвае** / на **электричке** / на **велосипеде** / на **метро** / на **такси**
2. на **самолёте** / на **вертолёте**
3. на **катере** / на **яхте** / на **корабле** / на **лодке**

37.c
1. в Росси**ю** / в Росси**и**
2. в комнат**у** / в комнат**е**
3. в столов**ую** / в столов**ой**
4. на концерт / на концерт**е**
5. в Европ**у** / в Европ**е**
6. в Петербург / в Петербург**е**
7. на вечеринк**у** / на вечеринк**е**

38.a
1. **ходить** (round trips)
2. **идти** (underway)
3. **ездить** (round trips)
4. **ехать** (underway)
5. **летать** (round trips)
6. **плавать** (around)
7. **бегать** (around)
8. **лететь** (underway)
9. **летать** (around)
10. **бежать** (underway)
11. **плыть** (underway)
12. **идти** (underway)

38.b
1. **идём**
2. **иду / идёшь**
3. **шли**
4. **едешь / еду**
5. **ехали**
6. **лечу / летят**
7. **плывёт**
8. **бегут**

38.c
1. **в Москву**
2. **на вечеринку**
3. **в клуб, на концерт**
4. **в столовую**
5. **из общежития**
6. **со скучной лекции**
7. **на Васильевский остров**
8. **из Петербурга**

38.d
1. [⬭⬭⬭]
2. [≡]
3. [⬭⬭⬭]
4. [≡ ≡]
5. [⬭⬭⬭]
6. [≡]
7. [⬭⬭⬭]

38.e
1. →
2. [⬭⬭⬭]
3. [⬭⬭⬭]
4. ↻
5. →
6. ↻
7. →
8. ↻
9. →
10. ↻ →
11. ≡
12. →
13. ↻
14. ≡

38.f
1. [⬭⬭⬭] ездить
2. → ехать
3. [⬭⬭⬭] ходить
4. → идти
5. → лететь
6. → идти
7. ↻ ходить
8. → бежать
9. ↻ бегать
10. ≡ идти

39.a
1. He said goodbye and **set off on foot**.
2. We **set off by water** along the canal on a tour boat.
3. Where is she? Where did she **set off to on foot**?
4. I don't know where they **set off to by vehicle**.
5. The plane **set off by air** for the south.
6. My dog **set off running** (ran off) into the park.
7. In an hour from now **I'll set off by foot** for the lecture.
8. Everything's ready. The boat **will soon set off by water**.

39.b
1. **в тренажёрном зале**
2. **на Земле**
3. **в России**
4. **в Америке**
5. **в магазине**
6. **в квартире**

39.c
1. ↦ поехать (ехать)
2. ↦ поехать
3. [⬭⬭⬭] ездить
4. [⬭⬭⬭] ездить
5. → лететь
6. ↦ пойти (идти)
7. [⬭⬭⬭] ходить
8. → идти

39.d
1. **Сначала я иду на лекцию, потом в кафе, и наконец (пойду) домой.**
2. **Вчера мы пошли (ходили) в магазин, потом в театр, потом в ресторан.**
3. **Завтра я пойду на занятие, потом в библиотеку, и наконец домой в общежитие.**
4. **Через месяц я полечу сначала во Францию, потом в Россию.**

39.e
1. Вы **ходили** на лекцию сегодня?
2. Каждое утро я **иду** (**хожу**) на лекцию.
3. Сначала я **пошёл** (**ходил**) на лекцию, и потом (я **пошёл**) домой.
4. Я **полечу** (**лечу**) в Москву на следующей неделе.
5. Я хочу **поехать** в Москву через неделю.
6. Я **буду** часто **летать** в Москву.
7. Куда он **бежал** вчера?
8. Куда он **побежал**?
9. Она любит **бегать** в парке.
10. Я обычно **иду** в театр пешком, но я **еду** домой на метро.
11. Я **ездила** в Нью-Йорк вчера.
12. Куда **плывёт** этот корабль / катер?

40.a
1. Я люблю **гулять** по городу.
2. Мы **погуляли**, потом пошли в кафе.
3. Ребёнок **прыгнул** в бассейн.
4. Не **прыгай** по (в) гостиной!
5. Замок сломался. Он не **движется**.

40.b
1. Я хочу пригласить тебя **на вечеринку**.
2. Мы вернулись **домой с вечеринки**.
3. Мне надо позвонить **в полицию**!
4. Ты всегда опаздываешь **на занятие**!
5. Мы не успеем **на поезд**!
6. Надо успевать **на занятие**.
7. Я спешу **на работу**!

40.c
1. из Москвы / в Москве
2. в Питер / в Питере
3. с вокзала / на вокзале
4. с лекции / на лекции
5. на стадион / на концерт
6. в библиотеку / в библиотеке
7. на урок / на уроке
8. на новоселье / на новоселье
9. в театр / в театре

40.d
1. Я часто **оставляю** студенческий билет дома.
2. Я **забыла** студенческий билет дома.
3. Я **оставлю** собаку у соседа.
4. Я **останусь** дома завтра.
5. Я решил **остаться** в России.
6. Наш сосед часто **остаётся** дома.

40.e
1. домой / дома
2. дома / из дома
3. здесь / отсюда
4. сюда / здесь
5. туда / там
6. оттуда / там

40.f
1. туда
2. сюда
3. отсюда
4. туда
5. отсюда
6. туда / домой

41.a
1. с большим ковром
2. с чистой кухней
3. с хорошей спальней
4. с огромным парком
5. с новой столовой
6. со вкусной едой
7. с красивым деревом
8. с новым платьем
9. с грязным бельём
10. с русской баней
11. с колбасой
12. с молоком
13. с сахаром
14. со сметаной
15. с лимоном

41.b
1. со старым другом
2. с новой подругой
3. с моим знакомым
4. с женой / с мужем
5. с сыном / с дочкой
6. с братом / с сестрой
7. с мамой / с папой
8. с большой группой
9. с профессором
10. с другим студентом
11. с другой студенткой
12. с этим человеком
13. с президентом США
14. с дядей / с тётей

41.c
1. с чувством юмора
2. карандашом
3. с отцом
4. с удовольствием
5. с сестрой и братом
6. книгой
7. с колбасой и сыром
8. с большим окном
9. мылом

41.d
С Днём Победы!
С Новым годом!
С Днём рождения!
С Рождеством!
С новосельем!
С победой!
С праздником!
С покупкой!

41.e
1. русской историей / литературой
2. футболом / баскетболом
3. математикой / лингвистикой
4. бегом / боксом / греблей

41.f
1. русский язык / русским языком
2. русская поэзия / русской поэзией
3. русское искусство / русским искусством
4. русская архитектура / русской архитектурой

41.g
1. Они занимают наш стол!
2. Пора занять моё место.
3. Он всегда интересовался Россией.
4. Ты заинтересуешься историей в Петербурге.

42.a
1. Где она **училась**?
2. Я не могу идти в кино. Мне надо **заниматься**.
3. Мы вчера весь день **занимались**.
4. Она **изучает** физику и русский язык.
5. Ты **учишься**? А что **изучаешь**?
6. Я хорошо **подготовилась** к экзамену по математике.

42.b
1. Я игра́ю в баскетбо́л.
2. Я занима́юсь гре́блей.
3. Я занима́юсь би́знесом.
4. Я занима́юсь бале́том
5. Я занима́юсь матема́тикой.
6. Я игра́ю на гита́ре.
7. Я игра́ю в хокке́й.
8. Я занима́юсь пе́нием.
9. Я игра́ю на трубе́.
10. Я занима́юсь лёгкой атле́тикой.

42.c
1. Наш оте́ц журнали́ст.
2. На́ша ма́ма профе́ссор.
3. Мой знако́мый бизнесме́н.
4. Моя́ знако́мая психо́лог.
5. Твой друг писа́тель.
6. Твоя́ подру́га врач.

Наш оте́ц рабо́тает журнали́стом.
На́ша ма́ма рабо́тает профе́ссором.
Мой знако́мый рабо́тает бизнесме́ном.
Моя́ знако́мая рабо́тает психо́логом.
Твой друг рабо́тает писа́телем.
Твоя́ подру́га рабо́тает врачо́м.

42.d
1. под дива́ном / на дива́не
2. с торго́вым це́нтром
3. пе́ред ле́кцией / по ру́сской исто́рии
4. за э́тим зда́нием / с фонта́ном
5. над мои́м пи́сьменным столо́м
6. на скаме́йке / пе́ред библио́текой
7. на ле́кции / по фи́зике
8. со ста́нцией

42.e
1. за хле́бом
2. за молоко́м
3. за колбасо́й
4. за шокола́дом
5. за пи́вом
6. за во́дкой

42.f
1. под стол
2. под столо́м
3. из-под стола́
4. за ба́рную сто́йку
5. за ба́рной сто́йкой
6. над ба́рной сто́йкой
7. из-за ба́рной сто́йки
8. пе́ред на́шей да́чей

42.g
1. из-за грани́цы
2. за грани́цей
3. за грани́цу
4. за столо́м
5. за стол
6. из-за стола́
7. за го́родом
8. за́ город
9. из-за го́рода

43.a
1. психо́логом
2. фило́софом
3. врачо́м
4. юри́стом
5. исто́риком
6. спорсме́ном
7. журнали́стом
8. певцо́м / певи́цей
9. футболи́стом
10. хоккеи́стом
11. био́логом

43.b
1. большо́й
2. стра́нным
3. интере́сной
4. гру́стным
5. просты́м
6. хоро́шей студе́нткой
7. изве́стным писа́телем

43.c
1. **Мы с сестро́й** ходи́ли в теа́тр. Мы с ней лю́бим о́перу.
2. **Мы с отцо́м** бы́ли на стадио́не. Мы с ним лю́бим смотре́ть футбо́л.
3. **Мы с сосе́дом** занима́лись весь ве́чер. Мы с ним изуча́ем фи́зику.
4. **Мы с жено́й** вме́сте учи́лись. Мы с ней там познако́мились.
5. **Мы с семьёй** бы́ли за го́родом, на да́че.

44.a
1. Здесь нет остано́вки авто́буса.
2. В э́том го́роде нет хоро́шего ба́ра.
3. В на́шем шта́те нет пля́жа.
4. У моего́ сосе́да не́ было велосипе́да.
5. У него́ не́ было туале́тной бума́ги.
6. У нас не бу́дет маши́ны.
7. Молоко́ есть.

44.b
1. но́вый журна́л
2. но́вого щенка́
3. дорого́е вино́
4. ба́нку икры́
5. ру́сскую газе́ту
6. Маяко́вского
7. ста́рого дру́га
8. ста́рую подру́гу
9. всю икру́
10. весь торт
11. це́лую буты́лку
12. всё молоко́
13. наш го́род
14. на́шего профе́ссора
15. на́шу сестру́
16. на́шего отца́
17. твою́ семью́
18. своего́ адвока́та
19. э́той тео́рии
20. ва́шего вопро́са

44.c
1. **Мы дадим ребёнку шоколад.**
2. **Они всегда давали нам вино.**
3. **Он нам очень помог.**
4. **Мы поможем бабушке.**
5. **Она мне показала собаку.**
6. **Он ей покажет кошку.**
7. **Они купили нам торт.**
8. **Я куплю ей икру.**

44.d
1. **Нам было скучно на лекции.**
2. **Ему было трудно читать.**
3. **Нам хотелось есть.**
4. **Нашему другу было плохо.**

Нам будет скучно на лекции.
Ему будет трудно читать.
Нам будет хотеться (захочется) есть.
Нашему другу будет плохо.

45.a
1. на диване / на полу
2. при бабушке
3. о футболе
4. в словаре
5. на лекции
6. в этом музее
7. на занятии
8. в рюкзаке
9. о его статье
10. при входе
11. на компьютере
12. в море / на берегу
13. на краю
14. при империи

45.b
1. с папой / за столом
2. с молоком
3. со сметаной
4. перед началом
5. с сестрой
6. под землёй
7. перед экзаменом
8. с балконом

45.c
1. по электронной почте
2. по моему мнению
3. к врачу
4. к дедушке
5. по русскому языку
6. по тротуару / по улице
7. по телевизору
8. по телефону

45.d
1. у дедушки
2. без компьютера
3. без словаря
4. после занятия
5. для соседа
6. с вокзала
7. из кофейни
8. машины
9. вместо того фильма
10. после экзамена

45.e
1. за пиво
2. за неделю
3. на месяц
4. через год
5. месяц назад
6. на вечеринку
7. на эту фотографию
8. в общежитие
9. под стол
10. за квартиру

45.f
1. в Москве / в Москву
2. на концерт / на концерте
3. за этой стеной / с фонтаном
4. под той книгой
5. в Петербург / с сестрой и братом
6. на берегу / на Неву
7. в Русском музее
8. в Эрмитаже
9. за еду / за пиво
10. на балет / на пятницу
11. с сыром / колбасой / луком
12. с молоком и сахаром
13. за шкаф

46.a
1. моя сестра / с новой русской студенткой
2. на кухне / рыбы / курицы / еды / еду
3. семьи / большая дача / в деревне / на дачу / каждую неделю
4. наша соседка / статью / чёрной ручкой
5. с подругой / в Москву / на прошлой неделе / банку икры
6. нашей тёте / недовольна / тётей
7. через неделю / эта студентка / русскую газету
8. литературой / в Второй мировой войне / блокаде

46.b
1. новый учебник / для сына / известным физиком
2. за домом / в котором / в Петербурге / большой, красивый парк
3. с отцом / целый час / по музею / по городу / в театр
4. из театра / на автобусе / одного автобуса
5. русским языком / такой трудный язык
6. щенка / старому другу / месяц / через год / нового
7. вашему знакомому / на автобусе / на трамвае
8. нет словаря / этот тескт / без словаря / со словарём

46.c
1. наш новый коллега / нового коллегу
2. с папой / нашим любимым дядей / любимого дядю

46.d
1. молок**а** / о молок**е** / молок**а**
2. морожен**ого** / французск**ое** вин**о**
3. на <u>о</u>зер**е** / дер<u>е</u>в**ом** / в эт**ом** дер<u>е</u>ве / за мо**им** окн**ом**
4. искусств**ом** / прав**ом** / прав**о**
5. печень**я** / печень**е** / яблок**о**
6. без хорош**его** одеял**а** / одеял**о**

46.e
1. меню / в меню
2. на метр<u>о</u> / метр<u>о</u>
3. пиан<u>и</u>но / кин<u>о</u> / в кафе
4. коф<u>е</u> / в каф<u>е</u> / коф<u>е</u>

46.f
1. в Росси**и** / в общеж<u>и</u>ти**и**
2. в Росси**ю** / из Росси**и**
3. г<u>е</u>ни**ем** / биол<u>о</u>ги**ей** / философи**ей**
4. фам<u>и</u>ли**ю** / фехтовани**ем** / хими**ю**
5. лекци**и** / по истори**и** / по хими**и**

46.g
1. нуж**ен** / нуж**на** / нуж**но**
2. трезв**ы** / пьян**ы** / жив**ы** / мертв**ы**
3. занят / занят**о** / занят**а**
4. дов<u>о</u>л**ен** / сч<u>а</u>стлив / недов<u>о</u>льн**а** / несч<u>а</u>стлив**а**

47.a
1. **Мая<u>ко</u>вская**
2. **Достоевская**
3. **Ч<u>е</u>ховская**
4. **Пушкинская**
5. **Чернышевская**
6. **Менделеевская**
7. **Г<u>о</u>рьковская**

47.b
Булгакова   **Толст<u>у</u>ю**   **Плат<u>о</u>нова**   <u>А</u>нну Андр<u>е</u>евну Ахм<u>а</u>тову
Пушкина   **Цвет<u>а</u>еву**   **Набокова**   Владимира Владимировича Маяковского
Бахтина   **Пастерн<u>а</u>ка**   **Ул<u>и</u>цкую**   Бор<u>и</u>са Леон<u>и</u>довича Пастерн<u>а</u>ка
Ахм<u>а</u>тову   **Г<u>о</u>рького**   **Шекспира**
Мая<u>ко</u>вского   **Толст<u>о</u>го**   **Джейн <u>О</u>стин**
Г<u>и</u>ппиус   **Солжен<u>и</u>цына**   **Достоевского**

47.c
1. **Александру Сергеевичу Пушкину**
2. **Никол<u>а</u>ю Вас<u>и</u>льевичу Г<u>о</u>голю**
3. **<u>А</u>нне Андр<u>е</u>евне Ахм<u>а</u>товой**
4. **Фёдору Мих<u>а</u>йловичу Достоевскому**
5. **Льву Никол<u>а</u>евичу Толст<u>о</u>му**
6. **Миха<u>и</u>лу Ив<u>а</u>новичу Гл<u>и</u>нке**
7. **Владимиру Ильичу Ленину**
8. **императр<u>и</u>це Екатер<u>и</u>не Втор<u>о</u>й**
9. **Владимиру Владимировичу Мая<u>ко</u>вскому**
10. **Александру П<u>у</u>шкину и Нат<u>а</u>лье Гончар<u>о</u>вой**
11. **носу М<u>а</u>йора Ковалёва**
12. **доброй соб<u>а</u>ке Гавр<u>ю</u>ше**

47.d
1. **Толст<u>о</u>го**
2. **Г<u>о</u>голя**
3. **Ахм<u>а</u>товой**
4. **Достоевского**
5. **Цвет<u>а</u>евой**
6. **Зам<u>я</u>тина**
7. **Мая<u>ко</u>вского**
8. **Бл<u>о</u>ка**

47.e
1. **Ир<u>и</u>не П<u>а</u>вловне**
2. **Мари<u>ю</u> Сергеевну**
3. **с <u>А</u>нной Ив<u>а</u>новной**
4. **Ив<u>а</u>ну Александровичу**
5. **Ол<u>е</u>га Серг<u>е</u>евича**
6. **Серг<u>е</u>ем Мих<u>а</u>йловичем**

47.f
1. **с Ч<u>е</u>ховым**
2. **с Толст<u>ы</u>м**
3. **Цвет<u>а</u>евой**
4. **Г<u>о</u>голем**
5. **П<u>у</u>шкиным**
6. **Гумилёвым**
7. **Андр<u>е</u>ем Б<u>е</u>лым**

47.g
1. **П<u>а</u>ше**
2. **с М<u>а</u>шей**
3. **Серёжу**
4. **Н<u>а</u>сте**
5. **Т<u>а</u>ни**
6. **<u>И</u>рой**
7. **Вол<u>о</u>дя**
8. **с К<u>о</u>лей**
9. **о Кс<u>ю</u>ше**
10. **Л<u>е</u>ну**

48.a
1. **кого**?
2. **ком**?
3. **чём**?
4. **что**?
5. **ком<u>у</u>**?
6. **кто**?
7. **к чему**?
8. **с кем**?

48.b
1. **отцу / ему**   **сестре / ей**   3. **о религии / о ней**   **о птице / о ней**
2. **с соседом / с ним**   **с дедушкой / с ним**   4. **на дерево / на него**   **на реку / на неё**

48.c
1. **меня**   4. **мне**   7. **тебя**   10. **тебе**   13. **вам**
2. **мне**   5. **мной**   8. **тобой**   11. **нами**   14. **вами**
3. **мне**   6. **тебе**   9. **тебя**   12. **нас**   15. **вас**

48.d
1. **всю**   4. **всей**   7. **всём**   10. **все**
2. **всё**   5. **всему**   8. **всей**   11. **всю**
3. **весь**   6. **всём**   9. **всё**   12. **всём**

48.e
1. **одну**   4. с **одной**
2. **одно**   5. в **одном**
3. **один**   6. на **одном**

48.f
1. **чей / чью**   4. **чьём**
2. **чьём / чьей**   5. **чьим**
3. **чьей**   6. **чьим**

48.g
1. **твою**   4. **моей**   7. **нашем**   10. **вашей**   13. **её**   16. **её**
2. **твоём**   5. **моём**   8. **нашим**   11. **его**   14. **его**
3. **твоему**   6. **моему**   9. **ваша**   12. **их**   15. **их**

49.a
1. нет скандала   4. нет скандала   7. есть скандал
2. нет скандала   5. нет скандала   8. нет скандала
3. есть скандал   6. нет скандала

49.b
1. Я работаю в **своей** комнате.   4. Ты всегда говоришь о **своей** собаке.
2. Мы любим **свой** город.   5. Я ненавижу **свою** работу.
3. Ты забыла **свой** ключ?

49.c
1. Он позвонил **своей** девушке.   4. Его сосед любит **его** собаку.
2. Его друг позвонил **его** девушке.   5. Они взяли **свой** зонт.
3. Боря любит **свою** собаку.   6. Их друг взял **их** зонт.

49.d
1. Он любит только **себя**.   4. Он написал **себе** письмо.
2. Он смотрит на **себя** в зеркале.   5. Он ведёт **себя** бесстыдно,
3. Он всегда думает только о **себе**.   6. но он всегда чувствует **себя** хорошо!

49.e
1. Он **сам** не понимает.   4. Я **сама** не знаю.
2. Они сделали работу **сами**.   5. Ребёнок сделает это **сам**.
3. Я всё делаю **сам**.

49.f
1. Они очень любят **друг друга**.   7. Они привыкли **друг к другу**.
2. Они всегда говорят **друг о друге**.   8. Они ездят **друг к другу**.
3. Они не могут жить **друг без друга**.   9. Они дают **друг другу** деньги.
4. Они всегда помогают **друг другу**.   10. Они говорят **друг другу** правду.
5. Они понимают **друг друга**.   11. Они знают всё **друг о друге**.
6. Они верят **друг другу**.   12. Они часто видят **друг друга**.

50.a
1. **Где нам раб_о_тать?**
2. **О чём мне говор_и_ть?**
3. **Что мне б_ы_ло д_у_мать?**
4. **Спрос_и_ть её, или нет?**
5. **Как_о_й фильм нам посмотр_е_ть?**
6. **Чью стат_ью_ нам чит_а_ть?**

50.b
1. **Чт_о_бы жить хорош_о_, н_а_до им_е_ть д_е_ньги.**
2. **Чт_о_бы им_е_ть д_е_ньги, надо раб_о_тать.**
3. **Чт_о_бы раб_о_тать, надо уч_и_ться.**

50.c
1. На пр_о_шлой нед_е_ле я отдых_а_ла в дер_е_вне.
2. З_а_втра я б_у_ду своб_о_дна. Если х_о_чешь, м_о_жно встр_е_титься.
3. Я пью в_о_ду, потом_у_ что пить х_о_чется.
4. Когда я г_о_лоден, я об_ы_чно ем шокол_а_д.
5. Они зн_а_ют, что я не любл_ю_ этого пис_а_теля.
6. Ты не ск_а_жешь, где он жив_ё_т?
7. Мы не зн_а_ем, когда он прид_ё_т.
8. В н_а_шем г_о_роде есть больш_о_й парк.

50.d
1. Он спр_а_шивал, **говор_и_т ли она по-р_у_сски.**
2. Она хот_е_ла знать, **будет ли у них телеф_о_н.**
3. Мы не поним_а_ем, **есть ли у нас экз_а_мен з_а_втра.**
4. Я не знал, **раб_о_тает ли он вообщ_е_.**
5. Как я мог_у_ знать, **где зонт?**
6. Он не сказ_а_л, **б_у_дем ли мы смотр_е_ть фильм.**
7. Мы заб_ы_ли спрос_и_ть, **должн_ы_ ли мы прочит_а_ть эту стать_ю_.**
8. Не зн_а_ю, **надо ли заплат_и_ть за эту газ_е_ту.**

50.e
1. **_Е_сли х_о_чешь н_о_вую маш_и_ну, ты д_о_лжен раб_о_тать.**
2. **Если он х_о_чет чит_а_ть, он д_о_лжен куп_и_ть книгу.**
3. **Хорош_о_, _е_сли у теб_я_ есть зонт.**
4. **_Е_сли л_ю_бишь м_а_му, ты к_у_пишь ей к_о_фе.**
5. **Куп_и_ билет в те_а_тр, если х_о_чешь.**
6. **Помог_и_ мне, _е_сли ты м_о_жешь.**

50.f
1. **_Е_сли ты меня спр_о_сишь, я теб_е_ отв_е_чу.**
2. **Б_у_дет хорош_о_, если у нас б_у_дет зонт.**
3. **_Е_сли мы б_у_дем своб_о_дны, мы см_о_жем пойт_и_ на бал_е_т з_а_втра.**
4. **Я купл_ю_ тебе бил_е_т, _е_сли я смог_у_.**

suffixed stems (both и and ё endings)

type	stem	non-past forms	infinitive	past forms
consonant stems + ё endings (-у/-ю, -ёшь, -ёт, -ём, -ёте, -ут/-ют)				
АЙ	чит-ай-	читаю, читаешь... читают	**читать**: read	читал, читала, читало, читали
ЕЙ	ум-ей-	умею, умеешь... умеют	**уметь**: know how	умел, умела, умело, умели
	стар-ей-	старею, стареешь... стареют	**стареть**: grow old	старел, старела, старело, старели
АВАЙ	дай-	даю, даёшь... дают (авай → а)	**давать**: give	давал, давала, давало, давали
(only 3 basic verbs)	у-знай-	узнаю, узнаёшь... узнают (авай → а)	**узнавать**: find out	узнавал, узнавала, узнавали
	в-стай-	встаю, встаёшь... встают (авай → а)	**вставать**: get up	вставал, вставала, вставали
vowel stems + и endings (-у/-ю, -ишь, -ит, -им, -ите, -ат/-ят)				
И	ответ-и-	отвечу*, ответишь... ответят	**ответить**: answer	ответил, ответила, ответили
(mutation in я form, when possible)	реш-и-	решу, решишь... решат	**решить**: solve	решил, решила, решили
	люб-и-	люблю*, любишь... любят	**любить**: love	любил, любила, любило, любили
	говор-и-	говорю, говоришь... говорят	**говорить**: say, speak	говорил, говорила, звонили
Е (like И)	сид-е-	сижу, сидишь... сидят	**сидеть**: sit	сидел, сидела, сидело, сидели
	смотр-е-	смотрю, смотришь... смотрят	**смотреть**: watch	смотрел, смотрела, смотрели
ЖА (ЙА)	леж-а-	лежу, лежишь... лежат	**лежать**: lie	лежал, лежала, лежало, лежали
	стой-а-	стою, стоишь... стоят	**стоять**: stand	стоял, стояла, стояло, стояли
vowel stems + ё endings (-у/-ю, -ёшь, -ёт, -ём, -ёте, -ут/-ют)				
А	пис-а-	пишу*, пишешь*... пишут*	**писать**: write	писал, писала, писало, писали
	смей-а-	смеюсь, смеёшься... смеются	**смеяться**: laugh	смеялся, смеялась, смеялись
n/sA	ж/д-а-	жду, ждёшь... ждут	**ждать**: wait	ждал, ждала, ждало, ждали
	з/в-а-	зову, зовёшь... зовут (inserted о)	**звать**: call, summon	звал, звала, звало, звали
	б/р-а-	беру, берёшь... берут (inserted е)	**брать**: take	брал, брала, брало, брали
ОВА (ЕВА)	рис-ова-	рисую, рисуешь... рисуют (ова → у)	**рисовать**: draw	рисовал, рисовала, рисовали
	танц-ева-	танцую, танцуешь... танцуют (ева → у)	**танцевать**: dance	танцевал, танцевала, танцевали
	с-ова-	сую, суёшь... суют (ова → у)	**совать**: stick, shove	совал, совала, совало, совали
	во-ева-	воюю, воюешь... воюют (ева → ю)	**воевать**: wage war	воевал, воевала, воевало, воевали
О	бор-о-	борюсь, борешься... борются	**бороться**: struggle	боролся, боролась, боролись
НУ	отдох-ну-	отдохну, отдохнёшь... отдохнут	**отдохнуть**: relax	отдохнул, отдохнула, отдохнули
(НУ)	при-вык-ну-	привыкну, привыкнешь... привыкнут	**привыкнуть**: get used	привык, привыкла, привыкли

non-suffixed stems (ё endings only!)

type	stem	non-past forms	infinitive	past forms
syllabic resonant stems				
В	жив-	живу, живёшь... живут	**жить**: live	жил, жила, жило, жили
Н	о-ден-	одену, оденешь... оденут	**одеть**: dress	одел, одела, одело, одели
Й	дуй-	дую, дуешь... дуют	**дуть**: blow	дул, дула, дуло, дули
ОЙ	мой-	мою, моешь... моют	**мыть**: wash	мыл, мыла, мыло, мыли
Ь	пь-	пью, пьёшь... пьют	**пить**: drink	пил, пила, пило, пили
non-syllabic resonant stems				
/Р	ум/р-	умру, умрёшь... умрут	**умереть**: die	умер, умерла, умерло, умерли
/М	ж/м-	жму, жмёшь... жмут	**жать**: squeeze	жал, жала, жало, жали
/Н	нач/н-	начну, начнёшь... начнут	**начать**: begin	начал, начала, начало, начали
Й/М	по-й/м-	пойму, поймёшь... поймут	**понять**: understand	понял, поняла, поняло, поняли
НИМ	с-ним-	сниму, снимешь... снимут	**снять**: take off	снял, сняла, сняло, сняли
obstruent stems (note past tense forms and infinitives in -сти / -чь)				
Д	вед-	веду, ведёшь... ведут	**вести**: lead	вёл, вела, вело, вели
Т	мет-	мету, метёшь... метут	**мести**: sweep	мел, мела, мело, мели
З	нес-	несу, несёшь... несут	**нести**: carry	нёс, несла, несло, несли
С	вез-	везу, везёшь... везут	**везти**: convey	вёз, везла, везло, везли
Г	мог-	могу, можешь*... могут (note г → ж)	**мочь**: be able	мог, могла, могло, могли
К	пек-	пеку, печёшь*... пекут (note к → ч)	**печь**: bake	пёк, пекла, пекло, пекли
Б	греб-	гребу, гребёшь... гребут	**грести**: rake, row	грёб, гребла, гребло, гребли

294   * asterisks mark a position where a mutation occurs, whenever possible

Verbs of motion (through Book 1)

	unprefixed verbs of motion		perfective
	two imperfective infinitives!		
	indeterminate	determinate	setting out / assumed arrival
	around / round trip ↺ 🗲	underway → ⇛	↦ ⇥
to go by foot	ход<u>и</u>ть И	идт<u>и</u> (иду, идёшь | шёл, шла, шли)	пойт<u>и</u>
to go by vehicle	<u>е</u>здить И	<u>е</u>хать (<u>е</u>ду, <u>е</u>дешь, <u>е</u>дят)	по<u>е</u>хать
to go by air, fly	лет<u>а</u>ть АЙ	лет<u>е</u>ть Е (леч<u>у</u>, лет<u>и</u>шь)	полет<u>е</u>ть
to run	б<u>е</u>гать АЙ	беж<u>а</u>ть (бег<u>у</u>, беж<u>и</u>шь, бег<u>у</u>т)	побеж<u>а</u>ть
to go by water	пл<u>а</u>вать АЙ	плыть В (плыв<u>у</u>, плыв<u>ё</u>шь)	попл<u>ы</u>ть

Noun and adjective endings: singular

masculine nouns

	special modifiers						adjectives	hard	soft		special soft
nom.	<u>э</u>т**от**	весь	од<u>и</u>н	чей	мой	наш	н<u>о</u>в**ый**	стол	словарь	муз<u>е</u>й	кафет<u>е</u>рий
gen.	<u>э</u>т**ого**	вс**его**	одн**ого**	чь**его**	мо**его**	н<u>а</u>ш**его**	н<u>о</u>в**ого**	стол<u>а</u>	словар<u>я</u>	муз<u>е</u>я	кафет<u>е</u>ри**я**
acc.	<u>э</u>т**от**	весь	од<u>и</u>н	чей	мой	наш	н<u>о</u>в**ый**	стол	словарь	муз<u>е</u>й	кафет<u>е</u>рий
animate:	<u>э</u>т**ого**	вс**его**	одн**ого**	чь**его**	мо**его**	н<u>а</u>ш**его**	н<u>о</u>в**ого**	студ<u>е</u>нт**а**	пис<u>а</u>тел**я**		г<u>е</u>ни**я**
dat.	<u>э</u>т**ому**	вс**ему**	одн**ому**	чь**ему**	мо**ему**	н<u>а</u>ш**ему**	н<u>о</u>в**ому**	стол<u>у</u>	словар<u>ю</u>	муз<u>е</u>ю	кафет<u>е</u>рию
prep.	<u>э</u>т**ом**	вс**ём**	одн**ом**	чь**ём**	мо**ём**	н<u>а</u>ш**ем**	н<u>о</u>в**ом**	стол<u>е</u>	словар<u>е</u>	муз<u>е</u>е	кафет<u>е</u>рии
instr.	<u>э</u>т**им**	вс**ем**	одн**им**	чь**им**	мо**им**	н<u>а</u>ш**им**	н<u>о</u>в**ым**	стол<u>о</u>м	словар<u>ё</u>м	муз<u>е</u>ем	кафет<u>е</u>рием

feminine nouns

	special modifiers						adjectives	hard	soft		special soft
nom.	<u>э</u>т**а**	вся	одн<u>а</u>	чья	мо**я**	н<u>а</u>ш**а**	н<u>о</u>в**ая**	газ<u>е</u>т**а**	нед<u>е</u>ля		фам<u>и</u>лия
gen.	<u>э</u>т**ой**	вс**ей**	одн**ой**	чь**ей**	мо**ей**	н<u>а</u>ш**ей**	н<u>о</u>в**ой**	газ<u>е</u>т**ы**	нед<u>е</u>ли		фам<u>и</u>лии
acc.	<u>э</u>т**у**	вс**ю**	одн**у**	чь**ю**	мо**ю**	н<u>а</u>ш**у**	н<u>о</u>в**ую**	газ<u>е</u>т**у**	нед<u>е</u>лю		фам<u>и</u>лию
dat.	<u>э</u>т**ой**	вс**ей**	одн**ой**	чь**ей**	мо**ей**	н<u>а</u>ш**ей**	н<u>о</u>в**ой**	газ<u>е</u>те	нед<u>е</u>ле		фам<u>и</u>лии
prep.	<u>э</u>т**ой**	вс**ей**	одн**ой**	чь**ей**	мо**ей**	н<u>а</u>ш**ей**	н<u>о</u>в**ой**	газ<u>е</u>те	нед<u>е</u>ле		фам<u>и</u>лии
instr.	<u>э</u>т**ой**	вс**ей**	одн**ой**	чь**ей**	мо**ей**	н<u>а</u>ш**ей**	н<u>о</u>в**ой**	газ<u>е</u>т**ой**	нед<u>е</u>лей	семь<u>ё</u>й	фам<u>и</u>ли**ей**

neuter nouns

	special modifiers						adjectives	hard	soft		special soft
nom.	<u>э</u>т**о**	вс**ё**	одн<u>о</u>	чь**ё**	мо**ё**	н<u>а</u>ш**е**	н<u>о</u>в**ое**	окн<u>о</u>	м<u>о</u>ре	бель<u>ё</u>	зад<u>а</u>ние
gen.	<u>э</u>т**ого**	вс**его**	одн**ого**	чь**его**	мо**его**	н<u>а</u>ш**его**	н<u>о</u>в**ого**	окн<u>а</u>	м<u>о</u>ря	бель<u>я</u>	зад<u>а</u>ния
acc.	<u>э</u>т**о**	вс**ё**	одн<u>о</u>	чь**ё**	мо**ё**	н<u>а</u>ш**е**	н<u>о</u>в**ое**	окн<u>о</u>	м<u>о</u>ре	бель<u>ё</u>	зад<u>а</u>ние
dat.	<u>э</u>т**ому**	вс**ему**	одн**ому**	чь**ему**	мо**ему**	н<u>а</u>ш**ему**	н<u>о</u>в**ому**	окн<u>у</u>	м<u>о</u>рю	бель<u>ю</u>	зад<u>а</u>нию
prep.	<u>э</u>т**ом**	вс**ём**	одн**ом**	чь**ём**	мо**ём**	н<u>а</u>ш**ем**	н<u>о</u>в**ом**	окн<u>е</u>	м<u>о</u>ре	бель<u>е</u>	зад<u>а</u>нии
instr.	<u>э</u>т**им**	вс**ем**	одн**им**	чь**им**	мо**им**	н<u>а</u>ш**им**	н<u>о</u>в**ым**	окн<u>о</u>м	м<u>о</u>рем	бель<u>ё</u>м	зад<u>а</u>нием

www.ingramcontent.com/pod-product-compliance
Lightning Source LLC
Chambersburg PA
CBHW061932260326
41798CB00034B/405